THIRD EDITION

PERSONNEL / HUMAN RESOURCE MANAGEMENT

David A. DeCenzo
Associate Professor of Management
Towson State University

Stephen P. Robbins
Professor of Management
San Diego State University

PRENTICE HALL
Englewood Cliffs, New Jersey 07632

Library of Congress Cataloging-in-Publication Data

DeCenzo, David A.
   Personnel/human resource management.

   Second ed. / Stephen P. Robbins.
   Includes bibliographies and index.
   1. Personnel management.   I. Robbins, Stephen R.
II. Title.
HF5549.D396 1988   658.3   87–6983
ISBN 0–13–657198–0

*In memory of Dee Earl Ezell,
who touched so many of our lives.*

Previously published under the title
PERSONNEL: The Management of Human Resources

Editorial/production supervision: Allison De Fren
Cover and interior design: Christine Gehring-Wolf
Cover photograph: Stan Wakefield
Manufacturing buyer: Harry Baisley

Printed in the United States of America
10 9 8 7 6 5 4 3 2

Prentice-Hall International (UK) Limited, *London*
Prentice-Hall of Australia Pty. Limited, *Sydney*
Prentice-Hall Canada Inc., *Toronto*
Prentice-Hall Hispanoamericana, S.A., *Mexico*
Prentice-Hall of India Private Limited, *New Delhi*
Prentice-Hall of Japan, Inc., *Tokyo*
Prentice-Hall of Southeast Asia Pte. Ltd., *Singapore*
Editora Prentice-Hall do Brasil, Ltda., *Rio de Janeiro*

Brief Contents

Contents

PART FIVE   MAINTENANCE OF HUMAN RESOURCES   *421*

16   *Compensation Administration   423*

17   *Benefits and Services   451*

Preface

Personnel/Human Resources Management, third edition, is a textbook for a one-term course in personnel or human resource management (HRM). As in the previous editions, we continue our commitment to provide readers with balanced coverage of the HRM field in a style that is both highly readable and relevant.

Balanced Coverage

As readers should expect in a dynamic field like HRM, we have completely updated the book's research base. That process, plus feedback from users of the second edition, revealed a number of topics that needed to be added or significantly expanded. For instance, there are now entire chapters on equal employment opportunity (Chapter 3), job analysis (Chapter 5), and labor relations (Chapter 20). In addition, a number of topics are new to this edition. Some of the more important include the impact of retrenchment on human resource planning (Chapter 4), employment-at-will (Chapter 18), stress and burnout (Chapter 19), and ergonomics (Chapter 23).

Readability

Our experience has led us to conclude that a text becomes highly readable when the writing is straightforward and conversational, the topics follow in a logical flow, and the authors make extensive use of examples to illustrate concepts. These factors have guided us as we have sought to make this text a highly effective learning tool. Of course, readability is a subjective concept. Previous users have regularly commented on how clearly the book presents ideas. We think this edition, too, is written in a clear, lively, concise, and conversational style. But only the reader can judge the accuracy of this claim.

We utilize two devices to facilitate the logical flow of the book. An integrative model, presented in Chapter 1, describes the key activities in HRM and how they interrelate. This model acts as a road map to guide readers as they proceed through the book. Additionally, each chapter has been individually organized to provide clarity and continuity.

Each chapter begins with "Learning Objectives," identifying specifically what the student should have learned after reading the chapter. This is followed by a short quotation and introduction designed to capture the student's interest in the chapter material. There is also a "Key Terms" section at the end of every chapter, and these terms are defined in the Glossary. To assist in capturing the most current information on a particular topic, a "Views in the News" report is included in each chapter. The chapter material concludes with a Summary section, indicating the learning experience that should have taken place. Review and Discussion questions follow the text material to reinforce the learning and to facilitate thought-provoking discussions. To complete each chapter, two cases are presented: One is a continuing case; the other is an application. The "Continuing Case: Concord General" is an ongoing story. The cast of characters, and the previous problems and solutions, are carried throughout the book. However, while each case is a continuation, the student can skip a chapter case and resume it in another chapter without damaging the learning experience. In addition, each chapter contains an independent case application that deals specifically with a major topic point of the chapter. These two cases together offer students an opportunity to apply what they have learned in each chapter. We have also included an "Additional Readings" section for students who wish to pursue a specific topic further.

Finally, in a quest for high readability, we have used a wealth of examples to clarify ideas. Our experience from the classroom demonstrates that students remember and understand concepts best when they are illustrated through examples. We have therefore made ample use of examples to make the concepts clear and pertinent.

Relevance

Human resource management, in contrast to disciplines like mathematics or philosophy, has the intrinsic potential to grab students' interest because of its relevance to their everyday lives. We have done our utmost to capitalize on this intrinsic interest. In addition to drawing upon examples from everyday life and organizations with which most students are familiar, we have developed cases that help students to link theory and practice, and guidelines for applying HRM concepts.

For instance, the chapter on recruiting sources includes an appendix that looks at recruitment from the student's or "recruit's" perspective. There are also sections that will help students perform better in interviews and a guide for careers in the 1990s. The discussion of performance appraisal presents techniques for improving appraisal systems. The chapters on socialization, training and development, and career development offer further guidance on how managers can design socialization experiences, training activities, and career programs that will enhance organizational effectiveness. Even the chapter on research—typically a dry and esoteric subject—has been written to show how managers can use research as a practical guide to making better human resource decisions. Throughout the book, you will find a liberal sprinkling of studies describing actual human resource management practices. When theory and practices differ, we sought to "tell it like it is." The end result is, we believe, a book that both enlightens and excites the reader.

Acknowledgments

At this point, we would like to move away from talking about the book and acknowledge some of the people who have made a major contribution to its development.

Authors rely heavily on the comments and suggestions of their reviewers. Ours were especially helpful. We want to express our thanks, in print, to: James W. Klinger, Villanova University; Bob S. Bulls, Reynolds Community College; Thomas N. Daymont, Temple University; David F. Caldwell, University of Santa Clara; Karl O. Mann, Rider College; and Marcus H. Sandver, Ohio State University. Any errors or omissions, of course, are fully our responsibility.

Many people at Prentice-Hall contributed to this book. We are particularly indebted to Alison Reeves, our acquisition editor; Allison De Fren, our production editor; Christine Gehring-Wolf our designer; and Marie Lines, our copy editor.

There are also a few others whose efforts should be recognized. Our deepest thanks go to Marilyn McMahon of Maryland Blue Cross and Blue Shield for her assistance on the compensation and benefits chapters. We also want to thank Tracy Diamond for her work on the "Additional Readings" sections.

Lastly, there are some personal acknowledgments that we want to make. Terri DeCenzo, Mark and Meredith DeCenzo, and Joan Rapp have missed many hours from their husband, dad, and POSSLQ, respectively. They have shown great patience over the past two years while we have worked on this revision. In some small way, we hope, the dedication of this book to them can acknowledge and offset the sacrifices they have had to make.

David A. DeCenzo
Baltimore, Maryland

Stephen P. Robbins
San Diego, California

CHAPTER 1

Introduction

to Human Resource

Management

AFTER READING THIS CHAPTER, YOU WILL BE ABLE TO:

1. Understand why the "people" dimension in an organization is important
2. Define *management*
3. Define *human resource management*
4. Identify the human resource outputs

I love mankind. It's people that I can't stand.

—Charlie Brown

Introduction

An organization is nothing without human resources. What is IBM without its employees? A lot of factories, expensive equipment, and some impressive bank balances. Similarly, if you remove the employees from such varied organizations as the Washington Redskins, the U.S. Army, the CIA, the Los Angeles Unified City Schools, or the Shell Oil Company, what would you have left? Not much.

The above paragraph is meant to dramatize something that most of us take for granted. When you think about the millions of organizations that provide us with goods and services, any one or more of which will probably employ you during your lifetime, how often do you explicitly consider that these organizations depend on people to make them operate? It is only under unusual circumstances, such as when the clerks go on strike at your local supermarket or the teachers walk out in your school district, that you recognize the important role that employees play in making organizations work. But how did these people come to be employees in their organizations? How were they found and selected? Why do they come to work on a regular basis? How do they know what to do on their jobs? How does management know if the employees are performing adequately? If they are not, what can be done about it? Will today's employees be prepared for the work the organization will require of them in ten, twenty, or thirty years?

These are some of the questions whose answers lie in the subject of human resource management (HRM). But before we attempt to understand how an organization should manage its human resources, we need to answer the generic question, What is management?

What is Management?

Management defined | *Management* is the process of efficiently getting activities completed with and through other people. The management process includes the planning, organizing, leading, and controlling activities that take place to accomplish objectives.

2

While an agreement on the exact definition of management has not been reached, any definition of management must include three common factors: goals, limited resources, and people. With reference to our definition, goals are the "activities completed," limited resources are implied in "efficiently," and people are those in "through other people."

First, goals are necessary because activities must be directed toward some end. There is considerable truth in the observation that "if you don't know where you're going, any road will take you there." The established goals may not be explicit, but where there are no goals, there may be a need for new managers or no need for managers at all.

Second, there are limited resources. Economic resources, by definition, are scarce; therefore, the manager is responsible for their allocation. This requires not only that managers be effective in achieving the goal or goals that are established but that they be efficient in relating output to input. They must seek a given output with a lower input than is now being used or, for a given input, strive for a greater output. Managers, then, are concerned with the attainment of goals, which makes them effective, and with the best allocation of scarce resources, which makes them efficient.

The need for two or more people is the third and last requisite for management. It is with and through people that managers perform their work. The legendary Robinson Crusoe could not become a manager until the man Friday's arrival.

In summary, managers are those who work with and through other people, allocating scarce resources, to achieve goals. If any one of these criteria is missing, there is less of a need for management.

Now let us move from the broad topic of management to the more specific topic of human resource management.

What is Human Resource Management

Human resource management defined

Human resource management (HRM) is concerned with the "people" dimension in management. Since every organization is made up of people, acquiring their services, developing their skills, motivating them to high levels of performance, and ensuring that they continue to maintain their commitment to the organization are essential to achieving organizational objectives. This is true regardless of the type of organization—government, business, education, health, recreation, or social action. Getting and keeping good people is critical to the success of every organization, whether profit or nonprofit, public or private.

Those organizations that are able to acquire, develop, stimulate, and keep outstanding workers will be both effective (able to achieve their goals) and efficient (expending the least amount of resources necessary). Those organizations that are ineffective or inefficient risk the

VIEWS IN THE NEWS

Activities Handled by Personnel Department

ACTIVITY

Personnel records/reports/information systems
EEO compliance/affirmative action
Insurance benefits administration
Unemployment compensation administration
Personnel research

Wage/salary administration
Workers' compensation administration
Job evaluation
Pre-employment testing
Promotion/transfer/separation processing

Induction/orientation
Retirement preparation programs
Health/medical services
Recruiting/interviewing/hiring
Vacation/leave processing

Pension/profit-sharing plan administration
Tuition aid/scholarships
Recreation/social/recognition programs
Complaint/disciplinary procedures
Employee assistance plan/counseling program

Human resource planning
Attitude surveys
College recruiting
Executive compensation administration
Union/labor relations

Outplacement services
Relocation services administration
Employee communications/publications
Safety programs/OSHA compliance
Performance evaluation, nonmanagement

Supervisory training
Thrift/savings plan administration
Management development
Career planning/development
Suggestion systems

Community relations/fund drives
Food services
Management appraisal/MBO
Organization development
Security measures/property protection

Stock plan administration
Skill training, nonmanagement
Productivity/motivation programs
Public relations
Payroll processing

Administrative services (mail, phone, messengers, etc.)
Library
Travel/transportation services administration
Maintenance/janitorial services

Reprinted by permission from *Bulletin to Management,* copyright 1985 by The Bureau of National Affairs, Inc., Washington, D.C.

hazards of stagnating or going out of business. Survival of an organization requires competent managers and workers coordinating their efforts toward an ultimate goal. While successful coordination cannot guarantee success, organizations that are unsuccessful in getting such coordination from managers and workers will ultimately fail!

To look at HRM more specifically, we suggest that it is a process consisting of four functions—acquisition, development, motivation, and maintenance—of human resources. In less-academic terms, we might describe these four functions as getting people, preparing them, activating them, and keeping them.

Acquisition function

The *acquisition* function begins with planning. Relative to human resource requirements, we need to know where we are going and how we are going to get there. This includes the estimating of demands and supplies of labor. Acquisition also includes the recruitment, selection, and socialization of employees.

Development function

The *development* function can be viewed along three dimensions. The first is employee training, which emphasizes skill development and the changing of attitudes among workers. The second is management development, which concerns itself primarily with knowledge acquisition and the enhancement of an executive's conceptual abilities. The third is career development, which is the continual effort to match long-term individual and organizational needs.

Motivation function

The *motivation* function begins with the recognition that individuals are unique and that motivation techniques must reflect the needs of each individual. Within the motivation function, alienation, job satisfaction, performance appraisal, behavioral and structural techniques for stimulating worker performance, the importance of linking rewards to performance, compensation and benefits administration, and how to handle problem employees are reviewed.

Maintenance function

The final function is *maintenance*. In contrast to the motivation function, which attempts to stimulate performance, the maintenance function is concerned with providing those working conditions that employees believe are necessary in order to maintain their commitment to the organization.

Within the confines of the four functions—acquisition, development, motivation, and maintenance—many changes have occurred over the years. What once was merely an activity to find a warm body to fill a vacancy has become a sophisticated process of finding, developing, and retaining the best-qualified person for the job. But this metamorphosis did not occur overnight. It is the result of many changes in management thought, society, and the workers themselves. Let us now look at this transition of personnel.

Personnel to HRM

Personnel departments were once called "Health and Happiness" departments. The people assigned to deal with personnel issues were often individuals who were past their prime. The personnel department was seen as a place where less-productive employees could be placed with minimal damage to the organization's ongoing operations. Individuals in the personnel department were perceived as those responsible for planning company picnics, vacation schedules, and retirement parties. Personnel, as an activity, was seen as a necessary, but unimportant, part of the organization.

Yet as the field of management began to mature, more emphasis was being placed on the workers. Various studies revealed that recognizing workers for the work they had done could influence their productivity (see Chapter 2). Workers were becoming more demanding in what they wanted from a job; and society, by means of laws and legislation, was placing new demands on employers. Figure 1-1 summarizes the historical events in the 1900s that have affected the changes in personnel. (Note: These events will be discussed in greater depth in Chapter 2.)

Events such as those listed in Figure 1-1 mandated changes in personnel practices. No longer could the personnel department be treated as a detour on the road to success. Organizations had to hire the best-qualified candidate without regard to race, religion, color, sex,

FIGURE 1-1

Historical Influences on Personnel: 1900–86

YEAR	HISTORICAL INFLUENCE
1900	B. F. Goodrich establishes the first employment department
1911	Frederick Taylor publishes *Principles of Professional Management*
1913	Hugo Munsterberg publishes *Psychology and Industrial Efficiency*
1931	Davis-Bacon Act
1935	National Labor Relations Act (Wagner Act)
1935	Congress of Industrial Organizations (CIO) founded
1938	Fair Labor Standards Act
1946	Employment Act
1947	Taft-Hartley Act
1959	Landrum-Griffin Act
1962	Manpower Development and Training Act
1963	Vocational Act
1963	Equal Pay Act
1964	Civil Rights Act (amended in 1972)
1964	Economic Opportunity Act
1965	Executive Order 11246 signed into law
1967	Age Discrimination in Employment Act (amended in 1978)
1970	Occupational Safety and Health Act
1971	Supreme Court rules in the *Griggs* v. *Duke Power* case
1973	Vocational Rehabilitation Act
1973	Health Maintenance Organization Act
1974	Employee Retirement Income Security Act
1974	Veteran's Readjustment Act
1978	Pregnancy Discrimination Act
1978	Civil Service Reform Act
1981	Tax Reform Act
1982	Tom Peters and Bob Waterman publish *In Search of Excellence*
1983	Job Training Partnership Act
1983	Social Security Reform Act
1986	Tax Reform Act

or national origin (see Chapter 3). The individuals hired needed to be trained to function effectively within the organization. Furthermore, once hired and trained, the organization had to provide a means of continuing the personal development of each employee. Practices were needed to ensure that these employees maintained their productive affiliation with the organization. Finally, work conditions had to be established such that the work environment induced workers to stay with the organization and simultaneously attracted new applicants to the organization.

These activities amounted to one conclusion—human resources of an organization must be managed. But what does this entail? In the next section, we will describe an HRM model and give a more specific outline of managing an organization's human resources.

HRM Model

In recent years there has been relative agreement among HRM specialists as to what constitutes the field of HRM. The model that provided the focus was developed by the American Society for Training and Development (ASTD).[1] In its study, ASTD identified nine human resource areas:

1. Training and Development
2. Organization and Development
3. Organization/Job Design
4. Human Resource Planning
5. Selection and Staffing
6. Personnel Research and Information Systems
7. Compensation/Benefits
8. Employee Assistance
9. Union/Labor Relations[2]

These nine areas have been termed spokes of the wheel in that each area impacts on the human resource outputs: quality of work life, productivity, and readiness for change.[3] Figure 1-2 is a representation of this model, and the focus of each spoke.

The outputs of this model—quality of work life, productivity, and readiness for change—warrant further exploration. Let us now take a closer look at each.

---

[1]American Society for Training and Development, *Models for Excellence* (ASTD, 1983).

[2]Ibid.

[3]Ibid.

FIGURE 1-2   Human Resource Wheel

SOURCE: American Society for Training and Development, *Models for Excellence* (ASTD, 1983), p. 23, with permission.

Quality of Work Life

Quality of work life is a multifaceted concept. The premise of quality of work life is having a work environment where an employee's activities become more important. This means implementing procedures or

Quality of work life

policies that make the work less routine and more rewarding for the employee. These procedures or policies include autonomy, recognition, belonging, progress and development, and external rewards.[4]

Autonomy deals with the amount of freedom that employees can exercise in their job. For example, if employees must get permission to purchase $2 in postage stamps to mail job-related material, the freedom to act is significantly reduced. However, in a position where employees can set their own hours, more autonomy exists. *Recognition* involves being valued by others in the company. An individual's contribution to the organization is noticed and appreciated. *Belonging* refers to being part of the organization. Closely tied to recognition, an individual who belongs to an organization is one who shares the organization's values and is regarded as being a valuable part of the firm. *Progress* and *development* refer to the "internal rewards available from the organization; challenge, and accomplishment."[5] And, finally, *external rewards*, which are usually in the form of salary and benefits but also include "promotion, rank, and status."[6]

Taken together, these components provide for the quality of work life for the individual. If the quality of work life is lacking, then worker productivity may suffer.

Productivity

Productivity

Productivity is the "quantity or volume of the major product or service that an organization provides."[7] In other words, it is the amount of work that is being produced in the organization, in terms of how much and how well. High productivity is what makes an organization thrive. Without a good product or service to sell, problems in an organization are sure to arise. Accordingly, productivity improvement programs are becoming more popular with organizations. Many components constitute the productivity factor; we can condense these components into four categories—capital investment, innovation, learning, and motivation.[8]

Capital investment includes having the best possible machinery available that will help improve the efficiency of the workers. This machinery, or equipment, can be in many forms—from robots to word processors. The concept behind capital investment is to provide the latest technologically advanced equipment that will help the workers to work smarter, not harder.

[4]Barry A. Stein, "Quality of Work Life in Action," American Management Association Management Briefing (New York, 1983), pp. 12–13.

[5]Ibid. p. 11.

[6]Ibid.

[7]Stephen P. Robbins, *Organization Theory* (Englewood Cliffs, N.J.: Prentice-Hall, 1983), p. 22.

[8]Stein, *Quality of Work Life*, pp. 10–11.

Innovation is a process whereby new and creative ideas are welcomed, studied for their feasibility, and, if feasible, implemented. Some of our better-selling products or larger cost savings have come from ideas submitted by employees. For example, the 3M Company's Post-it pad (the yellow pad with stickum on it) was developed from an idea of one of its employees, research scientist Art Fry. Fry, a singer in his church's choir, recognized the need for something to mark the pages of his hymnal so that he could easily turn to the next selection. The marking pad had to have two major attributes—it had to stick to a page and, when removed, cause no damage. As ideas for new products are being generated, they sometimes turn a problem into a success story. Art Fry, in looking for a way to find a hymnal marker, found that a batch of glue that 3M made was not up to its standards for adhesion. However, the below-standard adhesion had the properties required for his marker.

Art Fry's desire to develop a page marker has turned into a multimillion dollar product for 3M. Just about every secretary in every company in the United States uses the Post-it pad for making quick notes, attaching them to desks, phones, letters, memos, or anyplace necessary to get a message delivered.

On the cost savings side, one of the most notable employee suggestions program is the Lincoln Electric plan. This plan directs employees' efforts toward reducing operating costs and simultaneously rewards them with additional earnings. Success in the program rests on innovation, such as finding more expedient means of delivering raw materials in order to reduce the idle time associated with waiting for materials to be delivered. We will look closer at the Lincoln Electric plan in Chapter 16.

Learning looks at training issues. Not only do we want individuals to work effectively (doing the right things) but we want them to be efficient as well (doing the things right). To be effective and efficient in their work, employees must have the proper skills; and in many cases, these skills have to be taught—especially if we consider the skills needed to use a new piece of equipment.

Finally, productivity is contingent on an employee's *motivation.* The best-trained employee, one who not only has the ability but has access to the most-advanced piece of equipment, will not be productive if he or she is unwilling to be so. Attitude plays an important role as to whether an individual has the propensity to work. Accordingly, to increase productivity we must, in part, change an employee's attitude—or, in academic terms, increase his or her morale.

While productivity improvements can be achieved through a series of events—proper equipment, increased motivation—one common thread exists. That thread is a worker's ability to accept and implement changes.

Readiness for Change

Readiness for
change

If one thing in this world could be said that is always true, it would be that things will never remain the same. Change is a fact of life—in both our private and our work lives. At the work site, we must be aware that changes will occur. The change might be subtle, such as getting a new boss. Or it might be a major endeavor, such as an organization installing a computer system for the first time—automating many of the manual operations. But change rarely comes easily for everyone; in some cases, it is resisted. For example, imagine the fear that many secretaries experience when confronted by an office automation endeavor in the organization, especially the secretary who has had twenty-five years' experience. Going from a typewriter to a word processor could be traumatic and, accordingly, that change could be resisted. How do you overcome this resistance? There are a few ways, but probably the two greatest would be to inform the secretary that the word processor was designed to make her job more efficient; it was not designed to take over her job. The fear associated with a possible threat to job security could negate any advantage that might accrue by automating an office because this fear might manifest itself as decreased morale.

To reduce the fear associated with change, training is important. Once the secretary has been given time to learn how to use the new equipment, and to experience how efficient it is and how it makes her job easier, the fear of change can be reduced.

From an organizational perspective, employers must make changes to remain competitive. But it is also their responsibility to communicate the forthcoming changes to their employees, identify why the changes are necessary, and lend their total support in ensuring that the change takes place. This support can be in the form of time allowed to introduce a new system, time allowed for training, and decreased production allowed while one is in training, as well as supporting the change by budgeting monies so that the complete change can be made. Through this process, employers can create a work atmosphere that views change as a positive and progressive endeavor.

Summary

The outputs mentioned above—quality of work life, productivity, and readiness for change—are blended throughout this book. The remaining twenty-two chapters discuss the various activities involved in human resources necessary to achieve these outputs. However, before we take a closer look at what each chapter includes, let us consider the linkage between the model presented above and this text.

Linkage to Text

The HRM model shown in Figure 1-2 is generic in nature and is too broad for our purposes. Because of the interrelatedness of all the human resource functions and the impossible complexity of studying them in that state, more specificity is warranted.

To accomplish this objective, in Figure 1-3 we offer a model that represents a more manageable form.[9] This model reflects the major activities existing within the functions of acquisition, development, motivation, and maintenance.

At the hub of this model are the external influences—government regulations, labor unions, and management practice—that have an impact on HRM. Notice the overlap that these influences exhibit. As you proceed through the text, keep in mind that human resource activities in any of the four functions are constrained or guided by these external influences. The outer circles represent the flow of major activities included in HRM. There is no beginning or end to the HRM process; it is a continual process. Within each circle are the major subdivisions of each function.

It is with this model, as presented in Figure 1-3, that we constructed this book. In the following section, we will review the model further as it applies to the specific topic areas contained in the remaining chapters. The flow of the text can also be depicted as shown in Figure 1-4.

Part 1: Important Environmental Influences

Chapters 2 and 3 present important environmental influences on HRM practices—government regulations, labor unions, management practices, and Equal Employment Opportunity (EEO). It has been argued that these forces have a major impact on HRM by constraining the decision-making discretion of managers. Who can be hired and fired, how personnel information is disseminated, what methods can be used for evaluating jobs and employee performance, what equipment can and cannot be used, and how wage rates are determined are just a few of the issues that have constrained many, if not most, organizations. These environmental influences are discussed early in the book because their impact will be found repeatedly as HRM activities are being described.

Part 2: Acquisition of Human Resources

The discussion of the HRM process begins in Chapter 4 with human resource planning. It is here that management ensures that it has the right number and kinds of people, at the right places, at the right times,

---

[9]Adapted from Meg Issac Sternberg, ''Organizational Model for Human Resource Planning'' (Unpublished paper, Baltimore, 1984).

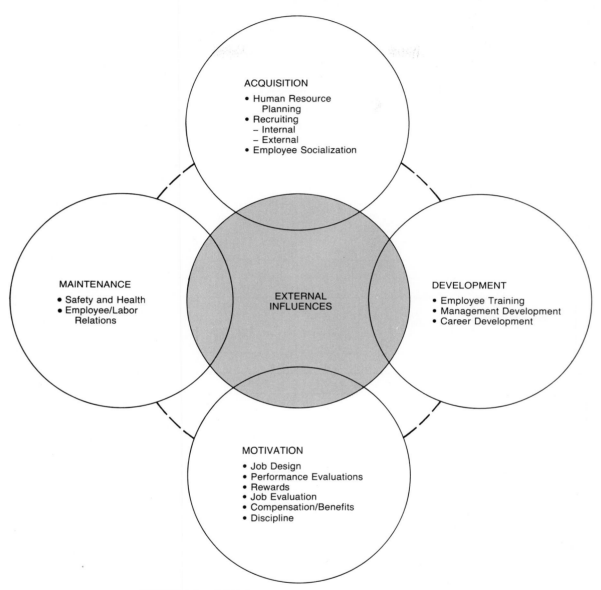

FIGURE 1-3   HRM Components

SOURCE: Adapted from Meg Isaac Sternberg, "Organizational Model for Human Resource Planning" (Unpublished paper, Baltimore, 1984).

capable of effectively and efficiently completing the work required so that the organization can achieve its overall objectives. The onset of much of the human resource planning process—job analysis—is explored further in Chapter 5.

If human resource planning uncovers the need to hire additional

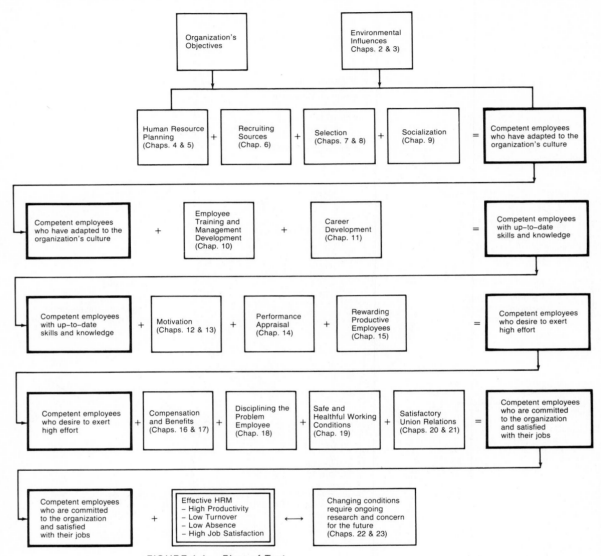

FIGURE 1-4   Flow of Text

employees, one must discover potential applicants. This requires locating candidates, the topic of Chapter 6. These potential applicants must be screened to identify job applicants who are likely to be successful if hired. This selection process is presented in Chapter 7. Specific selection devices are covered in Chapter 8.

The acquisition function is completed when the selected applicants have been placed in the organization and have adapted to the organization's culture and their work environment. The organization's culture conveys how things are done and what matters. When employees have adapted to the organization's culture, they have "learned the ropes." This adaptation process is discussed in Chapter 9, "Socializing the New Employee."

Part 3: Development of Human Resources

Competent employees will not remain competent forever. Some are minimally qualified upon entering the organization but require additional training or education. Others enter the organization capable of performing at an optimal level, but their skills become obsolete over time. And, of course, organizations change over time, and management must ensure that there is an appropriate match of individual abilities with organizational needs for the future. Each of these issues is considered in the development function.

Employee training gives individuals specific skills that they will use on the job; management development looks at practices for ensuring a continual flow of managers. These two topics—employee training and management development—are the focus of Chapter 10. Approaches to career development are presented in Chapter 11. When human resources have been developed effectively, one can expect to have competent employees with up-to-date skills and knowledge.

Part 4: Motivation of Human Resources

High performance depends on both ability and motivation. Many employees with extraordinary talents do not perform satisfactorily because they will not exert the necessary effort. Therefore, we desire to have capable employees who are also highly motivated.

If a person is to perform effectively, extrinsic factors such as job design, working conditions, job security, and supervision must be seen as satisfactory. But that alone is not enough. Many people also look for intrinsic factors such as achievement, recognition, and responsibility from their work. For individuals who place high value on intrinsic factors, the absence of these factors can reduce one's willingness to exert high degrees of effort. These topics are discussed in Chapters 12 and 13.

But other forces can influence motivation. The performance appraisal process and its outcome will affect an employee's motivation. People expect their work to be objectively evaluated. If they think their efforts will be unfairly judged, motivation will decrease. Performance appraisals, therefore, are considered in Chapter 14. Furthermore, the rewards or punishments that follow the appraisal will influence motivation. Rewards in general, and compensation administration and benefits in particular, are analyzed in Chapters 15, 16, and 17. Disciplining the problem employee and the effect of discipline on motivation are discused in Chapter 18.

At this juncture, if we have effectively motivated the individual who has up-to-date skills and knowledge, we can expect to have a competent employee who desires to exert a high level of effort.

Part 5: Maintenance of Human Resources

The objective of the last major function is to retain people who are performing at high levels. This requires that the organization provide safe and healthful working conditions (Chapter 19) and satisfactory labor relations (Chapters 20 and 21). If these activities are performed effectively, we can expect to have competent employees who are committed to the organization and satisfied with their jobs.

Part 6: Research and the Future

Since the effective management of human resources depends on refining HRM practices to changing conditions, we conclude with two chapters on the importance of managers' conducting research (Chapter 22) and keeping an eye on the future (Chapter 23). Research allows the manager to keep abreast of the latest findings in HRM and provides a framework by which solutions to unique HRM problems can be found. The last chapter looks at past trends and attempts to extend them to the end of this century. This is done in the belief that HRM is a dynamic and changing field. The successful manager will be at the forefront of these changes with new and relevant HRM practices.

SUMMARY

1. Organizations depend on people to make them operate.
2. Management is the process of getting activities completed with and through other people.
3. Human resource management (HRM) is a process consisting of the acquisition, development, motivation, and maintenance of human resources.
4. Human resource outputs are classified as quality of work life, productivity, and readiness for change.

KEY TERMS

Acquisition function
Autonomy
Development function

Human resource management
  (HRM)
Learning

Maintenance function
Management
Motivation

Motivation function
Productivity
Quality of work life

QUESTIONS FOR REVIEW

1. Contrast management, personnel, and HRM.
2. Why is the *acquisition* phase important in HRM?
3. Why is the *development* phase important in HRM?
4. Why is the *motivation* phase important in HRM?
5. Why is the *maintenance* phase important in HRM?
6. Compare a personnel department in the 1950s with one in the 1980s.
7. Identify and describe the nine areas in the ASTD HRM model. What is the focus of each?
8. Identify and describe the three HR outputs.
9. Identify and describe the major environmental influences on HRM practice.
10. What is the purpose of research with respect to HRM?

QUESTIONS FOR DISCUSSION

1. "The job of personnel manager is one that is given to an individual who has trouble performing in the mainstream of the organization's operations." Do you agree or disagree? Discuss.
2. Personnel and marketing courses are viewed as "soft" compared with accounting, finance, and statistics. Does that make personnel less relevant to business students? Discuss.
3. "A manager of marketing or production should not have to become involved in personnel activities. That is the job of the personnel department." Do you agree or disagree? Discuss.
4. In organizations in which you have worked, how have you seen the four functions of HRM being performed? Do you expect them to be consistent with those identified by your classmates? Discuss.
5. "The field of personnel changes so rapidly that it has become necessary for one to constantly review procedures and laws so that the practices will be effective and legal." Do you agree or disagree? Discuss.

CONTINUING CASE: Concord General

A New Beginning

Concord General is a 670-bed community hospital located in the Morgantown, West Virginia, metropolitan area. One of nine hospitals in the vicinity, Concord General has experienced constant growth over the past sixty years. During this period, new wings have been added to the hospital to provide a full array of health services, from cradle to grave so to speak. Currently the hospital employs nine hundred people which includes doctors, nurses, and support service personnel. The hospital has been managed by its president and CEO, Mr. John Michaels.

John Michaels is sixty years old. He has been with Concord General since 1960 and served in several capacities, such as director of hospital planning and chief financial officer, before ascending to the presidency in 1979. He has a master's degree in Finance and a similar degree in Hospital Administration. During the past three years his health has been failing, but he continues to conduct operations as if he were as young as he was on the day he became associated with the hospital.

John believed in adhering to the principles set by his predecessors. That is, good health care would be provided at all costs, services would be reasonably priced, and the necessary talent to perform these services would be hired. Concord General was progressive in its activities and sought to keep its health-care offerings current. This included purchasing new equipment whenever possible and being the forerunner in new medical techniques.

While many of these activities proved beneficial, one aspect seemed insurmountable. John Michaels, as did his predecessors, single-handedly ran the entire operation. He did the planning, the organizing, and the staffing and held a tight rein over all decision making. Anything that occurred regarding the hospital had to first clear his desk. The centralized nature of the hospital seemed to work well years ago, but lately John has been having problems, especially in the areas of motivation and employee unrest.

Being concerned about the events that had transpired, John decided to contact his longtime associate, Professor Williams, at the State University. After a discussion of the problems and a study of the organization, Professor Williams made his recommendations. Included in these recommendations were certain organizational structural changes, namely, a movement to a more functional structure (grouping similar activities together under a specific manager). The functional structure would foster the delegation of some of these activities. John agreed in part to these recommendations. He could see the benefits from having certain departments handle specific duties of the hospital and, accordingly, implemented these recommendations. There was now not only a department handling patient admission, a department handling patient billings, and an accounting department but also a marketing department. A doctor was appointed chief of medical affairs; his duties consisted of overseeing all the medical units in the hospital, such as the emergency room, the operating room, and the recovery room.

While the newly created departments appeared to be beneficial to the hospital, John Michaels refused to implement a recommendation that he delegate the personnel responsibilities. He believed that if people worked for his hospital, then he, and only he, could conduct this function. Thus a new set of problems emerged as the workers began to become more vocal about the autocratic nature of the hospital's president.

Feeling that something had to be done, John Michaels has hired you as a consultant to identify the causes of the problems and make recommendations for progressive change.

QUESTIONS

1. How would you describe the personnel function at Concord General? Discuss.
2. Prepare a list of pros and cons for John Michaels regarding the need for a human resource department. Have the pros outweighed the cons?
3. Let us suppose that John Michaels believes there is merit in your proposals but is not yet convinced that a human resource department is needed. Explain how you would persuade him that HRM is a necessity in his hospital. Describe the activities that you would recommend be included in the human resource department.

CASE APPLICATION

No More Books, No More Pencils

Paul Thomas had been teaching accounting at Parkville State College for the past four years. During that time, he had gained much respect from his students, his peers, and the college administration. He had twice been rated as one of the five best professors at Parkville State, a rating that carried with it an additional $1,000 stipend. He was active in the college, in the community, and in his own private consulting business. He had published a number of journal articles and was confident that he would be granted tenure and a promotion to full professor within three years.

In April, when the dean sent routine contract letters for the next academic year to each faculty member to sign, Paul Thomas returned his with a note saying that he would not be returning. Instead he was accepting a position in a CPA firm.

Shocked by the news, the dean called Dr. Thomas's department chairman to see why this sudden resignation had occurred. The department chairman, Mike Samuels, said that it was only a matter of time before it happened: "You see, dean, we cannot compete salary-wise with private industry. We need to make adjustments so that our salary compressions can be eliminated and those who are outstanding faculty members be encouraged to stay."

"You might be right, Mike, but we cannot go beyond our means. If we lose a few of the good ones, that is sad, but if we make concessions to keep Paul Thomas, what will that be opening us up to in the future?"

QUESTIONS

1. Describe how the four areas of HRM—acquisition, development, motivation, and maintenance—are affecting Parkville State.
2. Based on your understanding of these four HRM functions, how might they apply in the Dr. Thomas resignation case?
3. Suppose you are the dean and have just contacted Paul Thomas and have asked him to meet with you with regard to his resignation. How would you try to convince him to stay? Discuss.

ADDITIONAL READINGS

"Human Resource Managers Aren't Corporate Nobodies Anymore," *Business Week,* December 2, 1985, pp. 58–59.

MAHONEY, THOMAS A., and JOHN R. DECKOP, "Evolution of Concept and Practice in Personnel Administration/Human Resource Management," *1986 Yearly Review of the Journal of Management,* 12, No. 2 (1986), 223–41.

McDONOUGH, EDWARD F., III, "How Much Power Does HR Have, and What Can It Do to Win More?" *Personnel,* January 1986, pp. 18–25.

NURICK, AARON J., "The Paradox of Participation: Lessons from the Tennessee Valley Authority," *Human Resource Management,* 24, No. 3 (Fall 1985), 341–56.

ULRICH, DAVID O., BEVERLY A. CLARK, and LARRY DILLON, "Blue Cross of California: Human Resources in a Changing World," *Human Resource Management,* 24, No. 1 (Spring 1985), 69–80.

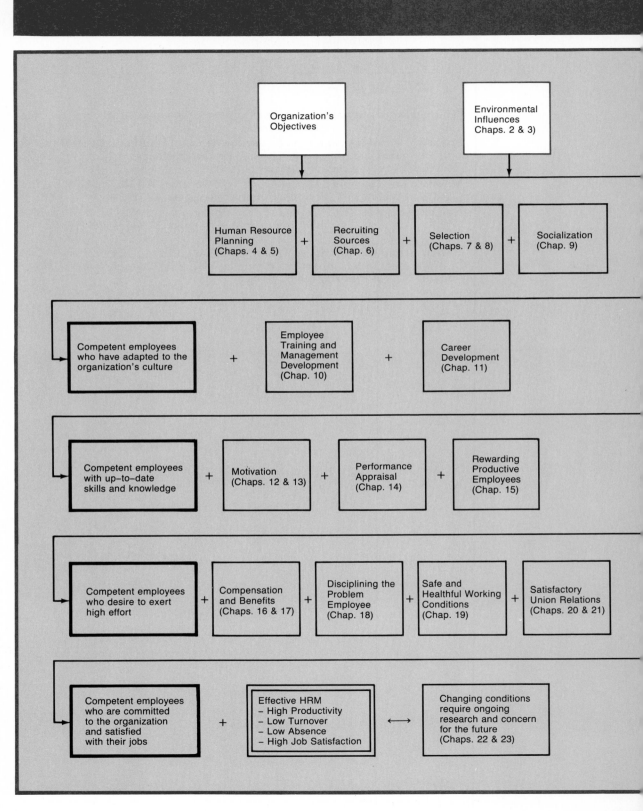

PART ONE

= Competent employees
who have adapted to the
organization's culture

= Competent employees
with up-to-date
skills and knowledge

= Competent employees
who desire to exert
high effort

= Competent employees
who are committed
to the organization
and satisfied
with their jobs

IMPORTANT ENVIRONMENTAL INFLUENCES

CHAPTER 2

Important

Environmental Influences

AFTER READING THIS CHAPTER, YOU WILL BE ABLE TO:

1. Identify the three major environmental influences on HRM
2. Describe the historical evolution of each environmental influence through four periods
3. Explain how the environmental influences have constrained HRM practices

When I want to understand what is happening today or try to decide what will happen tomorrow, I look back.

—Oliver Wendell Holmes, Jr.

Introduction

A large department store chain has decided to change its image. From a store that catered to the over-fifty population, the store's management has decided to focus on the under-thirty age group. In changing to its new "young and contemporary" image, the store has fired all of its older employees with no explanation, no severance pay, nor any right to their pensions. Some of the fired workers had almost twenty-five years of service with the store. Can department stores do this? No, not now; but in the 1950s, they could have, and some did!

The discussion in Chapter 1 focused on the model of HRM. This portrayal of the HRM functions as they exist today reflects a significant change since its primitive beginnings in the latter part of the 1930s. The external forces influencing much of the change can be reviewed from three perspectives: government regulation, labor relations, and management practice. To give you the background on how the concepts in HRM developed and to demonstrate how the three perspectives shaped many of the current theories and practices, the remainder of this chapter will explore HRM's historical evolution. We will look at these areas from four time periods: prior to 1932; 1932–46; 1946–70; and 1970 and beyond.

Government Regulation

Prior to 1932

The American economic system developed around the philosophy of a free and competitive market, laissez faire. Such a system implied the production and distribution of goods and services with an absence of regulation.[1] Government's role in the marketplace was expected to be

---

[1]Mitchell S. Novit, *Essentials of Personnel Management* (Englewood Cliffs, N.J.: Prentice-Hall, 1979), p. 21.

minimal, since a market free from external influences would be most efficient. These views dominated for over 150 years.

Free market philosophy

A free market philosophy meant that employers could hire, promote, and fire whom they wanted. Managers, who in business firms were usually also the owners, were all-powerful. They could, and often did, fire employees merely because they didn't like their looks. This power of management was further increased in the early 1900s because the many workers wanted jobs, and most of them were unskilled. The result was a labor force that was highly interchangeable and one that had little bargaining influence with management. When employees exist in large numbers, each anxious to hold a full-time job, and where an employee can easily be replaced with little cost to the employer, one should not be surprised to find worker exploitation. And this was prevalent during this period.

Prior to the early 1930s, employers were relatively free from outside influence when dealing with their employees. It is said to be "relatively free" because one can find instances of government influence, but it is of minor consequence. In the early 1800s, for instance, some states passed legislation that specified a minimum level of education for working children and limited the number of hours that they could work. And in the early 1900s, many states began to enact legislation requiring employers to insure workers against job-related injuries or death regardless of whether it was the employer's or the employee's fault. For the most part, however during the period ranging from the late 1700s to the middle 1930s, employers were generally free from outside interference in the management of their human resources.

1932–46

The end of the laissez-faire government can be traced to the impact of the 1930s. The "free" market approach had failed to create an economic system that could control the wild boom-bust cycles of the economy. The Great Depression was only one of many depressions. The "free" market didn't seem able to manage the economy into some equilibrium position that was stable. The Great Depression, along with the philosophical beliefs of Franklin Delano Roosevelt and his overwhelming success with Congress in getting his ideas turned into new legislation, provided the impetus for restructuring the labor force.

The Great Depression put more than one-quarter of the American labor force out of work. President Roosevelt did not believe that business alone could provide the stimulus to rejuvenate the economy. Such a posture would be too slow and uncertain. Roosevelt's answer was to use the federal government's resources to significantly increase the stimulus. While such an approach would certainly have been politically unacceptable a decade earlier, it met with little opposition. The American people and their legislators wanted a quick solution to the

Depression and therefore willingly supported the idea of a dramatically increased role for government in our economy.

Civilian Conservation Corps

Federal Emergency Relief Act

National Industrial Recovery Act

In quick succession, Congress established the Civilian Conservation Corps to put some of the unemployed to work on public projects; passed the Federal Emergency Relief Act, which required Washington to fund state-run welfare programs, and passed the National Industrial Recovery Act, the first major effort by the federal government to plan and regulate the economy and to establish collective bargaining and wage and hour regulations. But these actions were just the beginning. Legislation followed to prohibit unfair labor practices by employers and to establish our Social Security system.

The prosperity and optimism following World War II brought a reduction in government's involvement in personnel and labor relations matters. Although the frantic enactment of legislation that characterized the 1930s subsided, the commitment was made to a new era where there was a different relationship between government and business.

President Roosevelt's New Deal approach to reduce much of the distress of the Depression revealed renewed humanism and progressive legislation that affected the future of human resource programs in organizations.

1946–70

Employment Act of 1946

The governmental regulation continued with the Employment Act of 1946 and its statement that the federal government was committed to the protection of adequate job opportunities. While the act provided neither regulatory nor monitoring agencies, it indicated that the federal government was committed to taking actions necessary to maintain employment at high levels:

> The Act in effect pledged all future administrations to take an active role in economic affairs. It provided congressional sanction for a different role for government from the early philosophy of laissez-faire and it helped build the climate that would eventually result in such recent legislation as that dealing with equal employment opportunity.[2]

The unique feature of this period was the broad expansion of government intervention into every organization's HRM programs.

The transition continued throughout the 1950s. However, it would be the Kennedy and Johnson administrations in the 1960s that would accelerate the federal government's efforts to facilitate equal employment opportunities. The government was to accept the responsibility for ensuring that individuals had the skills to fit into the economic

[2]Ibid., p. 23.

mainstream. To facilitate this meant that the government would mount and run effective and massive training programs, people would show up willingly to be trained, and opportunities (i.e., jobs) would exist for the graduates of the programs. These new efforts meant that both private-and public-sector managers would have to understand and adjust to a myriad of new laws and regulations.

Manpower Development and Training Act

In 1962, the Manpower Development and Training Act (MDTA) was passed. This act established a three-year program for the training and retraining of unemployed workers and workers whose jobs were threatened because of automation and other technological advances. Two other manpower acts passed in the early 1960s had implications for employee development—the Vocational Education Act of 1963 and the Economic Opportunity Act of 1964. The former provided greatly increased support for education designed to prepare students for gainful employment in a broad selection of occupations. The latter act, which launched Lyndon Johnson's "War on Poverty" program, contained provisions with emphasis on training and work experience, especially for the young whose unemployment rates were in many cases triple those of older and more-experienced workers. The Economic Opportunity Act established a new job corps to provide basic education, training, and work in urban residential centers and rural conservation camps for unemployed youth in the sixteen to twenty-one age group; a work-training program to provide job experience for youths who drop out of school or need the incentive or financial assistance of this work to complete their high-school education; and a work-study program to help college students continue their education.

Vocational Education Act
Economic Opportunity Act

Civil Rights Act

Of all the laws passed during this period, none is more noteworthy than the Civil Rights Act of 1964. This act was probably the single most important piece of legislation during the 1960s in terms of affecting the reduction of discrimination. It is divided into a number of parts, or titles, each dealing with a particular facet of discrimination. For HRM purposes, Title VII is especially relevant.

Title VII prohibits discrimination in hiring, compensation, and terms, conditions, or privileges of employment based on race, religion, color, sex, or national origin. It covers companies, labor organizations, and employment agencies. Most important, it went further than merely stipulating that employers were to stop discriminatory practices. They were also supposed to actively recruit and give preference to minority group members in regard to hiring and other conditions of employment.

E.O. 11246

In the years between 1964 and 1972, there continued to be new laws and executive orders that sought to further fair employment practices. In 1965, President Johnson issued Executive Order 11246, which prohibited discrimination on the basis of race, religion, color, or national origin by federal agencies, as well as by contractors and subcontractors who worked under federal contracts. This was fol-

E.O. 11375   lowed in 1967 by Executive Order 11375, which added sex-based discrimination to the above criteria. Both of these executive orders are currently enforced by the Office of Federal Contract Compliance programs. Also in 1967, Congress passes the Age Discrimination in Employment Act. This act protected employees who are forty to sixty-five years of age (expanded to seventy years of age in 1979; uncapped in 1986) from discrimination unless the employer can demonstrate that age is a bona fide occupational qualification for the job in question. Compliance with this act is administered by the Equal Employment Opportunity Commission.

Age Discrimination Act

E.O. 11478   In 1969, President Richard Nixon issued Executive Order 11478 to supersede part of Executive Order 11246. It stated that employment practices in the federal government must be based on merit and must prohibit discrimination based on race, color, religion, sex, national origin, political affiliation, marital status, or physical handicap.

These antidiscrimination laws will be examined in Chapter 3.

VIEWS IN THE NEWS

Executive Order Options

Unable to agree on how to proceed with a revision of Executive Order 11246, President Reagan's advisers decide to offer him three options for setting his policy on federal contractors' affirmative action responsibilities.

The action is the latest in a series of events that began with a proposed revision to the executive order, prepared by some of the President's advisers in August, that would have banned the use of goals and timetables by federal contractors attempting to fulfill their EEO responsibilities (*FEP Summary*, August 22, 1985, page 24). Since that revision surfaced, several other draft proposals with modified language have been circulated, but no agreement has been reached (*FEP Summary*, Oct. 3, 1985, page 40, and Oct. 17, page 43).

The three options, agreed to at a meeting of the President's Domestic Policy Council, are:

- To issue a revised executive order that would allow contractors to set goals and timetables for employing minorities and women, as long as the goals do not discriminate, but that also would specify that nothing in the order may be interpreted as providing a legal basis for goals;
- To make no change to the existing executive order, but to issue new OFCCP regulations; and
- To issue a new executive order that would prohibit quotas and to promulgate new regulations that would deal with any problems in OFCCP enforcement.

1970 and Beyond

OSHA

The increasing number of accidents during the 1960s and the growing interest in environmental improvements gave rise to the passage of the Occupational Safety and Health Act (OSHA) in 1970. The act provided for various kinds of standards and aims to ensure safe and healthy working conditions for employees who had previously been inadequately covered by state safety legislation. The act also included stiff penalties and enforcement procedures to ensure complicance. Additionally, violators of the act could be imprisoned for certain violations. (We will take a closer look at OSHA in Chapter 19.)

Griggs v. Duke Power

One of the most important legal rulings affecting selection procedures occurred in 1971—the case of *Griggs* v. *Duke Power Company.* In the *Griggs* decision, the U.S. Supreme Court adopted the interpretive guidelines set out under Title VII, that is, tests must fairly measure the knowledge or skills required in a job in order not to discriminate unfairly against minorities. This action, single-handedly, made invalid any employment test or diploma requirement that disqualified blacks at a substantially higher rate than whites (even when this was not intended) if this differentiation could not be shown to be job related.

The *Griggs* decision had even wider implications. It made most intelligence and conceptual tests used in hiring illegal unless there was direct empirical evidence that the tests employed were valid. This crucial decision placed the burden of proof on the employer. It is now the responsibility of the employer to provide adequate support that any test used does not discriminate on the basis of non-job-related characteristics. For example, if an employer requires all applicants to take an IQ test, and the results of that test will be used in making the hiring decision, the burden of proof is on the employer to substantiate that individuals with higher scores outperform on the job those individuals with lower scores.

Note that nothing in the Court's decision precludes the use of testing or measuring procedures. What it did was to place the burden of proof on management to demonstrate, if challenged, that the tests used provided a reasonable measure of job performance.

Equal Employment Opportunity Act

In 1972, the Equal Employment Opportunity Act (EEOA) was passed, which provided a series of major amendments to Title VII of the Civil Rights Act. Probably of greatest consequence, the Equal Employment Opportunity Commission (EEOC) was given authority to effectively prohibit all forms of employment discrimination based on race, religion, color, sex, or national origin. The EEOC now had the power to file civil suits against organizations if the commission was unable to secure an acceptable resolution of discrimination charges within thirty days of its filing. The EEOC also expanded Title VII coverage to encompass employees of state and local governments, employees of educational institutions, and employers or labor organizations with fifteen or more employees or members (previously the law had covered only firms with twenty-five or more employees.

CETA

In 1973, the Comprehensive Employment and Training Act (CETA) passed, amending the Manpower Development and Training Act of 1962. In 1979 alone, CETA provided 725,000 public jobs, costing nearly $12 billion to operate. CETA lasted until 1982. Its success, at best, is questionable, for only a few people were permanently placed in organizations.

Legislation also passed to eliminate discrimination against handicapped people, protect and promote the rights of veterans, protect an individual's retirement, and extend the age for mandatory retirement.

Vocation Rehabilitation Act

The Vocational Rehabilitation Act of 1973 extended to the disabled the same protections afforded to racial minorities and women. The act requires companies receiving $2,500 or more annually in federal contracts to take affirmative action to recruit, employ, and advance all qualified handicapped individuals, including the making of reasonable accommodations to the physical and mental limitations of handicapped employees.

Veterans Readjustment Act

Congress has been concerned with the rights of veterans since World War II. There have been many Selective Service acts, and they reaffirm the right of a veteran to be hired into a former job or a similar position. More recently, the Veterans' Readjustment Act of 1974 specifically provided for employment opportunities for veterans of the Vietnam War.

ERISA

The Employee Retirement Income Security Act (ERISA) was passed in 1974. The purpose of the act was to deal with the largest problem posed by private pension plans—people were not getting their benefits. The design of private pension plans had almost always required a minimum tenure with the organization before the individual was guaranteed a right to pension benefits. Typically, employees had to be with the organization ten or more years before they gained a permanent right (called vesting) to those benefits, and in some cases, the only way employees could get their pensions was to stay until retirement. In the latter situation, an employee with twenty-five years' service who was discharged at the age of sixty would have no rights to pension benefits. The intent of ERISA was to correct these inconsistent and sometimes arbitrary practices. (We will revisit ERISA in Chapter 18.)

Albemarle Paper Company decision

In 1975, the Supreme Court decision in the case of *Albemarle Paper Company* v. *Moody* clarified the methodological requirements for using and validating tests in selection. Four black employees challenged their employer's use of tests for selecting candidates from the unskilled labor pool for promotion into skilled jobs. The Court endorsed the EEOC guidelines by noting that Albemarle's selection methodology was defective because (1) the tests had not been used solely for jobs on which they had previously been validated; (2) the tests were validated for upper-level jobs alone but were used for entry-level jobs; (3) subjective supervisory ratings were used for validating the tests, but the ratings had not been done with care; and (4) the tests had been validated on a group of job-experienced, white workers, whereas the tests were given to young inexperienced, and often nonwhite, candidates.

Age Discrimination Act

Possibly one of the most far-reaching pieces of legislation was the 1978 set of amendments to the Age Discrimination Act of 1967. The new bill outlawed the widespread practice of requiring workers to retire at the age of sixty-five. Under this law, most workers were not required to retire until they reach the age of seventy. (In 1986, this 70 age cap was eliminated, meaning there is now no mandatory retirement age.) Coverage of this act is widespread. It includes workers in private firms that have more than nineteen employees and nearly all state and local government workers except police officers and firefighters. The law eliminates, altogether, mandatory retirement based on age for most employees of the federal government.

Steelworkers v. Weber

The Supreme Court's decision (1979) in the case of the *United Steelworkers of America* v. *Weber* appears to have important implications for organizational training and development practices and for the larger issue of reverse discrimination. In 1974, Kaiser Aluminum and the United Steelworkers Union set up a temporary training program for higher-paying skilled trade jobs, such as electrician and repairer, at a Kaiser plant in Louisiana. Brian Weber, a white employee at the plant, who was not selected for the training program, sued on the grounds that he had been illegally discriminated against. He argued that blacks with less seniority were selected over him to attend the training due solely to their race. The question facing the Court was, Is it fair to discriminate against whites in order to help blacks who have been longtime victims of discrimination? The justices said that employers can choose to give special job preference to blacks without fear of being harassed by reverse discrimination suits brought by other employees. The ruling was a strong endorsement of voluntary affirmative action efforts—goals and timetables for bringing an organization's minority and female work force up to the percentages they represent in the available labor pool. Organizations can use this decision to justify giving special preference for jobs to blacks so as to correct racial imbalances in their work force without fear of being challenged in the courts.

Job Partnership Act

The Job Training Partnership Act of 1983 (which amended the 1973 Comprehensive Employment and Training Act) focuses on the issues of unemployment and underemployment. Its purpose, similar to the training acts before it, is to provide services for the economically disadvantaged individual. Through services such as training (provided at the federal, state, and local levels), disadvantaged individuals are helped to become more self-supporting.

A last point should be made before we move on. We have discussed only public policy actions by the federal government. In addition to the legislation and executive orders at the federal level, most states have laws similar to Title VII of the Civil Rights Act and additional legislation that affects local hiring and promotion policies. While we have not discussed these because of their number and diversity, you should be aware that there is another level of government that affects HRM practices.

FIGURE 2-1

Summary of Major Government Regulations

PERIOD	REGULATION	IMPACT
Prior to 1932	"Free" Market Philosophy	Employers could hire, fire, promote whom they wanted
1932–46	Civilian Conservation Corps	Put unemployed workers to work on public projects
	Federal Emergency Relief Act	Federal funding of state-run welfare programs
	National Industrial Recovery Act	Plan to regulate the economy; establish collective bargaining and wage and hour regulations
1946–70	Employment Act of 1946	Federal government commitment to the protection of adequate job opportunities
	Manpower Development and Training Act (1962)	Training and retraining unemployed and underemployed individuals
	Vocational Education Act of 1963	Support for education designed to prepare students for gainful employment
	Economic Opportunity Act of 1964	Emphasis on training and work experience for the young
	Civil Rights Act of 1964	Title VII prohibits discrimination in hiring, compensation and terms, conditions or privileges of employment based on race, religion, color, sex, or national origin
	Executive Order (E.O.) 11246	Prohibits discrimination on the basis of race, religion, color, and national origin, by federal agencies as well as those working under federal contracts

FIGURE 2-1 continued

PERIOD	REGULATION	IMPACT
1946–70	Executive Order 11375	Added sex-based discrimination to E.O. 11246
	Age Discrimination Act of 1967	Protects employees 40–65 years of age from discrimination
	Executive Order 11478	Amended part of E.O. 11246, stated practices in the federal government must be based on merit; also prohibits discrimination based on political affiliation, marital status, or physical handicap
1970 and Beyond	Occupational Safety and Health Act of 1970	Ensures safe and healthy working conditions for employees
	Griggs v. *Duke Power* decision	Tests must fairly measure the knowledge or skills required for a job; also validity of tests
	Equal Employment Opportunity Act	Empowered the EEOC to file suits against organizations that discriminate; expanded coverage of Title VII to include state and local governments, employees of educational institutions, and employers and labor organizations with 15 or more employees
	Comprehensive Employment and Training Act (1973)	Amended MDTA
	Vocational Rehabilitation Act of 1973	Extended to the disabled the same protection afforded to racial minorities and women
	Veterans Readjustment Act of 1974	Provided for equal employment opportunities for the Vietnam War veterans
	Employee Retirement and Income Security Act of 1974	Protection of employees' pensions
	Albermarle Paper Company decision	Clarified requirements for using and validating tests in selection
	Age Discrimination Act of 1978	Increased mandatory retirement age from 65 to 70
	United Steelworkers v. *Weber* decision	Endorsement of voluntary affirmative action efforts for bringing an organization's minority and female work force up to the percentages they represent in the available labor pool
	Job Training Partnership Act of 1983	Amended CETA

Labor Relations

Prior to 1932

The first labor unions were formed in America in the 1780s with the objective of increasing the workers' wages. But their growth in the early and middle 1800s was almost completely blocked by the courts' view of unionism. The courts followed England's precedent-setting criminal conspiracy doctrine. This doctrine proposed that any attempt by workers to band together with the objective of negotiating with an employer was illegal.

Commonwealth v.
Hunt

In 1842, however, a Massachusetts State court said in its decision in *Commonwealth* v. *Hunt* that a union was not illegal in and of itself. While this decision did not legalize the means of achieving unionization, the decision was important for not applying the doctrine to a labor matter. Even so, it would take nearly a hundred more years before unions would be fully recognized as legitimate collective-bargaining agents in dealing with management.

While the decision to not enforce the criminal conspiracy doctrine may have provided some hope for the workers, the hope was stifled by downturns in the economic cycle. In periods of recession or depression, workers were quick to drop their union affiliation, and any power that might accrue through coalition was overridden by fears of layoffs and unemployment.

The last quarter of the nineteenth century revealed the rapid growth of the factory system and the development of large industrial empires. As industries expanded, the formation of unions was sought to maintain a balance. In 1869, the Knights of Labor, a federation of local trade assemblies, was founded to achieve gains for workers through educational and political means. It grew to seven hundred thousand members by 1886, yet it failed in the late 1880s as a result of strike defeats and the collapse of its efforts to achieve an eight-hour workday. In this same period, however, the American Federation of Labor (AFL) was formed. The AFL was organized in 1886 with practical rather than idealistic objectives. While the Knights of Labor emphasized social reform, the AFL pressed ahead on bread-and-butter issues; essentially, wages and benefits. As a federation of craft unions—that is, unions that bring together closely related occupations and cut across many companies and industries—the AFL's major success was holding together during the depression of 1893.

AFL

The twentieth century began with the emergence of welfare secretaries to stem the growth of trade unionism. Welfare secretaries were supposed to assist workers by suggesting improvements in working conditions, housing, medical care, educational facilities, and recreation. These secretaries, who were the forerunners of the personnel manager, acted as a buffer between the organization and its employees.

In the period prior to World War I, the union movement could only be described as young and lacking broad base support. In 1916, for example, union membership totaled approximately 3 million. The prosperity of the war period swelled membership to nearly 6 million only four years later.

Any discussion of the modern union movement would probably begin with World War I and the favorable conditions it created for union development. The AFL supported President Woodrow Wilson's administration during the war and, in return, was allowed the right to organize and bargain collectively without government interference. After the war, however, these concessions were withdrawn. The rapid inflation of the 1920s brought about numerous strikes and increased antiunion sentiment. The 1920–22 depression hit unionized efforts hard, reducing membership rolls by approximately 30 percent. Once the recession had weathered, and the prosperity of the 1920s had accelerated, workers felt less inclined to join unions, and membership levels were generally stagnant.

At the start of the Great Depression in the early 1930s, management held an overwhelming advantage over unions. The legal environment was almost totally on management's side. Management could fire workers for joining unions, force them to sign a pledge not to join a union as a condition of employment, require them to belong to company unions, and spy on them to cut off any antagonistic union-organizing effort before it began.

Consistent with prior economic setbacks, the Depression resulted in a decline of union membership.

1932–46

Norris-LaGuardia Act

By 1932, union membership had declined to approximately 3 million. But legislation was beginning to be enacted that would change the public policy toward unionism. In 1932, the passage of the Norris-LaGuardia Act began to change how the courts acted in labor disputes. Norris-LaGuardia opened the door for allowing picketing and other union economic tactics against the employer. And, quite important, Norris-LaGuardia set the stage for permitting individuals full freedom to designate a representative of their own choosing to negotiate their terms and conditions of employment.

Wagner Act

Although this act served a major purpose in stimulating union growth, it did not constrain certain activities by the employers to fight union efforts. It was not until 1935, with the passage of the Wagner Act, that these activities by employers were curtailed. This piece of federal legislation was the most potent of any labor legislation that had ever been passed up to that time.

NLRB

The Wagner Act recognized unions as being authorized representatives of workers, able to bargain collectively with employers in the interests of their union members. The act also established the National Labor Relations Board, an organization that sets up the process for and conducts representation elections. The act further required employers to "bargain in good faith" and developed provisions for addressing unfair labor practices by the employer.

The Wagner Act legitimized the role of trade unions and gave much power to those unions. This act undoubtedly sparked the rapid growth in union membership for the next dozen years.

CIO

The year 1935 also marked the founding of the Congress of Industrial Organizations (CIO). The CIO was a federation of national unions having an industrial structure. In contrast to the AFL, the CIO included all workers from particular companies and industries, regardless of their occupation. The CIO's success was almost instantaneous. By 1937 it had 3.7 million members compared with the AFL's 3.5 million. The CIO sought unskilled industrial workers, signing up everyone in an industry. The existence of both the AFL and the CIO would prove to be a positive force in the rapidly expanding union movement.

1946–70

Taft-Hartley Act

To offset a pendulum that had swung too far *in favor of organized labor,* the Labor-Management Relations Act (also known as the Taft-Hartley Act) was passed in 1947 to amend the Wagner Act and prevent "unfair labor practices" on the part of unions. In contrast to the Wagner Act, which sought to protect the worker's right to join a union, the Taft-Hartley Act sought to protect the worker's right not to join a union and to protect employers from unfair labor practices. The act outlawed requiring employers to hire only union members; authorized the federal government to seek an injunction preventing any work stoppage for eighty days in a strike that was defined as imperiling the nation's health and welfare; prohibited unions from using union funds in connection with national elections; required union officers to swear that they were not members of the Communist party; required unions to file financial statements with the Department of Labor and with their membership; and authorized states to pass right-to-work laws, which make it illegal for any collective-bargaining agreement to contain clauses calling for compulsory union membership.

AFL–CIO

In 1955, the AFL and the CIO merged, creating the strongest federation of labor that had been experienced at any time before in U.S. labor history. But with its size also came its problems. Corruption had set in. Some of the largest unions during the period were being investigated by the U.S. Senate Labor Committee. The result of the investigations and subsequent congressional hearings was the passage of

Landrum-Griffin Act

the Landrum-Griffin Act, or the Labor and Management Reporting and Disclosure Act, in 1959. While the act contained many provisions, its thrust was to require all unions to disclose their financial statements. Similar to the Security and Exchange Commission requiring business organizations to file a 10–K report, the Landrum-Griffin Act requires all unions to file an LM–2 with the Department of Labor.

For the remainder of the period, union membership continued to grow. But it was increasing at a decreasing rate. From its peak of some 35 percent of the nonfarm work force, there was a steady decline in membership to just above 25 percent. While the percentage of the nonfarm work force that was unionized declined, this was primarily due to the increase in the labor force itself.

1970 and Beyond

There has been a continual decline not only in the percentage of the work force unionized but also in the absolute number of workers unionized. What has produced this phenomenon?

The answer to labor's stagnating union membership is not easily answered. The following hypotheses have been proposed: (1) The union movement is no longer a young, radical "cause." Unions have been victimized by their own success. Members no longer view themselves as the downtrodden. Most are middle-class citizens, more concerned with their taxes than with ideological issues or gaining legislation that will favor the union movement. (2) The most rapid growth in employment has occurred in white-collar and professional jobs, especially in government and among female workers, whereas union strength was traditionally built around appealing to and organizing male factory workers. The past twenty years have been characterized by growth in the wholesale and retail trade, service industries, and white-collar jobs, such as computer programmer. These are jobs in which unions have not focused their organizing efforts. Similarly, the rapid movement of women into the job market has hurt the union movement. Career-minded women, like white-collar workers generally, tended to identify with management goals rather than union goals. As one union executive concluded, "We have to get rid of the old baseball bat, T-shirt, tattooed image." (3) Unions have been adversely affected by the geographical shift in jobs to the Sunbelt. Union strongholds were in heavy industry that was substantially located in the Northeast and Middle West. The 1970s were characterized by thousands of jobs moving to the so-called right-to-work states (see Chapter 20). New and relocated businesses engaged in automobile, electric, furniture, glass, rubber, paint, and steel manufacturing have gone to the relatively nonunionized South or, in some cases, to foreign countries, where a history of low wages prevails.

It can be argued that the changing labor force, along with the growth in service industries and the shift of employment to the Sunbelt, represents new phenomena that lie outside the traditional scope of the union movement. Ironically, the original objectives of unions—to protect the worker from arbitrary abuse by employers and to provide a living wage and reasonable job security—when generally achieved for society as a whole, have undermined the union movement. So, paradoxically, one of the major problems that the union movement must confront is its own success. When an organization is successful in attaining its objectives, it must redefine itself and assume new directions. The March of Dimes, for example, whose objective was to find a cure for polio, redefined itself when this end was met so that its new direction would include other ailments, particularly birth defects. If the union movement is to resume its growth, it must likewise clarify its goal after determining the present needs of the work force and what functions the union movement can perform toward satisfying those needs.

One positive aspect for unions during this period was the growth of membership in the public sector. The relationship between the federal government and unions representing its employees was formally legislated in 1978 by the Civil Service Reform Act. Although the act prohibited unions from striking or making demands in the economic and staffing areas, it did two important things. First, it established the Federal Labor Relations Authority (FLRA) to monitor labor-mangement relations in the federal government. This unit would be the counterpart of the NLRB for the public sector. Second, the act required arbitration of unresolved contract grievances and made arbitration decisions binding on both labor and management.

The 1980s have witnessed even further decline in unions and in their power. Maybe this is most visible in concessionary bargaining, with workers "giving back" some of their gains from previous pacts. (For further discussion of this phenomenon, see Chapter 21.)

Management Practice

Prior to 1932

Prior to the twentieth century, there were unorganized and sporadic efforts at improving the management of people at work. In some instances, personnel specialists' positions were established in private industry to assist with hiring, safety, training, and health issues. However, these specialists were few, probably not encompassing more than several dozen firms in the United States.

The Industrial Revolution, which was well under way in the northeastern United States by 1870, initiated the movement of jobs away from homes and small shops to large factories. With the amalgamation of large numbers of people under one roof, there developed

FIGURE 2-2

Summary of Labor Relations

PERIOD	ACTIVITY	IMPACT
Prior to 1932	First labor unions formed circa 1780	
	Commonwealth v. *Hunt* decision in 1842	Unions not illegal in and of themselves; Criminal Conspiracy Doctrine not enforced
	Knights of Labor formed in 1869	
	American Federation of Labor formed in 1886	
	Emergence of Welfare Secretaries circa 1900	
1932–46	Passage of Norris-LaGuardia Act in 1932	Allowed employees freedom to choose representatives
	Passage of Wagner Act in 1935	Established the NLRB; required employers to bargain in good faith; identified employer unfair labor practices
	Congress of Industrial Organizations formed in 1935	
1946–70	Passage of Taft-Hartley Act in 1947	Protected workers' right not to join a union; identified union unfair labor practices
	American Federation of Labor and Congress of Industrial Organizations merge to form the AFL–CIO	
	Passage of Landrum-Griffin Act in 1959	Required unions to disclose their financial statements
1970 and beyond	Decline of unionized work force	
	Emergence of right-to-work states	
	Growth of unions in the public sector	

a greater need for planning, recruitment, selection, and placement. These activities were rarely formally instituted.

In 1900, however, B. F. Goodrich established the first employment department, but its responsibilities consisted only of hiring. Two years later, the National Cash Register Company established the first comprehensive labor department responsible for wage administration, grievances, employment and working conditions, health conditions, record keeping, and worker improvement.

Between 1910 and 1920, the placement theme "The right man in the right job" became familiar and popular. And it was during this same period that one of the most important movements in management was taking place: scientific management. The year 1911 marked the publication of Frederick W. Taylor's *Principles of Scientific Management.*

Scientific management

Taylor, an industrial engineer, advocated separate responsibilities for workers and management. It was management's responsibility to plan and the worker's responsibility to execute. Utilizing time studies toward the scientific determination of a proper job design, Taylor proposed methods and standards for performing each job, for training and supervising employees in the proper use of tools and equipment, and for evaluating each worker's performance. However, he had gone on record in 1903 about his belief in the uniqueness of each worker:

> *No system of management, however good, should be applied in a wooden way. The proper personal relations should always be maintained between the employers and men.*[3]

Taylor's philosophy that management should be viewed as a science strongly emphasized the importance of proper job selection, placement, and training so as to take maximum advantage of each employee's potential contribution.

During the same period, the impact of the social sciences was evident. The year 1913 marked the publication of Hugo Munsterberg's *Psychology and Industrial Efficiency.* This book ushered in the science of industrial psychology. Munsterberg and other industrial psychologists were able to make suggestions and improve methods of employment testing, training, performance evaluation, and job efficiency.

Industrial psychology

The outbreak of World War I brought about several new developments. The U.S. Army began to use tests on a large scale for selecting officers. Also, the war brought about an increase in apprenticeship training and the institution of widespread on-the-job training programs in factories.

By the early 1920s, employee counseling, paid holidays, vacations, and sick leave were evident. In the mid-1920s, objective systems for determining hourly wage rates were developed.

By the mid-1920s, because of successes that the U.S. Army had had with its personnel programs and because of the general economic prosperity in the nation, many businesses added personnel departments. In the late 1920s, a group of studies that would eventually have a major impact on personnel practices were beginning at the Hawthorne plant of the Western Electric Company, just outside of Chicago. These Hawthorne studies, which ran for nearly a decade, fostered the human relations movement. Emotional factors were found to influ-

Hawthorne studies

[3]Frederick W. Taylor, *Shop Management* (New York: Harper and Row, 1903), p. 184.

ence productivity to a greater extent than logical factors. The researchers found that informal work groups had a significant impact on worker productivity. Group standards and sentiments were more important determinants of a worker's output than the wage incentive plan. Results of the Hawthorne studies justified many of the paternalistic programs that personnel managers had instituted in their organizations. Personnel managers could point to these studies to defend and justify such benefits as good working conditions, as well as to support their contention that every manager must be concerned with human relations. Note that although there has been much criticism during the past decade regarding the conclusions drawn from the Hawthorne studies, this has in no way diminished the significance of the opinions they represent in the development of the field of human resource management. Whether founded or not, the conclusions of the Hawthorne studies rang the bell in American industry.

The Great Depression of the 1930s revealed the first major retrenchment in the growth of human resource activities. Since most of the expansion during the first quarter of the century had taken place within the maintenance function, these amenities were most vulnerable to cost-cutting efforts. Many benefits that grew out of the benevolent paternalism of the 1920s were eliminated. Although there had always been pressures to reduce costs and eliminate nonproductive activities, the 1930s were characterized by extensive efforts toward this end. Many of the paternalistic programs, which would have been difficult to justify in cost-benefit terms during prosperous times, became highly suspect and expendable as the United States incurred one of its worst economic depressions.

1932–46

The major influence on HRM practices during 1932–46 was undoubtedly World War II. Again, as during World War I, major studies were made in selection procedures and training methods. Among the most important war-instigated HRM developments were the Training within Industry (TWI) programs that were established to train supervisors to perform their jobs more effectively. The need for trained workers meant that there was a need for better trainers. As a result, supervisors were developed to prepare the unskilled for work in defense industries. World War II also brought increased use of films, discussion groups, and role playing as techniques for training.

Training within Industry

Immediately following the war, there was extensive interest in the management development area. This was predominantly a response to the wartime depletion of our "management stockpile." Additionally, the expanded optimism and prosperity following World War II resulted in reinstituting many of the benefits that had been eliminated during the financially troubled 1930s.

1946–70

The development of personnel continued to prosper during 1946–70. The field of human resource management continued to expand and gain in sophistication. If one theme could be identified to represent this time period, it would have to be motivation.

The 1950s and early 1960s marked a significant achievement in identifying what motivates workers. Realization that workers were human beings, not just mere pieces of equipment, promoted the humanism movement. Focus was placed on employee participation, especially on those decisions that directly affected the employees. This period also witnessed the movement of making jobs more important for the employees in the hope of increasing their job satisfaction and, ultimately, their productivity.

The 1960s also marked a decade in which the work ethic issue received much attention. As the work force moved to become predominantly white-collared, with young entrants to the work force being better educated than at any time previously, workers in general began to expect more from their jobs than just economic benefits. This sparked the increased efforts toward improving job content. Attention was focused on reducing or eliminating the boredom, fatigue, and stress that many behavioral scientists believed were primarily the cause of worker alienation and reduced job productivity. As a result, management redesigned jobs, experimented with nontraditional work schedules, increased employee benefits, and intensified efforts to treat employees in a fair and equitable manner. Much of our current knowledge on motivation and reward systems came out of this period.

The most important change, however, did not occur until the mid-to-late 1960s. In response to the new government regulations to reduce discrimination in regard to HRM practices, organizations had to revamp their personnel methods. They modified recruitment methods, sought new sources for employee candidates, heavily revamped selection and testing procedures, reassessed training needs and criteria, and moved to develop women and minorities for managerial positions. The governmental regulations certainly reshaped the methods of HRM.

1970 and Beyond

The last period we have isolated began in the early 1970s and has continued up to the present time. This transition period reflects a leveling off of the increase in government involvement: no less, but holding. However, the unique characteristic of this time interval is that it reflects a movement from the narrow view that human resources are something managed from within the personnel department to the wider recognition that the management of human resources is the responsibility of every manager.

The term *personnel management* became popular in the 1930s, and the topics in this book were traditionally covered in courses with this title. Personnel management was also used as the label for the discipline describing the functions and tasks of the specialized professionals who work on HRM activities in organizations. Personnel management was in a transition, both in practice and in academic curricula.

First, traditional personnel practices are becoming viewed in a wider and more complex perspective. Human resource management still includes such activities as hiring and firing, handling labor negotiations, determining proper compensation, and administering benefits. But heightened government regulations, increased awareness of the impact that people have on organizations, performance and the need to fully integrate personnel planning into an organization's total planning system—all have resulted in a broader interpretation of the traditional personnel role.

Personnel departments have assumed some of these new responsibilities, but not much has been delegated to operating managers. It is becoming increasingly popular, for example, for managers' appraisals to include an evaluation of how well they have been able to "grow" people who are under their supervision. This means that they must be concerned with the continual development and motivation of their subordinates. Furthermore, if key people in their units become disenchanted with their jobs, resulting in reduced levels of productivity and increased absenteeism or resignations, the managers' performance will come under close scrutiny. Even though many human resource activities occur in a separate personnel or human resources department, it is becoming more widely accepted that every manager has human resource responsibilities.

The move to the broader HRM view is also occurring in college and university curricula. The logic of such transition is self-evident. Consider the following: Most students who are studying marketing do not plan to pursue careers in marketing. They take a marketing course because they recognize that an understanding of marketing concepts is important for all business students. Similarly, all students of business and management study accounting, though not everyone intends to be an accountant or work in an accounting department. Why, then, should we approach the study of personnel in organizations from the sole perspective of what people in the personnel department do? All managers need to be concerned with the acquisition, development, motivation, and maintenance of people in their unit. It is true that some of the personnel activities discussed in this book relate directly to specialized jobs in human resource departments—such as labor relations specialist, negotiator, compensation analyst, employment interviewer, or training director—but all the managers in an organization must be familiar with HRM concepts, in the same way that they should under-

FIGURE 2-3

Summary of Management Practices

PERIOD	PRACTICE
Prior to 1932	First employment department in 1900 at B. F. Goodrich
	Frederick Taylor and scientific management in 1911
	Hugo Munsterberg and psychology and industrial efficiency in 1913
	Appearance of counseling, paid holidays, vacations, and sick leaves in the early 1920s
	Objective systems for determining hourly wage rates in the mid-1920s
	Hawthorne studies at Western Electric in the late 1920s
1932–46	Training within industry—training supervisors to perform jobs more effectively, in the 1940s
	Emphasis placed on management development in the 1940s
1946–70	Achievements in identifying what motivates workers, in the 1950s and 1960s
	Introduction of job design in the 1960s
1970 and beyond	"Personnel" changes to human resource management in the 1970s

stand marketing and accounting concepts. It only makes sense, and recent trends in college curricula concur, to design courses in personnel management around the management of human resources rather than from the perspective of activities performed by specialists in an organization's personnel department.

Conclusion

The three perspectives described in this chapter—government regulation, labor relations, and management practice—have broad implications for HRM. Certainly they are strong evidence that HRM is performed today in a constrained environment. The fact that many of these laws and policies conflict with one another further complicates the manager's task, as Sears and Roebuck has indicated. Accused of sexist promotion practices, Sears argued that it had adhered to the government's post–World War II policies, which gave preference to veterans. The government had encouraged firms to hire veterans. It had also provided substantial educational benefits to this group to make them attractive to employers. And of course, for the most part, these veterans were male. Twenty-five years later, Sears's management-level positions were largely filled with men, many of whom were these same veterans. But by the late 1970s, the government felt that Sears should have filled more of these positions with women. Sears's point was that the injustices that appear in the work force are as much due to previous government sanctions as they are to the practices of the accused firms. Similarly, many managers are currently asking how they are going to develop young people to meet their organization's future needs and, at the same time, ensure that older employees are not deprived of opportunities or adversely affected because of their age. The conflict exists because programs that emphasize the finding and developing of young people often result in de-emphasizing opportunities for older workers.

The laws, court decisions, and executive orders that were presented now require organizations to keep comprehensive personnel records to prove their compliance with government HRM policies. Employers are now on the defensive. If, for example, they administer tests as part of their selection process, they must be prepared to defend the validity of these tests in terms of job relatedness, should they be challenged. But that is only the tip of the iceberg. Employers must also ensure that their physical facilities meet specific OSHA regulations and can accommodate physically handicapped employees; that employees meet minimum wage and overtime rates after forty hours per week; that required contributions to Social Security are made; that the company's pension plan meets ERISA requirements; that the law is followed in recognizing and bargaining with organized labor unions—and the list goes on.

Unions have lost much of the power they enjoyed when they represented nearly one-third of the labor force and controlled the primary sectors of the economy. However, this loss has been somewhat offset by large gains in the public sector and a continued strong power base that comes from an effective lobbying organization.

For human resource managers, only the naive can afford to ignore the influence of unions. While the unions' relative power may have declined over the past generation, it remains a major constraint on HRM decisions in absolute terms. Both directly and indirectly, union successes and failures have an impact on all human resource managers. Union impact on managers operating in unionized organizations is obvious; but managers in nonunionized organizations, who desire to avoid unionization, can never ignore the demands and achievements that unions are making in other quarters.

CHAPTER SUMMARY

1. Government regulation, labor relations, and management practice have an impact on an organization's HRM practices.
2. Government regulation, labor relations, and management practice can be represented as evolving through four periods: prior to 1932, 1932–46, 1946–70, and 1970 and beyond.

3. Government regulation influences:
   a. Prior to 1932—Civil Service Commission established
   b. 1932–46—Roosevelt's New Deal—legislation supporting the union's right to bargain with employers
   c. 1946–70—reduced discrimination
   d. 1970 and beyond—worker protection

4. Labor relations influences:
   a. Prior to 1932—changes in the legal status of unions
   b. 1932–46—Wagner Act, National Labor Relations Board, and CIO
   c. 1946–70—Taft-Hartley, Landrum-Griffin, and AFL–CIO merger
   d. 1970 and beyond—decline in the power of organized labor

5. Management practice:
   a. Prior to 1932—Industrial Revolution, scientific management, and applied psychology
   b. 1932–46—World War II
   c. 1946–70—industrial humanism
   d. 1970 and beyond—broadening activities within HRM

6. The implications of government regulation, labor relations, and management practice have created constraints on HRM.

KEY TERMS

AFL
AFL–CIO
Age Discrimination in Employment Act
Albermarle Paper Company
CIO
Civilian Conservation Corps
Civil Rights Act
Commonwealth v. Hunt
Comprehensive Employment and Training Act (CETA)
Economic Opportunity Act
Employee Retirement Income Security Act (ERISA)
Employment Act of 1946
Equal Employment Opportunity Act (EEOA)
Executive Orders 11246, 11375, and 11478
Federal Emergency Relief Act
Griggs v. Duke Power
Hawthorne Studies

Industrial Revolution
Job Training Partnership Act
Laissez faire
Landrum-Griffin Act
Manpower Development and Training Act
National Industrial Recovery Act
National Labor Relations Board (NLRB)
Norris-LaGuardia Act
Occupational Safety and Health Act (OSHA)
Personnel management
Scientific management
Taft-Hartley Act
Training within Industry (TWI)
United Steelworkers v. Weber
Vocational Education Act
Vocational Rehabilitation Act

QUESTIONS FOR REVIEW

1. Contrast the ideal of "free enterprise" with the current description of the American economy.
2. How did the Great Depression change the role of governments' relation to the economy?
3. What implications does the Employment Act of 1946 have on HRM practices?
4. What implications does the Civil Rights Act of 1964 have on HRM practices?
5. "The federal government views itself as the employer of last resort." Do you agree or disagree? Why?
6. What implications does the *Griggs* v. *Duke Power* decision have on HRM practices?
7. Describe some instances where government policies create conflicting demands on employers.
8. How do unions constrain the HRM decisions of managers in a unionized organization? In a nonunionized organization?
9. Why does the management of most organizations resist unionization?
10. What forces have acted to stagnate union membership in the past decade?

QUESTIONS FOR DISCUSSION

1. "Executive positions in the personnel function are so complicated today that one needs to have both a graduate degree in employee relations and a law degree." Do you agree or disagree? Discuss.
2. "The government should not be so concerned with the personnel affairs of business. They should reduce some of their laws and let business police itself." Do you agree or disagree? Discuss.
3. "Unions have outlived their usefulness." Do you agree or disagree? Discuss.
4. "Government legislation in the area of HRM should not be a problem for managers, since it is requiring nothing more that what a good organization should be doing anyway." Do you agree or disagree? Discuss.
5. Describe how the four time periods identified in the chapter support the premise that HRM is a discipline within itself.

CONTINUING CASE: Concord General

The Times They Are A-Changin'

John Michaels was certainly convinced that he needed to hire a specialist to handle the myriad activities surrounding HRM. It was difficult to make the change, but he realized that the personnel job was too complicated for him to do alone.

"It was a lot easier thirty years ago," he said. "One only needed to find a woman dedicated to helping people with their suffering, train her, and call her a nurse. Now there are so many conditions placed on this hospital that the work is insurmountable. I wish we could return to the way it was thirty years ago."

"But John," remarked Jim Wilson, the new personnel specialist, "most of the changes have benefited the nurses and . . . "

"Yes," said John, "but why should something that benefits the nurses be so much of a constraint on us? We always treated our nurses fairly, and they respected us for that."

"That may be true, John, but in the short period of time since I've arrived, I've heard that some nurses are unhappy about their jobs. They are complaining that their pay is low and that there is neither upward mobility nor any incentive to motivate them."

"But they're nurses, working here because they want to help those less fortunate. Their pay is adequate, and with unemployment running so high, their incentive should be that they are in a service career."

"I see," said Jim. But what was Jim really thinking? "I've got my work cut out for me."

However, Jim felt confident. Even though he had had almost twelve years of experience in personnel matters since graduating from college, he had never worked for a hospital. The new constraints placed on him seemed unusual, but he was well aware of the politics involved in an organization. After serving as personnel assistant to Thomas Broady, personnel director at AT&T, he felt that not much more of a reality shock could come his way.

QUESTIONS

1. What impact has government legislation had on Concord General in the past thirty years? Management practice?
2. What are the possible implications to Jim Wilson and the organization if he doesn't solve some of the HRM problems?
3. What advice and/or strategies would you give Jim to help him solve these problems?

CASE APPLICATION

No Matter Where You Turn

John Carlos is a twenty-six-year-old white male who was honorably discharged from the service four years ago. Since that time, John has been attending a local college studying personnel management. Entering his last semester, John decided that he should be preparing for his job search. Putting together the necessary materials, he mailed his résumés to a number of companies. Six weeks later, he received a positive response from the Saturn Corporation, a large supplier of defense machinery to the federal government.

Interviewing for the position of personnel assistant, John knew that he had sound qualifications. He learned, however, that he was competing with Beverly Simpson, a twenty-two-year-old white female college classmate. During the interview process, it was determined that both John and Beverly were equally qualified. John, however, was given preference and was subsequently offered the job. Beverly, on the other hand, filed a suit against Saturn claiming that she was a victim of sex discrimination.

QUESTIONS

1. Do you believe that the Saturn Corporation discriminated against Beverly in giving preference to John? Discuss.
2. As a personnel specialist at Saturn, what explanation would you give to Beverly?
3. Are there any laws that would be supportive of John's hiring?

ADDITIONAL READINGS

BROWN, CLAIR, "Unemployment Theory and Policy," *Industrial Relations*, 22, No. 2 (Spring 1983), 164–85.

BROYCE, MICHAEL T., "Understanding the Guidelines: Knowing the Law Can Prevent Sexual Harassment Claims," *Management World*, 12, No. 5 (June 1983), 14.

KLERMAN, LAWRENCE S., and ROBERT H. FARLEY, "The Implications of Professional and Legal Guidelines for Court Decisions Involving Criterion-Related Validity: A Review and Analysis," *Personnel Psychology*, 38, No. 4 (Winter 1985), 803–33.

REDECKER, JAMES R., "The Supreme Court on Affirmative Action: Conflicting Opinions," *Personnel*, 63, No. 10 (October 1986), 8–14).

SCALESE, DAVID G., and DANIEL J. SMITH, "Legal Update: When Are Job Requirements Discriminatory?" *Personnel*, 63, No. 3 (March 1986), 41–48.

CHAPTER 3

Equal

Employment Opportunity

AFTER READING THIS CHAPTER, YOU WILL BE ABLE TO:

1. Describe the Civil Rights Act of 1964
2. Describe other federal legislation designed to prevent discrimination
3. Define *adverse impact*
4. Explain how organizations can comply with EEO guidelines
5. Identify the steps involved in filing an EEO complaint
6. Discuss the recent happenings regarding EEO
7. Explain sexual harassment, age discrimination, and comparable worth

A decision to hire someone carries a one-million-dollar impact to our company. I expect, then, that we discriminate on skills alone.

—Anonymous

Introduction

What do AT&T, the Detroit Edison Company, and the 3M Company have in common? Each has paid out over a million dollars for practices that allegedly discriminated against minorities.

In the preceding chapter, we briefly addressed the impact of the 1964 Civil Rights Act, Title VII, on employment practices. In this chapter, we will expand that discussion to provide a fuller understanding of this piece of legislation. Why? Because it is a fact of doing business. Almost every organization, both public and private, must abide by the guidelines established in Title VII, its subsequent amendment (1972), and other federal laws governing employment practices. The importance of these laws cannot be overstated, as they permeate all functions in the organization.

Federal Legislation

Important federal legislation

The beginnings of equal employment opportunity are usually related to the passage of the 1964 Civil Rights Act. While the main thrust of the activities we will explore are rooted in this 1964 act, equal employment's beginning goes back some two hundred years. Many of the amendments to the U.S. Constitution provided for freedom for U.S. citizens. These freedoms, as stated in the Fifth Amendment, stipulate that "no person shall be denied life, liberty, or the pursuit of happiness without due process." However, the Fifth Amendment is seldom used as a grounds for discrimination. Additionally, in 1866, a civil rights law was passed that stated that it was illegal to discriminate against individuals based on race. While this law is often overshadowed by the Civil Rights Act, it has gained prominence in recent years as being the law that "white male" workers can use to support claims of reverse discrimination, that is, arguments that minorities have been given treatment in employment decisions that favor these minorities over better-qualified white males.

Although these laws do exist, the most prominent piece of legislation on the topic remains Title VII of the Civil Rights Act. In the next section, we explore the act as it pertains to human resource management.

Title VII of the 1964 Civil Rights Act

Title VII of the Civil Rights Act states that it is illegal to discriminate against individuals based on race, religion, color, sex, or national origin. The law was very specific in that it was an attempt to eliminate the discriminatory practices in selection, placement, and promotion that organizations used to keep their work force homogeneous.

Title VII

All organizations, both public and private, including labor unions and employment agencies, are bound by the law.[1] However, the law does further specify compliance based on the number of employees/members in the organization. Generally, any organization with fifteen or more employees is covered by the act.[2] This minimum number of employees basically serves as a means of protecting, or removing from the law, small, family-owned businesses.

[1] *1981 Guidebook to Fair Employment Practices* (Commerce Clearing House, Chicago, 1980), p. 16.

[2] Ibid.

FIGURE 3-1

SOURCE: *Parade Magazine*, April 8, 1984. Reprinted by permission of Parade Publications, Inc., and the authors Irving Wallace, David Wallechinsky, and Amy Wallace.

The Conservative Who Gave Women Their Rights

The word "sex" was added to the equal employment clause of the 1964 Civil Rights Act by a conservative Congressman who did not believe in civil rights for women. He was Rep. Howard W. Smith (D., Va.), chairman of the House Rules Committee and arch foe of civil rights.

Smith was hoping his addition of equal rights for women would make the bill so radical that it would be voted down. When offering the amendment, he jocularly mentioned the "imbalance" in the population because of the nation's 2,661,000 spinsters and bemoaned the fact that if all women could not get husbands, they should at least have jobs with equal pay.

Rep. Howard W. Smith in 1961

Some conservatives concluded, however, that there was a good reason to include "sex" in the amendment: If it passed without the addition, the clause—which prohibited "color" discrimination—would protect black women but not white women, thus giving them an employment advantage. (Other conservatives fought the amendment for the standard reasons: Women would be forced into the military, they said, families would disintegrate, problems would arise with alimony and child custody.)

To Smith's astonishment, the amendment was approved. When the Civil Rights Act passed, it prohibited discrimination—whether based on race, color, religion, national origin or sex—by employers, labor unions and employment agencies. Smith, who didn't intend to, had helped to author one of the most radical civil rights amendments in U.S. history.

While the act served as a beginning for eliminating prejudice in selection, there were many loopholes that enabled companies to circumvent the intent of the law. These loopholes were in the area of employee testing. Many organizations used selection criteria that resulted in the elimination of minorities from the mainstream jobs in the organization. Employers claimed that "they could use any test which had been developed by a professional so long as they did not intend to exclude minorities, even if such exclusion was the consequence of the use of the test."[3]

The courts, however, took a different view. With the decisions rendered in the *Griggs* v. *Duke Power* case and the *Washington* v. *Davis* case, the Supreme Court held that if the results of "employer practices . . . had an adverse impact on minorities and were not justified by business necessity,"[4] then those practices were illegal. Unclear as to how this ruling was to be followed, how business necessity was to be established, and what constituted an adverse impact, four governmental agencies—the Department of Labor, the Department of Justice, the Equal Employment Opportunity Commission, and the Civil Service Commission (now the Office of Personnel Management)—established the *Uniform Guidelines on Employee Selection Procedures*. These guidelines were adopted by these agencies in September 1978 and have served as the rules governing employment practices. While interpretation of these guidelines is beyond the scope of this text and is often left to the lawyers and industrial psychologists to support or defend a particular practice, certain general aspects can be identified.[5]

Adverse Impact

Adverse impact The concept of adverse impact stems from the consequences of an employment practice, not solely on the intent of the practice. Overt practices such as barring blacks and women from certain jobs or segregating people, clearly point to practices that are based on the intent to discriminate. However, consequences of an employment practice may have the same result. As such, even though an employment practice does not have the "intent" to discriminate, if the practice results in a disparate rate of selection of minorities, the practice is said to have an adverse impact. Subsequently that action, if it cannot be shown to be necessary for successful performance on the job, is illegal.

For example, as noted in Chapter 2, the landmark case for adverse

[3]*Federal Register* (Department of Labor, Department of Justice, EEOC, and the Civil Service Commission, 1978), p. 38290.

[4]Ibid.

[5]The following information has been excerpted from the 1978 *Uniform Guidelines on Employee Selection Procedures*.

impact is *Griggs* v. *Duke Power.* Blacks in the Duke Power Plant, for the most part, were relegated to low-skilled jobs. The requirements for the higher-skilled jobs were a high-school diploma (or its equivalent) and satisfactory scores on a personality and mechanical test.[6] Most blacks in Duke Power either did not have the high-school diploma or had failed the tests more often than whites did.

The trials in the lower courts resulted in decisions favoring Duke Power. The courts' rationale was that the criteria had been applied equally, and therefore no indication of discrimination existed. However, the Supreme Court took a different view. In its decision, the Supreme Court noted that the tests required resulted in a greater proportion of blacks being rejected. Because of this higher rejection rate, the Court shifted the burden of proof to the company to prove that the tests were predictors of job performance. Duke Power was unable to provide the evidence.

The Supreme Court's ruling in *Griggs* v. *Duke Power* has had a major impact on HRM. The burden of proof in now placed on the employer to show that tests used are valid—that they measure job-related information. That is, the organization must ensure that the consequences of its practices do not result in adverse impacts.

Although the Supreme Court identified that adverse impacts might lead to discrimination, determining if an adverse impact has occurred is difficult. One way of beginning to do so, however, is the use of the *Uniform Guidelines on Employee Selection Procedures'* 4/5th rule. While this guideline is not a definition of discrimination, it is a "practical device to keep the attention of the enforcement agencies on serious discrepancies in hiring and promotion rates, or other employment decisions."[7] For example, assume that we have a pool of applicants, ten white males and ten members of the protected group. *Protected group,* in this context, is a term used to refer to those individuals

Protected group who are covered under EEO laws. This includes blacks, women, Hispanics, American Indians, handicapped individuals, veterans, individuals between the ages of forty and seventy, and Pacific Islanders. Back to our example.

If, in our employment decision, we hire six white males and three

4/5ths rule protected group members, we have not complied with the 4/5ths rule. Why? Because in our comparison, we see that while 60 percent of the white males were hired, only 30 percent of the protected group members were. That is, we have not hired as many protected group members to meet the 80 percent rule. To come into compliance in this simple example, we would need to hire at least five members of the

[6]Mitchell S. Novit, *Essentials of Personnel Management,* 2nd ed. (Englewood Cliffs, N.J.: Prentice-Hall, 1986), p. 105.

[7]*Federal Register.*

protected group (4.8 for those statistically inclined).

Note that the 4/5ths rule is only a rough indicator. More elaborate statistical tests are needed to confirm or reject that an adverse impact has occurred. Too many factors can enter into the picture. For instance, if Company 1 finds ways to keep most protected group members from applying in the first place, it will only need to hire a few of them to meet the 4/5ths rule-of-thumb measure. Conversely, if Company 2 actively seeks numerous applications from protected group members and hires more members of this group than Company 1, it may still not meet the 4/5ths rule.[8] In such a case, it may be necessary to look at the total spectrum, or the bottom-line technique.

Bottom-Line Technique

Bottom line

The *Uniform Guidelines on Employment Selection* offers a bottom-line technique to assist in the compliance of companies. This technique recognizes that every component of an organization's selection process need not be validated. That is, so long as the overall practice (bottom line) is such that progress is being made to increase protected members at all levels in the organization, the organization is not in violation of Title VII.[9]

In other words, even though a test may result in an adverse impact, if during the other steps in the process and in the overall selection process an adverse impact is not identified, then the organization is in compliance. For example, earlier we identified a pool of applicants consisting of ten white males and ten protected members. If we used a test and six white males and three protected group members passed, then we have not met the 4/5ths rule. If we hired based solely on this test, all things being considered, it could have an adverse impact. But if the test is only one aspect of our hiring process, we will need to explore it further. If we also use an interview and subsequently hire all three members of the protected group, and only three of the six white males, we have not only met our 4/5ths rule at this stage but have brought the entire process under compliance (even though our test did not satisfy the 4/5ths rule). Compliance in this case has come about through the bottom-line technique. Figure 3-2 contains a mathematical representation of the process.

One last thing about the bottom-line technique. Although it can be used as a means of indicating compliance (and eliminating an adverse impact), if the practice can be shown to affect certain individu-

[8]Novit, *Essentials of Personnel Management*, p. 114.
[9]Ibid., p. 115.

FIGURE 3-2

Bottom-Line Technique

ACTIVITY	PROTECTED GROUP (PG)	WHITE MALES (W)	RATIO OF PG/W	COMPLIANCE WITH 4/5THS RULE
Passed test	3/10 = 30%	6/10 = 60%	30%/60% = 50%	No
Passed interview	3/3 = 100%	3/6 = 50%	100%/50% = 200%	Yes
Overall hiring process	3/10 = 30%	3/10 = 30%	30%/30% = 100%	Yes

NOTE: Based on 10 protected group member applicants and 10 white male applicants. Ratio of PG/W is the ratio of the percentage of protected group to the percentage of white males.

SOURCE: Adapted from James Ledvinka, *Federal Regulation of Personnel and Human Resource Management* (Boston: Kent Publishing Company, 1982), p. 108. © 1982 by Wadsworth, Inc. Reprinted by permission of Kent Publishing Company, a division of Wadsworth, Inc.

als, then the practice may have an adverse treatment. Adverse treatment occurs when a practice affects certain individuals more than others. For example, if two black females are being discriminated against, because of race or sex, the practice may have an adverse treatment toward them.[10] The distinction here, in a highly simplistic sense, is that an adverse impact affects a class of people, whereas an adverse treatment affects one or more individuals.

Compliance With the Guidelines

If an adverse impact is resulting from the practices in the organization, there are a few remedies for the employer. First and foremost, the employer should discontinue the practice. Only after careful study and validation should the practice, or a modified version, be reinstated. (We will examine validation procedures in Chapter 7.) As for other remedies, if an adverse impact has resulted, an employer can defend the discriminatory charges.

Defending Discriminatory Charges

Generally, there are two defenses an employer can use when confronted with a discrimination charge. The first of these is business necessity; the second is bona fide occupational qualifications (BFOQs).

An organization has the right to operate in a safe and efficient manner. This safe and efficient manner is a business necessity. With-

[10]Ibid., p. 106.

out it, the survival of the organization can be threatened. For example, a major airline's requirements include five hundred flight hours and a college degree for pilot applicants. These two requirements have an adverse impact on minority groups. However, the airline has claimed that the requirements are necessary for safety reasons. The costs of not having these requirements would be too great, as the lives of passengers could be at great risk if an unqualified individual were hired. In this instance, business necessity prevails.

BFOQs   BFOQs are defenses only when specific religion, sex, age, or national origin criteria are job related. Citing BFOQs, airlines once hired only females for the position of flight attendant. When challenged in court, the airlines had many reasons why flight attendants should be females. Unfortunately for the airlines, the courts did not hold the same view and overruled hiring only females as flight attendants as a BFOQ. The use of BFOQs, for the most part, is difficult to validate. However, in cases such as religious orders requiring all of its members to be of the same religion, BFOQs have been upheld.

Summary

Complying with the guidelines should be in the best interests of the organization. But discrimination based on factors other than being able to do the job still exist. Because organizations consist of people, individuals who have varied backgrounds and experiences, human nature becomes a vital part in the operations. And with this human nature element come prejudices—prejudices that are unfounded and unwarranted, but real. This alone can explain why, even in the face of lengthy and costly lawsuits, some organizations still adversely impact some groups. If that occurs, what can a person do?

Filing an EEO Complaint

When the Civil Rights Act first passed there were good intentions, but the enforcement arm of the act was virtually nonexistent. It was not until 1972, with the Amendment to the Civil Rights Act,[11] that the Equal Employment Opportunity Commission (EEOC) was empowered to enforce the intent of the law and police the activities when problems occurred.

---

[11]This amendment to the Civil Rights Act also expanded the coverage of Title VII and empowered the EEOC to sue on behalf of individuals who had been discriminated against.

The EEOC established a five-step process to handle discriminatory charges:[12]

Steps in filing an EEO complaint

1. Contact the Human Rights Commission (HRC) within 180 days of the alleged violation.
2. The HRC will investigate the charge to see if the complaint is valid.
3. If a valid complaint, the HRC will meet informally with the organization to try to correct the situation.
4. If unsuccessful at conciliation, the HRC will set up a hearing at the EEOC.
5. Appeals of this hearing are heard in civil court.

Therefore, when an alleged discriminatory act has occurred, the individual has 180 days to file charges. Once these charges have been filed, the investigation begins. The EEOC's initial action is to determine if, in fact, an act of discrimination did occur. At this time, it tries to determine probable cause. If the act of discrimination did not occur, then the EEOC advises the individual that the agency cannot proceed further with the case. However, that does not prevent the individual from seeking aid elsewhere. It only states that, according to the EEOC, the charge of discrimination is unfounded.

If probable cause is determined, the EEOC meets with the employer to seek a conciliation agreement in an effort to stop the alleged practices and to correct any wrong that has harmed the individual. If this is successful, all efforts stop. However, if a solution is not achieved, a hearing before the EEOC is set. At the completion of the hearing, a decision will be rendered. If either party is not satisfied with the decision, an appeal can be made. Following this appeal, the matter becomes one that must now be adjudicated in the courts. The term *de novo* is used to describe this court case, as it is now a new beginning. All prior efforts must now begin again. The investigation of the EEOC and its subsequent interpretation may not be entered as evidence in the court.

Other Legislation

While our discussion thus far has focused solely on Title VII, there are other laws governing the employment practices of organizations. Although many were described in the preceding chapter, some need to be put into focus. Figure 3-3 summarizes these laws, their jurisdiction, and their prohibitions.

---

[12]Adapted from the *1981 Guidebook to Fair Employment Practices*, pp. 123–61.

FIGURE 3-3

Summary of Legislation

LEGISLATION	JURISDICTION	PROHIBITIONS
Civil Rights Act, Public Law 88-352 (1964)	Employers with 25 or more employees; also covers labor unions.	Discrimination with respect to color, national origin, race, religion, and sex.
Equal Employment Opportunity Act (1972) (Amendment to Title VII of the Civil Rights Act)	Most employers with more than 15 employees.	Same as Civil Rights Act.
Age Discrimination in Employment Act (1967, amended in 1978)	Employers with more than 25 employees.	Age discrimination in employment decisions concerning individuals between 40 and 70 years old. (Age 70 cap is now repealed.)
Executive Order 11246 [sec. 201(1)], 1965; amended by Executive Order 11375, 1966	Federal contractors and subcontractors with contracts exceeding $50,000 and 50 or more employees.	Discrimination in employment decisions with respect to color, national origin, race, religion, and sex.
Vocational Rehabilitation Act (1973)	Government contractors and federal agencies.	Discrimination in employment decisions against people with physical and/or mental handicaps.
Pregnancy Discrimination Act of 1978 (Amendment to Civil Rights Act) Public Law 95-555	Same as Civil Rights Act.	Discrimination on the basis of pregnancy, childbirth, or related medical conditions in benefit administration and other employment decisions.

SOURCE: Reprinted, by permission of the publisher, from "EEO Alert: Watch Out for Discrimination in Discharge Decisions," by Janisee Klotchman and Linda L. Neider, PERSONNEL, January–February 1983, p. 62, © 1983 AMACOM Periodicals Division, American Management Association, New York. All rights reserved.

Where is EEO Now?

The early 1980s witnessed much concern about the future of equal employment opportunity. When costs were soaring, competition increasing, and the economy fluctuating, organizations began to lay off workers or, in some cases, close entire plants. The impact that this had on EEO was detrimental. Many organizations that had followed the last-in, first-out concept when it came to laying off employees found that they were laying off a disproportionate number of workers from the protected groups. Opponents of these layoffs condemned the practice as uprooting twenty years of progress.

Another area that came into the public forum was the affirmative

Affirmative
action

action plan. Established as a worthwhile goal for organizations, the Reagan administration "worried pointedly about Affirmative Action Plans that kept turning into quotas."[13] While the debate continued, and a new Civil Rights Commission was appointed, the intent appeared to be that "getting back to color blind hiring was the [administration's] goal."[14] Even Clarence Pendleton, Jr., the head of the Civil Rights Commission, viewed quotas as "not working. . . . When you are hired on a quota, you're automatically pointed to as an affirmative action person, and you carry that label around forever."[15]

Regardless of the changes that have occurred or may occur, it is probable that efforts will continue. Although the current state of affairs may need to be reviewed, there is no doubt that affirmative action has its place in America's industries. The March 1987 Supreme Court ruling, allowing preferential treatment for women, is a clear indication of this point.

Recent Phenomena in EEO

The names have changed over time, but the concept has not. There still exist decisions about employees based on factors other than their performance. In this section we will review three of these: sexual harassment, age discrimination, and comparable worth.

Sexual Harassment.

Sexual harassment

Sexual harassment can be defined as "unwelcome sexual advances, requests for sexual favors and other verbal or physical contact of a sexual nature."[16] While this definition is contained in the 1964 Civil Rights Act, it has not been until recent years that this problem gained recognition. Prior to 1980, sexual harassment was generally believed to be an isolated problem, with the individual committing the act being solely responsible for his or her actions. But vagueness plagued the interpretation of the act. It was difficult to differentiate between someone who was being friendly and someone who was sexually harassing another. For example, are the following situations sexual harassment?

1. A male supervisor compliments his secretary on her style of dress.
2. A female supervisor asks a male supervisor out to lunch.

---

[13]"Affirmative Action Is Here to Stay," *Fortune,* April 19, 1982, p. 144.
[14]Ibid.
[15]Ibid.
[16]Donna E. Ledgerwood and Sue Johnson-Dietz, "Sexual Harassment: Implications for Employer Liability," *Monthly Labor Review,* April 1981, p. 45.

3. A male employee is apt to touch people's arms and shoulders as he speaks.

4. A male manager tells off-color jokes in his office, within hearing distance of the secretaries.

5. A female employee offers sexual favors to a male manager for assistance in obtaining a promotion.

Are these incidents reflective of sexual harassment? There were no clear-cut answers. It was not until the decision in the *Miller* v. *Bank of America* case that specific guidelines about sexual harassment appeared.[17] These guidelines are threefold:[18]

1. Where sexual conduct is made a condition of an individual's employment

2. Where such conduct or condition creates an employment consequence

3. Where such condition creates an offensive environment or interferes with job performance

What these guidelines have done is to place the liability for sexual harassment occurrences on the employer. An employee who has been sexually harassed now has a recourse against the employer. This has resulted in new "policy statements, management and employee training, and communication of internal grievance procedures for harassment complaints."[19] Therefore, to revisit our five examples, if someone is offended by the action described in each situation, then sexual harassment may have occurred. Even though what constitutes sexual harassment is far from being objective and is ambiguous, employers must now recognize that they need to stop possible actions at the worksite that may be construed as being offensive to someone.

Age Discrimination

Age discrimination

The number of cases regarding age discrimination has been increasing. Individuals over forty years of age are protected under the Civil Rights Act, and decisions regarding their employment based on age are clearly discriminatory. The reasons for age discrimination appear to center on two themes. First is the youthful image. Some organizations like to remain attuned to the younger buying public, those under fifty years of age. Second is the money issue. In many organizations, the salary of senior employees is two or three times higher than that of younger workers performing similar jobs. Accordingly, if the

[17]Ibid.
[18]Ibid., p. 46.
[19]Ibid., p. 47.

younger worker can handle the senior worker's job, eliminating the senior worker will save money. In such cases, the focus is on "cutting salary costs and pension liabilities."[20]

The number of organizations that have lost age discrimination suits or have settled out of court reads like a "Who's Who" list. Recently a case that had lasted for seven years was settled. Eugene B. Goodman, an international marketing executive with Heublein, Inc., charged that the company had failed to promote him because of his age. He had shown that the promotions made in the organization went to younger individuals, and that was the key to his charge that age discrimination did occur. It met the three-point test currently used by the courts: Is the person qualified for the position? If qualified, was that person turned down? And if turned down, did the company continue to search for another candidate? The decision rendered in the Eugene Goodman case was that he had been discriminated against based on his age. He was awarded $450,000, which included his back pay, benefits, and damages he incurred.[21]

Comparable Worth/Pay Equity

Comparable worth

Many jobs were formerly seen as being male- or female-oriented jobs. For example, librarian, nurse, and elementary school teacher were considered jobs for females. In contrast, truck driver, police officer, and construction worker were considered male jobs. Historically, this has resulted in the traditional female-oriented jobs being paid significantly less than the traditional male-oriented jobs.

Comparable worth is one of the most complex issues to arise in recent years. The comparable worth issue estimates the importance of each job factor, within each job, in determining and equating pay structures. While the 1963 Equal Pay Act states that workers doing the same job must be paid the same salary, this has not posed the same problem as the comparable worth issue. Comparable worth takes equal pay one step further. It tries to equate those factors that are present in each job (skills, responsibility, working conditions, and effort) with the male-female pay discrepancy. This means paying similar jobs, not equal jobs, the same amount. For instance, a nurse may be judged to have a job comparable to that of a police officer. Both must be trained before practicing, both are licensed to practice, both work under stressful conditions, and both must exhibit high levels of effort. But they are not typically paid the same. The male-dominated job (police

---

[20]"Wounded Executives Fight Back on Age Bias," *Business Week*, July 21, 1980, p. 109.

[21]Ibid.

FIGURE 3-4

Comparable Worth

MALE-DOMINATED JOBS		Point Count	FEMALE-DOMINATED JOBS	
	Top Monthly Salary		Top Monthly Salary	
Truck Driver I	$1,574	97	$1,114	Laundry Worker
Equipment Operator II	1,738	155	1,200	Attendant Counselor
Electrician	1,918	197	1,324	Secretary III
Equipment Mechanic	2,015	209	1,392	Attendant Counselor Supervisor

SOURCE: Copyright 1984 Time Inc. All rights reserved. Reprinted by permission from TIME.

officer) is usually paid more than the female-dominated job (nurse).

Comparable worth proponents indicate that resolving the comparable worth issue would eliminate females making approximately seventy cents for every dollar that a male makes. For example, Figure 3-4 gives a breakdown of eight jobs, four dominated by males and four dominated by females. Evaluating each job using the point method of job evaluation (discussed in Chapter 16), and comparing top monthly salary figures for each, we can see a discrepancy. While the point counts are the same (meaning that skills, responsibility, working conditions, and efforts equate), the pay differential is as much as $623 per month. A bit of mathematical calculation indicates that in this instance, the female-dominated job is being short-changed about $7,500 per year.

The point of this issue revolves around the economic worth of jobs to employees. If jobs are similar, even though they involve different occupations, why shouldn't they be paid the same? Unfortunately, resolving the conflict is not that easy. Both sides to the argument have made valid points, but the outcome is far from clear. A decision to change, to pay comparable jobs equally, would cause a need to restructure our pay scales. And as one expert has stated, to make such changes would "cost some $320 billion in added annual wages and increase inflation by 10 percent" in the United States.[22] That decision does not appear to be forthcoming soon, as Congress, in 1985, decided to table the entire comparable worth issue. While isolated cases of the comparable worth issue do turn up, they do not appear to have much of an impact.

However, cost projections aside, we must attack the central issue—pay disparities. Women still earn less than men. While compa-

[22]"A Worthy but Knotty Question," *Time*, February 6, 1984, p. 30.

rable worth issues may be seen as an exercise in futility, their intent is to reduce the pay discrepancy. But other means may be available to achieve this goal, such as "eliminating the barriers to better paying jobs for women."[23] With a Supreme Court ruling as support, the preferential treatment for women might quite possibly assist in achieving pay equity.

VIEWS IN THE NEWS

Comparable Worth: Practical Advice from the Experts

Comparable worth—the theory that wages for a job should be based on the job's value to an organization—has been a controversial topic since it was first proposed as a means to remedy the persistent male-female wage gap. Proponents of the comparable worth theory maintain that sex discrimination is the cause of depressed wages in female-dominated jobs, while its opponents argue that the marketplace and the law of supply and demand are—and should be—responsible for employers' wage-setting practices. Maintaining, however, that the ideas behind comparable worth aren't revolutionary or even new, Alvin Bellak of Hay Associates offers employers some practical pointers on structuring solid, unbiased compensation systems that will withstand scrutiny.

THE STORY BEHIND THE STORY

In a Hay report, "Linking Employee Attitudes and Corporate Culture to Corporate Growth and Profitability," Bellak notes that the widely used Hay Guide Chart-Profile Method of Job Evaluation was created in the early 1950s, long before the Equal Pay Act of 1963 and the 1964 Civil Rights Act. A "fundamental principle" of that system, he observes, is that jobs should be evaluated "independent of any characteristics of the job-holders." A second principle, which was "quite revolutionary" when first proposed, he says, is that jobs can be evaluated independently of the existing pay scale or the labor market to form the basis for an "internally equitable compensation system."

"From the very beginning," Bellak stresses, Hay advised that "jobs should be priced in relation to their measured job content (i.e., points) without regard to the ability, performance, potential, education, sex, color or any other characteristic of the job-holder." Over the years, as pay scales in labor markets became more differentiated, Hay increasingly recommended that larger, more diversified companies should consider multiple pay structures, but always with the proviso that all jobs

[23]"The Non-Comparability of the "Comparable Worth" Doctrine," *Collegiate Forum*, Fall 1983, p. 1.

covered by each specific pay structure should be compensated in relation to relative job content.

According to Bellak, what's new about comparable worth is that pay equity advocates are challenging the "fairness and the heterogeneity of the labor market." While stressing that "any thoughtful person would have to wonder about the fairness of the pay of college-trained nurses and librarians versus the pay fo semi-skilled auto and steel workers," Bellak notes that in the nation's "haste to address the issue of fair pay for women, laws are being passed which may open a Pandora's box of serious new problems."

ADVICE TO EMPLOYERS

Although the climate surrounding the issue of comparable worth remains one of "uncertainty and controversy," Bellak says, there are some steps employers can take to protect their compensation systems from challenge, including:

- Base your compensation system upon clear and complete definitions of specific jobs. The jobs must not restrict participation for or to any protected class unless there is a "necessary and irrefutable occupational requirement."
- Identify the extent to which each job, job family, or occupational family is dominated by a protected class. Where domination—which generally means 70 percent or more—exists, determine whether it stems from business necessity or simply from "custom, convenience, or indifference."
- Where there are many employees holding the same job, make sure you are giving equal pay for equal work, regardless of whether the job is dominated by a protected class.
- If your company has no job evaluation plan and claims to use a strictly market-pricing system, determine whether your job descriptions suggest some de facto form of job measurement.
- Test your job evaluation process to see if the results are "repeatable" by committees with various combinations of memberships.
- Identity the labor markets from which you typically draw applicants and employees. If a protected class dominates the markets that you use as a basis for job pricing, make sure you have no reasonable alternatives to wage-setting.
- Test any compensation procedures that produce significantly different pay within a single pay structure for similar jobs. If the compensation system produces unsupportable adverse effects on protected classes, it should be changed.
- Document your compensation system and publicize it internally. If your program is sound, you have nothing to hide, Bellak says.
- Finally, make sure that all your jobs are open to qualified applicants. An affirmative action program, together with a well-conceived and supportable compensation program, is "the certain route to the elimination of pay discrimination," Bellak maintains. (The Hay report is available from the Center for Management Research, Inc., Executive Plaza, 850 Boylston Street, Chestnut Hill, Mass. 02167.)

Conclusion

Equal employment opportunity—the law, the practice—is something that all managers will face. This, however, will not be easy. Operating a personnel department today is more difficult because of the multifaceted nature of its activities. And as arguments pro and con EEO continue, two things should be kept in mind. You cannot break the law, and discrimination can reduce your organization's effectiveness.

As you proceed through this book, remember that EEO does not stop at the end of this chapter. Its importance and implications will permeate everything discussed in the following chapters.

SUMMARY

1. Title VII of the 1964 Civil Rights Act prohibits discrimination on the basis of race, religion, color, sex, or national origin.

2. Other pieces of federal legislation are also designed to protect against discrimination. Among them are
   a. The Fifth Amendment
   b. The 1866 Civil Rights Act
   c. The Age Discrimination in Employment Act
   d. The Vocational Rehabilitation Act
   e. The Pregnancy Discrimination Act

3. Discrimination can be overt or hidden. If an action by management affects a particular group disproportionately, the act may be illegal (adverse impact).

4. Organizations can comply with the EEO guidelines by stopping the practice, validating the practice, or proving that the practice is based on a bona fide occupational qualification (BFOQ).

5. Filing and processing an EEO complaint involves five general steps:
   a. Contact the Human Rights Commission within 180 days of the alleged violation.
   b. The HRC will investigate to see if the complaint is valid.
   c. If a valid complaint, the HRC will meet informally with the organization to try to correct the situation.
   d. If unsuccessful at conciliation, the HRC sets up a hearing at the EEOC.
   e. Appeals of this hearing are heard in civil court.

6. The EEO has been under severe attack during the past few years. Its activities and enforcement powers have been reduced. However, it still remains an active vehicle for victims of discrimination.

7. The newest and most controversial aspects of EEO are sexual harassment, age discrimination, and comparable worth.

KEY TERMS

Adverse impact
Affirmative action
Bona fide occupational
  qualification (BFOQ)
Bottom-line technique
Comparable worth

Equal Employment Opportunity
  Commission (EEOC)
4/5ths rule
Protected group
Sexual harassment
Title VII

QUESTIONS FOR REVIEW

1. What is Title VII of the Civil Rights Act? Whom does it protect?
2. What are the HRM implications of the *Griggs* v. *Duke Power* case?
3. What is an adverse impact?
4. Describe the 4/5ths rule on discrimination. Give an example of how the 4/5ths rule can be applied.
5. What is a protected group?
6. What is "business necessity"?
7. Describe the five steps involved in an EEO complaint.
8. Define *sexual harassment*. Identify and describe the three sexual harassment guidelines.
9. Describe the three factors used to determine if age discrimination exists.
10. What is comparable worth? How does it differ from 1963 Equal Pay Act?

QUESTIONS FOR DISCUSSION

1. "To eliminate any adverse impacts, companies should lay off workers, when needed, on a basis other than last in, first out." Discuss.
2. "Quotas do not work. When you're hired on a quota, you're automatically labeled as an affirmative action person and you carry that label around forever." Do you agree or disagree? Discuss.
3. "Sexual harassment occurs between two people only. The company should not be held liable." Do you agree or disagree? Discuss.

4. "The youth image is important for many companies. Therefore, letting individuals go because they have become old is a business necessity." Do you agree or disagree? Discuss.

5. "Equating salaries to comparable worth will only cause more harm than good in most companies." Do you agree or disagree? Discuss.

CONTINUING CASE: Concord General

Cry, Cry, Baby

Susan Chapman had been a nurse at Concord General for over eleven years. She had served as head nurse in the Cardiac Care Unit before resigning her management position to give her more time to be with her husband and family and to continue her pursuit of a law degree.

Shortly after stepping down as head nurse, Susan discovered that she was pregnant. However, she planned to work for as long as she physically could. In her eighth month of pregnancy, Susan's doctor advised her to stop working immediately and take it easy. It appeared that being on her feet for such long periods had caused a buildup of fluid in her legs. While not critical, this condition could cause one's blood pressure to rise significantly and, accordingly, affect the fetus. Based on that diagnosis, Dr. Martin called the hospital and stated that Nurse Chapman was unable to work and could not return until he considered it safe—estimated to be ten weeks after her delivery.

Susan agreed with her doctor's orders and proceeded to the personnel department to fill out her maternity leave papers. She was told that she was entitled to a total of 396 hours of leave, a combination of sick and vacation leave. Since her doctor had determined that an additional eight weeks might be necessary, she could take the time as leave without pay.

Susan did deliver a healthy baby boy early in her ninth month. However, she decided to stay off work for the total time allotted by the personnel department.

When Susan returned to work approximately twenty weeks after the day she left, she was met with unpleasant news. It appeared that her position in the Cardiac Care Unit was no longer available; it had been filled seven weeks earlier by a replacement. Susan was miffed. She stated that she had been on maternity leave, leave that was in accordance with the hospital's policy. There was no reason whatsoever to keep her from getting her old job back.

Angry, Susan went to the personnel director. "Why isn't my job available?" she asked. The answer was that the situation mandated hiring a full-time replacement, and, unfortunately, there were no openings at the present time.

"Not good enough," said Susan, "we'll see about this." At that point, she stormed out of the hospital and drove directly to the State Human Rights Commission to file a complaint.

QUESTIONS

1. Has Susan been discriminated against? Discuss.
2. Under what act does Susan have protection?
3. Is the hospital required to give Susan back her job in the CCU? Discuss.

CASE APPLICATION

But You Said Equal

The owners of health spas in the state of Michigan were being sued by their female employees because of the lower pay rates that these employees were receiving. In those health clubs, both men and women were hired as managers and assistant managers, and both were paid a commission as a percentage of sales on new memberships. But the percentage paid to females was less than that paid to males, and thus the reason for the suit.

The owners contended that they were doing what the law stipulated that they must do. According to the 1963 equal pay act, men and women doing the same jobs must be paid the same. In their defense, they were doing just that—paying both the same. The jobs of each were the same, as evidenced by the job descriptions. The only apparent difference was that the sales volume for the women was higher, roughly 50 percent higher. Accordingly, the only way to equate their pay was to give a woman a lower commission rate.

QUESTIONS

1. Do you believe that the females at the health spa were being discriminated against? Discuss the rationale for your decision and support your position.
2. Can you think of any advantages that might accrue to the health spa from this experience?

ADDITIONAL READINGS

BALEY, DANDRA, "The Legalities of Hiring in the 80s," *Personnel Journal,* November 1985, pp. 112–15.

"Comparable Worth: It's Already Happening," *Business Week,* April 28, 1986, pp. 52–56.

GREENE, RICHARD, "Over the Hill to the Courthouse," *Forbes,* January 24, 1986, pp. 72–73.

STRAYER, JACQUELINE F., and SANDRA E. RAPOPORT, "Sexual Harassment, 2: Limiting Corporate Liability," *Personnel,* April 1986, pp. 26–33.

SULLIVAN, JOHN F., "Comparable Worth and the Statistical Audit of Pay Programs for Illegal Systematic Discrimination." *Personnel Administrator,* March 1985, pp. 102–11.

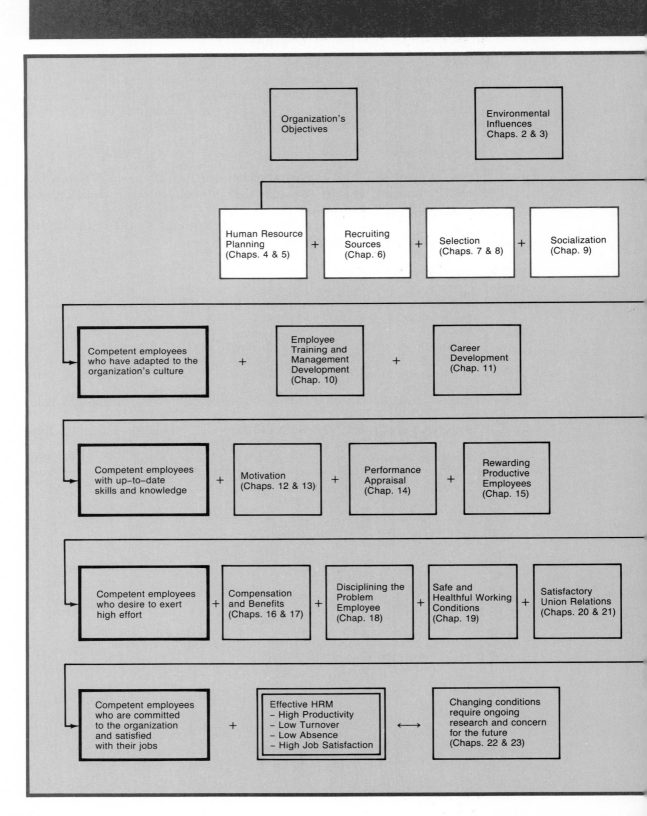

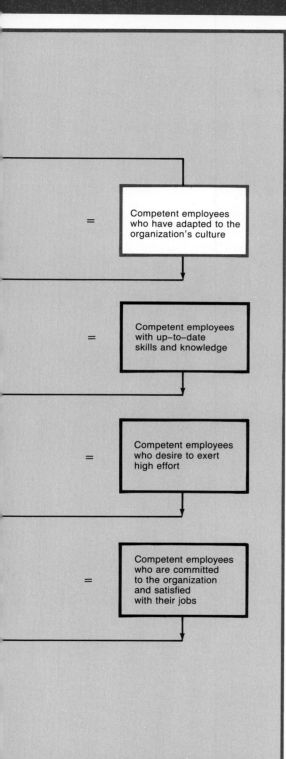

PART TWO

ACQUISITION OF HUMAN RESOURCES

CHAPTER 4

Human

Resource Planning

AFTER READING THIS CHAPTER, YOU WILL BE ABLE TO:

1. Define *human resource planning*
2. Identify the five steps involved in the human resource planning process
3. Describe how retrenchment affects human resource planning
4. Discuss the relevant retrenchment issues

Alice: Would you tell me, please, which way I ought to go from here?

Cheshire Cat: That depends a good deal on where you want to go.

Alice: I don't care where. . . .

Cheshire Cat: Then it doesn't matter which way you go.

—Lewis Carroll

Before you can depart on a journey, it is necessary to know your destination. The steps you take before beginning any trip appear quite simple: determining where you are; determining where you want to go; and, finally, suggesting a route that can take you from where you are to where you want to be. In an elementary form, this is what planning is all about—knowing where you are going and how you are going to get there.

Importance of Human Resource Planning

If an organization is to achieve its goals, it needs inputs: financial resources (such as money and credit), physical resources (such as buildings and equipment), and people. Too often, managers forget about how important that third factor, the people variable, is to the success of an organization. Many managers have failed because they have taken their human resources for granted.

To dramatize the value of the human factor, consider for a moment an organization like the Xerox Corporation, the duplicating machine company. It is a publicly held company whose stock is traded on the New York Stock Exchange, has sales of over $11 billion a year, and employs over 102,000 people. The hypothetical questions we propose are these: If these 102,000 people were to quit at once, what would happen to the organization? What would happen to the price of the company's stock? The answers are (1) the organization's survival would immediately be in jeopardy, and (2) the market price of the stock would plummet!

The point being made is simple: Organizations are composed of people, and these people represent one of the organization's most valuable assets. However, because the organization does not own people, as it does capital and physical assets, this resource is seldom given proper attention.

Its supply of human resources must be sufficient to ensure the healthy operation of the organization, whether it be a business firm, a government agency, a professional football team, or a university. Toward this objective of continuing healthy operations, the organization requires human resource planning.

A Definition

Human resource planning

Human resource planning is one of the most important elements in a successful HRM program. A survey of chief executives, for example, found that 85 percent listed human resource planning as one of the most critical management undertakings of this decade.[1] But what does the term *human resource planning* mean?

Specifically, human resource planning is the process by which an organization ensures that it has the right number and kinds of people, at the right places, at the right time, capable of effectively and efficiently completing those tasks that will help the organization achieve its overall objectives. Human resource planning, then, translates the organization's objectives and plans into the number of workers needed to meet those objectives. Without clear-cut planning, estimation of an organization's human resource need is reduced to mere guesswork.

In many organizations, few employees outside of the top executive group really know the short- and long-range objectives. It is not surprising, therefore, that management may find itself without the necessary human resources to fill unexpected vacancies, make replacements created by natural attrition, or meet opportunities created by the growth or development of new products or services because critical human resources are unavailable.

To ensure that people are available to provide the continued smooth development of an organization, organizations engage in human resource planning. The purpose of human resource planning is to assess where the organization is, where it is going, and what implications these assessments have on future supplies of and demands for human resources. Attempts must then be made to match supplies and demands, making them compatible with the achievement of the organization's future needs.

Assessing Current Human Resources

Human resource planning begins by developing a profile of the current status of human resources. Basically, this is an internal analysis that includes an inventory of the workers and skills already available within the organization and a comprehensive job analysis.

[1] "Wanted: A Manager to Fit Each Strategy," *Business Week*, February 25, 1980, p. 166.

Human Resource Inventory

Human resource inventory

In an era of complex computer systems, it is not too difficult for most organizations to generate a human resource inventory report. The input to this report would be derived from forms completed by employees and then checked by supervisors and the personnel department. Such reports would include a list of names, education, training, prior employment, current position, performance ratings, salary level, languages spoken, capabilities, and specialized skills for every employee in the organization.

From a human resource planning viewpoint, this input is valuable in determining what skills are currently available in the organization. It can act as a guide for considering new pursuits for the organization and can take advantage of opportunities to expand or alter the organization's strategies. This report also has value in other personnel activities, such as selecting individuals for training and executive development, for promotion, and for transfers.

The profile of the human resource inventory can provide crucial information for identifying current or future threats to the organization's ability to perform. For example, the organization can use this information to identify specific variables that are assumed to have a particular relationship to training needs, productivity improvements, and succession planning. A characteristic like technical obsolescence can, if it begins to permeate the entire organization, adversely affect the organization's performance.

HRIS

One of the newer devices for providing skills inventory information is the Human Resource Information System (HRIS). This system is designed to quickly fulfill the personnel informational needs of the organization with almost no additional expenditure of resources. Its highly technical features permit an organization to track most information about an employee and about jobs and retrieve that information when it is needed. HRIS has been useful for storing employment, training, and compensation information on each employee.

Succession planning

Some organizations also generate a separate executive inventory report (succession planning). This covers individuals in middle-management and top-executive positions. Such a report considers individual managers and the positions they occupy. When conducted solely on individual managers, the report is not unlike the general human resource inventory described above. However, when conducted with the position information, it adds a new dimension to the planning activity by highlighting those positions that may become vacant in the near future due to retirements, promotions, transfers, resignations, or death of the incumbent. Against this list of positions can be placed the individual manager's inventory to determine if there is sufficient managerial talent to cover both the expected and unexpected vacancies. When shortages are spotted, especially in the executive talent, the management can follow the suggestions outlined in Chapter 10 for developing managerial abilities.

Job Analysis

Job analysis

While the human resource inventory is concerned with telling us what individual employees can do, job analysis is more fundamental. It defines the jobs within the organization and the behaviors necessary to perform these jobs. For instance, what does a Court Reporter—Grade 2, who works for the City of Baltimore Municipal Court System, do? What minimal knowledge, skills, and abilities must an individual have to do a Court Reporter—Grade 2 job adequately? How do the requirements of a Court Reporter—Grade 2 job compare with those of a Court Reporter—Grade 3 or with the position of Court Stenographer? For compensation purposes, how does the Court Reporter—Grade 2 job compare with others in the City of Baltimore Municipal Court System? These are questions that job analysis can answer.

Job analysis obtains information about jobs, and it uses that information to develop job descriptions and job specifications and to conduct job evaluations (see Figure 4-1). These, in turn, are valuable in helping managers identify the kinds of individuals they should recruit, select, and develop, as well as providing guidance for decisions about training and career development, performance appraisal, and compensation administration.

Because of the importance of job analysis, we will examine it in the next chapter. The implications of the job analysis are many, as it is the framework on which all HRM activities are based.

Summary

The assessment of the organization's current human resource situation is based on a human resource inventory and a thorough job analysis. It should identify "where we are" by taking a close look at the jobs currently being done and the people doing those jobs. Because

FIGURE 4-1   The Purposes of Job Analysis

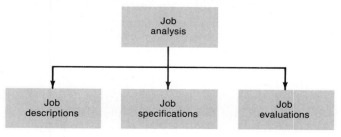

such jobs should be the result of previous human resource planning efforts, they should provide a fairly accurate reflection of what human resources the organization needs to achieve and what objectives the organization is currently seeking.

Assessing Where the Organization is Going

The organization's objectives and strategies for the future determine future human resource needs. That is, the number and mix of human resources are a reaction to the overall organizational strategy.

Demand for human resources is a result of demand for the organization's products or services. Based on its estimate of total revenue, the organization can attempt to establish the number and mix of human resources needed to reach these revenues. In some cases, however, the situation may be reversed. Where particular skills are necessary and the supply of these skills is scarce, the availability of satisfactory human resources will determine revenues. This might occur, for example, in a data-processing consulting firm that finds it has more business opportunities than it can handle. Its only limiting factor in building revenues may be its ability to locate and hire staff with the qualifications necessary to satisfy the consulting firm's clients. In most cases, however, the overall organizational goals and the resulting revenue forecast will provide the major input determining the organization's human resource demand requirements.

As a result, before we can estimate future human resource needs, some formal statement is required of what course the organization plans to take in the future, defined in terms of the sales or revenue forecast. This forecast should include not only a base dollar amount but a breakdown on how these dollars will be generated. The particular products that management expects to sell, or services that it expects to provide, will be important inputs in the determination of the employee mix necessary for the organization in future periods.

Demand for human resources

Implications of Future Demand

Once an assessment of the organization's current human resources situation has been made and the future direction of the organization in terms of revenue forecasts has been considered, a projection of future human resource needs can be developed.

It will be necessary to perform a year-by-year analysis for every significant job level and type. In effect, the result is a pro-forma human resource inventory covering specified years into the future. These pro-forma inventories must obviously be comprehensive and, therefore, complex. Organizations usually require a heterogeneous mix of people. Since people are not perfectly substitutable for each other within an organization, a shortage in engineering cannot necessarily be offset by transferring employees from the purchasing area where there is an oversupply. If accurate estimates are to be made of future demands in both qualitative and quantitative terms, more information is needed than just to determine that, for example, in eighteen months we will have to hire another 150 people. It is necessary to know what types of people are required. Accordingly, our forecasting methods must allow for the recognition of specific job needs as well as the total number of vacancies.

VIEWS IN THE NEWS

Temporary Help

It is estimated that 90 percent of all organizations use some type of temporary help services. This usage translates to approximately $7 billion in payroll expenses. The concept of temporary help services to complement an organization's staffing needs, however, is not new. It is, though, becoming more widely used for a number of reasons.

First, the use of temporary help reduces an organization's personnel fixed costs. Temporary employees are just that, temporary, and are not included as a permanent cost to an organization's payroll budget. Secondly, temporary personnel often bring higher skills and specialized services to an organization. Costs and time associated with training an employee to become fully functioning in a particular area are greater than the cost of the temporary help. This is especially true when variations in an organization's "production" cycle require immediate help.

With the advantages that are apparent in the temporary help services industry, advantages for both the company and the temporary help services firm, we can expect to see this concept expand as we enter the 1990s. More specifically, it has been suggested that we may see more of the following:

- Employee Leasing—A company terminates its employees and hires them back from an employee leasing firm.
- Full Service—Combining temporary help services with permanent placement services, to facilitate human resource planning. This gives an employer an opportunity to evaluate a temporary employee's performance. If the performance is good, then a permanent job offer could be made.
- Automation—Office automation requires a need for more highly skilled and trained workers. Temporary help services can supply these workers to an organization.

As organizations continue their plight to become "lean and mean," the availability of temporary help has assisted organizations in achieving this goal. This "pool of workers" too, can eliminate many problems associated with unexpected demands for labor.

Source: Walter W. Macauley, "Developing Trends in the Temporary Services Industry," *Personnel Administrator*, 31, No. 1 (January 1986), 61–68.

Implications of Future Supply

Estimating changes in internal supply requires the organization to look at those factors that can either increase or decrease its human resources. As previously noted in the discussion on estimating demand, the forecast must cover every level within the organization. Similarly, forecasting supply must also concern itself with the micro, or unit, level. For example, if one individual in Department X is demoted to a position in Department Y, and an individual in Department Y is promoted to a position in Department X, the net effect on the organization is zero. However, if an individual must be demoted, it is only through effective human resource planning that a competent replacement will be available to fill the recently vacated position.

Increasing Supply

Increasing supply of human resources

An increase in the supply of any unit's human resources can come from a combination of three sources: new hires, transfers-in, or individuals returning from leaves. The task of predicting these new inputs can range from simple to complex.

New hires are easy to predict, since they are self-initiated. A unit recruits to meet its needs, and hence, at least in the short term, the number and types of new hires that will be added can be determined with high accuracy.

It is more difficult, however, to predict transfers-in to a unit, since they often depend on concurrent action in other units. While the net effect to the total organization by a lateral transfer, demotion, or promotion may be zero, there are clear effects on individual departments and the mix within departments. If Mr. Smith is to be promoted from Department A to Department B, the disposition on the incumbent in Department B must be known.

Finally, the net effect on internal supply by people returning from leaves must be considered. This would include absences due to maternity, military, or sabbatical leaves. Such increases, however, are usually easy to estimate, since they are usually for some fixed duration—two months, six months, two years, and so forth. Note that the law currently requires that individuals who take maternity and military leaves be guaranteed that their job, or an equal position, will be available to them on their return.

Decreasing Supply

Decreasing supply of human resources

Decreases in the internal supply can come about through retirements, dismissals, transfers-out of the unit, layoffs, voluntary quits, sabbaticals, prolonged illnesses, or deaths. Some of these occurrences are easier to predict than others.

The easiest to forecast are retirements, assuming that a specific age criterion exists within the organization. If mandatory retirement occurs at age seventy, there is no difficulty in forecasting. Those individuals reaching their seventieth birthday will be required to terminate their ties with the organization. In some organizations, this can be modified by allowing the individual one-year delays—for example, up to age seventy-two. However, this can only be done with the agreement of both the employee and the organization. It is therefore totally controlled by management and easy to forecast accurately. At the other extreme, voluntary quits, prolonged illnesses, and deaths are difficult to forecast. Deaths of employees are the most difficult to forecast because they are usually unexpected. Although very large organizations can use probability techniques to estimate the number of deaths that will occur, such techniques are of course useless for forecasting the exact positions that will be affected. Voluntary quits can also be predicted by utilizing probabilities when the population size is fairly large. In other words, in a steel plant employing three thousand workers, one can estimate the approximate number of voluntary quits during any given year. In a department consisting of two or three workers, however, probability estimation is not a very effective tool. Weak predictive ability in small units is unfortunate, too, because voluntary quits have a major impact on supply in these units and are therefore a major concern to management.

In between the extremes, transfers, layoffs, sabbaticals, and dismissals can be forecast within reasonable limits of accuracy. Since all four of these types of actions are controllable by management—that is, they are either initiated by management or are within management's veto prerogative—each type can be reasonably predicted. Of the four, transfers out of the unit, such as lateral moves, demotions, or promotions up, are the most difficult to predict because they depend on openings in other units. Layoffs are more controllable and forecastable by management, especially in the short run. Sabbaticals, too, are reasonably easy to forecast, since most organizations' sabbatical policy requires a reasonable lead time between request and initiation of the leave. Dismissals, based on inadequate job performance, can usually be forecast in the same method as voluntary quits, using probabilities where large numbers of employees are involved. Additionally, performance evaluation reports are a reliable source for isolating the number of individuals whose employment might have to be terminated due to unsatisfactory work performance.

Estimated Changes in External Supply

The previous discussion on supply considered internal factors. We will now review those factors outside the organization that influence the supply of available workers.

Recent graduates from schools and colleges expand the supply of available human resources. This market is vast and includes everyone from high-school graduates to individuals who have received highly specialized training at the graduate level. Entrants to the work force from sources other than schools include housewives who are seeking full-time or part-time work to supplement the family income, women returning to work on a full-time basis in the capacity of primary bread-winner, students seeking part-time work, and individuals returning from military service. Of particular importance in this category are women. Past high levels of inflation and accelerating divorce rates, as well as changing attitudes, aspirations, and career expectations, have all acted as forces to increase the number of women entering the labor market.

Migration into a community, increases in the number of unemployed, and employed individuals who are seeking other employment opportunities all represent additional sources for the organization to consider as potential expanders of its labor supply.

Traditionally, it should be noted that consideration of only those supply sources identified above tends to understate the potential supply because many people can be retrained (formal or on-the-job training). Therefore the potential supply can differ from what one might conclude by looking at the obvious sources of supply. For example, with only a small amount of training, a journalist can become qualified to perform the tasks of a book editor. Thus an organization that is having difficulty securing individuals with skills and experience in book editing could consider those candidates who have had recent journalism or similar experience and were interested in being editors. In similar fashion, the potential supply for many other jobs can be expanded.

Matching Demand and Supply

The objective of human resource planning is to bring together our forecast of future demand and supply. The result of this effort will be to pinpoint shortages both in number and in kind; to highlight areas where overstaffing may exist (now or in the future); and to keep abreast of the opportunities that exist in the labor market to hire good people, either to satisfy current needs or to stockpile for the future.

Obviously, the most important concern must be given to the determination of shortages. Should an organization find that the demand for human resources will be increasing in the future, then it will have to hire additional staff or transfer people within the organization, or both, to balance the numbers, skills, mix, and quality of its human resources.

An action that is often overlooked, but may be necessary because of inadequate availability of human resources, is to change the organization's objectives. Just as inadequate financial resources can restrict the growth and opportunities available to an organization, the unavailability of the right type of people can also act as such a constraint.

A Special Case in HRP: Retrenchment

Much of the discussion in this chapter assumed that the organizations were operating in a growth mode. But many organizations today are facing a very different environment—one of decline. Not surprisingly, retrenchment carries with it different implications for HRP.

Retrenchment

The late 1970s were difficult for many organizations. There was a marked shrinkage of the once strong smokestack industries—steel, auto, and rubber. Competition in the high-tech industries soared, giving rise to massive layoffs at such companies as Apple, DEC, and Wang. Conglomerates were shedding less-profitable business units or closing down altogether. And foreign competition steadily increased, causing more problems for U.S. manufacturers.

Human resource planning tends to ignore issues resulting from managing in a declining organization. Going bankrupt, divesting holdings, or eliminating unprofitable product lines are activities that are not prevalent in a growing enterprise. As such, these activities have a major impact on the employee population. HRP, accordingly, must take a different focus.

Under retrenchment, certain topics associated with traditional HRP become irrelevant[2]—recruitment and selection. Both recruitment and selection become moot points. Finding the most productive workers for critical jobs that may need to be filled becomes a problem. Many candidates will rule out the possibility of working for an organization that is declining. Thus, at a time when the best employee is needed, a declining organization is in no position to be leading the industry in recruiting efforts. Unfortunately, this becomes a Catch–22 situation. The people who may best help a declining organization overlook the company as a possible place of employment.

Selection, too, has a much different focus. Job offers are seldom made. Little if any hiring is done; in fact, the converse is more prevalent—outplacement, layoffs, leaves of absence without pay, loaning, work sharing, reduced work hours, early retirements, and attrition. It is these areas that become critical HRP elements in organizations operating in a retrenchment mode.

Let us look at these further.

[2]This section has been adapted from Stephen P. Robbins, "The New Management: Managing Declining Organizations" (Presented at the Western Academy of Management Conference, Vancouver, Canada, April 1984).

Outplacement

Outplacement   Although outplacement services differ, they are intended to provide career guidance for displaced employees. Guidelines for such an activity include communicating what is to come; identifying the displaced employee; retraining those productive employees who can be placed elsewhere in the organization; and assisting with résumé writing, interviewing techniques, career counseling, and job searching.

Layoffs

Layoffs   Layoffs can take many forms. They can be temporary or permanent. Temporary layoffs usually occur during slack periods when the workloads do not warrant such a large work force. As soon as the work resumes to its normal level, workers are recalled. Although this is a cost-cutting measure, it can result in turning workers into cyclical employees and also increase a company's unemployment insurance premiums.

Proper human resource planning, leaving the work force at the proper staffing level, can help reduce this "yo-yo" effect. However, proper staffing may mean a permanent layoff for other employees. When this occurs, it is hoped that outplacement services are available. Unfortunately, many workers have been placed on permanent layoff and have joined countless others in periods of long unemployment.

Leaves of Absence Without Pay

Leaves of absence   One means of cutting labor costs temporarily is to give workers the opportunity to take leaves of absence without pay. This may provide time for an employee who is financially capable to leave the organization temporarily in pursuit of personal interests. These could range from attending college (to increase the employee's marketability and mobility) to engaging in a plethora of other endeavors. Individuals of-

---

FIGURE 4-2

The Problem of Job Security In a Declining Organization

Retrenchment takes its toll on chief executives. One study of nine companies facing cutbacks found that the board of directors in six of the companies chose a new CEO. Why? Certainly, the CEO's departure, in part, plays a scapegoat role. Someone has to die for the organization's sins and the CEO is the most visible. By replacing the CEO, the board indicates it is trying to correct the problem. Additionally, a new CEO may be less committed to previous decisions and, if chosen from the outside, less encumbered with political liabilities. This was certainly the case when International Harvester's Board fired Archie McCardell, the then CEO.

SOURCE: Veronique Bouchard and Larry Hirschhorn, "Cutbacks in the Private Sector," in *Cutting Back*, ed. Larry Hirschhorn and others (San Francisco: Jossey-Bass, 1983), pp. 270–71.

fered this leave are usually those whose jobs may be eliminated in the future. Thus this concept serves as a proactive method to help employees prepare for upcoming changes.

Loaning

Loaning

The loaning of valuable resources to other organizations is a means of keeping the "loaned" employees on the organization's payroll and bringing them back after the crisis has subsided. Under the loaning activity, usually higher-level managers are sent on special projects with government or quasi-government agencies (e.g., school boards, civic associations). The organization pays these "loaned" managers a reduced salary, with the difference usually paid by the agency. While an organization may ultimately lose some of these managers, some that have been "loaned" do return.

Work Sharing

Work sharing

Mike Malone, since becoming a father, has had child-care responsibilities. To meet these responsibilities, some organizations offer employees the opportunity to share jobs, or two people working one-half time, together constituting one full-time employee. Let us assume that Mike and his wife, Diane, are equally trained and skilled and hold the same job. Mike may work the first part of the day, go home, and fix lunch; and Diane then returns to the job to finish the day. While work sharing rarely consists of a husband-and-wife team, the concept is the same. Two people split an eight-hour workday, with the remaining time being spent on individual pursuits. Here two people hold one job, and the cost to the company is no greater than if only one person held the job. In retrenchment, this option may keep good employees from leaving the company. They may use the time to do some things they have wanted to do. And if the company recovers, it has not lost a valuable employee.

Reduced Work Hours

Reduced work hours

The retrenchment involving reduced work hours is based on the concept that there is only so much pie (payment to labor) and how it is split is up to the workers. For simplicity's sake, let us assume that we have $100,000 per year to spend for labor costs. We originally had ten workers with an annual income of $10,000. Now, as the company is experiencing economic hardships, only $80,000 per year is available to pay the workers. With no change in the hours worked, two employees would have to be laid off. To eliminate this dilemma, each worker agrees to work fewer hours, receiving less pay, so that the two jobs are saved. In this simplified case, instead of a forty-hour workweek, each employee is paid for only thirty-two hours of work. By working thirty-two hours each week, these ten employees will continue to be employed, but each will earn $2,000 less per year.

While the example is exaggerated, it does reveal an effort on behalf of employees to forgo some of their benefits in order to keep all the workers employed. The rationale is that receiving less is better than receiving nothing at all. However, it takes a strong personal conviction to accept that philosophy unless you are one of the two about to be laid off.

The work-sharing technique gained much popularity in the early 1980s. Many Japanese firms, as well as many progressive U.S. companies such as Hewlett-Packard, have used this technique to offset some of the problems brought about by economic downturns. The employees' morale flourishes in such cases, as the employees recognize the commitment that management has made to them. Again, similar to work sharing, in a retrenchment mode, it is possible to maintain an employee's skill and loyalty should the organization recover.

Early Retirement

Early retirement

Another retrenchment issue is the use of early retirement. Many of the industry giants have resorted to using early retirement inducements to reduce the number of workers, especially higher-level management personnel. Regardless of the specifics contained in these offers, the purpose is clear: buy out some of the highest-paid individuals in the organization and delegate their responsibilities to other employees making less money.

Usually the prime candidate for early retirement is an individual who is two or three years away from retiring. For this individual, the company offers a reduced retirement benefit until he or she reaches the normal retirement age or years of service.

Also, the option of buying the years of service remaining until normal retirement, for a sum of money equal to the amount that would have been contributed to the individual's retirement, may be available. In either case, the result is the same: a reduction in the cost of paying exorbitant salaries to those individuals. Although in retrenchment this is an effective cost savings plan, an organization may lose some key executives who just decide to "bail out."

Attrition

Attrition

The last retrenchment issue is attrition. *Attrition* is a process whereby as incumbents leave their jobs for any reason (retirement, resignations, transfers, etc.), those jobs will not be filled. Usually accompanying the process of attrition is a hiring freeze. Hiring freezes dictate that no recruiting will take place for jobs that are to be eliminated.

Attrition and hiring freezes can be implemented organization-wide (used to reduce overall employment numbers) or can be directed toward particular departments or jobs that may no longer be needed. The bottom-line result is that attrition with a hiring freeze is a short-term means of addressing a surplus of employees.

Summary

When an organization experiences retrenchment, human resources are going to be affected. Events surrounding the managing of a decline should be of concern to those conducting human resource planning.

Conclusion

By focusing on productivity, organizations are realizing that it is imperative to hire employees who can do the job and be successful at it. It behooves the organization to find these people, bring them into the organization, and maintain their services. That is sound human resource planning and implementation. In fact, it is the same thing we said regarding equal employment opportunity.

It is unfortunate that organizations had to suffer through poor economic times before they realized that many of their hiring practices and personnel philosophies were out of synchronization. They can no longer just hire to hire. And they can no longer rest on the belief that individuals will stay with a company through thick and thin. They must realize that training the new employee and updating training for current employees is necessary. And sound human resource planning is one means of ensuring this.

Human resource planning is full of "shoulds," but it is also influenced by "what is." Ideally, the "shoulds" should include an effective forecasting program that identifies the number of people needed in the years ahead, coupled with the skill levels required. Additionally, there should be a succession plan, whereby individuals are targeted to fill positions when the incumbent leaves.

But unfortunately, the "shoulds" do not dominate. Whereas long-term planning is the most effective, the short-term, informal human resource planning systems are the norm. In some organizations, organizational charts are color coded, with each color code referring to a name of an individual who is next in line for the position. While not scientific in nature, this system does provide a measure to see who is available at any time.

As technology keeps improving, more software will be developed to aid organizations in their human resource planning. The need is evident, as organizations must be able to plan for their future human resource requirements and ensure that a continual supply of talent is available and ready to move into managerial ranks when the time comes.

SUMMARY

1. *Human resource planning* is the process by which an organization ensures that it has the right number and kinds of people, at the right places, at the right time, capable of effectively and efficiently completing those tasks that will help the organization achieve its overall objectives.

2. The first step in the human resource planning process requires assessing the current status of the organization's resources:
   a. A human resource inventory describes skills available within the organization.
   b. A job analysis provides information about jobs currently being done. This information is the critical input for job descriptions, job specifications, and job evaluation.

3. The second step is to review the organization's overall objectives and revenue projections.

4. The third step translates the organization's revenue projections into a forecast of demand for human resources.

5. The fourth step involves an assessment and forecast of internal and external supply sources.

6. The final step in the human resource planning process consists of matching the forecasts of future demand and supply. This will highlight shortages and overstaff positions.

7. When an organization is in the midst of retrenchment, human resource planning takes on a different focus.

8. Relevant retrenchment issues include:
   a. Outplacement
   b. Layoffs
   c. Leaves of absence
   d. Loaning
   e. Work sharing
   f. Reduced work hours
   g. Early retirement
   h. Attrition

KEY TERMS

Attrition
Human Resource Information
  System (HRIS)
Human resource inventory
Human resource planning
Job analysis

Layoffs
Leaves of absence
Outplacement counseling
Retrenchment
Succession planning
Work sharing

QUESTIONS FOR REVIEW

1. Define *human resource planning.*
2. Outline the steps involved in the human resource planning process.
3. How can an organization's human resource supply be increased?
4. How can an organization's human resource supply be decreased?
5. Contrast human resource planning in theory with its actual practice.
6. How is organization-wide planning different from human resource planning? How is it similar?
7. How can organizations develop accurate human resource plans when there are so many rapidly changing environmental factors over which managers have little or no control?
8. What role does judgment play in making forecasts of future human resource demand and supply?
9. The text states that human resource planning is predominantly short term in nature. Why do you believe this is so?
10. Describe the implications on HRP when an organization is in a retrenchment mode.

QUESTIONS FOR DISCUSSION

1. "If people in our society are mobile and change jobs frequently, won't that detract from having an effective human resource planning system?" Discuss.
2. "More emphasis should be placed on the internal supply of employees for meeting future employee needs because these individuals already know the organization." Do you agree or disagree? Discuss.
3. Discuss the necessity for equating the demand for and supply of labor.
4. "The only fair way to lay off workers is on a last-in, first-out basis." Do you agree or disagree? Discuss.
5. "A retrenchment phase is short term. We must buckle down, sweat through it until we can resume operations as normal." Do you agree or disagree? Discuss.

The Road to Success

Concord General has decided to install a new Cardiac Surgery Unit. John Michaels has informed Jim Wilson that he is confident that the State Board of Health will approve the venture and that there are now staffing questions that need to be resolved.

Anticipating the authorization from the state, John instructed the physical plant manager to renovate the storage area adjacent to the Intensive Care Unit. He believed that this location was the most feasible, as the two units required many of the same pieces of equipment and some sharing could occur, but not at the expense of transferring machinery. With this in mind, John told Jim to make sure that the staffing levels would meet the state's requirements and to be prepared for full operation in six weeks.

The new unit was to be capable of handling three patients at a time, with each patient occupying a bed for two days. After this two-day recovery period, the patient would be transferred to a hospital floor bed where he or she would be cared for by the floor nurse. The preliminary reports revealed that there were enough patients to keep the Cardiac Surgery Unit operating seven days a week.

Furthermore, Jim was aware of the state's requirement that there be a patient-nurse ratio of one to one. Simple mathematics revealed that Jim would need three nurses for each eight-hour shift, totaling nine nurses, plus three more nurses to round out the staffing needs. (Three nurses would be off on any particular day.)

Jim realized that he had twenty-eight full-time nurses currently in the Intensive Care Unit. Although their skills were similar, in order to work in the Cardiac Surgery Unit, a nurse must be certified by the state. Certification could be obtained by attending a two-week workshop on cardiac surgery techniques and practices. Jim was stumped. He couldn't relinquish twelve nurses from Intensive Care for two weeks to be trained because that would cause staff shortages in the unit.

He proceeded to contact Judy Sapp, the hospital's nurse recruiter, to explain the situation. Judy stated that meeting the six-week deadline was nearly impossible, but she would help in any way she could. She told Jim that the average recruiting time for a specialized nurse was ten to twelve weeks, but she had some ideas on how to cut that time down. "However, it could be expensive," she remarked.

1. How has the proposed addition of the Cardiac Surgery Unit affected Concord General's human resource plans?
2. How would a human resource inventory assist in Jim and Judy's recruiting efforts to fill the Cardiac Surgery Unit nurse positions?
3. How could this staffing problem have been lessened? Anticipated?
4. What lessons can Concord General learn from this experience?

CASE APPLICATION

Pink Slips

In 1979, Edward L. Hennessey, Jr., became CEO of the Allied Corporation. Upon his taking over, he began to look for ways to make the organization more profitable. Throughout his investigation, he determined that the company's payroll was too high and, in part, the root of the problem.

Later that year, Mr. Hennessey instructed his personnel department to reduce the number of employees by 842, creating a savings of over $30 million. Realizing that this would be a shock, the company prepared to outplace the affected employees. An outplacement firm was hired to oversee the operations. The personnel director wrote letters to the CEOs of more than one hundred companies, trying to place these workers. Special offices were set up so that the terminated employees could make telephone contacts and work on their résumés. An array of services were available to the individuals, all leading to help them find new employment opportunities.

In the final review, almost all of the 842 workers were outplaced. Some, still upset about being terminated, complained that the new positions were lower than their current ones. Nonetheless, most were successfully outplaced, and severance from Allied was smoothly processed.

QUESTIONS

1. Discuss the advantages and disadvantages to using the company's premises for outplacement services.
2. What socially responsible behavior was exhibited by Allied? How might this help or hurt its image?

ADDITIONAL READINGS

CONNOLLY, PAUL M., "Clearing the Deadwood," *Training and Development Journal,* January 1986, pp. 58–61.

SPRUELL, GERALDINE, "Business Planning for Parenthood," *Training and Development Journal,* August 1986, pp. 30–35.

STONE, THOMAS H., and JACK FIORITO, "A Perceived Uncertainty Model of Human Resource Forecasting Technique Use," *Academy of Management Review,* 11, No. 3 (July 1986), 635–42.

"The End of Corporate Loyalty," *Business Week,* August 4, 1986, pp. 42–51.

WHEELOCK, KEITH, "No Fault Corporate Divorce," *Personnel Administrator,* March 1985, pp. 112–116.

CHAPTER 5

Job Analysis

AFTER READING THIS CHAPTER, YOU WILL BE ABLE TO:

1. Define *job analysis*
2. Explain the eight-step job analysis information hierarchy
3. Identify the six general techniques for obtaining job information
4. Describe the Department of Labor's Functional Job Analysis and Purdue University's Position Analysis Questionnaire
5. Distinguish between job descriptions, job specifications, and job evaluation

We analyze our jobs here once every ten years, whether we need to or not.

—Anonymous

The Hampstead Electronic Corporation has experienced a 30 percent turnover of computer programmers during the past three years. An analysis of the resignations has indicated that the average length of stay for the computer programmers in the company was eleven months. Perplexed by this dilemma and the resulting productivity losses, the president of Hampstead Electronics has insisted on an investigation to find out why such a high turnover rate exists.

Contacting most of the individuals who had resigned and asking them why they quit, the response was that what they were *hired* to do and what they were *required* to do were different things, the latter requiring different skills and aptitudes. Feeling frustrated and bored, they quit. Unfortunately, the company's training costs these past three years have run approximately 700 percent over budget. When the president of Hampstead asked what there was in the computer programmers' job that made it so difficult to properly match the job requirements with people skills, no one could give an answer. It appeared that no one took the time to find out what the computer programmer jobs were all about.

In the preceding chapter we alluded to the importance of the job analysis. This importance cannot be overstated, as most of the major activities involving employees are based on the job analysis. This means that recruiting, selecting, hiring, paying, and promoting employees, among other things, are procedurally defined by the results of the job analysis.

In the remainder of this chapter, we will explore job analysis, defining what job analysis is, how it is used, and what are the results of the action. We will also discuss the uses of job analysis in practice.

What Is Job Analysis?

Job analysis:
definition

A *job analysis* is a systematic exploration of the activities within a job. It is a basic technical procedure, one that is used to define the duties, responsibilities, and accountabilities of a job. This analysis *involves compiling a detailed description of tasks, determining the relationship of the job to technology and to other jobs and examining the knowledge, qualifications or employment standards accountabilities and other incumbent requirement.*[1]

In fewer words, we can say that a job analysis indicates what activities and accountabilities the job entails. There is no mystery to a job analysis; it is just an accurate recording of the activities involved.

In recording these activities, we are simply gathering information. And while every job is multifaceted, we must confine our information gathering to specific job attributes. What are these attributes? Figure 5-1 depicts the hierarchy of information that the job analysis seeks. Let us take a moment to define our terms. We begin with the smallest segment of information, which we call an element.[2] A job *element* is the smallest unit into which work can be divided. Putting the tomato on a hamburger is an example of an element in the job of a fry cook at McDonald's.

Task
A *task* is a distinct work activity carried out for a distinct purpose. Examples would include typing a letter, preparing a lecture, or unloading a mail truck.

Duty
A *duty* is a number of tasks. Counseling students is a duty of a college instructor. A general accounting clerk's duties might include preparing the monthly income statement and distributing the weekly payroll checks.

Position
A *position* refers to one or more duties performed by one person in an organization. There are at least as many positions as there are workers in the organization; vacancies may create more positions than

[1]Richard I. Henderson, *Compensation Management*, 3rd ed. (Reston, Va.: Reston Publishing Co., 1982), p. 121.

[2]The following material was adapted from Wayne Cascio, *Applied Psychology in Personnel Management* (Reston, Va.: Reston Publishing Co., 1978), p. 133.

FIGURE 5-1   *The Job Analysis Information Hierarchy*

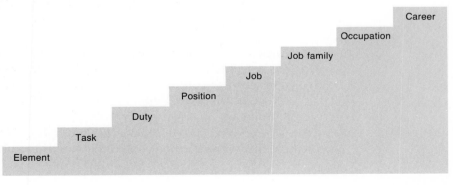

employees. Examples of positions include Supervisor—Grade IV; Accounts Payable Clerk I; and Assistant Professor, Level 2.

Job A *job* is a type of position within the organization. If a large insurance company employs sixty life insurance actuaries, then there are sixty positions, but just one life insurance actuary job.

Job family A *job family* is a group of two or more jobs that either call for similar worker characteristics or contain parallel work tasks as determined by job analysis. At the previously mentioned insurance company, service clerks and policy correspondents represent two jobs that frequently are placed in a common job family because they have many similar worker characteristics.

Occupation An *occupation* is a group of similar jobs found across organizations. Electrician, accountant, and service maintenance engineer are examples of occupations.

Career A *career* represents a sequence of positions, jobs, or occupations that a person has over his or her working life.

Why is it important to know the terms defined above? As we will show, job analysis begins at the level of the element and attempts to build understanding of jobs, occupations, and careers as components are combined. In other words, the previous definitions should help you to see how jobs evolve and develop.

Armed with this conceptual framework, let us now look at how to conduct the job analysis. The next section will explore the more widely used job analysis techniques.

Job Analysis Methods

Job analysis methods The methods that managers can use to determine job elements and the concomitant knowledge, skills, and abilities necessary for successful performance include the following:

1. *Observation method*—Using this method, a job analyst watches employees directly or reviews films of workers on the job. While the observation method provides firsthand information, workers in many cases do not function most efficiently when they are being watched. Thus distortions in the job analysis may occur. This method also requires that the entire range of activities be observable; possible with some jobs, but impossible for many—e.g., most managerial jobs.

2. *Individual interview method*—Using this method, job incumbents are selected and extensively interviewed. The results of these interviews are combined into a single job analysis. This method is effective for assessing what a job entails, but is very time-consuming.

3. *Group interview method*—This method is similar to the individual interview method except that a number of job incumbents are

interviewed simultaneously. Accuracy is increased in assessing jobs, but group dynamics may hinder its effectiveness.

4. *Structured questionnaire method*—Using this method, workers are sent a structured questionnaire on which they check or rate items they perform on their job from a long list of possible task items. This technique is excellent for gathering information about jobs. However, exceptions to a job may be overlooked, and feedback is often lacking.

5. *Technical conference method*—This method utilizes supervisors with extensive knowledge of the job. Here, specific characteristics of a job are obtained from the "experts." Although a good data-gathering method, it often overlooks the incumbent workers' perceptions about what they do on their job.

6. *Diary method*—This method requires job incumbents to record their daily activities. It provides much information but is seldom applicable to job activities. The diary method is the most intrusive of the job analysis methods, requiring much work on the part of the incumbent and, accordingly, requiring much time. To capture the entire range of work activities, this method may have to continue for long periods of time—all adding to its cost.

These six methods are not meant to be viewed as mutually exclusive. No one method is universally superior. Even obtaining job information from the incumbents may create a problem, especially if these individuals describe what they feel they should be doing rather than what they actually do. The best results, then, are usually achieved with some combination of methods—with information provided by individual employees, their immediate supervisors, a professional analyst, or an unobtrusive source such as filmed observations.

Realizing that a job analysis can occur in a number of ways, let us now consider two notable job analysis processes.

Functional Job Analysis

Functional job analysis

Functional job analysis was developed by the Department of Labor (DOL). This procedure describes what a worker does by having someone observe and interview the employee. This information is then cataloged into three general functions that exist in all jobs—data, people, and things (see Figure 5-2). An office receptionist clerk, for example, might be found to copy the data, speak with people, and handle things. The job would be coded as 5, 6, 7. This type of coding of key elements has already been done for over thirty thousand job titles listed in the *Dictionary of Occupational Titles*, readily available from the U.S. government. Use of this publication can significantly reduce the management's burden of gathering information on jobs for its organization. Additionally, the DOL job codes are supplemented with a detailed nar-

FIGURE 5-2

Work Functions

DATA	PEOPLE	THINGS
0 Synthesizing	0 Mentoring	0 Setting Up
1 Coordinating	1 Negotiating	1 Precision Working
2 Analyzing	2 Instructing	2 Operating–Controlling
3 Compiling	3 Supervising	3 Driving–Operating
4 Computing	4 Diverting	4 Manipulating
5 Copying	5 Persuading	5 Tending
6 Comparing	6 Speaking–Signaling	6 Feeding–Offbearing
	7 Serving	7 Handling
	8 Taking Instructions–Helping	

SOURCE: U.S. Department of Labor, *Dictionary of Occupational Titles*, 4th ed. (Washington, D.C.: (Government Printing Office, 1977).

rative. So the data on the office receptionist clerk job, described above, would also tell us exactly *what* data are copied, with *whom* the jobholder speaks, and *which* things are handled.

The DOL technique allows managers to group jobs into job families that require similar kinds of worker behavior. Candidates for these jobs, therefore, should hold similar worker traits. Obviously this information will benefit managers in identifying the kinds of people that the organization needs.

Position Analysis Questionnaire

PAQ   Developed by researchers at Purdue University, the Position Analysis Questionnaire (PAQ) generates job requirement information that is applicable to all types of jobs; but in contrast to the DOL approach, it presents a more quantitative and finely tuned description of jobs. The PAQ procedure involves "194 elements within 27 division job dimensions and five overall job dimensions."[3] These 194 elements represent six activity categories (see Figure 5-3). Jobs are rated by the degree to which these 194 elements are present.

By using statistical analysis on the PAQ, researchers have found that jobs tend to differ from each other on five dimensions. (In the DOL approach, by contrast, there were three key behavioral dimensions by which jobs differed—data, people, and things.) Analysis of the 194 elements in the PAQ, for more than five hundred different jobs, indicated that the important dimensions on which jobs differed from each other were the following:

1. *Having decision-making/communication/social responsibilities.* This dimension reflects activities involving considerable amounts

[3]Henderson, *Compensation Management*, p. 142.

FIGURE 5-3

Categories Comprising the PAQ's 194 Job Elements

CATEGORY	NUMBER OF JOB ELEMENTS
1. Information input. Where and how does the worker get the information he or she uses on the job?	35
2. Mental processes. What reasoning, decision making, planning, etc., are involved in the job?	14
3. Work output. What physical activities does the worker perform and what tools or devices are used?	49
4. Relationships with other persons. What relationships with other people are required in the job?	36
5. Job context. In what physical and social contexts is the work performed?	19
6. Other job characteristics.	41

SOURCE: Reprinted with permission from the Position Analysis Questionnaire, copyright 1969, Purdue Research Foundation.

of communication and interaction with people, as well as responsibilities associated with decision making and planning functions, such as might be the case with a general foreman.

2. *Performing skilled activities.* This dimension is characterized by activities of a skilled nature in which technical devices or tools tend to be used, and in which there is an emphasis on precision, recognizing differences, and manual control, such as in the case of tool and die makers.

3. *Being physically active/related environmental conditions.* This dimension is characterized by activities involving considerable movement of the entire body or major parts of it, and by environments such as those found in factories and shops.

4. *Operating vehicles/equipment.* This dimension is characterized by some aspect of the operation or use of vehicles or equipment, typically involving sensory and perceptual processes and physical functions.

5. *Processing information.* This dimension is characterized by a wide range of information-processing activities, such as those engaged in by budget officers or editors, in some instances accompanied by the use of machines such as office machines.[4]

The PAQ, in summary, allows management to scientifically and quantitatively group interrelated job elements into job dimensions. This, in turn, allows jobs to be compared with each other and similar

[4]Ernest J. McCormick and Joseph Tiffin, *Industrial Psychology,* 6th ed. (Englewood Cliffs, N.J.: Prentice-Hall, 1974), pp. 54–55.

jobs to be clustered into job families. Of course, the major use of this information is to develop job descriptions and job specifications, and to conduct job evaluation.

Note that although these techniques appear to be straightforward, some preparatory work is necessary before implementing one of them. Job analysis is not difficult per se, but detailed. To conduct the job analysis, you should gather as much background information as possible about the job to be analyzed. This information is readily available through old job descriptions and other literature, such as the organization chart. Once you have this information, you need to identify those particular jobs to be reviewed. Remember, all jobs need to be analyzed, but not all at one time. In identifying the job, you also identify those individuals with specific or expert relevant job information. Working with these individuals, you now employ one of the techniques described above. Once this has been accomplished, your data-gathering endeavor is over, but you are not finished. You must now analyze the information and produce the end results—the job description and the job specifications.

Purposes of Job Analysis

In the preceding chapter, we developed a schematic diagram of the purpose of the job analysis (Figure 4-1). Each of these categories—job descriptions, job specifications, and job evaluations—serves a distinct purpose in the job analysis process. Note that it is these three outcomes that are derived from the job analysis. The misconception about the job analysis is that it is a tangible product. It is not. The job analysis is the conceptual, analytical process or action from which we develop our tangible outcomes: job descriptions, job specifications, and job evaluations. Let us now explore these three outcomes.

Job Descriptions

Job descriptions

A job description is a written statement of what the jobholder does, how it is done, and why it is done. It should accurately portray job content, environment, and conditions of employment. A common format for a job description includes the job title, the duties to be performed, the distinguishing characteristics of the job, and the authority and responsibilities of the jobholder. An example of a job description for a record clerk at the Western Electric Company is provided in Figure 5-4.

When we discuss employee recruitment, selection, and appraisal, we will find that the job description acts as an important resource for (1) describing the job (either verbally by recruiters and interviewers or in written advertisements) to potential candidates, (2) guiding newly hired employees in what they are specifically expected to do, and (3)

VIEWS IN THE NEWS

Putting Action Into Your Job Description

If you've ever had to write a job description, with its very important list of responsibilities, you know that it's not an easy task. Conventional wisdom is that the writer use active verbs to describe the work to be done—words like "analyze," "direct," "sell," and the like. But sometimes even the best of writers find themselves at a loss for a verb to describe the tasks being considered.

To trigger your memory and help you get started on the next job description you have to write, here is a list of 110 verbs that are specific, precise, and rich in meaning.

Acquire	Deliver	List
Adjust	Demonstrate	Maintain
Administer	Design	Manage
Advise	Determine	Modify
Analyze	Develop	Monitor
Apply	Devise	Plan
Appraise	Direct	Prepare
Arrange	Draft	Present
Assess	Drive	Process
Assist	Edit	Program
Assure	Enlist	Prohibit
Brief	Ensure	Project
Bring	Establish	Purchase
Budget	Estimate	Qualify
Buy	Evaluate	Rate
Catalogue	Expand	Recommend
Chair	Expedite	Relate
Change	Explain	Report
Classify	Finance	Research
Close	Forecast	Review
Communicate	Formulate	Revise
Compare	Gather	Seek
Complete	Grade	Select
Conceive	Guide	Set
Conclude	Implement	Solve
Conduct	Improve	Specify
Contact	Initiate	Study
Continue	Inspect	Suggest
Control	Instruct	Summarize
Coordinate	Interpret	Target
Correct	Interview	Teach
Counsel	Introduce	Test
Critique	Investigate	Train
Deal	Join	Treat
Decide	Keep	Type
Define	Lead	Write
Delegate	License	

Source: Reprinted by permission of the publisher, from SUPERVISORY MANAGEMENT, January 1985 © 1985 American Management Association, New York. All rights reserved.

FIGURE 5-4

Example of a Job Description

JOB TITLE: Record Clerk   OCCUPATIONAL CODE NO. 3221
REPORTS TO: Record Supervisor   JOB NO. 01
SUPERVISES: None   GRADE LEVEL 20
                                   DATE: 2/21/88

FUNCTIONS: Originate, process, and maintain comprehensive records; implement required controls; collect and summarize data as requested.

DUTIES AND RESPONSIBILITIES:

Review a variety of documents, listings, summaries, etc., for completeness and accuracy.

Check records against other current sources such as reports or summaries; investigate differences and take required action to ensure that records are accurate and up to date; compile and summarize data into report format as required.

Implement controls for obtaining, perserving, and supplying a variety of information.

Prepare simple requisitions, forms, and other routine memoranda.

Furnish information upon request to interested personnel by selecting required data from records, reports, source documents, and similar papers.

Provide functional guidance to lower-level personnel as required.

May use a calculating machine, typewriter, or key punch machine to compile, type, or keypunch information.

JOB CHARACTERISTICS: Skilled operation of typewriter, calculating machine, or key punch machine is not necessarily a requirement of this job.

providing a point of comparison in appraising whether the actual activities of a job incumbent align with the stated duties.

Job Specifications

Job specifications   The job specification states the minimum acceptable qualifications that the incumbent must possess to perform the job successfully. Based on the information acquired through job analysis, the job specification identifies the knowledge, skills, and abilities needed to do the job effectively. Individuals possessing the personal characteristics identified in the job specification should perform the job more effectively than individuals lacking these personal characteristics. The job specification, therefore, is an important tool in the selection process, for it keeps the selector's attention on the list of qualifications necessary for an incumbent to perform the job and assists in determining whether candidates are qualified. An example of a job specification for a record clerk position is shown in Figure 5-5.

Job Evaluations

Job evaluations   In addition to providing data for job descriptions and specifications, job analysis is also valuable in providing the information that makes

FIGURE 5-5

Example of a Job Specification

JOB TITLE: Record Clerk.

EDUCATION: Minimum number of years of formal schooling: 12. Type of education: General with emphasis on business. Special subjects required: Some background and familiarity with accounting, office procedures, office machines, and the telecommunications industry.

PHYSICAL AND HEALTH: Good health; emotional stability.

APPEARANCE: Neat and clean.

MENTAL ABILITIES: Good with figures.

SPECIAL ABILITIES: Ability to work with others, manual dexterity.

PREVIOUS WORK EXPERIENCE: Minimum of one year, preferably in an industrial organization.

SPECIAL KNOWLEDGE OR SKILLS: Skilled in filing documents, checking records, compiling data, and initiating reports.

MATURITY: Must be capable of assuming increased responsibility within two years.

OTHER: Expect that incumbent would be ready for promotion (normally to the position of record supervisor or analyst) within 24 months.

comparison of jobs possible. If an organization is to have an equitable compensation program, jobs that have similar demands in terms of skills, education, and other personal characteristics should be placed in common compensation groups. Job evaluation contributes toward that end by specifying the relative value of each job in the organization. Job evaluation, therefore, is an important part of compensation administration, as will be discussed in detail in Chapter 16. In the meantime you should keep in mind that job evaluation is made possible by the data generated from job analysis.

Summary

What has been presented thus far is a recapitulation of the techniques, processes, and outcomes of the job analysis. Information that has been processed through the job analysis has implications reaching further than the organization. General job descriptions and specifications are widely used in the career counseling of potential and current employees.

With the use of the computer, individuals can obtain an overview of careers in the fields of their choice. This has been especially appealing for job seekers, as the information provides a current update of the job employment potential average salary and much more. Figures 5-6 and 5-7 are two examples of such use. Imagine how much easier it is to search career opportunities with this information as a guide.

FIGURE 5-6

PERSONNEL MANAGER

JOB DESCRIPTION:

Plans and carries out policies related to personnel management for a company. Recruits, interviews and selects workers for jobs. Informs new employees of company procedures and goals. Keeps record of insurance coverage, pension plan and hires, promotions, transfers and terminations. Investigates accidents and prepares reports for insurance company. Prepares budget of personnel operations.

School courses should include English, business, economics, sociology, and psychology. Usually requires a bachelor's degree. Graduate degrees preferred or required for some jobs. Training for this occupation is also available through the military. Personnel managers may be employed by all kinds of companies and businesses or federal, state and local government. A few are in business for themselves.

Indications are that through 1990, employment potential for this occupation will be good or stable in most states. Best opportunities will be in CA, FL, GA, NC, PA, SC, TX, and VA.

The national average starting salary is at least $24,900.

SPECIFIC OCCUPATIONAL REQUIREMENTS

INTERESTS RELATED TO THE OCCUPATION:
  Activities involving people and the communication of ideas
  Activities involving business contact with people
  Activities resulting in prestige or the esteem of others

APTITUDES RELATED TO THE OCCUPATION:
  Ability to understand and use words effectively
  Ability to do arithmetic quickly and accurately

PHYSICAL DEMANDS OF THE OCCUPATION:
  Sedentary: lifting up to 10 pounds occasionally
  Involves talking and hearing
  Involves both standing and sitting fairly equally

WORK CONDITIONS

WORK ENVIRONMENT:
  Mostly inside

WORK HOURS:
  Work customarily during weekdays
  35–40 hour work-week normal
  Occasional overtime
  Occasional travel

EMPLOYMENT POTENTIAL:
  Stable employment potential

EDUCATION AND TRAINING

HIGH SCHOOL:
  High school diploma

COLLEGE/UNIVERSITY:
  Bachelor's degree
  Master's or advanced degree
  Doctorate degree

FIGURE 5-6 (*continued*)

EDUCATION AND TRAINING

OTHER TRAINING ROUTES:
   Training available through the military

OCCUPATIONAL CLUSTERS:
   Business and Office

DOT OCCUPATIONAL CATEGORIES AND DIVISIONS

PROFESSIONAL, TECHNICAL AND MANAGERIAL OCCUPATIONS:
   Administrative specializations, managers and officials

INTEREST AREAS:
   Leader—Influencing

STANDARD OCCUPATIONAL CLASSIFICATION GROUPS

EXECUTIVE, ADMINISTRATIVE AND MANAGERIAL OCCUPATIONS:
   Officials and Administrators, other

SOURCE: The Guidance Information System™, Occupational File, Houghton Mifflin Company, Educational Software Division.

FIGURE 5-7

TELLER

Receives and pays out money and keeps records of money involved in banking and other financial transactions. Receives cash and checks for deposit. Examines endorsements, verifies amounts and enters in depositors' accounts. Cashes checks, pays out money and enters account withdrawals. Places holds on accounts for uncollected funds.

School courses in mathematics, bookkeeping and typing helpful. A high school diploma is required. Completion of college or business school courses helpful. Nearly all tellers are employed by banking institutions. Some may become head tellers or even bank officers.

Indications are that through 1990, employment potential for this occupation will be good or stable in most states in spite of the introduction of automated tellers.

The national average starting salary is at least $11,200.

SPECIFIC OCCUPATIONAL REQUIREMENTS

INTERESTS RELATED TO THE OCCUPATION:
   Activities involving business contact with people
   Activities of a routine, concrete, organized nature

APTITUDES RELATED TO THE OCCUPATION:
   Ability to do arithmetic quickly and accurately
   Ability to understand verbal/tabular material
   Ability to make precise movements with speed
   Ability to manipulate small objects with fingers

FIGURE 5-7 (*continued*)

SPECIFIC OCCUPATIONAL REQUIREMENTS

PHYSICAL DEMANDS OF THE OCCUPATION:
   Light: lifting up to twenty pounds
   Involves reaching, handling, feeling
   Involves talking and hearing
   Involves ability to see clearly
   Involves mostly standing

WORKING CONDITIONS

WORK ENVIRONMENT:
   Mostly inside

WORK HOURS:
   Work customarily during weekdays
   35–40 hour work-week normal
   Occasional night work
   Occasional weekend/holiday work

EMPLOYMENT POTENTIAL:
   Stable employment potential

EDUCATION AND TRAINING

HIGH SCHOOL:
   High School Diploma

VOCATIONAL TECHNICAL TRAINING, NON-DEGREE:
   Business school: 1–2 years

ON THE JOB TRAINING:
   OJT: unspecified length of time

OCCUPATIONAL CLUSTERS:
   Business and Office
   Public Services

DOT OCCUPATIONAL CATEGORIES AND DIVISIONS

CLERICAL AND SALES OCCUPATIONS:
   Computing and account-recording occupations

INTEREST AREAS:
   Business Detail

STANDARD OCCUPATIONAL CLASSIFICATION GROUPS:

ADMINISTRATIVE SUPPORT OCCUPATIONS, INCLUDING CLERICAL:
   Administrative Support Occupations, including Clerical

SOURCE: The Guidance Information System™, Occupational File, Houghton Mifflin Company, Educational Software Division.

Conclusion

Twenty-five years ago, job analysis was almost nonexistent. The major thrust behind job analysis has been the Civil Rights Act of 1964, specifically Title VII. As described in Chapter 3, the impact of Title VII was to require that the criteria used in hiring, firing, and promoting be job related (valid). The only means of establishing this job-relatedness factor has been to identify what the job entails and what an incumbent worker must possess to perform successfully on the job. Earlier in the chapter this was our definition of job analysis and job specifications.

But is job analysis being conducted? Conducted properly? The answers to these questions vary depending on the organization. Generally, most organizations do conduct some type of job analysis. This job analysis extends further than just meeting the federal requirement. It is used widely in organizations' compensation programs to ensure equity within the system.[5] More important, though, the more progressive organizations are using job analysis as a means of assessing what skills are needed to fulfill the requirements of the job. This is then followed by a human resource skills inventory that identifies what skills the employees possess and what skills are needed. This type of activity is paramount for training and development needs and for succession purposes.

While the uses of the job analysis appear to be plentiful, one problem that has been cited in seminars has focused on who conducts the job analysis. If such an activity were as important as we have indicated, the job analysis would undoubtedly be conducted by a highly trained specialist. But that is not necessarily the case. Many organizations place the responsibility for analyzing jobs on the newly hired college graduate. The job then becomes one of a training ground as well as an apprenticeship. Personnel managers appear to justify the delegating of this responsibility on the grounds that it serves as a good indoctrination for personnel specialists.

While not attempting to present an issue on the person selected to conduct a job analysis, we feel that it is imperative to have a knowledgeable person handling the activities. The consequences of these endeavors is such that it warrants putting the best available person into the position. Certainly analyzing jobs is not one of the glamorous aspects of HRM, but it is one of the more important activities that must be conducted and continually updated.

A Final Note

This chapter's point is clear: Job analysis is such that it should not be lightly addressed within the context of a broader topic but should stand

---

[5]Henderson, *Compensation Management*, p. 119.

on its own. We cannot overemphasize the importance of job analysis, as it permeates most of the organization's activities. If job analysis is not done well in an organization, it probably does not do any of its HR activities well. If individuals in the organization understood HR activities, they would understand the fundamental importance of job analysis.

The job analysis is the starting point of sound human resource management. Without knowing what the job entails, the material covered in the following chapters would merely be an effort in futility.

SUMMARY

1. *Job analysis* is a systematic exploration of the activities surrounding a job. It defines the job's
   a. Duties
   b. Responsibilities
   c. Accountabilities
2. The job analysis information hierarchy involves an eight-step process:
   a. Elements
   b. Tasks
   c. Duties
   d. Positions
   e. Jobs
   f. Job families
   g. Occupations
   h. Careers
3. Six general techniques exist for obtaining job information:
   a. Observation method
   b. Individual interview method
   c. Group interview method
   d. Structured interview method
   e. Technical conference method
   f. Diary method
4. Two special job analysis processes identified are
   a. The Department of Labor's Functional Job Analysis
   b. Purdue University's Position Analysis Questionnaire
5. In conducting a job analysis, one needs to collect background information about the job to be studied, select incumbent job experts, gather the data, analyze the data, and produce the end results
   a. Job descriptions—a written statement of what the jobholder does (duties and responsibilities of the job)

b. Job specifications—the personal characteristics needed to perform successfully on the job

c. Job evaluation—information used in developing a compensation package

KEY TERMS

Career	Job family
Duty	Job specification
Functional job analysis	Occupation
Job	Position
Job analysis	Position Analysis Questionnaire
Job description	(PAQ)
Job element	Task
Job evaluation	

QUESTIONS FOR REVIEW

1. What is job analysis?
2. Describe the job analysis information hierarchy.
3. Differentiate between a job, an occupation, and a career.
4. Compare and contrast the individual interview and the group interview methods of job analysis.
5. Identify the advantages and disadvantages of the following job analysis techniques: observation method, structured questionnaire method, and diary method.
6. Describe the functional job analysis.
7. Describe the Position Analysis Questionnaire.
8. What are job descriptions?
9. What are job specifications?
10. Describe the process involved in conducting a job analysis.

QUESTIONS FOR DISCUSSION

1. "Job analysis is just another burden placed on organizations through governmental legislation." Do you agree or disagree? Discuss.
2. When employees want to slow down their work effort they often "work to rule," which is a euphemism for doing only what one's job description says. What does this imply about job descriptions?

3. "Although systematic in nature, a job description is still at best a subjective result of a job analysis." Do you agree or disagree? Discuss.

4. How could it happen that an individual would be hired for a position and once in that position find out that the work he was asked to do was not the work he was hired to do? Discuss.

5. "Smaller organizations do not need a job analysis for their jobs because most of their employees are generalists and conduct a myriad of activities too far reaching for a standard job analysis." Do you agree or disagree? Discuss.

CONTINUING CASE: Concord General

What is a Nurse?

One of Judy Sapp's first tasks when she became Concord General's nurse recruiter was to familiarize herself with the duties and responsibilities of the nurses in each unit. Much to her dismay, however, she found that no such descriptions existed. What was on file were statements from 1940 medical operational procedures, which identified nurses' roles as being subservient to those of doctors.

Judy was not happy with this information. She realized that in order to recruit actively, she needed to know what the job she was filling entailed. Her previous work experience in the Intensive Care Unit was excellent, and she felt comfortable with the duties and responsibilities of the position. But beyond that, the scope of her activities was limited.

Judy wondered what differences there were with regard to nurses in pediatrics, maternity, surgery, recovery room, and so on. She knew that this information was needed, and needed quickly. To obtain such information, she has asked Jim Wilson to form committees in each unit and to supply formal job descriptions and job specifications. Unfortunately, one area was not included, that is, the position of general staff, or floor, nurse. Because this is considered to be the basic nursing position and an analysis that can be delegated, Judy has asked you for help.

1. What technique or techniques would you use to conduct the job analysis? Explain your rationale.
2. Using Figure 5-4 as a guide, write a job description for a general staff nurse. Later, when time permits, check your job description with that of the Department of Labor's *Dictionary of Occupational Titles.*
3. Using Figure 5-5 as a guide, develop a job specification for the job description written in Question 2.

CASE APPLICATION

And Leave the Driving to Us

The Boise City Transit System (BCTS) has been experiencing severe difficulties with its bus drivers. Consumer complaints have tripled during the past six months. These complaints have focused on drivers failing to make scheduled stops, buses being filthy, and drivers not enforcing the rules of conduct posted on the inside of the bus.

Fearing a loss of revenue and citizen support, Marshall Anson, the BCTS director, has called together members of both the supervisory ranks and the drivers. He wants to settle the ongoing problem and make amends so that full, courteous service can be restored immediately. During the meeting, Mr. Anson pinpointed the problem: The supervisors, as a group, had placed new demands on the drivers, demands that did not sit well with them. To retaliate, the drivers began their own show of strength. They invoked the letter of their job descriptions. Among these were statements such as the following: "The driver has the right to refuse to board any passenger he believes may cause disorder on the bus," "Drivers are responsible for ensuring that the seats are free from any debris," and "All drivers will report to the authorities any individual who disrupts the operation of the bus."

In better days, the drivers had handled almost everything themselves. If there was a problem such as the bus being dirty, they handled it. But not now. As one bus driver stated, "It's not my job!"

QUESTIONS

1. How could an accurate, updated, and well-defined job analysis have helped to prevent such a problem?
2. Realizing that every aspect of the job cannot be identified because exceptions do exist, how can a job description be written so that these exceptions cannot be referred to as "not my job"?

ADDITIONAL READINGS

FOURACRE, SANDRA and ANGELA WRIGHT, "New Factors in Job Evaluation," *Personnel Management*, May 1986, pp. 40–43.

FRASER, SCOTT L., STEPHEN F. CRONSHAW, and RALPH A. ALEXANDER, "Generalizability Analysis of a Point Method Job Evaluation Instrument: A Field Study," *Journal of Applied Psychology*, 69, No. 4 (1984), 643–47.

GARDNER, DONALD G., "Activation Theory and Task Design: An Empirical Test of Several New Predictions," *Journal of Applied Psychology*, 71, No. 3 (August 1986), 411–18.

MAURER, STEVEN D., and CHARLES H. FAY, "Legally Fair Hiring Practices for Small Business," *Journal of Small Business Management*, 24, No. 1 (January 1986), 47–52.

SCHUSTER, JAY R., "How to Control Job Evaluation Inflation," *Personnel Administrator*, 30, No. 6 (June 1985), 167–73.

CHAPTER 6

Recruiting Sources

AFTER READING THIS CHAPTER, YOU WILL BE ABLE TO:

1. Define *recruitment*
2. Explain what constrains managers in determining recruiting sources
3. Describe the principal sources involved in recruiting employees

"Is your advertising getting results?" "It sure is! Last week we advertised for a night watchman and the next night we were robbed."

—Anonymous

Successful human resource planning should identify our human resource needs. Once we know these needs, we will want to do something about meeting them. The next step in the acquisition function, therefore, is recruitment. This activity makes it possible for us to acquire the number and types of people necessary to ensure the continued operation of the organization. *Recruiting* is the discovering of potential candidates for actual or anticipated organizational vacancies. Or, from another perspective, it is a linking activity—bringing together those with jobs to fill and those seeking jobs.

The ideal recruitment effort will attract a large number of qualified applicants who will take the job if it is offered. It should also provide information so that unqualified applicants can self-select themselves out of job candidacy; that is, a good recruiting program should attract the qualified and not attract the unqualified. This dual objective will minimize the cost of processing unqualified candidates.

Factors Influencing Recruiting Efforts

Although all organizations will, at one time or another, engage in recruiting activity, some do so to a much larger extent than others. Obviously, size is one factor. An organization with one hundred thousand employees will find itself recruiting potential applicants much more often than will an organization with one hundred employees. However, certain other variables will influence the extent of recruiting. Employment conditions in the community where the organization is located will influence how much recruiting takes place. The effectiveness of past recruiting efforts will show itself in the organization's historical ability to locate and keep people who perform well. Working conditions and salary and benefit packages offered by the organization will influence turnover and, therefore, the need for future recruiting. Organizations that are not growing or those that are actually declining will find little need to recruit. On the other hand, organizations that are growing rapidly will find recruitment a major human resource activity.

Possible Constraints on Recruiting Sources, or Why You May Not Be Able to Attract the Person You Want

Constraints on recruiting

Before we discuss the sources of recruitment, the pragmatics in attempting to attract qualified applicants should be recognized. While the ideal recruitment effort will bring in a large number of qualified applicants who will take the job if it is offered, the realities cannot be ignored. For example, the pool of qualified applicants may not have included the "best" candidate; or the "best" candidate may not want to be employed by the organization; or such a candidate may be viewed as having lower priority than some other applicant because of criteria outside job performance. These and other constraints limit managers' freedom to recruit and select a candidate of their choice. We can narrow our focus by suggesting five specific constraints.

We noted that the prospective candidate may not be interested in pursuing job opportunities in the particular organization. The image of the organization, therefore, should be considered as a potential constraint. If that image is perceived to be low, then the likelihood of attracting a large number of applicants is reduced.[1] Many college graduates know that each of those individuals who occupy the top dozen spots at International Business Machines earn excellent salaries, are given a myriad of benefits, and are greatly respected in their communities. Among most college graduates, IBM has a positive image. The hope of having a shot at one of its top jobs, being in the spotlight, and having a position of power results in IBM having little trouble in attracting young college graduates into entry-level positions. But not all young graduates hold a positive image of large organizations. More specifically, their image of some organizations is pessimistic. In a number of communities, local firms have a reputation for being in a declining industry or for heavy pollution, poor-quality products, unsafe working conditions, or indifference to the needs of their employees. Such reputations can and do reduce these organizations' ability to attract the best personnel available.

Certainly if the job to be filled is unattractive, recruiting a large and qualified pool of applicants will be difficult. In recent years, for instance, many employers have been complaining about the difficulty

---

[1]Joseph G. P. Paolillo and John A. Belt, "The Influence of Corporate Image and Specificity of Candidate Qualifications on Response to Recruitment Advertisement" (Paper presented at the Western Academy of Management Conference, Monterey, Calif., April 1981).

of finding suitably qualified individuals for secretarial positions. Traditionally, these jobs appealed to females. Today, however, women have a wider selection of job opportunities, as well as heightened aspirations—a combination that has resulted in a severe shortage of qualified secretaries. Given the status, pay, and opportunities inherent in most secretarial jobs, many individuals who previously would have sought such positions now consider them unattractive. Any job that is viewed as boring, hazardous, anxiety creating, low pay, or lacking in promotion potential will seldom attract a qualified pool of applicants. Even during economic slumps, people have refused to take many of these jobs.

Internal organizational policies, such as "promote from within wherever possible," will give priority to individuals inside the organization. Such a policy, when followed, will usually ensure that all positions, other than the lowest-level entry positions, will be filled from within the ranks.

Union requirements can also restrict recruiting sources. In many of the trade industries, it is still common practice to have the union screen and approve those individuals who can be considered for employment. This determination of who can apply and who has the priority in selection, often a political process, restricts management's freedom to select those individuals who it believes would be the best performers if the candidate cannot meet the criteria stipulated by the union. For example, while the closed shop (which makes the union the only source of labor for the employer) is illegal in the United States, the union hiring hall is not. As a result, the union may give first preference to relatives or friends of current union members for union membership. If union membership is necessary in order to get into a company, management must recruit from a restricted supply.

The government's influence in the recruiting process should not be overlooked. An employer can no longer seek out preferred individuals based on non-job-related factors such as physical appearance, sex, or religious background. An airline that desires to staff all its flight attendant positions with attractive females will find itself breaking the law if comparably qualified male candidates are rejected on the basis of sex. The responsibility, in this case, would be on the airline to demonstrate that being female was a bona fide occupational qualification. However, as we noted in our discussion of BFOQs in Chapter 3, sex is not considered a BFOQ.

The last constraint, but certainly not the lowest in the priority of constraints, is one that centers on costs. Recruiting efforts by an organization are expensive. Sometimes continuing a search for long periods of time is not possible because of budget restrictions. Accordingly, when an organization considers various recruiting sources, it does so with some sense of effectiveness in mind. That is, recruiting expenditures are made where the best return on the "investment" can be realized. Unfortunately, because of limited resources, these expenditures need to be prioritized. Those lower in priority do not get the same resources, and this can ultimately constrain a recruiter's effort to attract the best person for the job.

Recruiting Sources

Recruitment is more likely to achieve its objective if recruiting sources reflect the type of position to be filled. For example, an ad in the Sunday *New York Times* business employment section is more likley to be read by a manager seeking an executive position in the $75,000-to-$100,000-a-year bracket than by a watch repairer seeking to find employment. Similarly, an interviewer who is seeking to fill a management training position and visits a two-year vocational school in search of a recent college graduate with undergraduate courses in engineering and a master's degree in business administration is looking "for the right person in the wrong place."

Certain recruiting sources are more effective than others for filling certain types of jobs. As we review each source in the following sections, the strengths and weaknesses in attempting to attract lower-level and managerial-level personnel will be emphasized.

Internal Search

Internal search

Most large organizations will attempt to develop their own employees for positions beyond the lowest level. The advantages from a "promote from within wherever possible" policy are that (1) it is good public relations; (2) it builds morale; (3) it encourages good individuals who are ambitious; (4) it improves the probability of a good selection, since information on the individual's performance is readily available; (5) it is less costly than going outside to recruit; (6) those chosen internally already know the organization; and (7) when carefully planned, promoting from within can also act as a training device for developing middle- and top-level managers.

There can be distinct disadvantages, however, to using internal sources. Obviously, it can be dysfunctional to the organization to utilize inferior internal sources only because they are there, when excellent candidates are available on the outside. However, an individual from the outside, in contrast with someone already employed in the organization, may appear more attractive because the recruiter is unaware of the outsider's faults.

The organization should avoid excessive inbreeding. Occasionally it may be necessary to bring in some "new blood" to broaden the present ideas, knowledge, and enthusiasm and to question the but-we've-always-done-it-that-way mentality.

As noted in the discussion of human resource inventories in Chapter 4, the organization's personnel files should provide information as to which employees might be considered for positions opening up within the organization. Most organizations can utilize their computer information system to generate an output of those individuals who have the desirable characteristics to potentially fill the vacant position.

In many organizations, it is standard procedure to "post" any new job openings and to allow any current employee to "bid" for the position. This action, too, receives favorable marks from the EEOC. The posting notification may be communicated on a central "positions open" bulletin board in the plants or offices, in the weekly or monthly organization newsletter, or, in some cases, in a specially prepared posting sheet from the personnel department outlining those positions currently available. A survey of company publicizing practices is shown in Figure 6-1. Even if current employees are not interested in the position, they can use these notices to recommend friends or associates for employment with the organization.

Advertisements

Advertisements   The sign outside the plant reads: "Now Hiring—Machinists." The newspaper advertisement reads: "Management Trainee. We are looking for someone who wants to assume responsibility and wishes to learn the women's retail shoe business. Minimum of two years' sales experience required. College degree or equivalent desired. Salary to $18,000. For appointment, call Ms. Resnick at 571-5060."

Most of us have seen both types of advertisements. When an organization desires to communicate to the public that it has a vacancy, advertisements are one of the most popular methods used. However, where the advertisement is placed is often determined by the type of job. Although it is not uncommon to see blue-collar jobs listed on

FIGURE 6-1

Publicizing Internal Vacancies

METHOD	TYPE OF JOB		
	Blue Collar	Office/ Clerical	Professional/ Technical
Posted on bulletin boards	82%	64%	48%
Circulated in memos to supervisors	12	12	20
Reported in employee publications	8	10	10
Publicized by other methods	10	15	12
Not publicized	8	20	30

SOURCE: *Employee Promotion and Transfer Policies*, Personnel Policies Forum, Survey No. 120 (Washington, D.C.: Bureau of National Affairs, January 1978), p. 2.

placards outside the plant gates, we would be surprised to find a vice-presidency listed in the same place.

The higher the position in the organization, the more specialized the skills, or the shorter the supply of that resource in the labor force, the more widely dispersed the advertisement is likely to be. The search for a top executive might include advertisements in a national periodical, for example. One the other hand, the advertisement of lower-level jobs is usually confined to the local daily newspaper or regional trade journals.

Recent legislation to ensure equal opportunity enforcement has resulted in a significant increase in the advertisement of all vacancies. Jobs can still be obtained through the "who-you-know" system, but many jobs that previously were never openly posted now must be. Unfortunately, it seems that many of these ads are listed only to meet the affirmative action requirements, and the applicants they generate will rarely be seriously considered.

A number of factors influence the response rate to advertisements. There are three important variables: identification of the organization, labor market conditions, and the degree to which specific requirements are included in the advertisement.

Many organizations place what is referred to as a blind ad, one in which there is no identification of the organization. Respondents are asked to reply to a post office box number or to a consulting firm that is acting as an intermediary between the applicant and the organization. Large organizations with a national reputation will seldom use blind advertisements to fill lower-level positions. However, when the organization does not wish to publicize the fact that it is seeking to fill an internal position, or when it seeks to recruit for a position where there is a soon-to-be-moved incumbent, a blind advertisement may be appropriate. This is especially true when the position that the organization wishes to fill is expected to draw an extraordinary number of applications. Using the blind ad relieves the organization from having to respond to any individual who applies. Only those individuals the organization wishes to see are notified; the remaining are not, as if the application was never received.

Although blind ads can assist personnel in finding qualified applicants, many individuals are reluctant to answer them. Obviously, there is the fear, usually unjustified, that the advertisement has been placed by the organization in which the individual is currently employed. Also, the organization itself is frequently a key determinant of whether the individual is interested; therefore, potential candidates are often reluctant to reply. Further deterrents are the bad reputation that blind advertisements have received because of organizations that place ads when no position exists in order to test the supply of workers in the community, to build a backlog of applicants, or to identify those current employees who are interested in finding a new position; or

Marketing

VICE PRESIDENT OF MARKETING

A Vice President of Marketing is being sought for a new health care corporation in the Tampa Bay area. This holding company is associated with a large hospital and affords the opportunity for a creative marketing manager to grow with the corporation. The position is considered one of the top four positions on the senior management team. Health care background is not a must, good marketing/planning skills are necessary.

REQUIREMENTS: Several years of excellent marketing experience, a creative mind, and competitive instincts. An MBA is preferred. Salary will be in the $60,000 range and is negotiable. Please send resume and salary history to:

FIGURE 6-2   Advertisement with High-Response Rate
SOURCE: *Wall Street Journal*, June 12, 1984.

DIRECTOR OF ADMINISTRATION

THE LATIN AMERICAN REGION OF DELTA STEAMSHIP CO. HAS A POSITION OPEN AS DIRECTOR OF ADMINISTRATION, LOCATED IN TEANECK, N.J., THE POSITION IS RESPONSIBLE FOR THE GENERAL ADMINISTRATIVE FUNCTIONS FOR ALL OF OUR SOUTH AMERICAN OPERATIONS INCLUDING ACCOUNTING, PERSONNEL, DATA PROCESSING, PAYROLL, AGENCY ACCOUNTING AND FOREIGN AUDITING. THE SUCCESSFUL CANDIDATE WILL HAVE A MINIMUM OF 5 YEARS EXPERIENCE WITH THE MARITIME INDUSTRY IN ACCOUNTING/ADMINISTRATION, BE BI-LINGUAL, POSSESS A DEGREE IN ACCOUNTING OR BUSINESS AND HAVE SOME EXPERIENCE WORKING WITH SOUTH AMERICAN OPERATIONS. THIS IS A GROWTH POSITION WITH EXCELLENT SALARY AND FRINGE BENEFITS.

FIGURE 6-3   Advertisement with Low-Response Rate
SOURCE: *Wall Street Journal*, June 12, 1984.

organizations that place the advertisement for affirmative action purposes only when the final decision, for the greater part, has already been made.

The job analysis process is the basic source for the information placed in the ad. A decision will need to be made as to whether the ad will focus on descriptive elements of the job (job description) or of the applicant (job specification). The choice made will often affect the number of replies received. If, for example, you are willing to sift through one thousand or more responses, you might place a national ad in the *Wall Street Journal* or the Sunday *New York Times* similar to the one in Figure 6-2. However, an advertisement in the same papers that looked like Figure 6-3 might attract less than a dozen replies.

The difference between Figures 6-2 and 6-3 is obvious. Figure 6-2 uses more applicant-centered criteria to describe the successful candidate. Most individuals perceive themselves as having creativity and competitive instincts. More important, how can an employer measure these qualities? "Excellent experience" and "good" marketing and planning skills are equally difficult to measure. The response rate should therefore be extremely high. In contrast, Figure 6-3 describes a job requiring precise abilities and experience. The requirements of at least "5 years experience with the maritime industry," bilingual skills, and experience with South American operations are certain to limit the respondents' pool.

Employee Referrals/Recommendations

Employee referrals/
recommendations

One of the best sources for individuals who will perform effectively on the job is a recommendation from a current employee. An employee will rarely recommend someone unless he or she believes that the individual can perform adequately. Such a recommendation reflects on the recommender, and when someone's reputation is at stake, we can expect the recommendation to be based on considered judgment. Employee referrals may also have acquired more accurate information about their potential jobs. The recommender often gives the applicant more realistic information about the job than could be conveyed through employment agencies or newspaper advertisements. This information reduces unrealistic expectations and increases job survival. As a result of these preselection factors, employee referrals tend to be more acceptable applicants, to be more likely to accept an offer if one is made, and, once employed, to have a higher job survival rate. Additionally, employee referrals are an excellent sourcing practice, especially in those hard-to-fill positions. For example, because of the difficulty in finding computer programmers with specific skills required by the organization, some organizations have turned to their employees and have asked for assistance. In one organization that the authors of this book contacted, these specifically identified hard-to-fill positions include a reward if an employee referral candidate is hired. In this case, both the organization and the employee benefit; the employee receives a monetary reward and the organization receives a qualified candidate without the major expense of an extensive recruiting search.

There are, of course, some potentially negative features of employee referral. For one thing, recommenders may confuse friendship with job performance competence. Individuals often like to have their friends join them at their place of employment for social and even economic reasons. For example, they may be able to share rides to and from work. As a result, a current employee may recommend a friend for a position without giving unbiased consideration to the friend's job-related competence.

Employee referrals may also lead to nepotism; that is, hiring individuals who are related to persons already employed by the organization. The hiring of relatives is particularly widespread in family-owned organizations. While such actions do not necessarily align with the objective of hiring the most-qualified applicant, interest in the organization and loyalty to it may be long-term advantages.

Employee referrals can also lead to an adverse impact. If a predominant white-male work force recommends other white-male acquaintances for the job and they are subsequently hired, this practice could be keeping minorities out. The organization could then be in violation of EEO laws.

Employee referrals do, however, appear to have universal application. Lower-level and managerial-level positions can, and often are, filled by the recommendation of a current employee. In higher-level positions, however, it is more likely that the referral will be a professional acquaintance rather than a friend with whom the recommender has close social contact. In jobs where specialized expertise is important, and where employees participate in professional organizations that foster the development of this expertise, it can be expected that current employees will be acquainted with, or know about, individuals who they think would make an excellent contribution to the organization.

Employment Agencies

We will describe three forms of employment agencies: public or state agencies, private employment agencies, and management consulting firms. The major difference between these three sources is the type of clientele served.

Public agencies

Public Agencies.   In 1933, a public employment service was established as a federal-state partnership. It was designed both to help job seekers find suitable employment and to help employers find suitable workers. In 1980, the twenty-six hundred local employment service offices throughout the United States processed more than 16 million applicants and close to 7 million job openings. The service took credit for placing approximately 6 million applicants in jobs.[2]

All states provide a public employment service. The main function of these agencies is closely tied to unemployment benefits, since benefits in some states are given only to individuals who are registered with their state employment agency. Accordingly, most public agencies tend to attract and list individuals who are unskilled or have had minimum training. This, of course, does not reflect on the agency's competence. Rather, it reflects the image of public agencies. State agencies are perceived by prospective applicants as having few high-skilled jobs, and employers tend to see such agencies as having few high-skilled applicants. Therefore public agencies tend to attract and place predominantly low-skilled workers. The agencies' image as perceived by both applicants and employers thus tends to result in a self-fulfilling

---

[2]"The U.S. Employment Service," *Employment and Training Report of the President* (Washington, D.C.: Government Printing Office, 1981), p. 47.

prophecy. That is, few high-skilled individuals place their names with public agencies, and, similarly, few employers seeking individuals with high skills list their vacancies or inquire about applicants at state agencies.

The United States Training and Employment Service (USTES) provides general control of the state agencies through its power over federal tax rebates. Currently, USTES is developing a nationwide computerized job bank to which all state employment offices can be connected. It is hoped that this job bank will be the link between job opportunities and applicants from all over the United States.

While such attempts are worthy in and of themselves, the problem is that many individuals who are seeking a job and cannot find one in their own community will not want to take a job in a distant community if it means permanent relocation. Geographical immobility is one of the major drawbacks to a nationwide job hookup system. For example, in the mid-1960s, when unemployment levels were disastrously high in Appalachia, attempts were made to move people to job opportunities that were available in other parts of the country. However, few would leave the area in which they, their parents, and their grandparents had been born and raised.

Despite increased attempts to develop a nationwide job clearinghouse, employers must be realistic and recognize that many job seekers do not view themselves as being geographically mobile and will accept unemployment compensation benefits rather than accept a job relocation.

Private agencies

Private Employment Agencies.   How does a private agency, which has to charge for its services, compete with state agencies that give their services away? Clearly, they must do something different from what the public agencies do, or at least give that impression.

The major difference between public and private employment agencies is their image. That is, private agencies are believed to offer positions and applicants of a higher caliber. Private agencies also provide a more complete line of services. They advertise the position, they screen applicants against the criteria specified by the employer, and they usually provide a guarantee covering six months or a year as protection to the employer should the applicant not perform satisfactorily.

The private employment agency's fee can be totally absorbed by either the employer or the employee, or it can be split. The alternative chosen usually depends on the demand-supply situation in the community involved.

Headhunters

Management Consultants.   The third agency source consists of the management consulting, executive search, or "headhunting" firms. Agencies of this type are actually specialized private employment agencies. They specialize in middle-level and top-level executive place-

"Miss Abbott, when you said there was a headhunter to see me, I thought ..."

FIGURE 6-4

SOURCE: Copyright © 1979 by NEA, Inc. Reprinted with permission.

ments.[3] In addition to the level at which they recruit, the features that distinguish executive search agencies from most private employment agencies are their fees, their nationwide contacts, and the thoroughness of their investigations. In searching for an individual of vice-president caliber, whose compensation package may be far in excess of $100,000 a year, the potential employer is often willing to pay a very high fee to locate exactly the right individual to fill the vacancy. A fee amounting to 30 percent of the executive's first-year salary is not unusual as a charge for finding and recruiting the individual.

Executive search firms canvass their contacts and do preliminary screening. They seek out highly effective executives who have the skills to do the job, can effectively adjust to the organization, and, most important, are willing to consider new challenges and opportunities. Possibly such individuals are frustrated by their inability to move up in their current organization at the pace at which they are capable, or

[3]Loretta D. Foxman and Walter L. Polsky, "Career, Q and A," *Personnel Journal,* November 1984, p. 27.

they may have recently been bypassed for a major promotion.

The executive search firm can act as a buffer for screening candidates and, at the same time, keep the prospective employer anonymous. In the final stages, senior executives in the prospective firm can move into the negotiations and determine the degree of mutual interest.

Temporary Help Services

Temporary help services

Organizations like the Kelly Temporary Services can be a source of employees when individuals are needed on a temporary basis. Temporary employees are particularly valuable in meeting short-term fluctuations in personnel needs. While traditionally developed in the office administration area, the temporary rental service has expanded its coverage to include a broad range of skills. It is now possible, for example, to hire a temporary nurse, computer programmer, or librarian, as well as a temporary secretary.

Schools, Colleges, and Universities

Educational institutions at all levels offer opportunities for recruiting recent graduates. Most educational institutions operate placement services where prospective employers can review credentials and interview graduates. Whether the educational level required for the job involves a high-school diploma, specific vocational training, or a college background with a bachelor's, master's, or doctoral degree, educational institutions are an excellent source of potential employees for entry-level positions in organizations.

Schools, colleges, and universities

High schools or vocational-technical schools can provide lower-level applicants; business or secretarial schools can provide administrative staff personnel; and two- and four-year colleges and graduate schools can often provide managerial-level personnel.

While educational institutions are usually viewed as sources for young, inexperienced entrants to the work force, it is not uncommon to find individuals with considerable work experience using an educational institution's placement service. They may be workers who have recently returned to school to upgrade their skills, or former graduates interested in changing jobs and utilizing their school's placement center. Thus employers seeking applicants can find not only new-diploma recipients at the school, college, or university placement bureau but also former graduates interested in pursuing other opportunities.

College placements, while a good source of applicants, are costly. An organization must weigh the benefits of this recruiting source with its costs, in many cases over $1,000 per school. This appears to be one of the reasons why, during economic downturns, interviews on campus severely declined.

VIEWS IN THE NEWS

What Do College Graduates Prefer?

Recruiting from various sources requires different recruiting strategies. Part of these strategies involves tailoring the recruiting effort to the targeted market. Often, however, recruiters do not understand the expectations of each target group, and accordingly, conduct their interviews with insufficient information.

In a study published in 1985, three researchers focused on this issue, emphasizing the compensation and benefit expectations of new college graduates entering the job market. The researchers sampled graduating seniors and recruiters alike, asking each to rank order eleven compensation and benefit items in a questionnaire. These items were:

- Cost-of-living increases of $1080 each year
- Early retirement at age 62
- Fifteen Fridays off each year with full pay
- Fifty percent increase in yearly pension payments
- Four day work week
- Flexible hours
- Health and life insurance coverage
- Company stock option plans
- Paid fifteen week leave of absence every five years
- Reduced length of work day
- Three weeks additional vacation each year

The study population consisted of 487 students, 81 percent male and 19 percent female; and 223 recruiters, 91 percent male, 9 percent female. The results of the students' ranking revealed a high preference given to cost-of-living increases and health and life insurance coverage; followed closely by company stock options and fifty percent yearly increase in pensions. In contrast, the recruiters tended to perceive new college graduates' preferences as those that provided more time off from work—four day work week, flexible hours and more vacations.

The researchers indicated that the implications of this study are far reaching. For instance, if recruiters are not aware of the needs of prospective employees, then "poor placement decisions, unrealistic employee expectations, and subsequent job dissatisfaction and turnover" may result.

How would you rank the eleven items?

Source: Kermit R. Davis, Jr., William F. Giles, and Hubert S. Field, Jr., "Compensation and Fringe Benefits: How Recruiters View New College Graduates' Preferences," *Personnel Administrator*, 30, No. 1, (January 1985), 43–50.

Professional Organizations

Many professional organizations, including labor unions, operate placement services for the benefit of their members. The professional organizations include such varied occupations as industrial engineer, psychologist, and seafarer.

Professional organizations

These organizations publish rosters of job vacancies and distribute these lists to members. It is also common practice to provide placement facilities at regional and national meetings where individuals looking for employment and companies looking for employees can find each other.

Professional organizations, however, can also apply sanctions to control the labor supply in their discipline. For example, although the law stipulates that unions cannot require employers to hire only union members, the mechanisms for ensuring that unions do not break this law are poorly enforced. As a result, it is not unusual for labor unions to control supply through their apprenticeship programs and through their labor agreements with employers. Of course, this tactic is not limited merely to blue-collar trade unions. In those professional organizations where the organization's placement service is the focal point for locating prospective employers, and where certain qualifications are necessary to become a member (such as special educational attainment or professional certification), then the professional organization can significantly influence and control the supply of prospective applicants.

Casual or Unsolicited Applicants

Walk-ins

"Walk-ins," whether they reach the employer by letter, telephone, or in person, can be a source of prospective applicants. Although the qualifications of unsolicited applicants will depend on economic conditions, the organization's image, and the job seeker's perception of the types of jobs that might be available, this source does provide an excellent supply of stockpiled applicants. Even if there are no particular openings when the applicant makes contact with the organization, the application can be kept on file for later needs.

Applications from individuals who are already employed can be referred to many months later and can provide applicants who (1) are interested in considering other employment opportunities and (2) regard the organization as a possible employer.

Unsolicited applications made by unemployed individuals, however, generally have a short life. Those individuals who have adequate skills and who would be prime candidates for a position in the organization if a position were currently available will usually find employment with some other organization that does have an opening. However, in times of economic stagnation, excellent prospects are often unable to locate the type of job they desire and may stay actively looking in the job market for many months.

Other Sources

In the search for particular types of applicants, nontraditional sources should be considered. For example, Employ the Handicapped associations can be a source of highly motivated workers; a Forty-Plus Club can be an excellent source of mature and experienced workers; and organizations like the National Organization for Women often provide placement services.

Conclusion

Although there is some support for the view that methods vary with economic conditions, it would appear that employers' efforts in recruiting are not totally rational and distinct. Many small employers keep no records of recruitment and use a variety of methods, whereas

FIGURE 6-5

Recruiting Sources Used by Skill and Level

SKILL/LEVEL	RECRUITING SOURCE	PERCENTAGE OF USE
Unskilled and Semiskilled	Informal Contacts	85
	Walk-ins	74
	Public Employment Agencies	66
	Want Ads	52
Skilled	Informal Contacts	88
	Walk-ins	66
	Public Employment Agencies	55
	Want Ads	55
Professional Employees	Internal Search	94
	Informal Contacts	92
	Walk-ins	71
	Public Employment Agencies	52
	Want Ads	48
	Private Employment Agencies	22
Managerial Level	Internal Search	100
	Informal Contacts	71
	Walk-ins	31
	Private Employment Agencies	20
	Want Ads	17
	Public Employment Agencies	12

SOURCE: Adapted from Stephen L. Mangum, "Recruitment and Job Search: The Recruitment Tactics of Employers," *Personnel Administrator*, June 1982, p. 102.

many large employers combine community relations and recruitment in a single endeavor.

Yet while no reason may be cited for using a particular recruiting source, certain sources appear to be used more frequently in specific cases. A study involving sixty-five manufacturing, commercial service, and heavy- and light-industry sectors revealed that specific sources were used when attempting to fill a position requiring a particular skill (see Figure 6-5).

In summary, Figure 6-5 indicates various uses of recruiting sources. At the lower levels in the organization, informal contacts appear to dominate, at the higher levels, internal search and informal contacts. In no case was one recruiting source used exclusively at all levels.

A Final Note

Throughout this chapter we have discussed recruiting from the organization's perspective. In the Appendix to this chapter, however, we look at recruiting from the applicant's perspective (see pp. 139–144). We hope you find the information useful.

SUMMARY

1. *Recruitment* is the discovering of potential applicants for actual or anticipated organizational vacancies.

2. Certain influences constrain managers in determining recruiting sources:
   a. Image of the organization
   b. Attractiveness of the job
   c. Internal policies
   d. Union requirements
   e. Government requirements
   f. Recruiting budgets

3. Popular sources of recruiting employees include
   a. Internal search
   b. Advertisements
   c. Employee referrals/recommendations
   d. Employment agencies
   e. Temporary rental services
   f. Schools, colleges, and universities
   g. Professional organizations
   h. Casual or unsolicited applicants

4. In practice, recruitment methods appear to vary according to job level and skill.

KEY TERMS

Advertisements
Blind advertisement
Constraints on recruiting
Employee referrals
Headhunters
Internal search

Private agencies
Professional organizations
Public agencies
Recruitment
Walk-ins

QUESTIONS FOR REVIEW

1. What is the "dual objective" of recruitment?
2. What factors influence the degree to which an organization will engage in recruiting?
3. What specific constraints may prevent a manager from hiring the best candidate?
4. What is a BFOQ? Why is it important?
5. What recruiting source gets the most acceptable candidates?
6. Why would a company pay a private employment agency to recruit candidates for a position when a public employment agency provides its services for free?
7. What are the advantages and disadvantages of recruiting through (a) internal search? (b) employee referrals? (c) casual or unsolicited applicants?
8. How can a professional association reduce the supply of qualified labor?
9. What are the most popular recruiting sources for unskilled jobs?
10. What are the most popular recruiting sources for managerial jobs?

QUESTIONS FOR DISCUSSION

1. "An organization should follow a promote-from-within policy." Do you agree or disagree?
2. When you go looking for a job upon college graduation, what sources do you expect to utilize? Why?
3. What improvements might you expect in the makeup of an organization's human resources as a result of having an affirmative action program?
4. "The best candidates are the ones who are hard to find. That is why it is imperative to pay a service to find these people." Do you agree or disagree? Discuss.

5. The philosophy behind the U.S. Training and Employment Service is that there is an opening for anyone who desires to work. The reason why there is unemployment is that there is just a mismatch between the jobs and the people. Do you believe that this system could work? What are the pros and cons of such a service?

CONTINUING CASE: Concord General

Hear Ye, Hear Ye, Hear Ye

After all the preliminaries had been established to staff Concord General's Cardiac Surgery Unit, it was still too early to fill the slots. Both Jim and Judy realized that the nurses needed to fill these positions were specialists. These nurses would usually have had four to six years of nursing experience to qualify to work in the Intensive Care Unit, and at least three years of progressive intensive care experience. Surgical experience is desirable but not mandatory.

Judy has contemplated cross-training all the nurses currently working in the Intensive Care Unit to handle the Cardiac Surgery Unit's staffing needs, but problems are anticipated. What if the nurses don't want to work in the Cardiac Surgery Unit? Should they be forced to expand their work activities? If the nurses do want to work in the CSU, will that cause a staffing shortage in the ICU? After some investigation, Judy found substance to her speculations. Only one-half of the ICU nurses want to be trained in the Cardiac Surgery Unit's techniques. And if they do want to be trained, a staffing shortage will result not only during the actual staffing of the Cardiac Surgery Unit but also during the training and orientation program to instruct the nurses.

The perplexities are real, but something must be done soon. The new unit is scheduled to open in a few weeks and is contingent on proper staffing.

QUESTIONS

1. How would you advertise the new positions to stimulate interest in them?
2. What sources would you use to attract qualified nurses? List the pros and cons of each.
3. Write a sample advertisement describing these positions, one that could be placed in the local Sunday paper.

CASE APPLICATION

Minorities and the ICC

The International Charcoal Corporation (ICC) had been accused of discriminating against minorities. For many decades, obtaining a job in ICC was contingent on two factors: know someone who is currently an employee and be a white male.

The organization was under governmental pressure to open its doors to minorities. In some cases this was done, but those employees were relegated to working in the poorest sections of town. Realizing that continued efforts needed to be made, the government placed pressure on the company to eliminate discrimination. The focal point of the pressure was the reliance ICC had on government contracts.

Shortly after the pressure was applied, ICC began to make an effort to recruit minorities into its organization. Yet, surprisingly, few minorities were applying. One requirement for the job was a high-school diploma or a G.E.D. However, the minorities who had the degree were going to college rather than work for the ICC. The federal government appreciated the open-door policy but mandated that the ICC find a method to actively recruit minorities and bring the composition of its work force into compliance with the composition of individuals in the surrounding community.

QUESTIONS

1. Where would you go to recruit the minorities? What recruiting sources would you use?
2. Realizing that many of the minorities who had a high-school diploma or its equivalent did not want to join the ICC, write an advertisement that could be placed in a newspaper and would attract these minorities.
3. If that does not work, what possibilities exist to recruit and retain minority employees?

ADDITIONAL READINGS

EDWARDS, CATHY, "Aggressive Recruitment: The Lessons of High-Tech Hiring," *Personnel Journal*, January 1986, pp. 40–48.
FREEDMAN, DANA E., "Child Care for Employees' Kids," *Harvard Business Review*, March-April 1986, pp. 28–33.

MAGNUS, MARGARET, "Recruitment Ad Advantages," *Personnel Journal,* August 1986, pp. 58–79.

MARCOUSE, IAN, "Giving Industry Career Credibility," *Management Today,* September 1986, pp. 37–40.

"Moving the Two-Career Couple," *Management Review,* September 1986, pp. 54–56.

APPENDIX TO CHAPTER 6

Recruitment from the Recruit's Perspective

One of the most trying and seemingly stressful situations that individuals face occurs when they begin the process of applying for a job. This is in part because there are no specific guidelines to follow to ensure success. However, we can offer some tips that could increase your chances of finding employment.

First and foremost, you need to have some idea of where you want to go. As the Cheshire cat said to Alice, if you don't know where you want to go, any road will get you there. What does this mean in recruiting? You will need to spend time thinking about your goals. You should be planning, charting a career path for at least the next five years. Just what is it you want to do? This plan serves as a guide—it is not something you must follow exactly. It just gives you some idea of what you want to accomplish, and something you can express in an interview if asked. And rest assured, almost all interviewers ask the question, "Where do you expect to be going in five years?" A realistic answer to this question reflects planning, initiative, and clear thinking on the part of the applicant. It surely has more of an impact than an "I don't know" response.

While interviews are an extremely important aspect of gaining employment, let's not focus all of our attention on specific questions in an interview. We explore that topic in Chapter 8. Let's go back to our tips.

Even though getting to the interview stage is a goal we all desire when we seek employment, obtaining that opportunity is not easy. As a rough rule of thumb, expect the following:

- 100 targeted résumés sent lead to
- 10 interviews, which lead to
- 1 job offer.

Now, don't hold us to these numbers. They are only a rule of thumb. The point that can be explicitly made, though, is that competition for jobs is fierce. Even so, there are things you can do to help increase your odds.

After you have given some thought to your employment goals (e.g., what type of work you want to do—sales, personnel, accounting, etc.), start your job hunting early. Give yourself at least seven to nine months' lead time. That is, if you are looking for a job after graduation (June), you should begin your job search sometime around September of your senior year. You may not need the entire time—but you don't want to wait until March to begin either. How is starting early helpful? In two ways. First, it shows that you are taking an interest and that you are planning. You are not waiting until the last minute to begin, and this reflects favorably on a candidate. Second, this period coincides with companies' recruiting cycles. If you wait until March to start, some job openings may have already been filled. For specific information regarding the company recruiting cycles in your area, see your career development center. It should be able to give you helpful information.

Our discussion so far has centered on getting to the interview. But let's digress for a moment. Before you go to an interview, you should have some information circulating that reflects positively on your strengths. This information is circulated in a résumé.

No matter who you are, or where you are in your career, you will need an updated résumé. Your résumé is the only information sheet that a recruiter has in determining whether to grant you an interview. As such, your résumé must be impeccable. That is, it must give accurate information that supports your candidacy. You must highlight your strengths. Identifying these strengths can take a long time, but you must give them much thought and express them in ways that speak well of you. The information in the résumé must also be listed in a way that is easy to read. An example of the type of information that should be included is shown in Figure 6A-1.

It is important to pinpoint a few key themes regarding résumés that may seem like common sense but are seldom followed. First of all, your résumé must be typed, professionally if possible, on an excellent typewriter. The style of type should be easy to read (e.g., Letter Gothic, Prestige Elite type fonts). Avoid any style that may be hard on the eyes, such as a script font. While the information may be the same, different reactions to a résumé may occur. Look at the résumé in Figure 6A-2. It is the same as the one in Figure 1, but what a difference! A recruiter who has to review two hundred résumés a day is not going to slow down and strain to read the script type. Valuable information may not come across. So, use an easy-to-read font and make the recruiter's job easier.

Second, your résumé should be copied on good-quality paper (no off-the-wall colors—use standard white or off-white). There are many definitions of good-quality paper, but you can't go wrong with a 20-

FIGURE 6A-1

Sample Résumé

```
                              SAMPLE RESUME

CONFIDENTIAL                      JUDY SAPP
RESUME OF                       21 Main Street
                              Anywhere, USA 10001
                           682-555-0028 (Residence)
                           682-555-8000 (Work)

CAREER OBJECTIVE:    Challenging opportunity to combine multidisciplinary skills
                     of nursing and management in a dynamic environment.

EXPERIENCE:          CONCORD GENERAL HOSPITAL

  5/84 to            Assistant Head Nurse, Intensive Care/Cardiac Care Unit.
  Present            Accountable to:  Director of Nursing, Speciality Units.

                     Primary Functions

                         Primary functions include clinical management of a ten-
                         bed combined Medical/Surgery Intensive Care Unit and a three
                         bed Cardiac Surgery Unit.  In addition to direct patient care
                         delivery, responsibilities include staffing, scheduling, and
                         assurance of quality patient care through development of an
                         eight week orientation/preceptorship program; ongoing
                         performance appraisals of nursing personnel and ancillary
                         support staff, and provision of staff development conferences
                         in areas of identified needs.  Also act as liaison between
                         general staff nurses and the Hospital's Administration.

                     Administrative Involvement

                         Quality Assurance Subcommittee to the Special Care Committee.
                         Quarterly meetings to report to Physician Unit Director and
                         Risk Management Team areas of identified deficiencies in
                         unit functioning.

                         Peer Review Committee.  Hospitalwide responsibilities,
                         reviewing randomly selected medical records to identify
                         nursing deficiencies.

                         Nurse Practice Committee.  Management resource person to
                         this twelve member non-management committee designed to
                         enhance professionalism and growth of staff level personnel.

  6/82 to            CONCORD GENERAL HOSPITAL
  5/84
                     General Staff Nurse, Intensive Care Unit.

EDUCATION:           STATE UNIVERSITY

                         Currently pursuing a management degree, with primary
                         focus on administrative management.  Expected graduation
                         date--May 1990

                     CONCORD GENERAL SCHOOL OF NURSING
                     B.A. Nursing, May 1982

REFERENCES:          Furnished on request.
```

bond-weight paper that contains some cotton content (about 20 percent). Don't send standard duplicating paper—it looks as if you are mass mailing résumés. You probably are mass mailing résumés (especially if you follow the "100 résumés" rule of thumb), but don't make it too obvious. To get your résumé in order, typed, and copied on good-quality paper, you should expect to spend about $20 (excluding envelope and postage costs). Typing costs about $4 per page, and the paper (including copying) will cost about $15. The cost might seem to be an expense you would rather not incur. But remember that your competition may be doing it, and if you have to spend a few dollars to make a few copies, consider it a wise investment.

FIGURE 6A-2

Sample Résumé

CONFIDENTIAL
RESUME OF

SAMPLE RESUME

JUDY SAPP
21 Main Street
Anywhere, U.S.A. 10001
682-555-0028 (Residence)
682-555-8000 (Work)

CAREER OBJECTIVE: Challenging opportunity to combine multidisciplinary skills of nursing and management in a dynamic environment.

EXPERIENCE: CONCORD GENERAL HOSPITAL

5/84 to Present

Assistant Head Nurse, Intensive Care/Cardiac Care Unit. Accountable to: Director of Nursing, Specialty Units.

Primary Functions

Primary functions include clinical management of a ten-bed combined Medical/Surgery Intensive Care Unit and a three bed Cardiac Surgery Unit. In addition to direct patient care delivery, responsibilities include staffing, scheduling, and assurance of quality patient care through development of an eight week orientation/preceptorship program; ongoing performance appraisals of nursing personnel and ancillary support staff, and provision of staff development conferences in areas of identified needs. Also act as liaison between general staff nurses and the Hospital's Administration.

Administrative Involvement

Quality Assurance Subcommittee to the Special Care Committee. Quarterly meetings to report to Physician Unit Director and Risk Management Team areas of identified deficiencies in unit functioning.

Peer Review Committee. Hospitalwide responsibilities, reviewing randomly selected medical records to identify nursing deficiencies.

Nurse Practice Committee. Management resource person to this twelve member non-management committee designed to enhance professionalism and growth of staff level personnel.

6/82 to 5/84

CONCORD GENERAL HOSPITAL
General Staff Nurse, Intensive Care Unit.

EDUCATION: STATE UNIVERSITY

Currently pursuing a management degree, with primary focus on administrative management. Expected graduation date—May 1990

CONCORD GENERAL SCHOOL OF NURSING
B.A. Nursing, May 1982

REFERENCES: Furnished on request.

The last point on résumés, one that shouldn't even have to be mentioned, relates to proofreading. Because the résumé is the only reflection of you that the recruiter has, a sloppy résumé can be deadly. If it contains misspelled words or is grammatically incorrect, your chances for an interview will be significantly reduced. Proofread your résumé, and if possible let others proofread it too.

In addition to your résumé, you need a covering letter. Your covering letter should contain information that tells the recruiter why you should be considered for the job. The covering letter should not be an "oversell" letter, but one that highlights your greatest strengths and indicates how these strengths can be useful to the company. Your covering letter should also contain some information citing why the organization getting your résumé is of interest to you. You may be stressing an important point here. Covering letters need to be tailored to the organization. Letters should be originals, not copies of a "To Whom It May Concern." (If you do use a standard letter, have it typed in a way that allows you to type in original names and addresses.)

One of the biggest turnoffs a recruiter experiences in reviewing résumés is the "To Whom It May Concern" letter. This tells the recruiter that you are on a fishing expedition and that you are sending hundreds of résumés out. This situation does not help your job hunting. A much greater impact is made when you write to a specific person. You may not always have the recruiter's name and title, but with some work you can get it. Telephone the company in question and ask for it. Most receptionists in personnel will give you the recruiter's name and title. The objective here is to use whatever resources you can. Be creative—you will be surprised at how much you can find out. If you just can't get a name, go to the library and locate a copy of the Standard and Poor's Register Manual. This reference lists the names and titles of companies' officers. If everything else fails, send your résumé to one of the officers, preferably the officer in charge of personnel or administration, or to the president. This is much better than a "To Whom It May Concern."

We won't belabor the point about typing and proofreading the covering letter except to say that it must also be impeccable. Finally, sign each letter individually. Real signatures carry more impact than a duplicate of a signature.

The last tip we would like to offer is what to do when you are granted an interview. It is important that you dress appropriately. Even though appearance is not supposed to enter into the hiring decision, it does make an impression. Be meticulous in your attire. Arrive early, not two hours early, but about thirty minutes ahead of your scheduled time. It is better for you to wait than to have something happen unexpectedly and cause you to be late. Arriving early also gives you a quick opportunity to survey the office environment and possibly gather some clues about the organization. For instance, if the atmosphere is friendly and cheerful, this may indicate that the organization puts considerable emphasis on employees' satisfaction. As you meet the recruiter, give a good firm handshake. This holds true for both men and women (recruiters as well as applicants). Make good eye contact, and maintain it throughout the interview. Finally, try to relax. You are going to be nervous, and recruiters know that. In fact, in most cases, the recruiter is responsible for making you feel at ease. Do your best to remain calm. To help you relax, you should not only be prepared but also have gone through several interviews. The more you go through an interview, the more skilled you will become. Practice with family, friends, or career counselors whenever possible.

After the interview is over, don't stop your "selling." As soon as you get home, type a thank-you letter and send it to the recruiter. This act of courtesy carries a big impact. Use it to your advantage.

We have tried to convey our experiences with the recruiting process in the hope that they will help you in your own job searches. If one theme runs throughout our message, it is that it takes long and hard work to get a job. But that time is well spent if you achieve your goal—employment.

CHAPTER 7

The Selection

Process

AFTER READING THIS CHAPTER, YOU WILL BE ABLE TO:

1. Discuss the benefits derived from a proper selection process
2. Identify the primary purpose of selection activities
3. Describe the discrete selection process
4. Describe the comprehensive selection process
5. Specify what a selection device must include if it is to be an effective predictor

We are not sure of the exact person to hire, but we know the one who makes it through this deserves the job on perseverance alone.

—Anonymous

In human resource planning we identified our personnel needs. Once these needs were established a job analysis was conducted, which clarified the characteristics of jobs being done and the individual qualities necessary to do these jobs successfully. This information was then used to recruit a pool of qualified applicants. We must now begin the process of thinning this set, which is one of the major objectives of selection. We want to assess our applicants against the criteria established in job analysis in order to predict which job applicants will be successful if hired. In this chapter, we will survey the selection process. In the following chapter, we will evaluate the major selection devices to determine how well they predict, and we will offer some suggestions on what managers can do to make selection as cost effective an activity as possible.

The Cost of Selection

The cost of selecting people who are inadequate performers or who leave the organization before contributing to profits is a major cost of doing business. The cost incurred in hiring and training any new employee is expensive, sometimes in the thousands of dollars. In 1983, the average cost per hire for exempt employees was more than $4,600; nearly $7,400 if there was a relocation.[1] These costs incurred by the organization suggest that hiring is a very expensive activity and that any efforts the organization can make toward minimizing turnover and hiring costs can pay dividends. Cost amounts and the representative category for hiring employees are shown in Figure 7-1.[2] Proper selection of personnel is obviously an area where effectiveness—choosing competent workers who perform well in their position—can result in large savings.

[1] "EMA 1983 National cost per Hire Survey," Wellesley, Mass., 1984.
[2] Ibid.

FIGURE 7-1

Cost Per Hire

EXPENSE	AMOUNT
Employment recruiting office	$ 669
Recruiting expenses	348
Company visit expenses	1,830
Direct fees (advertising agency, search)	1,792
Total recruitment costs (without relocation)	4,639
Relocation expenses	2,750
Total recruitment costs (with relocation)	$7,389

What Selection is All About

Selection All selection activities, from the initial screening interview to the physical examination if required, exist for the purpose of making effective selection decisions. Each activity is a step in the process that forms a predictive exercise—managerial decision makers seeking to predict which job applicants will be successful if hired. *Successful*, in this case, means performing well on the criteria the organization uses to evaluate personnel. For a sales position, for example, the criteria should be able to predict which applicants will generate a high volume of sales; for a teaching position as a university professor, they should predict which applicants will get high student evaluations or generate many high-quality publications or both.

Selection decision outcomes Consider, for a moment, that any selection decision can result in four possible outcomes. As shown in Figure 7-2, two of these outcomes would indicate correct decisions, but two would indicate errors.

Correct decisions are those where the applicant was predicted to be successful and later did prove to be successful on the job, or where the applicant was predicted to be unsuccessful and would have performed accordingly if hired. In the former case, we have successfully accepted; in the latter case, we have successfully rejected. Thus the purpose of selection activities is to develop outcomes shown as "correct decisions" in Figure 7-2.

Problems occur when we make errors—by rejecting candidates who would later perform successfully on the job (reject errors) or accepting those individuals who subsequently perform poorly on the job (accept errors). These problems are, unfortunately, far from insignificant. Reject errors historically meant that the costs in performing selection activities would be increased. Today, selection techniques that result in reject errors may open the employer to Title VII violation charges, especially if certain categories of applicants (such as women and minorities) are disproportionately rejected. Accept errors, on the other hand, have very obvious costs to the organization, including the

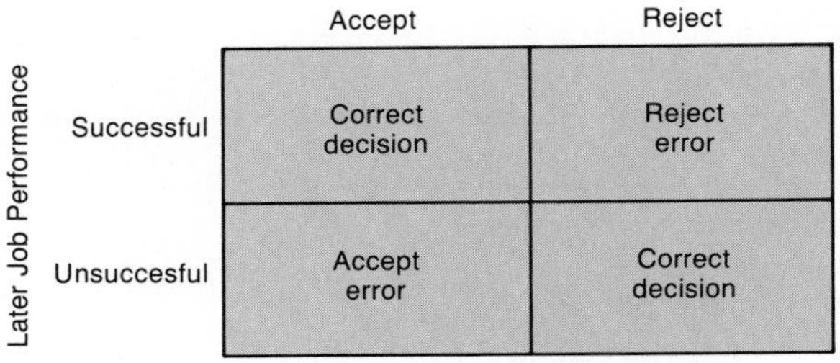

FIGURE 7-2   Selection Decision Outcomes

cost of training the employee, the costs generated (or profits forgone) due to the employee's incompetence, the cost of severance, and the subsequent costs of further recruiting and selection screening.[3] The major thrust of any selection activity, therefore, is to reduce the probability of making reject or accept errors while increasing the probability of making correct decisions.

Of lesser importance, but still an objective of the selection process, is informing and selling the candidate on the job and the organization. This secondary objective receives less attention, probably because it is so closely intertwined with recruitment, but it shows itself throughout the selection process.

In actuality, the selection process represents an effort to balance the objectives of evaluating and attracting. The interview is an obvious example of an activity where both objectives must be served. At the same time that the interviewer is attempting to acquire information about the candidate so an intelligent selection decision can be made, he or she is also informing the applicant about the job and the organization. This latter activity is critical if the organization is to be successful in "selling" itself to the candidate. If the organization fails in selling itself to the candidate, there is little likelihood that the applicant will accept the job even if it is offered. Additionally, this trading of information between applicant and interviewer can be valuable in allowing individuals with low chances of being chosen to self-select themselves *out* of the process. This saves both the organization and the applicant from "losing face" due to a rejection decision.

In summary, selection has two objectives: (1) to predict which job applicants would be successful if hired and (2) to inform and sell the candidate on the job and the organization. Unfortunately, these two objectives are not always compatible. Putting a job candidate through hours of filling out forms, taking tests, and completing interviews rarely endears the organization to the candidate. These are tiresome

[3]For a review of the costs of turnover, see Thomas F. Cawsey and William C. Wedley, "Labor Turnover Costs: Measurement and Control," *Personnel Journal*, February 1979, pp. 90–95.

and often stressful activities. Yet if the selection activities place too great an emphasis on public relations, obtaining the information needed to make successful selection decisions may be subordinated. Hence a manager's dilemma in selection is how to balance the desire to attract people with the desire to gather relevant selection data.

The Discrete Selection Process

The discrete selection process   Selection activities typically follow a standard pattern, beginning with an initial screening interview and concluding with the final employment decision. The selection process consists of seven steps: (1) initial screening interview, (2) completion of the application form, (3) employment tests, (4) comprehensive interview, (5) background investigation, (6) physical examination, and (7) final employment decision. Each of these steps represents a decision point requiring some affirmative feedback for the process to continue. Each step in the process seeks to expand the organization's knowledge about the applicant's background, abilities, and motivation, and it increases the information from which decision makers will make their predictions and final choice. However, some steps may be omitted if they do not yield data that will aid in predicting success, or if the cost of the step is not warranted. For example, the background investigation may not be used in all cases. For jobs where there are fuduciary responsibilities, the costs incurred conducting the background investigation might be cost effective. On the other hand, spending the same money on a background investigation for an assembly-line worker may not be the best use of that money.

Whether a step is omitted or not, it is beneficial to have some insight into how each works. The flow of these activities is depicted in Figure 7-3. Let us take a closer look at each.

Initial Screening

Initial screening   As a culmination of our recruiting efforts, we should be prepared to initiate a preliminary review of potentially acceptable candidates. This screening is, in effect, a two-step procedure: (1) the screening of inquiries and (2) the provision of screening interviews.

If our recruiting effort has been successful, we will be confronted with a number of potential applicants. Based on the job description and job specification, some of these respondents can be eliminated. Factors that might lead to a negative decision at this point include inadequate or inappropriate experience or, similarly, inadequate or inappropriate education. The screening interview is also an excellent opportunity for management to describe the job in enough detail so the candidates can consider whether they are really serious about making application. The sharing of job description information with the in-

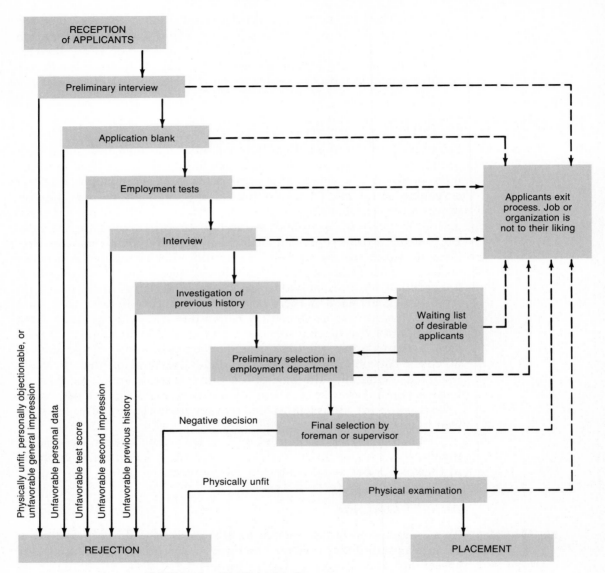

FIGURE 7-3   The Selection Process

FLOWCHART SOURCE: Thomas H. Patten, Jr., ''Personnel Management in the 1970's: The End of Laissez-Faire,'' *Human Resource Management,* Fall 1973, p. 9. With permission.

dividual can frequently encourage the unqualified or marginally qualified to voluntarily withdraw from candidacy—with a minimum of cost to the applicant or the organization. Another important point during the initial screening phase is to identify a salary range. Most workers are concerned about their salaries, and while a job opening may sound exciting, a low salary may preclude an organization from obtaining excellent talent. During this phase, if proper HRM activities have been conducted, there should be no need to masquerade the salary. Without the salary, only time and money are wasted.

Completion of Application Form

Completion of application form

Once the initial screening has been completed, applicants are asked to complete the organization's application form. The amount of information required may be only the applicant's name, address, and telephone number. Some organizations, on the other hand, may request the completion of a six- to ten-page comprehensive personal history profile. In general terms, the application form gives a synopsis of what applicants have been doing during their adult life, their skills, and their accomplishments. An example of the application form used by Blue Cross and Blue Shield of Maryland is shown in Figure 7-4.

Employment Tests

Employment tests

Organizations historically relied to a considerable extent on intelligence, aptitude, ability, and interest tests to provide major input to the selection process. Even handwriting analysis (graphology) and lie detector (polygraph) tests have been used in the attempt to learn more about the candidate—information that will supposedly lead to more effective selection.

In recent years, however, reliance on traditional written tests for selection purposes has decreased significantly. This can be attributed directly to legal rulings that now require the employer to justify as job related any test that is used. Given the historical difficulty and costs in substantiating this relationship, many organizations have merely eliminated employment testing as a selection device. Too many organizations found that charges of violating Title VII were being placed against them. Unfortunately, many of the general intelligence tests were declared to have a disparate impact on minorities. The only method to refute this allegation was through validity testing. However, when we consider that most tests are validated by industrial psychologist consultants who charge in excess of $600 per day plus expenses and that validating a test may take more than six months, it is not surprising that many organizations just scrapped these tests in lieu of other selection devices.

This should not discourage an organization from developing and using valid tests. To just scrap the employment test is, in our judgment, equivalent to "throwing the baby out with the bathwater." Valid tests can be extremely valuable tools in the selection process. This issue of validity will be discussed later in this chapter.

APPLICANT'S LAST NAME	FIRST	MIDDLE INITIAL

FOR EMPLOYMENT USE ONLY

DATE REC'D _____
DATE INPUT _____
CATEGORY _____

INTERVIEWED _____
_____
_____

OFFER DATE _____ START DATE _____ ☐ P/T ☐ F/T

**Blue Cross
Blue Shield**
of Maryland

700 East Joppa Road, Baltimore, Maryland 21204

EMPLOYMENT APPLICATION

INSTRUCTIONS:

PLEASE PRINT OR TYPE; ANSWER ALL QUESTIONS WHICH APPLY TO YOU; AND GIVE COMPLETE ADDRESSES INCLUDING ZIP CODES.

PERSONAL and GENERAL INFORMATION

LAST NAME	FIRST	MIDDLE INITIAL	SOCIAL SECURITY NUMBER

PRESENT ADDRESS (STREET, CITY, STATE AND ZIP CODE)		TELEPHONE	BUSINESS TELEPHONE NO.

ARE YOU UNDER 18 OR OVER 70 YEARS OF AGE	IF YOU ARE NOT A U.S. CITIZEN, GIVE VISA CLASS, NUMBER AND EXPIRATION DATE.	HAVE YOU EVER BEEN CONVICTED FOR OTHER THAN A MISDEMEANOR OR MINOR TRAFFIC VIOLATION? IF YES EXPLAIN.*

HOW WERE YOU REFERRED TO BLUE CROSS AND BLUE SHIELD OF MARYLAND?

NAME OF RELATIVES IN OUR EMPLOY (INDICATE RELATIONSHIP)

PREVIOUS EMPLOYMENT WITH BLUE CROSS AND BLUE SHIELD OF MARYLAND? ☐ NO ☐ YES	EMPLOYMENT DATES	DEPARTMENT	SUPERVISOR

POSITION APPLIED FOR	TYPE OF POSITION DESIRED: DAY PART TIME _____ OTHER _____ EVENING FULL TIME

SALARY REQUIRED	WHEN COULD YOU START WORK?	HOURS/DAYS AVAILABLE FOR WORK

*EXISTENCE OF A CRIMINAL RECORD DOES NOT CONSTITUTE AUTOMATIC BAR TO EMPLOYMENT.

EDUCATIONAL and PROFESSIONAL BACKGROUND

PLEASE CIRCLE HIGHEST GRADE COMPLETED   ELEMENTARY 1 2 3 4 5   JR. HIGH SCHOOL 7 8 9   SR. HIGH SCHOOL 10 11 12   COLLEGE 1 2 3 4   GRADUATE SCHOOL

SCHOOLS ATTENDED (Name, Address, State and Zip Code)	DATES ATTENDED FROM	TO	DAY OR NIGHT	YEARS COMPLETED	DID YOU GRADUATE	MAJOR SUBJECTS OR DEGREE CONFERRED
SENIOR HIGH SCHOOL						
COLLEGE						
GRADUATE SCHOOL						
OTHER SCHOOLS, IF ANY						

HONORS, PUBLICATIONS, PROFESSIONAL SOCIETIES

LISCENSURE, PROFESSIONAL REGISTRATION, OR CERTIFICATION

MILITARY BACKGROUND

HAVE YOU EVER SERVED IN THE ARMED FORCES? YES NO	BRANCH OF SERVICE	DATE ENTERED	DATE DISCHARGED	TYPE OF DISCHARGE

BRIEFLY DESCRIBE YOUR DUTIES IN THE SERVICE

FOR CLERICAL APPLICANTS ONLY

PLEASE LIST OFFICE MACHINES YOU CAN SKILLFULLY OPERATE:

APPROX. TYPING SPEED PER MINUTE _____

APPROX. SHORTHAND SPEED PER MINUTE _____

EMPLOYMENT RECORD

BEGIN WITH CURRENT OR MOST RECENT POSITION AND LIST PRIOR POSITIONS IN SEQUENCE. PLEASE COMPLETE IN DETAIL AND EXPLAIN ANY PERIODS OF UNEMPLOYMENT.

	WEEKLY SALARY	PERIOD EMPLOYED	FOR PERSONNEL USE ONLY
COMPANY NAME:	Final	Date Left	
ADDRESS, STATE, ZIP CODE:			
SUPERVISOR'S NAME, TITLE AND TELEPHONE:	Starting	Date Started	
REASON FOR LEAVING CURRENT POSITION:			
JOB TITLE:	DUTIES AND RESPONSIBILITIES:		

FIGURE 7-4   Sample Application Form

SOURCE: Blue Cross/Blue Shield of Maryland, Inc., Baltimore, Maryland, with permission.

		WEEKLY SALARY	PERIOD EMPLOYED	FOR PERSONNEL USE ONLY
COMPANY NAME:			Final	Date Left	
ADDRESS, STATE, ZIP CODE:				
SUPERVISOR'S NAME, TITLE AND TELEPHONE:		Starting	Date Started	
REASON FOR LEAVING CURRENT POSITION:				
JOB TITLE:	DUTIES AND RESPONSIBILITIES:			

		WEEKLY SALARY	PERIOD EMPLOYED	FOR PERSONNEL USE ONLY
COMPANY NAME:			Final	Date Left	
ADDRESS, STATE, ZIP CODE:				
SUPERVISOR'S NAME, TITLE AND TELEPHONE:		Starting	Date Started	
REASON FOR LEAVING CURRENT POSITION:				
JOB TITLE:	DUTIES AND RESPONSIBILITIES:			

		WEEKLY SALARY	PERIOD EMPLOYED	FOR PERSONNEL USE ONLY
COMPANY NAME:			Final	Date Left	
ADDRESS, STATE, ZIP CODE:				
SUPERVISOR'S NAME, TITLE AND TELEPHONE:		Starting	Date Started	
REASON FOR LEAVING CURRENT POSITION:				
JOB TITLE:	DUTIES AND RESPONSIBILITIES:			

		WEEKLY SALARY	PERIOD EMPLOYED	FOR PERSONNEL USE ONLY
COMPANY NAME:			Final	Date Left	
ADDRESS, STATE, ZIP CODE:				
SUPERVISOR'S NAME, TITLE AND TELEPHONE:			Date Started	
REASON FOR LEAVING CURRENT POSITION:				
JOB TITLE:	DUTIES AND RESPONSIBILITIES:			

PROVIDE ANY ADDITIONAL INFORMATION ABOUT YOURSELF WHICH WILL AID IN EVALUATING YOUR CAREER INTEREST AND ABILITIES

PLEASE READ THE FOLLOWING INFORMATION · SIGN WHERE INDICATED

Under Maryland Law an employer may not require or demand any applicant for employment or prospective employment or any employee to submit to or take a polygraph, lie detector or similar test or examination as a condition of employment or continued employment. Any employer who violates this provision is guilty of a misdemeanor and subject to a fine not to exceed $100.

The accuracy and completeness of all information on this application is of the utmost importance. Please read the following statements carefully before signing your name.

1. In consideration of my employment or continued employment by Blue Cross and Blue Shield of Maryland, I agree to perform the work which may be considered necessary by the corporations and to take physical and/or other examinations when required.

2. I certify that at the time of my application for employment I am not aware of any mental or physical reason which would prohibit me from performing the job for which I am applying.

3. I also agree to retain the confidentiality of medical, subscriber, provider, and company systems information to which I have access because of my work for the period of time that I am employed by the corporations.

4. I authorize the corporations to investigate all statements and references contained herein. I understand that misrepresentation or omission of facts in this application may be cause for immediate dismissal.

_____   _____
SIGNATURE   DATE

Blue Cross and Blue Shield of Maryland are Affirmative Action Employers. The elements of the corporate Affirmative Action Program will be made available upon request. All applicants for employment will be considered regardless of age, color, creed, sex, national origin, mental and/or physical handicap.

FIGURE 7-4 (continued)

Comprehensive Interview

Comprehensive
interview

Those individuals who are still viable applicants after the initial screening, application form, and required tests have been completed are then given a comprehensive interview. The applicant may be interviewed by personnel department interviewers, executives within the organization, a potential supervisor, potential colleagues, or some combination of these.

The comprehensive interview is designed to probe into areas that cannot be addressed by the application form or tests. These areas usually consist of assessing one's motivation, ability to work under pressure, and ability to "fit in" with the organization. However, this information, too, must be job related. The questions asked and the topics covered should reflect the specific characteristics of the job and the qualities sought for the job's incumbent. And above all, the questions should be structured so that applicants are asked the same questions. (The uses and advantages of the structured interview will be discussed in the next chapter.)

Background Investigation

Background
investigation

The next step in the selection process is to undertake an investigation of those applicants who appear to offer potential as employees. This may include contacting former employers to confirm the candidate's work record and to obtain their appraisal of his or her performance, contacting other job-related and personal references, and verifying the educational accomplishments shown on the application.

The background investigation has major implications. Every personnel administrator has the responsibility to investigate each potential applicant. In some organizations, failure to do so could result in the loss of his or her job. But many managers consider the background investigation data highly biased. Who would actually list a reference that would not give anything but the best possible recommendation? The seasoned personnel administrator expects this and delves deeper into the candidate's background. But that, too, may not prove to be beneficial. Many past employers are reluctant to give any information to another company other than factual information (e.g., dates of employment). Much of this reluctance comes as a result of the courts' actions against employers who gave unprovable information in response to background investigations.

Even though there is some reluctance to give this information, there are ways in which personnel administrators can obtain it. Sometimes, for instance, information can be obtained from references once removed. For example, the personnel administrator can ask a reference whose name has been provided on the application form to give another reference, someone who has knowledge of the candidate's work experience. By doing this, the administrator can eliminate the

FIGURE 7-5

By permission of Johnny Hart and Field Enterprises, Inc.

possibility of accepting an individual based on the employee's current employer's glowing recommendation when the motivation for such a positive recommendation was to get rid of the employee.

Many personnel administrators have horror stories about job applicants who are not the individuals they have represented themselves as being. In 1985, none was more notable than an East Coast college professor who taught simultaneously at a number of schools using thirty-three assumed identities. The embarrassment these schools incurred could have been eliminated if their administrators had done a bit of a background investigation.

Physical Examination

Physical examination The last step prior to the final "go—no go" decision may consist of having the applicant take a physical examination. For most jobs, this is a screening device in the selection process; that is, it can only act negatively on the applicant. It is assumed that the applicant can pass the physical examination; however, it is intended to screen out those individuals who are unable to comply physically with the requirements of the job and the organization. The vast majority of physical examinations are currently required to meet the minimum standards for the organization's group life and medical insurance programs and to provide base data in case of future worker's compensation claims. Exceptions would include such jobs as police officer, where rigorous physical qualifications are required.

While the physical examination may be used, it is coming under close scrutiny as a selection device by many state civil rights commissions. Before using a physical examination, an organization must check its state's interpretation of the legality of its use.

Final Employment Decision

Final employment decision
Those individuals who perform successfully on the employment tests and the comprehensive interview, and are not eliminated by the development of negative information on either the background investigation or the physical examination, are now considered to be eligible to receive an offer of employment. Who makes that employment offer? The answer is, it depends. For administrative purposes (processing salary forms, maintaining EEO statistics, etc.), the offer should be made by the personnel department. But their role should be only administrative. The actual hiring decision should be made by the manager in the department that had the position open. While this might not be the situation in all organizations, the manager of the department should have this authority. First of all, the applicant will eventually work for this manager and therefore a good "fit" between the boss and the employee is necessary. Second, if the decision made is not correct, the hiring manager has no one else to blame.

If the organization selection process has been effective in differentiating between those individuals who will make successful employees and those who will not, the thrust of the selection decision will now be in the hands of the applicant.

Is there anything management can do at this stage to increase the probability that the individual to whom an offer is made will accept? Assuming that the organization has not lost sight throughout the process of selection's dual objective—evaluation and attraction—we can expect that the potential employee has a solid understanding of the job being offered and what it would be like to work for the organization. Yet it might be of interest at this point to review what we know about how people choose a job. This subject—job choice—represents personnel selection from the perspective of the potential employee rather than the organization.

Research indicates that people gravitate toward jobs that are

FIGURE 7-6 "All right now, this is your application, so watch closely! . . . If it comes back through any of those windows you're just the man we're looking for."

SOURCE: WILLY 'N ETHEL by Joe Martin (C) Field Enterprises, Inc. 1984 Permission of News America Syndicate

compatible with their personal orientation.[4] Individuals appear to move toward matching their work with their personality. Social individuals lean toward jobs in clinical psychology, foreign service, social work, and the like. Investigative individuals are compatible with jobs in biology, mathematics, or oceanography. Careers in management, law, or public relations appeal to enterprising individuals. This approach to the matching of people and jobs would suggest that management can expect a greater proportion of acceptances if it has properly matched the candidate's personality to the job.

Most job choice studies indicate that an individual's perception of the attractiveness of a job is important.[5] People desire to work where their expectations are positive and where they believe their goals can be achieved. This, coupled with the previous research, should encourage management to ensure that those to whom offers are made can see that the job is compatible with their personality and goals (realistic preview). (We will take a closer look at realistic job previews (RJP) in the next chapter.)

[4]John L. Holland, *Making Vocational Choices: A Theory of Vocational Personalities and Work Environments*, 2nd ed. (Englewood Cliffs, N.J.: Prentice-Hall, 1985).

[5]Summarized in John P. Wanous, "Organizational Entry: The Individual's Viewpoint," in *Perspectives on Behavior in Organizations*, ed. J. R. Hackman, E. E. Lawler III, and L. Porter (New York: McGraw-Hill, 1977), p. 129.

Before we leave this last step in the selection process—the final employment decision—we should not hesitate to ask, What about those applicants to whom we did not make an offer? We argue that those involved in the selection process should carefully consider how rejected candidates are treated. What is communicated and how it is communicated will have a central bearing on the image that the rejected candidate will have of the organization. And that image may be carried for a lifetime. The young college graduate, rejected for a position by a major computer manufacturer, may a decade later be the influential decision maker for his or her current employer's computer purchase. The image formed many years earlier may play a key part in the decision. In this same vein, it was said that Richard Nixon never forgave FBI Director J. Edgar Hoover for the bureau's rejection of Nixon's application following his graduation from law school.

Summary

What we have presented in the previous pages is a synopsis of the selection process generally followed by most organizations. That is not to say that deviations do not occur or that steps are not occasionally omitted. Overall, however, the previously identified seven steps can be generalized to most organizations.

VIEWS IN THE NEWS

The Eighth Step?

The seven-step selection process you have just seen may one day be expanded to include an eighth step. That additional hurdle, however, is becoming one of the most highly debated issues in American corporations: Drug Testing. The late 1980s are witnessing tremendous attention to the possibility of this selection device, with support being generated from such high-ranking officials as the president of the United States. Although the issue is far from being settled, let us look at the two sides of drug-testing possibilities.

Substance abuse by employees in companies is resulting in losses estimated to be in the billions of dollars. This amount is not only associated with the costs of the health-related expenditures (e.g., increases in health care insurance premiums or worker compensation payments) but also related to the findings that substance abusers create an atmosphere at work that is more conducive to accidents; perform poorly and accordingly production is decreased; steal from the company to support their habits; and in some cases, sell drugs to other employees on company time.

The above-mentioned anomalies do substantiate a reason for implementing drug-screening tests, but too many feel that these actions are caused by the ''hard-core'' substance abusers. Unfortunately, that is not the case. Too many examples have been reported indicating that an infrequent or recreational user can cause as much damage in an organization. For example, in one defense-contracting organization, a worker whose job was to mix adhesives for use in fighter planes did so one day while he was high. His inability to do his job correctly cost this contractor approximately $100,000 to correct the situation. What might the loss have been if the company had not discovered that the glue didn't hold and had sent the planes out for use?

Because of incidents such as the one described above, many companies have begun to test employees, either current employees on a random or as-needed basis, or applicants as they move along the selection process. It has been estimated that approximately 150 of the Fortune 500 companies are currently testing for drugs, with more and more companies and governmental agencies expected to follow suit. The reasons for its increased usage appear evident, but drug screening is not without its critics.

First and foremost is the issue of accuracy of the tests. No drug-screening test to date can predict with 100 percent accuracy. This has led to major discussions on what happens if your test is positive (traces of drugs are found to be present) and you know that you have not taken drugs. For current employees, there might be a greater chance to retest and disprove the initial results. But this is generally left up to the employer to decide. If the employer is unwilling to give you another chance because of the costs associated with the test, you may have little recourse. If you are an applicant, the second chance is nonexistent. If you fail the drug-screening test, you are turned down for employment.

Cases regarding the inaccuracy of tests have been well cited. A Naval Academy midshipman was reinstated to the Academy after further tests could not substantiate an earlier positive result. In other cases, some of the employees have failed the drug-screening test because tne test indicated traces of barbiturates in their urine. In a few of these cases, it was found that an employee was taking a medically prescribed medication that contained a barbiturate, its content not known by the employee. Might something of this nature require doctors and pharmacists to label all components of the drugs they prescribe and fill to eliminate this occurrence? It's difficult to tell. Had these individuals not been given the opportunity to ''defend'' themselves, these readings could falsely label those workers and affect their careers.

The other issues in drug screening revolve around monitoring and the right to privacy. Every drug test administered must be monitored. Accordingly, as you give your urine sample, someone from the company must be with you to ensure that it's you who ''fills the bottle'' and that your sample is labeled and identified properly. This monitoring can be extremely uncomfortable for both the applicant/employee and the monitor. The right-to-privacy issue is based on ''alleged unreasonable intrusion, unreasonable discharge, or if test results go out (are made public), defamation or slander.''

Drug testing is by no means an easy issue to resolve. It is, at best, an extremely delicate process that must be handled with the utmost of care. But its implications are great for HRM. Will we see more testing in the mid-1990s, an increase in its use by more companies, and an eighth step in the selection process? The evidence so far indicates we will.

Source: Adapted from Mark Bomster. ''Drug Affecting Every Business,'' ''Drug Testing Increasing, Before and After Hiring,'' and ''Even the Pure Suffer the Taint of Examination,'' *Baltimore Evening Sun*, September 29–30, 1986, pp. A1, A8, amd A20.

An Alternative: The Comprehensive Approach

The comprehensive approach

We have presented the general selection process as being comprised of multiple hurdles—beginning with a screening interview and culminating with a final selection decision. This selection process is designed so that tripping over any hurdle puts one out of the race. This approach, however, may not be the most effective selection procedure for every job. If, for example, the application form shows that the candidate has had only two years of relevant experience but the job specification requires five years, the candidate is rejected without going any further in the process. Yet, in most jobs, negative factors can be counterbalanced by positive factors. Two years of experience, for example, may be offset by outstanding performance on a written test, or experience may be substituted for educational requirements. This suggests that sometimes it may be advantageous to do comprehensive rather than discrete selection. In comprehensive selection, all the applicants are put through every step in the selection process, and the final decision is based on a comprehensive evaluation of the results in each stage.

The comprehensive approach overcomes the major disadvantage of the discrete method: eliminating potentially good employees simply because they receive a poor evaluation at one selection step. The comprehensive method is more realistic—it recognizes that most applicants have weaknesses as well as strengths—but it is also more costly, since all the applicants must go through all the screening hurdles. Additionally, the method is more consuming of management's time and may demoralize many applicants by building up hope. Yet, in those instances where the job is important enough to justify the extra cost, where many qualities are needed for success in the job, and where acquiring candidates who are strong on all qualities is unlikely, the comprehensive approach is probably preferable to the typical discrete method.

No matter which approach is used or which steps are involved, one critical aspect must be present: The devices used must measure job-related criteria. That is, these devices must be able to predict how one would perform on the job.

Key Elements in Successful Predictors

We are concerned with selection activities that can help us predict which applicants will perform satisfactorily on the job. In this section, we want to explore the concepts of reliability, validity, and cut scores. For illustration purposes, we will emphasize these elements as they relate to employment tests, but they are relevant to any selection device.

Reliability

Reliability

For any predictor to be useful, it must possess an acceptable level of reliability or consistency of measurement. This means that the applicant's performance on any given selection device should produce consistent scores each time the device is used. For example, if you were to have your height measured every day with a wooden yardstick, you would get highly reliable results. On the other hand, if you were measured each day by an elastic tape measure, there would probably be considerable disparity between your height measurements from one to the next. Your height, of course, does not change from day to day. The variability is due to the unreliability of the measuring device.

Similarly, if an organization uses tests to provide input to the selection decision, the tests must give consistent results. If the test is reliable, any single individual's score should remain fairly stable over time, assuming that the characteristic it is measuring is also stable. An individual's intelligence, for example, is generally a stable characteristic, and if we give applicants an IQ test, we should expect that someone who scores 110 in March would score close to 110 if tested again in July. If, in July, the same applicant scored 85, the reliability of the test would be highly questionable.

Validity

Validity

High reliability may mean little if the selection device has low validity; that is, if the measures obtained are not related to some relevant criterion, such as job performance. For example, just because a test score is consistent is no indication that it is measuring important characteristics related to job behavior. It must also differentiate between satisfactory and unsatisfactory performance on the job. We should be aware of three specific types of validity: content, construct, and criterion related. For simplicity's sake, we will discuss each of these types of validity as it relates to employment tests, although the concepts also apply to the application form, interviews, or background investigation.

Content validity

Content validity is the degree to which the content of the test, as a sample, represents all the situations that could have been included: A simplified example of a content valid test is a typing test for a secretarial position. Such a test can approximate the work to be done on the job; the applicant can be given a typical sample of typing, and his or her performance can be evaluated based on that sample. Assuming that the tasks on the test constitute a random sample of the tasks on the job (ordinarily a dubious assumption at best), the test is content valid.[6]

[6]James Ledvinka, *Federal Regulation of Personnel and Human Resource Management* (Boston: Kent Publishing, 1982), p. 112.

VIEWS IN THE NEWS

Non-Standardized Selections

To what extent may an employer deviate from its standard procedures or use subjective criteria when it selects an employee for promotion and not run into discrimination charges? Two federal district courts provide very different answers.

OTHER FACTORS CONSIDERED

In the first case, the court holds that the Washington, D.C., fire department's promotion of a black employee over five whites—four of whom were senior in rank to the selected employee—was not discriminatory. Although acknowledging that the complainants' records generally were superior to the successful candidate's, the court accepts the statement of the fire department's chief that "he saw qualities" in the black employee "that he believed to be lacking" in the other applicants. For example, the court notes, "from his vantage point," the chief concluded that two of the applicants, despite their high ranks, were "indecisive and did not display the firmness" of the black employee.

Although each complainant showed "beyond dispute" that he was "a highly qualified candidate," the court stresses, they failed to show that the department discriminated on the basis of race "by giving greater weight in the selection process" to factors they "considered relatively unimportant." While acknowledging that under the criteria applied by the white candidates—seniority, education, breadth of experience—they normally would be rated as superior to the selected employee— the court points out that "no fire department policy mandated consideration of any of those criteria." (*Bishopp v. D.C.,* USDC DC, 1985, 37 FEP Cases 235)

PROCEDURAL DEVIATIONS

In the second case, however, the court finds that a U.S. Navy branch manipulated the selection process to ensure that a white candidate rather than a more qualified black candidate would be chosen as a department manager. The court cites several actions taken by the selecting officials that rendered the process discriminatory, including their:

- Using a nonvalidated, subjective test in place of an objective valuation when it appeared that the black candidate would be successful;
- Asking a number of questions during an interview that were designed to elicit "intangible" answers that could be used as a basis for denying the job to the black applicant;
- Emphasizing a particular experience requirement—in this case, budgetary— that the white applicant was known to possess, which, according to the court, supports "the possibility of pre-selection"; and
- Violating the federal government's guidelines on selection panels. According to the court, "deviations from normal procedures are themselves evidence of discrimination." (*Verdell v. Wilson,* USDC ENY, 1985, 37 FEP Cases 216)

Source: Reprinted by permission from *Bulletin to Management,* copyright 1985 by The Bureau of National Affairs, Inc., Washington, D.C.

Construct validity   *Construct validity* is the degree to which a particular trait is related to successful performance on the job. These traits are usually abstract in nature, such as a measure of intelligence. This type of validity is usually conducted by observing various behaviors of the applicant and measuring how these behaviors or traits relate to the job. If much of this sounds confusing, relax. It is. It takes the effort of a trained industrial psychologist to do this. In fact, it is the most difficult type of validity to prove because you are dealing with abstract measures.

Criterion-related validity   *Criterion-related validity* is the degree to which a particular selection device accurately predicts the important elements of work behavior. These measures reveal the relationship between some score (test) and job performance (e.g., production output or managerial effectiveness). To establish criterion-related validity, one of two measures can be used: predictive validity and concurrent validity.

Predictive validity   To validate the test *predictively,* an organization would give the test (invalidated at this time) to all prospective applicants. The test scores would be recorded and saved for future reference. The selection process would continue, the applicants being hired as a result of successfully completing the entire process; the test score would have no bearing on the case. At some prescribed date, usually one year from being hired, the new applicants would be evaluated by their supervisors. The ratings of the evaluations would then be compared with the initial test scores (stored in a file for over a year). At that time, an analysis would be conducted (we will look at this analysis in the next section) to see if there was any relationship between test scores and performance evaluation (the measure of success on the job). If no clear relationship exists, then the test may have to be revised. However, if the organization can statistically show that the employees who scored below some cut score (determined in the analysis) were unsuccessful performers (validity), then any future applicant scoring below the cut score would be ineligible for employment. What happens to those unsuccessful performers? They are handled like any other employee who has experienced poor evaluations: training, transfer, discipline, or discharge.

Concurrent validity   The *concurrent validity* method validates tests using current employees as the subjects. Given the test, the scores from the current employees are immediately analyzed, revealing a relationship between the test scores and their previous performance appraisals. Again, statistically speaking, if there is a relationship between test scores and performance, then a valid test has been found.

Predictive validity is clearly the preferred choice. Its advantage over concurrent validity is that it can be used as a screening device, whereas concurrent validity acts on current employees. Developing both types is similar with the exception of the people who are tested (see Figure 7-7).

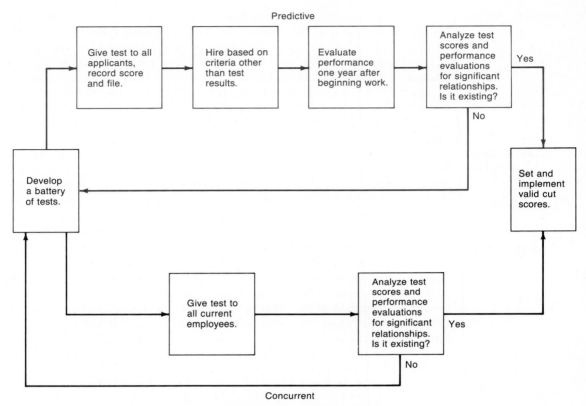

FIGURE 7-7   Predictive and Concurrent Validity

While the costs associated with each method are drastically different, the predictive validity method should be used if possible. Concurrent validity, although better than no validity at all, leaves many questions to be answered. Its usefulness has been challenged on the premise that current employees know the jobs already and that a learning process takes place. Thus there may be little similarity between the current employee and the applicant.

Analyses Used to Determine Validity

In both the predictive and concurrent validity methods discussed above, we alluded to an analysis that must be conducted to show that a relationship exists between test score and job performance. Two of the more popular analyses used to determine this relationship are the validity correlation coefficients and the expectancy diagrams.

Validity correlation coefficients

Validity Correlation Coefficients.   Validity correlation coefficients show the statistical relationships existing between an individual's test score and his or her job performance. Using a correlational analysis procedure, the results of the analysis can indicate a coefficient of −1 to +1. The closer the validity coefficient to +1, the better the test. That is, the test is a good predictor of job performance. For example, Figure 7-8 contains three diagrams. In each diagram, we are trying to determine if a positive relationship exists between test scores and successful job performance.

In diagram A, there is no relationship. Statistically speaking, a low test score predicts satisfactory job performance as well as a high test score, and vice versa. In this case, our test is not valid. That is, it does not help us distinguish between the successful and unsuccessful job performers.

Diagram B may be rare, but it too does not give support for our test. In this case, the results indicate that the lower the test score, the better the performance. This is somewhat counter to logical beliefs in testing. As such, this test, too, should not be used.

FIGURE 7-8   *Validity Correlational Analysis*

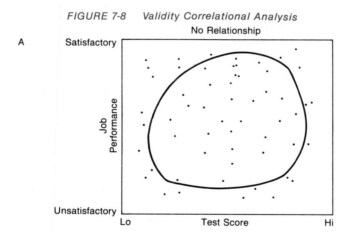

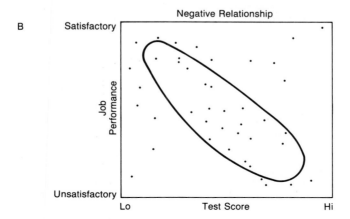

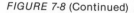

FIGURE 7-8 (Continued)

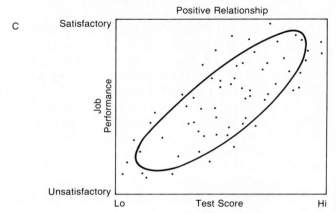

Diagram C reveals that there is a positive relationship between the test and an individual's job performance. Those individuals scoring higher on the test have a greater probability of being successful in their jobs than do those scoring lower. Based on this relationship, this test appears to be valid.

Expectancy diagrams. ***Expectancy Diagrams.*** The second method of determining the relationship between a test score and performance on the job involves the use of expectancy diagrams. Over a period of time, an organization compiles data regarding how well individuals did on a test, and after being hired, how well they are performing on the job. These data are then grouped into categories, indicating a relationship between a test score range and the probability of being successful on the job. An example of an expectancy diagram is shown in Figure 7-9.

Based on an applicant's score, and referencing it to the expectancy diagram, we can predict how well the applicant will do on the job. For example, in Figure 7-9 a score of 83 on a test would indicate that the applicant has an 87 percent probability of being successful on the job. A score of 43 would indicate that the probability is reduced to 31 percent.

Cut Scores and Their Impact on Hiring Decisions

Cut scores Throughout much of the validity discussion, we have been referring to test scores and their ability to predict successful job performance. By using our statistical analyses, we are able to generate a point at which applicants scoring below that point are rejected. This point is called the *cut score.* However, existing conditions (e.g., availability of applicants) may cause an organization to change the cut score. If cut scores do change, what impact will it have on hiring applicants who

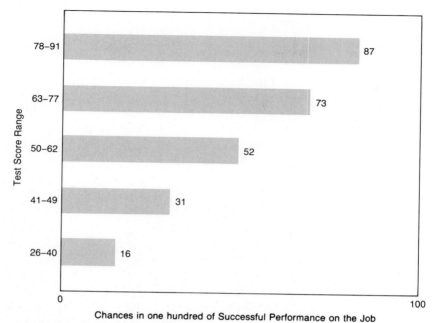

FIGURE 7-9   Expectancy Diagram

Source: Adapted from Ernest J. McCormick and Daniel R. Llgen, *Industrial Psychology* 7th ed. (Englewood Cliffs, N.J.: Prentice-Hall, 1980).

will be successful on the job? Let us again review the positive relationship we found in our validity correlation analysis. We have reproduced the main elements in the graph in Figure 7-10.

Let us assume that after our analysis, we determined that our cut score should be 70. At this cut score, we have shown that the majority of the applicants who scored above 70 have a greater probability of being successful performers on the job; the majority scoring below 70, unsuccessful performers. If we change our cut score, however, we alter the number of applicants in these categories. For example, suppose an organization faces a "buyer's" market for particular positions. Because of the many potential applicants, the organization can afford to be very selective. In a situation such as this, the organization may choose to hire only those applicants who meet the most extreme criteria. To achieve this goal, the organization increases its cut score to 98. By increasing the cut score from 70 to 98, the organization has rejected all but two candidates (areas A and B in the figure). However, many potentially successful job performers would also be rejected. These would be the individuals shown in area C. What has happened in this case is that the organization has become more selective. If there were one hundred applicants and only two were hired, we could say

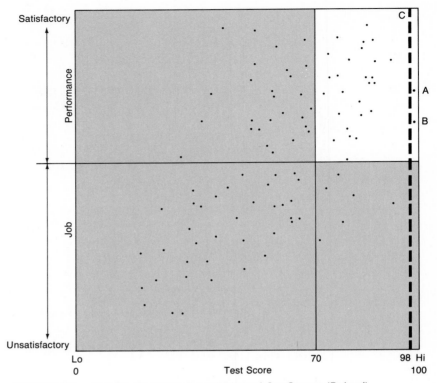

FIGURE 7-10   *Validity Correlation Analysis and Cut Scores (Raised)*

their selection ratio (the ratio of number hired to the number of applicants) is 2 percent. A 2 percent selection ratio means that the organization is very particular about who is hired.

Similar to raising the cut score, lowering the cut score has an impact. Taking our diagram from above, let us lower our cut score to 50 and see what results. We have graphically portrayed this in Figure 7-11.

By lowering the cut score from 70 to 50, we have increased our number of eligible hires who have a greater probability of being successful on the job (area D). But at the same time, we have also made eligible more applicants who could be unsuccessful on the job (area E). We hope, though, that we have hired more successful than unsuccessful applicants.

Although using a hiring process where we know that more unsuccessful applicants may be hired does not seem to make sense, conditions may necessitate the action. That is, labor market conditions may be such that there is a low supply of potential applicants who possess particular skills. For example, in some cities, finding a good

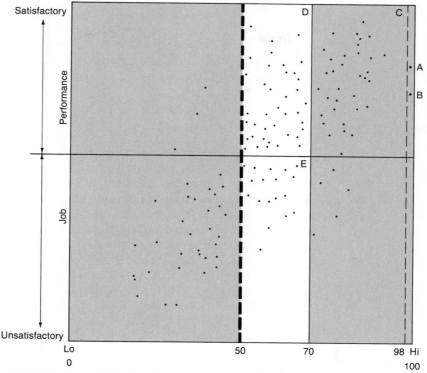

FIGURE 7-11   *Validity Correlation Analysis and Cut Scores (Lowered)*

computer programmer who can program a particular make of computer may be difficult. Because the supply is low, coupled with many openings, companies may hire individuals on the spot (more commonly referred to as an open-house recruiting effort). In this approach, the organization is hiring almost all the applicants who appear to have the skills needed (as reflected in a score of 50), putting them on the job, and filtering out the unsuccessful employees at a later date. While this may not appear to be effective, the organization is banking on the addition of individuals in area D of Figure 7-11.

The last important issue about cut scores is that there may be different cut scores for different groups. We may have one cut score for white males, and one cut score for minorities. Reasons for these different cut scores, called *differential validity*, stem from the cultural biases of some tests. If it is determined that minorities consistently score lower on tests than white males, and the reason for these lower scores is found to be a bias of the test, then the minorities may have a cut score that is lower. This, however, does not mean a difference in job performance level, but only a difference in the cut score.

Summary

We have tried to explain, as simply as possible, the topics of reliability and validity. Validating selection devices is a long and tedious process. Many variables enter into the picture, and many statistical techniques can be used. We hope our overview has provided some insight into the process.

Conclusion

In this chapter, we have described what selection is about, reviewed the selection process, proposed an alternative approach to selection, and considered the key elements that successful predictors should have. This last topic may appear unusually technical and you may even wonder why concepts like reliability and validity deserve attention. They were presented with a particular purpose in mind.

In the next chapter, we will carefully evaluate application forms, tests, interviews, background investigations, physical examinations, and other selection devices to determine how good each is in predicting job success. This analysis will rely heavily on concepts and terminology presented in the preceding section on successful predictors.

SUMMARY

1. Proper selection can minimize the costs of replacement and training, reduce legal challenges, and result in a more productive work force.

2. The primary purpose of selection activities is to predict which job applicant will be successful if hired. During the selection process, candidates are also informed about the job and organization.

3. The discrete selection process would include the following:
   a. Initial screening interview
   b. Completion of the application form
   c. Employment tests
   d. Comprehensive interview
   e. Background investigation
   f. Physical examination
   g. Final employment decision

4. In the discrete selection process, an unsuccessful performance at any stage results in rejection of the applicant.

5. An alternative to the discrete method of selection is the comprehensive approach, where all applicants go through every step in the selection process and the final decision is based on a comprehensive evaluation of the results of each stage.

6. To be an effective predictor, a selection device should
   a. Be reliable
   b. Be valid
   c. Predict a relevant criterion

KEY TERMS

Accept errors
Concurrent validity
Content validity
Construct validity
Criterion-related validity
Cut score
Discrete selection process

Expectancy diagram
Initial screening
Predictive validity
Reject errors
Reliability
Validity
Validity correlation coefficients

QUESTIONS FOR REVIEW

1. What is the relationship between selection, recruitment, and job analysis?

2. Contrast reject errors and accept errors. Which one is more likely to open an employer to charges of discrimination? Why?

3. What are the two objectives of selection? Why is it possible for them to conflict?

4. Describe the discrete selection process.

5. Is there anything management can do to increase the probability that an applicant to whom an offer has been made will accept?

6. Contrast discrete and comprehensive selection. Which is more typical in practice?

7. When might an employer choose to use the comprehensive rather than discrete approach?

8. Define the concepts of *reliability* and *validity*. What are the three types of validity? Why are we concerned about reliability and validity?

9. Describe the predictive and the concurrent methods of validation. Why is one preferred to the other?

10. How does the criterion chosen influence a predictor's effectiveness?

QUESTIONS FOR DISCUSSION

1. "EEO guidelines have resulted in a selection process that selects 'in' candidates rather than selecting 'out' applicants." Do you agree or disagree? Discuss.

2. "Since everyone has strengths and weaknesses, it is only logical that all selection should follow the comprehensive approach." Do you agree or disagree? Discuss.

3. Develop arguments about why the concurrent method of validation should be the preferred method.

4. "The responsibility for conducting a thorough background investigation lies with the personnel director. If someone is revealed at a later date as having misrepresented himself or herself, the personnel director must suffer the consequences." Do you agree or disagree? Discuss.

5. How much freedom should a personnel director have in gathering background information? Can't this be viewed as an invasion of privacy?

CONTINUING CASE: Concord General

One for You, One for Me

Judy Sapp has been actively recruiting nurses to fill the staffing needs of the new Cardiac Surgery Unit. With the pressure to hire very evident, Judy has primarily been checking to see if the nurses are currently registered in the state of West Virginia by the Board of Nursing and if they have the experience and desire to work in such a stressful unit.

One of the responsibilities of the cardiac surgery nurse is to ensure that proper drugs are obtained from the hospital pharmacy and stored in a locked cabinet in the unit. Many of these drugs are narcotics and are considered to be a controlled substance. Among them are morphine sulfate, demerol, codeine, and nembutol.

During a routine check of the drugs, it was found that some of the demerol was missing. After a thorough investigation, it was concluded that the drugs had been removed by an unauthorized individual. But only the new nurses had keys to the locked cabinet.

Sometime later, Judy was approached by Diane Stevens, an aspiring administrator and a close friend of Judy's. She told Judy in confidence that she suspected that Carla Ravensworth had stolen the drugs. She described Carla as an individual who in high school was "into the drug scene." Carla had also associated with an undesirable crowd and had evidently maintained many of her friendships. During the past few days, she was observed stocking the drug cabinet. (This information was correlated with the drug transfer slips that must be signed whenever someone handles the drugs.) In fact, three nurses in the unit had noticed that Carla often met her friends on the parking lot during her breaks and handed them small glass vials.

Armed with this information, Judy set up a conference with Carla, Jim Wilson, and John Michaels. At this time, Carla was informed of the purpose of the meeting and was asked to answer the accusations. Carla had nothing to say except that she had done nothing wrong but felt that she could no longer work with back-stabbing co-workers. Carla resigned, much to the pleasure of Judy, Jim, and John. Since her resignation, no other drugs have been missing. Acting on a hunch, Jim asked Judy to call the area hospitals to see if they had ever employed Carla and, if so, in what capacity, and why she had left. Two hospitals, not identified on Carla's application, had employed Carla, but they stated that she had resigned over a private matter. Judy, reading between the lines, went immediately to Jim to give her report.

QUESTIONS

1. What do you believe is the major problem in this case? How could Carla have slipped through the investigation?
2. If you were Jim, what would you instruct Judy to do (1) regarding Carla and (2) regarding future applicants?
3. How could Judy have overcome this embarrassment of hiring an individual who was suspected of stealing narcotics from the drug cabinet in the unit?
4. If Carla had maintained her innocence and refused to quit, what options would Judy have? What advice would you give Judy about the action she should take?

CASE APPLICATION

What Do You Mean, Bailey's Quit?

Susan Chapman is southern regional manager of Lucky Food Stores, a chain of supermarkets in the western United States. Five district supervisors report to her. Each of these district supervisors, in turn, oversees the activities of eight to twelve stores.

One spring morning as Susan was going over her morning reports, her secretary buzzed her on the intercom. "Ms. Chapman, did you see the business section in this morning's paper?" "No, why?" Susan answered. "Well, it says here that Chuck Bailey has accepted the position of Arizona regional manager for Safeway." Leaping to her feet, Susan quickly went to see the write-up for herself.

Susan's concern was not unwarranted. Chuck Bailey was one of her district supervisors. He had been with Lucky for four years in his current job. Lucky had hired him away from Alpha Beta Markets, where he had been a store manager. Susan felt hurt that she had to learn of Chuck's departure through the newspaper, but she knew she would soon get over that. What was more relevant was that Chuck was a very effective supervisor—his district consistently outperformed the other four. And where was she going to find a competent replacement?

Several days passed. Susan talked with Chuck and sincerely wished him well in his new job. She also discussed with him the problem of finding a replacement. Her final decision was to transfer one of the supervisors from a smaller district in her region into Chuck's district, and to begin an immediate search for someone to fill the smaller district's supervisor vacancy.

Susan went to her files and pulled out the job description for a district supervisor's position (no job specification was available). It described the job's duties: ensuring that corporate standards of cleanliness, service, and product quality are maintained; supervising store managers and evaluating their performance; preparing monthly, quarterly, and annual revenue and expense forecasts for the district; making cost savings suggestions to head office and/or store managers; coordinating buying; negotiating cooperative advertising programs with suppliers; and participating in union negotiations.

QUESTIONS

1. What recruitment sources do you think Susan should pursue? Why?
2. Would you recommend discrete or comprehensive selection? Explain.
3. Define the factors that should predict success on this job.

ADDITIONAL READINGS

ARTHUR, DIANE, "Preparing for the Interview," *Personnel,* 63, No 2 (February 1986), 37–49.

CORCORAN, VICTORIA, "Surviving Your Pre-employment Legal Minefield," *Management Review,* October 1986, pp. 36–38.

DANIEL, CHRISTOPHER, "Science, System or Hunch: Alternative Approaches to Improving Employee Selection," *Public Personnel Journal,* 15, No. 1 (Spring 1986), 1–10.

FARELL, BARRY M., "Recruitment: The Art of and Science of Employment Interviews," *Personnel Journal,* May 1986, pp. 91–94.

SUSSMANN, MARIO, and DONALD U. ROBERTSON, "The Validity of Validity: An Analysis of Validation Study Designs," *Journal of Applied Psychology,* 71, No 3 (August 1986), 461–68.

CHAPTER 8

Selection Devices

AFTER READING THIS CHAPTER, YOU WILL BE ABLE TO:

1. Explain the purpose of selection devices
2. Discuss the uses of application forms
3. Discuss the uses of tests that assess intelligence, ability, and personality traits
4. Discuss the uses of performance simulation tests
5. Discuss the uses of interviews
6. Describe the benefits derived from realistic job previews
7. Discuss the uses of background investigations
8. Discuss the uses of physical examinations

The closest to perfection a person ever comes is when he fills out a job application form.

—Stanley J. Randall

As we noted in Chapter 7, the selection process comprises a number of steps. Each of these steps provides managers with information that will help them predict whether an applicant will prove to be a successful job performer. One way to conceptualize this is to think of each step as a hurdle with a different selection device challenging the applicant. The able clear all the hurdles and win the race—victory being the receipt of a job offer.

The selection devices that were presented in Chapter 7 attempt to make predictions based either on evaluating the past or on sampling the present. The application form, background investigation, and comprehensive interview attempt to find out what the applicant has done in the past and then to project these past experiences and accomplishment into the future. You should be aware that this method of prediction implies certain assumptions concerning the relationship of the past to the future. Specifically, it assumes that a candidate's past behavior can be a guide for predicting future behavior, and that the candidate will remain the same person in the future that he or she was in the past. While these assumptions may be accurate and this approach satisfactory, it would appear that devices like job-related tests, where relevant, would be better predictors because they sample *present* behavior in order to predict future behavior.

It is logical that selection devices that simulate actual work behavior and that are as current as possible should stand the best chance for being good predictors. But is this true in practice? In the following pages, we will review the devices discussed in the previous chapter plus several new ones. Since each of these devices is a potential "tool" in the selector's "tool kit," we want to look carefully at each in the context of how good a tool it is and under what conditions it should be used.

Application Forms

Application forms

The 1964 Civil Rights Act and previous and subsequent executive orders, rulings, and legislation have made it illegal to discriminate on the basis of sex, race, color, religion, national origin, and age. The only major exceptions to those guidelines involving sex, age, and religion are cases where it can be shown that the sex, the age, or the religion of an applicant could prevent the applicant from performing successfully on the job; that is, where these characteristics are bona fide occupational qualifications (BFOQ).[1]

Many of the items that traditionally appeared on the application form—religion, age, marital status, occupation of spouse, number and ages of children, hobbies—may have been interesting to know, but they often could not be proved to be job related. Given this reality, it should not be surprising to find a trend toward shorter application forms. Since the onus is on management to demonstrate that information supplied by applicants is job related, items that cannot be demonstrated to be job related should be omitted.

The fact that application forms have had to be revised should not be interpreted as an indictment of the application form as an effective predictor. Such is not the case. In fact, the evidence indicates that hard and relevant biographical data that can be verified—for example, rank in high-school graduating class—may be a more valid measure of potential job performance than many of the intelligence, aptitude, interest, and personality items that have traditionally been used in the selection decision.[2] Additionally, when application form items have been appropriately weighted to reflect job relatedness, we find that the result can be a device that successfully predicts performance criteria for such diverse groups as salesclerks, engineers, factory workers, district managers, female clerical employees, draftsmen, and technicians.[3] A review of twenty-one studies using biographical data acquired from the application blank found that nineteen had at least one item that successfully predicted differences between short-tenure and long-tenure employees.[4]

The Weighted Application Form

Weighted application forms

The weighted application form appears to offer excellent potential. To create such a form, individual form items—such as number of years

---

[1]James Ledvinka, *Federal Regulation of Personnel and Human Resource Management* (Boston: Kent Publishing, 1982), p. 60.

[2]James J. Asher, "The Biographical Item: Can It Be Improved?" *Personnel Psychology,* Summer 1972, p. 266.

[3]George W. England, *Development and Use of Weighted Application Blanks,* rev. ed. (Minneapolis: Industrial Relations Center, University of Minnesota, 1971).

[4]Allan Schuh, "The Predictability of Employee Turnover: A Review of the Literature," *Personnel Psychology,* Spring 1967, pp. 133–52.

of schooling, number of previous jobs, number of months on last job, reason for leaving last job, salary increase over all previous jobs, and military experience—are validated against performance and turnover measures and given appropriate weights. Let us assume, for example, that management is interested in developing a weighted application form that would predict which applicants for the job of insurance claims adjuster will, if hired, stay with the company, They would select from their personnel files the application forms from each of two groups of previously hired adjusters—one, a group that had short tenure with the organization (adjusters that stayed, say, less than one year), and the other, a group with long tenure (say, five years or more). These old application forms would be screened, item by item, to determine how employees in each group responded. In this way, management would discover items that differentiate the groups. These items would then be weighted relative to their magnitude of differentiation. If 80 percent of the long-tenure group had a college degree while only 20 percent of the short-tenures had such a degree, then possession of a college degree might be given a weight of 4; but if 30 percent of the long-tenure group had prior experience in the insurance industry, while 20 percent of the short-tenure did, this item might be given a weight of only 1. Notice, of course, that this procedure would have to be done on every job. Items that predict long tenure for an insurance claims adjuster may be totally different from items that predict long tenure for a grocery clerk.

Some Successful Applications

The application form, as noted earlier, has had wide success in a number of diverse jobs. In a job as basic as door-to-door sales done by young boys, analysis of application form information has been valuable. It was shown for these jobs that owning a bicycle, receiving a newspaper at home, attending a show or circus with parents, and saving money earned were highly predictive of success.[5]

The evidence is generally supportive of the application form as providing relevant information for predicting job success across a broad range of jobs. Care must be taken to ensure that application items are validated for each job. Also, since the predictive ability of items may change over time, the items must be continuously reviewed and updated. Finally, management should be aware of the possibility that the application information given is erroneous. Follow-up through a background investigation can verify most of the application data.

[5]V. Appel and M. R. Feinberg, "Recruiting Door-to-Door Salesmen by Mail," *Journal of Applied Psychology*, August 1969, pp. 362–66.

Employment Tests

In this section we want to look at tests—the more well-known written tests that attempt to assess intelligence, abilities, and personality traits, as well as the lesser-known performance simulation tests, including work sampling and the tests administered at assessment centers. In addition, we will look at and evaluate the use of polygraph tests and handwriting analysis as valid selection devices.

Written Tests

Written tests   We noted in the previous chapter that written tests historically were a significant input to the selection decision. Recently, however, there has been a marked decline in their use. The reason for this decline is the fear that such tests may be judged as discriminating. Since the law now requires an employer to justify any test used as being job related, and since historically it has been difficult, even when employers were willing, to substantiate this relationship, many organizations have merely eliminated employment testing as a selection device.

Testing for purposes of hiring and promotion now entails considerable risk for an employer. With the extension of this fear of discrimination to other components in the selection process, such as application forms and interviews, some organizations are moving precipitously close to random hiring.[6] Tests that have been validated against job performance, when used with other selection tools, can significantly aid in the acquisition of efficient and effective workers, but now the burden of proof is placed on employers to justify any tests they use as fairly measuring the knowledge or skills actually required in a job.

Note that the intention of the law has never been to eliminate tests. Employers who have eliminated tests have done so predominantly in reaction to the uncertainty as to whether or not their tests are valid. The utilization by organizations of nonvalidated and improperly validated tests has gone a long way toward giving all tests a bad name.

> *Nothing in the Act precludes the use of testing or measuring procedures; obviously they are useful. What Congress has forbidden is giving these devices and mechanisms controlling force unless they are demonstrably a reasonable measure of job performance.*[7]

[6]John B. Miner, "Psychology Testing and Fair Employment Practices: A Testing Program That Does Not Discriminate," *Personnel Psychology*, Spring 1974, pp. 49–62.

[7]Griggs v. Duke Power Company (39 U.S.I., W., 4317), *Labor Law Reports*, 1971, p. 15.

Why are those committed to the elimination of discriminatory practices so concerned with testing? The answer lies in the historic importance of written tests in the selection process.

Minority candidates, as a group, score below the general population average on a number of selection tests. This should not be surprising, since almost all these tests were validated against white middle-class candidates. Minority candidates may score below whites, yet there may be no significant difference in their actual job performance.

By differentially validating tests for minority and culturally deprived population groups, such bias in the tests can be corrected. Unless such differential validation takes place, an employer risks taking the chance that candidates with an equal probability of success *on the job* will have an unequal probability of being *hired* for that job. Should that occur, the employer is guilty of practicing unfair discrimination.

Remember, that in the *Griggs* v. *Duke Power Company* case, the plaintiffs argued that the testing and educational background required by the organization restricted their opportunities for promotion to better jobs in other departments and constituted racial discrimination because of a previous discriminatory policy for hiring mostly blacks into entrance janitorial jobs. Even when employers have no intention of discriminating, if their actions are such as to discriminate, the courts have held them to have behaved outside the law.

Are aptitude tests valid measures for prediction? A thorough review of the research reveals some interesting findings.[8] The tests that were reviewed included intellectual, spatial, mechanical, and motor ability; perceptual accuracy; and personality and interests evaluations. It was observed that the prediction of training success is better for first-line supervisors than it is for middle- and top-level executives, while the reverse is true for prediction of job proficiency. Measures of personality and interests were of moderate value in predicting the level of proficiency that executives attain on their jobs, but much less useful for first-line supervisors. Success in training for clerical occupations is exceptionally well predicted by tests of intellectual ability, and nearly as well by those that measure perceptual accuracy. Tests of intellectual ability, spatial and mechanical ability, perceptual accuracy, and motor ability all appear to give approximately the same level of validity for proficiency criteria in many semiskilled and unskilled jobs in industrial organizations. The reviewer concluded that "these tests do give prediction of job proficiency which clearly are better than chance."[9] Figure 8-1 reviews job proficiency validity data for various types of jobs.

[8]Edwin E. Ghiselli, "The Validity of Aptitude Tests in Personnel Selection," *Personnel Psychology*, Winter 1973, pp. 461–77.

[9]Ibid., p. 475.

FIGURE 8-1

Validity of Various Tests as Predictive of Job Proficiency

JOB	TYPE OF TEST				
	Intellectual Ability	Spatial & Mechanical Ability	Perceptual Accuracy	Motor Ability	Personality Traits
Executive	Moderate	Moderate+	Moderate	Low	Moderate
Supervisor	Moderate	Moderate	Moderate+	Low/Moderate	Low
Clerical	Moderate	Low	Moderate	Low	Low/Moderate
Sales	Low	Low	Low	Low	Moderate+
Protective	Moderate	Low+	Low+	Low	Moderate
Service	Moderate	Low	Low	Low	Low
Vehicle operator	Low	Low+	Low/Moderate	Moderate	Moderate
Trade and crafts	Moderate	Moderate	Moderate	Low/Moderate	Low/Moderate
Industrial	Moderate	Moderate	Moderate	Moderate	High+

Low predictability: <.20
Moderate predictability: .20–.35
High predictability: .35–.50
High + predictability: >.50

SOURCE: Adapted from Edwin E. Ghiselli, "The Validity of Aptitude Tests in Personnel Selection," *Personnel Psychology*, Winter 1973, pp. 461–77. With permission.

There are literally hundreds of tests that can be used by organizations as selection tools. One can use tests that measure intellect, spatial ability, perception skills, mechanical comprehension, motor ability, and personality traits. It is not the purpose of this text to review each of these test categories. Such a review is the province of books on industrial psychology.[10]

Performance Simulation Tests

To avoid the criticism and potential liability that may result from the use of psychological, aptitude, and other types of written tests, there has been increasing interest in the past decade in developing performance simulation tests. The singular identifying characteristic of these tests is that they require the applicant to engage in specific behaviors which, based on job analysis data, have been shown to be key behaviors necessary for doing the job successfully. In contrast to the types

[10]Interested readers should review, for example, Ernest J. McCormick and Daniel Ilgen, *Industrial Psychology*, 7th ed. (Englewood Cliffs, N.J.: Prentice-Hall, Inc., 1980), Chaps. 8–9.

of tests discussed above, performance simulation tests should more easily meet the requirement of job-relatedness because they are made up of actual job behaviors rather than surrogates.

Work sampling   *Work Sampling.*   Work sampling is an effort to create a miniature replica of a job. Applicants demonstrate that they possess the necessary talents by actually doing the tasks. By carefully devising work samples based on job analysis data, the knowledge, skills, and abilities needed for each job are determined. Then each work sample element is matched with a corresponding job performance element. For example, a work sample for a job that involves computations on an adding machine would require the applicant to make similar computations. Ever wonder how a checkout clerk at K Mart is trained to ring up the prices of your purchases quickly and accurately? Most go through a similar work-sampling training session where supervisors check out carts of food. Work sampling provides actual "hands-on" experience.

The advantages of work sampling over traditional pencil-and-paper tests are obvious. Because content is essentially identical to job content, work sampling should be a better predictor and should minimize discrimination. Additionally, because of the nature of their content and the methods used to determine content, well-constructed work sample tests should easily meet EEOC content validity requirements.[11] The only disadvantages are the time and cost of doing job analysis and the difficulty in developing good work samples for each job.

The results from work sample experiments are impressive. One review of the literature showed that work samples have almost always yielded validities superior to those yielded by traditional tests.[12] Another review similarly found work samples to be better than written aptitude, personality, or intelligence tests.[13]

To show how a manager would go about creating work samples, we offer an illustration for the selection of maintenance mechanics in a food-processing company.[14]

Management began with a job analysis. The relevant data were obtained from several technical conferences with a group composed of an industrial engineer, who was an assistant to the plant mainte-

---

[11]Frank L. Schmidt, Alan L. Greenthal, John E. Hunter, John G. Berner, and Felecia W. Seaton, "Job-Sample vs. Paper-and-Pencil Trades and Technical Tests: Adverse Impact and Examinee Attitudes," *Personnel Psychology*, Summer 1977, p. 188.

[12]Marvin D. Dunnette and Walter C. Borman, "Personnel Selection and Classification Systems," in *Annual Review of Psychology*, ed. Mark R. Rosenzweig and Lyman W. Porter (Palo Alto, Calif.: Annual Reviews, Inc., 1979), XXX, 513.

[13]James J. Asher and James A. Sciarrino, "Realistic Work Sample Tests: A Review," *Personnel Psychology*, Winter 1974, pp. 519–33.

[14]This example is from James E. Campion, "Work Sampling for Personnel Selection," *Journal of Applied Psychology*, February 1972, pp. 40–44.

nance superintendent, and three foremen responsible for supervising the work of the maintenance mechanics. All were knowledgeable experts about the job. The experts began by listing all possible tasks in the job, then rated their frequency and importance. The list was then used to delineate the crucial dimensions of work behavior for maintenance mechanics. From these crucial dimensions came representative work sample measures. The experts identified four key tasks: installing pulleys and belts, disassembling and repairing a gearbox, installing and aligning a motor, and pressing a bushing into a sprocket and reaming it to fit a shaft. The last step in developing these work samples required that the four tasks be broken down into the steps logically required to complete them. Each step was analyzed in detail in order to determine the various approaches a job applicant might follow. The recordable behaviors related to these approaches were specified and weights assigned to them based on their correctness as judged by the job experts.

Applicants were required to complete standard paper-and-pencil tests that were traditionally used for selection of maintenance mechanics as well as the work sample test. The results showed that for all applicants, performance on the work sample measure was significantly and positively related to the foreman's evaluation of performance on the actual job. In contrast, none of the fifteen validity measures computed for the paper-and-pencil tests reached acceptable levels of statistical significance.

Based on the above discussion of work sampling, what conclusions can we draw? Certainly the evidence is strong in support of work samples being better predictors than traditional tests. Work sampling also appears to offer management a better defense against claims that selection may discriminate against women or minorities. Finally, research indicates that applicants perceive the work-sampling method as fairer, clearer, and of a more appropriate difficulty level than traditional tests.[15] The evidence, therefore, leads us to conclude that this method of selection deserves consideration by managers.

Unfortunately, though, work sampling is not applicable to all levels of the organization. It is often difficult to use for managerial jobs because it is difficult to create a work sample test that can address the full range of managerial activities. In the next section, we will look at a type of performance simulation test that is more directly related to managerial positions.

Asessment centers

Assessment Centers.   A more elaborate set of performance simulation tests, specifically designed to evaluate a candidate's managerial potential, is administered at the assessment center. Assessment centers involve procedures that incorporate group and individual ex-

[15]Schmidt et al., "Job-Sample vs. Paper-and-Pencil," p. 197.

ercises. Applicants go through a series of these exercises and are appraised by line executives, practicing supervisors, and/or trained psychologists as to how well they perform. As with work sampling, because these exercises are designed to simulate the work that managers actually do, they tend to be accurate predictors of later job performance. In some cases, however, the assessment center may also include traditional personality and aptitude tests.

How does an assessment center work? Essentially, the procedure follows something like this:[16]

1. A small group of applicants come to the assessment center.

2. The assessment center has approximately six to eight assessors, some of whom are trained psychologists, while others are managers who have been trained as assessors.

3. For about two to four days the assessees are asked to participate in exercises such as
   a. An interview
   b. An "in-basket" application, where applicants solve day-to-day problems that managers might find in their in-basket
   c. A case exercise
   d. A group discussion
   e. A business game
   f. A set of projective personality tests
   g. A set of general ability tests

4. Assessors, usually in pairs, observe and record the behavior of applicants in group and individual situational problems. A clinical psychologist summarizes the projective personality tests.

5. Each assessee is rated on twenty to twenty-five characteristics (such as organization and planning, decision making, creativity, resistance to stress, and oral communication skills).

6. A judgment is made about the assessee's potential for meeting the job requirements.

A typical two-day assessment center is described in Figure 8-2.

The evidence of the effectiveness of assessment centers is extremely impressive. They have consistently demonstrated results that predict later job performance in managerial positions.[17] This consistency in predicting, or validity, is based on the following four areas:[18]

1. Analysis of exhibited behavior—in observing an individual

---

[16]Adapted from Ann Howard, "An Assessment of Assessment Centers," *Academy of Management Journal*, March 1974, pp. 115–34.

[17]Stephen L. Cohen, "Pre-packaged vs. Tailor Made: The Assessment Center Debate," *Personnel Journal*, December 1980, p. 989.

[18]Ibid.

FIGURE 8-2

A Typical Two-Day Assessment Center

DAY 1

Orientation Meeting

Management Game: "Conglomerate." Forming different types of conglomerates is the goal with four-man teams of participants bartering companies to achieve their planned result. Teams set their own acquisition objectives and must plan and organize to meet them.

Background Interview: A 1½ hour interview conducted by an assessor.

Group Discussion: "Management Problems." Four short cases calling for various forms of management judgment are presented to groups of four participants. In one hour the group, acting as consultants, must resolve the cases and submit its recommendation in writing.

Individual Fact-Finding and Decision-Making Exercise: "The Research Budget." The participant is told that he has just taken over as division manager. He is given a brief description of an incident in which his predecessor has recently turned down a request for funds to continue a research project. The research director is appealing for a reversal of the decision. The participant is given 15 minutes to ask questions to dig out the facts in the case. Following this fact-finding period, he must present his decision orally with supporting reasoning and defend it under challenge.

DAY 2

In-Basket Exercise: "Section Manager's In-Basket." The contents of a section manager's in-basket are simulated. The participant is instructed to go through the contents, solving problems, answering questions, delegating, organizing, scheduling and planning, just as he might do if he were promoted suddenly to the position. An assessor reviews the contents of the completed in-basket and conducts a one-hour interview with the participant to gain further information.

Assigned Role Leaderless Group Discussion: "Compensation Committee." The Compensation Committee is meeting to allocate $8,000 in discretionary salary increases among six supervisory and managerial employees. Each member of the committee (participants) represents a department of the company and is instructed to "do the best he can" for the employee from his department.

Analysis, Presentation, and Group Discussion: "The Pretzel Factory." This financial analysis problem has the participant role-play a consultant called in to advise Carl Flowers of the C. F. Pretzel Company on two problems: what to do about a division of the company that has continually lost money, and whether the corporation should expand. Participants are given data on the company and are asked to recommend appropriate courses of action. They make their recommendation in a seven-minute presentation after which they are formed into a group to come up with a single set of recommendations.

Final Announcements

DAYS 3 and 4

Assessors meet to share their observations on each participant and to arrive at summary evaluations relative to each dimension sought and overall potential.

SOURCE: William C. Byham, "The Assessment Center as an Aid in Management Development." Reproduced by special permission from the December 1971 *Training and Development Journal.* Copyright 1971 by the American Society for Training and Development Inc.

2. Development of simulated exercises—that represent the work activities of the actual job

3. Determination of relative skill—strengths and weaknesses

4. Transmission of objective results—of the assessment of the individual

Even when the costs of conducting assessment center evaluations are taken into account—training of assessors, consultant fees, time away from the job, purchase of tests and exercises—the payoffs in terms of more effective selection are more than substantiated.[19] For instance, AT&T, which has assessed more than two hundred thousand employees, computes its costs at $800 to $1,500 per employee.

One note of caution has been offered concerning the impressive and consistent results from assessment center selection. It has been proposed that the measures of job performance may be contaminated.[20] Assessment center results may not be valid because they generally use the success measures of promotions and salary increases as determinants of "job performance." Given that promotions and salary increases are rarely based solely on performance (see Chapter 14), assessment evaluators will come up with effective results if they know what factors senior management actually uses to make advancement and salary increment decisions. The assessors may not be evaluating true performance but such non-performance-related factors as the candidate's social skills, likability, "proper" background, appearance, attitude, or just the fact that someone completed the assessment. For instance, assessors who correctly realize that upper-level managers like and tend to promote "yes types" and conformists may unintentionally assess candidates for these traits. Whenever assessment center ratings and success measures contain a common component unrelated to job performance, the results will be contaminated and the validity of the procedure questionable. Another major drawback of assessment centers is the purposes themselves. It appears to be an accepted practice in some organizations that the road to the top passes through an assessment center. Accordingly, never being selected to attend one of the assessment center sessions can prove demoralizing to the aspiring manager. The impact of this reduced job satisfaction can lead to increased turnover.

Other Tests

Two other types of tests—graphology (handwriting analysis) and polygraph (lie detector) tests—receive a disproportionate amount of me-

[19]Wayne F. Cascio and Val Silbey, "Utility of the Assessment Center as a Selection Device," *Journal of Applied Psychology*, April 1979, pp. 107–18.

[20]Richard L. Klimoski and William J. Strickland, "Assessment Centers—Valid or Merely Prescient," *Personnel Psychology*, Autumn 1977, pp. 353–61.

dia attention. Because of this attention, and the controversy surrounding their validity, we will conclude our discussion of tests with a brief review of these devices.

Graphology

Graphology.   It has been said that an individual's handwriting can suggest the degree of energy, inhibitions, and spontaneity to be found in the writer, disclosing idiosyncrasies and elements of balance and control from which many personality characteristics can be inferred.[21] Although most scientists doubt the validity of handwriting analysis, it is estimated that more than one thousand U.S. companies consult graphologists to supplement their usual personnel procedures.[22] When used as such, graphology can be considered as an employment test.

The argument is made that 70 to 85 percent of occupational failures are due to personality defects, not to lack of education or ability. Given the inadequacies of many standardized methods for assessing personality characteristics, handwriting analysis, if it really does tell us something about applicant's personality, might have validity.

> *Only with practice do we learn to write clusters of words without having to think of the individual lines. But once handwriting is mastered, it becomes an electrocardiogram of a person's moods, health, and personality; it indicates the pattern of his personal way of dealing with himself and the world. While different moods and circumstances may slightly alter the appearance of his writing from day to day, the basic characteristics remain constant for as long as the personality does. Qualities such as independence, maturity, sociability, social responsibility, and certain kinds of vocational and avocational interest can be as readily discovered in handwriting as in the* Individual Background Survey Analysis. [An IBS is a very complete biographical questionnaire.][23]

In spite of the relatively large number of organizations that admit to using graphology, there is little substantial evidence to support this method as a valid selection device. Of course, the organizations that have validated such a selection device may wish to keep it secret, for many reasons. The result is that there may be validated measures that have not been reported so that the firms using them will have a differential advantage over the firms that do not use the technique. Graphology may fall into this category.

---

[21]Jitendra M. Sharma and Harsh Vardhan, "Graphology: What Handwriting Can Tell You about an Applicant," *Personnel*, March–April 1975, pp. 57–63; and Ulrich Sonnerman and John R. Kernan, "Handwriting Analysis—A Valid Selection Tool?" *Personnel*, November–December 1962, p. 12.

[22]Sharma and Vardhan, "Graphology," pp. 57–63.

[23]Ibid., p. 60.

Polygraph tests

Polygraph Tests.   The use of lie detectors for verifying information on the application blank can also be considered as a form of employment test. Some organizations require all applicants to submit to polygraph tests as a security measure, and they follow up with occasional tests to randomly check on employee honesty. Other organizations use the tests only to confirm the accuracy of information given on the application.

While the polygraph is a reasonably accurate instrument when used by competently trained analysts, it can be abused when results are interpreted by the untrained. Because of these abuses, many states have passed laws prohibiting the use of polygraph tests as a prerequisite to employment.

What does the polygraph test actually measure? Contrary to popular belief, it does not actually pick out lies. Rather, the polygraph records physiological changes in blood pressure and skin sensitivity caused by stress. Importantly, stress may be caused by many factors besides lying, and lying is not necessarily stressful for everyone. Therefore some innocent persons may be falsely accused while some liars may beat the machine. These negative factors appear to be more than offset, at least in managers' minds, by the low cost of thirty ot fifty dollars per test, by the fact that results are achieved rapidly, and by the relatively accurate results.

The results of a survey revealed that approximately 20 percent of the largest companies in the United States use the polygraph test as a condition of employment. That figure increases drastically to almost 70 percent "in fiduciary positions, where one has access to pharmaceuticals or where one is employed in an organization that sells small consumer items."[24]

When a polygraph test is considered to be a condition of employment, there appears to be a subtle force placed on the applicant to subject himself or herself to the test. And while the courts have ruled that applicants cannot be forced to take a polygraph test, some organizations require that they sign a release, agreeing to a voluntary test.[25] Companies such as the Brinks Security Company, Central Intelligence Agency, and Zale Corporation (the Dallas-based retail jewelry chain) all require employees to sign an agreement to take the polygraph test as a condition of employment. The results of the voluntary polygraph have been helpful to the organization.

In the past, the "rule of thumb" regarding polygraphs was to take the test and give honest answers. The requirement of taking the test does not mean that an applicant is being suspected of any wrongdoing,

---

[24]"When a Lie Detector Is Part of the Job Interview," *Business Week*, July 27, 1981, p. 85.

[25]Ibid.

He says he has a Harvard M.B.A., a Yale LL.B., speaks four languages, and programs computers. He also lies.

FIGURE 8-3

SOURCE: National Association Specialist; Dept. 600-606-72, 200 Garden City Plaza, Garden City, N.Y. 11530. From *The New York Times*, June 27, 1976. p. F-13.

and the purpose is not to identify and hire only saints. The applicant is asked the questions prior to being hooked up to the polygraph machine and is then asked those questions again. The examiner is simply looking for consistency in the applicant's answers—his or her measure of truthfulness.

Keep in mind, however, that while there is nothing to be afraid of when routinely being scheduled for a polygraph test as a condition of employment, an individual can refuse. As a result of a 1982 court case, *Polsky* v. *Radio Shack,* an individual cannot be forced to sign the waiver agreeing to the test, nor is it legal for an organization to use a release form.[26]

[26]"Court Puts Curb on Polygraph Test Use," *Inc.*, April 1982, p. 33.

VIEWS IN THE NEWS

The issue about polygraphs (lie detectors) and their use in organizations has once again come to the forefront. The main concerns are people's willingness to submit to the test and the validity of the polygraphs.

In a poll taken recently, it was found that about 67 percent of the "respondents in a nationwide telephone poll said they would not object to taking a lie detector test as part of a job interview . . . or for a job they currently hold." While this poll indicated that many of the respondents understood the purposes of polygraph use and wouldn't object to being required to take the test, they "didn't think it was appropriate in general business circumstances." Part of this sentiment centered on whether polygraphs could actually determine if someone was lying.

The American Psychological Association (APA) has also recently issued new guidelines regarding polygraph use. The reasons for these new guidelines stem from its conclusion that "the scientific evidence [on polygraph use] is still unsatisfactory for the validity of psychophysiological indicators to infer deceptive behavior," and "those giving polygraphs often have limited training and expertise . . . in the interpretation of psychophysiological measures."

If polygraphs are used, however, the APA suggests that "their use be consistent with the Standards for Educational and Psychological Tests of the APA," and operated within the "Ethical Principles of Psychologists." Although the APA has issued its recommendations, it still concludes that polygraphs should be used only where it is absolutely appropriate.

Sources: "Most Aren't Scared of Polygraphs," *Evening Sun,* March 3, 1986, p. C-12; and "Doubts about Lie Detectors," *Baltimore Sun,* February 27, 1986, p. A-13.

Summary

While valid and reliable tests have proved to be effective selection devices, the possibility that tests may be challenged has frightened many employers. As a result, there has been a significant drop in test usage.

It may be dangerous to generalize about all tests. While the popularity of traditional personality and aptitude tests may be declining, this does not seem to be true of the assessment center test. The increased popularity of assessment centers seems to be a result of their high-validity ratings.

The assessment center is being used by such organizations as AT&T, Standard Oil, IBM, J. C. Penney, General Electric, and Sears, Roebuck, as well as the Social Security Administration and the Internal Revenue Service. Since word of the assessment center began to spread in the late 1960s, this concept is increasingly being used, primarily among larger organizations and those with more-sophisticated HRM practices.

The use of the polygraph, with the 1982 law change, is indeterminable at this time. However, there can be no doubt that employers in convenience stores, banks, treasury offices in organizations, and jewelry stores—that is, those highly vulnerable to employee theft—see tremendous uses of the polygraph as a means of protection.

Interviews

Whether we talk about initial screening interviews or comprehensive interviews, the issue is the same: Are interviews effective means for gathering accurate information from which selection decisions can be made?

The interview, along with the application form, has proved to be an almost universal selection tool. This is extremely interesting, given that the value of the interview to selection has been the subject of considerable debate, with most of the evidence stacking up against the interview as an effective predictive tool.

Are Interviews Effective?

Are interviews effective?

Surveys of research on interviewing have concluded that the reliability and validity of interviews are generally low.[27] It has been argued that despite its popularity, the interview is a "costly, inefficient and usually invalid procedure."[28] More specifically, a review of the research has generated the following conclusions:[29]

1. Prior knowledge about the applicant will bias the interviewer's evaluation.
2. The interviewer holds a stereotype of what represents a "good" applicant.
3. The interviewer tends to favor applicants who share his or her own attitudes.
4. The order in which applicants are interviewed will influence evaluations.
5. The order in which information is elicited will influence evaluations.
6. Negative information is given unduly high weight.
7. The interviewer makes a decision as to the applicant's suitability early in the interview.

[27]Milton D. Hakel, "Employment Interviewing," contributed paper in Kendrith M. Rowland and Gerald R. Ferris's *Personnel Management* (Boston: Allyn & Bacon, 1982), p. 131.

[28]Ibid., p. 130.

[29]See, for instance, Edward C. Webster, *Decision Making in the Employment Interview* (Montreal: Industrial Relations Center, McGill University, 1964); Eugene C. Mayfield in Neal Schmitt's "Social and Situational Determinants of Interview Decisions: Implications for Employment Interviews," *Personnel Psychology,* Spring 1976, p. 81; and Dunnette and Borman, "Personnel Selection and Classification Systems," pp. 505–9.

8. The interviewer forgets much of the interview's content within minutes after its conclusion.

9. Structured and well-organized interviews are more reliable.

10. The interview is most valid in determining an applicant's intelligence, level of motivation, and interpersonal skills.

These conclusions, although generated more than a decade ago, still hold today but require considerable elaboration. In the next several pages, therefore, we will examine those factors that reduce the effectiveness of interviews and will offer some suggestions on how their effectiveness might be improved. One point should be made, however, before we proceed. It is important to recognize that interviewing is relevant to performance appraisal as well as selection.

When an interviewer has already seen the candidate's application form, test scores, or appraisals of other interviewers, bias is introduced. The interviewer no longer relies on the data gained in the interview alone. Based on the data received prior to the interview, an image is created of the applicant. Much of the early part of the interview, then, becomes an exercise wherein the interviewer compares the actual applicant with the image formed earlier.

Studies of Canadian Army personnel officers concluded that personnel interviewers developed a stereotype of a good job applicant that is not unique to the individual interviewer but instead is commonly shared by all interviewers who have a reasonable amount of experience and who operate in a specific employment setting.[30] Other studies have tended to confirm the Canadian results.[31] Given identical applicant qualifications, and no explicit criteria relating to job requirements, subjects were influenced in their decisions by the proportion of shared (versus individual) attitudes and the sequence in which applicant qualifications were presented. Attitude similarities significantly influenced recommendations for the starting salary offer made to acceptable applicants.[32] Another study tried to isolate those items on which interviewers could develop high agreement. The researchers found that two clusters, personal relations variables and good citizens variables, were considered important by the interviewers.[33] Interviewers believed that it was desirable for an employer to have employees who are trustworthy, dependable, conscientious, responsible, stable, and so forth. "If the importance ratings can be taken as an index of what interviewers really look for in applicants, then

[30]Webster, *Decision Making.*

[31]Lawrence H. Peters and James R. Terborg, "The Effects of Temporal Placement of Unfavorable Information and of Attitudes Similarity on Personnel Selection Decisions," *Organizational Behavior and Human Performance*, April 1975, pp. 279–93.

[32]Ibid.

[33]Milton D. Hakel and Allan J. Schuh, "Job Applicant Attributes Judged Important Across Seven Diverse Occupations," *Personnel Psychology*, Spring 1971, pp. 45–52.

FIGURE 8-4   *"What we're really looking for is a not-too-bright young man with no ambition and who is content to stay on the bottom and not louse things up."*

SOURCE: Courtesy of Dick Lucas. With permission.

being a Boy Scout will get an applicant to first base in nearly any occupation."[34]

When interviewers are evaluating more than one applicant for a job, they use other applicants as a standard.[35] A candidate's appraisal may therefore be unjustly raised if he or she was directly preceded by two or three very poor candidates, or lowered if preceded by very strong candidates. Without an absolute standard, evaluations will tend to vary relative to the set of applicants against which the interviewer is most recently familiar.

The Canadian personnel study, which has become a classic in the interviewing field, reported that most interviewer decisions changed very little after the first four or five minutes of the interview. As a result, a "good applicant" is probably characterized more by the absence of unfavorable characteristics than by the presence of favorable characteristics. We can conclude, therefore, that negative information in an interview has a greater impact on assessment of evaluations than

[34]Ibid., p. 50.
[35]Hakel, "Employment Interviewing," p. 140.

does positive information. Additionally, while the evidence is not as fully supporting as that noted above, we might also state that (1) information elicited early in the assessment process has greater weight than does information elicited later, and (2) when the order of presentation and type of information are both varied, negative information has a greater and more permanent effect irrespective of its order of presentation.[36]

Interviewers have a remarkably short and inaccurate memory. In one interview simulation, a twenty-minute video tape of a selection interview was played for a group of forty managers. Following the playing of the tape, the managers were given a twenty-question test. Although all questions were straightforward and factual, the average number of wrong answers was ten. Thus, even in a short interview, the average manager remembers only half of the information.[37]

Evidence lends strong support to the view that structured and organized interviews are more valuable than unstructured interviews.[38] When two interviewers are allowed to use their own idiosyncratic patterns for questions and evaluation, they will frequently arrive at two different decisions. This happens, in part, because a different set of questions will elicit a different set of information from the same applicant. Unstructured interviews thus make for very low interrater reliability.

A final research finding points out that the interview offers the greatest value as a selection device in determining an applicant's intelligence, level of motivation, and interpersonal skills.[39] Other than these characteristics, few of the dimensions evaluated in an interview have much relationship to the work of most people. In how many jobs, for example, is "appearing comfortable in an interview" job related?

Toward More Effective Interviews

The problems we have pointed out may seem to cast a dark cloud over the interview. But the interview is far from worthless. It seems to be more of a problem with the interviewers than the interview itself. The interview is a valuable vehicle for relaying information to prospective employees and can, for certain jobs and with certain restrictions, provide reasonably valid data for selection decisions. What suggestions can we offer for improving the effectiveness of interviews? Unfortu-

---

[36]Ibid., pp. 136–41.

[37]Reported in Robert E. Carlson, Paul W. Thayer, Eugene C. Mayfield, and Donald A. Peterson, "Improvements in the Selection Interview," *Personnel Journal*, April 1971, p. 272.

[38]Ibid., p. 270.

[39]Mayfield, in Schmitt's "Social and Situational Determinants of Interview Decisions."

nately, there is at present no method for dramatically improving the reliability and validity of the interview. At best, we have some qualified suggestions.

Structure interviews   *Structure the interview so that the interviewer follows a set procedure.* Reliability is increased when the interview is designed along a constant pattern. A fixed set of questions should be presented to every applicant. In the trade-off between structure and consistency versus nonstructure and flexibility, it is structure and consistency that have proved to be of greater value for selection purposes.

Train interviewers   *Provide interviewers with training.* Structured interviews are more likely to be achieved when interviewers have been trained to follow similar patterns in their questioning and to evaluate responses using a common standard. This training would include awareness of the limitations and potential problems cited earlier, as well as the techniques we are presenting in this section.

Understand job   *Interviewers should have detailed information about the job for which applicants are interviewing.*[40] When interviewers are provided with a substantial amount of information about the job, they rely primarily on job-relevant factors in making selection decisions. When such information is unavailable, they rely more on factors less relevant to the job. The interviewer, therefore, should have a copy of the relevant job description at hand.

Avoid other information   *Keep other information away from the interviewer.* The interview should be conducted without foreknowledge by the interviewer of the candidate's background, experience, interests, test scores, or other characteristics. As noted earlier, this information biases the evaluation.

Standardize evaluation forms   *Standardize evaluation forms.* Along with a structured format should go a standardized evaluation form.[41] The interviewer should be required to complete this item-by-item form during the discussion. The information gathered can then be combined, tabulated, and summarized into an overall rating. This approach increases the likelihood that all interviewers will be applying the same frame of reference to each applicant.

Make notes   *Interviewers should take notes during the interview.*[42] Given the propensity for decision makers to forget what was actually said during

[40]A. Langdale and J. Weitz, "Estimating the Influence of Job Information on Interviewer Agreement," *Journal of Applied Psychology*, February 1973, pp. 23–27.

[41]Carlson et al., "Improvements in the Selection Interview," p. 272.

[42]Ibid.

the interview, notes should be taken. This will lead to increased accuracy in evaluation.

Avoid short interviews

Avoid very short interviews. Evidence indicates that extending interviews from, say, fifteen to thirty minutes will make the interviewer less likely to arrive at a premature decision.[43] Since there is a tendency to reach a decision early in the interview, the longer the time allocated for the interview, the less pressure the interviewer will feel to make such premature judgments.

Suggestions for Interviewing: Some Helpful Hints

What goes on in the interview is also important. Most applicants are nervous during the interview because they are seldom aware of what is ahead. There seems to be a set of questions that are most frequently asked by an interviewer. Figure 8-5 contains some of these questions and their intent. Consult your career development office for a more extensive listing before you go for an interview. Since you may be asked these questions, how do you answer them? The best advice we can give is to be yourself. Don't go into an interview with a prepared text and recite it as if you were a computer. Have an idea of what you would like to say, but don't rely on verbatim responses. They will only frustrate you when you lose your place and will ultimately make you look foolish.

The aspect you must be prepared for relates to the illegal questions. Yes, we said illegal questions. If you believe that they have ceased, you are mistaken. Interviewers are becoming increasingly clever, masking illegal questions so that they appear to be legal. But others are blatantly illegal. Questions about your marital status, number of dependents, and home life and sexual activities, among others, are clearly illegal but are sometimes asked. In fact, for women it is worse, as they are often faced with questions about when they plan to marry, the number of children they would like to have, or the type of birth control they practice. Being asked these questions is certainly demeaning. And in the past we simply advised applicants to answer with such a sentence as "I don't think that question is job related, but if you think so I'll answer it."

However, after contacting a few individuals who conducted interviews, it was easier to understand what they were assessing. Some began with clarifying statements such as "This is an illegal question, but . . . " Yet the intention was the same. The purpose of these questions is to assess how well you handle pressure and how dependable you are. So the next time you are asked one of these questions, pause

[43]William L. Tullar, Terry W. Mullins, and Sharon A. Caldwell, "Effects of Interview Length and Applicant Quality on Interview Decision Time," *Journal of Applied Psychology*, December 1979, pp. 669–74.

FIGURE 8-5

Interview Questions

QUESTION	WHAT IT IS TO ASSESS?
1 What are your greatest strengths?	How well you sell yourself. Give abstract qualities, expressed in concrete terms.
2. What are your greatest weaknesses?	Is hiring you a mistake? Give a weakness that reflects a professional strength.
3. Tell me about yourself.	Style and Poise. Give a synopsis of your skills.
4. Where do you hope to be in five years?	Realistic progression. With company knowledge you can provide a position reasonably achieved in five years.
5. Why did you leave your previous employer?	Honesty. Be pleasant and positive.
6. What do you do in your spare time?	Well-rounded individuals. Give hobbies that highlight aspects of the job.
7. What did you like most about your previous job?	Atmosphere and climate you seek. Be specific.
8. What do you think your employer's obligations are to you?	Willing to seek support and guidance, not dependency. Be positive and enthusiastic.
9. Are you applying for any other jobs?	Are you serious about changing jobs? Show how your skills are applicable to several types of jobs.
10. What type of salary did you have in mind?	Can the employer afford you? Deal with this at the end of the interview, if possible. Give a salary range.
11. Silence	Can you handle stress? Smile and keep quiet.
12. Personal Questions	Underlying motive. Be calm and collected.

SOURCE: "Interview Questions Designed to Destroy You," *Cosmopolitan*, April 1982, pp. 152–54.

a few moments and then tell the interviewer that if you are being asked such a personal question to reveal your dependability, assure him or her that you are. You will be amazed how that response is accepted and clears the climate for continuing the interview. Remember to stay calm. Under no circumstances should you get into a shouting match with the interviewer.

Summary

The most disturbing fact, given the interview's low validity and reliability, is not only the wide usage of interviews but also the weight placed on this tool in the selection decision. However, if interviews have a place in the selection decision, it appears to be more appropriate for the less-routine jobs, particularly middle- and upper-level managerial positions. As already noted, the interview has proved to be a reasonably effective method for discerning intelligence, level of motivation, and interpersonal skills. In jobs where these characteristics are important in determining success, the interview can be a valuable selection input. In nonroutine activities, especially senior managerial positions, failure (as measured by voluntary terminations) is more frequently caused by a poor fit between the individual and the organization than by lack of competence on the part of the individual. Interviewing can be useful, therefore, when it emphasizes the candidate's ability to fit into the organization rather than specific technical skills.

Realistic Job Previews

Realistic job
previews

John Lawson was a recent graduate from a master's program in industrial relations. During the recruiting process with one company, the aspiring labor relations specialist was guaranteed that he would be closely involved in upcoming contract negotiations. Impressed by the thought of having the opportunity to be an active part in contract negotiations within six months, a dream come true for an industrial relations graduate, the job offer seemed very appealing. He accepted the job and in six months was actively involved in contract negotiations. He saw that coffee was available for both the morning and afternoon breaks, and he made several trips a day to local fast-food restaurants to get food for the negotiators. This, he was told, was the closeness he had been promised. In frustration, John Lawson quit.

The primary purpose of selection devices is to identify individuals who will be effective performers. But it is not in management's interest to find good prospects, hire them, and then have them leave the organization. Therefore part of selection should be concerned with reducing voluntary turnover among those hired. Such a device is the realistic job preview (RJP). While RJP is not normally treated as a selection device, it does take place during the selection process and it has demonstrated effectiveness as a method for increasing job survival among new employees.

Every applicant acquires during the selection process a set of expectations about the organization and about the specific job the applicant is hoping to be offered. It is not unusual for these expectations to be excessively inflated as a result of receiving almost uniformly positive information about the organization and job during recruitment and selection activities. Evidence suggests, however, that managers may be erring by giving applicants only favorable information. More specifically, research leads us to conclude that applicants who have been given a realistic job preview hold lower and more realistic expectations about the job they will be doing and are better prepared for coping with the job and its frustrating elements. The result is lower turnover rates.[44] Of course, it is not unreasonable to suggest that ex-

[44]John P. Wanous, "Effects of a Realistic Job Preview on Job Acceptance, Job Attitudes, and Job Survival," *Journal of Applied Psychology,* June 1973, pp. 327–32; and D. R. Ilgen and W. Seely, "Realistic Expectations as an Aid in Reducing Voluntary Resignations," *Journal of Applied Psychology,* August 1974, pp. 452–55.

posing an applicant to RJP may also result in the hiring of a different type of person, or that better information may result in greater commitment on the part of new employees to their decision to come—and stay—aboard.

What is a realistic job preview? It may include brochures, films, plant tours, work sampling, or merely a short script made up of realistic statements that accurately portray the job. The key element in RJP is that unfavorable as well as favorable information about the job is shared. The concept has even been extended to the recruiting of students by college admissions offices. For instance, Barat College in Illinois sends all prospective students a candid thirty-two page, nine-by-fifteen-inch brochure that gives both the good and bad points about the college based on an accreditation report. An example: "The library cannot now provide the kind of service required by the educational goals of the college." School administrators find that this frankness has "brought in people who know more about the place and what to expect." It has also resulted in the college losing far fewer students before graduation.[45]

Most studies demonstrate that giving candidates a realistic job preview before offering them the job reduces turnover without lowering acceptance rates.[46] But the RJP is not a panacea for all turnover reduction. While the RJP is helpful and can create a more positive job-related attitude,[47] there is no indication that a general RJP procedure exists. What is of interest to one person may not be to another. However, the benefits from some type of RJP appear to outweigh its cost.

Background Investigation

How honest are the responses that individuals give in their application forms? While the research in this area is limited, several studies suggest that verifying the "facts" given on an application is an activity that pays dividends.

One study sampled one hundred applications made at Bulova, the watch company.[48] It was found that 24 percent of the returned reference checks had discrepancies in dates of employment, job title, past salary, or reasons for leaving a prior position. In the Bulova study,

[45] *Wall Street Journal*, April 15, 1980, p. 35.

[46] For example, see Marcia Parmelee Miceli, "Why Realistic Job Previews Cannot Meet Our Unrealistically High Expectations" (Academy of Management Proceedings, August 1983), pp. 282–286; Wanous, "Effects of a Realistic Job Preview on Job Acceptance," pp. 327–32; and Richard D. Scott, "Job Expectancy, An Important Factor in Labor Turnover," *Personnel Journal*, May 1972, pp. 360–63.

[47] Review of Richard R. Reilly et al., "The Effects of Realistic Previews: A Study and Discussion of the Literature," *Personnel Psychology*, 34, No. 4 (1981), 823–34.

[48] Robert Hershey, "The Application Form," *Personnel*, January–February 1971, pp. 36–39.

discrepancies were defined as deviations of two or more months of service and five or more dollars per week.

Another study looked at 111 subjects who aplied for positions as nurse's aides at a nursing home.[49] In verifying the responses made on the application blank with the applicant's previous employer, substantial disagreement was found in two categories: duration of previous employment and previous salary earned. The two sources disagreed in 57 percent of the cases. A typical applicant overstated both. There was also substantial disagreement on the reasons for leaving the previous job. This, however, is not surprising, for previous research has found that departing employees, in their exit interviews, are frequently noncommital or distort the actual reasons for departure. For example, one study revealed that 59 percent of a group sampled months after departure gave different reasons for leaving than they had given at the time of their exit interview.[50]

Two of the most startling findings from the nursing home study were that the average overestimation by former employees of time spent on their previous job was sixteen months and that 15 percent of the employers stated that the applicant had never worked for them. Two-thirds of the applicants whom the previous employer admitted to having employed disagreed with their employer's replies on two of the four categories (previous position held, duration of employment, previous salary earned, and reason for leaving).

In summary, it is generally acknowledged that the reference check, as a selection instrument, has little value. This is due to employers' reluctance to provide negative information about former employees to other employers. Since responses are almost universally positive, references do not provide the differentiating information necessary for selection decisions. On the other hand, checking with a former employer to confirm hard data on the application—such as previous job title, length of employment, and salary earned—is a worthwhile endeavor.

Concern by many employers over employee lawsuits[51] charging invasion of privacy, unlawful discrimination, or some similar impropriety has led them to simply refuse to give anything but the barest information: "Yes, the person worked here."[52] In such an environment, it seems unreasonable to expect too much in terms of valid information from the background investigation.

[49]Irwin L. Goldstein, "The Application Blank: How Honest Are the Responses?" *Journal of Applied Psychology*, October 1971, pp. 491–92.

[50]Joel Lefkowitz and Myron L. Katz, "Validity of Exit Interviews," *Personnel Psychology*, Winter 1969, pp. 445–55.

[51]*Wall Street Journal*, November 3, 1981, p. 1.

[52]"Coping with Employee Lawsuits," *Business Week*, August 27, 1979, p. 66.

Physical Examination

For jobs that require certain physical characteristics, the physical examination has some validity. However, this includes a very small proportion of jobs today.

In some instances, characteristics related to the physical examination can be used to screen out certain individuals. This is particularly true of jobs that historically have had minimum height and weight requirements. This would include such jobs as police officer, flight attendant, telephone line repairer, baseball umpire, and lifeguard as well as some production jobs. Recently these requirements have come under increasing attack for being a disguised form of sex discrimination:

> Even when neutrally applied to both sexes, such requirements are said to exclude a disproportionate number of women applicants from some jobs. Such requirements are often imposed without adequate inquiry into whether height and weight are related in any significant way to ability to do the type of work required by the job.[53]

Employers who have utilized minimum height and weight requirements have argued that only individuals who meet their standards will have the strength necessary to efficiently carry out the physical duties required of particular jobs. Unfortunately, these same employers often admit that they do not take height and weight as conclusive evidence of physical strength; separate tests for strength are often imposed on those applicants who have already met the specified height and weight requirements. Obviously, such practices are susceptible to attack as a form of sex discrimination. Although the law has not, at this time, specifically eliminated minimum height and weight requirements, such standards can be expected to be tested in the courts by individuals who believe that these requirements are discriminatory.

Conclusion

Research findings on major selection devices are often difficult to assimilate because of the technical issues involved. In this remaining section, we will briefly discuss why many human resource managers have detoured from the typical selection process described in the previous chapter, and then offer some practical advice to help you assess the value of each selection device in various situations.

It should not surprise you that the laws and requirements cur-

---

[53]Philip E. Callis, "Minimum Height and Weight Requirements as a Form of Sex Discrimination," *Labor Law Journal,* December 1974, p. 736.

rently affecting selection have confused many managers. The reasons for this confusion have been summarized as follows:

> Today, under the guidelines on Employee Selection Procedures issued by the Chairman of the Equal Opportunity Commission, the employer would have to validate all the "tests" used in the selection process. These tests would include the interviews and any personality, interests, or mental ability tests that were administered. These guidelines essentially gut the [typical] structure and leave little in its place. Employers are being encouraged to minimize the exclusion of employees from the work force based upon reference checks, and investigations of prior history when this means that ex-convicts, former mental patients, and drug addicts or alcoholics are actively being considered for positions. ... these kinds of applicants were considered far beyond the pale. It was thought that right-minded responsible employers would protect their employees from ever needing to associate with such people at work by screening them out quite early in the selection process. Employers have been encouraged for many years to hire the physically handicapped and to place them selectively. Thus many employers have long realized that the physical examination should not be used in a discriminating manner.
>
> But the new thrust of government intervention in the selection process is to change what was previously a process aimed at rejection of "undesirable" applications to one with a positive purpose of finding grounds for accepting any applicants.[54]

Even though conditions are not as bad as the above quote suggests, it is clear that a manager can no longer treat selection offhandedly. What advice can we offer?

First, since the validity of selection devices varies for different types of jobs, you should use only those devices that predict for the given job. Reference checks are generally worthless for almost all jobs unless you have the time to obtain further information. Weighted application forms can be valuable for lower-level jobs.

Interviews consistently get low marks for reliability and validity, yet they add relevant selection information whether interpersonal skills are a major determinant of job success. Figure 8-6 summarizes, in quantitative terms, the evidence we have found.

Second, since interviews will be used despite their weaknesses, try to make them as reliable as possible. Our suggestions on the previous pages offered guidelines for this activity.

Third, use performance simulation tests wherever it is practical

FIGURE 8-6

Quality of Selection Devices as Predictors

SELECTION DEVICE	POSITION			
	Senior Management	Middle & Lower Management	Complex Nonmanagerial	Routine Operative
Application form	2	2	3	4
Traditional paper-and-pencil tests	1	1	3	3
Work samples	—	—	4	4
Assessment center	5	5	—	—
Interviews	3	2	1	1
Verification of application data	3	3	3	3
Reference checks	1	1	1	1
Physical exam	1	1	1	2

NOTE: Quality is measured on a scale from 5 (highest) to 1 (lowest).

and cost effective to do so. They are better predictors than pencil-and-paper tests and reduce the organization's exposure to legal challenges.

Fourth, utilize realistic job previews, especially with introductory-level jobs. This should reduce the probability of surprise resignations when new hires suddenly confront the realities on the job.

Fifth, avoid using references that require judgments of the applicant's prior work performance, attitude, or character. Because physical examinations rarely provide any valid selection information, they, too, can usually be omitted from the selection process.

Finally, use a design strategy that makes sense for the job in question. This means that you should feel free to omit steps that do not provide valid information or that are found to be weak predictors.

SUMMARY

1. Selection devices provide managers with information that will help them predict whether an applicant will prove to be a successful job performer.

2. The application blank is effective for acquiring hard biographical data; the weighted application can provide relevant information for predicting job success.

3. Traditional tests that assess intelligence, abilities, and personality traits can predict job proficiency but many suffer from being non-job related.

4. Performance simulation tests require the applicant to engage in specific behaviors that have been demonstrated to be job related. Work sampling and the assessment center, which are performance simulations, receive high marks for their predictive capability.

5. Interviews consistently achieve low marks for reliability and validity.

6. Realistic job previews reduce turnover by giving the applicant both favorable and unfavorable information about the job.

7. Background investigations are valuable when they verify hard data from the application; they offer little practical values as a predictive selection device.

8. Physical examinations are valid when certain physical characteristics are required to be able to perform a job effectively.

KEY TERMS

Assessment center
Graphology
Polygraph
Realistic job preview (RJP)

Standardized evaluation form
Structured interview
Weighted application form
Work sampling

QUESTIONS FOR REVIEW

1. Which is preferable: a selection device that evaluates the past or one that samples the present? Explain.

2. Give four examples of items you can ask on an application form. Give four examples of items you cannot ask.

3. What is a weighted appliction form? How does it work?

4. What were the selection implications of the *Griggs* v. *Duke Power Company* case?

5. Contrast work samples with the assessment center.

6. How valid are the data obtained from the polygraph? When might you want to use the polygraph test?

7. What are the major problems of the interview as a selection device? What can management do to reduce some of these problems?

8. How should one prepare for an upcoming interview?

9. What effect should a realistic job preview have on a new hire's attitude and behavior?

10. Contrast the validity of background investigations that seek to verify application information with those that seek to obtain judgments about the applicant's character.

QUESTIONS FOR DISCUSSION

1. If you were the dean of a business college, what selection devices would you use to identify effective teachers?
2. What do you think of realistic job previews? Would you be more likely to choose a position where recruiters emphasized only the positive aspects of the job?
3. "Most testing devices for selection do not accurately assess the characteristics of the job. In fact, most people would say that the testing had no impact on future job performance." Do you agree or disagree? Discuss.
4. "Because of the law regarding employment questions, application forms provide limited information. Accordingly, they should not be used." Do you agree or disagree? Discuss.
5. "Even though interviews are not reliable, they are heavily used." Discuss why this selection device still rates very highly when it is known that it is unreliable.

CONTINUING CASE: Concord General

Who Are You Kidding?

Efforts to fill the Cardiac Surgery Unit with staff nurses have stalemated. It appears that in addition to receiving few applications from nurses in the area, some of the nurses who were currently in training for the position have resigned. With the opening only three weeks away serious problems have emerged.

To try to resolve the dilemma, Judy scheduled a conference with Jim, two nurses who have resigned, and herself. At that meeting, the resigning nurses were asked what had caused the early turnover. Kathy Morris, who has a reputation for being outspoken, stated:

"Judy, let me tell you. I've been in the Intensive Care Unit for three years now, and I felt that going to the new unit would be challenging. But there has been no challenge at all. First, the training course you set up for us is over one hundred miles from this hospital. You never mentioned that. And those of us with children at home simply cannot go through the distant training program. Second, as you have it set up, the cardiac surgery nurses will get no more reward nor any more incentives than those who work in the ICU unit. I enjoy the patient relationship in ICU and I resent being told after the fact that if I work in the Cardiac Surgery Unit, I'm unable to work in the ICU unit at any time. Cardiac surgery may be challenging, but you have to expect a lot of turnover, if you cannot rotate the nurses."

"And let me add this," said Cindy Jameson, a two-year veteran of a Cardiac Surgery Unit in a competitive hospital, "I'm being made to feel like trash. Other nurses resent my being chosen and receiving what they perceive to be preferential treatment. Preferential treatment, hogwash. The only nursing activities I've performed here during the past two weeks were punching in on the time clock. Imagine that, me a specialist, having to clock in like an . . . "

"Wait a minute, ladies," interrupted Jim. "Your point has been made. But please reconsider your resignations. We are pioneering this endeavor and Judy and I have made mistakes. Please give us a chance to correct the situation. You both are valued nurses and we don't want to lose you."

Questions

1. What issues have been raised in the case?
2. How could these issues have been prevented?

CASE APPLICATION

You Want Me to Do What?

David McClelland, the new personnel specialist at the First City Bank of Des Moines, has been assigned the task of revamping the bank's hiring procedures. Previously, if a prospective teller had a high-school diploma and passed a polygraph test, he or she was hired. Occasionally, however, the bank president had received complaints about tellers in some locations who were having difficulty in completing customers' transactions. When this occurred, the head teller would have to not only take over to settle the problem but also calm the angry customer.

After an investigation of the problem employees, it was revealed that the new hires who grew up in one section of the town were having the most difficulty. Unfortunately, this section was in the lower-income area, and now with a decision to not hire individuals from that area, discrimination charges have been filed by the rejected candidates.

The bank president has ordered David to correct this situation.

Questions

1. If you were David, what would you do about the discrimination charges levied against your organization?
2. What type of personnel selection practices might be used to demonstrate that the discrimination charges are unfounded?
3. Devise a work-sampling test that could validly be used in the bank.

ADDITIONAL READINGS

BRINKERHOFF, DAVID W., and ABBOTT P. SMITH, "Write a Resume, Not an Obituary," *Training*, (July 1986), pp. 37–39.

HIZER, DAVID, and ARTHUR D. ROSENBERG, "Answering Questions in Your Cover Letter," *National Business Employment Weekly*, June 16, 1986, pp. 9–10.

KNOUSE, STEPHEN B., "The Letter of Recommendation: Specificity and Favorability of Information," *Personnel Psychology*, 36, No. 2 (Summer 1983), 331–41.

REIBSTEIN, LARRY, "More Firms Use Personality Tests for Entry Level, Blue-Collar Jobs," *Wall Street Journal*, January 16, 1986, p. 27.

SAXE, LEONARD, DENISE DOUGHERTY, and THEODORE CROSS, "The Validity of Polygraph Testing," *American Psychologist*, (March 1985), pp. 355–66.

CHAPTER 9

Socializing

the New Employee

AFTER READING THIS CHAPTER, YOU WILL BE ABLE TO:

1. Define *socialization* in an organization
2. Explain the purpose of orientation programs
3. Describe how organizational socialization conveys the organization's culture
4. Describe how managers can influence the socialization process
5. Explain the reasons for socializing new employees
6. Identify the stages of the socialization process
7. Discuss the major considerations in the design of a socialization program

All marriages are happy. It's the living together afterward that causes all the trouble.

—Raymond Hull

Beth Carter, a thirty-year-old saleswoman, works in the fashion boutique of a large Atlanta department store. She recently commented on her work:

> *Ever since I got out of high school, twelve years ago, I've been in retail sales. I've worked for three different store chains. In the first two firms, I was judged solely on my sales performance. Then, six months ago, I took this job. Here, they really think it's important that salespeople look professional and keep busy. It didn't take me long to catch on. Sure, you gotta make sales, but I know that isn't enough to keep my job. Now, I take a lot more care in the way I dress, my hairstyle, and things like that. Also, if I'm on the floor and I'm not waiting on a customer, I sure don't stand around like I used to. Like the other salespeople here, I spend a lot of my time straightening merchandise.*

The comments of Beth Carter indicate an employee who has successfully "learned the ropes" on her new job. From the organization's standpoint, such learning is highly desirable. It means that people know and accept behaviors that the organization views as desirable. In this chapter, we will show how employees are socialized into their job environments, and the ways that management can influence the socialization process.

The Outsider–Insider Passage

Socialization   When we talk about *socialization*, we are talking about a process of adaption. In the context of organizations, the term refers to all passages undergone by employees. For instance, when you begin a new job, accept a lateral transfer, or get a promotion, you are required to make adjustments. You must adapt to a new environment—different work activities, a new boss, a different group of co-workers, and probably a different set of standards for what constitutes a good performance. While we recognize that this socialization will go on throughout our careers—within an organization as well as between organizations—the most profound adjustment will occur when we make the move into an organization—the move from being an outsider to being an insider. The following discussion, therefore, will limit itself to the outsider-insider passage, or what is more appropriately labeled organizational entry socialization.

Orientation

Orientation · It is not unusual to confuse a new employee's initial orientation on the job with the socialization process. In actuality, orientation is only a small part of the overall socialization of a new organizational member.

Orientation covers the activities involved in introducing a new employee to the organization and to his or her work unit. It expands upon the information received during the recruitment and selection stages and helps to reduce the initial anxiety we all feel when we first begin a new job. For example, an orientation program should familiarize the new member with the organization's objectives, history, philosophy, procedures, and rules; communicate relevant personnel policies such as hours of work, pay procedures, overtime requirements, and fringe benefits; review the specific duties and responsibilities of the new member's job; provide a tour of the organization's physical facilities; and introduce the employee to his or her superior and co-workers. Figure 9-1 illustrates an orientation program in one firm.

Who is responsible for orienting the new employee? This can be done either by the new employee's supervisor, by the people in personnel, or some combination thereof.

In many medium-sized and most large organizations, the personnel department takes charge of explaining such matters as overall organizational policies and employee benefits. In other medium-sized and most small firms, new employees will receive their entire orientation from their supervisor. Figure 9-1 demonstrates a situation where the process is shared between the personnel department staff and the new member's supervisor.

Of course, the new employee's orientation may not be formal at all. For instance, in many small organizations, orientation may mean the new member reports to her supervisor, who then assigns the new member to another employee who will introduce her to those persons with whom she will be closely working. This may then be followed by a "quickie" tour to show her where the lavatory is, how to make her way to the cafeteria, and how to find the coffee machine. Then, the new employee is shown her desk and left to fend for herself.

FIGURE 9-1

Orientation Schedule

NEW EMPLOYEE: Dana Hammond, B.S. in Marketing, Univ. of Oklahoma, 1988.
JOB TITLE: Assistant to the Manager
DEPARTMENT: Product Planning

8:00 A.M.	Report to Ms. Dennis in Personnel Office.
8:00–9:30 A.M.	Ms. Dennis will:
	—Distribute brochures describing the organization's history, products, and philosophy.
	—Review the organization's overall structure, and the authority structure within the Product Planning department.
	—Review personnel policies and practices.
9:30–10:30 A.M.	Mr. Phillips will discuss company benefits. New employee is to fill out health, tax, and other relevant forms.
10:30–11:30 A.M.	Tour of main building and auxiliary facilities with Ms. Dennis.
11:30 A.M.–12:30 P.M.	Lunch with personnel manager and Ms. Cosby (new employee's supervisor).
12:30–3:00 P.M.	Ms. Cosby will:
	—Provide a detailed tour of the Product Planning department.
	—Discuss daily job routine and departmental policies and rules.
	—Explain job expectations.
	—Introduce new employee to her co-workers.
3:00–5:00 P.M.	New employee is on her own to familiarize herself with her job.

Toward Understanding Socialization

We will begin examining the socialization process by proposing that every organization has a culture that defines appropriate behaviors for organizational members.

The Organizational Culture

The organization culture

Every organization has its own unique culture. This culture includes longstanding, and often unwritten, rules and regulations; a special language that facilitates communication among members; shared standards of relevance as to the critical aspects of the work that is to be done; matter-of-fact prejudices; standards for social etiquette and demeanor; established customs for how members should relate to peers, subordinates, superiors, and outsiders; and other traditions that clarify to members what is appropriate and "smart" behavior within the organization and what is not.[1] An employee who has been properly so-

[1]John Van Maanen and Edgar H. Schein, "Toward a Theory of Organizational Socialization," in *Research in Organizational Behavior*, ed. Barry M. Staw (Greenwich, Conn.: JAI Press, 1979), I, p. 210.

cialized to the organization's culture, then, has learned how things are done, what matters, and which work-related behaviors and perspectives are acceptable and desirable and which ones are not.

To better understand the concept of unique organizational cultures, we should look at the concepts of roles, values, and norms.

Roles   Every job requires the incumbent to behave in certain specified ways. These behaviors are more or less expected of persons who are identified with certain jobs. We call the set of such behaviors a *role*. Your instructor acts a certain way in the classroom, but that is not the way this individual behaves in a nightclub on Saturday night. Why? Because your instructor is probably not "playing teacher" on Saturday night.

Values   Employees do not play out their role in a vacuum. Their role is significantly influenced by the values and norms held by members of their work group. *Values* are basic convictions about what is right or wrong, good or bad, desirable or not. Every individual has a value system, rarely explicit, which represents a prioritizing or ranking of values in terms of their relative importance. A teacher of business subjects in a university finds that departmental colleagues identify with the values of competition, efficiency, free enterprise, and the profit ethic. On the other hand, they tend to denigrate values like socialism, rewarding employees based solely on seniority, and government intervention. What organizational members value, then, will significantly influence the behavior of new members.

Norms   The new employee's work group will have its own standards of acceptable behavior. These *norms* tell members what they ought or ought not to do under certain circumstances. They might include: not producing too little and thus drawing unnecessary attention to the work unit, defending your co-workers against attacks from the boss, or avoiding giving any assistance to "those idiots in the auditing department."

Note how the concepts of role, values, and norms interrelate. What a person does on the job depends on the standards that the organization and his or her work group convey as appropriate. Importantly the parameters of the role—whether one is an accountant, lawyer, teacher, librarian, or salesclerk—change in response to the values and norms in the environment where one performs that role. This explains, for instance, why almost all the management professors at the Harvard Business School wear suits and ties while their counterparts at U.C.L.A. do not.

You may be wondering how these concepts relate to the socialization process. The answer is that individuals, in their work roles, may accept all, some, or none of the organization's standards.[2] Individuals

---

[2]Edgar H. Schein, "Organizational Socialization and the Profession of Management," *Industrial Management Review*, Winter 1968, pp. 9–10.

who readily accept all of them become conformists. Their socialization, when complete, results in the infamous "yes man." At the other extreme is the rebel who rejects all the organization's standards. Such persons are usually quickly labeled as "misfits," since their actions seem to defeat the organization's goals. Rebels rarely last long, being expelled from the organization for their inability to adapt to "the way we do things here." In between, we get people who accept some standards, but not others. As long as these individuals accept at least the pivotal or key norms of the organization, there is no problem if they reject some of the relevant but nonpivotal norms. Pivotal norms are those deemed essential by the organization. Refraining from bad-mouthing the company in public, for example, is often considered a pivotal norm. Relevant norms, by contrast, are deemed desirable but not absolutely essential for success in the organization. Wearing a conservative three-piece suit, for example, may be a relevant norm for faculty at the Harvard Business School. People who are able to discriminate between key and relevant standards are often innovative and creative and perform the role of the healthy questioner. They have accepted those standards necessary to maintain membership in the organization. They are comfortable in their jobs and demonstrate commitment to the organization.

Clearly one objective of the socialization process is to ensure that rebellious, norm-rejecting types are either changed or expelled. But whether management considers most or only some of its standards as truly pivotal depends on management's objectives. If managers want people who are totally loyal to the organization and who will fight to maintain its traditions and customs, they will probably utilize different methods of socialization than if they seek highly creative, individualistic employees who accept only the pivotal standards and reject the rest. Later in this chapter we will present some of the methods used by management to effect these alternative types of socialization.

Learning the "Do's" and "Don'ts"

Do's and don'ts in an organization

Regardless of how tolerant management is of individualism, it is realistic to conclude that organizations, particularly large ones, do not enjoy having employees who continually attack the basic goals of the organization, the preferred means for the attainment of these goals, the underlying responsibilities inherent in each person's role, or the organization's basic rules and regulations. But the fact is that new people come into the organization with the potential to bring about change—change that can disturb the organization's "tried and true" ways of doing things.

It may not be management's desire to get every employee to accept all of the organization's standards. To do so may be to create a conforming and apathetic organizational environment. But the pivotal norms must be conveyed and accepted. Without this acceptance, new employees will lack commitment and loyalty to the interests of the organization and will pose a threat to management and experienced members. Furthermore, they will never be accepted as full-fledged members of the organization. "Put bluntly, new members must be taught to see the organizational world as do their more experienced colleagues if the traditions of the organization are to survive."[3] Successful socialization will mean having personnel who "fit in" by knowing the "do's and don'ts" of a "good employee."

Some Examples

Tenure is a familiar concept to academics. Teachers and professors who are granted tenure, in effect, are given permanent or lifetime employment. While procedures exist for removing tenure, they are time-consuming and difficult for an employer to execute. As a result, tenure is a highly prized possession. To achieve tenure, a prospect must endure the watchful eye of the "in-group"—those who are already tenured. This trial period, preceding the tenure decision, often lasts from three to seven years. Prospects who "measure up" will get tenure. Measuring up means, in actuality, that the individual has been well socialized to the norms of the tenured group. Prospects who accept and demonstrate, by their behavior, that they fit in with the tenured members are granted permanent employment. Those who fail are expelled from the organization.

For those who think this practice is some oddity, exclusive to only educational institutions, consider the process that exists in large accounting and law firms. New employees start out as associates, most with the goal of someday becoming partners in their firms. But partnership (which means owning a piece of the firm and enjoying permanent employment) is withheld for some extended period—usually five to fifteen years—while the associates prove to the current partners that they are worthy. This means that the potential partners must demonstrate through what they say and do that they know the ropes and can be trusted.

John DeLorean, a former executive at General Motors and developer of the now defunct DeLorean automobile, described how GM attempted to socialize its managers through pressuring deviants:

> *. . . The Corporate rule was dark suits, light shirts and muted ties. I followed the rule to the letter, only I wore stylish Italian-cut suits, wide-collared off-white shirts and wide ties.*

[3]Van Maanen and Schein, "Toward a Theory of Organizational Socialization," p. 211.

"Goddammit, John," he'd [DeLorean's boss] yell. "Can't you dress like a businessman? And get your hair cut, too."

My hair was ear length with sideburns. I felt both my clothes and hairstyle were contemporary but not radical, so I told him:

"General Motors' business—selling annual styling changes—makes this a fashion business. And what the hell do you know about fashion? Most of these guys around here wear narrow-lapelled suits and baggy pants with cuffs that are four inches above their shoes."

The fact that I had been divorced, was a health nut and dated generally younger actresses and models didn't set well with the corporate executives or their wives. And neither did my general disappearance from the corporate social scene. Dollie Cole, the second wife of then President Ed Cole, who himself was divorced, called me up after my second divorce when I was dating my wife Christina and told me, "They are all shook up on The Fourteenth Floor [where the top executives offices are located]. God! Don't get married again. You'd better cool it. All you've got to do is lay low and wait them out. Those guys will all be gone in five years. Don't kick away your career now."

Nevertheless, my clothing and lifestyle were increasingly rattling the cages of my superiors, as was the amount of publicity my personal and business lives were generating. I was being resented because my style of living violated an unwritten but widely revered precept that said no personality could outshine General Motors.[4]

Even though DeLorean had, at the age of forty-eight, risen to a position where he directed GM's Chevrolet, Buick, Oldsmobile, Pontiac, Cadillac, and GMC Truck and Coach Divisions—and was earning up to $650,000 a year—he quit in 1973. His complaint was that GM could not "accept or accommodate an executive who had made his mark in the corporation by being different and individualistic."[5] From another perspective, DeLorean's bosses felt that he had failed to accept GM's basic goals. As DeLorean himself admitted, "sometime in the late '60's, I cannot remember when, a nagging suspicion about the philosophy of General Motors and the automobile business began to overtake me . . . I found myself questioning a much bigger picture, the morality of the whole GM System."[6] The latter comment suggests that DeLorean had even rejected GM's pivotal standards, making his departure inevitable. The rest of the John DeLorean story has been well publicized.

[4]J. Patrick Wright, *On a Clear Day You Can See General Motors* (Grosse Point, Mich.: Wright Enterprises, 1979). p. 9.

[5]Ibid., p. 2.

[6]Ibid., pp. 4–5.

Of course, socialization is often more subtle. For instance, one man who decided on a career as a fireman said that he chose this job because he wanted something that provided a high degree of job security and made few demands on his off-work time. His first love was surfing and he thought the job of a fireman—with its schedule of working several days straight followed by several days off—would give him enough money to pay his bills and leave plenty of time to hit the beaches and be with his friends.

But after going through training school and being assigned to a firehouse, this person found that his colleagues on the job held different expectations.

I'll have to admit, I was really surprised with the esprit de corps *our firehouse had. I figured everyone would think like me. You know—put in your hours and do what ever was necessary to get by; certainly* no more *than was necessary. I thought they'd look forward to getting out of this place and spending time with their real friends. Well, it doesn't work that way here. We're a team—twenty-four hours a day, seven days a week. We take our work very seriously. If we have to put in extra hours to get the job done right, we do it and never think twice. We're a crack firehouse. You know we've been rated number one in the county for three straight years!*

After eighteen months in this job, it ain't nothing like I expected. I still surf a bit, but I take firefighting a whole lot more serious than I ever thought I would. And these guys are my friends—on and off the job. On our days off, we're always together. I guess the biggest shock to me is that I find myself talking about my work all the time. I had no intention of getting this involved in my job.

The Socialization Process

We will now turn our attention toward making some general assumptions about socialization and then toward constructing a model of the socialization process. This section will prepare us to consider the most relevant part in our discussion of socialization: What can managers do to effect the process?

Underlying Assumptions

The material presented in the remainder of this chapter is based on four assumptions.[7] We want to make explicit these assumptions about socialization.

[7]Adapted from Van Maanen and Schein, "Toward a Theory of Organizational Socialization," pp. 214–16.

Socialization
influences
performance

Socialization strongly influences employee performance and organizational stability. Your work performance depends to a considerable degree on knowing what you should or should not do. Understanding the right way to do a job indicates proper socialization. Furthermore, the appraisal of your performance includes how well you fit into the organization. Can you get along with your co-workers? Do you have acceptable work habits? Do you demonstrate the right attitude? These qualities differ between jobs and organizations. For instance, on some jobs you will be evaluated higher if you are aggressive and outwardly indicate that you are ambitious. On another job, or on the same job in another organization, such an approach may be evaluated negatively. As a result, proper socialization becomes a significant factor in influencing both your actual job performance and how it is perceived by others.

The stability of the organization is also increased through socialization. When, over many years, jobs are filled and vacated with a minimum of disruption, the organization will be more stable. Its objectives will be more smoothly transferred between generations. Loyalty and commitment to the organization should be easier to maintain because the organization's philosophy and objectives will appear consistent over time. Given that most managers value high employee performance and organizational stability, the proper socialization of employees should be important.

New employees
suffer from anxiety

New members suffer from anxiety. The outsider-insider passage is an anxiety-producing situation. Stress is high because the new member feels a lack of identification, if not with the work itself, certainly with a new superior, new co-workers, a new work location, and probably a new set of rules and regulations. Loneliness and a feeling of isolation are not unusual responses.

This anxiety state has at least two implications. First, new employees need special attention to put them at ease. This usually means providing an adequate amount of information to reduce uncertainties and ambiguities. Second, the existence of tension can be positive in that it often acts to motivate individuals to learn the values and norms of their newly assumed role as quickly as possible. We can conclude, therefore, that the new member is anxious about the new role but is motivated to learn the ropes and become an accepted member of the organization rapidly.

Socialization does
not occur in a
vacuum

Socialization does not occur in a vacuum. The learning associated with socialization goes beyond the formal job description and the expectations that may be made by people in the personnel office or by the new member's superior. Socialization will be influenced by clues given by colleagues, superiors, subordinates, clients, and other people with whom new members come in contact. In other words, regardless

Considerations in Developing a Socialization Program

Human resource managers must make decisions about how they want to socialize their new employees. We will, therefore, now direct our attention to the various alternatives that will influence the socialization process. The following discussion can be viewed as an assessment of the various alternatives managers should consider in designing the appropriate socialization program for their unit or organization.[10]

Formal or Informal?

New employees may be put directly into their jobs, with no effort made to differentiate them from those who have been doing the job for a considerable length of time. Such cases represent examples of informal socialization—it takes place on the job and the new member gets little or no special attention. In contrast, socialization can be formal. The more formal the program, the more the new employee is segregated from the ongoing work setting and differentiated in some way to make explicit his or her newcomer's role.

Formal socialization

The more formal a socialization program, the more likely it is that management has participated in its design and execution and, hence, the more likely that the recruit will experience the learning that management desires. In contrast, the more informal the program, the more success will depend on the new employee selecting the correct socialization agents. For example, if the new employee chooses a co-worker who is highly knowledgeable about the job and the system's values, and who is capable of transferring this knowledge, then socialization should be more successful than if the agent is marginally knowledgeable, a poor teacher, or holds deviant organizational values. In most circumstances, laissez-faire socialization will increase the influence of the immediate work group on the new member.[11]

Informal socialization

Whether a formal or an informal program is preferable will depend on management's goals. The more formal the program, the greater the likelihood that the recruit will acquire a known set of standards. That is, the new member is more likely to think and act like a GM executive, a management professor, or a U.S. Navy pilot. But an informal program is better for maintaining individual differences. Novel approaches to organizational problems and healthy questioning of the status quo are more likely to be generated by the person who has received informal socialization. And the informal program, be-

---

[10]This material is adapted with permission from John Van Maanen, "People Processing: Strategies of Organizational Socialization," *Organizational Dynamics,* Summer 1978. © 1978 by AMACOM, a division of American Management Associations, pp. 19–36.

[11]Ibid., p. 24.

cause it takes place on the job, does not require transference of knowledge. The more that new members are removed from the day-to-day realities of the organization as part of the formal socialization process, the less they will be able to carry over, generalize, and apply the skills and norms learned in the socialization setting to the new job itself. Thus there is likely to be more loss of learning from a formal program than from an informal program.

Of course, the idea of formal or informal programs represents two extremes along a continuum. Managers can make their programs more formal or more informal as they see necessary. In fact, a common practice in organizations is to use both. Employees begin with a relatively formal socialization to learn the pivotal standards of the organization. Then they begin the informal socialization process on the job, where they learn the norms of their work group. The Army recruit, for example, goes through six weeks of basic training—which is formal; followed up by the informal socialization that goes with becoming part of a working unit.

Individual or Collective?

Individual socialization

Another choice to be made by management is whether to socialize new members individually or to group them together and process them through an identical set of experiences.

The individual approach is likely to develop far less homogeneous views than collective socialization. As with the informal structure, individual socializing is more likely to preserve individual differences and perspectives. But socializing each person individually is expensive and time-consuming. It also fails to allow the new entrants to share their anxieties with others who are in similar circumstances.

Collective socialization

Processing new members in collective groups allows the recruits to form alliances with others who can empathize with their adjustment problems. The recruits have people with whom they can interact and share what they are learning. The group shares problems and usually develops similar solutions. Therefore collective socialization tends to form a common perspective on the organization among group members. College fraternity and sorority pledge classes are socialized collectively, and they tend to form consensus perspectives. Interestingly, because group socialization develops this consensual character, it allows the recruits, as a group, to deviate more from the standards held out by the organization than does the individual approach to socialization. It is easier for people to maintain a deviant position when they have others to support them. The group, therefore, is more likely than the individual to resist or redefine the organization's demands.

In practice, most large organizations find individual socialization impractical. They tend to rely on group socialization techniques. While small organizations, which have fewer new entrants to socialize, frequently use the individual approach, large organizations have moved to a collective approach because of its ease, efficiency, and predictability.

Fixed or Variable Time Period?

Fixed socialization

A third major consideration for management is whether the transition from outsider to insider should be done on a fixed or variable time period. A fixed schedule reduces uncertainty for the new members, since transition is standardized. New members know, for instance, that they are in a nine-month apprenticeship program. Each step of transition is clear. Successful completion of certain standardized steps means that they will be accepted to full-fledged membership. Variable schedules, in contrast, give no advanced notice of their transition time-table. Variability characterizes the socialization schedule for most professionals and managerial personnel.

Fixed schedules provide rigid conceptions of what is considered "normal" progress. Because the variable schedule does not, it requires new members to search for clues as to what is normal progress. They look for past patterns that might suggest when certain passages can and should be expected to take place or when tenure will be granted. Progress is then compared against these implied norms. Rumors and innuendos about who is going where and when characterize a variable schedule.

Variable socialization

Variable socialization processes give an administrator a powerful tool for influencing individual behavior. But the administration also risks creating an organizational situation marked by confusion and uncertainty among those concerned with their movement in the system. Fixed processes provide temporal reference points that allow people both to observe passages ceremonially and to hold together relationships forged during the socialization experiences. Variable processes, by contrast, tend to divide and drive apart people who might show much loyalty and cohesion if the process were fixed.[12]

Serial or Disjunctive?

When an experienced organizational member, familiar with the new member's job, guides or directs a new recruit, we call this serial socialization. In this process, the experienced member acts as a tutor and model for the new employee. When recruits do not have predecessors available to guide them or to model their behavior upon, we have disjunctive socialization.

Serial socialization

Like our previous choices, both serial and disjunctive strategies have distinct advantages and disadvantages. Serial socialization maintains traditions and customs. Consistent use of this strategy will ensure a minimum amount of change within the organization over time. It also allows new members a look into the future by seeing in their more experienced colleague an image of themselves later in their career. However, each of these advantages has accompanying disadvantages. Stability and conformity may be achieved at the cost of stagnation and pressures to adhere to the status quo, even when conditions suggest the need for change. Similarly, a look into the future will have a positive effect on new employees only if they like what is seen. If the more-experienced member is seen as frustrated, locked in, or caught up in some other negative context, the new employee may leave the

[12]Ibid., p. 29.

organization rather than face what seems to be an agonizing future. This latter point indicates the importance of the experienced tutor in the serial process. If the tutor is knowledgeable and enthusiastic, the recruit is likely to gain considerably from their working relationship. But if the tutor's morale is low, if he or she is a poor coach or feels threatened by the recruit, serial socialization may, at worst, result in the loss of the new member. At best, it might result in socializing the employee with organizational values that are counter to the interests of the organization.

The benefits and drawbacks to disjunctive socialization should be obvious from the above. It is likely to produce more inventive and creative employees because the recruit is not burdened by traditions. But this benefit must be weighed against the potential for creating deviants; that is, individuals who fail, due to an inadequate role model, to understand how their job is to be done and how it fits into the grand scheme of the organization.

Mentors   A special case of serial socialization has gained a great deal of attention recently. It is becoming increasingly evident that employees who aspire to reach the top echelons of management in an organization should acquire a mentor or sponsor. The road to the top in an organization requires gaining the favor of the dominant in-group which sets standards and priorities. In organizations that promote from within, those who aspire to succeed must win the favor of a sponsor who is part of the in-group.[13] The sponsor's role is to vouch for the candidate, answer for the candidate in the highest circles within the organization, make introductions, and advise and guide the candidate on how to move effectively through the system. A study of the sponsor's role in one large conglomerate found that sponsors specifically fought for their protégé (who, as we will see below, was generally a male), standing up for him in meetings, and promoting him into promising positions; offered inside information, not otherwise available; and provided a signal to others that the protégé had the resources of an important higher-up behind him.[14] A very interesting additional finding from this study was that women often find it difficult to get a sponsor and that this has hindered their movement into upper management. Sponsors usually select their protégé on the basis of seeing themselves, in their younger days, in the candidate. Since men can rarely identify with younger women, they are unwilling to play the part of a women's mentor. Of course, as women fight their way into the inner circle of organizational power, it will be only a matter of time

[13]Eugene E. Jennings, *Routes to the Executive Suite* (New York: McGraw-Hill, 1971), pp. 53–54.

[14]Rosabeth Moss Kanter, *Men and Women of the Corporation* (New York: Basic Books, 1977).

until women will be able to take equal advantage of the mentor form of serial socialization.

Investiture or Divestiture?

Investiture
socialization

Our final consideration concerns whether our goal is to confirm or dismantle the incoming identity of the new member. Investiture rites ratify the usefulness of the characteristics that the person brings to the new job. This describes most high-level appointments in the organization. These individuals were selected on the basis of what they can bring to the job. The organization does not want to change these recruits, so entry is made as smooth and trouble free as possible. If this is the goal, socialization efforts concentrate on reinforcing that "we like you just the way you are." This is frequently done by widely disseminating information on the new member's accomplishments. Recruits may be given a large degree of freedom to select their office furnishings and subordinates and to make other decisions that will reflect on their performance. Elaborate initiation rites to confirm the new person's characteristics and "track record" are not unusual: news conferences, formal introduction of the candidate to influencial groups in the community, or visits to key people in the organization for ceremonial introductions and handshakes.

Far more often is the desire to strip away certain entering characteristics of a recruit. The selection process identified the candidate as a potential high performer; now it is necessary to make those minor modifications to improve the fit between the candidate and the organization. This fine-tuning may take the shape of requiring the recruits to sever old friendships; accepting a different way of looking at their job, peers, or the organization's purpose; doing a number of demeaning jobs to prove their commitment; or even undergoing harassment and hazing by more-experienced personnel to verify that they fully accept their role in the organization. One writer describes how a manager in an engineering company deliberately put each of his new engineers through an "upending experience" for the purpose of reducing their arrogance and making the point that they didn't have all the answers:

He asked each new man to examine and diagnose a particular complex circuit, which happened to violate a number of textbook principles but actually worked very well. The new man would usually announce with confidence, even after an invitation to double-check, that the circuit could not possibly work. At this point the manager would demonstrate the circuit, tell the new man that they had been selling it for several years without customer complaint, and demand that the new man figure out why it did work. None of the men so far tested were able to do it, but all of them were thoroughly chastened and came to the manager anxious to learn where their knowledge was inadequate and needed supplementing. According to this manager, it was much easier from this point on to establish a good give-and-take relationship with his new man.[15]

Divestiture socialization

This example is not atypical. First-year college students are frequently given extremely heavy workloads to shock them into the world of higher education. Similar divestiture practices occur for those entering military basic training, professional football, police academies, fraternal groups, religious cults, and self-realization groups, to name the more obvious. Such tactics build on the premise that if the organization is to instill a new set of values or norms, it first must shake up and possibly destroy those that are already in place.

If the goal of management is to produce similar employees, a divestiture approach is likely to be used. It will achieve similar results with each recruit, and the process itself will promote a strong fellowship among those who have followed the same path to membership.

Conclusion

The five considerations we have discussed are largely controllable by management as they design and implement their socialization programs. But, as noted earlier, socialization does not take place in a vacuum. Many experiences of individuals are structured by others in the

---

FIGURE 9-3

The Problem of Socialization In a Declining Organization

As layoffs appear imminent, groups begin to form. These groups become self-serving rather than organization-serving. Problems can and do occur often. One group views another group as outsiders, and the entire climate in the organization becomes one of distrust and protect-your-own. The threat that the decline has brought permeates all levels of the organization. Job security is an issue, and change is likely to be vehemently resisted.

That change, however, is going to occur. But with that change comes a different environment. The climate created by the decline is obviously not conducive to initiating the behavioral changes that may be needed to help rebuild the organization. To do this requires trust, support, and humanistic values.* But these attributes are inconsistent with the climate within declining organizations. While change processes may be viewed as an opportunity during growth, they are more likely to be perceived as a threat during decline. Management's effort to initiate change, therefore, is much more likely to confront deeper and more persistent resistance during retrenchment.

---

*Stephen P. Robbins, "The New Management: Managing Declining Organizations" (Presented at the Western Academy of Management Conference, Vancouver, Canada, April 1984).

---

[15]Schein, "Organizational Socialization and the Profession of Management," p. 5.

organization—experiences that management cannot closely control. So we cannot be assured that we will always get the outcome that we want. But management can certainly control a number of the major socialization variables.

This last section has sought to demonstrate that while recruitment and selection identify acceptable candidates, by choosing appropriate socialization experiences for the new employee, we can further fine-tune the fit between the candidate's qualities and the organization's desires. The selection of the right entry socialization program, chosen from the mix of alternatives we have discussed, will go a long way toward developing members who meet the organization's definition of "a good employee."

It should be evident from this chapter that "organizational results are not simply the consequences of the work accomplished by people brought into the organization; rather, they are the consequences of the work these people accomplish after the organization itself has completed its work on them."[16] This should not be construed as implying that management is trying to create a *Brave New World* environment. The benefits from socialization flow to the organization and to the new employee. The organization gets higher productivity, greater employee commitment, and lower turnover rates. Employees achieve reduced anxiety, increased awareness of what is expected on the job, and an increased feeling of being accepted by their peers and bosses. When socialization works, employees receive the confidence and satisfaction that comes from feeling that they are members in good standing in the organization.

SUMMARY

1. Socialization is a process of adaption. Organization entry socialization refers to the adaption that takes place when an individual passes from outside the organization to the role of an inside member.

2. Orientation is part of socialization and covers the activities involved in introducing a new employee to the organization and to his or her work unit.

3. Organizational socialization attempts to adapt the new employee to the organization's culture by conveying to the employee how things are done and what matters.

4. It is imperative that the new employee accept the organization's pivotal standards.

[16]Van Maanen and Schein, "Toward a Theory of Organizational Socialization," p. 255.

5. Managers can significantly influence the degree to which new employees maintain their individuality and creativity or conform totally to the traditions and customs of the organization.

6. Evidence suggests the validity of the following assumptions:
   a. Socialization strongly influences employee performance and organizational stability.
   b. New members suffer from anxiety.
   c. Socialization does not occur in a vacuum.
   d. People adjust in similar ways.

7. The socialization process consists of three stages:
   a. Prearrival
   b. Encounter
   c. Metamorphosis

8. The major considerations in the design of a socialization program are concerned with whether the program
   a. Is formal or informal in structure
   b. Processes people individually or collectively
   c. Utilizes a fixed or variable time period
   d. Is serial or disjunctive
   e. Seeks investiture or divestiture

KEY TERMS

Collective socialization
Disjunctive socialization
Divestiture socialization
Encounter stage
Fixed socialization
Formal socialization
Individual socialization
Informal socialization
Investiture socialization
Mentor

Metamorphosis stage
Norms
Orientation
Prearrival stage
Protégé
Roles
Serial socialization
Socialization
Values
Variable socialization

QUESTIONS FOR REVIEW

1. Compare and contrast these terms: *socialization, organizational entry socialization,* and *orientation.*

2. What is an organizational role? What are values? Norms?

3. How do the concepts of role, values, and norms impact on socialization?

4. What makes a "conformist" or "rebel"?

5. Was John DeLorean's attitude and behavior good for General Motors? Explain.
6. What benefits can socialization provide for the organization?
7. What benefits can socialization provide for the new employee?
8. Explain the three stages in the socialization process.
9. What might a socialization program look like if management desired employees who were innovative and individualistic?
10. What might a socialization program look like if management desired employees who were totally loyal and committed to the organization's goals?

QUESTIONS FOR DISCUSSION

1. Individuals have values. Can we also say that organizations have values? Discuss.
2. Identify a social group that you are familiar with and describe its socialization process for new entrants.
3. "People are generally inflexible when confronted with change." Do you agree or disagree? What are the implications for socialization?
4. "Selection is a substitute for socialization." Do you agree or disagree? Discuss.
5. Compare the realistic job preview with socialization. Are they the same?

CONTINUING CASE: Concord General

Slim Pickins

Every nurse who is hired for the Intensive Care Unit at Concord General must attend a one-week seminar that explains the hospital's philosophy, rules, and regulations. After completing this one-week seminar, each nurse is assigned to a veteran ICU nurse for four weeks. These assignments are made on a rotating basis, with the seasoned nurse who oriented the last hired nurse being placed at the bottom of the assignment list.

Beth Needles has recently completed her week's orientation program and has been assigned to work with Roni Lewis, a four-year ICU veteran. Beth is anxiously awaiting her chance to work autonomously in the unit so that her lifelong ambition to be a humanitarian can be fulfilled. She had worked in a competing hospital's recovery unit during the past three years but left because she wanted the challenge of helping totally dependent, seriously ill patients.

After seven days of working with Roni, Beth has requested that another veteran nurse orient her. She has complained to the head nurse that instead of instructing her about the duties of an ICU nurse, Roni has used her as a personal sounding board and gofer.

Somewhat surprised by this information, the head nurse asked Beth to give it one more chance and if, after that time, there was no improvement, she would make the change.

For the next three days, Roni began to make matters worse, as the following indicates:

> I don't know why you want to work here, Beth. Our pay is no better than a floor nurse's. We have to put up with too much stress. The head nurse is a flake whose only concern is for herself and her career aspirations. Most of the doctors here treat us like playthings, and if you don't play their game, your patients will never get any attention. And, furthermore, you're now the low man on the totem pole. You know what that means—all the dirty jobs. I just can't stand this place, and I hate your better-than-thou, make-everything-great, attitude.

Losing control of her emotions, Beth said:

> I don't know why you treat me so rotten. I'm here to work, to help the sick. So far you have done nothing to make my life easier. I've seen the head nurse and have requested a change in assignments. And. . . .

Roni answered angrily:

> You've done what? You little troublemaker! Well, then, good; just get the hell away from me. You think anyone else is going to work for you after I tell them you're an "ear"? You're as good as gone if I can help it.

Beth just walked out of the unit in tears.

Questions

1. What types of orientation programs are identified in the case?
2. There seems to be a serious problem in the socialization process. What is it and how could it be remedied?
3. If you were the head nurse, how would you handle Roni? Beth?
4. Can you make recommendations for this orientation program that might avert any further incidents such as this?

CASE APPLICATION

Welcome to Desert National Bank

The Desert National Bank of Arizona is one of the largest banks in the western United States. It has fifty-five branches, with over two thousand employees. The bank's headquarters is in Phoenix.

Desert National regularly hires several dozen recent college graduates each year to participate in the bank's management training program. It is the objective of this program to prepare future lending officers and branch managers. In the summer of 1987, Marge Davis was promoted from her position as a compensation analyst to assistant personnel manager. The major responsibility of her new job would be to direct the bank's management training program.

Marge obtained all the information she could get on the training program and took it home one weekend. It made fascinating reading. The program had been in effect for sixteen years. Over that period, 221 individuals had been recruited for the program, all directly out of college. Approximately 10 percent of these entered with a master's degree, the rest with bachelor's degrees. With few exceptions, the latter had their degrees in business administration. As Marge dug deeper, she was taken aback by the statistics she computed. Of the 221 recruits, 47 were still working for Desert National. The average length of time recruits stayed with the bank was less than two years. More surprising was the fact that 34 of these 47 individuals had been hired within the past three years. A summary of her findings is shown below:

YEAR	NUMBER OF TRAINEES HIRED	STILL CURRENTLY EMPLOYED
1986	28	22
1985	24	9
1984	23	3
1983	18	2
1982	15	4
1981	15	1
1976–80	61	2
1970–75	37	4
	221	47

Marge was interested in how much of this turnover was attributed to voluntary resignations and how much was due to bank firings. A look through the personnel records indicated fewer than 15 percent of those who left were terminated because the bank was unhappy with their performance. At least, Marge thought, this suggested that the bank's selection procedure was effective in identifying people who would make good employees. But why were such a large percentage leaving the bank?

The management training program took thirty months to complete. All trainees went through a lock-step program which gave exposure to six main areas within the bank. It was estimated that those recruits who successfully completed the training program and sought to be branch managers should achieve their goal within four years after finishing the thirty-month program. In fact, every trainee hired prior to 1981 was either a lending officer, a branch manager, or a senior officer at the bank's headquarters.

Questions

1. What factors may be causing the low retention rate?
2. What evidence does Marge provide to support her contention that the bank's selection process is working effectively? Do you agree with her position?
3. How would you describe the bank's socialization program?
4. What changes might you consider to increase the retention rate?

ADDITIONAL READINGS

ADDAMS, H. LON, "Up to Speed in 90 Days," *Personnel Journal*, December 1985, pp. 35–38.

BEWAYO, EDWARD D., "What Employees Look For in First and Subsequent Employers," *Personnel*, 63, No. 4 (April 1986), 49–54.

HUBBARD, GHISLAINE, "How to Combat Culture Shock," *Management Today* September 1986, pp. 62–65.

OLDFIELD, KENNETH, and NANCY AYERS, "Avoid the New Job Blues," *Personnel Journal*, August 1986, pp. 48–56.

POSNER, BARRY Z., JAMES M. KOUZES, and WARREN H. SCHMIDT, "Shared Values Make a Difference: An Empirical Test of Corporate Culture," *Human Resource Management*, 24, No. 3 (Fall 1985), 293–309.

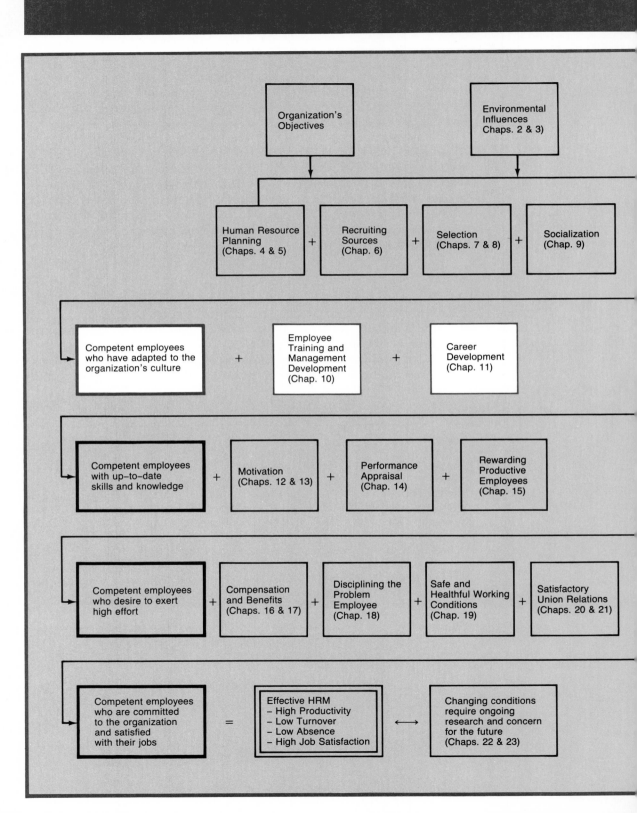

PART THREE

DEVELOPMENT OF HUMAN RESOURCES

= Competent employees who have adapted to the organization's culture

= Competent employees with up-to-date skills and knowledge

= Competent employees who desire to exert high effort

= Competent employees who are committed to the organization and satisfied with their jobs

CHAPTER 10

Employee Training

and Management

Development

AFTER READING THIS CHAPTER, YOU WILL BE ABLE TO:

1. Explain why employee training is important
2. Define *training*
3. Discuss the relationship between effective training programs and various learning principles
4. Describe how training needs evolve
5. Identify the two types of formal training methods
6. Define *management development*
7. Discuss the relationship between management development and motivation
8. Describe on-the-job and off-the-job management development techniques
9. Describe the methods and criteria involved in evaluating training programs

If you think education is expensive—try ignorance.

—Derek Bok

Every organization needs to have well-trained and experienced people to perform the activities that have to be done. If current or potential job occupants can meet this requirement, training is not important. When this is not the case, it is necessary to raise the skill levels and increase the versatility and adaptability of employees.

As jobs have become more complex, the importance of employee training has increased. When jobs were simple, easy to learn, and influenced to only a small degree by technological changes, there was little need for employees to upgrade or alter their skills. But the rapid changes taking place during the last quarter-century in our highly sophisticated and complex society have created increased pressures for organizations to readapt the products and services produced, the manner in which products and services are produced and offered, the types of jobs required, and the types of skills necessary to complete these jobs.

Nearly 50 percent of all jobs currently being done in the United States did not exist half a century ago. It is becoming increasingly common for individuals to "change careers" several times during their working lives. The probability of any young person learning a job today and having those skills go basically unchanged during the forty or so years of his or her career is extremely unlikely, maybe even impossible. In a rapidly changing society, employee training is not only an activity that is desirable but also an activity that an organization must commit resources to if it is to maintain a viable and knowledgeable work force.

What is Training?

Training defined
Training is a learning experience in that it seeks a relatively permanent change in an individual that will improve his or her ability to perform on the job. We typically say training can involve the changing of skills, knowledge, attitudes, or social behavior. It may mean chang-

ing what employees know, how they work, their attitudes toward their work, or their interactions with their co-workers or their supervisor.

For our purposes, training will be presented as it applies primarily to operative employees in the organization. By that we mean production, clerical, and maintenance workers. Our emphasis here is on the development of those employees who do *not* supervise the activities of others. What an organization can do to develop supervisory and managerial employees will be the subject of our next chapter.

Training and Learning

We have previously described training as a learning experience. Of course, a lot of an employee's learning about a job takes place outside of specific training activities. This was clearly demonstrated in our previous chapter on socialization. But if we are to understand what training techniques can do to improve an employee's job performance, we should begin by explaining how people learn. Later in this chapter, we will show how an understanding of learning principles should be valuable in structuring effective training experiences.

Theories of Learning

Learning is concerned with bringing about relatively permanent change as a result of experience. This can be done through direct experience—by doing—or indirectly, through observation. Regardless of the means by which learning takes place, we cannot measure learning per se. We can only measure the changes in attitudes and behavior that occur as a result of learning. For our discussion, we will emphasize *how* we learn rather than *what* we learn.

Two major theories have dominated learning research over the years. One position is the cognitive view. Its proponents argue that an individuals's purposes or intentions direct his or her actions.[1] The other position is the environmental perspective, whose proponents believe the individual is acted upon and his or her behavior is a function of its external consequences.[2]

More recently an approach has been offered that blends both of these theories—learning is a continuous interaction between the individual and the particular social environment in which he or she functions. This is called social-learning theory.[3] This theory acknowledges

[1]Edwin A. Locke, "Toward a Theory of Task Motivation and Incentives," *Organizational Behavior and Human Performance*, May 1968, pp. 157–89.

[2]B. F. Skinner, *Beyond Freedom and Dignity* (New York: Knopf, 1971).

[3]Albert Bandura, *Social Learning Theory* (Englewood Cliffs, N.J.: Prentice-Hall, 1977).

that we can learn by observing what happens to other people and just by being told about something, as well as by direct experiences. Since much of training is observational in nature, this theory would appear to have considerable application potential.

The influence of models is central to the social-learning viewpoint. Research indicates that much of what we have learned comes from watching models—parents, teachers, peers, motion picture and television performers, bosses, and so forth. Four processes have been found to determine the influence a model will have on an individual:

Attentional processes

1. *Attentional processes.* People only learn from a model when they recognize and pay attention to its critical features. We tend to be most influenced by models that are attractive, repeatedly available, that we think are important, or that we see as similar to us.

Retention processes

2. *Retention processes.* A model's influence will depend on how well the individual remembers the model's action, even after the model is no longer readily available.

Motor reproduction processes

3. *Motor reproduction processes.* After a person has seen a new behavior by observing the model, the watching must be converted to doing. This process then demonstrates that the individual can perform the modeled activities.

Reinforcement processes

4. *Reinforcement processes.* Individuals will be motivated to exhibit the modeled behavior if positive incentives or rewards are provided. Behaviors that are reinforced will be given more attention, learned better, and performed more often.

Social-learning theory offers us insights into what a training exercise should include. Specifically, it tells us training should provide a model; it must grab the trainee's attention; provide motivational properties; help the trainee file away what he or she has learned for later use; and if the training has taken place off the job, allow the trainee some opportunity to transfer what has been learned on the job.

Principles of Learning

The above processes derived from social-learning theory are frequently presented in more specific terms as principles of learning. In this section, we will briefly review these principles. You should, of course, be able to see how they closely align with social-learning theory.

Learning and motivation

Learning is enhanced when the learner is motivated. An individual must want to learn. When that desire exists, the learner will exert a high level of effort. There appears to be valid evidence to support the adage "You can take a horse to water, but you can't make him drink."

The learning experience, therefore, should be designed so learners can see how it will help them achieve those goals they have set for themselves. If, for example, the new trainee desires the security and fulfillment that comes from being a skilled computer word processor operator, he or she is more likely to be highly motivated to learn how to perform that job successfully.

Feedback and learning

Learning requires feedback. Feedback, or knowledge of results, is necessary so the learner can correct his mistakes. Only by getting information about how I am doing can I compare it against my goals and correct my deviations. And feedback is best when it is immediate rather than delayed. The sooner individuals have some knowledge of how well they are performing, the easier it is for them to correct their erroneous actions.

Additionally, feedback can provide intrinsic motivation. When individuals obtain information on their performance, the task becomes more intrinsically interesting and acts to motivate them.

Reinforcement and learning

Reinforcement increases the likelihood that a learned behavior will be repeated. The principle of reinforcement tells us that behaviors that are positively reinforced (rewarded) are encouraged and sustained. When the behavior is punished, it is temporarily suppressed but is unlikely to be extinguished. Punishment tells learners they are doing something wrong. What is desired, however, is to convey feedback to the learners when they are doing what is right to encourage them to keep doing it.

Learning will be facilitated by providing feedback through positive reinforcement. For instance, if workers are verbally praised when they have properly performed a task, they are likely to continue doing the task this way and be motivated to strive toward performing better work.

Practice and learning

Practice increases a learner's performance. When learners actually practice what they have read, heard, or seen, they gain confidence and are less likely to make errors or to forget what they have learned. Active involvement through practice, therefore, should be made part of the learning process.

There are three ways a worker can practice a job. One is to practice the whole job at once. The second is to break the job into parts and practice each part independently. The third is to break the job into two parts, then three and so on. Which way is best? The answer lies in the type of job being done. It appears that if the total work the person does is small and relatively simple, practice should cover the whole job. If the job is complicated, the independent part approach is best unless the parts are interdependent, in which case the progression approach will probably be most effective.

Learning curves

Learning begins rapidly, then plateaus. Learning rates can be expressed as a curve that usually begins with a sharp rise, then increases at a decreasing rate until a plateau is reached. Learning is very fast at the beginning, but then plateaus as opportunities for improvement are reduced.

The learning curve principle is illustrated by considering individuals who begin training to run the mile. At first, their time improves rapidly as they get into shape. Then, as their conditioning develops, their improvement plateaus. Obviously, knocking one minute off a ten-minute mile is a lot easier than knocking one minute off a five-minute mile. If you have ever learned to type, you may have had an experience that somewhat follows the pattern shown in Figure 10-1. The specific criterion is words typed per minute, and the time element is in months.

Note the shape of the curve in Figure 10-1. During the first three months, the rate of increase is slow as the subject learns the typing technique and becomes familiar with the keyboard. During the next three months, learning accelerates as the subject works on developing speed. After six months, learning slows as progress evolves into refinement of technique.

Transferring learning

Learning must be transferable to the job. It doesn't make much sense to perfect a skill in the classroom and then find that you can't successfully transfer it to the job. Therefore training should be designed to foster transferability.

Tansfer can be positive or negative. The ablity to type on a manual typewriter will aid in learning to type on an electric one. This is a positive transfer, for it improves performance. But knowledge of Spanish

FIGURE 10-1   Learning Curve for a Typist

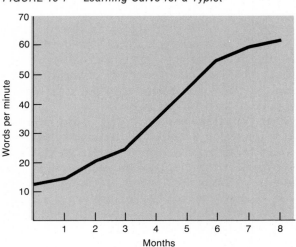

may impede students learning to speak French if the harsh pronunciations used in Spanish are carried over and attempted on the light pronunciations needed for French. This latter case is an illustration of negative transfer, which hampers performance. Management will obviously be concerned with maximizing positive transfer and minimizing negative transfer in any training activity.

Learning and Training: The Implications

The social-learning model and learning principles tell us training should provide the trainee with a given model to follow, specific goals to achieve, an opportunity to perfect the skill, feedback on how well the trainee is progressing, and praise for transferring the acquired skills to the job. These recommendations should guide the human resource manager in designing, implementing, and operating any employee training.

The value of these recommendations was shown in a training experiment at an international company in the northwestern United States.[4] Forty employees, all supervisors, were identified for the experiment—twenty assigned to the training group and twenty to the control group. The training focused on ways of orienting new employees, giving recognition, motivating a poor performer, correcting poor work habits, discussing potential disciplinary action, reducing absenteeism, handling a complaining employee, reducing turnover, and overcoming resistance to change. The training was done in nine two-hour sessions, one session taking place each week.

The training group received the following: introduction of the topic by two trainers; presentation of a film that depicted a supervisor-model effectively handling a situation by following a set of three to six learning points that were shown in the film immediately before and after the model was presented; group discussion of the effectiveness of the model in demonstrating the desired behaviors; practice in role playing the desired behaviors in front of the entire class; and feedback from the class on the effectiveness of each trainee in demonstrating the desired behaviors. Half of the control group were given only the set of learning points to see if knowledge alone of what one is "supposed to do" was sufficient to obtain the desired behaviors. The researchers argued that if giving the supervisors the learning points as guidelines to follow was as effective as requiring them to attend the nine training sessions, considerable time and expense could be saved by the company. The other half of the control group received no special information.

[4]Gary P. Latham and Lise M. Saari, "Application of Social-Learning Theory to Training Supervisors Through Behavioral Modeling," *Journal of Applied Psychology,* June 1979, pp. 239–46.

The results confirmed the value of training based on social-learning theory. Specifically, in independent evaluations of how all forty subjects responded to a set of tape-recorded role plays requiring the resolution of supervisor-employee problems, the trained group performed significantly better than either control group. Interestingly, there were no significant differences in the control groups. In other words, merely providing a list of desirable behaviors did not result in job-transferable learning. Futhermore, the researchers found that the performance appraisals of these supervisors, though similar before the experiment, differed significantly afterward. The supervisors who had the training received significantly higher performance appraisals than did those in the control groups.

Determining Training Needs and Priorities

Determining training needs

Now that we have an understanding of what training should include, we can look at how we assess whether there is a need for training. We propose that management can determine this by answering four questions: (1) What are the organization's goals? (2) What tasks must be completed to achieve these goals? (3) What behaviors are necessary for each job incumbent to complete his or her assigned tasks? (4) What deficiencies, if any, do incumbents have in the skills, knowledge, or attitudes required to perform the necessary behaviors? These questions demonstrate the close link between human resource planning and determination of training needs. Based on our determination of the organization's needs, the type of work that is to be done, and the type of skills necessary to complete this work, our training program should follow naturally. Once we can answer question 4, we have a grasp of the extent and nature of our training needs.

What kind of signals can warn a manager that employee training may be necessary? Clearly, the more obvious ones relate directly to productivity; inadequate job performance or a drop in productivity. The former is likely to occur in the early months on a new job. When a manager sees evidence of inadequate job performance, assuming the individual is making a satisfactory effort, attention should be given toward raising the skill level of the worker. When a manager is confronted with a drop in productivity, it may suggest that skills need to be "fine-tuned."

In addition to productivity measures, a high reject rate or larger than usual scrappage may indicate a need for employee training. A rise in the number of accidents reported also suggests some type of re-training is necessary. There is also the future element: changes that are being imposed on the worker as a result of a job redesign or a technological breakthrough. These types of job changes require a training effort that is less crisis oriented; that is, a preparation for planned change rather than a reaction to immediately unsatisfactory conditions.

Figure 10-2 shows the methods used for assessing training needs and their popularity among a large number of various-sized organizations. Note the dominant method, in practice, is observation and analysis of job performance.

If deficiencies in performance are uncovered, it need not necessarily follow that the manager should take corrective action. It is important to put training into perspective. It has costs, which are often high; and training should not be viewed as a panacea.

Training will be judged by its contribution to performance where *performance* is a function of skills, abilities, motivation, and the opportunity to perform. Managers must compare the value received from the increase in performance that can be attributed to training with the costs incurred in that training. The desire for improved worker productivity cannot be approached in a vacuum. The benefits that accrue from training must exceed the costs incurred. We must guard against those who rush about with $100,000 solutions to $10,000 problems. When inadequate performance results from a motivation problem rather than a skills problem, the rewards and disciplinary actions discussed in the next section may be of greater relevance. Nor would training be the answer if the problem lies outside the job activity itself. For example, if salaries are low, if supervision is poor, if worker benefits are inadequate, or if the physical work layout is deficient, spending on employee training may have little or no effect on productivity, since inadequate performance is due to conditions that training cannot remedy. Training experienced postal workers is not likely to increase productivity when you consider that many of these workers spend their entire workday punching the last two digits of the zip code into a sorting machine. Training can enhance skills but does nothing to relieve monotony.

FIGURE 10-2

Methods for Determining Training Needs

METHOD	PERCENTAGE*
Observation and analysis of job performance	49
Management and staff conferences and recommendations	24
Analysis of job requirements	19
Consideration of current and projected changes	16
Surveys, reports, and inventories	10
Interviews	6
Other	15

*Percentages exceed 100 because some organizations reported the use of more than one method.
SOURCE:*Training Employees.* Personnel Policies Forum, Survey No. 88 (Washington, D.C.: Bureau of National Affairs, November 1965), p. 5.

Once it has been determined that training is necessary, training goals must be established. Management should explicitly state what changes or results are sought for each employee. It is not adequate merely to say that change in employee knowledge, skills, attitudes, or social behavior is desirable; we must clarify what is to change, and by how much. We would argue that these goals should be tangible, verifiable, and measurable. They should be clear to both management and the employee. For instance, a firefighter might be expected to jump from a moving fire truck traveling at fifteen miles per hour, successfully hook up a four-inch hose to a hydrant, and turn on the hydrant, all in less than forty seconds. Such explicit goals ensure that both management and the employee know what is expected from the training effort.

Formal Employee-Training Methods

The most popular training methods used by organizations can be classified as either on-the-job or off-the-job training. In the following pages, we will briefly introduce the better-known techniques from each category.

On-the-Job Training

The most widely used methods of training take place on the job. This can be attributed to the simplicity of such methods and the impression that they are less costly to operate. On-the-job training places the employees in an actual work situation and makes them appear to be immediately productive. It is learning by doing. For jobs that either are difficult to simulate or can be learned quickly by watching and doing, on-the-job training makes sense.

One of the drawbacks to on-the-job training can be low productivity while the employees develop their skills. Another drawback can be the errors made by the trainees while they learn. However, when the damage the trainees can do is minimal, where training facilities and personnel are limited or costly, and where it is desirable for the workers to learn the job under normal working conditions, the benefits of on-the-job training frequently offset its drawbacks.

Apprenticeship programs

Apprenticeship Programs.   People seeking to enter skilled trades—to become, for example, plumbers, electricians, or ironworkers—are often required to undergo apprenticeship training before they are accepted to journeyman status. Typically, this apprenticeship period is from two to five years. For instance, a cosmetician's apprenticeship is two years, a bricklayer's is three years, machinists and printers spend four years, and a patternmaker requires five years. During the apprenticeship period, the trainee is paid less than a fully qualified worker.

Apprenticeship programs put the trainee under the guidance of a master worker. The argument for apprenticeship programs is that the required job knowledge and skills are so complex as to rule out anything less than a long time period where the trainee understudies a skilled master journeyman.

Job instruction training

Job Instruction Training.   During World War II, a systematic approach to on-the-job training was developed to prepare supervisors to train operatives. This approach, called job instruction training (JIT), was part of the Training within Industry program. JIT proved highly effective and became extremely popular. JIT consists of four basic steps: (1) preparing the trainees by telling them about the job and overcoming their uncertainties; (2) presenting the instruction, giving essential information in a clear manner; (3) having the trainees try out the job to demonstrate their understanding; and (4) placing the workers into the job, on their own, with a designated resource person to call upon should they need assistance. The sequence of these activities is shown in Figure 10-3.

A revival of JIT achieved impressive results.[5] When twenty supervisors who had received training for twenty-five hours over ten weeks in turn retrained their subordinates, all but three supervisors were able to show tangible results of job training in their areas. Productivity was significantly improved, and rejects were cut by approximately two-thirds.

Off-the-Job Training

Off-the-job training covers a number of techniques—classroom lectures, films, demonstrations, case studies and other simulation exercises, and programmed instruction. The facilities needed for each of these techniques vary from a small makeshift classroom to an elaborate development center with large lecture halls, supplemented by small conference rooms with sophisticated audiovisual equipment, two-way mirrors, and all the frills.

Classroom lectures/conferences

Classroom Lectures or Conferences.   The lecture or conference approach is well adapted to conveying specific information—rules, procedures, or methods. The use of audiovisuals or demonstrations can often make a formal classroom presentation more interesting while increasing retention and offering a vehicle for clarifying more difficult points. The lecture's liabilities include possible lack of feedback and the lack of active involvement by the trainees. However, this can be partially offset by reducing the structured lecture format and allowing

[5]James H. McCormick, "An Old Standby That Still Works," *Training and Development Journal,* October 1971, pp. 3–7.

FIGURE 10-3

JIT Instruction/Learning Sequence

BASICS OF INSTRUCTION	ESSENTIALS OF LEARNING
PREPARE	MOTIVATION
• Break down the job	
• Prepare an instruction plan	
• Put the learner at ease	
PRESENT	UNDERSTANDING
• Tell	
• Show	
• Demonstrate	
• Explain	
TRY OUT	PARTICIPATION
• Have the learner "talk through" the job.	
• Have the learner instruct the supervisor on how the job is done.	
• Let the learner do the job.	
• Provide feedback both positive and negative.	
• Let the learner practice.	
FOLLOW UP	APPLICATION
• Check progress frequently at first.	
• Tell the learner whom to go to for help.	
• Gradually taper off progress checks.	

SOURCE: Leon Gold, "Job Instruction: Four Steps to Success," *Training and Development Journal,* September 1981, p. 29.

trainees to provide feedback to the lecturer or creating discussion groups under the direction of a conference leader.

Films   *Films.*   Motion pictures can be a useful training technique. Whether purchased from standard film distributors or produced internally by the organization, they can provide information and explicitly demonstrate skills that are not easily presented by other techniques. Motion pictures are often used in conjunction with conference discussions to clarify and amplify those points that the film emphasized.

Simulation exercises   *Simulation Exercises.*   Any training activity that explicitly places the trainee in an artificial environment that closely mirrors actual working conditions can be considered a simulation. Simulation activities include case exercises, experiential exercises, complex computer modeling, and vestibule training.

Cases present an in-depth description of a particular problem an employee might encounter on the job. The employee attempts to find and analyze the problem, evaluate alternative courses of action, and decide what course of action would be most satisfactory.

Experiential exercises

Experiential exercises are usually short, structured learning experiences where individuals learn by doing. For instance, rather than talk about interpersonal conflicts and how to deal with them, an experiential exercise could be used to create a conflict situation where employees have to experience a conflict personally and work out its resolution. After completing the exercise, the facilitator or trainer typically discusses what happened and introduces theoretical concepts to help explain the members' behavior during the exercise.

Computer modeling

Complex computer modeling simulates the work environment by programming a computer to imitate some of the realities of the job. Computer modeling is widely used by airlines in the training of pilots. The computer simulates the number of critical job dimensions and allows learning to take place without the risk or high costs that would be incurred if a mistake were made in a real-life flying situation. An error during a simulation offers an opportunity to learn through one's mistakes. A similar error under real-life conditions might cost a number of lives and the loss of a multimillion-dollar aircraft—quite a high price for a learning exercise. Obviously, complex computer modeling is expensive and can be justified only where programs are formal, a number of trainees will be developed, and the costs of allowing the individual to learn on the job are prohibitive.

Vestibule training

In vestibule training, employees learn their jobs on the equipment they will be using, but the training is conducted away from the actual work floor. In the 1980s many large retail chains train cashiers on their new computer cash registers—which are much more complex because they control inventory and perform other functions in addition to ringing up orders—in specially created vestibule labs that simulated the actual checkout-counter environment. While expensive, vestibule training allows employees to get a full feel for doing tasks without "real-world" pressures. Additionally, it minimizes the problem of transferring learning to the job, since vestibule training uses the same equipment the trainee will use on the job.

Programmed Instruction

Programmed instruction

The programmed instruction technique can be in the form of programmed texts or manuals, while in some organizations teaching machines are utilized. All programmed instruction approaches have a common characteristic: They condense the material to be learned into highly organized, logical sequences, which require the trainee to respond. The ideal format provides for nearly instantaneous feedback that informs the trainee if his or her response is correct.

Summary

There is no training method that is right for all situations. A number of trade-offs must be made when actually making the choice of techniques and putting the program together—costs, time, and capacity of the trainer or trainees.

Figure 10-4 reviews the previously mentioned techniques by evaluating them against the major criteria we identified earlier as important in learning. Note that Figure 10-4 represents general estimates as they are normally practiced—certainly the trade-offs made about the technique will have an impact. As such, the estimates do not apply to all situations. But they should provide reasonable starting points for establishing a training program.

The implications of such programs have been studied by various researchers. A study conducted in the early 1980s concluded the following regarding training:[6]

- Informal on-the-job training costs may run as high as $100 billion.
- Formal employee training is concentrated in certain industries (service, manufacturing).

FIGURE 10-4

Comparison of Training Methods with Key Learning Criteria and Cost Estimates

METHOD	LEARNING CRITERIA			
	Feedback of Results to Trainee	Permits Practice During Training	Transfer of Learning to Job	Estimated Cost Per Trainee
Apprenticeship programs	Yes	Yes	High	Mod.-High
Job instruction training	Yes	Yes	High	Moderate
Classroom lectures or conferences	Varies	No	Low	Low
Films	No	No	Low	Low
Simulation exercises				
Cases	Some	No	Low	Moderate
Experiential exercises	Yes	Yes	Moderate	Low
Computer modeling	Yes	Yes	Mod.-High	High
Vestibule training	Yes	Yes	High	Mod.-High
Programmed instruction	Yes	No	Moderate	Moderate

[6]Elizabeth Gorovitz, "Employee Training: Current Trends, Future Challenges," *Training and Development Journal,* August 1983, p. 28.

- Formal employee training is concentrated by sex, age, and educational levels, tending toward males, the twenty-five to forty-four age group, and the more highly paid and educated.
- Informal employee training is more dispersed by sex and age, and it tends to be concentrated on lower-wage, blue-collar workers.
- Formal employee training is concentrated among occupations (professional, technical).
- Formal employee training is concentrated by subject matter (business, engineering).
- A large proportion of employee training is paid for by employees but provided by outside institutions.

Much of the discussion so far has focused on training and training methods. Generally we find that these areas focus on one segment of an organization—the employees. These training efforts emphasize the learning of routine and programmed behaviors that can immediately be applied to the job. Evaluation of these training programs becomes easier, as the trained employee can or cannot do the job after being trained. Whether this is measured by a test, by productivity gains, or by observation of the employee's work movements, we can assess whether the specific job-related tasks have been learned from the training program.

Personnel training is often treated as an activity that is universally applicable from the top of the organization to the bottom. However, as we look specifically at training management-level personnel, we will discover that it differs from employee training in many significant ways, including not only the job levels directly affected but also the kind of learning that is sought and the methods used to enable and enhance this learning process.

Management Development

Introduction

Management development defined
Management development is more future oriented, and more concerned with education, than is employee training, or assisting a person to become a better performer. By *education*, we mean that management development activities attempt to instill sound reasoning processes—to enhance one's ability to understand and interpret knowledge—rather than imparting a body of serial facts or teaching a specific set of motor skills. Development, therefore focuses more on the employee's personal growth.

Successful managers have analytical, human, conceptual, and specialized skills. They are able to think and understand. Training per se cannot overcome a manager's or potential manager's inability to understand cause-and-effect relationships, to synthesize from experience, to visualize relationships, or to think logically. As a result, we suggest that management development be predominantly an education process rather than a training process.

The words *predominantly an education process* should be noted. In contrast to what we have said above, certain activities that managers engage in are programmable, and training can be helpful. Managers need good listening skills, interviewing competence, and the ability to read, analyze, and classify types of employee behavior. Training can improve these types of skills. Unfortunately, effective management requires considerably more than the acquisition of any specific or specialized skills. For the most part, therefore, the methods for developing executives that we will consider are educational and are intended to foster the manager's analytical and conceptual abilities.

The Process

Organization's objective, and management development

Any effort toward developing managers must begin by looking at the organization's objectives. The objectives tell us where were are going and provide a framework from which our managerial needs can be determined.

Current management resources and management development

The second step is an appraisal of our current management resources. Based on information gathered from our human resource planning, we should have available an executive inventory. From the background and qualifications of our managers and a statement of the organization's objectives, we can begin the third step in the management development process: ascertaining the development activities necessary to ensure that we have adequate managerial talent to fulfill future managerial needs.

This comparative analysis will bring to our attention the potential obsolescence of some of our executives, the inexperience or shortage of managers in certain functions, and skill deficiencies relative to our future needs. The next step, then, is to determine individual development needs: skill development, changing attitudes, and knowledge acquisition. We can expect that most of our management development work will center on the changing of attitudes and the acquisition of knowledge in specific areas.

The assessment center, discussed in Chapter 8 as a selection device, can also be used as an effective tool to determine what specific development efforts our managers need. That is, assessment centers can be used not only to evaluate whether a job candidate can perform a job but also to assess current and potential managers, to find out what development activities might be necessary to improve their performance. Assessment centers thus become a definitive source for selecting and developing managers.[7]

Once we know our development needs, it is necessary to assess those types of development programs that can meet these needs. We will be looking for development activities that can meet the specific needs of each individual. This point cannot be overemphasized, since no development program can be adequate for all managers. Instead, programs must be uniquely tailored to the strengths and weaknesses of the individual manager.

No one development method is the most effective in all situations. Lectures, role plays, case studies, coaching, or any of the techniques we will present have an impact.

Finally, once managers have engaged in development activity, we evaluate—looking for changes in behavior and managerial performance. Just as with operative training programs, only through performing this final step can we fully appraise a program's effectiveness, highlight its weaknesses, and begin to develop information that will aid us in determining whether the development should be continued or how it can be improved.

The management development process reiterates a number of points that we have expanded on previously. Specifically, it depends on knowledge of the organization's objectives, development of management inventories, and evaluation of programs to appraise their effectiveness. The one issue we have not discussed, and which is obviously the central focus in the management development process, is the programs themselves. Let us now take a look at various methods for developing executives.

Methods For Developing Managers

On-the-Job Development

The development of a manager's abilities can take place on the job. We will review four popular on-the-job techniques: coaching, understudy assignments, job rotation, and committee assignments.

Coaching   *Coaching.*   When a manager takes an active role in guiding another manager, we refer to this activity as coaching. Just as track coaches observe, analyze, and attempt to improve the performance of their athletes, "coaches" on the job can do the same. The effective coach, whether on the track or in the corporate hierarchy, gives guid-

---

[7]George C. Thorton and William C. Byham, *Assessment Centers and Management Performance* (New York: Academic Press, 1982).

ance through direction, advice, criticism, and suggestions in an attempt to aid the growth of the employee.[8]

The technique of managers coaching other managers has the advantages that go with learning by doing, particularly the opportunities for high interaction and rapid feedback on performance. Unfortunately, its two strongest disadvantages are (1) its tendencies to perpetuate the current managerial styles and practices in the organization and (2) its heavy reliance on the coach's ability to be a good teacher. In the same way that we recognize that all excellent sprinters do not make outstanding coaches, we cannot expect that all excellent managers will be effective coaches. An individual can become a good manager without necessarily possessing the knack of creating a proper learning environment for others to do the same. Thus the effectiveness of this technique relies on the ability of the "coach."

Understudy assignments

Understudy Assignments.   The summer months in an organization are characterized by a particular phenomenon: a rapid rise in the usage of understudy assignments, as development technique, to replace vacationing managers. By *understudy assignments,* we mean potential managers are given the opportunity to relieve an experienced manager of his or her job and act as his or her substitute during the period. This label also describes permanent "assistant to" positions as well as temporary opportunities to assist managers in completing their jobs.

As a staff assistant to a manager, the understudy gets the opportunity to learn the manager's job. However, it is not unusual that this merely becomes the performing of "paper shuffling" chores. Should this be the case, or should the manager be threatened by the understudy, the learning experience becomes quite limited. In contrast, in those organizations where managers recognize that their own promotion and advancement depends on preparing underlings to satisfactorily move into their jobs, managers are motivated to prepare their understudies for their current jobs.

The understudy who is thrown into the job for a short period of time is given the opportunity to see the job in total. While there are opportunities for sizable errors, the technique is used predominantly in situations where major or critical decisions can be delayed until the manager returns or can be made in close consultation with the manager next up in line.

Job rotation

Job Rotation.   Job rotation can be either horizontal or vertical. Vertical rotation is nothing more than promoting a worker into a new position. In this chapter, we will emphasize the horizontal dimension of job rotation, or what may be better understood as *lateral transfer.*

---

[8]Woodlands Group, "Management Development: Coach, Sponsor and Mentor," *Personnel Journal,* 59 (November 1980), 918–21.

FIGURE 10-5   "Why complain now? You should have asked what 'Special Assistant to the President' meant before you took the job."

Job rotation represents an excellent method for broadening the manager or potential manager, and for turning specialists into generalists. In addition to increasing the manager's experience and allowing the manager to absorb new information, it can reduce boredom and stimulate the development of new ideas. It can also provide opportunities for a more comprehensive and reliable evaluation of the manager by his or her supervisors.

Horizontal job transfers can be instituted (1) on a planned basis— that is, by means of a development program whereby the worker spends two or three months in an activity and is then moved on; or (2) on a situational basis—that is, by moving the person to another activity when the first is no longer challenging to him or her, or to meet the needs of work scheduling. In other words, people may be put in a continual transfer mode. As employed by many large organizations in their programs to develop managerial talent, rotation may include moving people between line and staff positions, often closely coordinated with understudy assignments.

The advantages of job rotation are many. As already mentioned, it broadens employees and increases their experience. Boredom and monotony, which develop after a person has acquired the skills necessary to perform a task effectively, are reduced when transfers are made frequently. Additionally, since job rotation permits a greater understanding of other activities within the organization, people are prepared more rapidly to assume greater responsibility, especially at the upper echelons. As one moves up the organization, it becomes increasingly necessary to understand the intricacies and interrelationships of activities, and these abilities can be more quickly acquired by moving about within the organization.

On the other hand, job rotation is not without its drawbacks. Development costs are increased, and productivity is reduced by moving a worker into a new position just when his or her efficiency at the prior job was creating organizational economies. An extensive rotation program can result in having a vast number of employees situated in a position where their job knowledge is very limited. And even though there may be significant long-term benefits from the program, the oganization must be equipped to deal with the day-to-day problems that result when inexperienced personnel perform new tasks, and when rotated managers make decisions based on little knowledge of the activity at hand. Finally, job rotation can also demotivate intelligent and aggressive trainees who seek specific responsibility in their chosen specialty.

Committee assignments

Committee Assignments.   Assignment to a committee can provide an opportunity for the employee to share in managerial decision making, to learn by watching others, and to investigate specific organizational problems. When committees are of an "ad hoc" or temporary nature, they often take on task force activities designed to delve into a particular problem, ascertain alternative solutions, and make a recommendation for implementing a solution. These temporary assignments can be both interesting and rewarding to the employee's growth.

Appointment to permanent committees increases the employee's exposure to other members of the organization, broadens his or her understanding, and provides an opportunity to grow and make recommendations under the scrutiny of other committee members.

Off-the-Job Development

There are a wealth of management development techniques that personnel can partake in off the job. We will briefly discuss four of the more popular ones: sensitivity training, transactional analysis, lecture courses, and simulation exercises.

Sensitivity training

Sensitivity Training.   Sensitivity training in "encounter groups" became quite popular during the 1950s as a method of changing behavior through group processes. Often referred to as laboratory training, it influences the participants through unstructured group interaction. Members are brought together in a free and open environment in which participants discuss themselves and their interactive process, loosely facilitated by a professional behavioral scientist. This professional then creates the opportunity for the participants to express their ideas, beliefs, and attitudes. He or she does not accept—in fact, overtly rejects—any leadership role.

The objectives of sensitivity training are to provide managers with increased awareness of their own behavior and of how others perceive them, greater sensitivity to the behaviors of others, and increased understanding of group processes. Specific results sought include increased ability to empathize with others, improved listening skills, greater openness, increased tolerance for individual differences, and improved conflict resolution skills.

Our general conclusion regarding sensitivity training is that the process does change behavior. However, serious side effects, such as the weakest individual in the group bearing the brunt of the complaints, can result. And, too, much of it is attempted by people who are not trained professionals. There is also considerable doubt as to whether the skills acquired are transferable to the workplace.

Transactional analysis

Transactional Analysis.   Transactional analysis (TA) is both an approach for defining and analyzing communication interaction between people and a theory of personality. The fundamental theory underlying TA holds that an individual's personality consists of three ego states—the parent, the child, and the adult. These labels have nothing to do with age, but rather with aspects of the ego.

The parent state is made up of one's attitudes and behavior incorporated from external sources. It is an ego state of authority and superiority. A person acting in a parent state is usually dominant, scolding, and otherwise authoritative. The child contains all the impulses that are natural to an infant. Acting in this state, the person can be obedient or manipulative; charming at one moment and repulsive the next. Whereas the parent acts as he or she was taught, the child is emotional and acts according to how he or she feels at the moment. The adult state is objective and rational. It deals with reality and objectively gathers information. Since it reasons and is reasonable, its actions are almost computerlike—processing data, estimating probabilities, and making decisions. In TA theory, the parent and child ego states feel and react directly, while the adult state thinks or processes transactional data logically before acting. In most situations, therefore, the ideal interaction is an adult stimulus, followed by an adult response.

Courses in TA have been given to executives of many organizations, including American Airlines, the Bank of America, Westinghouse, the U.S. Postal Service, and the Bank of New York. Although little substantive research has as yet been conducted on TA's effectiveness, responses to the courses have generally been favorable. Al-

TRANSACTIONAL ANALYSIS
INTERACTIONS

Effective

Let's meet next week to begin your
performance review for the past 3 months.

ADULT

Certainly, and I'll supply you with
copies of major activities/accom-
plishments for the period.

ADULT

Ineffective

Let's meet next week to begin your
performance review for the past 3 months.

ADULT

Why now. We've just completed the last
one. If you'd leave me alone so I could
work, I'd get much more accomplished.

CHILD

FIGURE 10-6   Transactional Analysis Interactions

though much of the support for TA is based on intuitive feel rather than on hard evidence, the TA experience may help managers understand others better and assist them in altering their responses so as to produce more effective results.

Lecture courses

Lecture Courses.   Formal lecture courses offer an opportunity for managers or potential managers to acquire knowledge and develop their conceptual and analytical abilities. In large organizations, these lecture courses may be offered "in-house" by the organization itself and supported by outside college course work. Small organizations will utilize courses offered in development programs at universities and colleges, and through consulting organizations. Often, college and university faculty are willing to provide specific courses to deal with the unique needs of an organization.

Simulation exercises

Simulation Exercises.   Simulations were introduced as a training technique. They are probably even more popular for management development. The more widely used simulation exercises include case study, decision games, and role plays.

The *case study* analysis approach to management development was popularized at the Harvard Graduate School of Business. Taken from the actual experiences of organizations, these cases represent attempts to describe, as accurately as possible, real problems that managers have faced. Trainees study the cases to determine problems, analyze causes, develop alternative solutions, select what they believe to be the best solution, and implement it.

Case study can provide stimulating discussions among participants, as well as excellent opportunities for individuals to defend their analytical and judgmental abilities. It appears to be a rather effective method for improving decision-making abilities within the constraints of limited information.

Simulated *decision games* and role-playing exercises put individuals in the role of acting out managerial problems. Games, which are frequently played on an electronic computer that has been programmed for the particular game, provide opportunities for individuals to make decisions and to consider the implications of a decision on other segments of the organization, with no adverse effect should the decision be a poor one.

Role playing allows the participants to act out problems and to deal with real people. Participants are assigned roles and are asked to react to one another as they would have to do in their managerial jobs. Role playing, when combined with modeling as presented in social-learning theory, has become increasingly popular as a development technique.[9] Trainees receive a list of about six "learning points" that describe key words or phrases to use during a typical manager-subordinate encounter. The trainees attempt, with the assistance of videotapes, to improve their managerial abilities by imitating models who have successfully mastered the learning points. This role-play modeling is reported to be practiced in more than three hundred companies. "Ford Motor Co., for one, has made it mandatory for all new supervisors, Lukens Steel Co. credits it with more than $1 million a year in productivity savings, and Weyerhauser Co. judges its results as 'superlative.'"[10]

The advantages to simulation are the opportunities to attempt to "create an environment" similar to real situations the managers incur, without the high costs involved should the actions prove undesirable. Of course, the disadvantages are the reverse of this: It is difficult to duplicate the pressures and realities of actual decision making on the job; and individuals often act differently in real-life situations than they do in acting out a simulated exercise.

Summary

While the development of managerial personnel in the past closely paralleled the profit picture of the firm, management development has recently experienced a resurgence. Top officers in organizations have realized that sound training efforts are needed to continue the development of personnel for future managerial positions. The continuity

---

[9]"Imitating Models: A New Management Tool," *Business Week*, May 8, 1978, pp. 119–20.

[10]Ibid., p. 119.

of management practice alone has justified the need for training as well as the concern for developing more effective managers.

Programs that are now being offered by the larger organizations are building on the American Management Association's "Principles of Professional Management." Targeted to provide information concerning planning, organizing, leading, controlling, and decision making, these management development programs are serving as a means to ensure more effective management.

Additionally, many organizations are expanding their human resource development departments to provide in-house training programs for their managers. The focal point of these efforts is to produce managers who have the necessary skills to do their job, leading toward a more productive organization. These programs are usually offered in response to an assessed need for a particular skill. For example, Blue Cross and Blue Shield of Maryland has begun to work on more activities that require assistance from people from different departments. This project management approach identified a training need for project management skills, or working on a team project rather than a department project. The needs for managing the project, assigning task responsibilities, managing resources (especially those not directly under one's control), and influencing people became apparent. Subsequently, a training program was designed to meet this assessed need. Only by assessing the needs of the organization and designing training programs to meet those needs can a training department, and ultimately the organization, become more effective.

The designs of the management development programs vary widely, as do the employee training methods. But one point should be noted: Managers, for the most part, may be skeptical about the training. Thus the training design must be such that it encourages learning in a nonthreatening manner. Experiential learning exercises, cases, and role playing appear to meet the requirement. Note too that the programs must be geared toward the adult learner. In adult learning, the trainer provides some learning concept in such a way that the participants can experience the idea, analyze it, and ultimately put it into action. Accordingly, management development trainers do not train; they facilitate the enhancement of a manager's current skills.

Many of the programs designed for managers include some type of pencil-and-paper assessment of their personal styles. These assessments can focus on such areas as communications, openness for feedback, motivation, openness for change, or worker versus manager preference. Once the assessment has been made, the facilitator processes that information with each individual. The theory behind many of these assessments is that individuals must understand themselves before embarking on new avenues.

Note again that these development efforts are, or should be, the result of the assessed need. Our last point in this section is to identify

FIGURE 10-7

Sources of Developmental Needs	
Reaction to Problem Areas	81%
Projected Personnel Requirements	74%
Personnel changes, Promotions, etc.	70%
Unit Performance	64%
Internal changes	62%
External changes	55%
Established Development Policies	47%
Other	17%

SOURCE: L. A. Digman, "How Companies Assess Management Development Needs" (Detroit: Academy of Management Proceedings, 1980), p. 102.

how organizations determine the need for management development. Earlier we addressed a more comprehensive framework for determining the need of management development: reviewing organizational objectives, appraising current management resources, identifying development needs, and engaging in development activities. In practice, however, there seems to be less reliance on the comprehensive approach. A study published in 1980 indicated that organizations "rely on higher-level input, management judgment and performance appraisal data."[11] The areas that gained the most attention as a result of some problem are presented in Figure 10-7.

Therefore large organizations seem to be providing some form of management development. While we have little or no evidence concerning practices in small organizations, it is logical to surmise that development programs in these companies are predominantly restricted to on-the-job activities and formal courses offered through such institutions as colleges, universities, or the American Management Association. Finally, it appears that the decision for development needs may be more upper-management driven than based on the comprehensive framework described.

Evaluating Training Effectiveness

In Chapter 8, we discussed the effectiveness of selection devices. We were concerned, for example, with whether employment tests actually differentiated between satisfactory and unsatisfactory job performers. This same concern for effectiveness arises when we discuss training or development activities. It is not enough to merely assume that any training an organization offers is effective. We need to develop substantive data to determine whether our training effort is achieving

[11]L. A. Digman, "How Companies Assess Management Development Needs" (Detroit: Academy of Management Proceedings, 1980), p. 102.

its goals; that is, if it is correcting the deficiencies in skills, knowledge, or attitudes that were assessed as needing attention. Note too that the funding of training and development programs is expensive—estimated to exceed $100 billion annually for American workers.[12] The costs incurred alone justify evaluating the effectiveness.

It is often easy to generate a new training program, but if the training effort is not evaluated, it becomes possible to rationalize any employee-training efforts. To avoid the uncontrolled expansion of training costs, management must insist on a thorough cost-benefit evaluation to ensure that training dollars generate satisfactory returns.

Because of the assumption by many managers and training directors that any type of training is worthwhile, training programs may not be as effective as they could be. It is impossible to claim that training, in and of itself, is effective unless it is evaluated. If those responsible for training are convinced that every training program being offered is "good," it is a reasonable bet that little evaluation is taking place, and it is very possible that the actual training could be improved. While we know training *can be* effective in assisting management in attaining its goals, the issue of whether it *is* effective is often more a matter of opinion than of fact.

Can we generalize as to how training programs are typically evaluated? The following is probably generalizable across organizations: Several senior managers, a few managers in the field, and a group of workers who have recently completed a training program are asked for their opinions. If the comments are generally positive, the program gets a favorable evaluation and the organization continues it until someone in a position of authority decides, for whatever reason, it should be eliminated or replaced. Opinions and judgments dominate the evaluation.

There can be no question that training programs vary substantially in their effectiveness. Unfortunately, only a few of these programs are comprehensively appraised. That is, not enough evidence is developed in most cases to support or negate the value that training has had on worker performance.

We have argued the point that evaluation is important and opinions of trainees or managers appear to be more prevalent than rigorous evaluation. The reactions of participants or managers, while easy to acquire, are the least valid. These opinions are heavily influenced by factors that may have little to do with the training's effectiveness—things like difficulty, entertainment value, or personality characteristics of the instructor. Therefore let us direct our attention to three approaches, each of which offers improvement over subjective opinions.

[12]Wayne F. Casio and G. Ronald Gilbert, "Making Dollars and Sense out of Management Development" (Detroit: Academy of Management Proceedings, 1980), p. 95.

Test-retest method

The first approach is referred to as the test-retest method. Participants are given a test before they begin the program. After the program is completed, the participants retake the test. The difficulty arises in attempting to substantiate that changes in the test scores will be reflected in performance and that whatever change has occurred can be fully attributed to the instruction. The test may not be valid but, more importantly, increases in test scores may be due to causes other than the training given.

Pre-post performance method

The utilization of tests as proxies for job performance creates the opportunity for error. Our second approach, the *pre-post performance method*, is designed to correct this error. In this method, each participant is evaluated prior to training and rated on actual job performance. After instruction is completed, the participant is reevaluated. As with the test-retest method, the increase is assumed to be attributed to the instruction. However, in contrast to test-retest, the pre-post performance method deals directly with job behavior.

Experimental-control-group method

The most sophisticated evaluative approach is the *experimental control-group method*. Two groups are established—comparable as to skills, intelligence, and learning abilities—and evaluated on actual job performance. Members of the control group work on the job but do *not* undergo instruction. The experimental group is given the instruction. At the conclusion of training, the two groups are reevaluated. If the training is really effective, the experimental group's performance will have improved, and its performance will be substantially better than that of the control group. This approach attempts to correct for factors other than the instruction program that influence job performance.

Of the three methods mentioned, the experimental-control-group method is preferred. But costs, time, and questions about the ethical activity of withholding training from some employees may make this method inappropriate. Does this imply, then, that we should risk the evaluation of training effectiveness on subjective measures alone? No, but let us keep the opinions and build on them. Within the evaluation, we should assess four areas: trainee reaction, learning, behavior, and results.[13] The trainees' reaction includes our subjective assessment. In this phase, we need to know if the objectives of the program were consistent with the expectations of the participants. If the trainees perceive that the training program was ineffective, this should immediately raise a red flag about the program. As we stated earlier, an excellent reaction by the participants may indicate the session had an entertainment value, and therefore the excellent rating is not an accurate evaluation. However, a majority of the participants indicating that a program was a waste of time does, in fact, carry some weight

[13]Donald L. Kirkpatrick, "Evaluating In-House Training Programs," *Training and Development Journal*, 32 (September 1978), 6–9.

in determining effectiveness. If the participants were bored, or the material was not clearly taught, learning will not take place.

The learning criterion is an attempt to assess whether the skills and knowledge that were to have been taught were, in fact, acquired by the trainees. Testing may help to indicate if this occurred. The behavior change criterion attempts to look at how the trainee acts back on the job after training has taken place. Most learning results in some type of outward action, and this action is exemplified in one's behavior. For example, suppose a manager is having difficulty in giving feedback to his subordinates. This lack of communication has caused frustration among them. To help with this problem, the manager is enrolled in a communications course that trains participants in the act of giving and receiving feedback. The experiential approach is perceived as enjoyable by the manager, whose reaction to the program is positive. Has the program been effective? A follow-up evaluation on the manager's progress reveals that he is putting into practice (behavior) the skills he was taught in the training program (learning). Accordingly, the training program appears to have been effective so far.

Our last criterion is results. Here we try to measure those quantifiable factors that are attributable to the training program. In revisiting our manager, we find that the morale of his employees is better, productivity has increased, and complaints about the manager have decreased significantly (results).

Although this scenario is simplistic, its point is clear. Every training program can be evaluated by its effectiveness. We can also take the evaluation one step further and quantify the effectiveness of the training program.[14]

To conduct this analysis, we need to generate three measures: cost, change, and impact. The *costs* are those monetary outlays for providing the training—consultant fees, room rentals, supplies, salaries of the training department, and overhead. We can then determine a cost per trainee trained. The *change* factor looks at the difference between what one knew after the training as compared with before the training. This knowledge change can then be expressed as a ratio and can be obtained through pretesting and posttesting. The change factors could also be expressed in behavioral, attitude, or performance terms. The last factor, *impact*, tries to show what change was solely attributed to the training program. It measures "after training results" (i.e., results that can be measured—increased morale/productivity) to "before training status" (measured results prior to training).

This last ratio, impact, will determine the training effectiveness. If quantifiable differences are measured and recorded, and the ratio

---

[14]This material was adapted from the Saratoga Institute, "Quantifying Personnel's Return on Investment," American Society for Personnel Administration (Washington, D.C., 1979), Sec. T.

VIEWS IN THE NEWS

Evaluating Training: Common Problems

The costs associated with training and development warrants an accurate evaluation of the effectiveness of the training programs by human resources. Unfortunately, trainers often do not pay enough attention to this detail and, accordingly, cannot substantiate their training efforts. This can, and often does, lead to the reduction of training efforts when budgetary constraints dictate cutting costs. Many of these training cuts could be averted, if only human resources could show the worth of providing the workshops.

Even where some attempts at evaluating training programs are made, these evaluations often focus on criteria that do not provide an accurate picture of the benefits of training. Nine common errors that occur in evaluating training programs are listed below.

- Asking the Wrong Questions
  —Questions focusing on entertainment value of the program
  —Questions on skill gains that are not behaviorally identifiable
- Questioning the Wrong Areas
  —Obtaining information on a self appraisal basis may be unreliable or invalid
  —Failure to obtain input from superiors and subordinates on the behavioral changes noticed due to training
- Failure to Control for Extraneous Factors
  —Other factors can enter into, and distort the evaluation of training effectiveness
- Failure to Use Appropriate Control Group
  —Failure to randomly assign individuals to training programs may affect the evaluation
- Failure to Assure High Quality Data Collection Efforts
  —Non responses from participants results in missing data
- Failure to make Appropriate Statistical Adjustments
  —Evaluation may be biased
- Failure to Report the Results of the Evaluation in Terms that are Meaningful to the Intended Audience
  —Wrong information may have been collected
  —Report written in technical jargon
- Magnifying the Findings and Ignoring the Potential Problems
  —Reporting on the positive findings, not the areas that may be in need of improvement
- Over-generalizing the Findings
  —Implications that what works in one organization may work in another

Source: Darlene F. Russ-Eft and John H. Zenger, "Common Mistakes in Evaluating Training Effectiveness," *Personnel Administrator,* 30, No. 4 (April 1985), 57–62.

* * * * *

THE BEST MINUTE
I SPEND

IS THE ONE I INVEST
IN PEOPLE

* * * * *

FIGURE 10-8

SOURCE: Kenneth Blanchard and Spencer Johnson, *The One Minute Manager* (New York: Morrow, 1982).

is positive (remember that a reduction of a negative is a positive also), then the program is effective and a justifiable expenditure.

In summary, evaluating a training program's effectiveness need not be subjective only. There are means of making an objective assessment. However, the objective assessment takes time and energy if it is done correctly.

Conclusion

Throughout this chapter, we have discussed the need for training and development activities in organizations, as well as the expected outcomes from such endeavors. In practice, however, it is not uncommon for individuals to be sent to or to attend training and development events as a reward for past good work. While recognizing that good work has its merits, it is our premise that sending employees to a training program as a reward rather than to fulfill a training or development need undermines good training and development practices.

SUMMARY

1. Employee training has become increasingly important as jobs have become more sophisticated and influenced by technological changes.

2. Training is a learning experience that seeks a relatively permanent change in an individual that will improve his or her ability to perform on the job.

3. An effective training program should be consistent with the following learning principles:
   a. Learning is enhanced when the learner is motivated.
   b. Learning requires feedback.
   c. Reinforcement increases the likelihood that a learned behavior will be repeated.
   d. Practice increases a learner's performance.
   e. Learning begins rapidly, then plateaus.
   f. Learning must be transferable to the job.

4. An organization's training needs will evolve from asking these questions:
   a. What are the organization's goals?
   b. What tasks must be completed to achieve these goals?
   c. What behaviors are necessary for each job incumbent to complete his or her assigned tasks?
   d. What deficiencies, if any, do incumbents have in the skills, knowledge, or attitudes required to perform the necessary behaviors?

5. Formal training methods can be classified as
   a. *On-the-job training,* including apprenticeships and job instruction training
   b. *Off-the-job training,* including lectures, conferences, films, simulation exercises, and programmed instruction

6. Management development, in contrast to employee training, is more future oriented and concerned with education.

7. Management development expenditures may be for purposes other than those immediately apparent. In certain instances, development programs may be used to motivate managers or maintain their commitment.

8. On-the-job management development techniques include
   a. Coaching
   b. Understudy assignments
   c. Job rotation
   d. Committee assignments

9. Off-the-job management development techniques include
   a. Sensitivity training

  b. Transactional analysis
  c. Lecture courses
  d. Simulation exercises

10. Critical to any training activity is proper effectiveness evaluation. Evaluation methods can be classified as
  a. Reactions of participants or managers
  b. Test-retest method
  c. Pre-post performance method
  d. Experimental-control method

11. Evaluation criteria include reaction, learning, behavior, and results.

KEY TERMS

Apprenticeship
Coaching
Computer modeling
Experiential exercise
Feedback
Job instruction training (JIT)
Job rotation
Learning curve
Management development
Programmed instruction

Roles
Sensitivity training
Simulation
Social-learning theory
Training
Transactional analysis (TA)
Transfer learning
Understudy assignments
Vestibule training

QUESTIONS FOR REVIEW

1. What is social-learning theory? How does it relate to training?
2. What is a learning curve? What are its implications for training?
3. What kinds of signals can warn a manager that employee training may be necessary?
4. What role do goals play in training?
5. Contrast apprenticeship programs with job instructional training.
6. What is a simulation exercise? Give some examples.
7. Contrast employee training with management development training.
8. Contrast case studies, decision games, and role plays as development methods.
9. Why is the evaluation of training effectiveness necessary?
10. Define *reactions, learning, behavior,* and *results* as they apply to evaluating training effectiveness. Give an example of each.

QUESTIONS FOR DISCUSSION

1. Training programs are frequently the first items eliminated when management wants to cut costs. Why do you believe this occurs?

2. Describe how selection and training are related. Socialization and training.

3. "You can't develop managers. People either have the ability to manage or they don't." Do you agree or disagree? Discuss.

4. "Management development should downplay job knowledge and leadership abilities and emphasize the ethical issues in managerial decision making." Do you agree or disagree? Discuss.

5. What criteria would you use to determine whether a training program was effective?

CONTINUING CASE: Concord General

We Do It Our Way

John Michaels has decided that, in order to ensure a properly staffed Cardiac Surgery Unit, the hospital would have to provide its own training program. Jim and Judy have agreed that three nurses currently assigned to the area should be sent for a retraining of their skills and should then be utilized as in-house trainers. These nurses have agreed to assume the new duties and have also persuaded Dr. William Aorta, the chief cardiac surgery doctor, to participate.

Working with Dr. Aorta, Sally, Bonnie, and Jean were able to establish the procedures that he uses. They have also recently attended another hospital's training program and are ready to begin training the new nurses. Each, incidentally, has been certified by the State Board of Examiners as a qualified trainer.

With everything seemingly going as planned, Sally asked Bonnie, "Do you have any idea how we'll set this up? We know what to do and how to do it, but where and using what type of training approach is best?"

Before Bonnie had a chance to answer, Jean chimed in: "I overheard your concerns, Sally, and I think I have a solution. You see, my brother is the training director for Bethlehem Steel, and he has given me some advice. He suggests that we consider removing the trainees from the unit initially, for the formal education part of the session. Then we should provide actual hands-on experience for the nurses, each of us taking the trainee under our wing for six weeks while we perform the actual nursing duties."

"That sounds great, Jean," said Sally, "but what about the costs? This hospital will not go for six nurses working in a unit where only three are needed."

"You may be right, Sally, but they have to make that decision."

Questions

1. What types of training programs have been identified in the case?
2. How would you structure the sessions? What types of training do you believe would work best? Why?
3. Do you believe that the cost of Jean's proposed training method would be prohibitive? Discuss.
4. Justify your types of training (question 2) with regard to cost/benefit.

CASE APPLICATION

Management Stars Aren't Born— They're Nurtured!

The Barbara Wright story is in the true Hollywood tradition. After graduating from the University of Connecticut, Barbara married a young lawyer and taught high-school English. The marriage soon ended in divorce, and she began selling Avon products to support herself. In her late twenties, she went to New York and began her career in the computer industry as a five-dollar-an-hour keypunch operator. From there she progressed to computer analyst and computer programmer, and then to director of the company's electronic data processing. After six years as director, Barbara became one of the company's two senior vice-presidents. In June 1987, at the age of thirty-five, her ten-year climb up the executive ladder culminated in her being selected as president of the $150-million-a-year company, where she was responsible for making decisions. Her annual salary was $700,000, with bonus opportunities capable of pushing her yearly compensation toward $1 million.

How did Barbara Wright get so far so fast? Obviously, she has been successful at whatever she has undertaken. For instance, she was a major force in developing software packages that were IBM compatible. But she is also an effective manager. Her reputation for being highly organized is well known in the industry. She regularly handles about two hundred phone calls a day and reads several corporate reports each night before going to bed. Colleagues openly talk about her ability to pinpoint problems in a project and to offer solid solutions.

In an industry known for male domination, Barbara Wright's rise to head of a major computer company is remarkable. Of course, being bright, competent, and a hard worker is often not enough. In her case, some credit should be given to the support of Charlie Burnsides, her former college professor at the University of Connecticut. Professor Burnsides often advised and counseled Barbara. As her mentor, he could point out the "ropes to skip and the ropes to know."

Questions

1. How did Barbara Wright's background aid her progress up the executive ladder? How might it have hindered her?
2. If Barbara were concerned with bringing more women into top-management positions in the company, what actions might she take?
3. What advice would you give an aspiring female manager about climbing the corporate ladder?

ADDITIONAL READINGS

BOLT, JAMES F., "Taylor Executive Development to Strategy," *Harvard Business Review,* November–December 1985, pp. 168–76.

KIZILOS, TOLLY, and ROGER P. HEINISCH, "How a Management Team Selects Managers," *Harvard Business Review,* September–October 1986, pp. 6–12.

SULTON, CHARLOTTE DECKER, and KRIS K. MOORE, "Executive Women 20 Years Later," *Harvard Business Review,* September–October 1985, pp. 42–66.

TYSON, LYNNE A., and HERMAN BIRNBRAUER, "High Quality Evaluation," *Training and Development Journal,* September 1985, pp. 33–37.

WEXLEY, KENNETH N., and TIMOTHY T. BALDWIN, "Management Development," *1986 Yearly Review of Management of the Journal of Management,* 12, No. 2 (1986), 277–94.

CHAPTER 11

Career

Development

AFTER READING THIS CHAPTER, YOU WILL BE ABLE TO:

1. Define *career*
2. Discuss the outcomes of an effective organizational career development program
3. Identify the five stages involved in a career
4. Discuss career development techniques
5. Explain the three-step individual career development process
6. Analyze career opportunities for the post–baby boom group

Most college freshmen are majoring in initials—embarked on a course to gain an M.D., Ph.D., L.L.B., or C.P.A.

—Anonymous

Jack Phillips recently refused a promotion with his company because it would have meant he would have to move to another city. Maria Rodriguez similarly turned down a promotion with her firm, which would have meant significantly more responsibility and a $12,000-a-year pay increase, because her husband could not find an appropriate position in the new city. A major midwestern oil company executive recently remarked about the difficulty he was having in finding qualified minorities and women within his firm to fill anticipated vacancies in middle and upper management. An executive with a large government agency complains that she has a large number of stagnant personnel who not only have no potential for advancement but have difficulty performing their current jobs satisfactorily.

What do each of the above examples have in common? They reflect the new and unexpected complexities that managers must now confront in their efforts to mobilize and manage their human resources. The traditional views that every employee would jump at the chance for a promotion, that competent people would somehow emerge within the organization to fill vacancies that arose, or that a valuable employee would *always* be a valuable employee are no longer true. Lifestyles are changing. We are becoming increasingly aware of the different needs and aspirations of employees. If managers are to be assured that they will have competent and motivated people to fill the organization's future needs, they should be increasingly concerned with matching the career needs of employees with the requirements of the organization.

What Is A Career?

Definition

The term *career* has a number of meanings. In popular usage it can mean advancement ("his career is progressing nicely"), a profession ("she has chosen a career in medicine"), or a lifelong sequence of jobs ("his career has included fifteen jobs in six different organizations"). For our purposes, we will define *career* as "a sequence of positions occupied by a person during the course of a lifetime."[1] Utilizing this definition, it is apparent that we all have or will have careers. The concept is as relevant to transient, unskilled laborers as it is to engineers or physicians. Importantly, it does not imply advancement nor success or failure. For our purposes, therefore, *any* work, paid or unpaid, pursued over an extended period of time, can constitute a career. In addition to formal job work, it may include schoolwork, homemaking, or volunteer work.[2]

Individual versus Organizational Perspective

Careres

The study of careers takes on a very different orientation depending on whether it is viewed from the perspective of the organization or the individual. A key question in career development, then, is, With whose interests are we concerned?

Organization career development

From an organization or managerial standpoint, career development involves tracking career paths. Management seeks information so it can direct and monitor the progress of minorities and women, and to ensure capable managerial and technical talent will be available to meet the organization's needs.

Individual career development

In contrast, individual career development focuses on assisting individuals to identify their major career goals and to determine what they need to do to achieve these goals. Notice, in the latter case, the focus is entirely on the individual and includes his or her career outside the organization as well as inside. So while organizational career development looks at individuals filling the needs of the organization, individual career development addresses each individual's personal work career irrespective of where this work is performed. For instance, an excellent employee, when assisted in better understanding his or her needs and aspirations through interest inventories, life planning analysis, and counseling, may even decide to leave the organization if it becomes apparent that career aspirations can best be achieved outside the employing organization.

Both of these approaches have value. We would like to think that this chapter blends the interests of both the individual within the organization and the organization itself. However, since the primary orientation of human resource management is toward the interests of the organization, it is to the needs of the latter that we will tend to direct our attention.

[1] Donald E. Super and Douglas T. Hall, "Career Development: Exploration and Planning," in *Annual Review of Psychology*, Mark R. Rosenzweig and Lyman W. Porter (Palo Alto: Annual Reviews Inc., 1978), XXIX, 334.

[2] Douglas T. Hall, *Careers in Organizations* (Santa Monica, Calif.: Goodyear, 1976), pp. 3–4.

FIGURE 11-1

SOURCE: Copyright © 1977 United Feature Syndicate, Inc. With permission.

Career Development versus Personnel Development

Given the extensive discussion in the previous chapters on personnel development, you may be wondering what, if any, differences there are between career development and employee or management development. These topics have a common element, but there is one distinct difference—their time frame.

Career development

Career development looks at the long-term career effectiveness and success of organizational personnel. In contrast, the kinds of development discussed in the preceding chapter focus on work effectiveness or performance in the immediate or intermediate time frame.

Personnel development

These two chapters are closely linked; employee training and management development effort should be compatible with an individual's career development in the organization. But a successful career program should look toward developing people for the long-term needs of the organization and be capable of dealing with the dynamic changes that will take place, over time, in attempting to match individual abilities and aspirations with the needs of the organization.

The Value of Effective Career Development

Assuming that an organization already provides extensive employee and management development programs, why should it need to consider a career development program as well? A long-term career focus should increase the organization's effectiveness in managing its human resources. More specifically, we can identify several positive results that can accrue from a well-designed career development program.

Ensuring needed talent

Ensures Needed Talent Will Be Available.   Career development efforts are consistent with, and a natural extension of, human resource planning. Changing staff requirements over the intermediate and long term should be identified in human resource planning. Working with individual employees to help them better align their needs and aspirations with those of the organization will increase the probability that the right people will be available to meet the orgnization's changing staffing requirements.

Assisting in attracting and retaining personnel

Improves the Organization's Ability to Attract and Retain High-Talent Personnel.   Outstanding employees will always be scarce, and they usually find there is considerable competition to secure their services. Such individuals may give preference to employers who demonstrate a concern for their employees' future. If already employed by an organization that offers career advice, these people may exhibit greater loyalty and commitment to their employer. Importantly, career development appears to be a natural response to the rising concern by employees for the quality of work life and personal life planning. As more and more people seek jobs that offer challenge, responsibility, and opportunities for advancement, realistic career planning becomes increasingly necessary. Additionally, social values have changed so that a larger segment of the work force no longer look at their work in isolation. Their work must be compatible with their personal and family interests and commitments. Again, career development should result in a better individual-organization match for such individuals and lead to less turnover.

Ensuring growth opportunities for all employees

Ensures That Minorities and Women Get Opportunities for Growth and Development.   As discussed in previous chapters, equal employment opportunity legislation and affirmative action programs demand that minority groups and women get opportunities for growth and development that will prepare them for greater responsibilities within the organization. Minorities and women are asking for career development assistance. Furthermore, the courts frequently are looking at an organization's career development efforts with these groups in ruling on discrimination suits.

Reduces Employee Frustration.   As the educational level of the work force has risen, so has its occupational aspirations. Unfortunately, the late 1970s and early 1980s were characterized by a slowing of economic growth and reduced advancement opportunities. The result was increased frustration by employees when they saw a significant disparity between their aspirations and actual opportunities. Career counseling can result in more realistic, rather than raised, employee expectations.

External versus Internal Dimensions to a Career

Every individual's career has two dimensions or components. One, called the external dimension, is realistic and objective while the other, the internal dimension, represents the individual's subjective perceptions.[3] Let us briefly describe each, consider the value in distinguishing between the two, and the importance of achieving a successful match.

External dimensions in career development

The external dimension in a career represents the objective progression of steps through a given occupation. It may be very explicit, as it is for the physician who moves from an undergraduate program, to medical school, and then through an internship, residency, licensing, hospital affiliation or private practice, and so forth. But it need not be an upward progression. For instance, an automobile factory worker achieves visible progression, though not necessarily upward. He gets a higher rating or classification, an increase in pay, greater seniority, less physically demanding work, or the opportunity to train new employees. The relevant point is that each of these steps is objective and explicit.

Internal dimensions in career development

The internal dimension in a career is a subjective concept of progression. This concept of a career may be very vague, as when one has the general ambition to "get ahead." Of course, it might also be a very specific ambition of being a vice-president at Alcoa, making $100,000 a year by the age of forty. Importantly, the internal and external dimensions may equate; that is, one's perceptions align with reality. But the two frequently diverge.

What is the importance of viewing a career along these two dimensions? We have to recognize that the major influence on individuals' attitudes and behavior will not be objective reality, but rather their subjective perception of their career relative to their expectations. Complaining about one's work, demonstrating strong commitment, exhibiting high motivation, having a number of absences, or resigning from the organization are frequently responses to one's subjective perceptions about work and career development. The actual reality means little. The internal-external dichotomy can explain, for example, how one twenty-five-year-old woman can be enthusiastic and highly satisfied with a $20,000-a-year job as a cost accounting supervisor while another twenty-five-year-old woman, in the same job and earning the same pay, feels trapped. The first may perceive the job as a natural step in her long-term goal to senior management while the other perceives this same job as a dead end. Though both may have identical external career patterns, they react in response to the internal or subjective perception. So, regardless of what an organization may be objectively doing to develop the careers of its employees, successful career development demands that attention also be given to how employees perceive their career relative to their expectations.

A career development program must consider the aspirations of each employee and the organizational opportunities that realistically

[3]John Van Maanen and Edgar H. Schein, "Career Development," in *Improving Life at Work*, ed. J. Richard Hackman and J. Lloyd Suttle (Santa Monica, Calif.: Goodyear, 1977), pp. 46–54.

can be expected to evolve for each. Failure to match the internal career sought by the employee and the external career offered by the organization will result in suboptimal management of human resources. A twenty-one-year-old college graduate who joins General Motors with the aspiration of some day reaching the presidency will have to get a promotion every two or three years to achieve that end. General Motors has a responsibility to make this reality clear to ambitious junior employees. In contrast, another twenty-one-year-old entering a medium-sized supermarket chain with his eyes on the firm's presidency may need only three or four promotions to reach his goal. With realistic career counseling, the GM employee should understand that failure to obtain a promotion within three years may be a serious threat to his ultimate ambition. Similarly, realistic career counseling should indicate that the lack of a promotion within the same time period at the supermarket chain in no way hinders one's chances to reach the presidency. Since progression timetables differ from organization to organization, the successful matching of internal and external careers should result in the more effective management of human resources.

Career Stages

Career stages   The most popular way for analyzing and discussing careers is to look at them as made up of stages.[4] In this section, we will propose a five-stage model that is generalizable to most people during their adult years, regardless of the type of work they do.

We begin to form our careers during our elementary and secondary school years. Our careers begin to wind down as we reach retirement age. We can identify five career stages that most of us have gone through or will go through during these years: exploration, establishment, mid-career, late career, and decline. These stages are depicted in Figure 11-2.

For most of us, the age ranges for each stage in Figure 11-2 are generally accurate. Of course, for some individuals, pursuing certain careers, this model is too simplistic and must be significantly modified. The key is to give your primary attention to the stages rather than the age categories. For instance, someone who makes a dramatic change in a career to undertake a completely different line of work at age forty-five will have many of the same establishment-stage concerns as someone starting at age twenty-five. On the other hand, if the forty-

---

[4]See, for example, Donald E. Super, *The Psychology of Careers* (New York: Harper & Row, 1957); Edgar H. Schein, "The Individual, the Organization, and the Career: A Conceptual Scheme," *Journal of Applied Behavioral Science*, 7 (1971), 401–26; and Daniel J. Levinson, C. M. Darrow, E. B. Klein, M. H. Levinson, and B. McKee, "The Psychological Development of Men in Early Adulthood and the Mid-Life Transition," in *Life History Research in Psychopathology*, ed. D. F. Ricks, A. Thomas, and M. Roff (Minneapolis: University of Minnesota Press, 1974), Vol. 3.

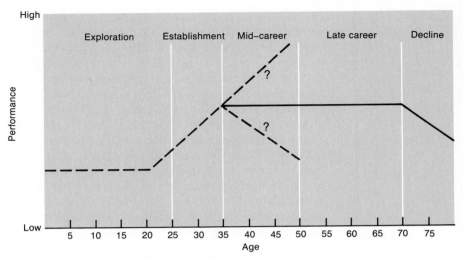

FIGURE 11-2   Stages in Career Development

SOURCE: Adapted from D. E. Super and D. T. Hall, "Career Development: Exploration and Planning," in *Annual Review of Psychology*, ed. M. R. Rosenzweig and L. W. Porter (Palo Alto, Calif.: Annual Reviews, Inc., 1978), XXIX, 35.

five-year-old first started working at age twenty-five, he or she now has twenty years experience as well as interests and expectations that differ from those of a peer who is just starting a career at middle-age. To illustrate, a thirty-five-year-old full professor is more like a fifty-five-year-old full professor than a thirty-five-year-old graduate student! However, for the large majority of us, the model in Figure 11-2 will have considerable relevancy.

Exploration

Exploration   Many of the critical choices individuals make about their careers are made prior to ever entering the work force on a paid basis. Our relatives, teachers, and friends, as well as what we see on television and in films, very early in our lives begin to narrow our alternatives and lead us in certain directions. Certainly the careers of our parents, their interests, their aspirations for their children, and their financial resources will be heavy factors in determining our perception of what careers are available or what schools, colleges, or universities we might consider.

The exploration period ends for most of us in our mid-twenties as we make the transition from school to work. From an organizational standpoint, therefore, this stage has the least relevance, since it occurs prior to employment. It is, of course, not *ir*relevant. The exploration period is a time when a number of expectations about one's career are developed, many of which are unrealistic. Such expectations, of course, may lie dormant for years and then pop up later to frustrate both the employee and the employer.

Establishment

Establishment

The establishment period begins with the search for work and includes getting your first job, being accepted by your peers, learning the job, and gaining the first tangible evidence of success or failure in the "real world." It is a time that begins with uncertainties and anxieties. Additionally, it is marked by the making of mistakes, the learning from these mistakes, and the gradual assumption of increased responsibilities. However, individuals in this stage have yet to reach their peak productivity, and rarely are they given work assignments that carry great power or high status.

Mid-Career

Mid-career

Most people do not face their first severe career dilemmas until they reach the mid-career stage. This is a time where individuals may continue their prior improvements in performance, level off, or begin to deteriorate. At this stage, the first dilemma is accepting that one is no longer seen as a "learner." Mistakes carry greater penalties. At this point in a career, one is expected to have moved beyond apprenticeship to journeyman status. To those who make the successful transition go greater responsibilities and rewards. For others, it may be a time of reassessment, job changes, adjustment of priorities, or the pursuit of alternative life styles (such as making a major geographical move or going back to college).

Late Career

Late career

For those who continue to grow through the mid-career stage, the late career usually is a pleasant time when one is allowed the luxury to relax a bit and enjoy playing the part of the elder statesman. It is a time where one can rest on one's laurels and bask in the respect given by younger employees. During the late career, individuals are no longer learning nor is it expected that they should be trying to outdo their levels of performance from previous years. Their value to the organization lies heavily in their judgment, built up over many years and through varied experiences, and sharing with and teaching others based on the knowledge they have gained.

For those who have stagnated or deteriorated during the previous stage, the late career brings the reality that they will not have an everlasting impact or change the world as they had once thought. It is a time when individuals recognize that they have decreased work mobility and may be locked into their current job. One begins to look forward to retirement and the opportunities of doing something different. Life off the job is likely to carry far greater importance than it did in earlier years.

Decline

Decline   The final stage in one's career is difficult for everyone but, ironically, is probably hardest on those who have had continued successes in the earlier stages. After several decades of continued achievements and high levels of performance, the time has come for retirement. These individuals are forced to step out of the limelight and give up a major component of their identity. For the modest performers or those who have seen their performance deteriorate over the years, it may be a pleasant time. The frustrations that have been associated with work will be left behind.

Adjustments, of course, will have to be made regardless of whether one is leaving a sparkling career or a dismal career. The regimentation that work provided will no longer be there. Responsibilities will be fewer and life will be less structured. As a result, it is a difficult stage for anyone to confront.

Linking Career Dimensions With Stages

We can link the previous material on external and internal dimensions of careers with the five-stage model. As shown in Figure 11-3, there are dominant activities and perceptions at each stage.

What value is it to the manager to look at careers as having two dimensions and five stages? The answer is that it can help us to identify potential problems and opportunities. For instance, it should direct us to spotting those individuals in mid-career who are deteriorating and need some specific job training. Similarly, other individuals at the same stage, but whose performance has leveled off, may present a problem because they hold the same high expectations that they held fifteen years earlier. Even if they have an adequate performance record, it may be insufficient to match their aspirations. The perceptive manager should be aware of the value of realistic career counseling at this point as a means toward improving the stagnant employee's attitudes and possibly preventing a resignation. Additionally, viewing careers as having stages should make clear that early career anxieties, mid-career crises, or late-career depressions are not that unusual and that progressive organizations should work closely with employees when these maladies strike. To ignore these frequent problems might result in a significant loss in an employee's productivity, or even an unexpected resignation.

FIGURE 11-3

Linking Career Dimensions with Stages

STAGE	EXTERNAL DIMENSION	INTERNAL DIMENSION
Exploration	Advice and examples of relatives, teachers, and friends Actual successes and failures in school, sports, and hobbies Actual choice of educational path—vocational school, college, major, professional school	Development of self-image of what one "might" be, what sort of work would be fun Self-assessment of own talents and limitations Development of ambitions, goals, motives Tentative choices and commitments
Establishment	Explicit search for a job Acceptance of a job Induction and orientation Assignment to further training or first job Acquiring visible job and organizational membership trappings (ID card, parking sticker, uniform, organizational manual) First job assignment, meeting the boss and co-workers Learning period, indoctrination Period of full performance—"doing the job" Leveling off, transfer, and/or promotion	Shock of entering the "real world" Insecurity around new tasks of interviewing, applying, being tested, facing being turned down Making a "real" choice; take a job or not; which job; first commitment Expectation of being tested for the first time under *real* conditions Reality shock—what the work is really like, doing "the dirty work" Forming a career strategy, how "to make it"—working hard, finding mentors, conforming to organization, making a contribution Feeling of success or failure Decision to leave organization if things do not look positive Feeling of being accepted fully by the organization, "having made it"
Mid-Career	Assignment of more crucial and important work of the organization Entering period of maximum productivity Becoming more of a teacher/mentor than a learner Explicit signs from boss and co-workers that one's progress has plateaued	Period of settling in or new ambitions based on self-assessment More feeling of security, relaxation, but danger of leveling off and stagnation Threat from younger, better trained, more energetic, and ambitious persons Possible thoughts of "new pastures" and new challenges Working through of mid-life crisis toward greater acceptance of oneself and others
Late Career	Job assignments drawing primarily on maturity of judgment More jobs involving teaching others	Psychological preparation for retirement Deceleration in momentum Finding new sources of self-improvement off the job
Decline	Formal preparation for retirement Retirement rituals	Learning to accept a reduced role and less responsibility Learning to live a less-structured life New accommodations to family and community

SOURCE: Adapted from John Van Maanen and Edgar H. Schein, "Career Development" in *Improving Life at Work,* ed. J. Richard Hackman and J. Lloyd Suttle (Santa Monica, Calif.: Goodyear, 1977), pp. 55–57.

Suggestions for More Effective Organizational Career Development

We will now consider the methods or tools that managers can utilize to better match the career needs of their subordinates with the requirements of their organization. While these suggestions are not proposed to be all-encompassing, they are a solid representation of the better-known career development methods.

Challenging Initial Jobs

Challenging jobs

There is an increasing body of evidence indicating that employees who receive especially challenging job assignments early in their careers do better on later jobs.[5] More specifically, the degree of stimulation and challenge in a person's initial job assignment tends to be significantly related to later career success and retention in the organization.[6] Apparently, initial challenges, particularly if they are successfully met, stimulate a person to perform well in subsequent years.

As we noted in Part 2 of this book in our discussion of human resource planning, job analysis recruitment, and selection, there are definite benefits for managers who correctly fill positions with individuals who have the appropriate abilities and interests to satisfy the job's demands. Given the prior evidence, managers should be even more concerned with the match for new employees and those just beginning their employment careers. Successful placement at this stage should provide significant advantages to both the organization and the individual.

Dissemination of Career Option Information

Understanding career options

Surprisingly, many employees lack any substantive information about career options. What they know is often a combination of myths and facts acquired through friends, co-workers, relatives, and the popular media.

As managers identify career paths that successful employees follow within the organization, they should make this information available. If, for example, the organization prefers candidates for middle-management positions to have had some job exposure in the manufacturing side of the business as well as experience dealing with budgets and financial issues, this information should be disseminated.

---

[5]D. E. Berlew and D. T. Hall, "The Socialization of Managers: Effects of Expectations on Performance," *Administrative Science Quarterly*, 11 (1966), 207–23; and D. W. Bray, R. J. Campbell, and D. L. Grant, *Formative Years in Business: A Long-Term A.T.&T. Study of Managerial Lives* (New York: John WIley, 1974).

[6]See Super and Hall, "Career Development," p. 362, for a review of the literature.

Such valid and reliable data will be of more help to the young, upwardly ambitious employee than, say, some co-worker's offhand comment that "this company favors well-rounded people for promotions."

Will the dissemination of career option information "turn off" the ambitious employee who finds that the organization desires skills that he or she lacks? There is the risk that it might. It may frighten you, if you aspire to a top-management position in your firm, to learn that your organization expects its senior executives to show outstanding abilities in meeting with the media, giving interviews, responding to questions without preparation, and testifying in front of congressional committees. However, it may be just the stimulus to direct you to take courses in public speaking and debate, to get involved in community affairs, or to seek out a one-year special assignment within the company to work on a public relations project. Just as the openness and truthfulness in realistic job previews help increase the job tenure of new employees, managers increase the probability of keeping good employees by making available to them realistic information about the successful career paths that past employees have followed and that future employees should consider.

Job Postings

Posting jobs
To provide information to all employees about job openings, managers can use job posting. Organizations that post jobs typically use bulletin board displays, but they may also use company publications and similar vehicles. The posting lists the abilities, experience, and seniority requirements to qualify for vacancies.

Consistent with the idea that full information on vacancies is a good human resource practice, job posting provides a channel by which the organization lets employees know what jobs are available and, for future reference, what requirements they will have to fulfill to achieve the promotions to which they may aspire. Additionally, a job-posting system is tangible evidence that the organization is notifying women and minorities of the availability of more desirable jobs.

Assessment Centers

Assessing personnel
We have discussed the assessment center both as a selection device and as a management development device. It also has relevance as a career development tool.

By putting people through assessment centers we obtain observable evidence of their ability to do a certain job. Additionally, and often overlooked, is the fact that this technique almost always uses internal supervisors and managers to do part of the appraisal. In this role as assessor, individuals learn how to observe behavior carefully, to make inferences from observations, and to give feedback to the assessee.

Therefore the process helps to build the important managerial skills necessary for performance appraisal. Even more important, it makes assessors more aware of what is involved in the process of development—and this awareness can provide valuable insights into their own career development.[7]

Career Counseling

Counseling programs   One of the most logical parts of a career development program is career counseling. This can appropriately be made part of an individual's annual performance review. What should take place in this encounter? It has been proposed that the dialogue contain the following four elements:[8]

1. The employee's goals, aspirations, and expectations with regard to his or her own career for the next five years or longer
2. The manager's view of the opportunities available and the degree to which the employee's aspirations are realistic and match up with the opportunities available
3. Identification of what the employee would have to do in the way of further self-development to qualify for new opportunities
4. Identification of the actual next steps in the form of plans for new development activities or new job assignments that would prepare the employee for further career growth

This career counseling process may not be easy for the manager. If the employee expresses unrealistic aspirations, the manager should be prepared to give a frank appraisal of where and how the individual falls short—an activity that is rarely enjoyable. The resulting dialogue may suggest that the employee needs further assessment and counseling, which should be offered by the organization. However, the final outcome should be a mutual understanding between the employee and the manager as to the realistic expectations the employee should hold about a career within the organization. The result, to the organization, will be employees with fewer false hopes and expectations about career opportunities. The key, again, is honesty and the conveying of realistic data. If we err, it should be on the side of communicating too much information even if the possibility exists of "turning off" an employee who has his or her unrealistic goals deflated. More employee "turnover, underutilization, and frustrated career development has assuredly resulted from too little realistic information, not too much of it."[9]

[7]Van Maanen and Schein, "Career Development," p. 87.

[8]Ibid., pp. 85–86.

[9]James W. Walker, "Let's Get Realistic about Career Paths," *Human Resource Management*, Fall 1976, p. 6.

FIGURE 11-4

SOURCE: Copyright © 1958 United Feature Syndicate, Inc. With permission.

Career Development Workshops

Career focus workshops Management should consider the value of group workshops to facilitate career development. By bringing together groups of employees with their supervisors and managers, problems and misperceptions can be identified and, it is hoped, resolved.

Entry workshops are a natural extension of realistic job previews and the orientation and socialization activities discussed earlier in this book. They provide the opportunity for groups of new employees and their supervisors to share their separate expectations. Discussion can then focus on those areas where mismatches are identified. Where incongruities are significant and not easily resolved, these entry workshops may be extended to work out procedures for reducing the differences by changing the employee's expectations, organizational practices, or both.

Mid-career workshops can be offered to help individuals with similar background and length of tenure in the organization to assess their career development. These workshops frequently include self-diagnostic activities for employees, diagnosis of the organization, and alignment of the separate diagnoses to identify potential mismatches. Where significant differences are found that may create obstacles or frustrations for employees, solutions may take the form of emphasizing the need for individuals to alter their career aspirations, altering the organization's career development practices, or some combination action.

Finally, the organization may provide late-career workshops. These would be particularly useful for employees preparing for retirement. However, they can also be used to deal with frustrations over unfulfilled career goals, the responsibilities and role expectations of mentors, developing new life interests, or coping with young and ambitious co-workers.

Continuing Education and Training

The training and educational development activities presented in Chapter 10 reduce the possibilities that employees will find themselves with obsolete skills. Additionally, when these development activities are carefully aligned with an individual's aspirations and anticipated future organizational needs, they become an essential element in an employee's career growth.

The education and training in an effective career development program could include on-the-job training; educational or skill courses offered by personnel within the organization; or outside courses provided by colleges, universities, or specialized consultants.

Periodic Job Changes

In addition to encouraging employees to continue their education and training so as to prevent obsolescence and stimulate career growth, managers should be aware that periodic job changes can achieve similar ends.[10] Job changes can take the form of vertical promotions, lateral transfers, or assignments organized around new tasks such as being made part of a special committee or task force.

Job changes

The important element in a job change that offers career development opportunities is the diverse and expanded range of experiences that new job tasks can provide. Varied experiences present new tests to the individual which, if successfully surmounted, build confidence and provide positive feedback that can encourage the undertaking of further new challenges and greater responsibilities. Of course, periodic job changes also provide management with more varied information as to the employee's potential to move higher in the organization. When four supervisors rate an employee as demonstrating high potential for promotion, management can be more assured it is receiving a reliable evaluation than when such appraisal comes from only one supervisor.

Sabbaticals

Leaves of absence

A final suggestion toward making career development more effective is to make use of sabbaticals or extended leaves of absence.[11] For senior executives, the traditional two-to-four-week vacation may be insufficient to offset the accumulated pressures from day-to-day work. An extended leave can allow time for attending executive development conferences, uninterrupted reading, accepting a visiting lectureship at a university, or other such activities that may enhance one's career development.

Middle managers and professional employees in mid-career may become stagnant and find that their performance levels have plateaued. This is frequently a response to the recognition that not many

[10]H. G. Kaufman, *Obsolescence and Professional Career Development* (New York: AMACOM, 1974).

[11]Van Maanen and Schein, "Career Development," p. 92.

more promotions can be anticipated. A period of time away from the organization may allow such individuals to develop new, non-work-related interests, to come to terms with the leveling off of their career, and to put their work into a life perspective. For employees at lower levels in the organization, the idea of sabbaticals ties in closely with continuing education and training to facilitate the learning of new skills that will make career advancement to higher levels feasible. Leaves of several months at a time can also be extended to all employees in the few years prior to their retirement. Such leaves allow the prospective retiree to begin to cultivate outside interests and to learn, gradually, how to adapt to life without formal work commitments.

Suggestions for an Individual's Career Development

As we pointed out at the beginning of this chapter, career development can be viewed from the perspective of the organization or of the individual. Our emphasis has been on the former. We can now focus briefly on individual career development. In this section, we want to identify what employees can do to better manage their own careers.

Career development suggestions

It is probably correct to state that once most individuals leave school and enter the world of work, they spend more time planning a two-week vacation than they spend planning a career that will span four decades. Yet the evidence demonstrates that those individuals who are most successful in their careers report more extensive career planning.[12] Assuming someone wants to take personal career development seriously, what should he or she do? The answer is to engage in self-assessment.

Individual career development requires people to become knowledgeable of their own needs, values, and personal goals. This can be achieved through a three-step, self-assessment process:[13]

1. Identify and organize your skills, interests, work-related needs, and values.
2. Convert these inventories into general career fields and specific job goals.
3. Test these possibilities against the realities of the organization or the job market.

Figure 11-5 provides a framework for engaging in this self-assessment process.

[12]Sam Gould, "Characteristics of Career Planners in Upwardly Mobile Occupations, *Academy of Management Journal*, September 1979, pp. 539–50.

[13]Irving R. Schwartz, "Self-Assessment and Career Planning: Matching Individuals and Organizational Goals," *Personnel*, January–February 1979, p. 48.

FIGURE 11-5

Individual Career Self-Assessment

EDUCATION:

Schools	Courses I Liked	Courses I Disliked	Academic Strengths	Academic Weaknesses	Extracurricular Activities
1.					
2.					
3.					

SKILLS:

1.
2.
3.

WORK EXPERIENCE:

Organization	Job	Degree of Satisfaction	What I Liked	What I Disliked	Why I Left
1.					
2.					
3.					

The most important needs I want to satisfy in my career are:

1.
2.
3.

These needs can be satisfied in the following general areas:

1.
2.
3.

Whatever job I have, the following values should not have to be compromised:

1.
2.
3.

The following constraints must be considered (minimum salary, geographical preferences, size of organization, etc.):

1.
2.
3.

Specific jobs that would be compatible with the above requirements are:

1.
2.
3.

Step 1: Identification and Organization

The best place to begin is by drawing up a profile of your educational record. List each school attended from high school on. What courses do you remember as liking most and least? In what courses did you score highest and lowest? In what extracurricular activities did you participate? Are there any specific skills that you acquired? Are there other skills you have gained proficiency in?

Next, begin to assess your occupational experience. List each job you have held, the organization you worked for, your overall level of satisfaction, what you liked most and least about the job, and why you left. It is important to be honest in covering each of these points. This is a *self*-assessment exercise, and you have no reason to share it with others. Therefore confront the facts and list them as such.

Step 2: Conversion into General Fields and a Specific Goal

If you have been honest in step 1, you should now have some genuine insights into your interests and abilities. What you need to do now is look at how these can be converted into the kind of organizational setting or field of endeavor where there will be a good match. Then you can become specific and identify distinct job goals.

What fields are available?—in business? government? nonprofit organizations? Your answer can be further delineated into areas such as manufacturing, banking, education, social services, and health services. Identifying areas of interest is usually far easier than pinpointing specific occupations. This is true, if for no other reason, because now you begin to recognize the sheer mass of alternatives. While you may be able to list several hundred different occupations, it might be worthwhile to casually flip through *The Dictionary of Occupational Titles*, which lists over twenty thousand different jobs, in order to expand your mind to the vast array of alternatives. Additionally, you should not fail to talk with several personnel managers for information on opportunities within their organization or industry, and friends and acquaintances who are already engaged in occupations that you think might be interesting.

When you are able to identify a limited set of occupations that have interest to you, you can start to align these with your abilities and skills. Will certain jobs require you to move? If so, would this be compatible with your geographic preferences? What type of people will be your co-workers? Do you have the educational requirements necessary for the job? If not, what additional schooling will be needed? Does the job offer the status and earning potential that you aspire to? What is the long-term outlook for jobs in this area? Does the career suffer from cyclical employment—up for a few years, followed by limited opportunities? Since no job is without its drawbacks, have you seriously considered *all* the negative aspects? When you have fully answered questions such as these, you should have a relatively short list of special job goals. For instance, you might have found that you would like to be working in the investment field, preferably for a large bank, where you will be employed as a bond trader.

Step 3: Testing Against Realities

The final step in this self-assessment process is testing your selection against the realities of the marketplace. This can be done by going out and talking with personnel specialists and knowledgeable people in the fields, organizations, or jobs you desire. This interaction should provide reliable feedback as to the accuracy of your self-assessment and the opportunities in the fields and jobs that interest you.

Summary

Career development programs are a relatively recent phenomenon. Although still not widely adopted, such programs were nonexistent a decade or more ago.

VIEWS IN THE NEWS

Career Guidance Sessions

Career guidance discussions between supervisors and subordinates are a key component of the employee development process and can produce big payoffs for both workers and employers, notes Richard Mirabile, vice-president for program development at Ward Associates, Menlo Park, Calif. A career guidance discussion is a formally structured meeting that focuses on the identification, development, and future use of a worker's skills and talents. Effective career guidance discussions not only help organizations to identify workers with high performance potential, but also assist employees in mapping out realistic career development plans.

PREPARATION AND SCHEDULING

Employees bear the "ultimate responsibility" for their career growth, Mirabile says, but "most managers and supervisors would probably agree that development of subordinates is a major part of their job." Since supervisors typically are more aware of the organization's staffing needs and job opportunities, Mirabile points out, they usually are in the best position to determine how workers' talents and skills can be used to the greatest advantage. Supervisors also are more apt to be familiar with available developmental resources, such as training programs.

Career guidance sessions should be conducted regularly. For most workers, once a year is appropriate, although once every two to three years may be sufficient in some cases. Before each session, the supervisor should ask the employee to put career accomplishments and aspirations in perspective by completing a self-assessment worksheet. The supervisor also should begin preparing for the session by thinking about the employee's:

- *Strengths and weaknesses*—What does the employee do well or poorly? What conditions (e.g., time pressures) affect the worker's performance? What changes can be made to improve those conditions?
- *Career objectives*—What promotional possibilities are in store for the employee? Where else in the organization could the employee make a contribution?
- *Developmental needs*—What kind of training is needed to improve the worker's current performance or chances for promotion?

CONDUCTING THE SESSION

For career guidance sessions to succeed, supervisors must be willing to understand, accept, and commit themselves to the role of helping employees grow and develop, Mirabile says. In addition to demonstrating an ability to understand employees' viewpoints and feelings, supervisors should be skilled in using probing, open-ended questions to solicit detailed information.

The career guidance interview can be divided into several stages, Mirabile says, offering supervisors the following guidelines for each step in the process:

- *Beginning the session*—It's important to establish rapport and to agree on the purpose of the session. Try to understand the employee's interests, objectives, and job criticisms.
- *Identifying strengths and weaknesses*—Discuss the worker's accomplishments, including obstacles that have been overcome. Ask the employee to identify areas requiring further development. Listen carefully and probe. If you agree with the self-assessment, reinforce the worker's perceptions by providing feedback in the form of examples of demonstrated talents. If you disagree, tactfully discuss your differences; remember that the employee may be right. If discussion reaches a stalemate, discontinue the meeting.
- *Identifying development opportunities*—Discuss your evaluation of the employee's potential and readiness for promotion. Be sure that the worker understands that your assessments are not decisions to promote or transfer at this time.
- *Mapping out a developmental action plan*—With the worker's help, draw up a plan that includes specific, achievable developmental objectives, then identify resources for achieving those goals. Be sure to translate the objectives into concrete action steps and to establish a realistic schedule for completing activities.
- *Closing*—Ask the employee to summarize the discussion; self-learning is the most useful outcome of career guidance sessions. Confirm a follow-up evaluation date, comment on the session's value for you, and praise the employee for investing time and energy in the development process. (*Career Guidance Discussions,* INFO-LINE No. 508, American Society for Training and Development, 1630 Duke St., Box 1443, Alexandria, Va. 22313)

Source: Reprinted by permission from *Bulletin to Management,* copyright 1985 by The Bureau of National Affairs, Inc., Washington, D.C.

There is a dearth of studies on career development in practice. What little evidence is available suggests that career development is informal in many organizations.[14] A survey of 142 organizations, all which had over three hundred employees, found that 35 percent had no formal policy concerning career development.[15] One expert who is familiar with career activities in many organizations believes that development of formal career programs has been hampered because many of the techniques are too sophisticated, and hence unsuitable, for the pragmatic needs of most organizations.

Although the evidence is scant, probably the most accurate conclusion regarding career development practices in organizations is that they tend to be informal and, where they are emerging, they are still "growing up piecemeal." However, we must remember that while organizations are taking more interest in developing employees' careers, the primary responsibility for managing a career rests with the individual. It is the individual who, as we noted at the beginning of this chapter, knows his or her own goals and aspirations and must therefore take charge of his or her career development.

Conclusion

This chapter focused on a number of aspects regarding career development. It also discussed the impact that a sound career development program has on an organization, as well as effective career development tehniques.

The appendix to this chapter explores personal opportunities with respect to careers and includes a career guide for the twelve most promising jobs in the next decade.[16] (See pp. 303–307.)

SUMMARY

1. A *career* is a sequence of positions occupied by a person during the course of a lifetime.
2. Effective organizational career development
   a. Ensures that needed talent will be available
   b. Improves the organization's ability to attract and retain high-talent personnel

[14]See Marilyn A. Morgan, Douglas T. Hall, and Alison Martier, "Career Development Strategies in Industry—Where Are We and Where Should We Be?" *Personnel*, March–April 1979, p. 22; and John W. Seybolt, "Career Development: The State of the Art Among the Grass Roots," *Training and Development Journal*, April 1979, p. 17.

[15]Marcia P. Kleiman, "Turning Career Development Lip Service into Action," *Training and Development Journal*, April 1984, p. 78.

[16]Douglas T. Hall, Marilyn A. Morgan, Alison Martier, and M. Blessington, *Surveys of Career Development Practices* (Evanston, Ill.: Northwestern University Mimeo, 1977).

    c. Ensures that minorities and women will have opportunities for growth and development

    d. Reduces employee frustrations

3. A career can be viewed as consisting of five stages:
   a. Exploration
   b. Establishment
   c. Mid-career
   d. Late career
   e. Decline

4. Effective organizational career development techniques include
   a. Challenging initial jobs
   b. Dissemination of career option information
   c. Job postings
   d. Assessment centers
   e. Career counseling
   f. Career development workshops
   g. Continuing education and training
   h. Periodic job changes
   i. Sabbaticals

5. Individual career development is a three-step self-assessment process:
   a. Identifying and organizing skills, interests, work-related needs, and values
   b. Converting these inventories into general career fields and specific job goals
   c. Testing these possibilities against the realities of the organization or the job market

6. Career opportunities appear to be good for the post–baby boom group:
   a. There are a variety of suggestions that one can follow to get ahead
   b. Mobility seems to be an issue
   c. Twelve careers have been identified as being promising in the next decade

KEY TERMS

Career
Career development workshop
Career stages
Decline phase
Establishment phase
Exploration phase

External dimension
Internal dimension
Late-career phase
Mid-career phase
Sabbatical

QUESTIONS FOR REVIEW

1. What is meant by the term *career*?

2. Which career perspective is more relevant to managers: the individual or the organizational? Why?

3. Contrast management development with career development.

4. How might a formal career development program be consistent with an organization's affirmative action programs?

5. Contrast the external and internal dimensions to a career. Which is more relevant in determining an employee's behavior?

6. Do you think that a person's age and career stage evolve together? Why?

7. Which of the five career stages is probably least relevant to managers? Why?

8. Describe the activities involved in career counseling.

9. Summarize the three steps in the self-assessment process.

10. Contrast human resource planning with career development.

QUESTIONS FOR DISCUSSION

1. "You can't be too open and honest with an employee when discussing his or her career." Do you agree or disagree? Discuss.

2. "Career development is a waste of money for a company. All it does is raise employees' expectations and then, frustrated, they quit." Do you agree or disagree? Discuss.

3. "Women and minorities require more career attention than do white males." Do you agree or disagree? Discuss.

4. "There are two ways to look at career development: (a) the organization is fixed and management's function is to advise employees about desirable paths to take and hurdles to avoid, or (b) the organization is dynamic and managers must initiate changes so as to open up career opportunities for ambitious employees." Discuss.

5. What role should the career development office play in today's colleges and universities? What do you expect from that office?

CONTINUING CASE: Concord General

To Dream the Impossible Dream

After hearing from John Michaels that he would appoint her to fill Jim Wilson's position (Jim had suddenly resigned), Judy began to wonder about her career. Confiding in John, Judy said:

> *John, I've been a nurse for some time now. Certainly I have enjoyed my administrative duties and I feel that I do them well, but I'm beginning to frighten myself. You see, John, I'm beginning to wonder if, in fact, a career move into administration is the best thing for me. When I took over as a nurse recruiter, I didn't mind because I was still close to the nurses. But in filling Jim's slot I'll be further removed, and that makes me feel as if I'm leaving what I love most: caring for the sick.*

John tried to soothe Judy because he realized that she was going through a decision crisis:

> *Judy, I believe that you are management material. And I'm sure that you're thinking that you won't be fulfilling your dream. But remember, Judy, only you can make that decision. I believe that you can combine the two, a managerial position and a concern for "caring for the sick."*

As the discussion progressed, it became apparent to John that Judy was being torn apart by what she regarded as a career change conflict. Trying to ease her mind, John has decided to begin career counseling with Judy in the hope of solving her dilemma.

Questions

1. How should John approach Judy regarding career counseling?
2. What advice should John give?
3. If you were Judy, what would you do to help make the decision?
4. How can personal conflicts affect one's career path?

CASE APPLICATION

A Funny Thing Happened On the Way to the Presidency

During the summer of 1982, Bob Williamson was described in an issue of *Business Week* as a person "on the move." The article described Williamson as "a winner," destined to assume the presidency of Consolidated Pharmaceuticals within several short years. One certainly could not argue with that conclusion.

Bob Williamson was a second-string All-American basketball player at the University of Denver in the mid-1950s. After graduating with academic honors, and an eighteen-month stay in the Army, Bob joined Miles Laboratories as a sales representative in 1958. He rapidly became one of Miles's best salesmen. In a five-year period, he took two marginal territories and increased sales in each by more than 150 percent. In 1963, he was promoted to district sales supervisor. Again, his performance sparkled. In addition to outperforming any other sales territory in the Miles organization, Bob also began studying for a M.B.A. degree at night. In 1966, after obtaining his degree, he rejected a promotion to regional sales manager at Miles, accepted a position as assistant to the vice-president for marketing at Consolidated Pharmaceuticals in New York City, and married Marie Flatley, whom he had met in his graduate program.

Bob and Marie agreed on their objectives—Bob should do whatever was necessary to get the top spot at Consolidated while Marie would stay home, at least for a few years, have several children, and return to full-time employment when their children had reached school age.

Everything seemed on track. Their first child arrived in 1968, and a second in 1969. Bob moved from his assistant-to position at Consolidated to vice-president of marketing in 1972 and to corporate executive vice-president in 1984.

But in early 1987 it became obvious to everyone at Consolidated that Bob was changing. Slacks and a sport shirt were frequently worn in place of the three-piece suit and shirt and tie. Gone was the Cadillac sedan, replaced by a red Porsche Targa. Williamson's hair had grown longer, he was sporting a beard, and the grapevine was saying he had filed for divorce from Marie and was living in the penthouse of a local hotel. Unfortunately, the changes went beyond alterations merely in lifestyle. Bob was frequently arriving late to work, taking two- and three-hour lunches, missing important committee meetings, and rarely returning from lunch on Fridays. Things looked as if they were coming to a head one August day in 1987 when the company president, Roland Houseman, came into Bob's office. Houseman asked the secretary if

Bob was in. She replied that she hadn't heard from him for three days. When Houseman asked if Bob had received any messages, she replied, "Only one. Mr. Williamson's lawyer called and told me to tell him that he had successfully concluded the deal to buy the two-thousand-acre ranch in Colorado that he wanted."

Questions

1. Trace Bob Williamson's career in terms of stages.
2. What do you think brought about these dramatic changes in Bob?
3. Is there anything Consolidated could have done early in Bob's career to have saved him from this loss of interest?
4. What do you think Bob's career plans are now?
5. Is there anything Consolidated can do now to make Bob a functional employee again?

ADDITIONAL READINGS

BOLTON, BRIAN, "Discriminant Analysis of Holland's Occupational Types Using the Sixteen Personality Factor Questionnaire," *Journal of Vocational Behavior,* 27, No. 2 (October 1985), 210–17.

CHALOFSKY, NEAL, "HRD Career Update," *Training and Development Journal,* 39, No. 5 (May 1985), 64–65.

FEUER, DALE, "Two Ways to Get to the Top," *Training,* February 1986, pp. 26–34.

JACOBSON, BETSY, and BEVERLY KAYE, "Career Development and Performance Appraisal: It Takes Two to Tango," *Performance and Development,* January 1986, pp. 26–32.

SLOCUM, JOHN W., and WILLIAM L. CRON, "Job Attitudes and Performance During Three Career Stages," *Journal of Vocational Behavior,* 26, No. 2 (April 1985), 126–45.

APPENDIX TO CHAPTER 11

Personal Opportunities

Introduction

The overview of career development presented in Chapter 11 has given you an opportunity to assess yourself. But by now you must be saying, Sure, the information is good to have, but what are my career prospects in the future? Although we cannot predict the future, we can give you some information regarding the best opportunities that appear to be available as we enter the 1990s.

Career Guide

How can you make yourself more attractive to an organization and in what areas are careers open? Despite the plethora of "how to" suggestions about getting to the top, none seem to be more important than doing good work, presenting the right image, learning the power structure, gaining control of organizational resources, staying visible, finding a mentor, supporting your boss, and staying mobile.[1] The last suggestion—staying mobile—appears to be one variable that has been changing rapidly. Evidently workers are not as willing to move today as they were two decades ago. "Tied down by dual-career marriages, rising housing costs, and a growing emphasis on leisure and community activities, and the quality of life, workers are resisting relocation."[2] For example:

> *An engineer with a major corporation in the midwest was delighted last winter when his company promoted him to the job of plant manager at one of its subsidiaries on Long Island. Then he discovered that the prices of homes at the new location were double what he could expect for his own. Moreover, he calculated that*

[1] Stephen P. Robbins, *Management: Concepts and Practices* (Englewood Cliffs, N.J.: Prentice-Hall, 1984), pp. 548–51.

[2] "America's New Immobile Society," *Business Week*, July 27, 1981, pp. 58–62.

a new mortgage of 13.5 percent, compared to the 7.5 percent he was paying on his existing mortgage, would cost him about $7,500 a year, wiping out his existing salary increase—and then some. He turned the job down.[3]

Years ago, turning down a promotion that included a transfer was not highly regarded by the company, but economic realities are causing companies to rethink their relocation policies. These policy changes reflect "seeking new incentives to move managers and other staffers."[4] Many of these incentives make such moving advantageous, especially for those trying to "grow" in the organization.

Mobility need not only imply a change in location. It could also imply a change in jobs or a change in organizations. People rarely stay in the first job they accept; they will change jobs a number of times. In fact, as Figure 11A-1 indicates, you may have ten or more jobs during your career. Many of those who change jobs use each job as a steppingstone toward their ultimate career goal. For example, suppose you would like to be vice-president of human resources in a major corporation. Chances are good that you will need ten to fifteen years of progressive experience in human resources, with exposure to employment, compensation, employee relations, and training and development. If that goal is to be achieved, you must strategize how you are going to get exposure in the four areas. This means targeting your sights on positions or organizations, spending a few years in each, and moving on to another.

Changing positions or organizations is not necessarily perceived negatively by others. The key, however, is performance. Whether you change jobs or not, it is your work history that counts. Solid performers are always sought by good companies. If that position of vice-president of human resources goal is to become a reality, you will need a proven track record to substantiate your being chosen to fill such an important position.

Where Are the Jobs?

By now you should have some indication of what type of general career you wish to pursue. Your attendance at college and your particular major field of study are reflections of that. But within any career field, there are many choices. As you proceed to make these career choices, we offer the following guidelines:

---

[3] Gerard Tavernier, "The High Cost and Stress of Relocation," *Management Review*, July 1980, pp. 18–19.

[4] Ibid., p. 18.

FIGURE 11A-1

The Job Hoppers
Cumulative number of employers by age group

AGE	MEN	WOMEN
16–17	0.7	0.8
18–19	1.9	1.8
20–24	4.1	3.8
25–29	5.8	5.2
30–34	7.0	6.4
35–39	7.9	7.4
40–44	8.7	8.3
45–49	9.3	9.0
50–54	9.8	9.4
55–59	10.2	9.8
60–64	10.5	10.0
65–69	10.7	10.2
70+	10.8	10.2

SOURCE: Robert E. Hall, "The importance of life time jobs in the United States economy," *New York Times*, November 23, 1980.

1. Assess your comparative advantage (what do you do better than others?).
2. What are your interests? What do you like doing? (Even if you are good at something doesn't mean much if you don't like it.)
3. Where are the opportunities? Assess the external environment to identify where opportunities are. (You may be an avid reader and want to be an English teacher in a college, but the market is not promising in that field at this time.)
4. Match your strengths, interests, and market opportunities to assess career directions.

Career Choices

While we cannot give you specific answers to guidelines 1 and 2, we can provide you with a list identifying where the opportunities have been during this decade. These career opportunities are listed in Figure 11-A2. Included within each major category are subdisciplines and their salary ranges. Even though these positions and salaries seem attractive, keep one consultant's advice in mind: "What is the best job of all? It is the one you are best fitted for, by dint of training and personality."[5]

[5] "Business Week's Guide to Careers," *Business Week*, Spring Edition, 1983, p. 9.

FIGURE 11A-2

12 Top Careers

	RANGE FOR TOP THIRD OF MANAGERS
Technical	
*R&D executive	60,000–79,000
*Corporate construction director	60,000–77,000
Chief industrial engineer	50,000–63,000
Finance	
*Security investments manager	50,000–76,000
*General accounting (report to controller)	45,000–68,000
*Tax compliance manager	50,000–66,000
Financial planning officer (report to controller)	50,000–62,000
Bank manager (at least $10 million deposits)	46,000–61,000
Chief internal auditor	40,000–53,000
Sales	
*National account manager	50,000–69,000
Brand manager (sales over $5 million)	30,000–63,000
International sales	45,000–59,000
Sales promotion	40,000–56,000
Personnel	
*Management training specialist/dept. head	50,000–76,000
*Personnel/human resources manager	50,000–68,000
*Labor relations executive	45,000–68,000
Employee training specialist/dept. head	35,000–47,000
Planning	
*Corporate strategic planner	50,000–70,000
Corporate economist	50,000–61,000
Manufacturing	
*Plant manager	40,000–69,000
Quality assurance & reliability	35,000–60,000
Other	
*Management Information Systems specialist/data proc.	45,000–77,000
Federal relations executive	50,000–64,000
Corp. insurance/risk manager	45,000–63,000
Contract administrator	40,000–54,000
Purchasing manager	35,000–53,000
Media manager	30,000–53,000

*The top dozen career slots for current middle managers of above-average abilities in medium and large-size companies.

Conclusion

In this appendix, we have endeavored to show where the best career opportunities can be found. We have also given you a guideline to follow to gain insight into career choices.

Competition for the better jobs in the 1990s will be fierce. The more you plan for and strive toward your goal, the more effective you will be in achieving that goal.

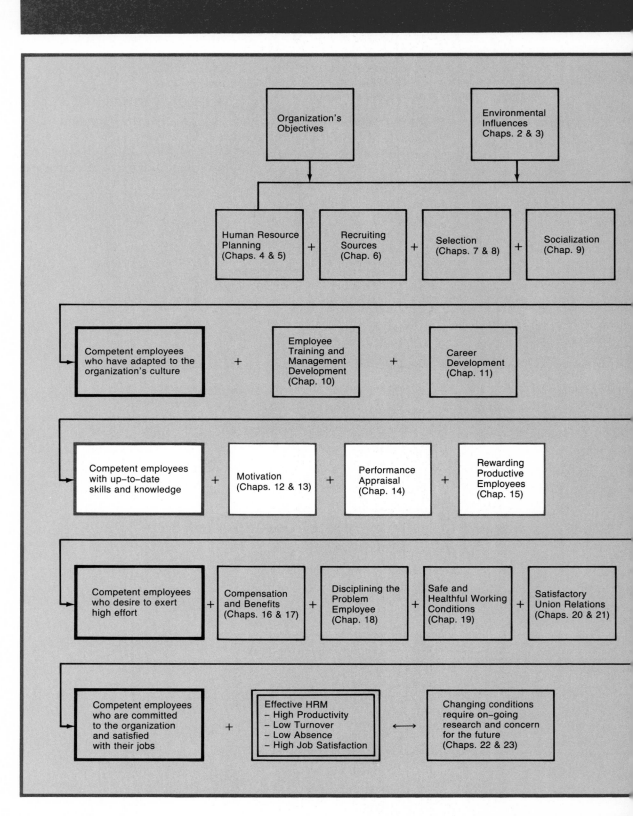

PART FOUR

= Competent employees who have adapted to the organization's culture

= Competent employees with up-to-date skills and knowledge

= Competent employees who desire to exert high effort

= Competent employees who are committed to the organization and satisfied with their jobs

MOTIVATION OF HUMAN RESOURCES

CHAPTER 12

Motivation

AFTER READING THIS CHAPTER, YOU WILL BE ABLE TO:

1. Define *motivation*
2. Describe Maslow's hierarchy of needs theory
3. Describe McGregor's Theory X; Theory Y
4. Describe Herzberg's two-factor motivation-hygiene theory
5. Describe McClelland's three needs theory
6. Describe expectancy theory
7. Identify the four personality types and discuss their implications for HRM

I asked a thief what motivated him to steal and he robbed me of six hundred dollars.

—Anonymous

Toward our goal of having a productive group of employees, we should not assume that the proper selection and development of our personnel will necessarily give us our desired result. We can hire individuals with extraordinary competence and develop these abilities, and still not be assured they will perform satisfactorily. A major missing ingredient is motivation, that is, activating the potential of our employees.

In simplistic terms, an employee's job performance can be defined as being determined by the level and interaction between ability and motivation:

$$\text{Job Performance} = \text{Ability} \times \text{Motivation}$$

This equation dramatizes the importance of not only having employees with the talent to do a good job but recognizing that human resource managers must be concerned with providing the stimulus that converts employee talent into successful job performance.

What is Motivation?

Motivation

We might define motivation in terms of some outward behavior. People who are "motivated" exert a greater effort to perform than those who are "not motivated." However, such a definition is relative and tells us little. A more descriptive definition would say *motivation* is the willingness to do something and is conditioned by this action's ability to satisfy some need for the individual. A *need*, in our terminology, means some internal state that makes certain outcomes appear attractive. This motivation process can be seen in Figure 12-1.

An unsatisfied need creates tension, which stimulates drives within the individual. These drives generate a search behavior to find particular goals that, if attained, satisfy the need and lead to the reduction of tension.

Motivated employees are in a state of tension. To relieve this ten-

FIGURE 12-1   Basic Motivational Process

sion, they engage in activity. The greater the tension, the greater the activity to bring about relief. Therefore when we see people working hard at some activity, we can conclude that they are driven by a desire to achieve some goal that they perceive as having value to them.

Some Early Motivation Theories

The previous description of the motivation process does little to specifically explain employee behavior. Let us therefore look at four theories that were formulated in the 1950s, received considerable attention, and are still frequently offered as explanations of, or approaches to, motivation. These theories were proposed by Abraham Maslow, Douglas McGregor, Frederick Herzberg, and David McClelland, respectively.

Maslow's Hierarchy of Needs

Maslow's hierarchy of needs theory

The best-known theory of motivation was proposed by Abraham Maslow.[1] He hypothesized that within every human being there exists a hierarchy of five needs. These needs are

1. Physiological: includes hunger, thirst, shelter, sex, and other bodily needs.
2. Safety: includes security and protection from physical and emotional harm.
3. Love: includes affection, belongingness, acceptance, and friendship.
4. Esteem: includes internal esteem factors such as self-respect, autonomy, and achievement; and external esteem factors such as status, recognition, and attention.
5. Self-actualization: the drive to become what one is capable of becoming; includes growth, achieving one's potential, self-fulfillment.

As each of these needs becomes substantially satisfied, the next need becomes dominant. In terms of Figure 12-2, the individual moves

[1]Abraham Maslow, *Motivation and Personality* (New York: Harper & Row, 1954).

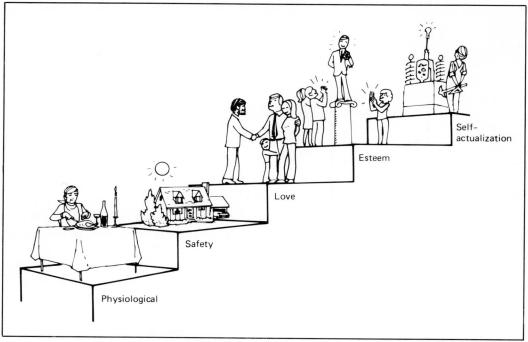

FIGURE 12-2   Maslow's Hierarchy of Needs

SOURCE: By permission of the Modular Project of Organizational Behavior and Instructional Communications Centre. McGill University, Montreal, Canada.

up the hierarchy. From the standpoint of motivation, the theory would say that although no need is ever fully gratified, a substantially satisfied need no longer motivates.

Maslow separated the five needs into higher and lower levels. Physiological and safety needs were described as lower-order needs, and love, esteem and self-actualization as higher-order needs. The differentiation between the two orders was made on the premise that higher-order needs are satisfied internally, whereas lower-order needs are predominantly satisfied externally (by such things as money wages, union contracts, tenure, and pleasant working conditions). In fact, the natural conclusion to be drawn from Maslow's classification is that in terms of economic plenty, which has generally described the North American society since the mid-1940s, almost all permanently employed workers have had their lower-order needs substantially met. But as the times changed, a renewed emphasis was revealed. As people become unemployed and their unemployment benefits ceased, their attention turned toward survival, a lower-order need. Therefore, according to Maslow, when a lower-level need is unsatisfied, we revert to that level.

Maslow's hierarchy of needs theory has received wide recognition, particularly among practicing managers. This can be attributed largely to the theory's intuitive logic and ease of understanding. Unfortunately, research does not generally validate the theory. Maslow provided no empirical substantiation, and several studies that sought to validate the theory found no support.[2]

McGregor's Theory X and Theory Y

McGregor's Theory X; Theory Y

After viewing the way managers dealt with subordinates, Douglas McGregor concluded that a manager's view of human nature is based on one of two sets of assumptions about people, and that managers tend to mold their behavior toward subordinates according to which set of assumptions they hold. The first set of assumptions, basically negative, McGregor labeled Theory X; and the second, basically positive, he labeled Theory Y.[3]

Under Theory X, four assumptions are held by the manager:

1. Employees inherently dislike work and, whenever possible, will attempt to avoid it.
2. Since employees dislike work, they must be coerced, controlled, or threatened with punishment to achieve desired goals.
3. Employees will shirk responsibilities and seek formal direction whenever possible.
4. Most workers place security above all other factors associated with work and will display little ambition.

In contrast to these negative views toward human nature, McGregor listed four other assumptions that he called Theory Y:

1. Employees can view work as being as natural as rest or play.
2. Employees will exercise self-direction and self-control if they are committed to the objectives.
3. The average person can learn to accept, even seek, responsibility.
4. Creativity—that is, the ability to make good decisions—is widely dispersed throughout the population, and not necessarily the sole province of those in managerial functions.

What are the motivational implications if you accept McGregor's analysis? The answer is best expressed in the framework presented by

[2]See, for example, Edward E. Lawler III and J. Lloyd Suttle, "A Casual Correlation Test of the Need Hierarchy Concept," *Organizational Behavior and Human Performance,* April 1972, pp. 265–87; and Douglas T. Hall and Khalil E. Nongaim, "An Examination of Maslow's Need Hierarchy in an Organizational Setting," *Organizational Behavior and Human Performance,* February 1968, pp. 12–35.

[3]Douglas McGregor, *The Human Side of Enterprise* (New York: McGraw-Hill, 1960).

Maslow. Theory X assumes that lower-order needs dominate individuals. Theory Y assumes that higher-order needs dominate. McGregor himself held to the belief that Theory Y assumptions were more valid than Theory X. Therefore he proposed ideas like participation in decision making, opportunities for responsible and challenging jobs, and good group relations as approaches that would maximize an employee's job motivation.

Unfortunately, there is no evidence to confirm that either set of assumptions is valid, or that acceptance of Theory Y assumptions and altering one's actions accordingly will lead to more-motivated workers. But you should not ignore the fact that most human resource managers are familiar with Theory X and Theory Y concepts, and that these labels are frequently used by practitioners when describing how a manager treats subordinates.

Herzberg's Motivation-Hygiene Theory

Herzberg's motivation-hygiene theory

In the belief that the relationship of people to their work is a basic one and that their attitude toward their work can very well determine their success or failure, Frederick Herzberg investigated the question, "What do people want from their jobs?"[4]

Herzberg asked people to describe, in detail, situations in which they felt exceptionally good or bad about their jobs. These responses were tabulated and categorized. Factors affecting job attitudes as reported in twelve investigations conducted by Herzberg are illustrated in Figure 12-3.

From the categorized responses, Herzberg concluded that the replies given when people feel good about their jobs are significantly different from the replies given when they feel bad. As seen in Figure 12-3, certain characteristics tend to be consistently related to job satisfaction, and others to job dissatisfaction. Intrinsic factors, such as achievement, recognition, the work itself, responsibility, and advancement, seem to be related to job satisfaction. When those questioned felt good about their work, they tended to attribute these characteristics to themselves. On the other hand, when they were dissatisfied, they tended to cite extrinsic factors, such as company policy and administration, supervision, interpersonal relations, and working conditions.

The data suggest, says Herzberg, that the opposite of satisfaction is not dissatisfaction, as was traditionally believed. In other words, removing dissatisfying characteristics from a job does not necessarily make the job satisfying, or vice versa. As illustrated in Figure 12-4, Herzberg interpreted his findings to propose the existence of a dual

---

[4]Frederick Herzberg, *Work and the Nature of Man* (New York: World Publishing, 1966).

Factors characterizing 1,753 events on the job that led to *extreme satisfaction*

Factors characterizing 1,844 events on the job that led to *extreme dissatisfaction*

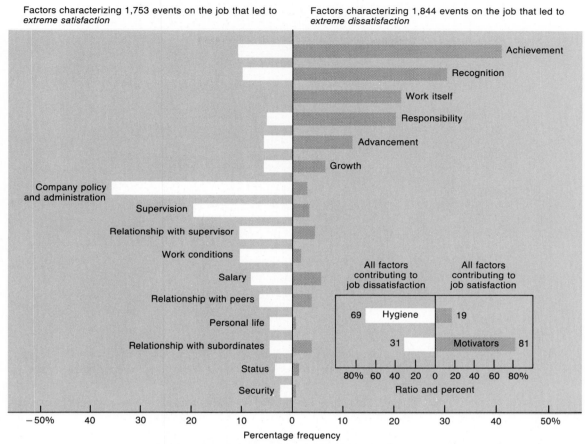

FIGURE 12-3   *Comparison of Satisfiers and Dissatisfiers*

SOURCE: Federick Herzberg, "One More Time: How Do You Motivate Employees?" *Harvard Business Review,* January–February 1968, p. 57. With permission, Copyright © 1967 by the President and Fellows of Harvard College; all rights reserved.

continuum, with the opposite of "satisfaction" being "no satisfaction," and the opposite of "dissatisfaction" being "no dissatisfaction."

According to Herzberg, the factors leading to job satisfaction are separate and distinct from those that lead to job dissatisfaction. Therefore, by acting to eliminate factors that can create job dissatisfaction, one can bring about peace, but not necessarily motivation. As a result, such characteristics as company policy and administration, supervision, interpersonal relations, working conditions, and salary have been categorized by Herzberg as hygiene factors. When they are satisfactorily maintained, people will not be dissatisfied; however, neither will they be satisfied. If we want to motivate employees, Herzberg suggests emphasizing achievement, recognition, the work itself, responsibility,

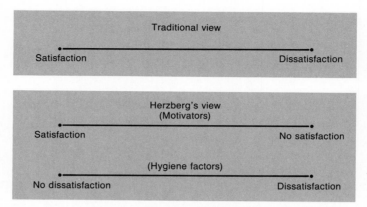

FIGURE 12-4   *Contrasting Views of Satisfaction-Dissatisfaction*

growth, and advancement. These are the characteristics that people find intrinsically rewarding.

The motivation-hygiene theory is not without its detractors however. The criticisms of the theory have been based on five suggested weaknesses:

1. The procedure that Herzberg used is limited by its methodology. When things are going well, people tend to take credit themselves. Contrarily, they blame failure on the extrinsic environment.

2. The reliability of Herzberg's methodology is questioned. Since raters have to make interpretations, it is possible that they may contaminate the findings by interpreting one response in one manner while treating another similar response differently.

3. No overall measure of satisfaction was utilized. In other words, a person may dislike part of her job, yet still think the job is acceptable.

4. The theory is inconsistent with previous research. The motivation-hygiene theory ignores situational variables.

5. Herzberg assumes that there is a relationship between satisfaction and productivity. But the research methodology he used looked only at satisfaction, not at productivity. To make such research relevant, one must assume a high relationship between satisfaction and productivity.[5]

[5]Robert J. House and Lawrence A. Wigdor, "Herzberg's Dual-Factor Theory of Job Satisfaction and Motivation: A Review of the Evidence and Criticism," *Personnel Psychology*, Winter 1967, pp. 369–89; and Donald P. Schwab and Larry L. Cummings, "Theories of Performance and Satisfaction: A Review," *Industrial Relations*, October 1970, pp. 408–30.

Regardless of the criticisms, Herzberg's theory has been widely read, and few managers are unfamiliar with his recommendations. The increased interest since the mid-1960s in vertically expanding jobs to allow workers greater responsibility in planning and controlling their work can probably be largely attributed to Herzberg's findings and recommendations.

From another perspective, Herzberg's findings appear consistent with general surveys made of workers' opinions about what they want from their job. Nationwide polls conducted by the National Opinion Research Center, for example, indicate that "more than half of the white, male work force in the United States believes the most important characteristic of a job is that it involve work that is important and provides a sense of accomplishment."[6] Meaningful work was rated "most important" three times more frequently than "opportunities for advancement" and "high income," and seven times more frequently than the desire for "shorter work hours and much free time." In terms of preference order, these polls found no difference between replies of white-collar and blue-collar workers.

McClelland's Achievement, Affiliation, and Power Motives

David McClelland has proposed that there are three major relevant motives or needs in workplace situations:

McClelland's three needs motivation theory

1. The need for achievement: the drive to excel, to achieve in relation to a set of standards, to strive to succeed
2. The need for affiliation: the desire for friendly and close interpersonal relationships
3. The need for power: the need to make others behave in a way that they would not have behaved otherwise

Some people have a compelling drive to succeed for the sake of success alone. McClelland calls this the drive for achievement, which he has abbreviated as *nAch*.[7] From his research into the achievement need, McClelland found that high achievers differentiate themselves from others by their desire to do things better. They seek situations where they can attain personal responsibility for finding solutions to problems, where they can receive rapid feedback on their performance, and where they can set moderately challenging goals. High achievers dislike succeeding by change. They like to keep score, they are

[6]Charles N. Weaver, "What Workers Want from Their Jobs," *Personnel*, May–June 1976, p. 49.

[7]David C. McClelland, *The Achieving Society* (New York: Van Nostrand Reinhold, 1961).

competitive, and they look for challenges. They avoid what they perceive to be very easy for very difficult tasks.

The characteristics of *nAch* closely align with qualities necessary for successful entrepreneurship. As a result, we should not be surprised to find high achievers attracted to business, and particularly to such fields as commissioned sales, where there are challenging risks, rapid feedback, and opportunities to influence outcomes through personal efforts.

The need for affiliation (*nAff*) and the need for power (*nPow*) tend to be closely related to managerial success, according to McClelland.[8] Research conducted by McClelland gives strong evidence that the best managers are high in their need for power and low in their need for affiliation.

Attempts to validate McClelland's research and conclusions have met with some success. However, practitioners have given greatest attention to the achievement need. Given that *nAch* drives people to act on the basis of an internally induced stimulus rather than relying on externally imposed motivators, there are several implications for managers. First, since the *nAch* attributes can be taught and have been positively related to higher work performance, managers can consider having employees undergo *nAch* training to stimulate this need. Second, the understanding of the concepts behind *nAch*, and the characteristics that individuals high in *nAch* seek in their jobs, can assist managers in designing jobs with maximum motivational properties.

Motivation Theory Today: An Expectancy Approach

Expectancy theory
Although the early motivation theories offer insights into motivation, no single one offers a valid explanation for why some people exert a high level of effort on their job while others do not. What is needed is an integrative theory—one that recognizes the importance of needs and their satisfaction but also considers the contingency aspects relevant to particular people in particular situations. Such a theory has been formulated and, though it has not been immune from attack,[9] it is currently the clearest and most valid explanation we have of individual motivation. We are referring to expectancy theory.[10]

---

[8]"McClelland: An Advocate of Power," *International Management*, July 1975, pp. 27–29.

[9]See, for example, Herbert G. Heneman III and Donald P. Schwab, "Evaluation of Research on Expectancy Theory Prediction of Employee Performance," *Psychological Bulletin*, July 1972, pp. 1–9; and Leon Reinharth and Mahmoud A. Wahba, "Expectancy Theory as a Predictor of Work Motivation, Effort Expenditure, and Job Performance," *Academy of Management Journal*, September 1975, pp. 520–37.

[10]Victor H. Vroom, *Work and Motivation* (New York: John Wiley, 1964).

Expectancy theory argues that the strength of a tendency to act in a certain way depends on the strength of an expectation that the act will be followed by a given outcome and on the attractiveness of the outcome to the individual. It includes, therefore, three variables:[11]

Attractiveness

1. Attractiveness: the importance that the individual places on the potential outcome or reward that can be achieved on the job. This considers the unsatisfied needs of the individual.

Performance/reward

2. Performance-reward linkage: the degree to which the individual believes that performing at a particular level will lead to the attainment of each job outcome.

Effort/performance

3. Effort-performance linkage: the perceived probability by the individual that exerting a given amount of effort will lead to performance.

While this may sound pretty complex, it really is not that difficult to visualize. Whether individuals have the desire to produce at any given time depends on their particular goals and their perception of the relative worth of performance as a path to the attainment of these goals.

Figure 12-5 is a considerable simplification of expectancy theory but expresses its major contentions. The strength of people's motivation to perform (effort) depends on how strongly they believe that they can achieve what they attempt. If they achieve this goal (performance), will they be adequately rewarded and, if they are rewarded by the organization, will the reward satisfy their individual goals? Let us consider the four steps inherent in the theory and then attempt to apply it.

FIGURE 12-5   *Simplified Expectancy Model*

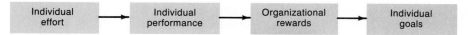

First, what outcomes does the job offer the employee? Outcomes may be positive: pay, security, companionship, trust, fringe benefits, a chance to use talent or skills, congenial relationships. On the other hand, employees may view outcomes as negative: fatigue, boredom, frustration, anxiety, harsh supervision, threat of dismissal. Note that reality is not important here; the critical issue is what the individual employee perceives the outcome to be, regardless of whether or not these perceptions are accurate.

Second, how attractive do employees view these outcomes as

[11]Vroom refers to these three variables as *valence, instrumentality, and expectancy,* respectively.

being? Are they valued positively, negatively, or neutrally? This obviously is an internal issue to the individual and depends on his or her personal values, personality, and needs. The individual who finds a particular outcome attractive—that is, positively valued—would prefer attaining it to not attaining it. If it is negative, the individual would prefer not attaining it to attaining it. Additionally, he or she may be neutral.

Third, what kind of behavior must the employee produce in order to achieve these outcomes? The outcomes are not likely to have any effect on the individual employee's performance unless the employee knows, clearly and unambiguously, what he or she must do in order to achieve them. For example, what is "doing well" in terms of performance appraisal? What are the criteria the employee's performance will be judged on?

Fourth and last, how do employees view their chances of doing what is asked of them? After the employees have considered their own competencies and their ability to control those variables that will determine their success, what probability do they place on successful attainment?[12]

Let us assume that Jill Jones, an employee of an organization, desires to buy a new home. Successful job performance should then ideally lead her toward that goal. If Jones perceives that her efforts will result in successful job performance, which, if rewarded by a significant pay raise, can satisfy her desire for a new home, we can expect her to be highly motivated. The key to the expectancy model, therefore, is the understanding of an individual's goals—and the linkage between effort and performance, between performance and rewards, and, finally, between rewards and individual-goal satisfaction.

The expectancy theory is a contingency model. It recognizes that there is no universal method for motivating people. Because we understand what needs an employee seeks to satisfy does not ensure that the employee herself perceives high job performance as necessarily leading to the satisfaction of these needs. If Beth Brown desires greater group acceptance, it is possible that more money, or even higher work performance, will not be important. More money cannot necessarily satisfy her social needs, and if the group norm reinforces low or moderate productivity, high productivity could be very detrimental to Brown's attaining greater group acceptance.

Let us summarize some of the issues this theory has brought forward. First, it emphasizes payoffs or rewards. As a result, we have to believe that the rewards the organization is offering align with what the employee wants. (This issue is discussed further in Chapter 15.)

---

[12]This four-step discussion was adapted from K. F. Taylor, "A 'Valence-Expectancy' Approach to Work Motivation," *Personnel Practice Bulletin*, June 1974, pp. 142–48.

Second, we have to be concerned with the attractiveness of rewards, which requires understanding and knowledge of what value the individual puts on organizational payoffs. We will want to reward the individual with those things he or she values positively. Third, expectancy theory emphasizes expected behaviors. Do employees know what is expected of them and how they will be appraised? (This issue will be discussed more fully in Chapter 14.) Finally, the theory is concerned with expectations. It implies that the manager should counsel subordinates to help them grasp a realistic view of their competencies. Furthermore, the manager should support the subordinate in developing those skills that are important in leading to better performance. These efforts are made because we want employees to be realistic in their perception of their efforts leading to a positive outcome.

Expectancy theory implies that we should make an extended effort to demonstrate confidence in individuals that they can perform well. Research tends to confirm that high expectancies of competence by others are positively related to performance.[13] In other words, we tend to perform based to some degree on the expectations others hold of our competency and our ability. Performance tends to follow a self-fulfilling prophecy; therefore, if we expect low performance, we increase the probability that the employee will perform at a low level.

Expectancy theory has been used to explain specific forms of employee behavior: for example, the turnover of hard-core unemployables.[14] After a review of twenty-four studies on hard-core unemployables, it was found that younger workers (those under twenty-one) have greater turnover during prejob training. These findings are explainable in expectancy terms.

Younger, hard-core, unemployable workers probably experience greater feelings of distrust toward the organization. Accordingly, they would perceive lower expectancies about the likelihood of receiving rewards and would be more likely to leave. On the other hand, older workers probably have higher expectancies and a greater desire for the rewards (a regular salary) that are contingent on attendance. There is a relationship between family responsibilities (such as marriage and home ownership) and retention. This probably reflects the greater need for job-related rewards. The greater the attraction of rewards related to holding a job, the higher the retention rates. Additionally, terminations are greater among those who have had a number of jobs in a short period of time. Evidently the inability to stay on past jobs leads to lower expectancies that rewards will follow from job attendance,

[13]Abraham K. Korman, "Expectations as Determinants of Performance," *Journal of Applied Psychology*, June 1971, pp. 218–22.

[14]Paul S. Goodman, Paul Salipante, and Harold Paransky, "Hiring, Training and Retraining the Hard-Core Unemployed: A Selected Review," *Journal of Applied Psychology*, August 1973, pp. 23–33.

and to lower expectancies by the individual that he or she will be capable of remaining on the job.

From management's viewpoint, the implications of the expectancy model are twofold. First, it is important to determine what needs each employee seeks to satisfy. This knowledge will be valuable to management in its attempt to align the rewards made available to the employee with the needs that the employee seeks to satisfy. Since rewards that are valuable to some employees may not be considered appealing to others, it is necessary to individualize rewards to each employee. Second, management should attempt to clarify the path for the worker between effort and need satisfaction. Individual motivation will be significantly determined by the probabilities the worker assigns to the following relationships: effort leading to performance, performance leading to rewards, and these rewards satisfying personal goals.

Summary

Of all the contemporary theories of motivation that exist, the expectancy theory, as discussed above, appears to be the one theory that encompasses the major aspects of all the motivational theories. Even so,

---

FIGURE 12-6

The Problem of Motivating Employees In a Declining Organization

---

Motivation takes on a different orientation during organization decline. Employees become primarily concerned with their basic security rather than challenging jobs. Under these conditions, wage and benefit givebacks become important as a means of preserving jobs. Similarly, programs designed to increase employee autonomy and job meaningfulness are likely to be replaced by stress management programs and the old scientific theme of efficiency through division of labor, with management doing the planning and the workers doing what they are told!

Levels of employee morale and commitment will typically be low. The work force suffers higher levels of stress and increased turnover. As slack resources dwindle, the margin for error decreases. The stakes for making good decisions increases; however, the penalties for a bad decision do too. As the tensions and pressures mount, morale tends to sag and the most mobile members within the organization look for new opportunities elsewhere.* Even managers are prone to jump ship. Thus a critical issue in managing the decline is not whether it can be done but whether the capable workers stay to get the job done.

The motivational issue becomes one of the strangest paradoxes in retrenchment. Part of the problem associated with the decline has been poor productivity—from managers in planning, organizing, leading, and controlling to workers in making the product. These problems, building over the years, have resulted in a condition that mandates immediate action. Unfortunately, based on the extent of the problems, the better employees begin to look for new opportunities to protect themselves. Thus, at a time when the best qualified are needed, many have departed from the organization and leave behind those whose actions have led, in part, to the decline. Many organizations never recover. Unfortunately, "when the going gets tough, the tough often get out."

---

*David A. Whetlen, "Sources Responses, and Effects of Organizational Decline," in *The Organization Life Cycle: Issues in the Creation in Transformation, and Decline of Organizations*, ed. John Kimberly and Robert H. Miles (San Francisco: Jossey-Bass, 1980), pp. 368–69.

expectancy theory is not without its limitations. Expectancy theory makes assumptions about people, the most important of which is that their motivation is a logical, thoughtful process. Since the array of outcomes and subjective probabilities that constitute the theory are known only to the individual, there can be little hope of accurately predicting individual behavior.

The Psychological Approach

Psychological approach to motivation

Some of the modern studies of motivation and productivity are finding that individuals do not fit nicely into the molds that many of the early motivational theorists proposed. In fact, more emphasis has been placed on the individual worker rather than on groups of workers. In many instances, group approaches to motivation have caused inconsistencies because "the motivationalists appear[ed] to have minimized the complexity and diversity of the motivational process and the influence and effects of numerous situational and contingency factors and circumstances in the workplace."[15] What has been needed is a more-tailored approach to motivation, one that takes each individual as an individual and treats him or her accordingly.

Because tailoring a specific job to a specific individual may be too costly or highly impractical, it was necessary to view motivation more from a set of factors that provide the basis of individuality. One such factor is personality type. Each one of us has a unique mixture of ingredients that make up our personality. However, we generally display one ingredient (personality type) predominantly. These predominant tendencies, while individualized, can be defined and separated into four categories: dominant, influencing, steady, and careful.[16]

Let us look at these four tendencies more closely.

The Four Personality Types

Dominant

Dominant. A dominant personality individual is someone who is forceful and domineering. These individuals are extremely confident in their actions and make a point of forcing their issues and concerns to the forefront. Dominant personality individuals make great leaders. They are good decision makers, have tremendous insight, and generate new and exciting ideas. For them, status and power are motivators. A good example of a dominant person is a CEO.

Influencing

Influencing. An influencing personality individual is someone who is outgoing and effervescent. These individuals are good talkers,

[15]E. S. Stanton, "A Critical Reevaluation of Motivation, Management and Productivity," *Personnel Journal*, March 1983, p. 211.

[16]John G. Geier, *The Performance Action System* (Minneapolis: Performax Systems International, 1983), p. 26.

striking conversations whenever they can. The extroverted influencing person works well with other people and enjoys entertaining others through the gift of communicating. For this person, popularity and social status are motivators. A good example of an influencing individual is a salesperson.

Steady
Steady.   A steady personality individual is someone who is extremely loyal to others. These individuals, in many cases, put the needs of others before their own. They are also very predictable because to do something differently might rock the boat. A steady person is someone with "stick-to-itiveness." He or she is able to remain relaxed in the worst of times and focus attention on details. For this person, job security and recognition are motivators. A good example of a steady person is a doctor.

Careful
Careful.   A careful personality individual is someone who is meticulous about details. These individuals analyze situations, and they check and recheck to ensure the accuracy of their decisions. They set high standards for themselves and identify specific actions to take, with checkpoints included to ensure that the achievements are attained. For this person, precision work and high quality of work are motivators. A good example of a careful person is an auditor.

Each of these four personality types has a distinct trait. While we cannot always identify an individual's mixture of the four personality types without extensive assessment, we can see the predominant type expressed behaviorally. For example, suppose we are outside a movie theater and are awaiting the arrival of our four personality individuals. This is what we may find: The dominant person arrives two minutes late for the feature film. Already past the cartoons, the dominant person yells to the usher to stop the film and rewind it. How dare the theater start anything before he arrives! The influencing individual is in the back of the theater, passing out free drinks and popcorn. He has many people laughing there, and you wonder if these people didn't come to see him instead of the movie. The influencer knows every joke in the movie and gives the punch line before it is said on the screen. The steady person was seated thirty minutes prior to the movie's starting. He wanted to make sure that he got a good seat, not too close so as to cramp his neck nor too far away so as to strain his eyes; just the right seat. He has been reading the latest movie review while waiting for the movie to start. And, finally, the careful person. You can't find him. Why? He is already inside. He came two hours early, just in case there might have been traffic to contend with. He didn't want to miss this movie. In fact, he was so early that he decided to go into the theater and watch the first showing. Now he is ready to sit through it again, to make sure he heard every line that was uttered.

While this parody has poked some fun at the four personality types, we can see a bit of ourselves in each of them. In fact, we take these same behaviors to the job and act accordingly. For instance, have you ever seen that steady, careful secretary so loyal to the boss and so accurate in typing and proofreading? What a wonderful combination of personality types!

In the next section, we will explore more of the implications of personality types on human resource management.

Implications of Personality Types For HRM

Personality types and HRM
The identification of personality types has many implications for human resource management. Among them are recruiting, career planning, and motivation.

From a recruiting perspective, personality typing allows the proper matching of an individual to a specific job. As individuals have personalities, so too do jobs. A unique feature of personality typing is that we can match those tendencies required for the job with those of the individual. For example, earlier we mentioned the job of a secretary, classifying that position as one that requires a steady and careful personality type. Imagine how much of a mismatch there would be if someone with a dominant personality were put into the position. The characteristics and traits of the dominant personality would be incongruent with the personality expectations of the position. And with this incongruency would come boredom, distaste, decreased motivation, and lower productivity.

To reduce these possibilities, we must analyze each job in terms of those job factors required for successful performance. One instrument, the "Job Factor Analysis System,"[17] provides twenty-four statements that, when evaluated as to their importance to the job, identify the specific personality typing needed for the position. If managers conducted these analyses prior to filling their positions, they would be better able to place someone into a position where personality typings match.

What makes this process interesting is that managers have the opportunity to analyze the jobs under their control and supervision and to develop individual profiles. Thus, if a manager firmly believes, because of the circumstances of the job, that a dominant personality is needed for a secretarial position, then that information is known prior to recruiting. Armed with this information, the manager can eliminate or significantly reduce poor-hiring decisions.

Keep in mind that although you may not be able to test a candidate to ascertain his or her personality, behaviors will indicate the individual's predominant personality type. Remember the movie theater?

---

[17]Ibid.

Career planning is enhanced from two perspectives. First, it gives you an opportunity to obtain an assessment of yourself. Knowing yourself, and where you desire to go in an organization, is the first step. Second, and more important, career planning provides information on how to reward people in the organization. With each personality type having different motivational desires, the company can more closely tailor its rewards. For example, promoting a careful, steady type into a sales position, where influencing personalities are needed, may be a wrong decision. In this case, frustration may set in from two perspectives: (1) the company loses in productivity from not having properly matched the person with the job, and (2) the individual is placed in a position without the proper tools (skills). Demotivation and lower productivity would probably result. Accordingly, personality typing becomes important in career planning as companies try to advance individuals in areas where they best fit. This may be one means of eliminating the Peter principle—promoting an individual to his or her highest level of incompetence.

Motivation suggestions   The third implication, and the focus of this chapter, is motivation. Employees are happier and more productive when they are placed into jobs that are related to their skills, abilities, and desires. Personality typing permits the tailoring of rewards to meet the specific wants of the individual. For example, if the steady employee values job security, then one means of motivating that individual would be to reinforce his or her security with the organization. Certainly other requirements must be met (we will discuss these later), but offering what is truly desired will have the greatest impact. Figure 12-7 is a composite of the four personality types and their respective motivators.

FIGURE 12-7

Motivators

DOMINANT	INFLUENCING
Power	Popularity
Authority	Recognition
Control over Results	Contact with People
Freedom from Restraint	Freedom of Expression
Wide Scope of Operations	Favorable Relationships
STEADY	CAREFUL
Stability	Personal Autonomy
Planned Change	Think Time
Conflict-Free Environment	Freedom from Pressure
Clear Responsibilities	Personal Achievements
Concrete Results	Quality Standards

SOURCE: John G. Geier, *The Action Projection System* (Minneapolis: Performax Systems International, 1983.) With permission.

Summary

Assessing personality types of both the employee and the job is becoming increasingly popular in today's organizations. With more focus being placed on making the environment at the worksite more conducive to productive work, placing individuals in jobs that match their makeup and fulfilling our basic premise of tailoring rewards to each individual will inevitably produce a motivated employee.

Even though this process seems logical and is becoming popular, we do not find that this or other motivational processes are being properly implemented. In the next section, we will explore motivation in practice and offer some suggestions for motivating employees.

Conclusion

If organizations were widely practicing the theories of Maslow, McGregor, Herzberg, and McClelland, we should expect to see extensive implementation of participative decision making, creation of autonomous and challenging jobs, and workers with greater responsibility in planning and controlling their work. Generally speaking, this is not the case. Managers still rely heavily on money as a motivator. Similarly, personnel departments tend to emphasize wages, hours, and working conditions—all hygiene factors.

It has been suggested that managers, for whatever reasons, are not providing accurate open feedback to individuals about their performance. Managers find that identifying group task goals and linking them to task responsibilities of individual members is a time-consuming operation. Mutual goal setting (the sharing of the goal-setting task with the subordinate) is avoided by some managers because they believe this is an infringement of management prerogatives. In some cases, task goals are identified, performance is evaluated, and the results are conveyed to the employee; yet the employee remains unsure of management's view of his or her accomplishments in terms of preestablished goals. In summary, it appears that many managers have failed to recognize the importance of establishing goals and performance feedback as would be suggested by expectancy theory.

Furthermore, expectancy theory suggests that managers should ensure that high productivity and good work performance lead to the achievement of personal goals. Again a review of actual organizational practices reveals many exceptions. Organizations seldom allocate rewards in such a way as to optimize motivation, per the expectancy model. While individual performances tend to be widely divergent— that is, a few outstanding, a few very poor, and the majority surrounding the average—rewards tend to be allocated more uniformly. The result is the overrewarding of incompetence and the underrewarding of superior performance. Organizations, generally speaking, do not necessarily reward "Protestant ethic" behavior. Hard work does not

MOTIVATION DEVICE

In need of motivation, Zeno goes to window (**A**), raising blind (**B**), allowing sun to melt block of ice (**C**). Water drips into pan (**D**) and through tube (**E**) into bucket (**F**). Weight of bucket pulls cord (**G**), driving hammer (**H**) into scissors (**I**) and cutting string (**J**) causing weight (**K**) to drop into net (**L**). Handle of net swings up into bullseye (**M**) making cactus (**N**) fall on and burst water-filled balloon (**O**). Water douses cat (**P**) who leaps forward, pulling on string (**Q**) attached to lever (**R**), causing boot (**S**) to swing up and suddenly motivate Zeno.

FIGURE 12-8

SOURCE: This article has been reprinted/republished through the courtesy of Halsey Publishing Co., publishers of Delta Air Lines' *Sky* magazine.

necessarily pay off; and therefore many workers place low probability on its leading to organizational rewards, and eventually the attainment of personal goals.

Internal politics is a vital determinant of who and what will be rewarded. For example, group acceptance may be a personal goal, and high productivity may hinder rather than support achievement of this goal. As a result, workers will reduce output and gain approval. The failing of our motivational theories tends to lie in their overemphasis on the rationality of managers in allocating rewards while understating the influence of politics in their distribution.

While the above discussion presents a rather pessimistic view, some suggestions can be offered to help us motivate employees. Such variables as recognizing individual differences, matching people to

VIEWS IN THE NEWS

Praise and Its Impact on Motivation

For years, we have been inundated with articles on how to motivate. Each article, in its own right, has laid more of a foundation that focuses on treating employees as people, not machines. One of the major themes included in most of the articles is the idea of recognition—giving praise for a job well done.

There's no doubt that recognition is important. But to simply state that we should recognize our employees leaves too much left unsaid. Offering praise to an employee is "an art." Recognition needs to be tailored to each employee's needs, for each is different and will react differently to the amount of praise received. For instance, while the praise may be genuine, if it's overused or perceived as insincere, its impact will be lost.

To avoid pitfalls that may occur in using praise as a motivator, the following guidelines are suggested:

- The Praiser Must Be Credible—Praise must come from someone knowledgeable about the job (e.g., supervisor). It must be given freely, with no strings attached or activities expected in return. Also, praise must be used only where appropriate so as not to lose its impact.
- Praise Should Fit the Situation—Praising an outstanding job should be noticeably different from praise given to a good job. Failure to do so may negate the impact of the intended praise.
- Praise Should Not Be Routine—If praise is used too much, or for the wrong activities, it too will lose its impact.
- Praise Should Not Reach a Saturation Point—Not all employees have the same need for praise; some need it frequently, while others don't. Accordingly, praise should be used in accordance with performance and individual need.

Praising an employee is an activity that should be encouraged in every organization. Its impact on motivation can be great—many studies have shown that to be the case. But there's a time and a place for praise, and a technique in using it that should be followed. A good motivational "tool" should not have its impact diminished by improper use.

Source: Adapted from David Engler, "Supervision Today: The Art of Praise," *Professional Trainer*, 6, No. 1 (Winter 1986), 7.

jobs, using goals, ensuring that goals are perceived as attainable, individualizing rewards, linking rewards to performance, and checking the system for equity can result in a more motivated employee, thereby increasing productivity.[18]

As employers, we must realize that each employee has different interests. We must find out what those interests are and try to develop a system of rewards to fulfill them. This may include career counseling to assess whether individuals are in positions in which they have the aptitudes necessary to do the work involved. Employees need to know what is expected of them. To achieve this end, we must establish and implement challenging goals for them to attain. Finally, we must meet periodically with our employees to provide them with feedback on how they are doing—which goals are on target, and which ones are not. For those goals that are not on target, we must work with the employee to discover why they are not and seek remedies for putting the employee back on the right track. Once these goals have been met, we must reinforce the employee's behavior with rewards, rewards tailored to meet his or her interests. We must also ensure that the rewards are fair and equitably distributed.

Much has been said about people looking for other rewarding factors in their jobs, but still the number one reason they work is for *money.* Once the pay becomes, or is perceived as being inadequate, very little can be done to help increase job satisfaction.

Every manager eventually experiences problems with subordinates who are not motivated or satisfied with their job. And every time this occurs, there is a cry for a motivational theory or process that can correct the situation. During the past few decades, we have witnessed the development of many theories that endeavor to explain motivation. In this chapter, we have provided an overview of these theories and offered a guideline vis-à-vis the expectancy theory as an approach to motivation.

We have come a long way in trying to identify how to motivate employees, but there appears to be even a longer road ahead. In the next chapter, we will review various structural changes that can be established to affect employees' motivation.

SUMMARY

1. Motivation is the willingness to do something, conditioned by this action's ability to satisfy some need.

2. Maslow, in his hierarchy of needs theory, said there are five needs.

[18]Stephen P. Robbins, *Management: Concepts and Practices* (Englewood Cliffs, N.J.: Prentice-Hall, 1984), pp. 322–24.

These needs are, in ascending order, physiological, safety, love, esteem, and self-actualization. When each need becomes substantially satisfied, it no longer motivates.

3. McGregor proposed two alternative sets of assumptions that managers hold about human motivation: one, basically negative, he labeled Theory X; and the other, basically positive, he labeled Theory Y. He argued that Theory Y assumptions are more valid than Theory X, and that employee motivation would be maximized by giving workers greater job involvement and autonomy.

4. Herzberg offers a two-factor motivation-hygiene theory of motivation. He argues that intrinsic job factors motivate, whereas extrinsic factors only placate employees.

5. McClelland proposed that there are three major relevant needs in workplace situations: achievement, affiliation, and power. A high need to achieve has been positively related to higher work performance.

6. The most accurate model for explaining motivation is expectancy theory. This theory states that an individual's desire to produce at any given time depends on his or her particular goals and perception of the relative worth of performance as a path to the attainment of these goals.

7. Certain personality types have been identified regarding how individuals react and what they expect from a job. The four types of personalities discussed are: dominant, influencing, steady, and careful.

KEY TERMS

Achievement need
Careful personality type
Dominant personality type
Expectancy theory
Herzberg's motivation-hygiene theory
Influencing personality type

Maslow's hierarchy of needs theory
McClelland's three needs theory
Motivation theory
Self-actualization
Steady personality type
Theory X and Theory Y

QUESTIONS FOR REVIEW

1. Define *motivation*. Describe the motivation process.

2. Contrast the hierarchy of needs theory with the motivation-hygiene theory.

3. What role would money play in the hierarchy of needs theory? In the motivation-hygiene theory? In expectancy theory? For the individual with a high *nAch*?

4. What role would self-actualization play in the hierarchy of needs theory? In the motivation-hygiene theory? In expectancy theory? For the individual with a high *nAch*?

5. What specific characteristics do high achievers tend to possess?

6. Contrast expectancy theory with research on *nAch*.

7. Describe personality types as they relate to motivation. How can motivation be increased by proper job matching?

8. What motivators would you use to motivate a *dominant* personality type? *Influencing? Steady? Careful?*

9. What role does money play as a motivator?

10. List and explain the ways in which one can promote a motivational atmosphere.

QUESTIONS FOR DISCUSSION

1. "Every individual can be classified as either Theory X or Theory Y." Do you agree or disagree? Discuss.

2. The owner of a Massachusetts electronics firm rewarded his thousand employees by closing the plant for a week and taking everyone on an all-expense-paid trip to Rome. What are the motivational implications of this action?

3. Think of the students you know who consistently make excellent grades. Are they more likely to be high achievers? Think of the successful athletes you know. Are they more likely to be high achievers? Should there be a positive relationship between academic success and athletic success?

4. "If you want to know if an employee is satisfied with her job, just ask her." Do you agree or disagree? Discuss.

5. "If pay is a prime motivator, one should not expect there to be a poorly motivated union member." Do you agree or disagree? Discuss.

CONTINUING CASE: Concord General

Behind Closed Doors

Last winter Concord General experienced an outbreak of a severe infection in the hospital. While only a few people were seriously ill, word spread that the hospital had a problem. Even though the problem was not isolated to Concord General and was not out of control, the community was apprehensive. Patients stopped coming to the hospital, which ultimately resulted in over $500,000 in lost revenues.

Not being able to recoup these losses in the short term, the hospital decided to change certain personnel policies. Effective immediately, no one was permitted to work overtime. Certain paid holidays were eliminated, and a severe reduction in benefits was implemented. There was also a hiring freeze, and cost-of-living adjustments were temporarily postponed until the hospital could recoup its losses. And some units experienced layoffs.

Within three weeks after these actions had been implemented, turnover in the nursing staff was insignificant. This low-turnover rate amazed Judy, as nurse openings in other hospitals were being advertised at substantially higher rates of pay and with greater benefits. Something, she assumed, was working for the hospital.

Questions

1. What motivational theory best describes the action of those who stayed? Those who left? What role did money play in motivating these nurses?
2. Is it safe to assume that the nurses who stayed were not motivated by money and that these tactics might be useful for future cutbacks? Discuss.
3. Would you have stayed? Why?
4. Identify those variables that may be keeping the nurses from resigning.

CASE APPLICATION

Below Sea Level

Dave Singleton and Steve Crenshah were close friends and both were college seniors. They enjoyed doing collaborative work and, for the most part, did very well. A few weeks prior to an exam, Dave and Steve would meet and identify the material that was to be covered on the exam. Each would then take one-half of the material, review it, and condense it into relevant study notes. After a week of preparing the notes, the two would meet again and exchange copies of their respective work. They would then set aside three hours each night for the remainder of the time before the exam to study, each quizzing the other on the material until they were both confident that they understood it.

Their system was successful. On seven previous exams, they scored within five points of each other. Deciding that this was a desirable learning mechanism, they continued. However, the results began to change significantly. Steve was now constantly scoring the highest marks on the exams in the class while Dave was just making D's. The two were astounded, and after reviewing each other's tests, could not believe that such a difference was possible. But this occurred in all the classes that the two took together, so the possibility that there was a personality difference with the professor was highly unlikely.

Dave is depressed. He doesn't know what to do. Evidently his studying is not paying off. He has decided to complete the remainder of the semester studying on his own.

Dave finished the semester with a 1.9 GPA (on a scale of 4.0). Demoralized about being placed on probation, he has decided to leave school.

Questions

1. Analyze Dave's behavior in terms of the expectancy theory.
2. What should Dave have done prior to taking a semester off from school?
3. If you were Dave's guidance counselor, how would you motivate him to return to school?
4. How could such a discrepancy exist between Dave's and Steve's grades?

ADDITIONAL READINGS

BERMAN, FREDERIC E., and JOHN B. MINER, "Motivation to Manage at the Top Executive Level: A Test of the Hierarchic Role-Motivation Theory," *Personnel Psychology*, 38, No. 2 (Autumn 1985), 377–91.

JORDAN, PAUL C., "Effects of Extrinsic Reward on Intrinsic Motivation: A Field Experiment," *Academy of Management Journal*, 29, No. 2 (January 1986), 405–11.

KAFKA, VINCENT W., "A New Look at Motivation—For Productivity Improvement," *Supervisory Management*, 31, No. 4 (April 1986), 19–24.

NIEHOUSE, OLIVER, "Job Satisfaction: How to Motivate Today's Workers," *Supervisory Management*, 31, No. 2 (February 1986), 8–11.

STAW, BARRY M., "Organizational Psychology and the Pursuit of the Happy/ Productive Worker," *California Management Review*, 28, No. 4 (Summer 1986), 40–53.

CHAPTER 13

Job Design,

Work Scheduling,

and Motivation

AFTER READING THIS CHAPTER, YOU WILL BE ABLE TO:

1. Explain how job design and work scheduling affect motivation
2. Describe the job characteristics model
3. Define *job enrichment*
4. Explain how job rotation can motivate workers
5. Discuss the scheduling of work modules
6. Discuss the shorter workweek
7. Explain how flex-time affects motivation
8. Explain the purpose of home work
9. Discuss work sharing

You can't eat for eight hours a day, nor make love for eight hours a day—all you can do for eight hours a day is work. Which is the reason why man makes himself and everyone else so miserable and unhappy.

—William Faulkner

One of the more important factors that influence an employee's motivational level is the structure of his or her work. Is there a lot of variety or is the job repetitive? Is the work closely supervised? Does the job allow the employee discretion? The answers to questions like these will have a major impact on the motivational properties inherent in the job and hence the level of productivity that an employee can expect to achieve. In this chapter, we will discuss a few job design issues and developments that can make jobs more attractive and motivating to employees.

Design, Scheduling, and Expectancy Theory

There are no explicit elements in expectancy theory to suggest that the way tasks are designed or scheduled will affect performance. However, the model takes into account various needs that workers seek to satisfy. Some of these can be, and should be, satisfied off the job. Since the time a person puts into a job represents about 35 percent of his or her waking hours, there are ample opportunities for finding fulfillment and satisfaction from non-job-related activities. It can be argued that if jobs are a bore, there are sufficient opportunities for finding excitement off the job. On the other hand, it can also be argued that jobs that are intrinsically rewarding—those that offer challenge and greater freedom, and that employees find interesting—will provide motivation in themselves and will permit substantially less reliance on externally initiated motivators.

It is no secret that the vast majority of jobs in the United States today are highly specialized. Activities are broken down into smaller and smaller tasks resulting in a large segment of the work force doing routine and repetitive activities eight hours a day, five days a week, forty-eight to fifty weeks a year. To many people, this way of organiz-

FIGURE 13-1

SOURCE: Copyright 1973, G. B. Trudeau. Distributed by Universal Press Syndicate.

ing work leaves a lot to be desired. This becomes relevant when we see that employees place a great deal of importance on the type of work they do.

The Job Characteristics Model

If the type of work a person does is so important, can we identify those specific job characteristics that affect productivity, motivation, and satisfaction? A model has been developed that identifies five such job factors and their interrelationship. It is called the job characteristics model.[1] The early research with this model indicates that it can be a useful guide in redesigning the jobs of individuals.

The model specifies five core characteristics or dimensions:

Skill variety
1. *Skill variety*—the degree to which a job requires a variety of different activities so one can use a number of different skills and talents

Task identity
2. *Task identity*—the degree to which the job requires completion of a whole and identifiable piece of work

Task significance
3. *Task significance*—the degree to which the job has a substantial impact on the lives or work of other people

Autonomy
4. *Autonomy*—the degree to which the job provides substantial freedom, independence, and discretion to the individual in scheduling the work and in determining the procedures to be used in carrying it out

Feedback
5. *Feedback*—the degree to which carrying out the work activities required by the job results in the individual obtaining direct and

[1] J. Richard Hackman and Greg R. Oldham, "Development of the Job Diagnostic Survey," *Journal of Applied Psychology*, April 1975, pp. 159–70.

clear information about the effectiveness of his or her performance

Figure 13-2 presents the model. Notice how the first three dimensions—skill variety, task identity, and task significance—combine to create meaningful work. That is, if these three characteristics exist in a job, we can predict the incumbents will view their job as being important, valuable, and worthwhile. Notice, too, that jobs that possess autonomy give the job incumbents a feeling of personal responsibility for the results; and that if a job provides feedback, the employees will know how effectively they are performing. From a motivational standpoint, the model says that internal rewards are obtained by individuals when they *learn* (knowledge of results) that they *personally* (experienced responsibility) have performed well on a task that they *care about* (experienced meaningfulness).[2] The more that these three conditions are present, the greater will be the employees' motivation, performance, and satisfaction; and the lower their absenteeism and likelihood of turnover. As the model shows, the links between the job dimensions and the outcomes are moderated, or adjusted for, by the strength of the individual's growth need; that is, the

FIGURE 13-2   *The Job Characteristics Model of Work Motivation*

SOURCE: J. Richard Hackman, "Work Design," in *Improving Life At Work*, ed. J. R. Hackman and J. L. Suttle (Santa Monica, Calif.: Goodyear 1977), p. 129.

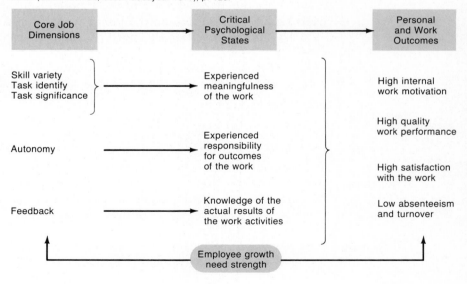

[2]J. Richard Hackman, "Work Design," in *Improving Life At Work*, ed. J. R. Hackman and J. L. Suttle (Santa Monica, Calif.: Goodyear, 1977), p. 129.

$$\text{Motivating potential score} = \left[\frac{\text{Skill variety} + \text{Task identity} + \text{Task significance}}{3} \right] \times \text{Autonomy} \times \text{Job feedback}$$

FIGURE 13-3   Computing a Motivating Potential Score

employee's desire for self-esteem and self-actualization. This means that individuals with a high growth need are more likely than their low-growth-need counterparts to experience the critical psychological states when their jobs are enriched, and to respond more positively to the psychological states when they are present.

The core job dimensions have been analyzed and combined into a single index, as shown in Figure 13-3. Jobs that are high on motivating potential must be high on at least one of the three factors that lead to experiencing meaningfulness, and they must be high on both autonomy and feedback. If jobs score high on motivating potential, the model predicts that motivation, performance, and satisfaction will be positively affected, while the likelihood of absence and turnover is lessened.

While the job characteristics model is still undergoing testing, the preliminary results have been supportive:

1. People who work on jobs with high core job dimensions are more motivated, satisfied, and productive than those who do not.
2. People with strong growth needs respond more positively to jobs that are high in motivating potential than do those with weak growth needs.
3. Job dimensions operate through the psychological states in influencing personal and work outcome variables, rather than influencing them directly.[3]

These findings support our position that the structure of work is an important influence on an employee's motivation level. Certainly the decision about how a job is to be structured reflects other considerations (such as technology, the environment, plant and equipment, and skill levels) besides its motivational potential. But the design of a job and the way work is scheduled are variables that (1) management can readily influence and (2) do affect an employee's motivation. Therefore we have committed a chapter to reviewing some of the more frequently suggested structural modifications for making jobs more meaningful and interesting.

[3]Ibid., pp. 132–33.

Job Enrichment

Job enrichment The most popularly advocated structural technique for increasing an employee's motivational potential is job enrichment. To enrich a job, management allows the worker to assume some of the tasks executed by his or her supervisor. Enrichment requires that workers do increased planning and controlling of their work, usually with less supervision and more self-evaluation. From the standpoint of increasing the internal motivation from doing a job, it has been proposed that job enrichment offers great potential.[4] However, job enrichment is successful only when it increases responsibility, increases the employee's freedom and independence, organizes tasks so as to allow workers to do a complete activity, and provides feedback to allow individuals to correct their own performance. Furthermore, job enrichment efforts will only be successful if the individuals in the enriched job find that their needs are met by the "enrichment." If these individuals did not want increased responsibility, for example, then increasing responsibility will not have the desired effect. Successful job enrichment, then, is contingent on worker input.

A successful job enrichment program should ideally increase employee satisfaction. But since organizations do not exist to create employee satisfaction as an end, there must also be direct benefits to the organization. There is evidence that job enrichment produces lower absenteeism and reduced turnover costs; but on the critical issue of productivity, the evidence is inconclusive. In some situations, job enrichment has increased productivity; in others, productivity has been decreased. However, when it decreases, there does appear to be consistently conscientious use of resources and a higher quality of product or service. In other words, in terms of efficiency, for the same input a higher quality of output is obtained.

Job Rotation

Job rotation In Chapter 10 we discussed job rotation as an on-the-job management development technique. Job rotation also offers a potential for dealing with the problem of general worker dissatisfaction caused by overstructuring. It allows employees to diversify their activities and offset the occurrence of boredom.

Horizontal job transfers can break up the monotony inherent in almost any job after the employee's skills have been refined and the newness has worn off. In some cases this may be after only a few weeks,

---

[4]See, for example, F. Herzberg, B. Mausner, and B. Snyderman, *The Motivation to Work* (New York: John Wiley, 1959); Louis E. Davis, *Design of Jobs* (London: Penguin, 1972); R. N. Ford, *Motivation through the Work Itself* (New York: American Management Association, 1969); and John R. Turney and Stanley L. Cohen, "Alternative Work Schedules Increase Employee Satisfaction," *Personnel Journal*, 62, No. 3 (March 1983), 202.

while in other cases it may be years. Opportunities for diversity, to learn new skills, change supervisors, relocate, or make new job acquaintances, can deter or slow up the onset of boredom from jobs that have become habitual. Job rotation, therefore, can renew enthusiasm for learning and motivate workers to higher performance.

Work Modules

Work modules If you can conceive of extremely rapid job rotation, to the point where one would assume new activities every few hours, you can comprehend the technique of work modules. It has been suggested as a solution to meet the problem of fractionated, boring, and programmed work, at an acceptable price, with undiminished quality and quantity of product.[5]

Robert Kahn, of the University of Michigan, has defined a work module as a time task unit, equal to approximately two hours of work at a given task. A normal forty-hour-a-week job would then be defined in terms of four modules a day, five days a week, for between forty-eight and fifty weeks a year.

Through the use of modules, it would be possible to increase diversity for workers. Undesirable work could be spread about, for example, by having everyone take a module or two each day. The result would be that people would change activities through changing work modules.

The benefits of work modules lie in increasing diversity for the employees, by dividing up and sharing the undesirable work activities, expanding work independence to the bottom of the hierarchy, and constructing the job to meet the needs of the individual, rather than forcing people to fit a particularly defined job.

However, work modules do present some problems. Considerable time and money are involved in planning and executing the change-over. Dysfunctional conflicts can develop over the question of equity and the allocation of modules. Bookkeeping and payroll-computation costs increase. Finally, as we noted with a rotation program, there is a loss of expertise, and with it, an increased possibility of errors.

Shorter Workweek

Shorter workweek The 1970s saw an increasing interest by employers in developing shorter workweeks for employees. Experiments have generally covered workweeks of three twelve-hour days, four nine-hour days, and four ten-hour days with the latter receiving the greatest attention.[6] For

---

[5]Robert L. Kahn, "The Work Module," *Psychology Today,* February 1973, pp. 35–39.

[6]James A. Breaugh, "The 12 Hour Work Day: Differing Employee Reactions," *Personnel Psychology,* 36 (Summer 1983), 278.

our discussion, we will limit our scope to the four ten-hour-days program.

Proponents of the four-day, forty-hour workweek have argued that in addition to having a favorable effect on employee absenteeism, job satisfaction, and productivity, a four-day workweek provides employees with more leisure time, decreases commuting time, decreases requests for time off for personal matters, makes it easier for the organization to recruit employees, and decreases time spent on tasks such as setting up equipment. Others, however, have noted some potential disadvantages. Among these are a decrease in workers' productivity near the end of the longer workday, low job satisfaction, and underutilization of equipment.[7] While the evidence does generally support that the shorter workweek increases employee enthusiasm and morale and reduces turnover and absenteeism, the evidence is mixed on the issue of productivity.[8]

It appears that there is a long-term and short-term impact of the shorter workweek.[9] When first implemented, the shorter workweek achieves many of the results claimed by its advocates: improved morale, reduced dissatisfaction, and reduced absenteeism and turnover figures. However, after approximately one year, many of these advantages disappear. Employees then begin to complain about increased fatigue and the difficulty of coordinating their jobs with their personal lives—the latter a particular problem for working mothers. Managers also find drawbacks. More scheduling of work is involved, overtime rates must frequently be paid for the hours worked over eight during the workday, and general difficulties arise in coordinating work. Additionally, managers still tell employees when to arrive and when to leave, so the shorter workweek does little to increase the workers' freedom, specifically in selecting the work hours that suit them best.

Flex-Time

Flex-time

Another approach toward increasing workers' freedom and their motivation is flex-time. *Flex-time* is a system whereby employees contract to work a specific number of hours a week but are free to vary the hours of work within certain limits. Each day consists of a common core, usually six hours, with a flexibility band surrounding the core. For example, the core may be 10:00 A.M. to 4:00 P.M., with the office

---

[7]Ibid.; and Simcha Ronen and Sophie B. Primps, "The Compressed Work Week as Organizational Change: Behavioral and Attitudinal Outcome," *Academy of Management Review,* 6, No. 1 (1981), 61–74.

[8]Ronen and Primps, "Compressed Work Week," p. 71.

[9]John M. Ivancevich and Herbert L. Lyon, "The Shortened Workweek: A Field Experiment," *Journal of Applied Psychology,* February 1977, pp. 34–37.

actually opening at 7:30 A.M. and closing at 6:00 P.M. All employees are required to be at their jobs during the common core period, but they are allowed to accumulate their other two hours from before and/or after the core time. Some flex-time programs allow extra hours to be accumulated and turned into a free day off each month.

Under flex-time, employees assume responsibility for completing a specific job, and that increases their feeling of self-worth. It is consistent with the view that people are paid for producing work, not for being at their job stations for a set period of hours; hence its motivational aspects.

Flex-time has been implemented in a number of diverse organizations, and the response has generally been favorable. In the United States, approximately 13 percent of all organizations use some variant of flex-time—amounting to between 3 and 4 million workers, mostly white-collar.[10] More specifically, we find an evaluation of Mutual of New York's flex-time program rated it very successful. There was an increase in employee productivity, fewer errors, improved employee morale, and a significant reduction in lateness and absenteeism.[11] A flex-time program initiated in several administrative departments at a large General Motors of Canada plant received similarly favorable notices.[12] Workers liked the program, and the company found that lateness and absences were reduced, offices were staffed for a longer period each day, and overtime costs were reduced. The State of New York's Commerce Department has also given its flex-time experiment high ratings.[13] Based on use by over 150 employees, the program has been described as "an astounding success," with improvements in departmental productivity and worker morale. Said one executive, "The idea is to treat state employees like civilized adult people instead of like kindergarteners. It's very simple: If you treat people with maturity, they respond with maturity. But if you treat them like children, then the game becomes how to cheat the system.[14]

On the plus side, flex-time appears to contribute toward decreased tardiness, reduced absenteeism, less job fatigue, increased organizational loyalty, and improved recruitment. However, it produces problems for managers in directing subordinates outside the core time period, causes confusion where there is shift work or interdependen-

[10]Stanley D. Nollen, "Does Flex-time Improve Productivity?" *Harvard Business Review*, September–October 1979, pp. 12, 16–18, 22.

[11]Cynthia J. Fields, "Variable Work Hours—the MONY Experience," *Personnel Journal*, September 1974, pp. 675–78.

[12]"Flexitime at GM of Canada." *Personnel*, January–February 1978, pp. 41–43.

[13]Molly Ivins, "Bill in Albany Asks Flexible Work Time," *New York Times*, March 13, 1977, p. 45.

[14]Ibid.

cies between functions, increases difficulties when someone with a particular skill or knowledge is not available, and makes planning and controlling of work more cumbersome and costly for managers.[15]

In summary, flex-time has been a popular technique that has been instituted easily and at a relatively low cost. It has offered strong motivational potential by increasing worker freedom and allowing workers to assume greater responsibility through creating opportunities for them to make decisions about their work schedule. Note, however, that while flex-time has offered greater flexibility, many of the workers continue to arrive and depart according to their pre-flex-time patterns.[16] But, by the same token, most later arrivals are eliminated.[17]

New Trends in Work Scheduling

Until the 1980s, most of the changes that we have described occurred inside the organization and deviated very little from the traditional work patterns that had existed since the 1930s. However, with the changes that have taken place in both the organization and the home, we are finding new alternatives to the classic working day. The two that appear to be the most drastic are home work and job sharing.

Home work   *Home Work.*   With the advent of technological breakthroughs and changing family needs, there has been a surge in the number of individuals doing work at home for their employer. Home work was prominent during the early 1900s and is again becoming a national phenomenon. The jobs most affected by this transition are those that have some relationship to information processing, such as computer programming, financial analysis, writing, and clerical services. While there are only thirty-five known work programs involving six hundred employees at such companies as Aetna Life and Casualty, Investors Diversified Services, and Blue Cross/Blue Shield of South Carolina, it is estimated that in the 1990s more than 15 million people will be involved in home work.[18]

The advantages from home work appear to be numerous. It will allow employers to tap an expanded work force, namely, people who have small children at home and those who are handicapped. It is also believed that such a work relationship will build more trust—an honor system between the employer and the employee. Yet this same honor system could also be the major drawback. It will become more diffi-

---

[15]J. Carrol Swart, "What Time Shall I Go to Work Today?" *Business Horizons*, October 1974, pp. 19–26.

[16]Simcha Ronen, "Arrival and Departure Patterns of Public Sector Employees Before and After Implementation of Flextime," *Personnel Psychology*, 34 (Winter 1981), 817–22.

[17]Ibid.

[18]"If Home Is Where the Work Is," *Business Week*, May 3, 1982, p. 66.

VIEWS IN THE NEWS

Working Parents: Issues for Employers

Working parents miss about one week of work each year because of child care problems, according to a survey of 1,243 working parents that was conducted by Child Care Systems, Inc., a child care information and referral services firm. The study finds that, to accommodate such problems as sick children, ill child-care providers, holidays, and transportation problems, working parents miss an average of 5.4 work days annually. To receive compensation for this time off, the study notes, responding employees most often report missed days to their employers as vacation days (34 percent), sick days (30 percent), or personal days (25 percent).

Child care problems also cause the typical working parent to lose slightly more than eight hours of working time per year because of early departures from or late arrivals to the job, the study finds. Nearly one-third (30 percent) of the employees with children said they leave work early or arrive late at least twice a month, and 27 percent of the respondents indicated that, during work hours, they call or are called at least once a week to answer questions about their children, receive calls from their children, or arrange for child care adjustments. The study also finds that:

- Selecting appropriate child care arrangements takes an average of 8.8 hours each time changes are made.
- Thirty-nine percent of the working parents have considered leaving their jobs because of child care problems.
- Thirty percent of employees with children favor family day care homes, 28 percent prefer either center-based care or care in their own homes, and the remainder are partial to school-based care. ("Workplace Impact of Working Parents," Child Care Systems, Inc., 329 W. Main St., Lansdale, Penn. 19446)

Source: Reprinted by permission from *Bulletin to Management,* copyright 1985 by The Bureau of National Affairs, Inc., Washington, D.C.

cult for managers to manage their subordinates. That, in addition to developing new compensation packages and performance evaluation, may hinder home work's growth.

Work sharing

Work Sharing. With the increase of two-career families that have small children, work sharing allows one or both parents to be at home with the child during the formative years. Years ago, parents had to make a decision—would one of them quit work (primarily the wife/mother) to raise the child or would the child be sent to a day-care center? Perplexed by these questions and desiring to maintain both a family and a career, many sought a job that would allow both. Work sharing was that alternative. In work sharing, two people share one full-time job. One person may work in the morning; the other in the afternoon. Each person is compensated according to his or her share of the work. Whom one shares the work with is contingent on factors too numerous to elaborate here. Usually, though, we find a woman sharing her job with another woman; both of them are parents and work for the same organization. However, fathers, too, have been known to work share.

Work sharing has been predominant in the school system. Teachers who are also mothers work part of the day in their classroom and then leave to go home to their child. Another teacher/mother then replaces the morning teacher. In one county school system in Maryland, work sharing has worked well by providing not only the flexibility that the worker needs but also the skilled teaching that the school and the pupils need.

Whether work sharing will continue to grow cannot be determined at this time. The point that is being stressed, however, is that careers and family life can be combined. If an employer values the services of an employee and if variations are possible, then the two can work together to develop a viable alternative. Forcing a good employee to choose between work and home provides no choice, as this will only result in the loss of a good worker.

Conclusion

We have discussed various aspects of jobs as they relate to increased worker satisfaction. Workers need to be challenged at work, and the job itself must be one that the worker values. Jobs must include skill variety, task identity, and task significance. A number of alternatives are available to the organization to make jobs more interesting. Among these are job enrichment, job rotation, work modules, shorter workweeks, flex-time, home work, and work sharing.

SUMMARY

1. The manner in which job tasks are designed and work is scheduled can influence the motivational level of employees.

2. The job characteristics model demonstrates that jobs that rate high on motivating potential must be high on at least one of the following three factors—skill variety, task identity, and task significance—and they must score high on both autonomy and feedback.

3. Job enrichment allows workers to assume increased responsibility for planning and self-evaluation of their work.

4. Job rotation can act to motivate workers by diversifying their activities and offsetting the occurrence of boredom.

5. Work modules are two-hour work units, the scheduling of which can be moved about to increase diversity and reduce opportunities for workers to become bored.

6. The shorter workweek—particularly the four-day, forty-hour work-week—is designed to improve worker satisfaction and productivity by increasing employee enthusiasm and morale.

7. Flex-time increases motivation by allowing workers greater freedom in deciding when they will arrive at or depart from work.

8. Home work is designed to provide work for those individuals who would otherwise be out of the labor force. Home work allows these individuals to work for an employer within the confines of their home.

9. Work sharing is designed to give flexibility to those people who for some reason cannot work a full day. This has been effective in the school system and has enabled parents to have more time at home with their children.

KEY TERMS

Autonomy	Job design
Flex-time	Job enrichment
Home work	Work modules
Job characteristics model	Work sharing

QUESTIONS FOR REVIEW

1. What is the relationship, if any, between the way tasks are designed or work scheduled and expectancy theory?

2. Is job redesign concerned with intrinsic or extrinsic motivation? Explain.

3. What is the job characteristics model?

4. To score high on motivating potential, why must a job have both high autonomy and job feedback?

5. What is job enrichment? When is it likely to be effective?

6. Explain how job rotation can be both a development and a motivation technique.

7. What are the advantages and disadvantages of the shorter workweek?

8. What are the advantages and disadvantages of flex-time?

9. Compare the approximate costs to management of implementing (a) job enrichment, (b) a shorter workweek, and (c) flex-time.

10. Describe home work and work sharing. What ingredients are necessary for both to work?

QUESTIONS FOR DISCUSSION

1. Which one of the following work schedules would you prefer: (a) 8 hours a day, 5 days a week; (b) 10 hours a day, 4 days a week; (c) 12 hours a day, 3 days a week; or (d) 10 hours a day for 5 straight days, followed by 5 days off? Why?

2. "Want to find out if a person likes his job? Ask him if he would stay with it if he inherited five million dollars tomorrow!" What percentage of today's labor force do you think would continue working in their present job if they were suddenly independently wealthy? Do you see any common characteristics in either the persons or the jobs of those who would choose to continue their present work?

3. "Employees should have jobs that give them autonomy and diversity." Build an argument in favor of this statement. Then build an argument against this statement.

4. Which of the core job dimensions do you value most? Do you think most of your friends would give a similar answer? How about your parents or grandparents?

5. "Careers and family life are not compatible. You have to have either one or the other." Do you agree or disagree with this statement? Discuss.

CONTINUING CASE: Concord General

Forty by Twenty-Four

To become a leader in nurse recruiting, Judy has decided to offer a new program that would not only attract excellent personnel but also serve as a motivational tool for the current nurses. This new program is a weekend option—working two twelve-hour shifts, one on Saturday and one on Sunday, and being paid for forty hours of work. Included in this option will be all the benefits that the full-time employees now receive.

Response to this option has been phenomenal. Not only have there been a multitude of applications from individuals outside the hospital but the internal applications have also been overwhelming. In fact, response has been so good that Judy has anticipated offering the twenty-four hour option to all nurses, working two twelve-hour shifts and being paid for forty. However, John Michaels believes that the twenty-four-hour option is too costly. Even though a device may be motivational, he believes that any cost-prohibitive measure must be avoided. The weekend option is excellent, but that is as far as it would extend.

Questions

1. Discuss the advantages and disadvantages of Judy's weekend option.
2. How can this option be motivational for current employees who do not want to work two twelve-hour shifts?
3. If the weekend option is beneficial for the weekends, why is it not beneficial during the week?
4. Do you believe it to be discriminatory for Concord General to offer the weekend option to a select few, paying them for forty hours of work when other nurses must work forty hours to be paid for forty? Justify your answer.

CASE APPLICATION

The Rites of Spring

"It happens around here every spring," Ryan Gabriel began. "I've been an electrician here at Republic Mills for ten years. Got my ten-year pin, in fact, last month. Every spring, those hotshots up in the administrative offices come up with some harebrained scheme they think is going to get us to work harder. Those people up there think we're a bunch of idiots. Well, I've got news for them—they're the idiots. Just look at their record.

"Back in 1982, it was their suggestion system. The 'brains' came down and told us that we were important, that we knew our jobs better than anyone, and they encouraged us to come up with better ways of doing our jobs. They set up some committee to review our suggestions and gave out bonuses to the ones they liked. I heard some people got as much as $500 for a suggestion, but the only person I know who got any money was Adele over in design. She got a big $25 bucks.

"They had some scheme in 1983, but I forget what it was. In 1984, though, the new answer was called profit sharing. Management had some incredible bonus system based on this plant's productivity. It was ridiculous! You had to have a Ph.D. to figure the damn thing out. We used to joke that if you took your age, multiplied it by the number of kids you had, and divided it by your wife's age, you'd get the amount due you. Well, it didn't work out too well. None of us got a nickel out of it.

"In 1985, MBO was the 'in' thing. I think it means management by objectives. Whatever, the big brass had us all establishing objectives with our supervisors, setting specific goals, and junk like that. In the fall of that year, the board of directors canned the president. When the new honcho came in, he wasn't too impressed with all the paper work that MBO required. We haven't heard about MBO since.

"In 1986, quality circles were on everyone's tongue. We were all supposed to be like the Japanese. We were told by top management to meet occasionally and discuss everything. The only thing we accomplished was a two-hour break each week for a useless meeting.

"Last year, management decided that what we needed were enriched jobs. Can you believe they started changing all our jobs around? Hell, they had me filling out purchase requisitions for electrical cable, inspecting my own work, and a bunch of other stuff. Don't those idiots up on top realize that if I wanted to do management work, I'd be a manager? Most of us told our bosses we liked our jobs just the way they were. Don't bog us down with increased responsibilities.

"Here it is springtime again and, sure as hell, the bozos upstairs have got a new brainchild. Something called flex-time. Do they really think we are going to buy another one of their hocus-pocus tricks? They haven't had one yet that has worked. They're on a real hot streak—about zero for ten. Why doesn't management just leave us alone to do our jobs and stop trying to manipulate us with these motivational tricks?"

Questions

1. What effect on employees does introducing a motivational technique and then dropping it have?
2. Does Gabriel's perception of job enrichment suggest anything about implementing this technique?
3. Is there any way to increase Gabriel's motivation?

ADDITIONAL READINGS

BANKS, WILLIAM C., "The Way We'll Work: Shorter Hours, Bigger Bonuses," *Money*, November 1985, pp. 153–70.

BUREAU OF NATIONAL AFFAIRS, "Scheduling Study: Flextime Flourishing," *Bulletin to Management*, 37, No. 16 (April 17, 1986), 125.

CROSBY, BOB, "Employee Involvement: Why It Fails, What It Takes to Succeed," *Personnel Administrator,* February 1986, pp. 95–106.

MARKS, MITCHELL LEE, "The Question of Quality Circles," *Psychology Today,* March 1986, pp. 36–46.

WALTON, RICHARD E., "From Control to Commitment in the Workplace," *Harvard Business Review,* March–April 1985, pp. 77–84.

and 8. The reason is that the problems inherent in rating individuals and controlling for evaluator error are just as critical in performance appraisal as they are in selection. In this chapter, we will be emphasizing rating and ranking problems rather than, say, interviewing bias; however, it should be evident that in attempting to reach a selection decision about a potential candidate, the primary motive of the selection process is to gain information in order to reach a decision. Similarly, in performance appraisal, information is accumulated in order to reach a decision. The only difference is that the former attempts to reach a decision about an individual's potential performance, while the latter looks at actual performance. The techniques are really quite alike; it is only their use that is different.

Performance Appraisal and Expectancy Theory

As we argued at the beginning of Chapter 12, just because employees have ability does not ensure that they will perform satisfactorily on the job. The other critical dimension is motivation. Theoretically, as managers we should be interested in ends; that is, getting the job done! As one football coach remarked in appraising his ungraceful, but effective, field goal kicker: "It ain't pictures, it's numbers." Similarly, managers shoud be concerned with results—it's performance that counts! It may be difficult for some managers to accept, but they should not be appraising personnel on how they look (means), but rather on whether they can score (end results). We propose, therefore, that organizations exist to "score," rather than to provide an environment for individuals to "look like players." Just like the previously cited football coach, managers must be concerned with evaluating their personnel on "numbers" and not on "pictures."

Performance is a vital component of expectancy theory. Specifically, we must be concerned with the linkage between effort and performance, and between performance and rewards. Do people see effort leading to performance, and performance to the rewards that they value? Clearly, they have to know what is expected of them. They need to know how their performance will be measured. Furthermore, they must feel confident that if they exert an effort within their capabilities, it will result in a satisfactory performance as defined by the criteria by which they are being measured. Finally, they must feel confident that if they perform as they are being asked, they will achieve the rewards they value.

In summary, it is obvious that performance appraisal plays a vital part in the expectancy model of motivation. If the objectives that individual employees are seeking are unclear, if the criteria for measuring that objective attainment are vague, and if employees lack confidence that their efforts will lead to a satisfactory appraisal of their performance or feel that there will be an unsatisfactory payoff by the organization when their performance objectives are achieved, we can expect individuals to work considerably below their potential. If we have done our job to acquire capable people and develop their basic abilities to do the job, we must also make sure that they know what behaviors are required of them, understand how they are going to be appraised, believe that the appraisal will be conducted in a fair and equitable manner, and can expect their performance to be recognized by proper rewards. But what is performance?

Defining the "Performance" in Performance Appraisal

Defining
performance

We talk about *performance* a lot, but what does the term actually mean? Employees are performing well when they are productive. Yet productivity itself implies both concern for effectiveness and efficiency, so let us begin there.

As noted in Chapter 1, *effectiveness* refers to goal accomplishment. If Mike is supposed to haul his fully loaded rig from New York to its destination in Los Angeles in sixty-eight hours or less, he is effective if he makes the three-thousand-mile trip within this time frame. But effectiveness doesn't speak to the costs incurred in reaching the goal. That is where efficiency comes in. *Efficiency* evaluates the ratio of inputs consumed to outputs achieved. The greater the output for a given input, the more efficient you are. Similarly, if output is a given, the lower input consumed to get that output results in greater efficiency. So, Mike might make the New York to Los Angeles trip in sixty-seven hours and average seven miles per gallon. Allison, on the other hand, made the trip in sixty-seven hours but averaged nine miles per gallon. Both Mike and Allison were effective—they accomplished their goal—but Allison was more efficient than Mike. She consumed less gas (the input) to reach Los Angeles (the output).

It is most desirable to have objective measures of productivity—hard data on effectiveness (such as number of units produced, dollar volume of sales, or percent of crimes solved) and hard data on efficiency (average cost per unit, ratio of sales volume to number of calls made, or number of traffic tickets issued per full-time traffic officer). Yet there are a vast number of jobs where there are no good measures of either effectiveness, efficiency, or both. Mary works as an inspector for Hathaway. She checks on shirts and pulls defective ones from the assembly line prior to folding and packing. Mary is considered efficient when she inspects an average of 120 shirts per hour. She is effective when less than .01 percent of all the shirts she inspects and puts her inspection tag on are returned as blemished by retailers. But consider the case of a classroom instructor in college. An instructor's classroom efficiency can be computed by calculating the average number of students taught per term. An instructor who teaches two hundred students per term is more efficient than one who teaches one hundred. But how do we measure effectiveness? Is a teacher effective when all her students pass? When students say she is doing a good job? If all get jobs upon graduation? If they go on to graduate school? If they can score well on a retention test a year after the course is over? The point here should be evident—there are no generally agreed upon measures of effectiveness for college teachers. That doesn't mean that college administrators don't try to measure the effectiveness of their teachers, only that objective data are absent. So they substitute subjective measures such as student opinions on factors like promptness in returning papers, accessibility during office hours, enthusiasm about the subject matter, and willingness to answer student questions in class.

In addition to productivity, as measured in terms of effectiveness and efficiency, performance also includes personnel data such as measures of accidents, turnover, absences, and tardiness. That is, a good employee is one who not only performs well in terms of productivity but also minimizes problems for the organization by being to work on time, by not missing days, and by minimizing the number of work-related accidents.

In summary, satisfactory performance implies a combination of things. It means doing a job effectively and efficiently, with a minimum degree of employee-created disruptions. Now that we have an understanding of the term *performance*, we can turn to the subject of the performance appraisal process. We will demonstrate how the process should be constructed so as to uphold the components and linkages in expectancy theory.

The Appraisal Process

The appraisal process   The appraisal process (see Figure 14-1) begins with the establishment of performance standards. These should have evolved out of job analysis and the job description discussed under human resource planning. These performance standards should also be clear and objective enough to be understood and measured. Too often, these standards are articulated in some such phrase as "a full day's work" or "a good job." Vague phrases tell us nothing. The expectations a manager has in terms of work performance by her subordinates must be clear enough in her mind so that she will be able to, at some later date, communicate these expectations to her subordinates and appraise their performance against these previously established standards.

Once performance standards are established, it is necessary to communicate these expectations. It should not be part of the employees' job to guess what is expected of them. Unfortunately, too many jobs have vague performance standards. The problem is compounded when these standards are not communicated to the employee. It is im-

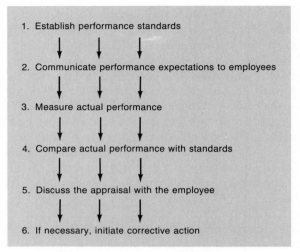

FIGURE 14-1   The Appraisal Process

portant to note that communication is a two-way street. Mere transference of information from the manager to the subordinate regarding expectations is not communication! Communication only takes place when the transference of information has taken place and has been *received and understood* by the subordinate. Therefore feedback is necessary from the subordinate to the manager. Satisfactory feedback ensures that the information communicated by the manager has been received and understood in the way it was intended.

The third step in the appraisal process is the measurement of performance. To determine what actual performance is, it is necessary to acquire information about it. We should be concerned with *how* we measure and *what* we measure.

Four measures of performance

Four common sources of information are frequently used by managers to measure actual performance: personal observation, statistical reports, oral reports, and written reports. Each has its strengths and weaknesses; however, a combination of them increases both the number of input sources and the probability of receiving reliable information.

What we measure is probably more critical to the evaluation process than *how* we measure, since the selection of the wrong criteria can result in serious dysfunctional consequences. And what we measure determines, to a great extent, what people in the organization will attempt to excel at.

The criteria we choose to measure must represent performance as it was stated and articulated in the first two steps of the appraisal process. When we tell an employee that she will be evaluated based on criterion X and then appraise her performance based on criterion

Performance Appraisal Goals

Conducting performance appraisals on employees' performance should be more than a simple checklist of "do's and don'ts." Performance evaluations should serve as a vital component, one that is of interest to both the organization and the employee. From the organizational perspective, sound performance appraisals can assure that the correct work is being done, work that assists in meeting department goals. In a simplistic rendition, each employee's work should support the activities on his or her boss's performance objectives. This should ultimately continue up the hierarchy, with all efforts supporting corporate strategic goals.

From the employee perspective, properly operating performance appraisal systems provide a clear communication of worker expectations. Knowing what is expected is a first step in helping one to cope better with the stress usually associated with a lack of clear direction. Secondly, properly designed performance appraisals should also serve as a means of assisting an employee's personal development.

To make effective performance appraisals a reality, four criteria need to be present. These are:

- Employees should be actively involved in the evaluation and development process.
- Bosses need to enter performance appraisals with a constructive and helpful attitude.
- Realistic goals must be mutually set.
- Bosses must be aware, and have knowledge of the employee's job and performance.

If these criteria are present, the performance appraisal process now becomes a communications meeting. With both parties well prepared for the performance review, the two discuss the total performance of the employee; addressing both the strengths and weaknesses of the employee, and how these attributes led to the attainment of the mutually agreed on goals. While at this stage, one is not only addressing past performance, but also areas for continued development have been identified. The next step, then, is to meet and plan for the employee's development.

Performance appraisals need not be as stressful or threatening as they are. With proper preparation and a few key criteria in place, the performance appraisal process can be enhanced. However, we can expect to reap this enhancement only after we make this transition towards more participative performance appraisals; ones that focus not solely on performance, but also on personal development.

Source: Adapted form H. Kent Baker, "Two Goals in Every Performance Appraisal," *Personnel Journal* 63, No. 9 (September 1984) 74–78.

Y, we can expect her effort to do a good job to decline, and *we can expect her to behave in such a manner that she will look good on criterion Y.*

The fourth step in the appraisal process is the comparison of actual performance with standards. The attempt in this step is to note deviations between standard performance and actual performance so that we can proceed to the fifth step in the process—the discussion of the appraisal with the employee.

One of the most challenging tasks facing managers is to present an accurate appraisal to the subordinate and then have the subordinate accept the appraisal in a constructive manner. Appraising performance touches on one of the most emotionally charged activities—the assessment of another individual's contribution and ability. The impression that subordinates receive about their assessment has a strong impact on their self-esteem and, very important, on their subsequent performance. Of course, conveying good news is considerably less difficult for both the manager and the subordinates than conveying the bad news that performance has been below expectations. In this context, the discussion of the appraisal can have negative as well as positive motivational consequences. This is reinforced, for example, when we recognize that statistically speaking, half of all employees are below average.

A survey of over eight hundred thousand high-school seniors found that people seem to see themselves as better than average. Seventy percent rated themselves above average on leadership; and when asked to rate themselves on "ability to get along with others," none rated themselves below average, 60 percent rated themselves in the top 10 percent, and 25 percent saw themselves among the top one percent.[1]

The above survey indicates that truthful appraisals will frequently place the manager in a situation where the subordinate's perception of his or her own performance overstates the manager's appraisal. While there is no easy answer to this problem, the issue will be explored later in this chapter, along with methods for overcoming the problem.

The final step in the appraisal is the initiation of corrective action when necessary. Corrective action can be of two types. One is immediate and deals predominantly with symptoms. The other is basic and delves into causes. Immediate corrective action is often described as "putting out fires," whereas basic corrective action gets to the source of deviation and seeks to adjust the difference permanently.

Immediate action corrects something right now and gets things back on track. Basic action asks how and why performance deviated. In some instances, managers may rationalize that they do not have the time to take basic corrective action and therefore must be content to "perpetually put out fires." Good managers recognize that they must find the time to analyze deviations and, in situations where the benefits justify such action, permanently correct significant differences between standard and actual performance.

---

[1] "How Do I Love Me? Let Me Count the Ways," *Psychology Today,* May 1980, p. 16.

Appraisal Methods

The previous section described the appraisal process in general terms. We now want to move from the general to the specific. In this section, we will look at how management can actually establish performance standards and devise instruments that can be used to measure and appraise an employee's performance. Three different approaches exist for doing appraisals. Employees can be appraised against (1) absolute standards, (2) relative standards, or (3) objectives. No one approach is always best. Each has its strengths and weaknesses.

Absolute Standards

Our first group of appraisal methods use absolute standards. This means that subjects are not compared with any other person. Included in this group are the following methods: the essay appraisal, the critical incident appraisal, the checklist, the graphic rating scale, forced choice, and behaviorally anchored rating scales (BARS).

Essay appraisal

Essay Appraisal.   Probably the simplest method of appraisal is to have the rater write a narrative describing an employee's strengths, weaknesses, past performance, potential, and suggestions for improvement.

The strength of the essay appraisal lies in its simplicity. It requires no complex forms or extensive training to complete. But its weaknesses are many. Because the essays are unstructured, they are likely to vary widely in terms of length and content. This makes it difficult to compare individuals across the organization. And, of course, some raters are better writers than others. So a "good" or "bad" evaluation may be determined as much by the rater's writing skill as by the employee's actual level of performance.

However, the essay appraisal can provide considerable information, much of which can easily be fed back and assimilated by the employee. But this method provides only qualitative data, and HRM decisions improve when useful quantitative data are generated. The latter can be compared and ranked more objectively. However, the essay appraisal is a good start and is beneficial if used in conjunction with other appraisal methods.

Critical incident appraisal

Critical Incident Appraisal.   Critical incident appraisal focuses the rater's attention on those critical or key behaviors that make the difference between doing a job effectively and doing it ineffectively. What the appraiser does is write down little anecdotes that describe what the employee did that was especially effective or ineffective. For example, the college dean might write the following critical incident about one of her instructors: "Outlined the day's lecture on the chalkboard at the beginning of class." Note that with this approach to appraisal, specific behaviors are cited, not vaguely defined personality traits. A behaviorally based appraisal such as this should be more valid than trait-based appraisals because it is clearly more job related. It is one thing to say that an employee is "aggressive" or "imaginative" or "relaxed," but that does not tell us anything about how well the job is being done. Critical incidents, with their focus on behaviors, judge performance rather than personalities.

The strength of the critical incident method is that it looks at behaviors. Additionally, a list of critical incidents on a given employee provides a rich set of examples from which the employee can be shown which of his or her behaviors are desirable and which ones call for improvement. Its drawbacks are basically that (1) appraisers are required to regularly write these incidents down, but doing this on a daily or even weekly basis for all of their subordinates is time-consuming and burdensome for managers; and (2) critical incidents suffer from the same comparison problem found in essays; mainly, they do not lend themselves to quantification. Therefore the comparison and ranking of subordinates is difficult.

Checklist

Checklist.   In the checklist, the evaluator uses a list of behavioral descriptions and checks off those behaviors that apply to the employee. As Figure 14-2 illustrates, the evaluator merely goes down the list and gives "yes" or "no" responses.

Once the checklist is complete, it is usually evaluated by the staff personnel department, not the manager doing the checklist. Therefore the rater does not actually evaluate the employee's performance; he or she merely records it. An analyst in the personnel department then scores the checklist, often weighting the factors in relationship to their importance. The final evaluation can then be returned to the rating manager for discussion with the subordinate, or someone from the personnel department can provide the feedback to the subordinate.

The checklist reduces some bias, since the rater and the scorer

FIGURE 14-2

Sample of Checklist Items for Appraising Salesclerks

	YES	NO
1. Are supervisor's orders usually followed?	___	___
2. Does the individual approach customers promptly?	___	___
3. Does the individual suggest additional merchandise to customers?	___	___
4. Does the individual keep busy when not servicing a customer?	___	___
5. Does the individual lose his or her temper in public?	___	___
6. Does the individual volunteer to help other employees?	___	___

are different, but the rater can usually pick up the positive and negative implications in each item so bias can still be introduced. From a cost standpoint, this appraisal method may be inefficient if there are a number of job categories, because a checklist of items must be prepared for each category.

Graphic rating scale

Graphic Rating Scale.   One of the oldest and most popular methods of appraisal is the graphic rating scale. An example of some graphic rating scale items is shown in Figure 14-3.

Graphic rating scales can be used to assess factors such as quantity and quality of work, job knowledge, cooperation, loyalty, dependability, attendance, honesty, integrity, attitudes, and initiative. However, this method is most valid when abstract traits like loyalty or integrity are avoided unless they can be defined in more specific behavioral terms. The assessor goes down the list of factors and notes that point along the scale or continuum that best describes the employee. There are typically five to ten points on the continuum. In the design of the graphic scale, the challenge is to ensure that both the factors evaluated and the scale points are clearly understood and unambiguous to the rater. Should ambiguity occur, bias is introduced.

Why are graphic rating scales popular? Though they do not provide the depth of information that essays or critical incidents do, they are less time-consuming to develop and administer, they permit quan-

FIGURE 14-3

Sample of Graphic Rating Scale Items and Format

PERFORMANCE FACTOR	PERFORMANCE RATING				
Quality of work is the accuracy, skill, and completeness of work.	☐ Consistently unsatisfactory	☐ Occasionally unsatisfactory	☐ Consistently satisfactory	☐ Sometimes superior	☐ Consistently superior
Quantity of work is the volume of work done in a normal workday.	☐ Consistently unsatisfactory	☐ Consistently unsatisfactory	☐ Consistently satisfactory	☐ Sometimes superior	☐ Consistently superior
Job knowledge is information pertinent to the job that an individual should have for satisfactory job performance.	☐ Poorly informed about work duties	☐ Occasionally unsatisfactory	☐ Can answer most questions about the job	☐ Understands all phases of the job	☐ Has complete mastery of all phases of the job
Dependability is following directions and company policies without supervision.	☐ Requires constant supervision	☐ Requires occasional follow-up	☐ Usually can be counted on	☐ Requires very little supervision	☐ Requires absolute minimum of supervision

titative analysis and comparison, and, in contrast to the checklist, there is greater standardization of items so comparability with other individuals in diverse job categories is possible.[2]

Forced choice

Forced Choice. When you were in elementary or secondary school, did you ever complete one of those tests that presumably was to give you insights into what kind of career you should pursue? They had questions like: "Would you rather go to a football game with a group of your friends or stay home and read a nonfiction book in your room?" If so, then you are familiar with the forced choice format.

The forced choice appraisal is a special type of checklist, but the rater has to choose between two or more statements, all of which may be favorable or unfavorable. The appraiser's job is to identify which statement is most (or in some cases least) descriptive of the individual being evaluated. For instance, students evaluating their college instructor might have to choose between

a. Patient with slow learners
b. Lectures with confidence
c. Keeps interest and attention of class
d. Acquaints classes in advance with objectives for each class

All the above statements are favorable. However, the choices might all be unfavorable. As with the checklist method, to reduce bias, the right answers are not known to the rater. Someone in the personnel department scores the answers based on the key. This key should be validated so management is in a position to say that individuals with higher scores are better-performing employees.

The major advantage to the forced choice method is that since the appraiser does not know the "right" answers, it reduces bias and distortion. The appraiser may, for example, like a certain employee and intentionally want to give her a favorable evaluation, but this becomes difficult if one is not sure which response is most preferred. On the negative side, this method tends to be disliked by appraisers. Many do not like being forced to make distinctions between statements that are difficult to differentiate between. Raters also may become frustrated with a system where they do not know what represents a "good" or "bad" answer; hence they may be relegated to trying to second-guess the key in order to get the formal appraisal to align with their intuitive appraisal.

BARS

Behaviorally Anchored Rating Scales. An approach that has received considerable attention by academics in recent years involves behaviorally anchored rating scales. These scales combine major elements from the critical incident and graphic rating scale approaches:

[2]Richard I. Henderson, *Performance Appraisal*, 2nd ed. (Reston, Va: Reston Publishing Co., 1984), p. 175.

The appraiser rates the employees based on items along a continuum, but the points are examples of actual behavior on the given job rather than general descriptions or traits. The enthusiasm surrounding BARS grew from the belief that the use of specific behaviors, derived for each job, should produce relatively error-free and reliable ratings. Though this promise has not been fulfilled,[3] it has been argued that this may be partly due to departures from careful methodology in the development of the specific scales themselves rather than to inadequacies in the concept.[4]

Behaviorally anchored rating scales specify definite, observable, and measurable job behavior. Examples of job-related behavior and performance dimensions are generated by asking participants to give specific illustrations of effective and ineffective behavior regarding each performance dimension. These behavioral examples are then retranslated into appropriate performance dimensions. Those that are sorted into the dimension for which they were generated are retained. The final group of behavior incidents are then numerically scaled to a level of performance that each is perceived to represent. The incidents that are retranslated and have high rater agreement on performance effectiveness are retained for use as anchors on the performance dimension. The results of the above processes are behavioral descriptions, such as anticipates, plans, executes, solves immediate problems, carries out orders, and handles emergency situations. Figure 14-4 is an example of a BARS for a grocery clerk's "organization of checkstand" scale.

The research on BARS indicates that while it is far from perfect, it does tend to reduce rating errors. But possibly its major advantage stems from the dimensions generated rather than from any particular superiority of behavior over trait anchors.[5] The process of developing the behavioral scales is valuable in and of itself for clarifying to both the employee and the rater which behaviors connote good performance and which connote bad. Unfortunately, it too suffers from the distortions inherent in most rating methods.[6] These distortions will be discussed later in this chapter.

[3]See, for example, W. C. Borman and M. D. Dunnette, "Behavior-based versus Trait-oriented Performance Ratings: An Empirical Study," *Journal of Applied Psychology*, October 1975, pp. 561–65; T. J. Keaveny and A. F. McGann, "A Comparison of Behavioral Expectation Scales," *Journal of Applied Psychology*, December 1975, pp. 695–703; and J. M. Ivancevich, "A Longitudinal Study of Behavioral Expectation Scales: Attitudes and Performance," *Journal of Applied Psychology*, April 1980, pp. 139–46.

[4]Donald P. Schwab, Herbert Heneman III, and Thomas DeCotiis, "Behaviorally Anchored Rating Scales: A Review of the Literature," *Personnel Psychology*, Autumn 1975, pp. 549–62.

[5]Ibid.

[6]Paul O. Kingstrom and Alan R. Bass, "A Critical Analysis of Studies Comparing Behaviorally Anchored Rating Scales (BARS) and Other Rating Formats," *Personnel Psychology*, 34, No. 2 (Summer 1981), 263–89.

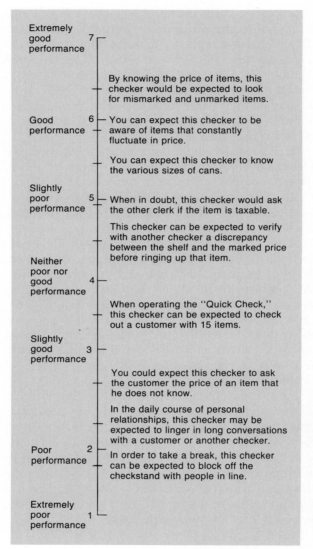

FIGURE 14-4 Behaviorally Anchored Rating Scale for Appraising the Organization of a Grocery Clerk's Checkstand

SOURCE: Adapted from Lawrence Fogli, Charles W. Hulin, and Milton R. Blood, "Development of First-Level, Behavioral Job Criteria," *Journal of Applied Psychology*, February 1971, pp. 3–8. Copyright 1971 by the American Psychological Association. Reprinted by permission.

Relative Standards

In the second general category of appraisal methods, individuals are compared against other individuals. These methods are relative rather than absolute measuring devices. The more popular of the relative methods are group order ranking, individual ranking, and paired comparison.

Group order ranking

Group Order Ranking.

The group order ranking requires the evaluator to place employees into a particular classification, such as "top one-fifth" or "second one-fifth." This method is often used in recommending students to graduate schools. Evaluators are asked to rank the student in the top 5 percent, the next 5 percent, the next 15 percent, and so forth. But when used by managers to appraise subordinates, managers deal with all their subordinates. So if a rater has twenty subordinates, only four can be in the top fifth and, of course, four must also be relegated to the bottom fifth.

The advantage to this group ordering is that it prevents raters from inflating their evaluations so everyone looks good or from homogenizing the evaluations so everyone is rated near the average—outcomes that are not unusual with the graphic rating scale. The predominant disadvantage surfaces when the number of employees being compared is small. At the extreme, if the evaluator is looking at only four employees, it is very possible that they may all be excellent, yet the evaluator may be forced to rank them into top quarter, second quarter, third quarter, and low quarter! Theoretically, as the sample size increases, the validity of relative scores as an accurate measure increases; but occasionally the technique is implemented with a small group, utilizing assumptions that apply to large groups. Another disadvantage, which plagues all relative measures, is the "zero-sum game" consideration. This means, any change must add up to zero. For example, if there are twelve employees in a department performing at different levels of effectiveness, by definition, three are in the top quarter, three in the second quarter, and so forth. The sixth-best employee, for instance, would be in the second quartile. Ironically, if two of the workers in the third or fourth quartiles leave the department and are not replaced, then our sixth best employee now falls into the third quarter. Because comparisons are relative, an employee who is mediocre may score high only because her or she is the "best of the worst." In contrast, an excellent performer who is matched against "stiff" competition may be evaluated poorly, when in absolute terms his or her performance is outstanding.

Individual ranking

Individual Ranking.

The individual ranking method requires the evaluator merely to list the employees in an order from highest to lowest. Only one can be "best." If the evaluator is required to appraise thirty individuals, this method assumes that the difference between the first and second employee is the same as that between the twenty-first and twenty-second. Even though some of these employees may be closely grouped, this method allows for no ties.

In terms of advantages and disadvantages, the individual ranking method carries the same pluses and minuses as group order ranking.

Paired comparison   *Paired Comparison.*   The paired comparison method is calculated by taking the total of $[n \ (n \ - \ 1)]/2$ comparisons. A score is obtained for each employee by simply counting the number of pairs in which the individual is the preferred member. It ranks each individual in relationship to all others on a one-on-one basis. If ten people are being evaluated, the first person is compared, one by one, with each of the other nine, and the number of times this person is preferred in any of the nine pairs is tabulated. Each of the remaining nine persons, in turn, is compared in the same way, and a ranking is evolved by the greatest number of preferred "victories." This method ensures that each employee is compared against every other, but the method can become unwieldly when large numbers of employees are being compared.

Objectives

The third approach to appraisal makes use of objectives. Employees are evaluated by how well they accomplish a specific set of objectives that have been determined to be critical in the successful completion of their job. This approach is frequently referred to as management by objectives (MBO).[7]

Management by objectives   Management by objectives is a process that converts organizational objectives into individual objectives. It can be thought of as consisting of four steps: goal setting, action planning, self-control, and periodic reviews.

In goal setting, the organization's overall objectives are used as guidelines from which departmental and individual objectives are set. At the individual level, the manager and subordinate jointly identify those goals that are critical for the subordinate to achieve in order to fulfill the requirements of the job as determined in job analysis. These goals are agreed upon and then become the standards by which the employee's results will be evaluated.

In action planning, the means are determined for achieving the ends established in goal setting. That is, realistic plans are developed to attain the objectives. This step includes identifying the activities necessary to accomplish the objective, establishing the critical relationships between these activities, estimating the time requirements for each activity, and determining the resources required to complete each activity.

Self-control refers to the systematic monitoring and measuring of performance—ideally, by having the individual review his or her own performance. Inherent in allowing individuals to control their own

---

[7]For a comprehensive treatment of MBO and its advantages, disadvantages, and effectiveness, see H. John Bernardin and Richard W. Beatty, *Performance Appraisal: Assessing Human Behavior at Work* (Boston: Kent Publishing, 1984), Chaps. 4 and 6.

performance is a positive image of human nature. The MBO philosophy is built on the assumptions that individuals can be responsible, can exercise self-direction, and do not require external controls and threats of punishment to motivate them to work toward their objectives. This from a motivational point of view would be representative of McGregor's theories.

Finally, with periodic progress reviews, corrective action is initiated when behavior deviates from the standards established in the goal-setting phase. Again, consistent with the MBO philosophy, these manager-subordinate reviews are conducted in a constructive rather than punitive manner. Reviews are not meant to degrade the individual but to aid in future performance. These reviews should take place at least two or three times a year.

What will these objectives look like? It is important that they be tangible, verifiable, and measurable. This means that, wherever possible, we should avoid qualitative objectives and substitute quantifiable statements. For example, a quantitative objective might be "to cut, each day, 3,500 yards of cable to standard five-foot lengths, with a maximum scrap of 50 yards," or "to prepare, process, and transfer to the treasurer's office, all accounts payable vouchers within three working days from the receipt of the invoice."

The advantages of MBO lie in its results-oriented emphasis. It assists the planning and control functions and provides motivation, as well as being an approach to performance appraisal, because employees know exactly what is expected of them and how they will be evaluated, and that their evaluation will be based on their success in achieving their objectives. Additionally, employees should have a greater commitment to objectives they have participated in developing than to those unilaterally set by their boss. The major disadvantage to MBO is that it is unlikely to be effective in an environment where management has little trust in its employees, that is, where management makes decisions autocratically and relies heavily on external controls. The amount of time needed to implement and maintain an MBO process may also cause problems. Many activities must occur, such as a manager meeting with all of his or her subordinates to set and monitor objectives. These meetings take an inordinate amount of the manager's time. Additionally, it may be difficult to measure whether the MBO activities are being carried out properly. The difficulty involved in properly appraising the managers' efforts and performance as they carry out their MBO activities may cause it to fail.

Summary

The evidence indicates that most organizations have a formal performance appraisal system. An exact percentage is difficult to give, but most studies find that between 50 and 75 percent of all organizations have a formal system. A summary of some representative studies will support this conclusion.

Data from Prentice-Hall's *Personnel Management: Policy and Practices* indicate that 95 percent of all the organizations they studied used some form of performance appraisal.[8] However, these instruments were used predominantly on lower-level individuals, up to middle-manager levels in the organization. Less than one-half of these companies studied had performance evaluations for top management. For those that did, the criterion measured was financial success.[9]

Uses of performance appraisals

Performance appraisals have many uses. While their initial thrust is focused on evaluating an employee's performance, the instrument also serves as a means of conducting further analysis. A recent study concluded that a performance appraisal had seven subsequent uses. These uses and their percentage of use are as follows: compensation (86%), counseling (65%), training and development (64%), promotion (45%), planning (43%), retention and discharge (30%), and validation (17%).[10] Accordingly, we can see the importance of the performance evaluation. Its application to other areas and its usefulness warrants an instrument that is free from bias, one that is objective.

But what do we usually find is the most popular appraisal method? Generally, rating scales.[11] Why? Because they appear to be the easiest to use. But being the easiest isn't always the most correct. While tabulation of the data and standardization are advantages of the rating scale method, their validity is questioned;[12] coupled with the fact that behavior and attitude are vaguely defined.[13] Taking this information into consideration, the rating scales may provide information that may be less than effective.

While there is an indication that many types of performance appraisals exist and are used to varying degrees in organizations, one central theme appears to permeate these appraisals: "Most systems are poorly designed because of a lack of clear objectives."[14]

The thrust behind any performance appraisal should be to identify the major areas of accountability (objectives) and to set plans for meeting these. Unfortunately, this is not done, and single-criterion ratings flourish in organizations. One attempt was made to counter this single focus, and that was MBO. But MBO had its problems, its critics,

---

[8]*Personnel Management: Policy and Practices* (Englewood Cliffs, N.J.: Prentice-Hall, 1984), p. 160.

[9]Ibid., p. 161.

[10]Ibid., p. 465.

[11]Bernardin and Beatty, *Performance Appraisal*, p. 144.

[12]*Personnel Management: Policies and Practices*, p. 898.

[13]Ibid.

[14]Ed Yager, "A Critique of Performance Appraisal Systems," *Personnel Journal*, February 1981, p. 129.

and its downfall because "MBO forces employees to be more concerned with how time is spent, rather than with real accomplishments."[15]

What can we conclude from these reports about performance appraisals? Performance appraisal systems probably exist in most organizations. They are more likely to be used with nonunion than union workers. Where unions exist, rewards are substantially determined by seniority, so the benefits of a merit appraisal system may not justify the costs. Within the management ranks, appraisal evaluations are significantly more likely to be done for lower- and middle-level than for top-level managers.

As to the type of appraisal used, evaluations tend to emphasize the personality characteristics of ratees rather than their specific job behaviors. Techniques such as critical incidents, BARS, and MBO, which emphasize behaviors and results, appear to be in the minority.

Factors that can Distort Appraisals

The performance appraisal process and techniques that we have suggested present an objective system in which the evaluator is free from personal biases, prejudices, and idiosyncrasies. This is defended on the basis that objectivity minimizes the potential capricious and dysfunctional behavior of the evaluator, which may be detrimental to the achievement of the organizational goals. It would be naive to assume, however, that all practicing managers impartially interpret and standardize the criteria upon which their subordinates will be appraised. This is particularly true of those jobs that are not easily programmable and for which developing hard performance standards is most difficult if not impossible. These would include, but are certainly not limited to, such jobs as researcher, teacher, engineer, and consultant. In the place of such standards, we can expect managers to utilize nonperformance or subjective criteria against which to evaluate individuals. Our goal should be to utilize direct performance criteria in appraising individuals wherever possible.

In spite of our recognition that a completely error-free performance appraisal can only be an idealized model,[16] with all actual appraisals being something less than this optimum, we can isolate a number of factors that significantly impede objective evaluation. In this section, we will briefly review the more significant of these factors.

Leniency Error

Every evaluator has his or her own value system which acts as a standard against which appraisals are made. Relative to the true or actual

[15]Ibid., p. 133.
[16]Henderson, *Performance Appraisal*, pp. 1–18.

Leniency error

performance an individual exhibits, some evaluators mark high and others low. The former is referred to as positive leniency error, and the latter as negative leniency error. When evaluators are positively lenient in their appraisal, an individual's performance becomes over-stated; that is, rated higher than it actually should. Similarly, a neg-ative leniency error understates performance, giving the individual a lower appraisal.

If all individuals in an organization were appraised by the same person, there would be no problem. Although there would be an error factor, it would be applied equally to everyone. The difficulty arises when we have different raters with different leniency errors making judgments. For example, assume a situation where both Jones and Smith are performing the same job for a different supervisor, but they have absolutely identical job performance. If Jones's supervisor tends to err toward positive leniency while Smith's supervisor errs toward negative leniency, we might be confronted with two dramatically dif-ferent evaluations.

Halo Error

Halo error

The halo effect or error is a "tendency to rate high or low on all factors due to the impression of a high or low rating on some specific fac-tor."[17] For example, if an employee tends to be conscientious and de-pendable, we might become biased toward that individual to the extent that we will rate him or her high on many desirable attributes.

People who design teaching appraisal forms for college students to fill out in evaluating the effectiveness of their instructor each se-mester must confront the halo effect. Students tend to rate a faculty member as outstanding on *all* criteria when they are particularly ap-preciative of a few things he or she does in the classroom. Similarly, a few bad habits—like showing up late for lectures, being slow in re-turning papers, or assigning an extremely demanding reading require-ment—might result in students' evaluating the instructor as "lousy" across the board.

One method frequently used to deal with this error is to stagger the questions on the evaluation so that a favorable answer for, say, question number 17 might be five on a scale of one through five, while a favorable answer for question number 18 might be one on a scale of one through five. Structuring the questions in this manner seeks to reduce the halo effect by requiring the evaluator to consider each ques-tion independently. Another method, which can be used where there is more than one person to be evaluated, is to have the evaluator ap-praise all ratees on each dimension before going on to the next di-mension.

[17]Bernardin and Beatty, *Performance Appraisal*, p. 140.

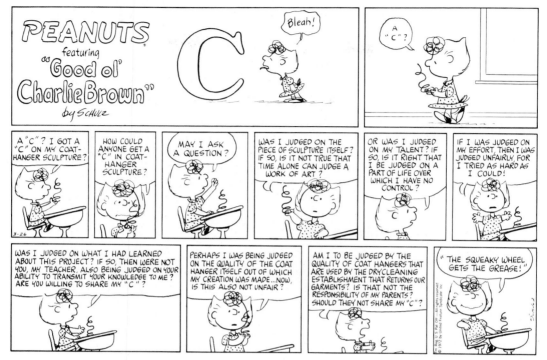

FIGURE 14-5

Similarity Error

Similarity error

When evaluators rate other people in the same way that the evaluators perceive themselves, they are making a similarity error. Based on the perception that evaluators have of themselves, they project those perceptions onto others. For example, the evaluator who perceives himself or herself as aggressive may evaluate others by looking for aggressiveness. Those who demonstrate this characteristic tend to benefit, while others are penalized.

Again, this error would tend to wash out if the same evaluator appraised all the people in the organization. Interrater reliability obviously suffers when various evaluators are utilizing their own similarity criteria.

Low Appraiser Motivation

Low appraiser motivation

What are the consequences of the appraisal? If the evaluator knows that a poor appraisal could significantly hurt the employee's future—particularly opportunities for promotion or a salary increase—the evaluator may be reluctant to give a realistic appraisal. There is evidence that it is more difficult to obtain accurate appraisals when important rewards depend on the results.[18]

It has been argued that performance appraisals that are used as the determinant for rewards can be viewed as analogous to the proverbial forward pass in football.[19] The appraisal can lead to three outcomes, two of which are inherently bad; specifically, the employee is rewarded, not rewarded, or punished. As a result, most consequences for the appraiser of assigning accurate performance ratings are negative. Not surprisingly, then, many managers approach the performance appraisal event with reluctance and assign inaccurate ratings simply because there are so few benefits inherent in giving accurate ratings and so few penalties for assigning inaccurate ratings.[20]

Central Tendency

Central tendency

It is possible that regardless of whom the appraiser evaluates and what traits are used, the pattern of evaluation remains the same. It is also possible that the evaluator's ability to appraise objectively and accurately has been impeded by a failure to use the extremes of the scale, that is, central tendency. Central tendency is "the reluctance to make extreme ratings (in either direction); the inability to distinguish between and among ratees; a form of range restriction."[21] Raters who are prone to the central tendency error are those who continually rate all employees as average. For example, if a manager rates all subordinates as 3, on a scale of 1 to 5, then no differentiation among the subordinates exists. Failure to rate subordinates as 5, for those who deserve that rating, and as 1, if the case warrants it, will only create problems, especially if this information is used for pay increases.

Forcing Information to Match Nonperformance Criteria

While rarely advocated, it is not a totally infrequent practice to find the formal appraisal taking place *following* the decision as to how the individual has been performing! This may sound illogical, but it merely recognizes that subjective, yet formal, decisions are often arrived at prior to the gathering of objective information to support that decision. For example, if evaluators believe that the evaluation should not

---

[18]Ibid., p. 270.

[19]Henderson, *Performance Appraisal*, pp. 201–204, and Thomas Decotiis and André Petit, "The Performance Appraisal Process: A Model and Some Testable Propositions," *Academy of Management Review*, July 1978, pp. 635–46.

[20]Ibid.

[21]Bernardin and Beatty, *Performance Appraisal*, p. 139.

be based on performance, but rather seniority, they may be unknowingly adjusting each "performance" evaluation so as to bring it into line with the employee's seniority rank. In this and other similar cases, the evaluator is increasing or decreasing performance appraisals to align with the nonperformance criteria actually being utilized.

Inflationary Pressures

A U.S. Army captain could not understand why he had been passed over for promotion. He had seen his file and knew that his average rating by his supervisor was 86. Given his knowledge that the appraisal system defined "outstanding performance" as 90 or above, "good" as 80 or above, "average" as 70 or above, and "inadequate performance" as anything below 70, he was at a loss to understand why he had not been promoted, with his near-outstanding performance appraisal. The officer's confusion was somewhat resolved when he found out that the "average" rating of captains in the U.S. Army is 92.

This example addresses a major potential problem in appraisals—inflationary pressures. This, in effect, is a specific case of low differentiation within the upper range of the rating choices.

Inflationary pressures have always existed but appear to have increased as a problem since the 1960s. As "equality" values have grown in importance in our society, there has been a tendency for evaluation to be less rigorous and negative repercussions from the evaluation reduced by generally inflating or upgrading appraisals.

Inappropriate Substitutes for Performance

It is the unusual job where the definition of performance is absolutely clear and direct measures are available for appraising the incumbent. In many jobs it is difficult to get consensus on what is "a good job," and it is even more difficult to get agreement on what criteria will determine performance. For a saleswoman the criterion may be the dollar sales in her territory, but even this criterion is affected by factors such as economic conditions and actions of competitors—factors outside the saleswoman's control.

As a result, the appraisal is frequently made by using substitutes for performance; criteria that, it is hoped, closely approximate performance and act in its place. Many of these substitutes are well chosen and give a good approximation of actual performance. However, the substitutes chosen are not always appropriate. It is not unusual, for example, to find organizations using criteria such as enthusiasm, neatness, positive attitudes, conscientiousness, promptness, and congeniality as substitutes for performance. In some jobs, one or more of the criteria listed in the previous sentence *are* part of performance. Obviously, enthusiasm does enhance the effectiveness of a teacher. You are more likely to listen to and be motivated by a teacher who is enthusiastic than one who is not. And increased attentiveness and motivation typically lead to increased learning. But enthusiasm may in no way be relevant to effective performance for many accountants, watch repairers, or copyeditors. So what may be an appropriate substitute for performance in one job may be totally inappropriate in another.

Attribution Theory

Attribution theory

A newer field of study surrounding performance evaluations has been called *attribution theory*. In attribution theory, it is suggested that "employee evaluations are directly mediated by managers' attributions as to who is perceived to be in control of the employee's performance—the employer or the manager."[22] Much of attribution theory is consistent with McGregor's Theory X, Theory Y. That is, if a manager has more of a Theory Y orientation and uses a more democratic and participative approach, there is a tendency for that manager to rate the subordinates higher. This higher rating appears to be attributed solely to the manager's perception of worker initiative. Conversely, a more Theory X-oriented manager, one who is more autocratic and makes unilateral decisions, is likely to rate his subordinates lower. In this sequence, such managers feel that they controlled the work and, accordingly, performance is poorer.

One research study mentioned that the two generalizations regarding attribution theory were supported:[23]

1. When managers attribute an employee's poor performance to the employee's own motivations, the judgments are harsher than when the same poor performance is attributed to external factors.
2. When an employee is performing satisfactorily, managers will evaluate the employee favorably if the performance is attributed to the employee's own efforts than if the performance is attributed to outside forces.[24]

While extremely interesting and shedding new light on rater affects on performance evaluations, much more study of the topic is needed. Yet it does provide much insight on why unbiased performance evaluations are important.

[22]David Kipnis, Karl Price, Stuart Schmidt, and Christopher Stitt, "Why Do I Like Thee: Is It Your Performance or My Orders?" *Journal of Applied Psychology*, June 1981, pp. 324–28.

[23]Ibid.

[24]Ibid.

Suggestions for Improved Performance Appraisals

Improving
performance
appraisals

The fact that managers frequently encounter problems with performance appraisals should not lead you to throw up your hands and give up on the concept. There are things that can be done to make performance appraisals more effective. In this section, we offer some suggestions that can be considered individually or in combination.

Behaviorally Based Measures

Measure behaviors

As we have pointed out, the evidence strongly favors behaviorally based measures over those developed around traits. Many traits often considered to be related to good performance may, in fact, have little or no performance relationship. Traits like loyalty, initiative, courage, reliability, and self-expression are intuitively appealing as desirable characteristics in employees. But the relevant question is, Are individuals who are evaluated as high on those traits higher performers than those who rate low? We cannot answer this question. We know that there are employees who rate high on these characteristics and are poor performers. We can find others who are excellent performers but do not score well on traits such as these. Our conclusion is that traits like loyalty and initiative may be prized by managers, but there is no evidence to support that certain traits will be adequate synonyms for performance in a large cross-section of jobs.

A second weakness in traits is the judgment itself. What is "loyalty"? When is an employee "reliable"? What you consider "loyalty," I may not. So traits suffer from weak interrater agreement.

Behaviorally derived measures can deal with both of these objections. Because they deal with specific examples of performance—both good and bad—we avoid the problem of using inappropriate substitutes. Additionally, because we are evaluating specific behaviors, we increase the likelihood that two or more evaluators will see the same thing. You might consider a given employee as "friendly" while I rate her "standoffish." But when asked to rate her in terms of specific behaviors, we might both agree that she "frequently says 'Good morning' to customers," "rarely gives advice or assistance to co-workers," and "almost always avoids idle chatter with co-workers."

Combine Absolute and Relative Standards

Use absolute and
relative standards

A major drawback to individual or absolute standards is that they tend to be biased by positive leniency; that is, evaluators lean toward packing their subjects into the high part of the rankings. On the other hand, relative standards suffer when the number of individuals being appraised is small and when there is little actual variability among the subjects.

The obvious solution is to consider using appraisal methods that combine both absolute and relative standards. For example, you might want to use the graphic rating scale and the individual ranking method. This dual method of appraisal, incidentally, has been instituted at some universities to deal with the problem of grade inflation. Students get an absolute grade—A, B, C, D, or F—and next to it is a relative mark showing how this student ranked in the class. A prospective employer or graduate school admissions committee can look at two students who each got a "B" in their cost accounting course and draw considerably different conclusions about each when, next to one grade it says "ranked 4th out of 26," while the other says "ranked 17th out of 30." Obviously, the latter instructor gave out a lot more high grades!

Ongoing Feedback

Provide feedback

One nationwide motel chain has advertised that "the best surprise is no surprise." This logic also holds for performance appraisals.

Employees like to know how they are doing. The "annual review," where the manager shares the subordinates' evaluations with them, can become a problem. In some cases, it is a problem merely because managers put off such reviews. This is particularly likely if the appraisal is negative. But the annual review is additionally troublesome if the manager "saves up" performance-related information and unloads it during the appraisal review. This creates an extremely trying experience for both evaluator and employee. In such instances it is not surprising that the manager may attempt to avoid confronting uncomfortable issues which, even if confronted, may only be denied or rationalized by the subordinates.[25]

The solution lies in having the manager share with the subordinate both expectations and disappointments on a day-to-day basis. By providing the employee with frequent opportunities to discuss performance before any reward or punishment consequences occur, there will be no surprises at the time of the annual formal review. In fact, where ongoing feedback has been provided, the formal sitting down step should not be particularly traumatic for either party. Additionally, in an MBO system that actually works, ongoing feedback is the critical element.

Multiple Raters

Have many raters

As the number of raters increases, the probability of attaining more accurate information increases. If rater error tends to follow a normal curve, an increase in the number of raters will tend to find the majority congregating about the middle. If a person has had ten super-

[25]Henderson, *Performance Appraisals*, pp. 284–89.

visors, nine having rated him or her excellent and one poor, we can discount the value of the one poor evaluation. Therefore, by moving employees about within the organization so as to gain a number of evaluations, we increase the probability of achieving more valid and reliable evaluations.

The U.S. Army has made good use of this technique. For individuals who have received ten or fifteen appraisals during their first five or six years in the service, there is less chance that one or two "slanted" evaluations will seriously influence decisions made on the basis of these performance appraisals.

Selective Rating

Rate on areas where job knowledge exists

It has been suggested that appraisers should rate in those areas in which they have significant job knowledge. If raters make evaluations on only those dimensions on which they are in a good position to rate, we increase the interrater agreement and make the evaluation a more valid process. This approach also recognizes that different organizational levels often have different orientations toward ratees and observe them in different settings. In general, therefore, we would recommend that appraisers should be as close as possible, in terms of organizational level, to the individual being evaluated. Conversely, the more levels that separate the evaluator and evaluatee, the less opportunity the evaluator has to observe the individual's behavior and, not surprisingly, the greater the possibility for inaccuracies.

The specific application of these concepts would result in having immediate supervisors or co-workers as the major input into the appraisal and having them evaluate those factors that they are best qualified to judge. For example, it has been suggested that when professors are evaluating secretaries within a university, they use such criteria as judgment, technical competence, and conscientiousness; whereas peers (other secretaries) use such criteria as job knowledge, organization, cooperation with co-workers, and responsibility.[26] Such an approach appears both logical and more reliable, since people are appraising only those dimensions on which they are in a good position to make judgments.

In addition to taking into account where the rater is in the organization or what he or she is allowed to evaluate, selective rating should also consider the characteristics of the rater. If appraisers differ in traits, and if certain of these traits are correlated with accurate appraisals while others are correlated with inaccurate appraisals, then it seems logical to attempt to identify effective raters. Those identified as especially effective could be given sole responsibility for doing ap-

[26]W. C. Borman, "The Rating of Individuals in Organizations: An Alternative Approach," *Organizational Behavior and Human Performance*, August 1974, pp. 105–24.

praisals, or greater weight could be given to their observations. It has been demonstrated that 17 percent of the variance in the accuracy of ratings can be attributed to the characteristics of the person doing the rating.[27] We should therefore be concerned with those characteristics that differentiate effective and ineffective raters. First, we can test to determine if an evaluator is a high or a low differentiator. Appraisals should ideally be done only by high differentiators or those who use the entire scale when rating employees. Second, research has found that the effectiveness of individual managers is correlated with the criteria they tend to rate high in evaluations.[28] More effective managers tend to value initiative, persistence, broad knowledge, and planning ability. Less effective managers tend to value cooperation, company loyalty, good teamwork, tact, and consideration. This might suggest that if you are going to have performance appraisals evaluate job competence, have effective managers do the appraising. If you want the performance appraisal to emphasize the subordinate's interpersonal relations, then have less effective managers do the evaluations.

Trained Appraisers

Train appraisers   If you cannot find good raters, the alternative is to make good raters. Evidence indicates that the training of appraisers can make them more accurate raters.[29]

Common errors such as halo and leniency have been minimized or eliminated in workshops where managers can practice observing and rating behaviors. These workshops would typically run from one to three days, but allocating many hours to training may not always be necessary. One case has been cited where both halo and leniency errors were decreased immediately after exposing evaluators to explanatory training sessions lasting only five minutes.[30] But the effects of training do appear to diminish over time.[31] This suggests the need for regular training refresher sessions.

[27]W. C. Borman. "Some Raters Are Simply Better Than Others at Evaluating Performance: Individual Differences Correlates of Rating Accuracy Using Behavioral Scales" (Paper presented at the 85th Annual Meeting of the American Psychological Association, San Francisco, August 1977).

[28]W. K. Kirchner and D. J. Reisberg, "Differences between Better and Less Effective Supervisors in Appraisals of Subordinates," *Personnel Psychology*, Autumn 1962, pp. 295–302.

[29]Bernardin and Beatty, *Performance Appraisal*, pp. 254–58, and Henderson, pp. 305–309.

[30]H. J. Bernardin, "The Effects of Rater Training on Leniency and Halo Errors in Student Rating of Instructors," *Journal of Applied Psychology*, June 1978, pp. 301–8.

[31]Ibid., and John M. Ivancevich, "Longitudinal Study of the Effects of Rater Training on Psychometric Error in Ratings," *Journal of Applied Psychology*, October 1979, pp. 502–5.

Peer Evaluations

Have peers evaluate   Periodically, managers find it difficult to evaluate their subordinates' performance because they are not working with them every day. Unfortunately, unless they have this information, they may not be making an accurate assessment. And if their goal of the performance evaluation is to identify deficient areas and provide constructive feedback to their subordinates, they may be providing a disservice to these subordinates by not having all the information. Yet, how do they get this information? One of the easiest means is through peer evaluations. Peer evaluations are conducted by employees' co-workers, people explicitly familiar with the jobs involved mainly because they too are doing the same thing. They are the ones most aware of co-workers' day-to-day work behavior and should be given the opportunity to provide the management with some feedback.

The rationale behind peer assessment is similar to that of the U.S. Constitution guaranteeing every citizen the right to be judged by his or her peers. Certainly there are disadvantages to peer assessments. For instance, if the members of a work group decide that they would like to "get someone," then all they need to do is give consistently poor evaluations. That would clearly indicate group alienation. But there are safeguards to this. Remember that no single evaluation should be used. Multiple ratings provide a better picture, and if the case exists where a peer evaluation is skewed, the multiple evaluation rating system would detect it.

The main advantages to peer evaluation are that (1) there is a tendency for co-workers to offer more constructive insight to each other so that, as a unit, each will improve; and (2) their recommendations tend to be more specific regarding job behaviors—unless specificity exists, constructive measures are hard to gain.

Whether peer assessment will ever expand to its potential is yet to be seen. Opponents criticize its time-consuming nature, but even in the most rigid of performance evaluation systems, some informal peer assessment is evident—in that case, it is called "advice" from a friend. However, for peer assessments to function properly, the environment in the organization must be such that politics and competition for promotions are minimized. This environment can only be found in the most "mature" organizations.

Postappraisal Interview

Have follow-up   Although we have alluded to it at various times in this chapter, the
appraisal interview   *communications* aspect of the performance appraisal system cannot be overemphasized. A performance evaluation system is only as effective as the manager is in communications. If managers feel that their objective is to just go through the hassle of filling out reports on their

subordinates, then they should just scrap the performance evaluation because the outcome will be the same—no value.

Unfortunately, too many managers follow the above routine. Performance evaluations are conducted and placed in the employee's personnel file. No constructive feedback is given, and if there are problems, they will continue.

What is needed is a more comprehensive system for using the performance appraisal data. The information obtained must serve a purpose. That purpose is to communicate to employees how they have performed. To meet this need, managers must take the time to schedule a meeting with their subordinates to discuss the results of the performance evaluation. While this certainly becomes time-consuming, the result should be increased productivity. Employees need to know how they are doing, be recognized for outstanding achievements, and be notified about where there is room for improvement. Associated with this postappraisal would be a self-assessment by each employee. This self-assessment serves two purposes: It requires the employee to address previous performance and it serves as a future goal orientation.

Organizations such as Mattel Toys have had great success with the postappraisal interview. Individuals are allowed to explain any circumstances that may have inpinged on their productivity. More important, the postassessment interview reveals an interest in employees. A well-designed appraisal process, one with explicit performance criteria and reasonably reliable measures, can set up the interview in a favorable, constructive light. In essence, the tension that may be experienced during the interview process can be designed out up front. In many cases, this approach is enough to spur increased productivity.

Rewards to Accurate Appraisers

Reward accurate appraisers

Our final suggestion is obvious but is frequently overlooked when organizations establish a performance appraisal system. The managers doing the evaluating must perceive that it is in their personal and career interests to conduct accurate appraisals. If they are not properly rewarded for doing effective appraisals, they will take the easy way out—trying first to avoid the process entirely. If pushed, they will complete the appraisals, but such appraisals can be expected to suffer from positive leniency and low differentiation. Finally, if push comes to shove and the manager has to develop accurate and differentiating evaluations, we can expect a minimum amount of feedback to subordinates, especially to those who were evaluated poorly. We noted earlier in the chapter that in most organizations, the consequences for the appraiser of assigning accurate performance ratings to poor performers are negative. This must be overcome by encouraging and rewarding accurate appraisers.

* * * * *

HELP PEOPLE REACH THEIR FULL POTENTIAL

CATCH THEM DOING SOMETHING RIGHT

* * * * *

FIGURE 14-6

SOURCE: Kenneth Blanchard and Spencer Johnson, *The One Minute Manager* (New York: Morrow, 1982).

Conclusion

Throughout much of the discussion thus far, we have advocated the use of quantifiable, objective performance measures. These, as the literature has revealed, provide direction for the employees and act as goals for which they strive. MBO, as presented, was the classic example of performance evaluation by means of meeting one's objective.

But objective setting itself can have severe drawbacks. If we could set objectives in a vacuum, then there would be no possibility for distortions. However, when we put two individuals together and have them attempt to set "realistic" goals, the goals that are set are more a result of negotiation than realism. Consider, for example, the sales representative who must set her sales objectives for the upcoming year. A realistic sales increase may be approximately 14 percent. But this saleswoman knows that external factors might have an impact on how she sells her product and, ultimately, her 14 percent goal. This is compounded if there is also a penalty for not meeting her stated goals. Realizing what she could sell with minimal effort, she meets with her superior and claims that she will increase her sales by 4 percent next year. The superior, on the other hand, is aware of what is taking place. If he says that he wants a 14 percent increase, then he would be establishing a ceiling on productivity. Not wanting to establish a low ceiling, he confronts the saleswoman with a request for a 20 percent increase in sales. If the two simply split the difference, the saleswoman would be required to increase sales by 12 percent, 2 percent less than the "realistic estimate."

Actions such as these can undermine the theory of objective setting. Accordingly, some subjective measures must be added to assess workers' performance. These subjective measures become even more

---

A Sample Performance Agreement for a Training Specialist

FINANCIAL

- Provide recommendations for software and/or other training products, accompanied by a detailed cost estimate and cost/benefit assessments.
- Reduce and/or control program expenses where possible.

CUSTOMER SERVICE

- Design and deliver state-of-the-art training programs that support the Corporate Training Catalog, for employees of the corporation.
- Provide dedicated training programs for specific departments on an as needed basis.
- Develop a posttraining evaluation strategy.
- Manage and coordinate next year's Corporate Training Catalog project. Have catalog ready for distribution by October of this year.
- Manage and coordinate training scheduling. Schedules are to be ready for distribution when catalogs are distributed.
- Coordinate and host the socialization program for new employees.
- Conduct other duties, as assigned.

OUTSIDE ACTIVITIES

- Provide community service while serving on the Board of Education's Advisory Council.
- Provide community service by participating in company's "Walk-for-Life" marathon.

SELF-DEVELOPMENT

- Pursue efforts to enhance training program delivery skills.
- Participate in local Human Resources Professional Association meetings.
- Keep abreast of current literature in field.

---

important when deficiencies occur in establishing specific outcomes. While objective measures are clearly preferred, a subjective measure is better than no measure at all.

A Final Note

Performance evaluations are an integral part of every organization. Properly developed and implemented, the performance evaluation can help an organization achieve its goals by developing productive employees. While there are many types of performance evaluation systems, each having its own advantages and disadvantages, we offer the following suggestions: Evaluate employees on behaviorally desired measures, use multiple raters, include peer assessments and self-assessments, reward accurate appraisers, and, above all, communicate the results of the evaluation to the employee.

SUMMARY

1. Performance appraisals have many uses, such as allocating rewards, identifying areas where development efforts are needed, and identifying criteria against which selection and development programs are validated.

2. Performance is defined in terms of effectiveness, efficiency, and personal data, such as measures of accidents, turnover, absences, and tardiness.

3. The appraisal process consists of six steps:
    a. Establish performance standards
    b. Communicate performance expectations to employees
    c. Measure actual performance
    d. Compare actual performance with standards
    e. Discuss the appraisal with the employee
    f. If necessary, initiate corrective action

4. Employees can be appraised against
    a. Absolute standards
    b. Relative standards
    c. Objectives

5. Appraisals can be distorted by
    a. Leniency error
    b. Halo error
    c. Similarity error
    d. Central tendency
    e. Forcing information to match performance criteria
    f. Low appraiser motivation

   g. Inflationary pressure
   h. Inappropriate substitutes for performance
   i. Attribution theory
6. More effective appraisals can be achieved with
   a. Behaviorally based measures
   b. Combination of absolute and relative ratings
   c. Ongoing feedback
   d. Multiple raters
   e. Selective rating
   f. Trained appraisers
   g. Peer assessment
   h. Postappraisal interview
   i. Rewards to accurate appraisers

KEY TERMS

Absolute standards
Attribution theory
Behaviorally anchored rating
  scales (BARS)
Critical incidents
Effectiveness
Efficiency
Graphic rating scale
Group order ranking
Halo error

Individual ranking
Leniency error
Management by Objectives
  (MBO)
Paired comparison
Performance
Performance appraisal process
Relative standards
Similarity error

QUESTIONS FOR REVIEW

1. To what three purposes can performance appraisal be applied?
2. What role does performance appraisal play in expectancy theory?
3. Describe the appraisal process.
4. Compare the essay appraisal with the critical incident appraisal.
5. Contrast the advantages and disadvantages of (1) absolute standards and (2) relative standards.
6. What is BARS? Why might BARS be better than trait-oriented measures?
7. What is MBO?
8. What are some of the major factors that distort performance appraisals?

9. What is peer assessment? How can it affect a good performance evaluation?

10. Describe the usefulness of the postassessment interview.

QUESTIONS FOR DISCUSSION

1. "Good raters are born, not made." Do you agree or disagree? Discuss.

2. "Performance appraisal should be a two-way street. Supervisors evaluate their subordinates, and subordinates should evaluate their supervisors." Do you agree or disagree? Discuss.

3. "The higher the position an employee occupies in an organization, the easier it is to appraise his or her performance objectively." Do you agree or disagree? Discuss.

4. Describe an optimum performance appraisal system.

5. "Using a performance evaluation instrument that is not valid is a waste of time." Do you agree or disagree? Discuss.

CONTINUING CASE: Concord General

Nobody Knows The Trouble I've Seen

Judy has been trying to correct a problem with respect to performance evaluations conducted at Concord General. She has found that the evaluations have traditionally been conducted by an administrator, someone who does not have the clinical knowledge to assess the nurses' performance accurately. Evaluations are conducted once a year, and there are no follow-ups. If an individual is experiencing problems in either practice or judgment, no correction is made or identified until the annual review. And finally, the evaluations are subjective; no objective measures are used.

Judy has been meeting with various nurse committees in an attempt to correct the troubled performance evaluation system. But she has had some difficulty. She has received so many suggestions that she is inundated with ideas. However, she knows that out of these ideas may come a solution. Realizing that performance differs in the various units, she has established ad hoc committees in each unit to develop a realistic performance evaluation instrument and a timetable for implementing it.

Each group is obligated to find a viable system that will work within the respective unit.

Questions

1. What must each ad hoc committee do before developing a performance evaluation instrument?
2. On what criteria should a nurse in the Intensive Care Unit be evaluated? How could that be measured?
3. Although each unit will have specifics regarding its respective procedures, list a standard set of procedures that each should follow.

CASE APPLICATION

You Get What You Pay For

Frank Henderson is the manager of General Electric's Appliance Division. Each April, he must evaluate all of his subordinates to decide who is to receive a merit increase for the upcoming fiscal year. But each year these employees complain about how they are evaluated, how merit money is dispersed, and what criteria are used for the evaluations. However, during the past two years there has been a tremendous emphasis on quality of production. A review of the merit recipients reveals that these people were the ones who had the best quality records. But many of the employees felt that quality should not be the determining factor. At an employee forum, one of the senior members remarked: "How can Frank now reward quality? What has happened to production numbers?"

Another employee agreed and stated: "This quality game is okay for some, but what about overall production? It seems to me that if I will only be rewarded for quality, then I should produce a few items but make them perfect."

After hearing such criticism, Frank was quite upset. He was not trying to cause chaos in his evaluations, nor was he attempting to hurt anyone. Unfortunately, what was originally intended to be an evaluation system had just become a nuisance.

Questions

1. What is the major problem with Frank's evaluation system?
2. Describe a performance evaluation system that you could recommend to Frank for evaluating a worker on the production line.
3. If no changes are made in the current system that Frank is using, what do you expect will occur regarding future production performance of the employees?
4. What does this case tell us about the impact of performance appraisals on employee motivation?

ADDITIONAL READINGS

BUREAU OF NATIONAL AFFAIRS, "Performance Appraisals: Making Them Work," *Bulletin to Management*, 37, No. 9 (February 27, 1986), 66–71.

DEETS, NORMAN R., and D. TIMOTHY TYLER, "How Xerox Improved Its Performance Appraisals," *Personnel Journal*, April 1986, pp. 50–56.

GOMEZ-MEJIA, LUIS R., RONALD C. PAGE, and WALTER W. TORNOW, "Improving the Effectiveness of Performance Appraisal," *Personnel Administrator*, January 1985, pp. 74–82.

HOWE, TERRY R., "Eight Ways to Ruin a Job Performance Review," *Personnel Journal*, January 1986, pp. 60–63.

KINICKI, ANGELO J., BRENDAN BANNISTER, PETER HAM, and ANGELO S. DENISI, "Behaviorally Anchored Rating Scales vs. Summated Rating Scales: Psychometric Properties and Susceptibility to Rating Bias," *Educational and Psychometric Measurement*, 45, No. 3 (Fall 1985), 535–49.

CHAPTER 15

Rewarding

the Productive

Employee

AFTER READING THIS CHAPTER, YOU WILL BE ABLE TO:

1. Classify rewards
2. Identify the components of effective rewards
3. Describe the criteria that influence the distribution of rewards

What's worth doing is worth doing for money.

—Joseph Donohue

"What's in it for me?" That is a queston every person consciously or unconsciously asks before engaging in any form of behavior. Obviously, then, it applies to all employees in an organization. Our knowledge of motivation tells us that people do what they do to satisfy some need. Before they do anything, therefore, they look for a payoff or reward:

> *Whether dealing with monkeys, rats, or human beings, it is hardly controversial to state that most organisms seek information concerning what activities are rewarded, and then seek to do (or at least pretend to do) those things, often to the virtual exclusion of activities not rewarded. The extent to which this occurs of course will depend on the perceived attractiveness of the rewards offered . . .* [1]

The most obvious reward employees get from work is pay, and we will spend the major part of this chapter addressing pay as a reward. However, rewards also include promotions, desirable work assignments, and a host of other less obvious payoffs—a smile, acceptance by a peer, a covert or overt implication that you are doing a good job, or a kind word of recognition.

Rewards and Expectancy Theory

The place of rewards in expectancy theory was made clear in Chapter 12. Since people behave in ways that they believe are in their best interests, they constantly look for payoffs for their efforts. They expect good job performance to lead to organizational rewards, and they further seek rewards that will satisfy their individual goals or needs.

[1]Steven Kerr, "On the Folly of Rewarding A, While Hoping for B," *Academy of Management Journal*, December 1975, p. 769.

Organizations, then, use rewards to motivate people. They rely on rewards to motivate job candidates to join the organization. They certainly rely on rewards to get employees to come to work and perform effectively once they are hired.

In this chapter, we will review the various types of rewards over which managers have discretion; look at the properties of effective rewards, with particular emphasis on using rewards in ways that are consistent with expectancy theory; and outline the various criteria on which rewards can be distributed.

Types of Rewards

There are a number of ways to classify rewards. We have selected three of the more typical dichotomies: intrinsic versus extrinsic rewards, financial versus nonfinancial rewards, and performance-based versus membership-based rewards. As you will see, these categories are far from being mutually exclusive.

Intrinsic versus Extrinsic Rewards

Intrinsic rewards
Intrinsic rewards are the satisfactions one gets from the job itself. These satisfactions are self-initiated rewards, such as having pride in one's work, having a feeling of accomplishment, or being part of a team. The techniques of job enrichment, shorter work-weeks, flex-time, and job rotation, as discussed in Chapter 13, can offer intrinsic rewards by providing interesting and challenging jobs and allowing the employee greater freedom. *Extrinsic rewards* include money, promotions, and fringe benefits. Their common thread is that they are external to the job and come from an outside source, mainly, management. Thus, if an employee experiences feelings of achievement or personal growth from a job, we would label such rewards as intrinsic. If the employee receives a salary increase or a write-up in the company magazine, we would label those rewards as extrinsic.

While we have stressed the role of extrinsic rewards in motivation, we should point out that intrinsic and extrinsic rewards may be closely linked. Let us expand this point a bit.

Extrinsic rewards
Motivational researchers had generally assumed that intrinsic and extrinsic rewards were independent; that is, the stimulation of one would not affect the other. However, research conducted in the late 1960s and early 1970s suggested that this assumption might be in error.

Early experiments designed to test the independence assumption tended to support the proposition that when extrinsic rewards like money, promotions, or fringe benefits were used as payoffs for superior performance, the internal rewards, which are derived from the individual doing what he or she likes, were reduced.[2] The explanation for this occurrence went something like this. For money or other extrinsic rewards to be used as effective motivators, they should be made contingent on the employee's performance. But when this is done, it decreases the internal satisfaction the employee gets from doing the job. What has happened is that an external stimulus had been substituted for an internal one.

If this proposition were true, the implication for rewards should be obvious. An individual's pay should be noncontingent on performance in order to avoid decreasing intrinsic motivation. If paying someone directly for the performance of a task decreases the intrinsic interest in the task itself, the compensation of subordinates should not be a major concern of managers. Ironically, if this proposition were valid, the more success management achieved in linking compensation to performance, the greater the decrease in intrinsic desire to do the job.

Is the proposition valid? A summary of more than two dozen studies that have researched the argument finds a substantial mix of support and refutation for the proposition.[3] The evidence indicates the proposition may be true in certain highly specific conditions, but it appears that these conditions "are so restrictive that the proposition is without utility for understanding work rewards and motivation."[4] We conclude, therefore, that extrinsic rewards should continue to be considered a major influence on employee performance, and viewed as independent of the intrinsic rewards the employee obtains from the work itself.

Financial versus Nonfinancial Rewards

Rewards may or may not enhance the employee's financial well-being. If they do, they can do this directly—through wages, bonuses, profit sharing, and the like; or indirectly—through supportive benefits such as pension plans, paid vacations, paid sick leaves, and purchase discounts.

Nonfinancial rewards

Nonfinancial rewards cover a smorgasbord of desirable "things" that are potentially at the disposal of the organization. Their common link is that they do not increase the employee's financial position. Instead of making the employee's life better off the job, nonfinancial rewards emphasize making life on the job more attractive. The nonfinancial rewards that we will identify represent a few of the more

---

[2]Edward L. Deci, "Paying People Doesn't Always Work the Way You Expect It To," *Human Resource Management*, Summer 1973, pp. 28–32.

[3]Richard A. Guzzo, "Types of Rewards, Cognitions, and Work Motivation," *Academy of Management Review*, January 1979, pp. 75–86.

[4]Ibid., p. 78

obvious; however, the creation of these rewards is limited only by managers' ingenuity and ability to assess "payoffs" within their jurisdiction that individuals within the organization find desirable.

The old saying "one man's food is another man's poison" applies to the entire subject of rewards, but specifically to the area of nonfinancial rewards. What one employee views as "something I've always wanted," another finds superfluous. Therefore care must be taken in providing the "right" nonfinancial reward for each person; yet where selection has been done assiduously, the benefits to the organization should be impressive.

Some workers are very status conscious. A paneled office, a carpeted floor, a large walnut desk, or a private bathroom may be just the office furnishing that stimulates an employee toward top performance. Similarly, status-oriented employees may value an impressive job title, their own business cards, their own secretary, or a well-located parking space with their name clearly painted underneath the "Reserved" sign.

Some employees value having their lunch between one and two o'clock in the afternoon. If lunch is normally from eleven in the morning until noon, the benefit of being able to take their lunch at another, more preferred, time can be viewed as a reward. Having a chance to work with congenial colleagues, and achieving a desired work assignment or an assignment where the worker can operate without close supervision, are all nonfinancial rewards that are within the discretion of management and, when carefully used, can provide stimulus for improved performance.

Performance-Based versus Membership-Based Rewards

The rewards that the organization allocates can be said to be based on either performance criteria or membership criteria. While the managers in most organizations will vigorously argue that their reward system pays off for performance, you should recognize that this is almost invariably not the case. Few organizations actually reward employees based on performance, a point we will discuss more extensively later in this chapter. Without question, the dominant basis for reward allocations in organizations is membership.

Performance-based rewards

Performance-based rewards are exemplified by the use of commissions, piecework pay plans, incentive systems, group bonuses, or other forms of merit pay plans. On the other hand, membership-based rewards include cost-of-living increases, profit sharing, benefits, and salary increases attributable to labor-market conditions, seniority or time in rank, credentials (such as a college degree or a graduate diploma), or future potential (the recent M.B.A. out of a prestigious university). The demarcation between the two is not always obvious. For instance, company-paid membership in a country club or use of company-owned automobiles and aircraft by executives may be given for membership or performance. If they are available to, say, all middle- and upper-level executives, then they are membership based. However, if they are made available selectively to certain managers based on their performance rather than their "entitlement," which, of course, implies they can also be taken away, we should treat them as performance-based rewards for those who might deem them attractive.

Membership-based rewards

For practical purposes, we need to break membership-based rewards into two groups. One group is made up of benefits and services that go to all employees regardless of their performance level. All nurses at a certain hospital, for instance, get ten days' sick leave, $25,000 worth of life insurance, paid hospitalization coverage, access to the credit union, and a host of other benefits and services regardless of whether they do an outstanding job or a barely acceptable one. Because benefits and services are explicitly acknowledged to be allocated on the basis of membership, we will call them *explicit* membership-based rewards. All the other membership-based rewards will be thrown into the second group which we will call *implied*. You may wonder why the need to differentiate two groups?

We have separated the membership-based rewards into two groups to clarify what is often confusing in practice. Most organizations treat benefits and services as the only membership-based rewards. All other rewards are traditionally treated as performance based. This, of course, is both incorrect and misleading labeling. In

FIGURE 15-1

ZIGGY   TOM WILSON

practice, as we will show later, performance is only a minor determinant of rewards. This is true despite academic theories holding that high motivation depends on performance-based rewards. In practice, a lot of lip service is given to the value of good job performance, but the organization's rewards do not closely parallel employee performance.

In summary, you should recognize that there are performance-based rewards; there are explicit membership-based rewards, which we call benefits and services; and there are implied membership-based rewards. Practicing managers often call the latter group "performance based," but they are not.

Summary

The general structure of rewards is summarized in Figure 15-2. We have separated rewards, first, into two categories—intrinsic and extrinsic. The former group are obtained as a result of the work itself. By the way management structures and schedules work, it is possible to provide intrinsic rewards to employees. This point was the main theme of Chapter 13.

The focus in this chapter will be on extrinsic rewards, but not *all* extrinsic rewards. Here we will emphasize financial rewards, excluding benefits and services. Why are they excluded? Because they are explicitly acknowledged to be given out to all employees regardless of their level of performance, we treat them separately, in Chapter 17, as part of the maintenance function.

You may now be thinking, "Wait! Why aren't implied membership-based rewards also relegated to the maintenance function? After all, they aren't allocated on the basis of performance, either!" If you see this contradiction, then you are paying close attention.

The reason we will cover implied membership-based rewards in this chapter is pragmatic. They are a major component of compensation administration. Since an understanding of compensation is a major objective of Chapter 16, we must address both the performance and membership sides of wage and salary administration. However, since rewards like cost-of-living increases or pay adjustments based on seniority are distributed on nonperformance criteria, they contribute more toward keeping people in the organization than toward stimulating them to high levels of effort. This distinction will become clearer as you proceed through the following pages.

Qualities of Effective Rewards

We can identify qualities that an effective reward system should have. Research indicates that rewards work best when they are individualized to reflect differences in what employees consider important, are

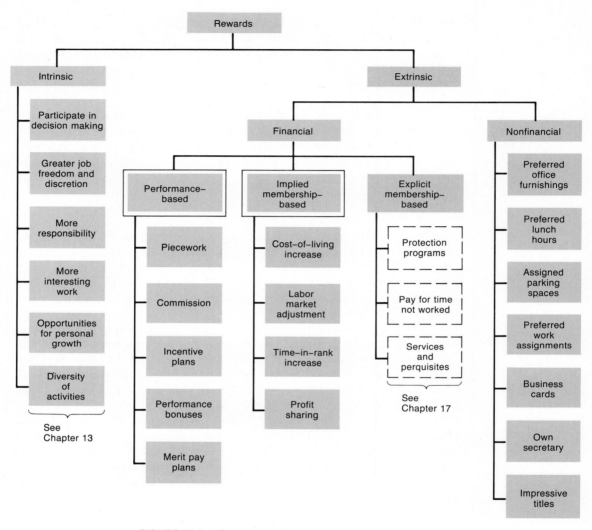

FIGURE 15-2   Structure of Rewards

perceived as equitable, are visible and flexible, and can be allocated at a relatively low cost.[5] We will expand on each of these properties.

Importance

Rewards should be important to person receiving them

Never assume a particular reward is universally important to all employees. Money, for example, can have a very different meaning to different people. It may represent basic security and love, power, a measure of one's achievements, or merely the means to a comfortable life style. To some employees, a $100-a-month raise would be very important. Other employees, in the same job and at the same salary level, might far prefer an extra week of vacation.

This difference among employees was substantiated in a study undertaken at a public utility.[6] One hundred and fifty employees were asked to rank their preference for rewards. It was found that the employees, in general, rated extra vacation as most preferred, followed by pay, a pension increase, paid family dental insurance, early retirement, and work schedule rearrangements, in decreasing order. But this ranking varied among different employee groups. For instance, the preference for the dental plan decreased with age, while desire for more pension benefits increased. Married employees also valued the dental plan far more than single employees, and this preference increased with the number of dependents.

Research indicates that the preference for rewards will be significantly affected by age, marital status, and the number of children the employee has.[7] It should not surprise you to find that young unmarried men desire more time off the job and young married men rated more vacation lower than family health coverage; or that older employees seek increased retirement benefits while younger workers opt for more cash.

In expectancy theory terms, motivation is optimized when employees see rewards satisfying their individual needs. Therefore a good reward system should be designed to offer heterogeneous rewards to a heterogeneous labor force. Employees should be rewarded with what they individually consider important.

One effort to broaden the idea of individualizing rewards has been labeled *cafeteria compensation*. In contrast to the traditional manner in which fringe benefits are allocated—all employees get the same package—cafeteria compensation allows each employee to choose that total compensation package which best satisfies his or her current needs. Specifically, where cafeteria-type flexible compensation exists, employees are told what their total compensation is, and they can choose a mix of salary, life insurance, deferred compensation, and other benefits to suit their particular needs. Assuming James Douglas currently earns $30,000 and his employer spends another 35 percent on traditional benefits, he now has $40,500 to spend at the "cafeteria" counter. Every reward has a price tag, and Douglas can select—up to

---

[6] J. Brad Chapman and Robert Ottemann, "Employee Preferences for Various Compensation and Fringe Benefits Options," in *Policy Issues in Contemporary Personnel and Industrial Relations,* ed. Mary G. Miner and John B. Miner (New York: Macmillan, 1977), pp. 549–58.

[7] Lawler, "Reward Systems," p. 180.

Another Look, Another View: How to Motivate with Rewards

Almost a day doesn't go by in which a manager asks "Just how do I motivate my employees?" And almost as frequently as we hear this question, we can find some reference that suggests what to do.

But too frequently, we look for quick fixes, trying to find "rewards" that will motivate the masses. Unfortunately, these techniques are for the most part, not long term solutions. Implementing a quick fix strategy will not bring about the desired change managers want. Why? Because managers often try to reward employees with those things that "excite" them, the managers. This practice, however, is backwards. "Employees do things for their reasons, not the manager's," and accordingly, the "manager's job is to create enthusiasm," so the employees will want to produce. In order to establish an environment in which enthusiasm can be created, several criteria must be present. These are:

Adequate Pay Levels
Job Security
Interaction with Fellow Employees
Adequate Working Conditions
Personal Growth
Recognition for a Job Well Done

To help a manager to ensure that these criteria are present, the following acronym has been proposed.

G—Growth, company and employee
R—Recognition, identify good work
A—Achievement, innovative ideas to get the job done
P—Participation, listening to employees
E—Execution, practicing what you preach
S—Several, use the above routinely

Following the GRAPES philosophy may help a manager to motivate employees. These rewards, if used properly, can "turn on" employees and lead to many benefits; benefits for both the company and the employee.

Source: William H. Scott, "Motivating the Right Employees," *In Business*, 8, No. 1 (January–February 1986), 24.

a value of $40,500—those items that he deems important in suiting his personal needs.

The advantages of flexible compensation go beyond merely allowing employees to customize their own compensation package. This method involves little in additional direct costs, it makes clear to employees exactly how much the organization is actually spending to compensate them, and it ensures that the money will be spent only on the rewards the employees want. On the negative side, there is the tendency for employees to think in short-range rather than long-range terms. Most organizations that have instituted a cafeteria plan actually provide all employees with minimum insurance and pension benefits and let each employee select the additional rewards to suit his or her own needs. This overcomes the dilemma of management having to tell a widow that her husband chose to receive longer vacation periods in lieu of life insurance coverage. The biggest drawback, however, stems from the fact that the costs and availability of many benefits are based on the number of people who subscribe to them and may be reduced if that number decreases. For example, many large corporations are able to provide life insurance at a fraction of the cost that an individual within the corporation would have to pay personally because they have the clout that comes when coverage extends to tens of thousands of employees. If only a fraction of all employees choose life insurance, the cost of the firm's group policy can be expected to rise considerably. When this happens across the board, many of the advantages of a cafeteria plan are lost, since the higher price for individual benefits means fewer benefits can be purchased. And last, the start-up costs. It has been estimated that the start-up costs "can run from $500,000 to $1.5 million, for a complicated computer program to keep track of all the trading of benefit options.[8]

In spite of the drawbacks from cafeteria compensation, there are several visible examples where it has been introduced. Companies that offer flexible compensation include the American Can Company and TRW.[9] At American Can, all employees get core coverage and then choose from optional benefits, the amount of which is determined on the "basis from benefit reductions in medical coverage and the pension plan, and from a service factor.[10] The TRW plan allows employees to restructure their reward package each year, and it offers a very diverse set of choices. For instance, employees can choose among four hospitalization options and eight death benefit options.[11]

Equitable Distribution

Rewards must be fairly distributed

Employees desire rewards that are distributed in what seems to be an equitable manner. This means fairness among the organization's employees and fairness relative to what people get for doing a similar job

[8]"Cafeteria Benefits Plans Let Employees Fill Their Plates, Then Pay with Tax Free Dollars," *Wall Street Journal*, May 9, 1983, p. 58.

[9]Mitchell Meyers, *Flexible Employee Benefit Plans: Companies' Experience*, Report No. 831 (New York: The Conference Board, 1983), p. 8.

[10]Ibid, p. 9.

[11]Ibid, p. 24.

in another organization. *Equity theory* has been proposed to explain what happens when individuals perceive an imbalance between what they put into a job and what they get out of it relative to others' give-and-get ratio.[12]

It is no secret that employees make comparisons between themselves and their peers. Employees perceive what they get from a job situation (outcomes) in relation to what they must put into (inputs). They also compare their input-outcome ratio with the input-outcome ratio of their peers. If a person's ratio and that of others are perceived to be equal, a state of equity is said to exist. If they are unequal, inequity exists. That is, the individual views himself or herself as underrewarded or overrewarded. Equity theory argues that when an inequity is seen as aversive, the individual will attempt to correct it.

Evidence indicates that the referent chosen by the employee is an important variable in equity theory.[13] The three referent categories have been classified as "other," "system," and "self." The "other" category includes other individuals with similar jobs in the same organization, as well as friends, neighbors, or professional associates. Based on information that employees receive through word of mouth or through newspapers and magazines on such issues as executive salaries or a recent union contract, employees can compare their pay relative to that of others.

The "system" category considers organizational pay policies and procedures, and the administration of this system. It considers organizationwide, implied and explicit, pay policies. Organization precedents in terms of allocation of pay would be a major determinant in this category.

The "self" category refers to input-outcome ratios unique to the individual that differ from the individual's current input-outcome ratio. This category is influenced by such criteria as past jobs or commitments that must be met in terms of family role.

The choice of a particular set of referents is related to the information available about referents as well as their perceived relevance. Based on equity theory, we might suggest that when employees envision an inequity, they may choose one or more of five alternatives:

1. Distort either their own or others' inputs or outcomes
2. Behave in some way so as to induce others to change their inputs or outcomes
3. Behave in some way as to change their own inputs or outcomes

[12]J. S. Adams, "Inequity in Social Exchanges," in *Advances in Experimental Social Psychology,* ed. Leonard Berkowitz (New York: Academic Press, 1965), pp. 267–300.

[13]Paul S. Goodman, "An Examination of Referents Used in the Evaluation of Pay," *Organizational Behavior and Human Performance,* October 1974, pp. 170–95.

4. Choose a different comparison referent

5. Leave the organization

Equity theory recognizes that individuals are concerned not only with the absolute amount of money they are paid for their efforts but also with the relationship of this amount to what others are paid. They make judgments as to the relationship between their inputs and outcomes and the inputs and outcomes of others. Based on their own inputs, such as effort, education, and competence, they compare outcomes such as salary levels, raises, and other factors. When people perceive an imbalance in their input-outcome ratio relative to others, tension is created. This tension provides the basis for motivation as people strive for what they perceive as equity and fairness. Perceptions of overreward seem to be easily reduced by individuals and, therefore, are infrequent. Surveys often show that about 5 percent of an employee group feel overpaid.[14] When people feel overrewarded, they usually bring about equity by changing their perceptions of the situation. For example, they increase their perceptions of their worth or their perception of the amount of pay deserved. Perceptions of underreward are less easily corrected. These are likely to result in reducing effort, fighting the system, engaging in increased absenteeism, or performing other undesirable behaviors. The implications of equity theory for managers should be clear. The absolute rewards that employees receive are not the sole influence on motivation; relative rewards are also critical. Where employees perceive inequity, it can result in lower productivity, more absenteeism, or an increase in resignations. However, managers can only have control over the "system" referent, not referents outside of the workplace, such as "what the neighbors have."

Visibility

Rewards should be visible

A reward that is not visible to the employee may fail to get the desired motivating effect from the employee. On the other hand, a truly visible reward gets the attention not only of individual employees but also of their peers. This latter quality means visible rewards can contribute to satisfying an employee's esteem and recognition needs.

In what ways can managers increase the visibility of rewards? Possibilities include well-publicized bonuses, allocating annual salary increases in a lump sum rather than spreading them out over the entire year, and eliminating the secrecy surrounding pay by openly communicating everyone's compensation.

Some organizations have successfully maximized the value of rewards by making them both impressive in size and highly visible. For

---

[14]Lawler, "Reward Systems," p. 164.

instance, the Suave Shoe Corporation of Miami, Florida, paid its general manager of manufacturing a salary of $33,000, but he made headlines when he earned an additional $438,290 performance bonus.[15] This bonus was the result of successfully cutting manufacturing costs, allowing Suave to go from a $1.1 million loss to a $3.1 million profit in three years. Data Terminal Systems, a Massachusetts manufacturer of electronic cash register systems, spreads the wealth. All employees—from the president to the lowliest assembler—participate in travel bonuses.[16] For example, the factory was shut down for a week and employees could choose a company-paid trip to either London, England, or Disneyworld in Florida. A year later, the company did it again—this time, however, the trip was to Rome. Both trips were rewards to employees for having doubled sales and earnings in a year. Such trips obviously meet our criterion that rewards be visible.

It has been suggested that lump-sum salary increases can be a successful device for increasing a reward's visibility.[17] Use of this approach means that employees are given the option of having their annual raises presented in a single lump sum as soon as the increases are granted, rather than parceled out in paychecks through the year. An increase presented as a lump sum is obviously more visible than one divided up into small amounts and buried in, say, twenty-six regular paychecks. After deductions for taxes, even the most generous salary increase usually means very little change in an employee's regular take-home pay, so the lump sum tends to ensure maximum impact for the raise. Of course, while a large raise tends to come across clearly as a large amount of money, a small raise tends to come across as just what it is—a small increase. The lump-sum option is reported to have been introduced at Westinghouse and Equitable Life Assurance Society.[18]

Probably the most widely discussed and controversial approach to increasing the visibility of rewards is to eliminate the traditional secrecy surrounding pay. The proponents of openness argue that pay secrecy actually demotivates employees. Secrecy may tend to work to the disadvantage of using money to motivate managers because even the most carefully derived pay schedule and differentials may be seen as potentially less rewarding than they actually are. The misperception of pay contributes to dissatisfaction with pay, and secrecy regarding pay contributes to this misperception.

Complete openness about pay policies is indeed rare in organizations. If such information were common knowledge, employees

---

[15]"This Bonus Is a Real Incentive," *Business Week*, March 14, 1977, pp. 54, 58.

[16]Stephen Solomon, "How a Whole Company Earned Itself a Roman Holiday," *Fortune*, January 5, 1979, pp. 80–83.

[17]Edward E. Lawler III, "New Approaches to Pay Administration," *Personnel*, September–October 1976, pp. 11–23.

[18]"Compensation Woe: How to Pay?" *Time*, October 15, 1979, p. 110.

would undertake to compare their salaries with those of everyone else, and the inevitability of human error would reveal any inequities in the pay system. There would be misunderstandings, petty complaints, increased dissatisfaction, and perceived if not real inequities. Whether it is true or not, almost everyone thinks he or she is worth more than the next person. On the other hand, an open pay system demonstrates confidence by management in the structure of compensation, and hence it should increase the trust individuals have in the organization.

Flexibility

An effective reward is one that has the flexibility to vary with changes in performance. If an employee's job performance declines in 1987, the rewards he received in 1986 should ideally have downside adjustment capability.

An effective reward would be flexible in terms of the amount given and whether it is given to everyone in the organization. The annual performance bonus, for instance, offers high flexibility. It can be adjusted upward or downward, or eliminated, each year depending on some measure of performance. Additionally, it can be given selectively to those employees who have done a superior job.

Another attribute of a flexible reward is that it be given frequently without losing importance. Giving rewards frequently is often helpful for sustaining extrinsic motivation, yet some rewards diminish in importance when used over time. As a case in point, praise is a flexible reward in that its amount can be varied in allocations to and among individuals. However, it suffers from diminishing returns. Continued use of praise results in the reward losing its importance.

Low Cost

Rewards should be low in cost

The final quality of an effective reward is low cost. Rewards are not free goods, and the organization must consider the costs along with the benefits from any reward. A high-cost reward simply cannot be given out as often, and when it is, it reduces organizational effectiveness as a result of its cost. All other factors equal, the lowest-cost reward should be preferable to management.

Summary

A careful review of the criteria we have identified for effective rewards brings one to the conclusion that no organizational reward is ideal on all dimensions. Figure 15-3 makes this point by evaluating a number of the more common extrinsic rewards.

Pay possesses all the characteristics of the perfect reward except one—it is not low in cost. Promotions and permanent employment

FIGURE 15-3

Evaluation of Extrinsic Rewards

REWARD	QUALITY				
	Important	Equitable	Visible	Flexible	Cost
Pay	High	High	Potentially High	High	High
Promotion	High	High	High	Low	High
Permanent employment (tenure)	Moderate	High	High	Low	High
Status symbols	Moderate	High	High	High	Moderate
Special awards, certificates, and medals	Low	High	High	High	Low
Benefits	High	Moderate	Moderate	Moderate	High

SOURCE: Adapted from Edward E. Lawler III, "Reward Systems," in *Improving Life at Work*, ed. J. Richard Hackman and J. Lloyd Suttle (Santa Monica, Calif.: Goodyear, 1977), p. 174.

score low on flexibility and high in cost. Promotions cannot be given regularly and are a scarce commodity. The guarantee of permanent employment is a one-shot motivator that, once given, loses all ability to motivate. Furthermore, it commits the organization to paying the salaries of tenured employees for the rest of their working lives. Special awards, certificates, and medals are low in cost, but also low in importance. Fringe benefits suffer from high cost and the fact that they are made available to everyone, regardless of job performance.

Because no reward is perfect, managers must carefully assess what they expect from their reward system and structure it so it provides the maximum in motivation potential. Each organization is unique, so the rewards that work in one firm may be ineffective in another. Similarly, jobs within each organization differ, and the rewards made available to incumbents of each job should reflect this fact.

Criteria On Which Rewards Can Be Distributed

Let us now consider the realities of reward distribution. So far, we have presumed that management allocates rewards based solely on employee performance, though we noted in our discussion of performance-based rewards that this is a fallacy. Most organizations believe their rewards system is designed to pay off for merit. The problem is that we find differing definitions of *merit*. Deserving rewards may take into consideration such factors as intelligence, effort, or seniority. The problem is that what is deserving may differ from what is excellent. A major contributor to the problem is undoubtedly the difficulty of defining *excellence*. If excellence is performance, we concede how unsatisfactory our efforts have been at trying to measure performance. Creation of quantifiable and appropriate performance measures of almost all white-collar and service jobs, and many bluecollar jobs, has eluded us. While few will disagree with the viewpoint that the merit concept for distributing rewards is desirable, what constitutes merit is highly debatable.

Our position that performance and rewards must be closely linked has evolved from the importance attached to this relationship in expectancy theory. In the following pages, we will assess the role of performance as a prerequisite for rewards, then discuss other popular criteria by which rewards are distributed.

Performance

Rewards distributed based on performance

The principle of paying for performance is so logical and so deeply instilled in our value system that few attack it. Like apple pie, motherhood, and the flag, the allocation of rewards on the basis of performance is a revered concept in organizations. But, as described above, there are major difficulties in measuring performance.

Performance is concerned with results. Performance measurement asks the question, Did you get the job done? To reward people in the organization based on performance, therefore, requires some agreed-upon criterion for defining performance. Whether this criterion is valid or not in representing performance is not relevant to our definition; as long as rewards are allocated based on job productivity, we are using performance as the determinant.

Another difficulty in measuring performance is differentiating between *quantity* and *quality*. For example, an individual may generate a high output, but his or her performance standards may be quite low. Hence, where controls are not instituted to protect against such abuses, we often find quantity replacing quality. A case in point is reflected by the senior university faculty member who takes the junior faculty member aside and cautions him against maintaining such high standards in his publications. "You won't survive around here by generating only two articles a year. No one cares about quality, it's numbers that matter. Remember, deans can't read, but they can count!"

A problem that has played havoc with performance-based rewards during the past decade has been inflation. Organizations find that, in times of inflation, by the time they have allocated membership-based rewards, there is little or nothing left to reward performance. In the late 1970s, when inflation rates were in the high teens, it took raises in the 16 to 19 percent range just to keep an employee's spending power constant. High inflation generally acts to limit funds available for performance-based rewards.

Effort

It is not uncommon for a report card in grammar school to include *effort* as one of the categories used in grading students. Organizations rarely make their rewarding of effort that explicit, yet it is certainly a major determinant in the reward distribution.

The rewarding of effort represents the classical example of rewarding means rather than ends. In organizations where performance is generally of a low caliber, rewarding of effort may be the only criterion by which to differentiate rewards. For example, a major eastern university was attempting to increase its research efforts and had designated the objective of obtaining grants or funded research as a critical benchmark toward that end. Upon selection of this objective, all faculty members were informed that rewards for the coming year were going to be based on performance in obtaining grants. Unfortunately, after the first year of the program, even though approximately 20 percent of the faculty had made grant applications, none were approved. When the time came for performance appraisal and the distribution of rewards, the dean chose to give the majority of the funds available for pay raises to those faculty members who had applied for grants. Here is a case where performance defined in terms of obtaining funded research grants was zero, so the dean chose to allocate rewards based on effort.

The above example is much less rare than one might think. On the assumption tht those who try should be encouraged, in many cases, effort can count *more than* actual performance. Employees who are clearly perceived by their superiors to be working at less than their optimum can often expect to be rewarded less than other employees who, while producing less, are giving out a greater effort. Even where it is clearly stated that performance is what will be rewarded, people who make appraisals and distribute rewards are only human. Therefore they are not immune to showing compassion for those who try hard, but with minimal success, and allowing this to influence their appraisal and reward decisions.

Seniority

Seniority, job rights, and tenure dominate most civil service systems in the United States, and while they do not play as important a role in business organizations, there is evidence that length of time on the job is a major factor in determining the allocation of rewards. Seniority's greatest virtue is that, relative to other criteria, it is easy to determine. We may disagree as to whether the quality of Smith's work is higher or lower than Jones's, but we would probably not have much debate over who has been with the organization longer. So seniority represents an easily quantifiable criterion that can be substituted for performance.

Skills Held

Rewards distributed
based on skills held

Another practice that is not uncommon in organizations is to allocate rewards based on the skills of the employee. Regardless of whether the skills are used, those individuals who possess the highest skills or talents will be rewarded commensurately. Where such practices are used, it is not unusual to see individuals become "credential crazy." The requirement that an individual needs a college degree in order to attain a certain level within the organization is utilizing skills as a determinant of rewards. Similarly, the requirement that an individual has to pass certain skill tasks by demonstrating an acceptable score in order to maintain a particular position in the organization is again using skills as a reward criterion. If it is necessary for a secretary to demonstrate that she can take shorthand at 120 words per minute to be eligible for consideration as a secretary to a department head, and if department heads do all their dictating into a dictating machine rather than giving it directly to the secretary, we see an example of a skill being utilized as a reward criterion when, in effect, it is irrelevant.

When individuals enter an organization, their skill level is usually a major determinant of the compensation they will receive. In this case, the marketplace or competition has acted to make skills a major element in the reward package. These externally imposed standards can evolve from the community or from occupational categories themselves. In other words, the relationship of demand and supply for particular skills in the community can significantly influence the rewards the organization must expend to acquire particular skills. Also, the demand-supply relationship for an entire occupational category throughout the United States can affect rewards.

The rewards that the organization will have to distribute to hire a physical therapist will depend on both the market for physical therapists in the local community and the market for physical therapists nationwide. If the two markets are out of balance, there will be pressures to equalize them. Most often, however, we find they are fairly well in agreement. Those skills that are in short supply on a national basis are usually also in short supply in the local communities. Therefore, to acquire individuals with those skills, we are required to pay more. If we want all the accountants in our accounting department to have a CPA certificate, we are going to have to upgrade our reward package in order to attract these higher skills. On the other hand, if we set our minimum skill level as a high-school education plus one year of business school, we can expect to find a greater supply of candidates available, requiring a lower initial compensation.

Job Difficulty

Rewards distributed based on job difficulty

The complexity of the job can be a criterion by which rewards are distributed. For example, those jobs that are highly repetitive and can be learned quickly may be viewed as less deserving in rewards than those that are more complex and sophisticated. Jobs that are difficult to perform, require working odd hours, or are undesirable due to stress or unpleasant working conditions, may have to carry with them rewards that are higher in order to attract workers to these activities.

Discretionary Time

Rewards distributed based on discretionary time

The greater the discretion called for on a job, all other things being equal, the greater the impact of mistakes and the greater the need for good judgment. In a job that has been completely programmed—that is, where each step has been procedurized and there is no room for decision making by the incumbent—there is little discretionary time. Such jobs require less judgment, and lower rewards can be offered to attract people to take these positions. As discretion time increases, greater judgmental abilities are needed, and rewards must commensurately be expanded.

A derivative of rewarding employees based on discretionary time is Elliot Jaques's theory of equitable payment.[19] This theory argues that fair and equitable compensation should reflect the maximum time during which the employee exercises discretion without the results being reviewed. It says people should be rewarded for the weight of responsibility they assume. Probably the most important evidence in support of Jaques's theory is the finding that in jobs where the level of responsibility is measured in terms of time span of discretion, employees at the same level state a very similar wage and salary bracket to be fair for the work they do.[20] In other words, employees see the use of the time-span concept as the fairest way to differentiate pay differences.

Conclusion

In this chapter, we have discussed the rewarding of performance so that productivity gains will continue. However, while this would represent the ideal situation, we have to realize that, in practice, organizations reward other factors. We have attempted to review those other factors by describing their impact on both the organization and the employee.

[19]Elliott Jaques, *Equitable Payment* (New York: John Wiley, 1961).

[20]Elliott Jaques, "Taking Time Seriously in Evaluating Jobs," *Harvard Business Review*, September–October 1979, pp. 124–32.

FIGURE 15-4

Ranking of Factors Determining Pay Increases in 493 Companies

FACTORS DETERMINING PAY INCREASES	EMPLOYEE CATEGORY				
	Officers and Executives	Exempt Salaried	Nonexempt Salaried	Nonunion Hourly	Union Hourly
Worker productivity	4	7	5	3	9
Company's financial results	1	2	3	5	7
Company's financial prospects	2	3	4	4	5
Internal equity among groups	6	5	6	6	8
Increases of industry leaders	5	6	8	7	4
Area surveys	3	1	1	1	6
Ability to hire	7	8	7	10	10
National bargaining settlements	9	10	10	8	2
Union demands	10	9	9	9	1
Cost-of-living index	8	4	2	2	3

NOTE: Importance rating determined by frequency of mentions in first, second, or third place in a ranking from 1 to 10. Sample composed of manufacturing (44%), banking and insurance (38%), utility (15%), and retail (3%) firms.

SOURCE: Adapted from David A. Weeks, *Compensating Employees: Lessons of the 1970's*, Report No. 707 (New York: The Conference Board, 1976), pp. 12–14.

Our next step is to develop a compensation system. While rewards in many cases are given in various ways, the compensation system is something that must be established according to the worth of a job. This worth is considered to be the framework on which we establish the pay structure. Keep in mind that although we reward people for their work, we pay a job. How we determine this pay is the focus of the next chapter.

SUMMARY

1. Rewards can be classified as
   a. Intrinsic or extrinsic
   b. Financial or nonfinancial
   c. Performance-based or membership-based
2. Effective rewards are
   a. Individualized to reflect differences in what employees consider important
   b. Perceived as equitable
   c. Visible
   d. Flexible
   e. Allocated at a relatively low cost

3. Popular criteria that influence the distribution of rewards are
   a. Performance
   b. Effort
   c. Seniority
   d. Skills held
   e. Job difficulty
   f. Discretionary time

KEY TERMS

Cafeteria compensation
Equity theory
Extrinsic rewards
Intrinsic rewards

Jaques's theory
Membership-based rewards
Peformance-based rewards

QUESTIONS FOR REVIEW

1. What role do rewards play in expectancy theory?

2. Contrast intrinsic and extrinsic rewards.

3. Describe the qualities that an effective reward would contain.

4. What is "cafeteria compensation"?

5. What is equity theory? What are its implications for compensation administration?

6. What is Jaques's theory of equitable payment? How does it relate to job evaluation and compensation?

7. Contrast financial and nonfinancial rewards.

8. What is a membership-based reward? How does it differ from a performance-based reward?

9. What are the advantages and disadvantages of an open distribution of rewards?

10. How does one reward discretionary time? Job difficulty? Seniority?

QUESTIONS FOR DISCUSSION

1. "Organizations reward employees based on performance." Do you agree or disagree? Discuss.

2. Would you rather work for an organization where everyone knew what others were earning or would you prefer an organization where this information was kept secret? Why?

3. "Cost determinations should be management's only concern when

contemplating a reward system." Do you agree or disagree? Discuss.

4. "Cafeteria benefits are detrimental to employees. Employees do not have the hindsight to know what they need." Do you agree or disagree? Discuss.

5. "As long as we continue to reward people for activities other than performance, productivity gains will be slow in coming." Do you agree or disagree? Discuss.

CONTINUING CASE: Concord General

A Raise, Not Praise

Nurses at Concord General have been complaining about the way the hospital administration treats them. On most occasions, an activity that goes beyond the call of duty is recognized with an "Attaboy" certificate signed by John Michaels. It is also apparent that most activities are regarded as being beyond the call of duty. Every year the hospital orders thousands of "Attaboy" certificates and distributes them to each department head. How they are then used depends on each unit.

While the idea might be considered a good one, it has led to much frustration. As one nurse put it:

> I got four "Attaboys" yesterday. Big deal. It seems whatever we do, we get these things. They are supposed to be a reward. The only thing they are is a waste of time and money. I'd rather have nothing. I feel like a rabbit with a carrot dangling in front of me. Besides, what will they get me anyway?

Realizing that most of the nurses felt the same way, Judy has put an end to the use of "Attaboys."

Questions

1. What went wrong with this type of reward system? How could the problem have been prevented?
2. Develop a procedure that would be conducive and provide meaning to the use of "Attaboys."
3. How should praise be used as a reward in an organization? What must be recognized by the employees before recognition will be beneficial?

CASE APPLICATION

There's No Accounting For Accountants

Don Parce is dean of the College of Business Administration at Metro University, a large, publicly supported, urban college in the northern part of the United States. Don is new to his job, having arrived only three months ago from a professorship in the Midwest. One of the first issues Don has confronted is the hiring of new accounting professors. Don summarized the problem this way:

> Accounting is one of our hottest majors. Nearly 40 percent of our undergraduates are now majoring in the area. And this popularity is widespread. Enrollments in accounting programs throughout North America are expanding rapidly. The dilemma is that there are less than sixty new Ph.D.'s in accounting being produced each year. National figures currently show that the ratio of jobs to people is more than twelve to one. The result has been an unbelievable bidding up of new accounting professors' salaries.

> Don has just revealed the salary structure within Metro's College of Business Administration. Following are the university's floors or minimum salaries for each rank, and the current range (low to high) within the business college:

Instructor	$17,290; $20,692–$26,718
Assistant Professor	$22,290; $25,692–$31,718
Associate Professor	$27,290; $30,692–$38,718
Full Professor	$32,290; $38,692–$59,718

The chairman of Metro's accounting department has told Don that the market in accounting demands that if new people are to be hired, their starting salaries have to be in the $34,000 to $37,000 range. Don is concerned that if such salaries are paid, they will distort the college's salary structure.

Don decided to survey other business schools within his region. Based on the replies from eight institutions, he compiled the following comparative data (figures represent ranges for business faculty only):

Instructor	$14,800–$23,000
Assistant Professor	$21,700–$31,400
Associate Professor	$26,800–$37,300
Full Professor	$35,000–$57,200

The survey revealed that these other schools were also having considerable difficulty staffing their accounting vacancies. What were they doing? The data indicated that many schools were bringing in new people at a higher rank than they deserved in order to be able to pay them more. For example, one school had hired a twenty-six-year-old accountant, who had both a Ph.D. and a CPA, at the high associate professor level—paying $36,000. Other schools had lowered their requirements from the Ph.D. and CPA to only the M.B.A. and CPA.

Don concluded that in spite of his school's paying the top salaries in his region, he would have to do something out of the ordinary if he was going to hire accounting faculty. But what should he do? If he pays $36,000 or so, he will destroy his present salary structure. Furthermore, what are the long-term implications when the demand-supply of accountants moves closer to balance? (Experts expect this to happen by the early 1990s.) Don is reluctant to lower hiring standards to meet the problem. He knows that if he does lower them, in ten years or so he will be stuck with tenured professors whose credentials are below what the college demands. Finally, he realizes that if new faculty are brought in at the higher ranks, their salaries will be the same as those of colleagues who have had five or ten or more years' experience. In addition to creating morale problems, this action would mean that new hires could not expect a promotion for possibly ten years and could receive only minimum raises if salary ranges are to be maintained.

Questions

1. What advice would you give Don?
2. Can you see any parallels between this case and the problems a human resource manager in industry might encounter?
3. What would be the equity theory implications for current Metro University faculty?

ADDITIONAL READINGS

BROWN, ABBY, "Today's Employees Choose Their Own Recognition Award," *Personnel Administrator,* 31, No. 8 (August 1986), 51–58.

FEENEY, EDWARD J., "Modifying Employee Behavior: Making Rewards Pay Off," *Supervisory Management,* 30, No. 12 (December 1985), 25–27.

NORDSTROM, RODNEY, and R. VANCE HALL, "How to Develop and Implement an Employee Incentive Program," *Management Solutions* (September 1986), pp. 40–43.

SOLOMON, BARBARA, "When Incentives Add Punch to Production-Line Pay," *Personnel,* 62, No. 9 (September 1985), 4–6.

WRIGHT, MARTIN, "Helping Employees Speak Out about Their Jobs and the Workplace," *Personnel,* 63, No. 9 (September 1986), 56–60.

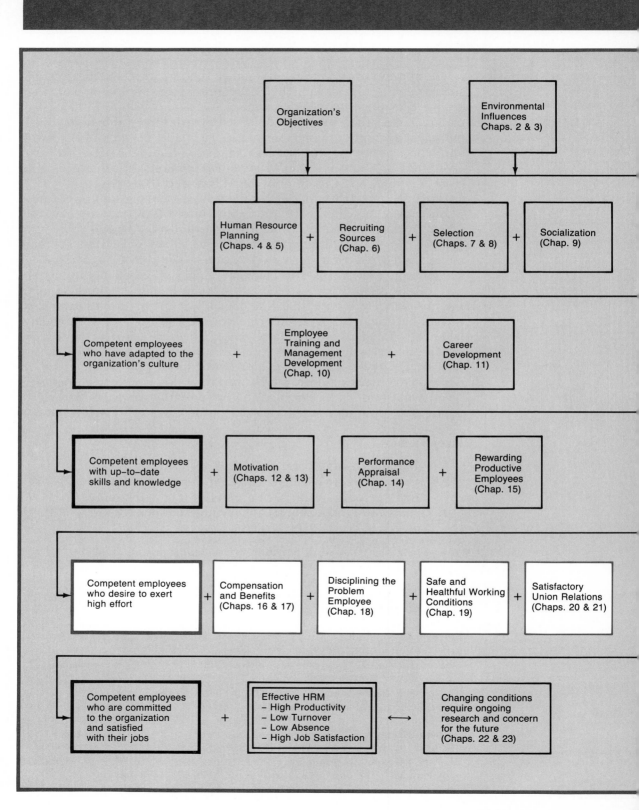

PART FIVE

MAINTENANCE OF HUMAN RESOURCES

= Competent employees who have adapted to the organization's culture

= Competent employees with up–to–date skills and knowledge

= Competent employees who desire to exert high effort

= Competent employees who are committed to the organization and satisfied with their jobs

CHAPTER 16

Compensation

Administration

AFTER READING THIS CHAPTER, YOU WILL BE ABLE TO:

1. Define the goal of compensation administration
2. Discuss job evaluation and its four basic approaches
3. Explain the evolution of the final wage structure
4. Describe incentive compensation
5. Describe executive compensation

If the love of money is the root of all evil, why are rich people so happy?

—Anonymous

Why do electricians at Georgia Power and Light earn more than security guards? Intuitively, you would say that electricians are more skilled, so they should earn more. But how about pollution engineers at GP&L? Should they make more or less than electricians? The answer to questions such as these lies in job evaluation.

Job evaluation is the process whereby an organization systematically establishes its compensation program. In this process, jobs are ranked in order to arrive at each job's appropriate worth. In this chapter, we will discuss the broader topic of compensation, narrow our discussion to job evaluation methods, and conclude with a review of an increasingly controversial topic—executive compensation.

What Is Compensation Administration?

Compensation administration defined

Employees exchange work for rewards. Probably the most important reward, and certainly the most obvious, is money. In this section we want to answer the question, How much should an employee be paid? The search for this answer throws us directly into the topic of compensation administration.

The goals of compensation administration are to design the lowest-cost pay structure that will attract, motivate, and retain competent employees, and that also will be perceived as fair by these employees. *Fairness* is a term that frequently arises in the administration of an organization's compensation program. Organizations generally seek to pay the least that they have to in order to minimize costs. So fairness means a wage or salary that is adequate for the demands and requirements of the job. But, of course, fairness is a two-way street. Employees also want fair compensation. As we pointed out earlier in our discussion of equity theory, if employees perceive an imbalance in the relation of their input-outcome ratio to some comparative standard, they will act to correct the inequity. So the search for fairness is pursued by both employers and employees.

How do managers know if they have a fair compensation plan? How do they know if it is actually effective in motivating employees? One author offers the manager a simple approach:

> *I would suggest that he or she start the review by going out and asking the people who are part of the plan one simple question, "What do you have to do around here in order to make more money?" If the answer to that question was anything other than "Work hard and effectively and perform well in these and these areas," then I would say to the person, "Your pay system is in trouble. It is not motivating performance, and you are not getting a good return on your investment in pay. It's time for a change."*[1]

As you read the following pages, keep in mind that we are concerned with determining a fair compensation plan for an organization. Also, recognize that while we pay *employees*, compensation systems are predominantly designed around *jobs*. That is, the responsibilities and demands of the *job* determine a pay range. The actual performance of incumbents determines where within the pay range they are placed. Also, governmental influences on compensation systems are such that they must be incorporated into the overall scheme of determining pay ranges.

Government Influences on Compensation Administration

In Chapters 2 and 3, we described how government policies influence HRM. This influence, however, is not equally felt in all areas. For example, collective bargaining and the selection process are heavily constrained by government rules and regulations. In contrast, this influence is minimum in the areas of human resource planning and socialization. Compensation administration falls into the former category. Government policies set minimum wages and benefits that employers must meet, and these policies provide protection for certain groups.

Fair Labor Standards Act The Fair Labor Standards Act stipulates that nonexempt employees must be paid time-and-one-half for overtime work beyond forty hours a week. This act, when coupled with protective state laws, also establishes that organizations must pay at least the minimum wage. For instance, in 1987, all employers but the smallest businesses and a few exempt classes had to pay their employees at least $3.35 an hour.

---

[1]"Effective Pay Programs—An Interview with Edward E. Lawler III," *Compensation Review,* Third Quarter, 1976, p. 27.

Both federal and state governments have enacted laws that require employers who contract with the government to pay prevailing rates. The secretary of labor is required to review industry rates in the specific locality to set a prevailing rate which becomes the minimum under the contract. The Walsh–Healy Act also stipulates that government contractors must pay time-and-one-half for all work in excess of eight hours a day or forty hours a week.

The Civil Rights Act and the Equal Pay Act protect employees from discrimination. Just as it is illegal to discriminate in hiring, organizations may not discriminate in pay on the basis of race, color, creed, age, or sex.

In times of wage controls, as prevailed sporadically during the 1970s, the federal government dictates ceilings on wages. During periods of controls, organizations must limit pay increases to those levels sanctioned by the control authorities.

In Chapter 17, we will discuss benefits and services in detail. Benefits such as Social Security protection, pensions, or unemployment compensation are heavily interlaced with government regulations. The Social Security Act, the Employment Retirement Income Security Act, and state workers' compensation laws dictate that organizations provide their employees with basic social insurance.

The laws and regulations discussed above are not meant to comprehensively cover government's influence on compensation administration. Rather, they are presented as highlights. The point of these highlights should be to make you aware that government constraints reduce management's discretion on compensation decisions. An abundance of laws and regulations define the general parameters within which managers decide what is fair compensation.

Job Evaluation and Pay Structure

The essence of compensation administration is job evaluation and the establishment of a pay structure. Let us turn, therefore, to a definition of job evaluation and a discussion of how it is done.

What is Job Evaluation?

Job evaluation defined

In Chapter 5, we introduced job analysis as the process of describing the duties of a job, authority relationships, skills required, conditions of work, and additional relevant information. We stated that the data generated from job analysis could be used to develop job descriptions and specifications, as well as to do job evaluation. By *job evaluation*, we mean using the information in job analysis to systematically determine the value of each job in relation to all jobs within the organization. In short, job evaluation seeks to rank all the jobs in the organization and place them in a hierarchy that will reflect the relative worth of each. Importantly, this is a ranking of jobs, not people. Job evaluation assumes normal performance of the job by a typical worker. So, in effect, the process ignores individual abilities or the performance of the jobholder.

The ranking that results from job evaluation is the means to an end, not an end in itself. It should be used to determine the organization's pay structure. Note that we say "should." In practice, we will find that this is not always the case. External labor market conditions, collective bargaining, and individual differences may require a compromise between the job evaluation ranking and the actual pay structure. Yet even when such compromises are necessary, job evaluation can provide an objective standard from which modifications can be made.

Isolating Job Evaluation Criteria

The heart of job evaluation is the determination of what criteria will be used to arrive at the ranking. It is easy to say that jobs are valued and ranked by their relative job worth, but there is far more ambiguity when we attempt to state what it is that makes one job higher than another in the job structure hierarchy.

Most job evaluation plans use responsibility, skill, effort, and working conditions as major criteria. But each of these, in turn, can be broken down into more specific terms. "Skill, for example, is often measured by education and experience; mental effort is often differentiated from physical effort; responsibility of various kinds is delineated."[2] But other criteria can and have been used, including difficulty, time span of discretion, size of subordinate staff, and degree of creativity needed.

You should not expect the criteria to be constant across jobs. Since jobs differ, it is traditional to separate jobs into common groups. This usually means that production, clerical, sales, and managerial jobs are evaluated separately. Treating like groups separately allows for more valid rankings within categories but still leaves unsettled the importance of criteria between categories. Separation by groups may permit us to say the position of die-design engineer in the production group requires more mental effort than that of a production supervisor, and hence gets a higher ranking; but it does not readily resolve whether greater mental effort is necessary for die-design engineers than for office managers.

---

[2]David W. Belcher, *Compensation Administration* (Englewood Cliffs, N.J.: Prentice-Hall, 1974), p. 90.

Methods of Job Evaluation

These are four basic methods of job evaluation currently in use: ranking, classification, factor comparison, and point method.

Ranking method of job evaluation

Ranking Method.   The ranking method requires a committee typically composed of both management and employee representatives to arrange jobs in a simple rank order, from highest to lowest. No attempt is made to break the jobs down by specific weighted criteria. The committee members merely compare two jobs and judge which one is more important or difficult. Then they compare another job with the first two, and so on until all the jobs have been evaluated and ranked.

The most obvious limitation to the ranking method is its sheer unmanageability when there are a large number of jobs. Imagine the difficulty of trying to rank hundreds or thousands of jobs. Other drawbacks to be considered are the subjectivity of the method—there are no definite or consistent standards by which to justify the rankings—and because jobs are only ranked in terms of order, we have no knowledge of the distance between the ranks.

Classification method of job evaluation

Classification Method.   The classification method was made popular by the U.S. Civil Service Commission. The commission requires that classification grades be established. These classifications are created by identifying some common denominator—skills, knowledge, responsibilities—with the desired goal being the creation of a number of distinct classes or grades of jobs. Examples might include shop jobs, clerical jobs, sales jobs, and so on, depending, of course, on the type of jobs the organization requires.

Once the classifications are established, they are ranked in an overall order of importance according to the criteria chosen, and each job is placed in its appropriate classification. This latter action is generally done by comparing each position's job description against the classification description. In the civil service, for example, evaluators have classified both Accounting Clerk I and Typists II positions as GS–3 grades, while Engineer VI and Attorney IV jobs have both been graded as GS–13.

The classification method shares most of the disadvantages of the ranking approach, plus the difficulty of writing classification descriptions, judging which jobs go where, and dealing with jobs that appear to fall into more than one classification. On the plus side is the fact that the classification method has proved itself successful and viable in classifying millions of kinds and levels of jobs in the civil service.

Factor comparison method of job evaluation

Factor Comparison Method.   Factor comparison is a sophisticated and quantitative ranking method. The evaluators select key jobs in the organization as standards. Those jobs chosen should be well known, with established pay rates in the community, and they should

FIGURE 16-1

Factor Comparison Method

JOB	HOURLY PAY	MENTAL REQUIRE- MENTS	SKILL REQUIRE- MENTS	PHYSICAL REQUIRE- MENTS	RESPON- SIBILITY	WORKING CONDITIONS
Inventory Control Specialist	$13.65	$4.00	$4.40	$1.25	$3.00	$1.00
Job Maintenance Electrician	13.40	3.00	4.40	1.80	2.30	1.90
Warehouse Stocker	11.10	2.25	3.00	1.80	2.30	1.75
Secretary	8.65	3.00	2.00	.50	2.15	1.00
Maintenance Electrician Helper	8.45	2.25	1.50	1.70	1.10	1.90

consist of a representative cross-section of all jobs that are being evaluated—"from the lowest to the highest paid job, from the most important to the least important—and cover the full range of requirements of each factor, as agreed upon by a committee representing workers and management."[3] Typically, ten to twenty-five key jobs are selected by the committee.

What factors in the key jobs will the other jobs be compared against? These criteria are usually mental requirements, skill requirements, physical requirements, responsibility, and working conditions. Once the key jobs are identified and the criteria chosen, committee members rank the key jobs on the criteria.

The next step is the most interesting dimension in the factor comparison method. The committee agrees upon the base rate (usually expressed on an hourly basis) for each of the key jobs and then allocates this base rate among the five criteria. To illustrate, in one organization the job of maintenance electrician was chosen as a key job and had an hourly rate of $13.40. The committee then allocated $3.00 to mental effort, $4.40 for skill, $1.80 for physical effort, $2.30 to responsibility, and $1.90 for working conditions. These amounts then became standards by which other jobs in the organization could be evaluated. That is, all other jobs with similar responsibilities were assigned $2.30 for that criterion.

The final step in factor comparison requires the committee to compare its overall judgments and resolve any discrepancies. The system is in place when the allocations to the key jobs are clear and understood, and high agreement has been achieved in committee members' judgments about how much of each criteria every job has.

Drawbacks to factor comparison include its complexity; its use of the same five criteria to assess all jobs when, in fact, jobs differ across and within organizations; and its dependence on key jobs as

---

[3]Wayne F. Cascio, *Applied Psychology in Personnel Management* (Reston, Va.: Reston Publishing Co., 1978), p. 150.

anchor points. "To the extent that one or more key jobs change over time either without detection or without correction of the scale, users of the job comparison scale are basing decisions on what might be described figuratively as a badly warped ruler."[4] On the positive side, factor comparison requires a unique set of standard jobs for each organization, so it is a tailor-made approach. As such, it is automatically designed to meet the specific needs of each organization. Another advantage is that jobs are compared with other jobs to determine a relative value, and since relative job values are what job evaluation seeks, the method is logical.

Point method of job evaluation

Point Method.   The last method we will present breaks jobs down based on various identifiable criteria (such as skill, effort, and responsibility) and then allocates points to each of these criteria. Depending on the importance of each criterion to performing the job, appropriate weights are given, points are summed, and jobs with similar point totals are placed in similar pay grades.

An excerpt from a point method chart for clerical positions is shown in Figure 16-2. Each clerical job would be evaluated by deciding, for example, the degree of education required to satisfactorily perform the job. First degree might require the equivalent of skill competencies associated with ten years of elementary and secondary education; second degree might require competencies associated with four years of high school; and so forth.

The point method offers the greatest stability of the four approaches we have presented. Jobs may change over time, but the rating scales established under the point method stay intact. Additionally, the methodology underlying the approach contributes to a minimum of rating error. On the other hand, the point method is complex, making it costly and time-consuming to develop. The key criteria have to be

FIGURE 16-2

Excerpts from a Point Method Chart

	JOB CLASS: CLERK				
Factor	1st Degree	2nd Degree	3rd Degree	4th Degree	5th Degree
Skill					
1. Education	22	44	66	88	110
2. Initiative	14	28	42	56	70
Responsibility					
3. Safety of others	5	10	15	20	25
4. Work of others	7	14	21	28	35

[4]Belcher, *Compensation Administration*, p. 157.

carefully and clearly identified, degrees of factors have to be agreed upon in terms that mean the same for all raters, the weight of each criterion must be established, and point values must be assigned to degrees. While it is expensive and time-consuming to both implement and maintain, the point method appears to be the most widely used method.

Establishing the Pay Structure

Once the job evaluation is complete, its data become the nucleus for the development of the organization's pay structure.[5] This means establishing pay rates or ranges that are compatible with the ranks, classifications, or points arrived at through job evaluation.

Any of the four job evaluation methods can provide the necessary input for developing the organization's overall pay structure. Each has its strengths and weaknesses, but because of its wide use, we will use the point method to show how point totals are combined with wage survey data to form wage curves.

Wage surveys *Wage Surveys.* Most organizations use surveys to gather factual information on pay practices within specific communities and among firms in their industry. This information is used for comparison purposes. It can tell management if the organization's wages are in line with those of other employers and, in cases where there is a short supply of individuals to fill certain positions, may be used to actually set wage levels.

Where does an organization get wage survey data? The U.S. Department of Labor, through its Bureau of Labor Statistics, regularly publishes a vast amount of wage data broken down by geographic area, industry, and occupation. Many industry and employee associations also conduct surveys and make their results available. But organizations can conduct their own surveys, and most large ones do.

It would not be unusual, for instance, for the personnel manager at a General Electric plant in Los Angeles to regularly share wage data on key positions. Jobs such as maintenance engineer, electrical engineer, keypunch operator, or clerk-typist would be identified, and comprehensive descriptions of these jobs would be given to firms in the community like TRW, Litton, Hewlett-Packard, NCR, Control Data, and Motorola. This is most often done by way of a mailed questionnaire, but personal interviews and telephone interviews can also be used. When organizations do their own wage surveys, they are not limited in what they can ask. In addition to the average wage level for a specific job, other information frequently requested includes entry-level

---

[5]For a thorough mathematical discussion of various methods of determining the pay structure, see Richard I. Henderson, *Compensation Management* (Reston, Va.: Reston Publishing Co., 1982), pp. 262–301.

and maximum wage rates, shift differentials, overtime pay practices, vacation and holiday allowances, the number of pay periods, and the length of the normal workday and workweek.

Wage curves   *Wage Curves.*   When management arrives at point totals from job evaluation and obtains survey data on what comparable organizations are paying for similar jobs, then a wage curve can be fitted to the data. An example of a wage curve is shown in Figure 16-3. This example assumes usage of the point method and plots point totals and wage data. A separate wage curve can be constructed based on survey data and compared for discrepancies.

A completed wage curve tells management the average relationship between points of established pay grades and wage base rates. Importantly, it can identify jobs whose pay is out of the trend line. When a job's pay rate is too high, it should be identified as a "red circle" rate. This means that pay is frozen or below-average increases are granted until the structure is adjusted upward to put the circled rate within the normal range. There will, of course, be times when a wage rate is out of line but not red circled. The need to attract or keep individuals with specific skills may require a wage rate outside the normal range. To continue attracting these individuals however, may ultimately upset the internal consistencies supposedly inherent in the wage structure. It should also be pointed out that a wage rate may be *too low*. Such undervalued jobs carry a "green circle" rate and attempts should be made to grant these jobs above average pay increases.

FIGURE 16-3   Wage Curve

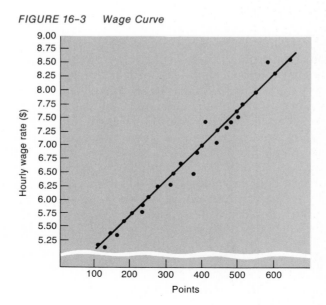

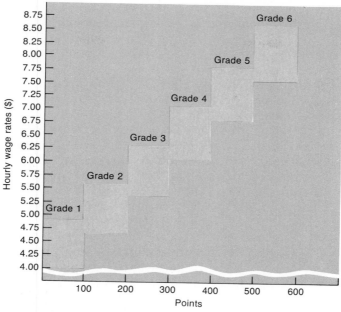

FIGURE 16-4   Wage Structure

Wage structure   *The Wage Structure.*   It is only a short step from plotting a wage curve to developing the organization's wage structure. Jobs that are similar—in terms of classes, grades, or points—are grouped together. For instance, pay grade 1 may cover the range from 0 to 100 points, pay grade 2 from 101 to 200 points, and so on. As shown in Figure 16-4, the result is a logical hierarchy of wages. The more important jobs are paid more; and as individuals assume jobs of greater importance, they rise within the wage hierarchy. Notice that each pay grade has a range and that the ranges overlap. Typically, organizations design their wage structure with ranges in each grade to reflect different tenure in positions, as well as levels of performance. Additionally, while most organizations create a degree of overlap between grades, employees who reach the top of their grade can only increase their pay by moving to a higher grade.

Incentive Compensation Plans

In addition to the basic wage structure, organizations that are sincerely committed to developing a compensation system that is designed around performance will want to consider the use of incentive pay. Typically given in addition to—rather than in place of—the basic wage, incentive plans should be viewed as an additional dimension to the wage structure we have described. Incentives can be paid based on individual, group, or organizationwide performance.

Individual Incentives

Individual incentives

Individual incentive plans pay off for individual performance. Popular approaches include piecework plans, time-savings bonuses, and commissions.

The best-known incentive is undoubtedly piecework. Under a straight piecework plan, the employee is typically guaranteed a minimal hourly rate for meeting some preestablished standard output. For output over this standard, the employee earns so much for each piece produced. Differential piecerate plans establish two rates—one up to standard and another when the employee exceeds the standard. The latter rate, of course, is higher so as to encourage the employee to "beat standard."

Individual incentives can be based on time saved as well as output generated. As with piecework, the employee can expect a minimal guaranteed hourly rate, but in this case, the bonus is achieved for doing a standard hour's work in less than sixty minutes. Employees who can do an hour's work in fifty minutes obtain a bonus that is some percentage (say 50 percent) of the labor saved.

Sales personnel frequently work on a commission basis. In addition to a low wage rate, they get an amount that represents a percentage of the sales price. On encyclopedias, it may be a hefty 25 or 30 percent. On sales of multimillion-dollar aircraft or computer systems, commissions are frequently 1 percent or less.

Individual incentives work best where clear performance objectives can be set and where tasks are independent (see Figure 16-5). If these conditions are not met, individual incentives can create dysfunctional competition or encourage workers to "cut corners." Coworkers become the enemy, individuals create inflated perceptions of their own work while deflating the work of others, and the work environment becomes characterized by reduced interaction and communications between employees. And if corners are cut, quality and safety may be affected. What can happen is explained by a former National Football League linebacker, whose contract paid for individual performance although the team's objective was to win its division championship. The two goals were not always compatible, such as when he was able to pick up a particular tip on the opposition. Should he, for example, share it with the other linebackers on his team, individuals whom he was competing with for playing time?

Coaches constantly talk about team spirit, but I've always wondered how the hell there can be team spirit if I know that the more the other linebackers screw up, the more I'll be able to play and

FIGURE 16–5   *Example of Performance-Based Compensation*

John Jefferson — 1980 Contract:

	Deferred	Current	Total
Salary	$25,000	75,000	100,000
Bonuses		82,500	82,500
*Division Playoffs		5,000	5,000
*AFC Championship		9,000	9,000
*Pro Bowl		2,500	2,500
**Preseason		2,870	2,870
Totals	**25,000**	**176,870**	**201,870**

*Paid by NFL
**Rate stipulated by Collective Bargaining Agreement

Charger Performance Bonuses

	Potential	Earned
1. Pro Bowl Section	10,000	10,000
2. All AFC		
—1st Team	10,000	10,000
—2nd Team	5,000	
3. All NFL		
—1st Team	15,000	15,000
—2nd Team	7,500	
4. Pass receptions (excludes running backs)		
—Top 5	12,000	
—Top 3	15,000	15,000
—No. 1	20,000	
5. TD receptions (excludes running backs)		
—Top 5	7,500	
—Top 3	10,000	
—No. 1	12,500	12,500
6. Pass reception yards (excludes running backs)		
—Top 5	12,500	
—Top 3	15,000	
—No. 1	20,000	20,000
Totals		**82,500**

NOTE — On July 19, 1980, an interest free loan of $75,000 was made to Jefferson. Provisions of advance call for repayment based on 75% of bonus clauses earned each year. Per the bookkeeper, the 1980 repayment was based on 25% of bonuses earned (no documentation of this was seen).

The original contract (standard NFL player agreement form) called for $100,000 total compensation; $55,000 payable currently, the balance deferred. On July 19, 1980, the agreement was amended to increase the current portion to $75,000 with no change in the total compensation amount. The deferred portion is payable in 10 equal installments, beginning Sept. 1, 1986. There is no provision for the payment of interest on the referred portion.

SOURCE: *San Diego Union*, October 7, 1981, p. D-1

the more I play, the more money I make. Owners keep writing contracts with performance clauses such as the one I had, though these can only work to create defensiveness on the team, for these clauses create a situation where the amount of money a player gets is dependent on how badly his teammates at his position play. A second string player who will not get his bonus unless he plays at least 40 percent of the plays will not be upset if the guy ahead of him screws up badly. The owners introduced these bonuses with the idea that they would extract better performance from the players and result in more victories. In reality, just the opposite usually happens.[6]

A potentially negative effect with incentives for performance is that you may "get what you pay for." Since the incentives are tied to specific goals (which are only part of the total outcomes expected from a job), people may not perform the not measured, and thus not rewarded, activities in favor of the measured, rewarded ones. For example, if your school held a colloquium, bringing in a guest speaker, and your instructor decided to take your class, would you go? Your response might be contingent on whether the colloquium was a requirement, the content of which could be included on an exam, and where attendance was taken. But if it was just for your information, attending might not be as high a priority.

In spite of the potential negative repercussions that individual incentives can cause in inappropriate situations, they are undoubtedly widespread in practice.

Group Incentives

Each of the individual incentives we described can also be used on a group basis. That is, two or more employees can be paid for their combined performance.

When are group incentives desirable? They make the most sense where employees' tasks are interdependent and thus require cooperation. This would describe, for example, the conditions that exist in an automobile assembly line.

Group incentives

One problem with group incentives is that employees do not see them as being directly linked to their own behavior. The pay of the employee under group incentives is influenced by the behavior of others with whom that employee works. Another problem is the self-deception phenomenon.[7] People claim more responsibility for their

[6]Dave Meggyesy, *Out of Their League* (Palo Alto, Calif.: Ramparts Press, 1970).

[7]Barry R. Schlenker and Rowland S. Miller, "Egocentrism in Groups: Self Serving Biases or Logical Information Processing? *Journal of Personality and Social Psychology,* October 1977, pp. 755–64.

group's successful performance than they would if the group failed. Additionally, when a group performs well, most people present themselves as contributing more than other members to the group's success. This suggests that group members expect greater than average rewards when their group does well, creating internal conflict.

Organizationwide Incentives

Organizationwide
incentives

The goal of organizationwide incentives is to direct the efforts of all employees toward achieving overall organizational effectiveness. This type of incentive produces rewards for all employees based on organizationwide cost reduction or profit sharing.

Kaiser Steel, for example, developed in one of its plants a cost reduction plan that provides monthly bonuses to employees.[8] The amount of the bonus was determined by computing one-third of all increases in productivity attributable to cost savings as a result of technological change or increased effort. Additionally, Lincoln Electric has had a year-end bonus system for decades, which in some years has provided an annual bonus "ranging from a low of 88 percent to a high of 115 percent of annual earnings."[9] The Lincoln Electric plan pays off handsomely for employees' beating previous years' performance standards. Since this bonus is added to the employees' salary, it has made the Lincoln Electric workers the highest-paid electrical workers in the United States.

One of the better-known organizationwide incentive systems is the Scanlon Plan.[10] It seeks to bring about cooperation between management and employees through the sharing of problems, goals, and ideas. Under Scanlon, each department in the organization has a committee composed of the supervisor and employee representatives. Suggestions for labor-saving improvements are funneled to the committee and, if accepted, cost savings and productivity gains are shared by all employees, not just the individual who made the suggestion. Typically, about 80 percent of the suggestions prove practical and are adopted.

Profit-sharing plans are also organizationwide incentives. They allow employees to share in the success of a firm by distributing part of the company's profits back to the workers. The logic behind profit-sharing plans is that they increase commitment and loyalty to the organization. You are more likely to be cost conscious if you share in the benefits. On the negative side, employees often find it difficult to relate their efforts to the profit-sharing bonus. Their individual impact on

[8]Harold Stieglitz, "The Kaiser Steel Union Sharing Plan," National Industrial Conference Board Studies in Personnel Policy Number 187 (New York, 1963).

[9]Richard I. Henderson, *Compensation Management*, 3rd ed. (Reston, Va.: Reston Publishing Co., 1982), p. 363.

[10]Ibid, pp. 360–61.

VIEWS IN THE NEWS

Pay Equity News

Under settlements reached in Washington State and the City of Chicago, government workers in female-dominated job classifications will receive pay increases to bring their wages into parity with amounts paid to employees in male-dominated jobs. On the private-sector side, New York unions file suit under Title VII for sex-based wage discrimination against female workers in the hotel industry.

IN THE PUBLIC EYE

The Washington settlement effectively ends the "comparable worth" case filed against the state by the American Federation of State, County and Municipal Employees (421:617). The agreement, announced by the union Dec. 31, calls for pay raises over the next seven years to 35,000 employees in female-dominated job classifications, and an additional $10 million in annual pay equity adjustments through July 1, 1992. The total amount of the settlement is approximately $482 million, according to a spokesman for the state. The settlement, which must still be reviewed by the Washington legislature and a federal court, does not provide for back pay.

In Chicago, a pay equity provision for 3,500 workers in female-dominated jobs is a feature of the city's first collective bargaining agreement covering white collar workers. The provision, which settles sex discrimination charges filed against the city by AFSCME in 1982, is hailed by AFSCME Illinois Director Steve Culen as "a major comparable worth settlement."

Under the three-year contract, which was signed Dec. 13 and still must be approved by the Chicago city council, 79 predominantly female city job classifications will be upgraded by one pay grade effective July 1, 1986. The 3,500 incumbents in those grades will be placed on the appropriate salary step representing a 5 percent salary boost in addition to other contract increases.

Meanwhile, New York unions file a class action suit under Title VII for sex-based wage discrimination against female workers in the hotel industry. Through this legal action and a previously filed Equal Pay Act lawsuit, the New York Hotel and Motel Trades Council is attempting to equalize the pay of female room attendants and bath attendants with that of male house attendants in New York city hotels. (*New York Motel and Hotel Trades Council v. Hotel Association of New York City,* USDC SNY, filed Dec. 18, 1985)

Source: Reprinted by permission from *Fair Employment Practices,* copyright 1986 by The Bureau of National Affairs, Inc., Washington, D.C.

the organization's profitability is usually miniscule. Additionally, outside factors such as economic conditions and actions of competitors—which are outside the control of the employees—may have a far greater impact on the company's profitability than any actions of the employees themselves.

All the organizationwide incentives suffer from a dilution effect. It is hard for employees to see how their efforts result in the organization's overall performance. These plans also tend to distribute their payoffs at wide intervals. A bonus paid in March 1988 for your efforts in 1987 loses a lot of its reinforcement capabilities. Finally, we should not overlook what happens when organizationwide incentives become both large and recurrent. When this happens, it is not unusual for the employee to begin to anticipate and expect the bonus. Employees may adjust their spending patterns as if the bonus were a certainty. As such, the bonus loses some of its motivating properties, for it becomes perceived as a membership-based reward.

Executive Compensation

The pay of executives is merely a special case within the topic of compensation, but it does have several twists that deserve attention. First, the base salaries of executives are higher than those of low-level managers or operative personnel. We want to explain why this fact exists. Second, executives frequently operate under bonus and stock option plans that can dramatically increase their total compensation. A senior executive at General Motors, IBM, Data General, or General Electric may in a good year earn $500,000 or $1,000,000 or more on top of his base salary. We want to briefly look at how such compensations come about and why. Finally, executives receive perquisites or special benefits that others do not. What are these and how do they impact on executive motivation? These are the topics in this final section on compensation.

Executive Salaries

Executive salaries

In the early 1980s, executives in the public service generally earned yearly salaries in the $40,000-to-$65,000 range. At the extreme, the president of the United States earns approximately $200,000 annually. In contrast, it is well known that executives in the private sector receive considerably higher compensation. Middle-level executives regularly earn base salaries of $50,000 to $80,000. The chief executive officer of a billion-dollar corporation can expect a minimum salary in excess of $300,000, while base salaries of $700,000 or more are not unusual among senior management of Fortune 100 firms. In fact, in 259 of the largest U.S. corporations, forty executives had base salaries in excess of $1 million.[11]

How do organizations justify such extraordinary salaries for their executives? The answer is quite simple: economics and motivation. In economic terms, we know that top managers are expected to demonstrate good decision-making abilities. This skill is not widely held in our society. As a result, the supply of qualified senior executives is scarce, and organizations have bid up the price for this talent. They

[11]"Executive Compensation Scoreboard," *Business Week*, May 6, 1985, pp. 89–100.

too must keep their salaries in line with the competition or potentially lose an executive to another organization. High salaries also act to motivate both top executives and lower-level managers. High pay encourages top-level managers to perform well in order to keep their jobs. But high pay also acts to stimulate lower-level managers to work hard so that they can someday move up the ladder to "the big money."

Supplemental Financial Compensation

Supplemental executive compensation

Financial incentives, like bonuses or stock option plans, are the exception among rank and file workers, but it is the rare senior business executive whose compensation does not include such incentives.

In 1984, the average compensation for executives in the largest 259 companies in the United States was $1.1 million.[12] Figure 16-6 shows the top twenty-five executives with respect to total compensation. Notice how bonuses and stock options dramatically increase the total compensation that executives received.

Deferred bonus

Much of this additional compensation is obtained through a deferred bonus. That is, the executive's bonus is computed on the basis of some formula, usually taking into account increases in sales and profits. This bonus, although earned in the current period, is distributed over several future periods. Therefore it is not unusual for an executive to earn a $1 million bonus but have it paid out at $50,000 a year for twenty years. The major purpose of such deferred compensation is to increase the cost to the executive of leaving the organization. In almost all cases, executives who voluntarily terminate their employment must forfeit their deferred bonuses. It is well known, for example, that one of the main reasons why there are so few voluntary resignations among the ranks of senior management at General Motors is that these executives would lose hundreds of thousands of dollars of deferred income.

Interestingly, another form of bonus has arisen in the last decade, purposely designed to help senior executives defray the loss of deferred income. This is the "hiring bonus." It is now becoming increasingly popular to pay senior executives a hiring bonus to sweeten the incentive for them to leave their current employer, forfeiting their deferred bonuses and pension rights. These bonuses often do provide deferred income to compensate for loss of pension rights. For example, Chrysler paid Lee Iacocca $1.5 million to compensate him for giving up his deferred compensation and pension and retirement rights at Ford.[13]

Stock options

Stock options have been a common incentive offered to executives. They generally allow executives to purchase, at some time in the

[12]Ibid.

[13]Lee Iacocca, *Iacocca: An Autobiography* (New York: Bantam Books, 1984), p. 146.

FIGURE 16-6

The 25 Highest-Paid Executives

		ANNUAL TOTAL COMPENSATION	LONG-TERM COMPENSATION	TOTAL COMPENSATION
			Thousands of Dollars	
1. T. Boone Pickens Jr., chmn, & pres.	Mesa Petroleum	$4,223	$18,600	$22,823
2. David A. Jones, chmn.	Humana	722	17,394	18,116
3. Edson D. deCastro, chmn. & pres.	Data General	436	7,529	7,965
4. Herbert J. Richman, exec. v-p.	Data General	336	6,962	7,298
5. Lee A. Iacocca, chmn.	Chrysler	1,195	4,315	5,510
6. Sidney J. Sheinberg, pres.	MCA	500	4,138	4,638
7. An Wang, chmn.	Wang Labs	606	3,814	4,420
8. Philip Caldwell, chmn.	Ford Motor	1,575	2,485	4,060
9. Thomas D. O'Malley, vice-chmn.	Philbro-Salomon	2,514	1,395	3,909
10. John R. Opel, chmn.	IBM	1,034	2,807	3,841
11. Anthony R. Hamilton, chmn.	Avnet	1,049	2,773	3,822
12. Gerald Greenwald, vice-chmn.	Chrysler	877	2,419	3,296
13. Frank D. Trznadel Jr., senior v-p.	Comdisco	1,602	1,561	3,163
14. Paul J. Rizzo, vice-chmn.	IBM	767	2,120	2,887
15. Harold K. Sperlich, pres.	Chrysler	828	2,040	2,868
16. Barry Diller, senior exec. v-p.	Gulf & Western	2,866	0	2,866
17. Kenneth N. Pontikes, chmn. & pres.	Comdisco	1,239	1,593	2,832
18. Oliver C. Boileau, pres.	General Dynamics	643	2,127	2,770
19. John G. Breen, chmn. & pres.	Sherwin-Williams	772	1,849	2,621
20. Clifton C. Garvin Jr., chmn.	Exxon	1,350	1,236	2,586
21. Howard H. Kehrl, vice-chmn.	General Motors	1,269	1,253	2,522
22. Harrington Drake, chmn.	Dun & Bradstreet	975	1,459	2,434
23. Donald E. Petersen, pres.	Ford Motor	1,229	1,184	2,413
24. John H. Gutfreund, chmn.	Philbro-Salomon	2,379	0	2,379
25. John F. Burlingame, vice-chmn.	General Electric	932	1,408	2,340

DATA: SIBSON & CO. AND STANDARD & POOR'S COMPUSTAT SERVICES INC.

SOURCE: Reprinted from the May 6, 1985 issue of *Business Week* by special permission, © 1985 by McGraw-Hill, Inc.

future, a specific amount of the company's stock at a fixed price. Under the assumption that good management will increase the company's profitability and, therefore, the price of the stock, stock options are viewed as performance-based incentives. Suppose the stock of a given company is selling for $45 a share. If the company's current net earnings per share is $4.50, the stock is selling at ten times its earnings. The executive who is given a five-year option to purchase ten thousand shares of stock at $50 a share should be motivated to increase net earnings per share. If the price-earnings ratio stayed at ten to one, and this executive could get earnings up to, say, $7 a share before his options expired, he could earn an additional $200,000 from the exercise of his options. It should be pointed out that the use of stock options is heavily influenced by the current status of the tax laws. In recent years, tax reform legislation has taken away many of the tax benefits that could accrue through the issuance of stock options. As a result, the use of stock options as incentive compensation has been decreasing.

Supplemental Nonfinancial Compensation: Perquisites

Perquisites

Executives are frequently offered a smorgasbord of perquisites not offered to other employees. The logic of offering these "perks," from the organization's perspective, is to attract and keep good managers and to motivate them to work hard in the organization's interests.

In addition to the standard benefits offered to all employees (see Chapter 17), some benefits are reserved for privileged executives. They range from an annual physical examination, worth several hundred dollars, to interest-free loans of millions of dollars, which can be worth $100,000 a year or more. Popular perks include the payment of life insurance premiums (current tax laws require that tax be paid on that amount of life insurance over $50,000), club memberships, company automobiles, liberal expense accounts, supplemental disability insurance, supplemental retirement accounts, postretirement consulting contracts, and personal financial, tax, and legal counseling. In past times of high inflation and tight money, it was also popular to offer transferred executives the opportunity to sell their home at the appraised value to the company and have the company assume the increased interest expense resulting from giving up a low-cost 7 or 8 percent mortgage and having had to assume a new one at 12 to 16 percent.[14]

Golden parachute

Finally, a popular benefit that accrued to top executives in the early 1980s was the "golden parachute." The golden parachute was designed by top executives as a means of protecting themselves if a

---

[14]"It Takes Big Benefits to Recruit Executives Who Have to Relocate," *Wall Street Journal*, June 3, 1980, p. 25.

merger took place. These parachutes provide either a severance salary to the departing executive or a guaranteed position in the newly created (merged) organization. While their popularity has been diminishing, none was so notable as William Agee's, the then chairman of Bendix, who exercised his golden parachute when Allied Chemical took over the Bendix Corporation. Agee received benefits amounting to more than $4 million. While the debate is still ongoing as to whether a golden parachute lessens an executive's efforts to fight an acquisition, the fact remains that this elite benefit has provided a comfortable cushion for an outgoing executive to fall back on.

The logic of offering salaries, incentives, and perks to executives has been debated. In the next section, we will look closer at this controversy.

The Controversy

Pay levels for some of the top executives in many U.S. corporations appear to be exceeding the $1 million mark. We also find that overall, top executives' salaries increased by 12.7 percent in 1984.[15] Three of the more dramatic and noteworthy executive salary increases were those of MESA's chairman and president, T. Boone Pickens; Chrysler's chairman, Lee Iacocca; and Cummins Engine's chairman, Henry B. Schact. In 1984, their salaries increased by 789 percent, 152 percent, and 144 percent, respectively.[16] These increases are highlighted by the fact that the average worker's salary increased by 6.5 percent during the same period.

Newspapers have had such headlines as "John Doe, President of XYZ Company, Was Paid $XX Million Last Year." These stories have stirred controversy in the more economically depressed areas; especially in those towns where workers have experienced increased unemployment. The automobile industry in Detroit is just one example. Although many people may resent such high executive compensation packages, we must ask ourselves, Are they worth it?

Are executives worth their salaries

No one could possibly prove that the executives are or are not worth a million dollars in salary. However, if we systematically review the measures for judging the executive's performance, evidence may be revealed that will help us answer the question.

If we compare the executive's total compensation with his performance, we get mixed results; some highly paid executives performed better than others. For example, take the Lee Iacocca case. His rebuilding of the Chrysler Corporation, and saving it from bankruptcy, was a tremendous feat. The articles and books written about Iacocca's endeavors—his dealings with the federal government, the United Auto

[15]"Executive Compensation Scoreboard," p. 78.
[16]Ibid.

Workers, and the financial institutions—document his story well. There seems to be no doubt that the new Chrysler Corporation has justified every penny that he has earned. But what about the rest, and how can we measure whether an executive is appropriately paid?

Performance index

A set of measures that have been used to determine whether an executive is appropriately paid are the company's size, its profitability, its return on equity, and its return to stockholders (stock appreciation plus dividends).[17] These figures have been used to determine a "pay for performance index," showing "whether an executive was paid salary plus bonus commensurate with his company's relative performance."[18] (Note: "Annual compensation as a percent of industry standard is compared with the company's return on equity as a percent of industry standard. The industry standards are the average measures within each group.")[19] In short, the lower the pay for performance index, the more the company's performance exceeded the executive's total compensation. Conversely, the higher the index, the lower the percentage of performance to pay. If the two equate (performance and pay), the index would be 100.

Best executive performers

Using this index as a guide, in the study of the 259 largest U.S. corporations, approximately 50 percent of the executives had a pay for performance index of 100 or less.[20] This indicates that for those executives, their company's excellent performance justified their total compensation. Who were these top performers? Figure 16-7 lists the top eleven executives who had the best performance ratings. How did Lee Iacocca do? According to the study, his performance index was 61.[21]

While this pay for performance index gives a good estimation of how executives are doing, it is not enough to settle the controversy. Therefore many factors that go into the total compensation of an executive can affect the pay for performance index. For example, exercising stock options could cause the pay level to be out of proportion. Whatever the case may be, the pay for performance index cannot solely provide a definitive answer to the controversial question, Are executives worth their pay? But it does offer some evidence that many executives justify their compensation packages.

Conclusion

Compensation administration is part of every organization. These systems must be tailored to meet the objectives and needs of the company. While exact techniques are offered for developing salary ranges, com-

[17]Ibid., p. 80.
[18]Ibid., p. 88.
[19]Ibid.
[20]Ibid., p. 80.
[21]Ibid., pp. 89–100.

FIGURE 16-7

The Most Productive Executives 1984

NAME	COMPANY	PRODUCTIVITY MEASURE*
C. M. Browning	Dresser Industries	38
R. W. Allan	Delta Airlines	40
L. E. Karmas	Ralston Purina	42
L. E. Azzato	Foster Wheeler	47
S. M. Bateman	Whirlpool	48
D. C. Garrett, Jr.	Delta Airlines	50
R. J. Ferris	UAL, Inc.	51
G. L. Crenshaw	Universal Leaf Tobacco	54
R. A. Hanson	Deere	56
D. H. Chookaszian	CNA Financial	57
J. J. Hartigan	United Airlines	57

SOURCE: Based on an article from Business Week, "Executive Compensation Scoreboard," May 6, 1985, pp. 89–100.

*The lower the score, the more productive the executive.

FIGURE 16-8

SOURCE: "Reprinted by permission: Tribune Media Services.

═══CLYDE═══

I got a raise today!...

Now I'm at a new poverty level.

pensation systems in practice may differ in scope. We have reviewed these aspects of compensation and have endeavored to explain the controversy regarding the salaries of top-level managers.

Regardless of the system used, the bottom line still holds: People work for money, and money is used to attract, motivate, and retain the best employees. Because of this bottom line, the importance of compensation cannot be overstated. None of us need what Figure 16-8 implies.

SUMMARY

1. Compensation administration seeks to design the lowest-cost pay structure that will not only attract, motivate, and retain competent employees but also be perceived as fair by these employees.

2. Job evaluation systematically determines the value of each job in relation to all jobs within the organization. The four basic approaches to job evaluation are
   a. The ranking method
   b. The classification method
   c. The factor comparison method
   d. The point method

3. The final wage structure evolves from job evaluation input, wage survey data, and the creation of wage grades.

4. In addition to a basic wage structure, some organizations offer incentive compensation. Incentives can be designed around the individual, the group, or the organization.

5. Executive compensation is higher than that of rank-and-file personnel and also includes other financial and nonfinancial benefits not otherwise available to operative employees.

KEY TERMS

Compensation administration
Equal Pay Act
Fair Labor Standards Act
Golden parachute
Incentive compensation plans
Job evaluation

Performance index
Perquisites
Piecework
Wage curve
Wage structure

QUESTIONS FOR REVIEW

1. What is compensation administration? What does it entail?

2. How have governmental influences affected compensation administration?

3. What is job evaluation? Discuss the four basic methods of job evaluation.

4. Differentiate between wage surveys, wage curves, and wage structures.

5. Describe the use of job evaluations in practice. Why is there such a difference between theory and practice?

6. What are the advantages and disadvantages of (a) individual incentives? (b) group incentives? and (c) organizationwide incentives?

7. If we pay predominantly for jobs rather than people, how can we reward the truly exceptional performing employee?

8. What differentiates the subject of executive compensation from the general subject of compensation?

9. Describe the uses of bonuses and stock options for executive compensation.

10. Identify and describe five perquisites that are offered to executives.

QUESTIONS FOR DISCUSSION

1. It is not unusual for college students to dislike being assigned group projects. They frequently complain that some group members will loaf and that allocating the same grade to all members is not fair. Compare this situation with the use of group incentives in industry.

2. How can subjectivity be successfully removed from compensation administration?

3. "Unions typically object to the use of incentive plans because they are an attempt by management to undermine the collective-bargaining process." Do you agree or disagree? Discuss.

4. Do you think the senior executives in major U.S. corporations are overpaid? Discuss.

5. "When considering wage givebacks, executives should make the first move. They are the ones who can best afford a pay cut." Do you agree or disagree? Discuss.

One for the Heart

Since the inception of the Cardiac Surgery Unit (CSU), animosities have been growing between the nurses who exclusively work there and the nurses who work in both the Intensive Care Unit and the Cardiac Surgery Unit. It appears that somewhere along the line pay differentials have been established for the CSU-only nurse, amounting to $1.80 extra per hour. The nurses in ICU have been complaining bitterly and have asked Judy to review the matter.

After studying the problem, Judy felt that the wage differential was justified. This differential was based on the added shifts necessary to function solely in the CSU. Judy certainly recognized that the ICU nurses who temporarily staffed CSU had many of the same skills. She justified the differential, not on the skill level, but on the working conditions. Full-time CSU nurses worked twelve-to-fourteen-hour shifts and had to be on call for a postoperative patient. Because surgery was scheduled every other day, and because a person's stay in CSU was only three days, these nurses had no set schedule. They would work three days on, two off, three on, and so forth.

On the other hand, ICU nurses worked eight-hour days and were scheduled in accordance with hospital rules. This meant that while their days might fluctuate, each ICU nurse was required to work only one weekend per month. Even then if the nurse worked in CSU, it was done on her regularly scheduled workday.

Additionally, to attract and retain qualified CSU nurses, Judy had to meet what the market required. She sympathized with the ICU nurses but reminded them that each had had an opportunity to work full time in CSU but had opted not to do so.

Questions

1. If skills are similar in the two positions, is it permissible for the hospital to offer the differential to attract and retain qualified personnel?
2. What could Judy do to alleviate some of the aggravation shared by the ICU nurses, short of a pay raise?
3. What impact do you foresee on performance and productivity regarding ICU nurses working in CSU?

CASE APPLICATION

Perk Up

Last year, and in three of the five preceding years, Smithson Industries lost millions of dollars. Although a large conglomerate, Smithson has found these losses hard to accept and has sought to place a freeze on wage increases for its executives. However, after conferring with the president of the corporation, the chairman of the board has decided to offer nonfinancial incentives. His reasoning was that the competition was headhunting, and to make such a blatant no-increase statement might cause the more-promising executives to leave the organization. This, he felt, would be extremely detrimental. He believed that when times were tough, as they had been, that is when excellent managers are needed. Losing them now could only snowball the decline.

Accordingly, the board of directors has voted to provide each executive with a membership in the local health spa. While considered a permanent perk and in lieu of a raise this year, the board rationalized that managing the corporation in the months ahead would be extremely stressful and that this membership would be a means of reducing the stress while enabling the executives to become healthier.

Unfortunately, however, the perk was not enough. Grumbling about the chain of events, two executives jumped ship. The ones that stayed did so because of their time invested in the company's pension. However, they too were upset over the board's decision.

Questions

1. How could this perk have been offered or marketed better to these executives?
2. What do you believe is the reason why most of the executives did not find the perk rewarding?
3. Faced with a similar dilemma, what would you have done if you had been the chairman of the board? What would you do now that the executives are upset?

ADDITIONAL READINGS

MURRAY, THOMAS J., "Checking Out the New Corporate Wife," *Dun's Business Monthly,* September 1986, pp. 50–51.

O'BRIEN, JOAN C., and ROBERT A. ZAWACKI, "Salary Surveys: Are They Worth the Effort?" *Personnel,* 62, No. 10 (October 1985), 70–74.

REICHENBURG, NEIL E., "Pay Equity in Review," *Public Personnel Management*, 15, No. 3 (Fall 1986), 211–31.

RYNES, SARA L., and GEORGE T. MILKOVICH, "Wage Surveys: Dispelling Some Myths about the Market Wage," *Personnel Psychology*, 39, No. 1 (1986), 71–89.

SYER, GREGORY A., "The Exempt Salary Survey, Part 2: Analyzing and Reporting Data, *Personnel*, 63, No. 7 (July 1986), 24–31.

CHAPTER 17

Benefits

and Services

AFTER READING THIS CHAPTER, YOU WILL BE ABLE TO:

1. Discuss benefits and services and their impact on motivation
2. Describe the addition to the direct wage bill
3. Discuss the legally required benefits
4. Identify the benefits often provided by organizations
5. Identify the services often provided by organizations
6. Discuss the current trends regarding benefits and services

I'd like to live like a poor man with lots of money.

—*Pablo Picasso*

Individuals expect more than wages or salary from their employers. The amount of paid vacation, the number of sick-leave days, and insurance and pension programs are factors that will influence whether applicants accept employment with a given organization or, once employed, whether they continue working for that organization.

Do benefits motivate employees to higher performance? The answer is probably no. Since benefits are membership-based rewards—offered to all employees regardless of performance—they should not be expected to motivate employees. However, there is evidence that the absence of adequate benefits and services can contribute to employee dissatisfaction and increased absenteeism and turnover.[1] The billions of dollars spent each year by organizations for benefits are not altruistically motivated—these dollars are meant to attract and keep good employees. A good benefits package is, in some cases, a primary reason why some job seekers choose certain organizations. Thus the subject of organizationally provided benefits and services is important to the field of human resource management.

Benefits: Something for Everybody

Most of us are aware of inflation and the impact that it has had on the wages and salaries of every American. It seems incredible that only forty years ago, a worker earning $100 a week was ranked among the top 10 percent of the wage earners in the United States. Although hourly wages and monthly salaries have consistently increased in recent years, we often overlook the more rapid growth in benefits offered employees. Since the cost of employing any worker includes both direct wage or salary and those benefits and services the organization provides him or her, the growth in both benefits and services has resulted in dramatic increases in labor costs to organizations.

452

[1]Frederick Herzberg, *Work and the Nature of Man* (New York: World, 1966).

Since the late 1920s, management has been steadily increasing the "pot" by providing greater benefits to its employees. Much of this increase was directly a result of management's desire to counteract the unions' efforts to organize company personnel. In 1929, benefits cost the average employer approximately 3 percent of total wages and salaries. Twenty years later, this was up to 16 percent. Currently, benefits range from 8 percent to over 60 percent of total wages and salaries, with the current average approximately 37 to 40 percent of direct compensation.[2]

Cost of benefits

When you consider that organizations are paying $1.40 for every $1.00 in direct salary, there must be a good reason. Generally, as we mentioned above, offering good benefits serves as a tool to attract and retain good employees. While simply offering benefits is no guarantee that employees will stay with the organization, the lack of benefits will surely cause some people to leave. Offering many benefits is often based on a total compensation philosophy. If an organization expects to get the "best," then it must pay for the "best." In return, organization performance improves. Competition, too, for employees can cause an organization to rethink its benefits package, because if the decision to join an organization is split between one with good benefits and one without, the decision becomes an easy one to make. Organizations survey other companies to determine not only their wage structure but also their benefits package. Deciding what to offer will often depend more on the "going" job market benefits offered than on any other factor.

Employers have also found that benefits present attractive areas of negotiation when large wage and salary increases are not feasible. Both the employers and the employees realize, too, that benefits are not altruistically motivated. For example, if employees were to purchase life insurance on their own, they would have to pay for it with net dollars, that is, with what they have left after paying taxes. If the organization pays for it, the benefit is nontaxable (up to $50,000) for each employee, who therefore considers it more attractive.

In the remainder of this chapter, we will look at both the legally required and the voluntary benefits that organizations can provide their employees, and the types of services that are increasingly being offered by organizations to their employees. Keep in mind that the executive "perks" we mentioned in Chapter 16 would be provided to executives, in addition to the benefits and services discussed.

Legally Required Benefits

Certain benefits must be supplied by the organization for its employees, regardless of whether it wants to or not. With a few exceptions

---

[2]*Wall Street Journal,* June 10, 1980, p. 1.

that we will note, the hiring of any employee will require the organization to pay Social Security premiums, unemployment compensation, worker's compensation, and state disability premiums. Similarly, the payment of these costs by the organization provides the employee with financial protection at retirement, termination, or as a result of injury; and it also provides benefits to the worker's dependents in case of his or her death.

Social Security

Social Security.   The major source of income for American retirees has been the benefits provided by Social Security insurance. In 1980, these benefits exceeded $75 billion a year.

Social Security insurance is financed by contributions made by the employee and matched by the employer, computed as a percentage of the employee's earnings. Figure 17-1 shows the tax rate and benefit schedule as approved by Congress. In 1986, for instance, the rate was 7.15 percent (levied on both the employee and the employer) of the worker's earnings up to $42,000 a year, or a maximum levy of $3,003. This cost has risen rapidly for both employers and employees. As recently as 1965, the maximum was only $174 a year. Prior to 1983, employees became eligible for full benefits at the age of sixty-five. With the revisions placed into law since that time, anyone born after 1938 will have to wait up to two additional years before receiving full benefits. Survivor benefits are also administered through this program should an employee die. Should the employee become too disabled to engage in gainful employment, the Social Security program will provide benefits.

The Social Security tax places a proportionately larger burden on the poor and middle class. In 1986, an executive earning $100,000 paid $3,003 into Social Security, only about $1,300 more than an electrician making one-fourth of the executive's salary. In lower income

FIGURE 17-1

Social Security Taxes 1985–90

YEAR	TAX RATE (%)	WAGE BASE ($)	MINIMUM TAX ($)	MAXIMUM BENEFIT* ($)
1985	7.05	39,600	2,792	12,957
1986	7.15	42,000	3,003	13,475
1988†	7.51	42,000	3,154	14,014
1990†	7.65	42,000	3,213	14,575

SOURCE: Hay/Huggins, "Social Security Incorporating Changes to December 31, 1984" (December 1984), p. 24 and updated.

*Maximum benefit is calculated using a 4 percent cost-of-living adjustment.

†Years 1988 and 1990 are estimates and do not include an increase in the wage base.

brackets, some employees find that they pay more in Social Security taxes than they do federal income taxes.

Social Security is undoubtedly an important part of America's attempt to protect and care for the aged and ensure a minimum living standard for them. However, because of serious financial problems the Social Security law was revised in 1983. The law aimed at increasing the time period before younger workers are eligible to receive full benefits. It also increased the contributions that all employees and employers will be making over the next ten years. These changes should ensure the viability of the system through the twenty-first century.

Social Security has traditionally been referred to as an insurance program. This is a misnomer. Under a straight insurance program, the insured pays premiums and in return receives a promise to pay, from the insurer, a certain sum to the insured's heirs if he dies, or to the insured himself if he lives long enough to retire. The amount of premiums paid will determine the policy payoff. But Social Security pays off depending on need—those with dependents collect more. Furthermore, there is a minimum level of benefits available to everyone, but unlike pension benefits, Social Security benefits are reduced if the recipient is between sixty-five and seventy and earns in excess of $7,000 a year.

In reality, Social Security is a transfer program of funds from one generation to another. Today's workers pay taxes to support yesterday's workers who are disabled or retired. Our children and grandchildren will, in theory, provide our benefits from payroll taxes they will pay when they join the work force. This is necessary because the trust fund that has accumulated, from which future benefits will be paid, would be totally consumed in a little over a year if current payroll tax inputs were to stop. So, more correctly, Social Security is a pay-as-you-go program rather than an insurance program. It is largely a tax-financed welfare program which is an essential part of our total social programs.

What are the implications of Social Security's financial problems for managers and their organizations? Further changes are being made which will increase both the tax rate and the maximum income. This provides greater resources for Social Security but also raises the cost of both the employee's and the employer's contributions. If, for example, the rate for employers increased to 12 percent, and the maximum wage base increased to $60,000, the maximum cost to the employer would jump from $3,003 to $7,200 a year. Although a considerable part of this jump would reflect inflation, it would also represent a significant increase in the smorgasbord of benefits that politicians have deemed desirable to provide through Social Security. While this appears to be a large increase, such a rate will arise out of necessity if political forces seek to continue expansion of Social Security benefits and if these costs, or a large part of them, cannot be absorbed through general tax revenues.

Unemployment compensation

Unemployment Compensation.   Unemployment compensation laws provide benefits to employees who are without a job, who have worked a minimum number of weeks, who submit an application for unemployment compensation to their State Employment Agency, who register for available work, and who are willing to accept any suitable employment offered them through their State Unemployment Compensation Commission. The premise behind unemployment compensation is to provide an income to individuals who have lost a job through no fault of their own (e.g., layoffs, plant closings).

The funds for paying unemployment compensation are derived from a combined federal and state tax imposed on the employer, typically 0.4 percent of the employer's wage payroll.[3] Eligible unemployed workers receive an amount that varies from state to state but is determined by the worker's previous wage rate and the length of previous employment. Benefits commonly range from $50 to $75 a week but may run to $150 a week or higher. This compensation is provided for only a limited period—typically, the base is twenty-six weeks but may be extended by the state another twenty-six weeks in unusual situations. This extension was witnessed in the recession of the early 1980s, especially in the hardest-hit areas where auto workers and steel workers constituted a large percentage of the unemployed.

Unemployment compensation and parallel programs for railroad, federal government, and military employees cover more than 75 percent of all members in the work force. Major groups that are excluded include self-employed workers, employees who work for organizations that employ less than four individuals, household domestics, farm employees, state and local government employees, and employees of nonprofit institutions.

As recent recessions have demonstrated, unemployment compensation provides stable spending power throughout the nation. In contrast to the early 1930s, when millions of workers lost their jobs and had no compensatory income, unemployment compensation provides a floor that allows individuals to continue looking for work while receiving assistance through the transitory period from one job to the next.

Worker's compensation

Worker's Compensation.   Every state currently has some type of worker's compensation to compensate employees or their families

---

[3]The tax imposed on the employees is reflective of the number of workers that the company laid off, its "experience rating." The tax is generally 3.4 percent of the first $6,000 earned by the worker. Lower rates are charged to those organizations with low experiences. The intent of the increased rate is to discourage employers from overhiring and laying off when they choose. Proper personnel practices can help to reduce the imposed unemployment tax.

for death or permanent or total disability resulting from job-related endeavors. Federal employees and others not working within the states are covered by separate legislation.

The rationale for worker's compensation protection is to protect employees and to attribute the cost for occupational accidents to the employing organization. This accountability factor considers worker's compensation costs as part of the labor expenses incurred in meeting the organization's objectives.

Worker's compensation benefits are based on fixed schedules of minimum and maximum payments. For example, the loss of an index finger may be calculated at $400, or the loss of an entire foot at $5,000. When comprehensive disability payments are required, the amount of compensation is computed by considering the employee's current earnings, future earnings, and financial responsibilities.

The entire cost of worker's compensation is borne by the organization. The organization, then, protects itself by covering its risks through public, private-external, or private-internal insurance programs. Some states provide an insurance system for the handling of worker's compensation. These may be voluntary or required. Some organizations cover their worker's compensation risks by purchasing insurance from private insurance companies. Finally, some states allow employers to be self-insurers. Self-insuring, while usually limited to large organizations, requires the employer to maintain a fund from which benefits can be paid.

Most of the worker's compensation laws stipulate that the injured employee will be compensated either by a monetary allocation or by the payment of medical expenses, or a combination of the two. Almost all worker's compensation insurance programs, whether publicly or privately controlled, provide incentives for employers to maintain good safety records. Insurance rates are computed based on the organization's accident experience. Hence employers are motivated to keep accident rates low.

Although worker's compensation has generally represented less than 1 percent of total compensation by an organization, the costs have skyrocketed. In 1983, employers paid about $10 billion in insurance premiums, compared with about $2 billion in 1964.[4] The bulk of this increase can be directly attributed to decisions handed down by worker's compensation commissions, which have been established to adjudicate claims. These commissions have greatly expanded the scope of compensation awards made to injured employees. A generation ago, these awards were almost entirely for employees who had incurred physical impairments, but awards have increasingly been made for emotional illnesses. Even emotional illnesses that occur prior to a

---

[4]"The Hot Battle Over Workers' Comp.," *Business Week,* March 22, 1976, p. 42; and updated by an interview with a benefits specialist, June 1985.

physical injury have been found to be compensable. Stress or anxiety that can be attributed to job conditions that lead to neuroses or heart attacks can result in compensation.

Attention has recently been focused on certain industries where health hazards are potentially high. Specifically, fear of physical damage from radiation and respiratory problems in the asbestos and coal-mining industries have resulted in large costs to employers.

State disability laws

State Disability Laws.   For some individuals, state disability laws provide income supplements for short-term illnesses. These payments are designed to continue to provide a portion of income should an employee have an illness or injury that prevents him or her from working beyond the period that would be covered under a sick-leave plan. State disability plans are totally funded by employer contributions.

Summary

The preceding discussion focused on the increasing costs associated with required benefits. Not only the tax rates imposed on employers appear to be increasing, but also the costs of the voluntary benefits offered. In the next section, we will discuss the major voluntary benefits offered by employers.

Voluntary Benefits

One of the costs of "doing business," which can frequently be overlooked, is payment to employees for time spent off the job. This includes rest periods, holidays, vacations, sick leaves, and leaves of absence. While some employers also compensate employees for time spent in changing clothes, attending funerals, or performing jury duty, the following classification represents the major categories, each of which costs American employers billions of dollars annually.

Rest periods

Rest Periods.   Particularly popular among office jobs and those jobs requiring heavy exertion, high repetition, or diligent concentration are breaks during the day to allow the worker to rest. Whether it is called a rest period or a "coffee break," the intent is the same: to allow workers some mental and physical diversion from their work. Rest periods, however, are not free to the employer. The absolute cost to U.S. employers if every employee were permitted a twenty-minute rest period each day would exceed $62 billion a year.[5]

Holidays

Holidays.   Certain days of the year are stipulated as paid holidays. Most organizations define these days to include the Fourth of

[5]Computed on an assumed average wage of $7.50 an hour for 100 million workers: $2.50 per day × 250 days × 100 million workers.

July, Labor Day, Thanksgiving, Christmas, and New Year's, plus others that act to break up the workweek. Some industries acknowledge special days as ones for which employees are paid but do not have to work, such as Columbus Day in the banking industry.

The number of paid holidays varies, but within a relatively narrow range. Virtually all employees receive this benefit—usually nine to eleven holidays are provided each year regardless of the employee's length of service.[6]

If hourly employees are required to work on paid holidays, a premium is paid—for example, double time for Thanksgiving or triple time for Christmas. Among salaried employees, compensatory time off is frequently substituted for premium pay.

Vacations   *Vacations.*   After employees have been with an organization for a specified period of time, they usually become eligible for a paid vacation. Common practice is to relate the length of vacation to the length of tenure and job classification in the organization. For example, after six months' service with the organization, an employee may be eligible for one week's vacation; after a year, two weeks; after five years, three weeks; and after ten or more years, four weeks. If the individual is an executive, the vacation time is usually doubled.

One survey found that 50 percent of the companies studied provided one week's vacation for employees after a year's service; 66 percent provided two weeks after five years; 69 percent, three weeks after ten years; and 59 percent, four weeks after twenty or more years.[7] Obtaining current information in this area, however, is important, since the trend in recent years has been toward the expansion of paid vacations. Most of this expansion has involved three- and four-week vacation periods for individuals with fewer years of service. A generation ago, vacation periods that extended beyond two weeks were predominantly reserved for individuals with fifteen, twenty, or more years of service. As already noted, more than 69 percent of companies provide three weeks' vacation after ten years, and we might predict that this will become more liberal in the future. The five-week vacation, unknown a generation ago, has become increasingly pupular during the past decade and its popularity will undoubtedly continue. Figure 17-2 is a recapitulation of paid vacations by length of service.

The rationale behind the paid vacation is to provide a break in which employees can refresh themselves. This rationale is an important concept, but one that in some situations may be overlooked. For example, in a situation where employees accrue a certain amount of vacation time and can sell back to the company any unused vacation days, the regenerative "battery charging" intent is lost. While the cost

[6]"Labor Month in Review," *Monthly Labor Review,* July 1980, p. 2.

[7]*Personnel Management: Practices and Policies* (Englewood Cliffs, N.J.: Prentice-Hall, 1984), pp. 225–26.

FIGURE 17-2

Paid Vacations by Length of Service

LENGTH OF SERVICE	VACATION				
	1 Week (%)	2 Weeks (%)	3 Weeks (%)	4 Weeks (%)	5 Weeks (%)
6 months	76.2	7.1	—	—	—
1 year	32.2	66.0	—	—	—
2 years	8.0	90.1	—	—	—
3 years	2.9	93.1	2.0	—	—
5 years	1.0	59.6	36.5	—	—
8 years	0.9	37.5	53.8	2.0	—
10 years	—	10.8	71.6	14.7	—
15 years	—	7.9	39.6	47.5	1.9
20 years	—	6.9	19.6	58.9	13.7
25 years	—	6.7	16.3	49.0	27.0

SOURCE: *Personnel Management: Practices and Policies* (Englewood Cliffs, N.J.: Prentice-Hall, 1984), p. 244.

may be the same to the employer whether the employee takes the time off from work or not, the employee does not get a break from the job from selling back his or her time. This lack of recharging may ultimately lead to burnout.

Those organizations that offer progressively longer vacations as the length of service increases may find that vacations develop employee loyalty. Employees who, because of their years of service with the organization, are currently entitled to five weeks of paid vacation annually may be reluctant to leave their present employer to accept a more-challenging and better-paying position elsewhere that would begin with a two-week vacation period.

A recent phenomenon has been the extended vacation covering ten- to thirteen-week period. This has become a focal point by some unions in their negotiations. In contrast to normal paid vacations, the extended vacation is made available to employees every five to seven years, depending on the terms of the negotiation. Unions argue that this long vacation is necessary to allow individual workers an opportunity to partake in activities that cannot be completed in the normal two- to four-week period. The extended vacation is also attractive to the union because, when it is implemented, more workers are needed to do the same amount of work and hence the extended vacation acts to expand union ranks.

Sick leave   *Sick Leaves.*   Most organizations provide their employees with pay for days not worked because of illness. Sick leave is allocated on the basis of so many days a year, accrued on a cumulative basis, or expanded relative to years of service with the organization. In the first case, an individual may take up to a specific maximum number of days off due to illness, say five days a year, and still receive full pay. The cumulative accrual basis calculates sick-leave days as so many a year, less those used up. For example, if 10 days a year are accrued, and an employee with fifteen years of service never missed a day due to illness, the employee would have accumulated 150 days of sick leave with tenure. Finally, some organizations expand their sick leave with tenure. Each year of employment might entitle the worker to two days' leave. Regardless of whether sick leave is used of not, it would continue to accumulate. Those individuals who had been with the company longest would have accumulated the largest sick-leave credit. This last approach recognizes that those employees with the longest tenure tend to be older and thus have a greater probability of incurring a long-term illness.

One of the problems with a liberal sick-leave program is abuse. Employees may perceive this benefit to be something they have earned and therefore have coming to them. This perception is also compounded by the belief that you "use them or lose them." It does not take long for that perception to permeate an organization. Take, for example, two workers, both receiving the same number of sick days per year. Let us suppose that after five years both leave the organization. Employee one has no accumulated sick days, so he is not upset. But employee two has sixty days, twelve days for each year of service. On separating from the company, employee two gives back these sixty days. In essence, he has been punished for not taking those days off. With all things being equal, employee one has had an additional twelve weeks of leave with pay. The belief that one should accumulate sick days for use later in life is quickly diminishing. That belief may have prospered when a person joined an organization early in life and retired from that company, but with today's mobility, a long-term focus has no meaning, especially when we consider that the sick days are not usually transferable to other organizations. Thus the "use them or lose them" concept only hinders productivity.

Recently companies have been giving financial incentives to individuals who do not fully consume their sick leave for the year. In one instance, a company provides ten days of sick leave to each employee and then gives a ten-dollar-a-day premium for each day not taken. Thus an employee who uses only three sick days would receive a seventy-dollar-a-year-end bonus. This may sometimes mean that employees will come to work ill so as not to lose their bonuses. Thus we reward people for not taking sick leave, but that may result in longer periods of illness, or the infecting of others in the unit. It is not uncommon to find many people in one department out sick at one time, especially when something is "going around."

Other attempts have been made to pay an employee, at the time

FIGURE 17-3

SOURCE: The Wizard of Id, by permission of Johnny Hart and Field Enterprises, Inc.

of resignation or retirement, a lump sum for the unused sick days on a two-for-one basis. One problem here, however, is that sick days earned at a lower salary years ago are now being paid off at one's current higher salary. This increases the cost for management.

Nonetheless, although attempts are being made to correct the abuse of sick leave, as long as workers perceive the reward for not using a sick day to be less than the benefit of an additional day off, abuses will continue. Employees may do so until employers are ready to pay for sick days not used, day for day. For example, in some manufacturing firms, employers are offering to buy back unused sick leave from their employees. This incentive serves as an "end-of-the-year" bonus and encourages judicious use of sick time.

Finally, some organizations provide their employees with accident insurance to cover loss of income brought about by a long-term illness or disability. The amount of this coverage varies, but a popular range is between 40 to 60 percent of an individual's weekly wage or salary. The majority of these plans provide coverage for up to sixteen weeks. However, where the disability is permanent, coverage may include benefits up to the normal retirement age when pension benefits will be available to provide financial security.

Leave of absence

Leaves of Absence.   A miscellaneous category includes leaves of absence for which pay is provided. This category would embrace absences for jury duty, military service, or extended education.

Educational leaves, where full pay is maintained, are the usual province of managers or management trainees. These forms of leave may vary from permission to be exempt from work for one-half day a week in order to attend a particularly difficult-to-schedule afternoon class to time off for a nine-month executive development program where full attention must be given to the educational endeavor.

A more recent phenomenon has been the corporate sabbatical, utilized by such organizations as IBM and Xerox, which permits employees to take a paid six-month or one-year leave in order to engage in community service. For example, since its inception in 1971, about five hundred IBM employees have taken a paid social service leave. Usually confined to the executive level, the intent is to bring the skills of top-level managers to bear on the problems facing the community. Since the net effect of such leaves is to enhance the organization's image within the community, such activities can appropriately be charged against the organization's public relations outlay.

Finally, employees in the organization who are active in their union are frequently given periods of time off each week, with pay, in which they can engage in union administrative activities. For example, service on the union's grievance committee usually entails time off from the job so that grievances can be heard and resolved, and it is not unusual to have this time away from the job compensated by the employer. And depending on the size of the certified bargaining unit, some union-bargaining representatives tend to union affairs on a full-time basis. These shop stewards continue to be paid by the employer, but handle only union-related matters.

Pension programs

Pension Programs.   The single largest source of income for retired workers in the past was Social Security benefits. Most workers in the public sector today, however, rely on some form of pension plan to cover their financial needs in retirement. Many workers in the private sector also have their Social Security benefits supplemented through private pension plans, which are operated through their employers. Pension funds, with assets in excess of one-quarter of a trillion dollars, now represent one of the most influential bodies of financial power in America.

A pension represents a fixed payment, other than wages, made regularly to former employees or their surviving dependents. To qualify, employees are required to fulfill certain conditions of employment for a specific length of time. The most popular method for determining the amount of an employee's pension is to base payment on a percentage of the employee's earnings, usually computed on an average over several years, multiplied by the number of years he or she has been employed by the organization. The next most popular method is one in which payment is based on some percentage of the employee's income, usually for a particular period of time.

In 1974, the Employee Retirement Income Security Act (ERISA) was passed for the purpose of dealing with the largest problem of private pension plans: Only a fraction of the 30 million plus workers covered by private pension plans could expect to collect any payment when they left work. This was due to the design of private pension plans, which almost always required a minimum tenure with the organization before individuals were guaranteed a right to pension benefits regardless of whether they stayed with the organization. These permanent benefits, referred to as vesting, were traditionally withheld until employees had served ten to fifteen years with the organization, and in some cases, there were no vesting provisions. If there were no vesting provisions, an employee with, for example, twenty-five years of service who was discharged at the age of sixty would have no rights to pension benefits. As noted in Chapter 2, ERISA has corrected major abuses in private pension plans. Pension funds are now insured, and vesting schedules can no longer be arbitrary. Furthermore, if a pension plan is terminated for any reason and the company's pension fund is inadequate, ERISA allows the federal government through the Pension Benefit Guarantee Corporation (PBGC) to lay claim directly on corporate assets—up to 30 percent of net worth—to pay benefits that had been promised to employees.

Pensions are expensive benefits for organizations to provide but are necessary if organizations are to attract and keep valuable employees. The inflation of the early 1980s made it more important than ever for older workers to have some assurance that their financial needs in their retirement years would be taken care of. However, there is little evidence to indicate that employees are motivated by pension plans. The reasons are that pension plans are only remotely tied to an individual's performance, and the payoff, especially for the worker under forty-five years of age, is far into the future. Pensions must therefore be viewed as membership-based rewards that are provided to develop loyalty, especially where vesting is withheld for the full ten years.

The passage of federal legislation in the early 1980s provided the opportunity for each worker to open an Individual Retirement Account (IRA). This was done to lessen the impact of ensuring that older workers would have their financial needs met. While an IRA was voluntary, it did provide certain tax advantages for workers and gave each worker an opportunity to save for old age. The IRA's impact on company pension plans was negligible. IRAs did not eliminate a company's responsibility for a pension program, nor did they serve as incentives for company retention. IRAs made the employee realize that saving for retirement was something in which he or she must participate. The employee could no longer rely on the company pension or Social Security for financial security. While IRAs did serve a useful purpose for many employees, the 1986 tax reform bill drastically decreased the tax advantage, and eligibility, for many workers. IRAs are now geared toward those employees who do not have a company pension program, and those with a household income under a specified amount. IRAs still retain a tax deferment on interest earned on the accounts.

Capital accumulation plans

Capital Accumulation Plans.   Both employees and employers have found that there are advantages to offering capital accumulation plans. The cost to provide these plans is low for employers, and employees can supplement their retirement program and dabble in investments.

Many companies have offered their employees savings plans through payroll deductions. During the past twenty years, some employers have added a matching feature to their plans. Under this arrangement, the employee could receive up to an additional 50 percent which was contributed by the company to the employee's account. For example, an employee who has a weekly gross salary of $500 decides that he wishes to put 6 percent of the gross into his capital accumulation fund, or $30. The company, by agreeing to match 50 percent of the employee's contribution, would place $15 into the account. Accordingly, each payday, $45 is deposited into the employee's account. However, if the employee should leave the organization prior to a specified period of time (usually two to five years), he may forfeit all or part of the employer's contributions. The amount in the account that was deposited by the employee is always 100 percent vested. Another important feature of the capital accumulation account is that the employee can withdraw the monies at any time.

Changes in tax laws during the early 1980s resulted in the use of pretax savings plans. Commonly known under the label of 401–K programs for the section of the IRS code that they represent, these plans have seen tremendous growth since 1982. Over 80 percent of employers with 401–K plans also offer a matching provision.[8]

---

[8] "Capital Accumulation Plans," Hay/Huggins Benefits Comparison 1984, October 1984, p. VI–1.

Stock ownership plans (ESOP, PAYSOP, and TRASOP) are popular with utilities and manufacturing concerns. Under these plans, an individual can purchase company stock through payroll deductions. Stock is generally sold at a discount or straight market value without the use of, or commissions for, a broker.

Insurance.   One of the most popular benefits offered employees today is the provision of insurance—life, health, and accident. While life insurance is probably one of the oldest benefits offered employees, the skyrocketing cost of medical and hospital care has resulted in health insurance becoming a necessity for workers and their families. The economies that can be obtained by organizations purchasing group health plans have shifted the health insurance burden progressively more toward the employer.

Group life insurance

Group life insurance plans offer a distinct advantage to employees: low-cost coverage without a physical examination. Whether the employer absorbs the full cost of the life insurance for employees or whether it is shared between the employer and the employee, the fact that the plan covers a large number of employees allows the insurer to provide coverage at low cost. Rather than premiums being determined on the individual characteristics of each member in the organization, the characteristics of the group as a whole are the determinant.

Life insurance coverage is a frequent point of negotiation by unions. For the most part, employers absorb the full premium cost for basic life policies. Among operative workers, the most popular form of life insurance coverage is based on a flat rate, such as $15,000. Administrative and executive personnel usually have their coverage based on some multiple of their annual earnings. For example, if a manager is provided life insurance equal to four times his current salary, and his salary is $45,000 a year, this coverage amounts to $180,000. Evidence provided by the Bureau of Labor Statistics suggests that the popular multiple for computing life insurance is between two and four times an employee's annual salary.[9]

One interesting note with respect to life insurance is that it has declined in relation to other benefits offered by the organization. A study published in the *Monthly Labor Review* indicated that "fewer workers were concerned about life insurance and more interested in health and retirement benefits."[10]

If one major illness can bring financial ruin to a family and therefore undermine years of effort to strive for financial security, the provision of health care becomes a natural target for government influence. Since high-quality, comprehensive health care should be available

[9]Ibid, p. II-1.

[10]Allan P. Blostin, "Is Employer-Sponsored Life Insurance Declining Relative to Other Benefits," *Monthly Labor Review,* September 1981, p. 31.

to everyone in the United States, many believe that some form of socialized health insurance, such as that currently provided in Canada and Great Britain, is necessary. However, it does not appear that the United States will embark in the near future on a federal form of health-care insurance, other than the government funding of Medicare (which covers the disabled, the retired, and dependents) and Medicaid (which covers below-poverty families).

Health insurance

At a time when a bed in a hospital can cost $600 per day, and routine surgery can cost in excess of $2,500, no individual can justify the risk of not having a comprehensive health insurance program to cover hospital and medical expenses. As a result, more than 70 percent of those individuals employed by private organizations receive hospital and medical benefits.[11]

Health maintenance organizations

Associations such as Blue Cross and Blue Shield have been factors in the health insurance industry for several decades. A recent alternative has been the emergence of health maintenance organizations (HMOs). There are now more than three hundred HMOs in the United States that provide 15 million subscribers with a comprehensive range of health services for a flat fee—everything from eye examinations and advice for the common cold to heart surgery.[12] Because they emphasize preventive care and operate on a flat-fee formula, HMOs have been successful in drastically cutting the number and length of hospital stays. In 1985, most companies offered some type of HMO health insurance option to their employees through cosponsorships or federal mandate.

Preferred Provider Organizations

Another alternative, Preferred Provider Organizations (PPOs), emerged during the 1980s. A PPO involves the use of specific physicians and health-care facilities to contain the rising costs of health care. Generally, those physicians or hospitals belonging to a PPO agree to accept a lower fixed cost for services rendered in the anticipation of receiving a greater number of patient referrals.

Services

In addition to benefits, organizations can offer a wealth of services that employees find desirable. These services can be provided by the organization at no cost to the employee or at significant reduction from what might have to be paid without the organization's support.

Social and Recreational Events

The company picnic, the Christmas dance, award banquets, and the company golf tournament are all examples of services that most large

[11]Hay/Huggins Benefits Comparison, IV-18.

[12]"What to Know Before You Go HMO," *Changing Times*, November 1984, p. 53.

organizations and many small organizations provide for employees, their spouses, or their entire families.

Company-sponsored events

The motivation behind management's offering social and recreational programs is to develop cohesiveness among employees, as well as commitment and loyalty to the organization. For example, the organization's sponsorship of a team to compete in the community bowling league provides employee recreation, offers a diversionary outlet, and builds *esprit de corps*.

These programs may fill the void left by an unchallenging and repetitive job. The opportunity to participate in the planning and coordinating of social and recreational activities, where the organization merely provides the funds, is usually the way these programs are handled. By taking an active role, employees develop their loyalty to the organization and relieve management of much of the burden of planning these programs. Employees who participate in the planning and coordinating stage are also more likely to get involved in the programs themselves.

Counseling

Counseling.   Every manager has a responsibility to counsel his subordinates. When individual managers are unable to deal with specific problems requiring the counseling services of a professional, organizations can either offer the services of a full-time, in-house counselor or refer the employee to a community counseling service.

The counseling need not be limited to work-related issues. Marital problems, problems with the children, financial difficulties, or general psychiatric problems may not be directly related to the job; however, we recognize that individuals cannot completely separate their life away from the job from their life on the job. Therefore personal problems do affect a worker's job performance. An increasingly popular form of counseling involves employees who are about ready to retire. Preretirement counseling prepares individuals to deal with the realities of leisure, as well as outlining details about Social Security benefits and company pension provisions.

Cultural activities

Cultural Activities.   In an effort to broaden the interests and assist in the overall growth of employees, organizations may provide cultural benefits such as free tickets to plays or operas, participation in a company Great Books Club, or creation and use of a company library. The costs of such benefits are usually minimal, yet they provide an opportunity for the employee to grow and develop. These benefits, while paternalistic in nature, can produce closer ties between employee and employer.

Credit unions

Credit Unions.   Many organizations have established credit unions to serve both the savings and lending needs of their employees. Credit unions usually lend money at rates that are competitive with or lower than those otherwise available outside. They also assume marginally higher risks than will other forms of financial institutions, and they offer the benefit of payroll deduction. Deposits put into savings in credit unions (called share accounts) usually offer a higher rate of interest than that paid by commercial banks on a passbook or statement savings account.

The direct cost to the employer is usually minimal. Income provided from loans made by the credit union provides adequate resources to pay all costs involved in the services provided.

Housing   *Housing.*   Organizations with facilities in isolated areas, where housing is scarce, where costs are unusually high, or where there is a high risk in ownership, may provide employees with the option of organization-supported and -supplemented housing.

Mining towns in Montana and Arizona are often labeled "company towns" because the mining companies operating in the communities own almost all the property, including stores, restaurants, apartments, and houses. Individuals working for these companies are often provided with low-cost company-owned housing.

Top executives in some organizations are provided free housing. For example, most university presidents are provided with a home in which they and their family may reside as long as they are incumbent. Similarly, business executives may be provided with a home or free use of an apartment.

The practice of providing free or subsidized housing to top executives is defended on the grounds that they are required to do considerable entertaining and require appropriate facilities. A prestigious home can also be an attractive benefit when attempting to recruit top executives.

Other Services.   The list of services that an organization can provide its employees is only limited by the imagination of management. Retail stores, for example, usually provide some form of discount to employees when they buy goods in their store. The vast majority of large organizations provide some form of educational assistance, traditionally in the form of tuition refunds, for employees who take job-related courses or are working toward a degree in an accredited college or university. Tuition refunds are usually geared to pay some percentage of reimbursement based on the relevance of the course to an individual's work and whether it is part of a degree program, and they are usually contingent on the attainment of some satisfactory grade in the course.

Free coffee, a company cafeteria, company-provided transportation to and from the job, and child-care centers represent only a few of the types of services that some organizations provide for their employees. Not all of these are free, and some may only represent a benefit to the employee in terms of convenience; however, others go beyond that and offer financial benefits. For example, a government agency in Montreal provides its employees with a full four-course lunch each day, available to all employees for only sixty cents. The remaining costs are paid by the employer.

Trends in Benefits and Services

Benefits have become something other than the once thought of "fringe." Employees expect certain extras to be the norm rather than the exception. Cognizant of these requirements and competition from other business, management has had to develop cost-effective methods to offer and service these benefits. The most widely used prescription has been the cafeteria style of benefits. The cafeteria approach allows employees to pick and choose those benefits that are desirable. The use of the cafeteria style approach to benefits will undoubtedly continue, with the most popular offering being some core benefits that are required for all employees, and the remainder of the monies to be spent on benefits left to the decision of each employee. The advantages of the cafeteria approach to benefits has been supported by many research studies, as we can show that

> *people do have different needs according to their age, financial and family position, attitudes, and life style. Younger employees tend to favor benefits that can be of frequent or immediate use, such as vacation days, holidays, and flexible working hours. Older employees are usually security conscious, preferring life insurance and retirement related benefits.*[13]

As for the other trends, we can expect the burden of paying for these benefits to shift to one that is more equitably shared between the employee and the employer. Health care is a primary example. While it may cost more to subscribe to health coverage, the cost is still minimal compared with the costs of a disastrous illness.

Finally, we must realize that employees may be paying more for or getting less of the benefits that employers offer. Economic hardships are a reality, and cost-cutting measures are mandated. Employees must be willing to accept less if they are to progress in the future. The paternalistic perception of an organization must be changed, and employees must be willing to share more responsibility for their well-being.

Conclusion

Organizations have been offering a plethora of benefits as a means of "sweetening the pot." Employees have become accustomed to these

[13]Kenneth A. Kovach, "New Directions in Fringe Benefits," *Academy of Management Journal*, Summer 1983, p. 63.

benefits and find it difficult to accept less or pay more for what they have. Companies are still offering many of the benefits discussed in this chapter, but skyrocketing costs are causing them to rethink the process. Benefits serve a valuable purpose for both the employer and the employee, but continual growth may only lead to more problems than benefits.

SUMMARY

1. Benefits and services do not motivate employees because they tend to be offered to all workers and are not contingent on performance.

2. Benefits are a major HRM expense, adding approximately 40 percent to the direct wage bill.

3. Most organizations are required by law to provide Social Security insurance, unemployment compensation, worker's compensation, and state disability plans.

4. Additional benefits that employers often provide include
   a. Pay for rest periods
   b. Pay for holidays
   c. Pay for vacations
   d. Pay for sick leaves
   e. Pay for leaves of absence
   f. Pension programs
   g. Capital accumulation programs
   h. Accident insurance
   i. Life insurance
   j. Health insurance

5. Other services that many employers provide include
   a. Social and recreational events
   b. Counseling
   c. Cultural activities
   d. Credit unions
   e. Housing
   f. Discounts on purchases
   g. Tuition refunds for educational courses

6. Current trends focus on benefits being offered on a cafeteria style. This provides the opportunity for employees to get what they want while simultaneously providing a cost-effective measure for the employer.

KEY TERMS

Benefits
Capital accumulation programs
Credit union
Health maintenance organizations (HMOs)
Individual Retirement Account (IRA)
Pension

Pension Benefit Guarantee Corporation (PBGC)
Preferred Provider Organization (PPO)
Social Security
Vesting
Worker's compensation

QUESTIONS FOR REVIEW

1. Why are benefits described as being membership-based rewards?

2. Why might employees choose to have their employer purchase benefits for them rather than receive cash and make the purchase themselves?

3. What benefits are provided by Social Security?

4. How are Social Security benefits financed?

5. How can unemployment compensation benefits act as a counterforce during periods of recession and high unemployment?

6. In what three ways can employers protect themselves against worker's compensation claims?

7. What benefits accrue to an organization that offers a liberal sick-leave policy and liberal vacation and holiday schedules?

8. Describe the abuses of sick leave. How can these abuses be overcome?

9. What is ERISA? What factors brought about its creation?

10. What are HMOs? How do they differ from traditional health insurance like Blue Cross?

QUESTIONS FOR DISCUSSION

1. "As employees' wages have risen during the past several decades, the percentage of these wages that is expended on benefits has been decreasing." Do you agree or disagree? Discuss.

2. If you had your choice of an additional $100 a month in salary or the equivalent of $200 a month in benefits, which would you choose? Why? What do you think most employees would choose? What implications do these answers have on HRM?

3. With regard to employees, what are the advantages and disadvantages of Social Security insurance? Are you in favor of it? Why?

4. "An organization could not attract competent employees today without a competitive benefit program." Do you agree or disagree? Discuss.

5. Do you believe that benefits and services should be considered a part of compensation that employees have earned by working at their jobs, or do they represent something extra that employers are giving their employees? Support your position.

CONTINUING CASE: Concord General

A Case of the Freebies

After consulting with John Michaels, Judy has decided that in order to cut costs, some of the nurses' benefits have to be cut. The following memorandum has been sent to each nurse with her last paycheck:

Dear Staff Nurse:

Due to the decrease in our daily census at the hospital, it has become imperative that we implement cost-cutting measures. To be as fair as we possibly can, and to avoid any unnecessary or undue hardship to any one person or unit, we have decided to reduce the hospital's contributions made for certain benefits. Effective two pay periods from now, Concord General will only pay one-half of your hospitalization. This is a change from the 100 percent that it has been paying. Additionally, tuition reimbursements will cease. However, those currently enrolled this semester will be reimbursed. We will also be eliminating our cafeteria subsidy for employees. Employees using the cafeteria will be expected to pay full price for their meals. Finally, we have decided to eliminate all unnecessary overtime. Overtime must first be approved by a department head.

We realize that these cuts are upsetting to you but hope that you understand the seriousness of our financial difficulties. By cutting benefits, we spread the burden among all staff members. We also hope that as our financial picture improves, we can reinstate these benefits.

If you have any questions, please do not hesitate to contact me.

Sincerely,
Judy Sapp

1. What reaction do you expect this memorandum will generate from the staff nurses? Discuss.
2. If you were faced with similar circumstances, how would you react if you were Judy? The staff nurse?
3. What impact do you believe this memorandum will have on motivation? Recruiting? What information is needed to assess the impact?
4. Should the staff nurses be responsible for sharing the hospital's financial difficulties? Explain your position.

CASE APPLICATION

Hunter Hunts for College Grads

Woody Hunter had been an HRM analyst with Control Data Corporation (CDC) for three years but was recently reassigned to the college recruitment staff. The basic duties in his new job were to visit college and university campuses and interview seniors in order to identify individuals who could fill entry-level positions at CDC in accounting, engineering, and marketing.

After three months' traveling on the road, Woody received a report summarizing his performance to date. The figures showed he had conducted 540 preliminary interviews on 18 different campuses. Woody had had follow-up interviews with 136 of these students, or approximately 25 percent. Based on these second interviews, Woody recommended to his supervisor that 71 candidates be invited for company-paid visits to appropriate CDC manufacturing and administrative facilities where new college graduates were needed. All of Woody's selectees were offered visits.

What concerned Woody and his supervisor was this statistic: Only four of the seventy-one candidates accepted the CDC invitation. Based on over seven years of recruiting experience with CDC, Woody's supervisor said that the company traditionally had better than a 60 percent acceptance rate. Woody's boss knew there was something seriously wrong. He asked Woody to summarize how he described opportunities at CDC to the recruits.

"I ask the students if they have read the CDC literature in the placement office," replied Woody. "Most usually have, but if they haven't I highlight what we do at CDC, the kind of entry-level positions we have to fill, and the kind of people we're looking for. But I know that these students have heard similar propaganda from a dozen other big company recruiters. So I emphasize the things CDC has that others don't. One thing I never fail to mention is our benefit package. It is superior to anybody else's. I tell students about our tuition-reimbursement plan, our comprehensive health insurance program, and our pension system. I tell them that our pension plan vests after only five years. I point out that the employee pays nothing into it—that all the costs are paid by CDC. Most important, I emphasize that they can retire at age fifty-five and receive 80 percent of the salary they were making in their last year. There's not a pension plan anywhere that attractive. I even take the time to show the students how, with inflation figured in, they can probably expect a pension of $200,000 or $300,000 a year if they come to work for CDC."

Questions

1. What role do you think benefits play in the employment decision of a new college graduate?
2. What role do you think the beginning salary plays in the employment decision of a new college graduate?
3. What suggestions would you make that might improve Woody's acceptance ratio?

ADDITIONAL READINGS

"Benefits Are Getting More Flexible, But Caveat Emptor," *Business Week*, September 8, 1986, pp. 65–66.

HERZLINGER, REGINA E., "How Companies Tackle Health Care Costs: Part II," *Harvard Business Review*, September–October 1985, pp. 108–20.

KLEIN, DANIEL L., and JEFFREY PETERTIL, "Health Coverage for Retirees: A Timebomb," *Personnel*, 63, No. 8 (August 1986), 54–62.

KRUPP, NEIL B., "Managing Benefits in Multinational Organizations," *Personnel4*, 63, No. 9 (September 1986), 76–78.

ROSEN, BENSON, and THOMAS H. JERDEE, "Retirement Policies for the 21st Century," *Human Resource Management*, 25, No. 3 (Fall 1986), 405–20.

CHAPTER 18

Disciplining

the Problem

Employee

AFTER READING THIS CHAPTER, YOU WILL BE ABLE TO:

1. Define *discipline*
2. Describe the most frequent discipline problems
3. Identify the contingency factors that determine the severity of the discipline
4. Discuss the general guidelines for administering discipline
5. Describe the disciplinary actions available to managers
6. Explain employment-at-will
7. Discuss the implications of employment-at-will
8. Discuss the special discipline problems created when unionized or professional employees are involved

Gross incompetence: 144 times worse than ordinary incompetence.

—Anonymous

There are employees who—regardless of what the organization has done in terms of its efforts at selection, socialization, job design, performance standards, and reward practices—create discipline problems for management. These problem employees may be chronically late for work, have excessive absences, fight with their co-workers, consume drugs on the job, refuse to obey their boss's orders, break safety rules, or engage in other similar digressions. A review of these problems, and what managers can do about them, will be the major concern of this chapter.

What Is Discipline?

Discipline defined   The term *discipline* refers to a condition in the organization when employees conduct themselves in accordance with the organization's rules and standards of acceptable behavior. For the most part, employees discipline themselves. By that we mean that members conform with what is considered proper behavior because they believe it is the right thing to do. Once they are made aware of what is expected of them, and assuming they find these standards or rules to be reasonable, they seek to meet those expectations.

But not all employees will accept the responsibility of self-discipline. There are some employees for whom the motivational concepts discussed in previous chapters are not enough to elicit the accepted norms of responsible employee behavior. These employees will require some degree of extrinsic disciplinary action. This extrinsic action is frequently labeled punishment. It is this need to impose extrinsic disciplinary action that we will address in the remainder of this chapter.

Types of Discipline Problems

With little difficulty, we could list several dozen or more infractions that management might believe require disciplinary action. For simplicity's sake, we have classified the more frequent violations into four categories: attendance, on-the-job behaviors, dishonesty, and outside activities.

Attendance

Attendance problems

A serious disciplinary problem facing managers undoubtedly involves attendance. For instance, a study of two hundred organizations, 60 percent of which employed over one thousand workers, found that absenteeism, tardiness, abuse of sick leave, and other aspects of attendance were rated as the foremost problems by 79 percent of the respondents.[1] Importantly, attendance problems appear to be even more widespread than those related to productivity—such as carelessness in doing work, neglect of duty, and not following established procedures.

Why is attendance such a serious problem? While there is no simple or clear answer, we might postulate several reasons. First, many organizations have failed to align workers' goals with those of the organization. When employees cannot relate to their work or to the organization, the result is usually a decline in attendance. A second reason may be a changing attitude toward employment. For many people, work is not their central life interest, and hence the desire to conscientiously be at their jobs regularly, and on time, is not of primary importance. A third reason may be the different backgrounds of new entrants into the work force during the 1970s. In the 1970s, we saw a rapid movement of minorities and women into the job market, and many of these new entrants had little previous experience. Their values and attitudes toward attendance differed from those of the new entrants of the 1950s and 1960s. Fourth, it is obvious that many employees believe that earned sick-leave days have to be consumed, regardless of whether they are ill or not. As organizations have increased their paid sick-leave benefits, as part of expanded benefit packages, many employees have merely treated these days as just more earned time off. This is especially true of the organizations that imply "use them or lose them." A final reason is the greater difficulty involved in firing an employee, especially those union members protected by a collective-bargaining agreement. As noted in Chapter 2, government regulations and union power have decreased the discretion once held by management. In such a climate, workers may be more apt to take advantage of management's restricted options. However, keep in mind that no union or government legislation will protect a worker who is a disciplinary problem. The intent of the above is only to ensure that the action that takes place is fair and unbiased.

[1] *Employee Conduct and Discipline*, Personnel Policies Forum, Survey No. 102 (Washington, D.C.: Bureau of National Affairs, August 1973).

On-the-Job Behaviors

Infractions of
company rules

Our second category of discipline problems covers on-the-job behaviors. This blanket label includes insubordination, horseplay, fighting, gambling, failure to use safety devices, carelessness, and two of the most widely discussed problems in organizations today—abuse of alcohol and drugs.

Most of the above actions reflect direct infractions of organization rules. For instance, refusing to obey a boss's orders, ignoring safety procedures, or being intoxicated on the job are all behaviors that are usually expressly forbidden. As a result, these infractions are rarely difficult to identify. Furthermore, because they represent a clear violation of an organization's acceptable standards of behavior, corrective action should be taken immediately. In contrast to ambiguous infractions (such as taking an unnecessary sick-day leave), fighting, gambling, or safety infractions represent clear rule violations. The relative absence of ambiguity surrounding such violations will prove important later in this chapter when we consider the degree of discipline to administer and whether the discipline handed out is perceived by employees to be commensurate with the action. We will find that the greater the ambiguity surrounding the infraction, the more likely others are to see it as inequitable.

Arriving at work drunk or consuming alcoholic drinks on the job is an age-old problem. Many organizations now consider alcoholism a treatable illness and have established programs to cure alcoholic employees (see Chapter 20). The use of drugs on the job is a newer problem, one that much greater than it was a generation ago. More and more employees have experimented with drugs off the job, and there has been a carryover of drug abuse onto the job.

Dishonesty

Dishonesty

Although not one of the more widespread employee problems confronting management, dishonesty has traditionally resulted in the most severe disciplinary actions. One study found that 90 percent of the surveyed organizations would discharge an employee for theft, even if it was only a first offense.[2] Similarly, 88 percent would discharge those employees who were found to have falsified information on their employment application.[3]

These findings reflect the strong cultural norms held in North America against dishonesty. More than with any other type of behavior, evidence that one has engaged in a single dishonest act reflects directly on the employee's character. Furthermore, it is assumed, rightly or wrongly, that an employee who lies or steals once cannot be

[2]Ibid.
[3]Ibid.

trusted and must therefore be separated from the organization. Evidence of this practice appears in the media on an almost regular basis. Recent headlines tell us of a meteorologist who had been with an eastern television station for over a decade. When it was discovered that he had lied about his having earned several advanced degrees, his outstanding record as a weatherman at the station became incidental. He was fired. Similarly, when it became known that a dean of a major Colorado university had plagiarized a major part of his doctoral thesis, the evidence that he had performed admirably as an academic administrator was dwarfed by the fact that he had broken a cardinal rule within the academic community. Under pressure from colleagues, university board members, and the media, he "voluntarily" resigned. The public's treatment of Richard Nixon attests to our society's strongly held conviction that dishonesty must be severely punished.

Outside Activities

External activities Our final problem category covers activities that employees engage in outside of their work, but which either effect their on-the-job performance or generally reflect negatively on the organization's image. Included here are unauthorized strike activity, having one's wages garnisheed, outside criminal activities, and working for a competing organization. Among managerial personnel, this category would also include bad-mouthing the organization or questioning the organization's key values in public.

An individual may be on the job only forty hours a week, but that does not exclude the organization from disciplining employees when their behavior off the job embarrasses the organization. While the courts have recently acted to greatly protect employees from arbitrary punishment by management for a worker's action off the job, it would be naive to assume that the organization ignores the behavior of employees in their off-the-job hours. This is most evident in managerial positions. The line between managers speaking or acting for themselves and speaking or acting for their organization becomes less clear as one rises in the organization. For senior executives, what they say or do twenty-four hours a day, seven days a week, reflects on the organization. Hence their off-the-job activities must fall within the acceptable standards of the organization or they will be subjected to disciplinary action by their organization.

Before Disciplinary Action: Put the Problem in Perspective

The above discussion reflects that there are a wide range of problems that might require disciplinary action. More important, however, we should recognize that infractions vary greatly in terms of severity. Therefore, before we review the types of discipline available to managers, we should look at the major factors that need to be considered if we are to have fair and equitable disciplinary practices.

The following nine contingency factors have been proposed to help us analyze a discipline problem:[4]

Seriousness of the problem

1. *Seriousness of the problem.* How severe is the problem? As noted previously, dishonesty is usually considered as a more serious infraction than reporting to work twenty minutes late.

Duration of the problem

2. *Duration of the problem.* Have there been other discipline problems in the past, and over how long a time span? The violation does not take place in a vacuum. A first occurrence is usually viewed differently than a third or fourth offense.

Frequency and nature of the problem

3. *Frequency and nature of the problem.* Is the current problem part of an emerging or continuing pattern of discipline infractions?

[4]Wallace Wohlking, "Effective Discipline in Employee Relations," *Personnel Journal*, September 1975, pp. 491–92.

We are concerned with not only the duration but also the pattern of the problem. Continual infractions may require a different type of discipline from that applied to isolated instances of misconduct. They may also point out a direction that demands far more severe discipline in order to prevent a minor problem from becoming a major one.

Employee's work history

4. *Employee's work history.* How long has the employee worked for the organization, and what has been the quality of his or her performance? For many violations, the punishment will be less severe for those employees who have developed a strong track record. Equity would suggest that a violation incurred by employee A, who has been with the organization for three months, be treated differently from a similar violation incurred by employee B, who has proved to be an excellent employee for more than twenty years. However, EEO considerations must be recognized.

Extenuating factors

5. *Extenuating factors.* Are there extenuating circumstances related to the problem? The student who fails to turn in her term paper by the deadline date because of the death of her grandfather is likely to have her violation assessed more leniently than will her peer who missed the deadline because she overslept.

Degree of socialization

6. *Degree of socialization.* To what extent has management made an earlier effort to educate the person causing the problem about the existing discipline rules and procedures and the consequences of violations? Discipline severity must reflect the degree of knowledge that the violator holds of the organization's standards of acceptable behavior. In contrast to point 4, the new employee is less likely to have been socialized to these standards than the twenty-year veteran. Additionally, the organization that has formalized written rules governing employee conduct is more justified in aggressively enforcing violations of these rules than is the organization whose rules are informal or vague.

History of organization's discipline practices

7. *History of the organization's discipline practices.* How have similar infractions been dealt with in the past within the department? Within the entire organization? Has there been consistency in the application of discipline procedures? Equitable treatment of employees must take into consideration precedents within the unit where the infraction occurs, as well as previous disciplinary actions taken in other units within the organization. Equity demands consistency against some relevant benchmark.

Implications for other employees

8. *Implications for other employees.* What impact will the discipline selected have on other workers in the unit? There is little point to taking a certain action against an employee if it has a major dysfunctional effect on others within the unit. The end result may be only to convert a narrow and single disciplinary problem into a widespread headache for management.

Management
backing

9. *Management backing.* If employees decide to take their case to a higher level in management, will you have reasonable evidence to justify your decision? Should the employee challenge your disciplinary action, it is important that you have the data to back up the necessity and equity of the action taken and feel confident that your superiors will support your decision. No disciplinary action is likely to carry much weight if violators believe that they can challenge and successfully override their manager's decision.

Now that we have identified major factors that can influence the disciplinary decision, let us review some general guidelines in administering discipline.

General Guidelines in Administering Discipline

The human resource manager should be aware that, over time, we have developed some guidelines to indicate how discipline should be administered. In this section, we will briefly describe these guidelines.

Discipline should be
corrective

Make Disciplinary Action Corrective Rather Than Punitive.   The objective of disciplinary action is not to deal out punishment. The objective is to correct an employee's undesirable behavior. While punishment may be a necessary means to that end, one should never lose sight of the eventual objective.

Discipline should be
progressive

Make Disciplinary Action Progressive.   Although the type of disciplinary action that is appropriate may vary depending on the situation, it is generally desirable for discipline to be progressive. Only for the most serious violations will an employee be dismissed after a first offense. Typically, progressive disciplinary action begins with an oral warning and proceeds through a written warning, suspension, and, only in the most serious cases, dismissal. The progressive approach will be followed in our next section.

Discipline should
follow the "Hot
stove" rule

Follow the "Hot Stove" Rule.   Administering discipline can be viewed as analogous to touching a hot stove. While both are painful to the recipient, the analogy goes further. When you touch a hot stove you get an *immediate* response. The burn you receive is instantaneous, leaving no question of cause and effect. You have ample *warning.* You know what happens if you touch a red-hot stove. Furthermore, the result is *consistent.* Every time you touch a hot stove, you get the same response—you get burned. Finally, the result is *impersonal.* Regardless of who you are, if you touch a hot stove you will be burned. The comparison between touching a hot stove and administering discipline should be apparent, but let us briefly expand on each of the four points in the analogy.

The impact of a disciplinary action will be reduced as the time between the infraction and the penalty's implementation lengthens. The more quickly the discipline follows the offense, the more likely it is that the employee will associate the discipline with the offense rather than with the manager imposing the discipline. As a result, it is best that the disciplinary process begin as soon as possible after the violation is noticed. Of course, this desire for immediacy should not result in undue haste. If all the facts are not in, managers will often invoke a temporary suspension, pending a final decision in the case.

The manager has an obligation to give advance warning prior to initiating formal disciplinary action. This means the employee must be aware of the organization's rules and accept its standards of behavior. Disciplinary action is more likely to be interpreted as fair by employees when there is clear warning that a given violation will lead to discipline and when it is known what that discipline will be.

Fair treatment of employees also demands that disciplinary action be consistent. When rule violations are enforced in an inconsistent manner, the rules lose their impact. Morale will decline and employees will question the competence of management. Productivity will suffer as a result of employee insecurity and anxiety. All employees want to know the limits of permissible behavior, and they look to the actions of their managers for such feedback. If John is reprimanded today for an action that he did last week, for which nothing was said, these limits become blurry. Similarly, if Sally and Barbara are both goofing around at their desks and Sally is reprimanded and Barbara is not, Sally is likely to question the fairness of the action. The point, then, is that discipline should be consistent. This need not result in treating everyone exactly alike, because that ignores the contingency factors we discussed earlier. But it does put the responsibility on management to clearly justify disciplinary actions that may appear inconsistent to employees.

The last guideline that flows from the "hot stove" rule is keep the discipline impersonal. Penalties should be connected with a given violation, not with the personality of the violator. That is, discipline should be directed at what an employee has done, not the employee herself. As a manager, you should make it clear that you are avoiding personal judgments about the employee's character. You are penalizing the rule violation, not the individual. And all employees committing the violation can be expected to be penalized. Furthermore, once the penalty has been imposed, the manager must make every effort to forget the incident. She should attempt to treat the employee in the same manner as she had prior to the infraction. Figure 18-1 summarizes the discipline process. Again, note the objective. We want to correct the behavior, not personally attack the employee.

Let us now specifically look at the various disciplinary actions that the manager may want to take.

FIGURE 18-1

The Reprimand Process

The One Minute Reprimand works well when you:

1. Tell people beforehand that you are going to let them know how they are doing and in no uncertain terms.

the first half of the reprimand:

2. Reprimand people immediately.
3. Tell people what they did wrong—be specific.
4. Tell people how you feel about what they did wrong—and in no uncertain terms.
5. Stop for a few seconds of uncomfortable silence to let them *feel* how you feel.

the second half of the reprimand:

6. Shake hands, or touch them in a way that lets them know you are honestly on their side.
7. Remind them how much you value them.
8. Reaffirm that you think well of them but not of their performance in this situation.
9. Realize that when the reprimand is over, it's over.

SOURCE: "The One Minute Reprimand," from THE ONE MINUTE MANAGER by Kenneth Blanchard and Spencer Johnson. Copyright © 1981, 1982 by Blanchard Family Partnership and Candle Communications Corporation. By permission of William Morrow and Company.

Disciplinary Actions

Discipline generally follows a typical sequence of four steps: oral warning, written warning, suspension, and dismissal. Two additional steps, which would logically follow suspension—demotion and pay cuts—are less popular in practice but are important enough to justify discussion. These six steps, then, are the topic of this section.

Oral Warning

Oral warnings

The mildest form of discipline is the oral warning. This reprimand is best achieved if completed in a private and informal environment. The manager should begin by clearly informing the employee of the rule that has been violated and the problem that this infraction has caused. For instance, if the employee has been late several times, the manager would reiterate the organization's rule that employees are to be at their desks by 8:00 A.M., and then proceed to give specific evidence of how violation of this rule has resulted in an increase in workload for others and has lowered departmental morale. After the problem has been made clear, the manager should then allow the employee to respond. Is she aware of the problem? Are there extenuating circumstances that justify her behavior? What does she plan to do to correct her behavior?

After the employee has been given the opportunity to make her case, the manager must determine if the employee has proposed an adequate solution to the problem. If this has not been done, then the manager should direct the discussion toward helping the employee figure out ways to prevent the trouble from recurring. Once a solution has been agreed upon, the manager should ensure that the employee understands what, if any, follow-up action will be taken if the problem recurs.

If the oral warning is effective, further official disciplinary action can be avoided. If the employee fails to improve, the manager will need to consider more severe action. A final point on the oral warning: It is a good idea to make a temporary record of this reprimand and place it in the employee's file. It should state the purpose, date, and outcome of the interview with the employee. Once the employee has demonstrated that she has corrected the problem, the record of the oral reprimand can be removed from her file.

Written Warning

Written warnings

The second step in progressive discipline is the written warning. In effect, it is the first formal stage of the discipline procedure. This is true because the written warning becomes part of the employee's official file. This is achieved by not only giving the warning to the employee but sending a copy to the personnel department to be inserted in the employee's permanent record. In all other ways, however, the procedure preceding the writing of the warning is the same as the oral warning. That is, the employee is advised of the violation, its effect, and potential consequences of future violations. The only difference is that the discussion concludes with the employee being told that a written warning will be issued. Then the manager writes up the warning—stating the problem, the rule that has been violated, any acknowledgement by the employee to correct her behavior, and the consequences from a recurrence of the deviant behavior.

While written warnings are more severe, many organizations are allowing employees to purge their personnel files of these warnings after a period of time (usually two years of proper work behavior).

Suspension

Suspensions

A suspension or layoff would be the next disciplinary step, usually taken only if the prior steps have been implemented without the desired outcome. Exceptions—where suspension is given without any prior oral or written warning—occasionally occur if the infraction is of a serious enough nature. We will discuss this possibility later in this section.

A suspension may be for one day or several weeks. Disciplinary layoffs in excess of a month are rare. Some organizations skip this step completely because it can have negative consequences for both the company and the employee. From the organization's perspective, a suspension means the loss of the employee for the layoff period. If the person has unique skills or is a vital part of a complex process, her loss during the suspension period may severely impact on her department or the organization's performance if a suitable replacement cannot be located. From the employee's standpoint, a suspension can result in the employee returning in a more unpleasant and negative frame of mind than before the layoff.

Then why should management consider suspending employees as a disciplinary measure? The answer is that a short layoff, without pay, has the potential to be a rude awakening to problem employees. It may convince them that management is serious and shock them back to accepting responsibility for following the organization's rules.

Demotion

Demotions

If suspension has not been effective and management wants to strongly avoid dismissing the problem employee, demotion may be an alternative. However, we should point out that few organizations use demotion as a discipline measure, probably because it tends to demoralize not only the employee but the co-workers as well. Also, in contrast to the previous actions, it is not temporary. A demotion is a constant punishment to the demoted employee and hence has broad motivation implications.

If demotion has a place as a disciplinary action, if probably is where (1) the employee clearly has the ability to perform the job, (2) management perceives itself legally or ethically constrained from firing the employee (for example, an employee with thirty years of tenure in the organization), and (3) it is believed that a blatant demotion will awaken the employee. In such instances, demotion is a loud message that such employees will have to shape up radically if they want their old job back, and that management has no intention of letting them "get away" with chronic abuses of the organization's rules.

Pay Cut

Pay cuts

Another alternative, also rarely applied in practice, is cutting the problem employee's pay. Certainly, this approach usually has a demoralizing effect on the employee, but it has been suggested as a rational action by management if the only other alternative is dismissal.[5]

From management's perspective, dismissal means losing the individual's experience and background. A replacement will be hired in at a lower salary but still has to be trained to do the job. In cost-benefit terms, it may be to management's advantage to save the hiring and training costs incurred with a new employee. This can be done by cutting the pay of the problem employee and saving the investment the organization has already made in that person. And, of course, if the problem employee alters her behavior, the pay cut can always be rescinded.

Dismissal

Dismissals

Management's ultimate disciplinary punishment is dismissing the problem employee. Dismissal should be used only for the most serious offenses. Yet it may be the only feasible alternative when an employee's behavior is so bad as to seriously interfere with a department or the organization's operation.

A dismissal decision should be given long and hard consideration. For almost all individuals, being fired from a job is an emotional trauma. For employees who have been with the organization for many years and for those over fifty years of age, it may make it difficult to obtain new employment or require the individual to undergo extensive retraining. In addition, management should consider the possibility that a dismissed employee will take legal action to fight the decision. Recent court cases indicate that juries are cautiously building a list of conditions under which employees may not be lawfully discharged.

[5]"Effective Pay Programs—An Interview with Edward E. Lawler III," *Compensation Review.* Third Quarter, 1976, p. 23.

FIGURE 18-2   *"One nice thing about this company, though. They almost never fire anybody."*

SOURCE: *Wall Street Journal*, June 27, 1980. With permission.

In the next section, we look at employment-at-will and some of its limitations.

Employment-at-Will Doctrine

Background

History of employment-at-will

The concept of the employment-at-will doctrine is rooted in nineteenth-century common law, which permitted employers to discipline or discharge an employee at their discretion. We can define *employment-at-will* as the process whereby "employees may be discharged for whatever reason the employer may elect."[6] This means that employers "may dismiss their employees at will . . . for good cause, for no cause or even for cause morally wrong, without being guilty of legal wrong."[7]

[6]Stephen J. Holoviak, Jerry Weigle, and Thomas Bright, "Employment-at-Will: A Legal Area That Merits Attention for the Small Business Person," *American Journal of Small Business*, IX, No. 1 (Summer 1984), 58.

[7]Marie Leonard, "Challenges to the Termination-at-Will Doctrine, *Personnel Administrator*, February 1983, p. 49. (Quoted from Lawrence E. Blades, *Columbia Law Review*, 67 (1967), 1405.)

The common law practice of employment-at-will has heavily influenced the courts' interpretation of employee discharge. However, certain protections have been imposed. The Wagner Act "prohibited employers from discharging workers because of union membership or union activities and gave employees dismissed in violation of the statute the right to reinstatement with back pay."[8] This action reinforced the concept that the common law interpretation of the employment-at-will doctrine could be changed by means of a contractual or collective agreement.

Additionally, the Civil Rights Act of 1964 had an impact on protecting employees from wrongful discharge. The Civil Rights Act curtailed the use and made it illegal to discharge an employee on the basis of race, color, religion, sex, or national origin. Subsequent acts have expanded this coverage,[9] such as the Age Discrimination in Employment Act of 1967 (making it illegal to discharge an employee based solely on age), the Occupational Safety and Health Act of 1970 (making it illegal to discharge an employee for identifying safety and health violations), and the Rehabilitation Act of 1973 (making it illegal to discharge an employee because of physical handicaps). In addition to these acts, federal or state statutes may further curtail at-will discharges.

Just cause dismissals   The overriding theme is to ensure that the firing of an employee who may be covered by the legislation or a contractual arrangement be for "just cause." Having just cause to discharge an employee sounds rational, but what is *just cause?* While no specific definition exists, there are some guidelines for which the employer can show "just cause":[10]

1. Was there adequate warning of consequences of the worker's behavior?
2. Are the rules reasonable and related to safe and efficient operations of the business?
3. Before discipline was rendered, did a fair investigation of the violation occur?
4. Did the investigation yield definite proof of worker activity and wrongdoing?
5. Have similar occurrences, both prior and subsequent to this event, been handled the same and without discrimination?
6. Was the penalty in line with the seriousness of the offense and in reason with the worker's past employment record?

[8]Ibid., p. 50.

[9]Holoviak, Weigle, and Bright, "Employment-at-Will," p. 59.

[10]Ibid. Adapted from Stephen Rosen, Industrial Relations Research Association (Proceedings, 35th Annual Meeting, New York 1982).

Implied Employment Contracts

Implied employment
contracts

While the employment-at-will doctrine is still very much alive in organizations today, even though it has been curtailed by pieces of legislation, recent court interpretations may have begun to curb its use even further. This has occurred when there is an implied contract between the organization and an employee. This implied contract can be generated at many stages, but it is primarily found during interviewing activity. If, during an interview, any "organizational guarantees or promises about job security were made by the company, or written statements in policy manuals or employee handbooks implying or stating that an employee would be terminated only for just cause,"[11] these statements may have become legally binding contracts. For example, one noteworthy case related to this topic was *Toussant* v. *Blue Cross and Blue Shield of Michigan*. In this case, Mr. Toussant claimed that he was improperly discharged, for unjust causes, by the defendant. He asserted that he was told "he'd be with the company until age 65 as long as he did his job."[12] Delving further into the matter, it was also apparent that the employees' handbook reinforced this tenure with statements reflective of discharge for just cause, only and then, after progressive disciplinary processes had been followed. In this case, the court determined that the discharge was improper,[13] because permanence of his position was implied by the organization.

Implications for HRM

Actions such as the above indicate that human resource managers must ensure proper wording in their policy manuals and employee handbooks. Any reference to a binding contract or permanance should be removed, otherwise at-will discharges may be overturned. In fact, such disclaimers as "This handbook is not a contract of employment" or "Employment in the organization is at the will of the employer" should be included on the covers of the handbooks or manuals.

Employers must also ensure consistency in their disciplinary process. As mentioned earlier in this chapter, discipline must be progressive and follow the "hot stove" rule. Anything else may lead to problems if a discharge is questioned. Finally, in administering personnel performance evaluations, employers need to furnish documentary evidence when the employee's behavior is not what is expected. They must address these behaviors with the employee and have the employee "sign off" to the fact that the undesired behaviors were discussed and that he or she understands the consequences that may oc-

[11]Leonard, "Challenges," p. 52.
[12]Ibid., p. 50.
[13]Ibid.

cur if the behaviors continue. Sound documentation is a good defense if questions arise later.

Disciplining Special Employee Groups

To this point, we have treated all employees alike. Yet certain employee groups require special attention because they have unique characteristics. In this section, we will consider some modifications in disciplinary action necessary when dealing with unionized and professional employees.

Unionized Employees

Where employees belong to a union, there will be a collective-bargaining agreement. This agreement, among other things, will outline rules governing the behavior of union members. It will also identify disciplinary procedures and clarify the steps members are to follow if they believe that they are receiving arbitrary or unfair treatment.

Although we will discuss collective bargaining at length in Chapter 21, it is our purpose here to acknowledge that this process does influence management's handling of disciplinary problems among unionized personnel. It usually defines what represents a rule violation and what penalties are applicable. Very importantly, the more serious actions—to suspend or dismiss an employee—can usually be expected to be vigorously opposed by the employee and the union.

Most collective-bargaining agreements stipulate that employees can only be disciplined for "just cause," and they provide a grievance procedure and opportunities for third-party arbitration if employees believe they have been wronged. Disciplining a unionized employee thus tends to be a more formal or quasi-legal undertaking than the disciplining of nonunion employees. The bargaining contract, the existence of a grievance procedure, the right to arbitrate differences, and the whole quasi-legal management-labor relationship—all act to reduce management's discretion in taking disciplinary action.

Professional Employees

Professional employees—engineers, computer specialists, accountants, scientists, health-care specialists, and so forth—also present unique disciplinary problems. Because they hold high skills and frequently possess important and valuable information about the organization, they are more difficult to replace if dismissed and can discredit the organization with competitors, suppliers, customers or clients, government agencies, or other constituencies.

These factors suggest that management must take greater care in disciplining professional employees than it might take with nonunionized operative employees. They may also explain the replacement of traditional dismissal actions with the practice of dehiring and offering outplacement services.

Dehiring seeks to get the employee to quit voluntarily. If the employee is not performing adequately and corrective attempts have proved unsuccessful, management can begin sending out clues that the professional's services are no longer needed. Excluding such employees from important meetings, bypassing them on key memos, and reassigning them to boring and unchallenging tasks are examples of actions that should convey the message. If their actions are successful, the employees find another job and give their notice. The end result is the same as if the professional had been outrightly fired; however, face is saved by both the employee and the organization.

Another approach that replaces the traditional dismissal action is outplacement counseling. Also used for nondisciplinary purposes—during cutbacks or redundancies caused by mergers—outplacement counseling is usually provided free of cost to the professionals by their employer for the purpose of assisting the employees in marketing their services. Counselors provide guidance in designing and updating one's résumé and making lists of contacts, coaching in how to go out on interviews, and advice on how to follow up on leads and how to evaluate any job offers that are received.

It is not unusual for the employee to continue on the payroll for several months while, in effect, searching full time for a new job. Again, like dehiring, outplacement makes the employee's severance a lot easier. However, in contrast to dehiring, outplacement requires management to become a partner in helping the professional find new employment. It is expensive for the organization—fees usually run 10 to 15 percent of the employee's annual salary plus out-of-pocket expenses—but it is a definite step forward in the humanistic treatment of employees. For individuals who have prepared themselves through years of education and made a strong commitment to a professional career, outplacement sure beats a boss saying, "You're fired! Get out!"

Conclusion

We have considered a number of aspects regarding disciplining the problem employee. Our discussion focused on a disciplinary process that was fair, equitable, and consistently practiced. The typical progression of discipline moves from an oral warning, to a written warning, to suspension, and, if necessary, to dismissal. Management might also consider the use of demotion and paycuts as an alternative to dismissal.

While we have presented these steps in a sequential manner—the severity of the penalty is increased as the offense is repeated—it is not unusual for a first offense to result immediately in a suspension or even dismissal. This obviously depends on the infraction. Since some violations are much more severe than others, if the punishment is to fit the crime, we can expect that the early steps may sometimes be skipped.

Figure 18-3 separates offenses into minor and serious categories. By making such a distinction, management can begin to establish a consistent and equitable discipline policy. For instance, employees who experience their first minor offense might generally expect an oral warning. A second offense might result in a written warning, and so forth. In contrast, the first occurrence of a serious offense might mean an immediate suspension, the length on the circumstances surrounding the violation.

Finally, we made suggestions about how the discipline problem workers, discussed employment-at-will and implied employment contracts, and offered some considerations that must be recognized for special employee groups. Above all, we discussed the purpose of disciplining. That purpose is to correct a particular behavior that is misaligned. We do not attack people when disciplining but instead address some aspects of their work behaviors.

FIGURE 18-3

Categorizing Specific Discipline Problems

TYPE OF PROBLEM	MINOR OFFENSES	SERIOUS OFFENSES
Attendance	Habitual tardiness Unexcused absence Leaving without permission	
On-the-job behaviors	Failure to obey safety rules Drunk on the job Defective work Sleeping on the job Failure to report accidents Loafing Gambling on the job Fighting Horseplay	Malicious destruction of organizational property Gross insubordination Carrying a concealed weapon Attacking another employee with intent to seriously harm
Dishonesty	Clock-punching another's timecard Concealing defective work Subversive activity	Stealing Deliberate falsification of employment record
Outside activities	Wage garnishment Working for a competing company	Unauthorized strike activity Outside criminal activities

SUMMARY

1. *Discipline* is a condition in the organization when employees conduct themselves in accordance with the organization's rules and standards of acceptable behavior.

2. The most frequent discipline problems can be classified as related to
   a. Attendance
   b. On-the-job behavior
   c. Dishonesty
   d. Outside activities

3. Whether discipline is imposed and the severity of the action chosen should reflect the following contingency factors:
   a. Seriousness of the problem
   b. Duration of the problem
   c. Frequency and nature of the problem
   d. Employee's work history
   e. Extenuating circumstances
   f. Degree of socialization
   g. History of the organization's discipline practices
   h. Implications of other employees
   i. Management backing

4. General guidelines in administering discipline include
   a. Making disciplinary action corrective
   b. Making disciplinary action progressive
   c. Following the "hot stove" rule—discipline should be immediate, provide ample warning, be consistent, and be impersonal.

5. Disciplinary actions available to the manager include
   a. Oral warning
   b. Written warning
   c. Suspension
   d. Demotion
   e. Pay cut
   f. Dismissal

6. Employment-at-will has changed significantly since its nineteenth-century common law roots. Employers may have to fire an employee for "just cause."

7. The implications of employment-at-will are many. References to permanent employment agreements in personnel handbooks may specify whether an employer has the right to discharge an employee.

8. Unionized employees create special discipline problems because the quasi-legal relationship developing out of collective bargaining acts to reduce management's discretion in taking disciplinary action.

9. Professional employees create special discipline problems because they are more difficult to replace if dismissed and can discredit the organization with important constituencies.

KEY TERMS

Discipline
Employment-at-will
Hot stove rule

Implied employment contract
"Just cause" dismissals
Suspension

QUESTIONS FOR REVIEW

1. Why is discipline necessary?
2. Contrast self-discipline with extrinsic discipline.
3. What type of discipline problems is most prevalent?
4. What type of discipline problem traditionally results in the most severe disciplinary actions?
5. Why are penalties often imposed progressively?
6. Under what conditions should dismissal be used as a penalty?
7. How does collective bargaining influence management's discipline practices?
8. Are the goals of "consistency" and having the "punishment fit the crime" incompatible? Why?
9. What is the purpose of discipline? How can we ensure that this purpose is achieved?
10. What is employment-at-will? How has it changed since its nineteenth-century beginning? What implications does it have for HRM in the 1990s?

QUESTIONS FOR DISCUSSION

1. Are the goals of "consistency" and acknowledging "extenuating circumstances" incompatible? Discuss.
2. Should an organization adopt a uniform hierarchy of penalties for all offenses? Discuss.
3. "You can't discipline employees today the way you could a generation ago." Do you agree or disagree? Discuss.

4. What should be the rights of an employee who has been charged with a rules violation by his or her supervisor?

5. Two shipping clerks report back to their jobs following lunch, heavily intoxicated. One has been employed for three months and is under the usual six-month probation that all new employees undergo. The other has been with the company for sixteen years, is a good worker, and except for a two-day suspension for telling off his old boss a few years ago, has a spotless record. As their supervisor, what would you do?

CONTINUING CASE: Concord General

Flaunting the Ware

Last Thursday during the 11:00 P.M. to 7:00 A.M. shift, security officers responded to a complaint regarding unusual noises coming from the blood laboratory. When they arrived and entered the lab, they found a doctor and a nurse making love. Requesting that both get dressed immediately, the security officers told both individuals that a report would be submitted to Mr. Michaels in the morning.

When John Michaels got to his office later that morning and read the report, he was furious. "I run a hospital here, not a love den," he told his secretary. "Get me the chief of surgery and the vice-president of nursing immediately."

When these two administrators arrived in John's office, they suspected what he wanted. The rumors throughout the hospital about Dr. Tate and Nurse Crabits had been quite rampant. Before either of the two administrators had a chance to even greet John Michaels, he just waved the officers' report in front of them and said, "Do something about this, NOW!!!"

The chief of surgery was not at a loss as to how to handle the incident. Dr. Tate had been reported twice before for his nighttime extracurricular activities with nurses. In each case he had counseled Dr. Tate, explaining that what he did away from the job was his own business, but that in the hospital this type of action was both unacceptable and deplorable: "Just because you are one of the best gastrointestinal surgeons in the state, Chester," said the chief of surgery, "we are not going to put up with this kind of behavior. I have warned you before that this was not acceptable, and if it happens in the hospital again, you are finished. Leave the nurses alone."

Dr. Tate apologized to his boss and to John Michaels and left for the day.

Nurse Crabits was not as fortunate. She was cited for leaving her work unit and for actions unbecoming a professional nurse: "I am sorry, Susan," said the vice-president of nursing, but I cannot tolerate this behavior. You knew what you were doing, and because of that I have no recourse other than to dismiss you. You have given the nursing profession a bad name. Imagine two married people carrying on like that! Adultery is not what we consider to be consistent with professionalism. Please get out of my sight—you disgust me!"

Susan cleaned out her locker, said goodbye to a few friends, and went home.

Questions

1. Was the discipline administered in this case fair, equitable, and consistent? Why or why not?
2. If Nurse Crabits or Dr. Tate filed a complaint about the discipline received, how could the discipline be justified by the vice-president of nursing? By the chief of surgery?
3. If you had to make the decision regarding disciplining either Dr. Tate or Nurse Crabits, what action would you take?
4. Identify any discrepancies regarding the discussion between the chief of surgery and Dr. Tate and between the vice-president of nursing and Nurse Crabits and the discipline process proposed in your text.

CASE APPLICATION

You Know the Rules, Brenda!

"But Ms. Gilbert, this just isn't fair! I'm away from the conveyor belt for five minutes and you're going to suspend me for two weeks? Aw, come on, Ms. Gilbert."

"Listen," replied Nancy Gilbert, "you know the rules, Brenda! No one is allowed to leave their work station without permission from their supervisor. I'm your supervisor and you left your job without permission. And don't give me that 'five minute' crap! I glanced at my watch when you left—it was 10:20. You came back at 10:40!"

"That's not right, Ms. Gilbert," retorted Brenda. "I had to check with my daughter's nursery school. She's been sick for the past few days. I was away less than five minutes. Hell, everyone around here leaves their jobs for a few minutes without getting permission. This just isn't fair. I've been here for two years and I know I didn't do anything wrong!"

"Look, Brenda. That's the whole problem around here. I may have only been a supervisor for a few months, but I'm not stupid. People around here get away with murder. You break the rules and your boss looks the other way. Well, no more! We're going to shape up this department!"

"But why me, Ms. Gilbert? You know how I need this job. I just can't afford two weeks without pay," explained Brenda.

"Well, that's too bad. You should have thought about that before you broke the rule. No, Brenda. You knew the rules around here. You left your work station without permission. The suspension stands."

Questions

1. Has Nancy Gilbert treated Brenda fairly?
2. Contrast Gilbert's disciplinary action with the "hot stove" rules.
3. How would you have handled this situation?

ADDITIONAL READINGS

BELCHAV, JAMES A., "A Comparative View of Employee Disciplinary Practices," *Public Personnel Management*, 14, No. 13 (Fall 1985), 245–51.

Bureau of National Affairs, "Erosion of Employment-at-Will Doctrine Seen Decreasing Employer Protections," *White Collar Report*, 59, No. 17 (April 30, 1986), 424–25.

CONDON, THOMAS J., and RICHARD H. WOLFF, "Procedures That Safeguard Your Right to Fire," *Harvard Business Review*, November-December 1985, pp. 16–19.

MATEJKA, J. KENNETH, D. NEIL ASHWORTH, and DIANE DODD-McCUE, "Managing Difficult Employees: Challenge or Curse?" *Personnel*, 63, No. 7 (July 1986), 43–46.

PULICH, MARCIA ANN, "What to Do with Incompetent Employees," *Supervisory Mangement*, 31, No. 3 (March 1986), 10–16.

CHAPTER 19

Safety

and Health

AFTER READING THIS CHAPTER, YOU WILL BE ABLE TO:

1. Describe the Occupational Safety and Health Act (OSHA)
2. Discuss OSHA's impact on organizations
3. Explain the leading causes of safety and health accidents
4. Discuss accident prevention measures
5. Explain what determines whether an organization will have formal medical and health facilities
6. Discuss alcoholism and drug abuse
7. Identify the trends in employee health care
8. Define *stress*
9. Identify the causes of stress and explain its symptoms
10. Define *burnout*
11. Explain what causes burnout
12. Describe the results of burnout
13. Discuss how to reduce burnout
14. Discuss how organizations are dealing with burnout

Even hypochondriacs can get sick.

—*S. P. R.*

Management has a responsibility to ensure that the workplace is free from unnecessary hazards and that conditions surrounding the workplace are not hazardous to employees' physical or mental health. Of course, accidents can and do occur on many jobs, and the severity of these may astound you. There are approximately 20 million work-related injuries each year, 390,000 work-related illnesses, and 100,000 work-related deaths.[1] These numbers have an even greater impact when you consider that 48,380 individuals died a violent death in 1983 as a result of a crime,[2] or that 47,318 individuals were killed in combat during the entire Vietnam War period, 1959–83.[3] So, while it may sound heartless, all employers are concerned about employees' health and safety if for no other reason than accidents cost money. However, from a moral standpoint, employers have an obligation to maintain a workplace that will facilitate the operation of the work tasks employees are assigned and will minimize any negative aspects of situations affecting the employees' health and safety.

From the turn of the century through the late 1960s, remarkable progress was made in reducing the rate and severity of job-related accidents and diseases. Yet the most significant piece of federal legislation in the area of employee health and safety was not enacted until 1970.

The Occupational Safety and Health Act

OSHA Any discussion of employee health and safety is clearly different today from what it would have been thirty years ago. The passage of the

[1]Barry S. Levy and David H. Wegman, eds., *Occupational Health* (Boston: Little, Brown, 1983), p. 10.

[2]*Reader's Digest 1985 Almanac and Yearbook* (New York: Reader's Digest Association, 1985), p. 464.

[3]Bureau of the Census, *National Data Book and Guide: Statistical Abstracts of the United States*, 105th ed. (Washington, D.C., 1985), p. 342.

Occupational Safety and Health Act (OSHA) in 1970 dramatically changed the role that management must play in ensuring that the physical working conditions meet adequate standards. What the Civil Rights Act did to alter the organization's commitment to affirmative action OSHA has done to alter the organization's health and safety programs.

The OSHA legislation established comprehensive and specific health standards, authorized inspections to ensure the standards are met, empowered the Occupational Safety and Health administration to police the organization's compliance, and required employers to keep records of illness and injuries and to calculate accident ratios. The act applies to almost every business engaged in interstate commerce, which means that five million workplaces employing approximately 64 million workers are covered. Those organizations not meeting the interstate commerce criteria are covered by state occupational safety and health laws.

The safety and health standards OSHA established are incredibly extensive, complex, and in some cases contradictory. Standards exist for such diverse conditions as noise levels, air impurities, physical protection equipment, the height of toilet partitions, and the correct size of ladders. The initial standards consumed 350 pages in the *Federal Register*, and some of the annual revisions and interpretations have exceeded 500 pages. Yet, in spite of such volume, employers are responsible for knowing these standards and ensuring that those that do apply to them are followed.

Enforcement

Enforcement procedures of the OSHA standards vary depending on the nature of the event and the organization. Typically, the Occupational Safety and Health administration enforces the standards based on a five-item priority listing. These are, in descending priority: imminent danger; serious accidents that have occurred within the past forty-eight hours; a current employee complaint; inspections of target industries with a high injury ratio; and, finally, random inspections.

Imminent danger

Imminent danger refers to a condition where an accident is about to occur. Although this is given top priority and acts as a preventive measure, imminent danger situations are hard to define. In fact, in some cases, the definition of imminent danger appears to be an accident in progress. Interpretation leaves much to the imagination. For example, a leading OSHA union-management liaison described the following situation of imminent danger. Suppose you were leaving school and, on the way to your dormitory, someone stopped you, put a gun to your head, and demanded your money: Are you in imminent danger? No, according to one interpretation of imminent danger, not until the trigger is pulled and the bullet is rifling through the barrel are you in imminent danger. By that time it is obviously too late, and as some individuals claim, this gives rise to priority two—accidents that have led to serious injuries or death.

Catastrophes

Under the law, an organization must report these *serious accidents* to the Occupational Safety and Health Administration field office within forty-eight hours of their occurrence. This permits the investigators to review the scene and try to determine the cause of the accident. Unfortunately, many disasters have occurred (see Figure 19-1), and in each case, OSHA officials responded. Some of the more notable cases have been coal mine disasters and construction accidents.

Employee complaints

The third priority item, and one that many managers are concerned about, is *employee complaints.* If an employee sees a violation of the OSHA standards, that employee has the right to call OSHA and have it respond. During this time the worker can refuse to work on the item in question until OSHA has investigated the complaint. This is especially true when there is a union present. In some union contracts, workers may legally refuse to work if conditions are below standard and they may stay off the job with pay until OSHA arrives and either finds the complaint invalid or cites the company and mandates compliance.

Targeted inspections

The next priority for enforcement is the *inspection of targeted industries.* Earlier we stated that more than five million workplaces are covered under OSHA. To investigate each would require several hundred thousand full-time inspectors. However, OSHA only employs about eleven hundred inspectors. So in order to have the largest impact, OSHA began to direct its attention to those industries with the highest injury rates: roofing and sheet metal, meat processing, lumber and wood products, mobile homes and campers, and stevedoring.

Random inspections

The final item is *random inspection.* Originally, OSHA inspectors were authorized to enter any work area premise, without notice, to ensure that the workplace was in compliance. In 1978, however, the

FIGURE 19-1

Workers Killed or Disabled on the Job, 1980–84   (000s)

	TOTAL	MANUFACTURING	NON-MANUFACTURING
1980	13.2	1.7	11.5
1981	12.4	1.5	10.9
1982	11.5	1.1	10.4
1983	11.2	1.2	10.0
1984	11.3	1.2	10.1

SOURCE: *Statistical Abstracts of the U.S., 1986,* 106th ed. (U.S. Department of Commerce, Bureau of the Census), p. 425.

Supreme Court ruled in *Marshall* v. *Barlow's Inc.* that employers do not have to let OSHA inspectors enter their premises unless the inspectors have search warrants. This decision, while not destroying OSHA's ability to conduct inspections, forces inspectors to justify their choice of inspection sites more rigorously. That is, rather than trying to oversee health and safety standards in all of their jurisdictions, OSHA inspectors find it easier to justify their actions and obtain search warrants if they appear to be pursuing specific problem areas.

Fines

Maximum fine An OSHA inspector has the right to levy a fine against an organization for noncompliance. While levying the fine is more complicated than described here, if an organization does not bring into compliance a "red-flagged" item, it can be assessed up to a maximum of $10,000 per day per violation. Refusing to come into compliance could prove costly. However, the maximum fine is rarely levied, and if levied, there are loopholes enabling the organization to circumvent the standard. Once a fine has been levied, if the organization files an appeal, the fine does not increase daily. Thus a $10,000 fine, if appealed, could take five years to be adjudicated. Meanwhile the infraction continues. However, where a union exists, this may not be beneficial, for as we discussed earlier, the workers can remain off the job with pay. Finally, note that most organizations are safety conscious and make every attempt to ensure compliance.

To comply with OSHA standards, many large organizations have had to undertake extensive efforts at a cost of millions of dollars. However, the impact has been even greater on small businesses, which are less able to financially absorb the costs involved. A number have argued that if they have to meet the letter of the law, they will be driven out of business. In contrast, unions have argued that enforcement efforts have not been extensive enough. They cite thousands of examples of firms that have not yet complied with OSHA's standards and have not been penalized for this neglect. Finally, OSHA itself has had to adjust as the transition is made from stipulations of the law to operationalizing the intent of the law. Hundreds of OSHA standards have had to be modified because many businesses complained that they could not understand the highly complex and technical rules. Standards have also been expanded to give greater emphasis to health issues, which during the first four years took a back seat to safety issues. Meanwhile OSHA is attempting to meet its objectives while being attacked by a vocal minority who believe that many of the standards are unnecessary and argue that the costs exceed the benefits.

Has OSHA worked? The answer is a qualified yes. In fact, OSHA has had a direct and significant impact on almost every business or-

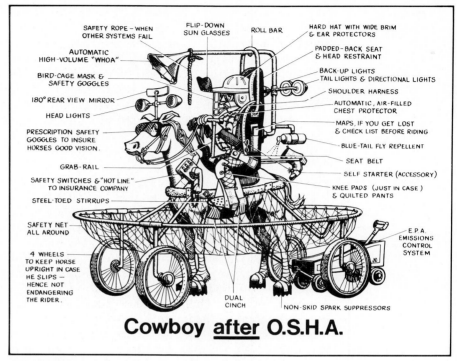

FIGURE 19-2

SOURCE: James N. Devin, Independence, Mo. Reprinted by permission of the author.

ganization in the United States. In some of the largest organizations, an additional administrator has been created who is solely responsible for safety.

The impact of OSHA standards has made organizations more aware of health and safety. The standards may have been initially extreme in their specificity, but that has been changing. Modifications in recent years have made them more realistic.

The preceding information suggests that OSHA has been effective at cutting on-the-job injuries and illnesses, but not without high costs for both business firms (in their efforts to conform to OSHA standards) and government (in its efforts to enforce the standards).

Trends for OSHA

While OSHA has been effective in reducing health and safety problems in organizations, there have been complaints from organizations that OSHA was not needed. Instead each organization should police itself in providing an environment that is conducive to productive work. This self-service method came to fruition in 1981.[4]

Although there are opponents to this new approach, this concept has generally been accepted. Placing health and safety responsibilities on joint labor-management teams would serve as a means of increasing worker participation while attacking those areas that appear to be hazardous.

This new decentralized approach is a means of expanding health and safety consciousness, but OSHA would still be investigating problem areas. However, with more in-house programs, this will give OSHA inspectors more opportunity to address more problematic health issues, such as the long-term health effects of chemicals (e.g., asbestos) in the workplace.

Safety Programs

Safety programs
Managers are not exempt from acting within the law. As a result, they must ensure that the physical working conditions in their organizations meet the minimum standards of the law. Specifically, this includes OSHA's standards, plus all state and community requirements that may exist. On close examination we find that a vast number of organizations go considerably beyond the minimum standards of the law.

If businesses are concerned with efficiency and profits, you may ask, why would they spend money to create conditions that exceed those required by law? The answer is the profit motive itself. The cost of accidents can be, and for many organizations is, a substantial additional cost of doing business.

The direct cost of an accident to an employer shows itself in the organization's worker's compensation premium. This cost, as noted in the preceding chapter, is determined by the insured's accident history. Indirect costs, which generally far exceed direct costs, must also be borne by the employer. These include wages paid for time lost due to injury, damage to equipment and materials, personnel to investigate and report on accidents, and lost production due to work stoppages and personnel changeover. The impact of these indirect costs can be seen from statistics that describe the costs of accidents for American industry as a whole.[5] In 1983, worker's compensation cost employers approximately $18 billion. Accidents additionally cost employers billions in wages and lost production. The significance of this latter fig-

[4]"OSHA's Controversial Do-It-Yourself Approach," *Business Week*, July 19, 1982, p. 60.

[5]Statistical Abstracts of the U.S., 1986, 106 ed. (U.S. Department of Commerce, Bureau of the Census), p. 375.

ure is emphasized when we note that this cost is approximately ten times greater than losses caused by strikes, an issue that has historically received much more public attention.

Causes of Accidents

Causes of accidents

The cause of an accident can be generally classified as either human or environmental. Human causes are directly attributable to human error brought about by carelessness, intoxication, daydreaming, inability to do the job, or other human deficiency. Environmental causes, in contrast, are attributable to the workplace and include the tools, equipment, physical plant, and general work environment. Both these sources are important, but in terms of numbers, the human factor is responsible for the vast majority of accidents. No matter how much effort is made to create a work environment that is accident free, a low accident rate record can only be achieved by concentrating on the human element.

One of the main objectives of safety engineers is to scrutinize the work environment to locate sources of potential accidents. In addition to looking for such obvious factors as loose steps, oil on the walkways, or a sharp protrusion on a piece of equipment at eye level, they will seek those that are less obvious. Standards established by OSHA provide an excellent reference to guide the search for potential hazards.

As we noted, human deficiencies are the predominant cause of accidents. This may be due to irresponsible behavior by the employee, physiological deficiencies, or both.

Preventive Measures

What traditional measures can we look to for preventing accidents? The answer lies in education, skill training, engineering, protection devices, and regulation enforcement.

Education

Education.   To induce people to "think safety," it is necessary to create safety awareness. That is the objective of safety education. Popular methods for creating safety awareness include exhibiting easily visible signs that proclaim safety slogans; placing articles on accident prevention in organization newsletters; or, a technique popular in manufacturing facilities, exhibiting a sign proclaiming "This plant has operated for xx days without a lost-day accident."

Skill training

Skill Training.   When employees undergo training (see Chapter 10), safety issues and preventive techniques should be discussed. Incorporating accident prevention measures into the learning process, rather than at some later date, makes them a natural part of the job activity. If putting on safety goggles is described as the step that always precedes turning on the machine, we have integrated safety measures into the job itself.

Engineering

Engineering. It is possible to utilize engineering methods to prevent accidents through both the design of the equipment and the design of the jobs themselves. When equipment is being ordered, the type that will best minimize accident rates should be selected. For example, because of the layout of traffic patterns within the working facility, we can have particular features of the machine redesigned so as not to cause a hazard to people walking by. Or if the plant is old and the lighting poor, specific lighting features may be designed into the machine in order to make the operation safer. Equipment design can also consider those elements about the process that can reduce operator fatigue, boredom, and daydreaming—all factors that can increase accident rates.

Engineering can also consider the worker-machine interplay in the design of jobs. Whether the operators stand or sit, and their position relative to the control devices that they must monitor, are examples of factors that affect the amount of stooping, twisting, tension, and so forth—factors that can and do increase accident rates.

Protection

Protection. People should of course be provided with protective equipment where necessary. Safety shoes, gloves, hard hats, safety glasses, and noise mufflers are some of the more popular protective devices that organizations may require their employees to wear. But protection is not limited to the employees. Protection of machinery, too, can pay dividends in fewer accidents. Obviously, preventive maintenance of machinery can avoid fires, explosions, and oil leakages.

Regulation enforcement

Regulation Enforcement. The best rules and regulations will not be effective in reducing accidents if they are not enforced. Management must ensure that people do not smoke in "No Smoking" areas, that people not operating machines stay behind demarcated safety lines that encircle the work area, and that safety helmets are always worn in the plant if that is the rule of the land. If not enforced, the employer may be liable for any injuries that occur.

Inspection of Work Surroundings

The only way management can be assured that rules and regulations are being enforced is to develop some type of feedback system. This can be provided by inspection of the work surroundings.

Management can rely on oral or written reports for information on enforcement. Another approach is to get firsthand information by periodically walking through the work areas to make observations. Ideally, managers will rely on reports from supervisors on the floor, supported by their own personal observations.

Health Programs

Health programs Almost all large organizations and many small ones provide a medical unit to service the needs of employees. These units are available to deal with illnesses or injuries incurred by workers on the job. Additionally, they often provide physical examinations for new employees; and they work closely with those directly responsible for safety in the organization, for example the safety director, to advise of potential work-related hazards.

Whether or not an organization has medical and health facilities, and the extent to which they are offered, can usually be determined by the number of workers the organization employs and the type of work involved. The larger the organization, the greater the probability that such facilities will be needed. The greater the job-related hazards, the greater the need for facilities. The headquarters of a large multi-branch bank, for example, while often employing several thousand employees, usually has a minimum medical unit—possibly only one full-time nurse. In contrast, a mining operation, with the same number of employees, might require two full-time doctors, four full-time nurses, and a physical facility looking very much like a small hospital.

In addition to the provision of physical health programs, increasing attention is being directed to psychological problems. Two of the most widespread are alcoholism and drug abuse. Because the abuse of alcohol and drugs is seldom restricted to an employee's off-the-job activities, these problems require management's attention and action.

Alcoholism

Alcoholism Alcoholism is the nation's fourth largest health problem—after cancer, heart disease, and mental illness. It is estimated that there are approximately 10 million alcoholics in the United States, that is, individuals whose addiction to alcohol causes chronic incapacitation. Approximately one-half of these alcoholics are employed in some type of

FIGURE 19-3

SOURCE: The Wizard of Id, by permission of Johnny Hart and Field Enterprises, Inc.

work capacity.[6] The National Council on Alcoholism estimates that alcoholic employees in the United States cost industry billions of dollars a year. This sum is calculated by including reduction in employee productivity, increased absenteeism, more on-the-job accidents, and higher health-care costs. These activities, taken in the aggregate, cost industry almost $20 billion annually.[7] Even though the costs are high, identifying employees and helping them is not easy. Why?

Two myths about alcoholic employees persist. The first is that they are predominantly blue-collar and low-skilled workers. The second is that it is easy to spot the alcoholic on the job.

In fact, alcoholics are distributed in proportion to employment groups in the work force. Professional, managerial, and white-collar employees are about as likely as those in blue-collar and operative jobs to be alcoholics.[8] So the problem of alcoholism has ramifications for all levels in the organization. The risk of losing managerial and professional employees through alcoholism is equal to the risk of losing workers in the lower ranks.

It is often believed that alcoholics are easy to spot. This is rarely the case. Why? Because the symptoms resemble other problems. Also, alcoholism follows growth stages. In the early development stage, symptoms are almost nonexistent. Corrective efforts of a preventive nature can be used at this point. In the second, or disruptive, stage, the symptoms become visible, and early detection can prevent alcoholism from developing further. The third stage is fully developed alcoholism. Here, intensive treatment will be required to cure addiction.

What can management do to deal with the problem? The answer lies in awareness and an action-oriented program to deal with each stage of affliction.

Alcoholism is an illness, and employees with the problem should be treated as they would be for any other illness. Management must educate supervisory personnel to detect the early signs of the disease and train them to counsel employees. Employees already in the second or third stage may have to be referred to a rehabilitation program. More than twelve hundred organizations now have in-house alcoholism programs. These include such firms as the Bank of America, CBS, DuPont, Eastman Kodak, General Motors, Inland Steel, and Illinois Bell.[9]

Do these rehabilitation programs work? Their success record is good. Precise data are not available, but estimates of successes rates

[6]Gopal C. Pati and John I. Adkins, Jr., "The Employer's Role in Alcoholism Assistance," *Personnel Journal*, July 1983, p. 659.

[7]*Personnel Management: Policy and Practices* (Englewood Cliffs, N.J.: Prentice-Hall, 1982), p. 257.

[8]Ibid.

[9]Pati and Adkins, "Employer's Role," p. 569.

range from 65 to 85 percent.[10] But what can management do about the other 15 to 35 percent, or those who refuse to participate in rehabilitation programs? The organization has an obligation to be supportive of employees as long as they are cooperative in trying to beat alcoholism. If an employee fails to cooperate, the disciplinary process should be followed. This includes the use of suspensions and discharge.

Drug Abuse

Drug abuse

Alcoholism and drug abuse are often seen as similar problems. Both cause increased absenteeism and accident rates. While they do have commonalities, they also have some important differences. First, alcohol can be legally obtained while drugs are frequently illegal. Drug abuse, therefore, may mean involvement with law enforcement agencies. Also, detection of drug abusers is complicated because of possession and use laws, which encourage secrecy. Second, society is more tolerant of alcohol abuse than drug abuse. We tend to be more sympathetic to the alcoholic than to the drug abuser, although both are suffering from an illness. Alcoholism is a problem that is most widespread among employees in their forties and fifties, while drug abuse is most prevalent among employees under thirty years of age. Finally, drug abuse is more likely to be accompanied by theft than is alcoholism, because users need to raise money to buy drugs.

Employers should generally pursue the same road with the employee who suffers from drug abuse problems as they would with the alcoholic, with the following modifications. First, careful selection can increase the likelihood that drug abusers can be detected and screened out. Second, detection among employees will require closer scrutiny because individuals are more likely to hide their drug habit. Supervisors should be particularly knowledgeable of drug paraphernalia so they can be on the lookout for it. Lastly, organizations may want to establish more severe discipline for the drug abuser. This can be justified alone on illegality of many popularly abused drugs such as marijuana, heroin, and cocaine.

Trends in Health Programs

Companies have found that providing health programs can be rewarding. Besides programs that deal with alcohol and drug abuse, organizations have been implementing fitness centers, providing health club memberships, and sponsoring in-house sports programs. Programs

[10]*Personnel Management: Policy and Practices*, p. 257.

such as these not only increase worker morale but drastically reduce health insurance claims.[11]

Many of the progressive companies implementing the programs are doing so to make the employees more aware of their health. These organizations realize that they have made an investment in their employees and desire to continue their efforts to protect their investment. Certainly there are costs associated with health programs, but the increase in productivity and the reduction in human error accidents have outweighed the costs. In one organization, these programs have saved roughly $26 million. To make that much in net sales, the organization would have to increase its sales by approximately $500 million.[12]

The following programs appear to be most successful for the continuing health of employees: the cessation of smoking; the detection and control of high blood pressure; the control of lipid levels, such as cholesterol and triglyceride; weight control and fitness; and stress management.[13] This last topic, stress management, has become increasingly important because of the burnout issue. In the next section, we will focus on stress and on how it may lead to burnout.

What is Stress?

Stress defined   *Stress* is a dynamic condition in which an individual is confronted with an opportunity, constraint, or demand, related to what he or she desires, and for which the outcome is perceived to be both uncertain and important.[14] This definition is complicated, so let us look at it more closely.

Stress can manifest itself in both a positive and a negative way. Stress is said to be positive when the situation offers an opportunity for one to gain something. The "psyching-up" that an athlete goes through can be stressful, but this can lead to maximum performance. It is when constraints of demands are placed on us that stress can become negative. Let us explore those two features—constraints and demands.

Constraints are things that keep us from doing what we desire. Purchasing a new car may be your desire, but if you cannot afford $11,000 for a car, you are constrained from purchasing it. Accordingly, constraints inhibit us in ways that take control of the situation out of

---

[11]"Employers Try In-House Fitness Centers to Lift Morale, Cut Cost of Health Claims," *Wall Street Journal*, November 10, 1981, p. 25.

[12]"When Accidents Don't Happen," *Fortune*, September 6, 1982, p. 68.

[13]Andrew J. J. Brennan, "Worksite Health Promotion Can Be Cost-Effective," *Personnel Administrator*, April 1983, p. 39.

[14]Adapted from Randall S. Schuler, "Definition and Conceptualization of Stress in Organizations," *Organizational Behavior and Human Performance*, April 1980, p. 189.

our hands. If you cannot afford the car, you cannot get it. *Demands,* on the other hand, cause us to lose something we desire. If we desire to attend a fabulous party on campus Wednesday night but have a major examination Thursday morning, the examination may take precedence. Thus demands preoccupy our time and force us to shift priorities.

Constraints and demands can lead to potential stress. When they are coupled with uncertainty of the outcome and importance of the outcome, potential stress becomes actual stress.[15] Regardless of the situation, if you remove the uncertainty or the importance, you remove stress. For instance, you may have been constrained from purchasing the car because of your budget, but if you know you will get one for graduating from college, the uncertainty element is significantly reduced. Accordingly, if you are auditing a class, for no grade, the importance of the major examination is also reduced. However, when constraints or demands have an impact on an important event and the outcome is unknown, pressure is added—pressure resulting in stress.

Causes of Stress

Causes of stress

Stress can be caused by a number of factors called *stressors.* These stressors can be grouped into two major categories—personal factors and organizational factors. Both of these areas directly affect the person and, ultimately, the job. For that reason, we will postpone our discussion of organizational factors and cover them in the "burnout" section of this chapter. However, because personal factors affect and are affected by organizational factors, we will address them now.

Almost anything can cause stress for an individual. We all have our levels of resistance, but once the stressors become too great, we exhibit some different behavior. The main fact to remember about stress from personal factors is that the good can cause as much stress as the bad. Certainly we all know that the death of a family member, a divorce, or being fired from work can cause undue stress, but so can the birth of a child, getting married, or landing that new job. For example, remember the time you finally got that date with the person of your dreams? A happy time? Yes. But what did you go through to get ready for it? You debated over what clothes to wear, where to go, whether you looked good, and so on. You were nervous when you finally arrived to get your date, or when the doorbell rang and your date arrived. At the end it was such a good time, but this good time caused you a lot of stress.

If we are under stress, we can exhibit one or more of three symptoms: physiological, psychological, or behavioral.[16]

---

[15]Ibid., p. 191.
[16]Ibid., pp. 200–205.

Symptoms of Stress

Because stress can show itself in many ways, it is important for us to recognize how stress can be identified.

Physiological symptoms
Physiological Symptoms.   This type of stress is difficult to detect with the naked eye. It relates to the medical changes that can occur internally in the individual. Such changes as increased heart and breath rates, higher blood pressure, headaches, and heart attacks can be brought on by stress but are not easy for us to spot early. Accordingly, they become less important for us with respect to helping individuals change their actions.

Psychological symptoms
Psychological Symptoms.   This type of stress can cause harm in an organization because it leads to significant dissatisfaction with the job. This symptom manifests itself as tension, anxiety, irritability, boredom, and procrastination.

Behavioral symptoms
Behavioral symptoms.   This type of stress has the greatest impact on the organization. It produces productivity changes, absenteeism, turnover, and increased smoking and alcohol consumption.

If you are in an organization where these symptoms are evident, there may be some action you can take to help reduce these levels. For personal factors, we can try to get people to recognize the need for assistance and provide that assistance for them. This may include special programs such as stress management or sponsoring physical activities. Whatever is chosen, the emphasis on the result should be the same—try to keep the employees healthy.

Let us now consider the more specific organizational effects of stress—burnout.

What is Burnout?

Burnout defined
Between 1974 and 1982, forty-eight attempts were made to define burnout.[17] While each of these attempts focused on a specific aspect of burnout, it was not until 1982 that a coalesced definition appeared. This definition views burnout as a function of three concerns: "chronic emotional stress with (a) emotional and/or physical exhaustion, (b) lowered job productivity, and (c) overdepersonalization."[18] Note that none of the three concerns include long-term boredom. While this is often referred to as burnout, it is not. Let us look at these three concerns in more depth.

Emotional and/or physical exhaustion is an inner condition caused by various personal and organizational factors. Personal fac-

[17]Baron Perlman and E. Alan Hartman, "Burnout: Summary and Future Research," *Human Relations*, 35, No. 4 (1982), 284–92.

[18]Ibid., p. 293.

tors, such as marital, legal, or financial problems, may become so paramount in a worker's life that he or she tends to give up. As these problems become manifest, the worker begins to feel even more helpless and loses sight of reality, resulting in a change of behavior. Emotional exhaustion can also manifest itself when workers who are in the business of dealing with other people lose their ability to be at peak performance in dealing with others.[19] When this results, they begin to feel inadequate in handling various situations and ultimately change their behavior. Physical exhaustion, on the other hand, speaks for itself. When high energy is needed but lacking, performance will be affected. Think of the professional boxer who, in order to get a title shot, schedules one fight after another. This physical torture, whether the fighter wins or not, may take its toll and affect the final goal.

Lowered job productivity can be a cause and a result. As a cause, it becomes demeaning. Workers generally like to produce. When workers keep busy, they find they can achieve positive results—salary increases, recognition, advancement—and the time spent at work seems shorter. The adage that productive workers are happy workers has an impact, as workers are motivated by the challenge. However, as constraints and demands emerge and lower this productivity, problems occur. These constraints and demands impinge on the workers' welfare, making them less productive, less happy, and, ultimately, less motivated.

The final concern is overdepersonalization. After years of technological advancements, we are finding that by dehumanizing jobs we are causing an undue hardship on the remaining workers. This automation, coupled with many rules and regulations and lack of interpersonal relationships, has led to the early burnout of workers.

Causes of Burnout

Causes of burnout   While there have been many attempts to define burnout, there have also been an equal number of attempts to determine the cause of such occurrences. Generally, the factors contributing to burnout can be identified as follows: organization characteristics, perceptions of organization, perceptions of role, individual characteristics, and outcome.[20] Figure 19-4 summarizes these variables.

While these variables can lead to burnout, their presence does not guarantee that burnout will occur. Much of that outcome is contingent on the individual's capability to work under and handle stress. Because of this contingency, stressful conditions result in a two-phased outcome—the first level being the stress itself, and the second level

---

[19]Christina Maslach and Susan E. Jackson, "The Measurement of Burnout," *Journal of Occupational Behavior*, 2 (1981), 99.

[20]Perlman and Hartman, "Burnout," p. 294.

FIGURE 19-4

Variables Found to be Significantly Related to Burnout

ORGANIZATION CHARACTER- ISTICS	PERCEPTIONS OF ORGANIZATION	PERCEPTIONS OF ROLE	INDIVIDUAL CHARACTER- ISTICS	OUTCOME
Caseload	Leadership	Autonomy	Family/friends support	Satisfaction
Formalization	Communication	Job involvement	Sex	Turnover
Turnover rate	Staff support	Being supervised	Age	
Staff size	Peers	Work pressure	Tenure	
	Clarity	Feedback	Ego level	
	Rules and procedures	Accomplishment		
	Innovation	Meaningfulness		
	Administrative support			

SOURCE: Baron Perlman and E. Alan Hartman, "Burnout: Summary and Future Research," *Human Relations*, 25, No. 4 (1982), 294. Reprinted by permission of Plenum Publishing Corporation.

being the problems that arise from the manifestation of this stress.[21] Figure 19-5 contains a schematic representation of this two-phase stress outcome.

Symptoms of Burnout

Symptoms of burnout

Once stress has reached the second phase of the continuum, severe changes begin to appear in the individual. These changes can occur in the worker's health, attitude, emotions, or relations with others; or the changes can result in excessive behaviors.[22] Figure 19-6 summarizes these burnout indicators.

Summary of Burnout and Its Causes

Burnout by workers is costing U.S. industry billions of dollars. One estimate revealed that more than $77 billion is lost each year due to burnout and its related implications.[23] But putting a finger on the cause is like plugging the hole in the dam with your thumb. Burnout is a multifacted phenomenon, the byproduct of both personal variables and organizational variables.

[21]Donald F. Parker and Thomas A. DeCotiis, "Organizational Determinants of Job Stress," *Organizational Behavior and Human Performance*, 32 (1983), 166.

[22]Whiton Stewart Paine, ed. *Job Stress and Burnout*, (Beverly Hills, Calif.: Sage Publications, 1982), p. 44.

[23]"Study Shows Firms Lose $77 Billion Yearly to Stress," *San Diego Union*, May 24, 1982, p. C-11.

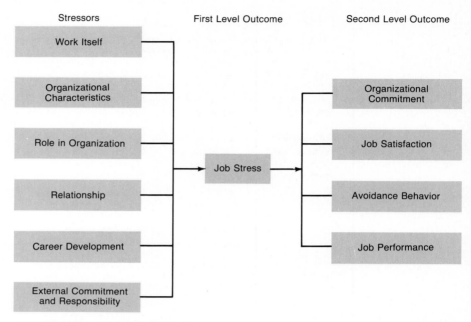

FIGURE 19-5   A Model of Job Stress

SOURCE: Donald F. Parker and Thomas A. Decotiis, "Organizational Determinants of Job Stress," *Organizational Behavior and Human Performance*, 32 (1983), p. 166. Reprinted by permission.

Many of these causes and their indicators are recapitulated in Figure 19-7.

Reducing Burnout

Realizing that stress is a fact of life and must be channeled properly, organizations must establish procedures for reducing these stress levels before workers burn out. Although no clear-cut remedies are available, four techniques have been proposed:

Identification
1. *Identification:* techniques for the analysis of the incidence, prevalence, and characteristics of burnout in individuals, work groups, subunits, or organizations

Prevention
2. *Prevention:* attempts to prevent the burnout process before it begins

Mediation
3. *Mediation:* procedures for slowing, halting, or reversing the burnout process

Remediation
4. *Remediation:* techniques for individuals who already burned out or are rapidly approaching the end stages of this process[24]

[24]Paine, *Job Stress,* p. 19.

FIGURE 19-6

Personal Indicators of Staff Burnout

HEALTH INDICATORS	EXCESSIVE BEHAVIOR INDICATORS	EMOTIONAL ADJUSTMENT INDICATORS	RELATIONSHIP INDICATORS	ATTITUDE INDICATORS	VALUE INDICATORS
Fatigue and chronic exhaustion	Increased consumption of caffeine, tobacco, alcohol, over-the-counter medications, psychoactive prescription drugs, illicit drugs	Emotional distancing	Isolation from or overbonding with other staff	Grandiosity	Sudden and often dramatic changes in values and beliefs
Frequent and prolonged colds		Paranoia	Responding to clients in mechanical manner	Boredom	
Headaches		Depression: loss of meaning, loss of hope		Cynicism	
Sleep disturbances: insomnia, nightmares, excessive sleeping	High-risk-taking behavior: auto/cycle accidents, falls, "high-risk" hobbies, general proneness to accidents and injuries, gambling, extreme mood and behavioral changes	Decreased emotional control	Increased isolation from clients	Sick humor—aimed particularly at clients	
Ulcers		Martyrdom	Increased expressions of anger and/or mistrust	Distrust of management, supervisors, peers	
Gastrointestinal disorders		Fear of "going crazy"	Increased interpersonal conflicts with other staff	Air of righteousness	
Sudden losses or gains in weight		Increased amount of time daydreaming/ fantasizing		Hypercritical attitude toward institution and/or peers	
Flare-ups of preexisting medical disorders: diabetes, high blood pressure, asthma, etc.	Increased propensity for violent and aggressive behavior	Constant feelings of being "trapped"	Increased problems in marital and other interpersonal relationships away from work, including relationships with one's children	Expressions of hopelessness, powerlessness, meaninglessness	
Injuries from high-risk behavior	Over-and undereating	Nervous ticks			
Muscular pain, particularly in lower back and neck	Hyperactivity	Undefined fears	Social isolation: overinvolvement with clients, using clients to meet personal and social needs		
Increased premenstrual tension		Inability to concentrate			
Missed menstrual cycles		Intellectualization			
		Increased anger			
		Increased tension			

SOURCE: Whiton Stewart Paine, ed., *Job Stress and Burnout* (Beverly Hills, Calif.: Sage Publications, © 1982), p. 44. Reprinted by permission of Sage Publications, Inc.

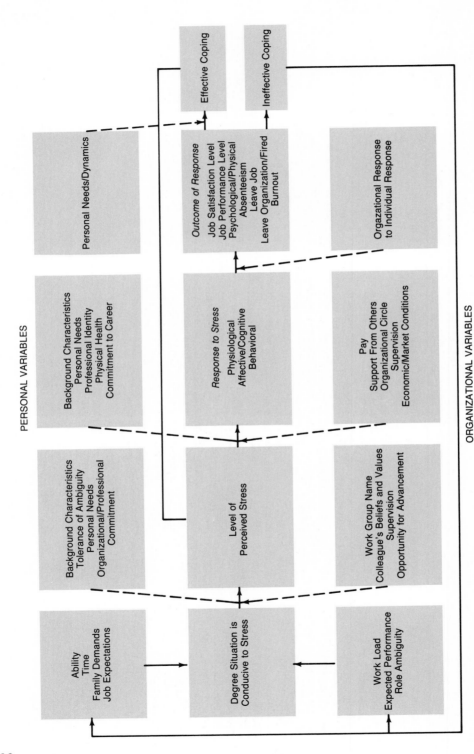

FIGURE 19-7   *Factors Causing Burnout*

SOURCE: Adapted from Baron Perlman and E. Alan Hartman, "Burnout: Summary and Future Research," *Human Relations*, 35, No. 4 (1982), 297. Reprinted by permission of Plenum Publishing Corporation.

FIGURE 19-8

Illustrative Burnout Interventions

Site Intervention	GOAL OF INTERVENTION			
	Identification	Prevention	Mediation	Remediation
Personal	Self-evaluation	⟷ Professional training/orientation	⟷ Stress management	⟷ Individual counseling
Interpersonal	Peer feedback	⟷ Support groups	⟷ Creative supervision	⟷ Group counseling
Workplace	Formal surveys	⟷ Professional development	⟷ Job redesign	⟷ Job/Career changes
Organizational	Performance monitoring	⟷ Organizational development	⟷ Quality assurance	⟷ Employee assistance

SOURCE: Whiton Stewart Paine, ed., *Job Stress and Burnout* (Beverly Hills, Calif.: Sage Publications, © 1982), p. 20. Reprinted by permission of Sage Publications, Inc.

These four techniques are then coupled with the four specific areas of concentration. These four areas focus on the individual, interpersonal relations, the workplace, and the organization.[25]

Matching these ideas, we can create a 4 × 4 matrix designed to specify which technique best fits which level. Figure 19-8 is a summary of that matrix.

The key point here is that accurate identification is made and then, and only then, is a program tailored to meet that need. However, keep in mind that the changes rarely concentrate on one factor. Chances are great that when you try to bring about change in one area, it will spill over and affect other areas. For example, any type of job redesign will surely affect the workers personally. Thus you cannot put all your efforts into job redesign and forget about the human element. New training programs may need to be developed and implemented to enable the changes to occur.

Summary

Because of the costs associated with burnout, many companies are implementing a full array of programs to help alleviate the problem. Many of these programs are designed to do two things: increase productivity and make the job more pleasant for the worker.

To achieve these ends, organizations are systematically studying each job in the organization in an effort to redefine the jobs in such a manner that if proper equipment and working conditions exist, a more productive work force will result. But to effect these changes requires

[25]Ibid., p. 20.

VIEWS IN THE NEWS

Burnout

The term "burnout" is quickly becoming part of an organization's vocabulary. The severe stress associated with burnout is causing great harm to workers and, too, to an organization's productivity. But burnout need not be totally associated with negative stressors in one's life. People's dreams and ambitions, and how they attempt to fulfill them, often cause many of the symptoms associated with burnout. "Burning Out in America: When Success Is Overwhelming" specifically addresses such a phenomenon. This article focuses on how our goals and achievements may be the leading causes of our stress. For example, the author identifies three "facts of life" that are "major causal factors of burnout":

1. The responsibilities of a solid middle-class lifestyle are exceptionally high.
2. These days, work is much more mental than physical.
3. The health link between mental and physical well-being is clearly established.

How these factors affect each of us differs, but those suffering from the effects of burnout usually exhibit the following symptoms:

1. You ask, Why am I doing this?
2. You have a bad case of the "Its."
3. You have a dragging, tired feeling.
4. You have a strong need to be left alone.
5. You use tremendous energy just to get up in the morning.
6. You watch television indiscriminately.
7. You don't enjoy leisure life these days.
8. You're not as emotionally close to others as you used to be.
9. You are experiencing physical symptoms of stress.
10. You feel out of control of your life.

If many of the above symptoms are present, the author found that four outcomes were probable:

1. You begin to job hop.
2. You retreat to a quiet, simple life.
3. You escape through alcoholism or drug abuse.
4. You leave your marriage.

But, as the author points out, all is not lost. Those suffering from the effects of burnout need to recognize what has caused the problems and turn it around. The author calls the approach to achieving this "lifestyle management." Lifestyle management includes

1. Making a commitment to oneself to reverse the obsession of work.
2. Make a commitment to oneself to define yourself from within.
3. Make a commitment to oneself to better personal health.

These behavioral changes are neither easy nor achievable overnight. But failure to do so could ultimately prove disastrous.

Source: Bruce A. Baldwin, "Burning Out in America: When Success Is Overwhelming," *Piedmont Airlines Magazine,* March 1985, pp. 12–15.

a concerted effort on the part of personnel. Personnel must ensure that the compensation for these redefined jobs is competitive and equitable. This entails a rewriting of job descriptions and a systematic process of job evaluation. Training must be a vital part of this process, helping the employees adapt to their new endeavors. We also find that employment concerns must be addressed. Good employees who may be displaced by the redesign should be given the first opportunity to retrain for other positions in the organization. If this is not possible, outplacement services should be offered.

Finally, programs available for employees to reduce their stress must be offered. These may include diet control programs, aerobic exercises, health screenings, smoking cessation, and assistance for the employee addicted to drugs or alcohol. It is these programs that are available in the more progressive companies. They recognize that stress exists in their jobs but deal with it proactively rather than reactively.

Conclusion

We have discussed many aspects of safety- and health-related issues. From OSHA to in-house programs to stress management, all are intended to make employees' work more enjoyable. By offering an environment that is conducive to productive work, many organizations are reaping the benefits and, simultaneously, the workers are being treated humanely.

SUMMARY

1. The Occupational Safety and Health Act (OSHA) outlines comprehensive and specific safety and health standards.
2. OSHA has had a profound impact on organizations, as they have had to bring their workplaces up to OSHA standards.
3. Human factors are the predominant causes of accidents.
4. Accident prevention measures include
   a. Education
   b. Skill training
   c. Engineering
   d. Protection
   e. Regulation enforcement

5. The extent to which an organization will have formal medical and health facilities is influenced by
   a. The number of employees
   b. The type of work that employees perform

6. Two health problems requiring management's attention and action are
   a. Alcoholism
   b. Drug abuse

7. Trends in health care reveal a tendency for organizations to offer in-house programs designed to make the employees less stressful and more productive.

8. Stress is a dynamic condition in which an individual is confronted with an opportunity, constraint, or demand:
   a. The outcome must be perceived as important and uncertain
   b. Stress can be positive or negative

9. Stress is caused by personal factors and organizational factors, and its symptoms are
   a. Physiological
   b. Psychological
   c. Behavioral

10. Burnout is a combination of
    a. Emotional and/or physical exhaustion
    b. Lowered job productivity
    c. Overdepersonalization

11. Burnout is caused by
    a. Organizational characteristics
    b. Perceptions of organization
    c. Perceptions of role
    d. Individual characteristics
    e. Outcome

12. Burnout can affect the following:
    a. Health
    b. Attitude
    c. Emotions
    d. Relations with others
    e. Behavior

13. Burnout can be reduced through identification, prevention, mediation, and remediation:
    a. Coupling these techniques with focus on the individual, interpersonal relations, the workplace, and the organization.
    b. Accurate identification must be made and programs tailored to meet the need.

14. The more progressive organizations are attacking burnout proactively, rather than reactively.

KEY TERMS

Burnout
Constraints
Imminent danger
Occupational Safety and Health
  Act (OSHA)

Stress
Stressors
Targeted industries

QUESTIONS FOR REVIEW

1. What are the objectives of the Occupational Safety and Health Act?
2. Describe the priority of OSHA investigations.
3. Identify three methods for preventing accidents.
4. Differentiate between drug abusers and alcoholics.
5. What is stress? How can it be positive?
6. What conditions are necessary for stress to be negative?
7. Differentiate between physiological, psychological, and behavioral stress symptoms.
8. What is burnout? List and describe the causes of burnout.
9. How does lowered job productivity affect burnout?
10. Describe the process of reducing burnout.

QUESTIONS FOR DISCUSSION

1. If a supervisor is aware that one of his or her subordinates has a drinking problem, but it is having no adverse effect on the subordinate's performance or attendance, should the supervisor take any action? Are there moral implications involved in this situation? Discuss.

2. Should employers be concerned with helping employees cope with stress? Do you differentiate between job-related stress and off-the-job-related stress? Discuss.

3. Some medical experts believe that regular daily exercise results in individuals' having better health, improved conditioning, and greater tolerance of stressful situations. What would you think about being employed by a company that required you to work out daily on company time? Do you think this would help or hurt the company's recruiting ability? Discuss.

4. At what point would you say that stress becomes less positive and more negative? Cite examples.

5. "Automation and technological advancements are causing more stress and burnout among workers, which results in negating some of the benefits that can be achieved through automation." Do you agree or disagree? Discuss.

CONTINUING CASE: Concord General

I'm OK, You're Not

John Michaels has become aware of some peculiar changes in the nurses in the Intensive Care and Cardiac Care units. During his normal rounds throughout the hospital, he has noticed that the nurses in these units have been quarreling much more than usual, that most have been rude to the families of patients in the units, and that their overall demeanor has deteriorated. Worried about these nurses, John Michaels has asked Theresa Margaret, the hospital's psychologist, to visit the units, talk to the nurses, and report back to him.

Dr. Margaret decided to do some research prior to her meeting with the nurses. In her investigation, she found that absenteeism rates had nearly tripled in two months, more vacation days were being scheduled, more nurses appeared to be smoking, coffee consumption had doubled, and complaints about some nurses' attitudes toward patients' families had increased. To complicate matters, she also found that there had been a significant reduction in the number of staff available for each shift. It seemed that seven nurses had left the unit on maternity leave, and none of the seven would be back for at least eight more weeks. This, coupled with the hospital policy that you cannot replace workers who are out on maternity leave, was causing severe staff shortages.

When Dr. Margaret met with the nurses, she was inundated with complaints. The nurses complained that they were being overworked because the hospital's administration was not being supportive about alleviating staffing shortages. They also felt that during the past few months, some of the sickest people had been placed in the units. The nurses prided themselves on low death rates, but nearly 60 percent of the patients admitted to either unit during the past few months had died. And the patients' families and friends expected them to be supernurses, complaining that it was the nurses' duty to keep their loved ones alive.

As one nurse stated, "We need help!" That summarized statement was reported back to John Michaels.

Questions

1. What appears to be the main problem with the nurses?
2. How could this be overcome in the short run? The long run?
3. What type of stress management programs would you design for these nurses?

CASE APPLICATION

Bend Me, Shake Me

The Japanese style of management has permeated all aspects of the management literature. Their participative style has been labeled successful because they have been able to increase worker morale, satisfaction, and productivity. Although much attention has been paid to their quality of work life programs, one aspect seems to generate less attention: exercise.

In many Japanese-run organizations, each day starts with a period of calisthenics. Here the employees forgo their worries and participate in a series of stretching exercises designed to make them healthy and ready to work. The Japanese belief that exercise gives the employee an opportunity to reduce stress and strengthen the cardiovascular system has proved to be accurate. The productivity of the Japanese during the past twenty years has been unbeatable.

While the Japanese have found these calisthenic periods useful, they have not become as popular as expected in many U.S. organizations. Even though the in-house programs in the United States have increased, many of these have been oriented toward the executives rather than the hourly workers. This is obviously a step in the right direction, but there seems to be a need to include all the company members, especially those directly involved in the day-to-day production of the organization's products.

Questions

1. What are the hurdles for in-house programs for hourly workers?
2. Describe what an exercise program for hourly workers might look like.
3. What assumptions would you make regarding in-house training programs with respect to employee participation? How can one ensure that these assumptions hold?

ADDITIONAL READINGS

BALDWIN, DR. BRUCE A., "Burning Out in America: When Success Is Overwhelming," *Piedmont Airlines Magazine*, March 1985, pp. 11–16.

GLOGOW, ELI, "Research Note: Burnout and Locus of Control," *Public Personnel Management*, 15, No. 1 (Spring 1986), 75–83.

IVANCEVICH, JOHN M., MICHAEL T. MATTESON, and EDWARD P. RICHARDS III, "Who's Liable for Stress on the Job?" *Harvard Business Review*, March–April 1985, pp. 60–72.

KLEIN, ALFRED, "Employees under the Influence, Outside the Law," *Personnel Journal*, September 1986, pp. 57–71.

OSTELL, ALISTAR, "Where Stress Screening Falls Short," *Personnel Management*, September 1986, pp. 34–37.

CHAPTER 20

Labor Relations

AFTER READING THIS CHAPTER, YOU WILL BE ABLE TO:

1. Define *union* as it applies to labor relations
2. Describe how unions constrain managerial discretion
3. Discuss the major labor legislation
4. Explain why management is prone to fight unions
5. Describe the professional occupational associations
6. Identify the goals of group representation
7. Describe the public's perception of the union movement and labor leaders
8. Determine whether union influence is on the decline

The union organizer's best weapon is poor management.

—Anonymous

A *union* is an organization of workers acting collectively, who seek to protect and promote their mutual interests through collective bargaining. However, before we can examine the collective-bargaining process (Chapter 21), we need to introduce unions, review their goals, and identify the laws that govern the labor relations process. As we progress through the following pages, one major aspect should be noted. That is, as we demonstrate how unions and occupational associations pursue their goals, realize that these pursuits impose significant constraints on HRM decision makers in many organizations. The following section will discuss specific constraints on managerial discretion.

How Unions Constrain Managerial Discretion

Unions constrain managerial discretion

Although less than 20 percent of the total labor force is currently represented by unions, union efforts—both successes and failures—affect all segments of the work force in two important ways. First, since major industries in the United States, such as automobile, steel, and electrical manufacturers as well as all branches of transportation, are unionized, unions have a major impact on key sectors of the economy. Second, the gains made by unions tend to have a spillover effect, impacting the wages, hours, and working conditions offered by employers of nonunionized workers.

For many managers, the practice of HRM is largely composed of following procedures and policies laid out in the labor contract, agreed to by both management and labor, which stipulate the wage rate, the hours of work, and the terms and conditions of employment for those covered by the labor agreement. Decisions about where recruitment is done, how employees are selected, who is trained, how compensation is determined, and what benefits are offered employees are no longer unilateral prerogatives of management for jobs within the union's province. Such decisions are substantially made at the time the labor contract is negotiated. Also, as noted in Chapter 18, the major means of limiting employment-at-will is the union contract, along with the grievance procedure that more than 90 percent of the contracts contain. Not surprisingly, there is almost a universal effort by employers to resist unionization of their organizations, in spite of the fact that a unionized labor force can provide some advantages to employers—for instance, eliminating the problems and costs involved with individual bargaining and minimizing labor problems during the life of the contract. Let us briefly outline some of the major reasons why employers fight unions.

Reduction in management's power

1. Reduction of Management's Power.   When an organization's employees are unionized, HRM decisions become open to close scrutiny and possible challenge. The written labor contract specifies rules that govern key HRM issues and greatly reduce the individual manager's discretion. Unions also create more problems for management by introducing outsiders into the organization's labor relations.

Potential for strikes

2. Potential for Strikes.   The ultimate weapon of a union in its efforts to gain concessions from management is to bring about a strike or work stoppage. Without its unionized employees, the organization is forced either to close down its operations completely or to operate with a skeleton staff of administrators trying to keep the organization functioning as normally as possible. This latter approach has been attempted in Chicago, where administrators within the city's fire department filled in as best as they could when unionized firefighters went on strike. Similarly, telephone supervisors at Chesapeake and Potomac Telephone attempted to keep telephone service operating in Baltimore despite a strike by telephone operators. However, lost time due to strikes is costly and does affect productivity (see Figure 20-1).

Fear of increased costs

3. Fear of Increased Costs.   Union efforts to improve employee pay and working conditions, increase paid holidays and benefits, provide better pensions, and so forth, all imply higher costs to manage-

FIGURE 20-1

Work Stoppages 1980–84

	# STOPPAGES	# WORKERS INVOLVED	IDLE DAYS	% WORK TIME
1980	187	795,000	20,844	.09
1981	145	729,000	16,908	.07
1982	96	656,000	9,061	.04
1983	81	909,000	17,461	.08
1984	62	376,000	8,499	.04

SOURCE: *Statistical Abstracts of the U.S., 1986,* 106th ed. (U.S. Department of Commerce, Bureau of the Census), p. 424.

ment. Unless these costs are offset by increases in employee productivity, management must raise the prices charged for its goods and services, accept a lower profit margin, or accept lower wages for the nonunionized employees in the firm (e.g., managerial and executive salaries or wages paid to unorganized nonmanagerial employees). Obviously, higher costs are not desirable from management's perspective, especially when the organization's goods and services face strong competition, and potential customers' decisions are sensitive to price increases.

Threats to efficiency

4. *Threats to Efficiency.* Unions occasionally seek to reduce productivity through featherbedding. Union efforts to obtain payment for work not performed, refusal to allow the adoption of labor-saving equipment, and creation of nonessential jobs are examples of actions that management would correctly perceive as threats to the organization's efficiency. Featherbedding, however, is not necessarily directed toward unions' propensity for inefficiency, as it is a means of increasing union security.

Loss of employee commitment

5. *Loss of Employee Commitment.* Management frequently resists unionization for fear that the union will redirect employee loyalties and allegiances from the organization to the union. Employees may associate themselves more with the interests of their union than with their employing organization. This can result in reduced employee commitment, lower morale, resistance to change, and sublimation of the organization's goals to those of the union.

Union review of HRM policies

6. *Union Review of HRM Policies.* Management has to exercise greater care in developing its HRM policies, for these policies will be under constant assessment by the union membership. If the policies prove to increase employee dissatisfaction, the union can be expected to impose pressures on management to correct them when the current contract expires.

Management might want to resist unionization efforts for any or all of the reasons listed above. But wanting to operate in a union-free environment and achieving this goal may be two different things. Although most employers desire to keep their organizations nonunion, literally millions of managers in hundreds of thousands of organizations find themselves having to recognize unions, engage in collective bargaining, and live under the terms of a labor-management contract. How did unions come to achieve this power to negotiate with management? It was a long drawn out process. Recall from Chapter 2 the historical labor movements. Prior to the mid-1930s, union advances were negligible. The courts, the people in power, and the general public did not approve of unionism. However, as the years progressed, labor organizations became more powerful through legislative support and changing public sentiment. In the following section, we will review the major laws surrounding labor relations and discuss their impact on union growth.

Major Labor Legislation

Labor-management relationships today are significantly different from what they were more than a century ago. Association in a union or attempting to organize workers was then deemed a violation of law. For years the courts suppressed unionization, and they, together with the "big bosses," were successful in keeping union organizers in their place. But many of these suppressive actions were the same things that had propelled the union cause. Workers were treated as pieces of equipment. If the equipment became costly, it was simply replaced. Organizations made unilateral decisions regarding the workers, and in most cases, these decisions worsened the workers' rights. Undoubtedly workers were upset and demanded that changes occur so that workers would be recognized. However, before this could occur on a large-scale basis, help was needed from a third party, namely, federal government legislation.

Although identifying all the laws that have affected labor-management relationships would be exhaustive and beyond our purpose, it is important to identify the major legislation, especially the laws giving rise to union efforts. These would include the Railway Labor Act of 1926; the National Labor Relations Act of 1935 (the Wagner Act); the Labor-Management Relations Act of 1947 (the Taft-Hartley Act); Presidential Executive Orders 10988 (1962) and 11491 (1969); and the Civil Service Reform Act of 1978.

Railway Labor Act

Railway Labor Act (1926).   The *Railway Labor Act* provided the initial impetus to widespread collective bargaining. Although the act covered only the transportation industry, it is important because it guaranteed workers in this industry the right to organize and to bargain collectively with employers.

Between 1926 and 1935, a few pieces of federal legislation were passed, but none was more notable than the National Labor Relations Act of 1935, more popularly called the Wagner Act. The Wagner Act, often referred to as the "Union Bible," was the first piece of federal legislation that was totally in favor of labor. The act made the refusal to bargain collectively with employee representatives an unfair labor practice for most private-sector employers. Let us now consider the Wagner Act and its major amendment, the Taft-Hartley Act (1947) in more detail.

Wagner Act

The Wagner Act (1935).   As you may recall from Chapter 2, the *Wagner Act* guaranteed workers the right to organize and join unions, to bargain collectively, and to act in concert in pursuit of their objectives. In terms of collective bargaining, the act specifically requires employers to bargain in good faith over wages, hours, and terms and conditions of employement. Note that we said *employers*, employers only. The Wagner Act shifted the pendulum of power to favor the unions. According to the act, unions could do no wrong. All the components of the act addressed those things that employers must or must not do—or otherwise face an unfair labor practice charge.

These actions can be summarized as follows:

1. Interfering with, restraining, or coercing employees in the exercise of the rights to join unions and bargain collectively
2. Dominating or interfering with the formation or administration of any labor organization
3. Discriminating against anyone because of union activity
4. Discharging or otherwise discriminating against any employee because he filed charges or gave testimony under the act
5. Refusing to bargain collectively with the representatives chosen by the employees

NLRB

To police this law and enforce its requirements, the Wagner Act established the National Labor Relations Board (NLRB). The NLRB has the responsibility for conducting elections to determine union representation and to interpret and apply the law against the above-stated unfair labor practices.

The association between the passage of the Wagner Act and the tremendous growth period of unions is evident. However, employers were not happy. For twelve years unions could obtain what they wanted from employers and had the backing of the federal government to do so. To help curtail this unbalance of power, the Taft-Hartley Act was passed.

Taft-Hartley

Taft-Hartley (1947).   Officially called the Labor-Management Relations Act, *Taft-Hartley* addressed activities unions must or must not do. In essence, Taft-Hartley addressed union unfair labor practices. This means the union must now bargain in good faith and must curtail certain activities that appear to threaten, coerce, or cause an organization to discriminate in employment.

With the passage of Taft-Hartley, both parties must now negotiate in good faith. Although the negotiation process is described in more detail in the next chapter, it is important to discuss "bargaining in good faith" as it applies to both laws. Bargaining in good faith does not mean reaching an agreement. No law can force that. What it does mean, however, is that both parties must try to work together toward reaching an agreement. The working together comes about from the effort both parties expend. It is the effort that is enforced, not its outcome.

FMCS

Realizing that unions and employers might not reach an agreement and that a work stoppage might be imminent, Taft-Hartley created the Federal Mediation and Conciliation Service (FMCS). The FMCS is a neutral third party that sends a representative to the negotiations to help both parties overcome the impasse. While not empowered to force the parties to reach an agreement, the skillful FMCS mediator gains the confidence of both groups and helps them to return to the negotiation table and work out their difficulties. Probably the most publicity the FMCS has received during the past few years was its part in settling two strikes when it brought the Baseball Players Association and the Football Players Association to an agreement with their respective employers.

While the Wagner Act and its Taft-Hartley amendment have paved the road for current labor management philosophies in the private sector, Executive Orders 10988 and 11491 and the Civil Service Reform Act have done so in the public sector.

Executive Orders 10988 and 11491 and the Civil Service Reform Act

E.O. 10988

Executive Orders 10988 and 11491   In 1962, President John F. Kennedy issued *Executive Order 10988*, which affirmed the right of federal government employees to join unions and granted restricted bargaining rights to these employees. The order required agency heads to bargain in good faith, defined unfair labor practices, and specified the code of conduct to which labor organizations must adhere. In addition, the order prohibited strikes by federal employees. Accordingly, any federal employee engaging in strike activities could be dismissed. This was well understood and enforced when President Reagan fired the striking air traffic controllers.

While Executive Order 10988 was effective in granting organizing rights to federal employees, areas for improvement were identified. To make these changes, *Executive Order 11491* was signed into law by President Richard M. Nixon in 1969.

E.O. 11491

The objectives of E.O. 11491 were to make federal labor relations more like those in the private sector and to standardize procedures among federal agencies. It defined the assistant secretary of labor as the authority to determine appropriate bargaining units, to oversee recognition procedures, to rule on unfair labor practices, and to enforce standards of conduct on labor organization. It also established the Federal Labor Relations Council to supervise the implementation of E.O. 11491 provisions, handle appeals from decisions of the assistant secretary of labor, and rule on questionable issues. This council is, in effect, the counterpart to the NLRB for the public sector.

Civil Service Reform Act

Civil Service Reform Act (1978).   The *Civil Service Reform Act* replaced E.O. 11491 as the basic law governing labor relations for federal employees. The act gave labor-management relations in the federal government a statutory base, which means they are no longer subject to change and refinement by the president.

The Civil Service Reform Act established the Federal Labor Relations Authority as an independent agency within the executive branch to carry out the major functions previously performed by the Federal Labor Relations Council. The FLRA was given the authority to decide representation and unfair labor practice cases, negotiability disputes, and appeals from arbitration awards, and to provide leadership in establishing policies and guidance under the statute. An additional feature of the Civil Service Reform Act is mandatory binding arbitration. All negotiated grievance procedures for federal units now require binding arbitration as the final step. Under E.O. 11491, arbitration had been optional.

None of the acts and executive orders we have discussed deal with state or local collective bargaining. In 1970, it was estimated that only about one-third of these public-sector units require or permit their employees to organize and bargain collectively. Recently, more states have been allowing public-sector employees to engage in collective bargaining, but almost always with the proviso that applies to federal employees—that they do not have the power to strike.

Summary

During the past fifty years, many of the laws enacted have focused on labor-management relationships. Certainly the laws themselves have helped to expand the growth of unionism, but they have included a check and balance system. The laws on the books for labor and management are plentiful, but all have one common theme. That is, the laws work toward harmony in the labor-management environment.

Along with more favorable legislation toward unionism, we are experiencing union growth in the nontraditional jobs. Once perceived as a blue-collar emphasis, more and more professional associations are emerging. In the next section we will discuss this new growth area, its goals, and the public's perception of white-collar unionism.

Growth of Professional Occupational Associations

Growth
of occupational
associations

When one thinks of unions, one usually thinks of manual workers. While this generalization was fairly accurate in the early years of the union movement, more recently the concept of unionization has spread to include white-collar occupations, a broad spectrum of professionals, and even executives.[1] In addition to the growth in unionization of

[1]William H. Holley and Kenneth M. Jennings, *The Labor Relations Process*, 2nd ed. (New York: Dryden Press, 1984), p. 430.

professional groups, we must consider the expansion of professional occupational associations, many of which, while adamant in their desire not to be considered as unions, perform many of the same functions.

Since the early 1960s, the growth of jobs at the municipal, county, state, and federal government levels has far outstripped the creation of jobs in the private sector. The rapid expansion in public-sector jobs has been a major contributing factor in making the United States the first country to have more than 50 percent of its work force engaged in service-related jobs. This situation, when combined with the changes we noted previously in the makeup of the work force, would suggest potentially large opportunities for unionization among professional groups. The evidence seems to support such a conclusion. For example, two of the fastest-growing unions in the United States are the American Federation of Teachers and the American Federation of State, County, and Municipal Employees.

Why would teachers, engineers, librarians, nurses, and other professionals be interested in joining a union? The answer lies in the benefits that derive from the power of coalitions and the gains that can be achieved through more aggressive and militant behavior. While one of the major problems that the union movement must confront is the negative connotation of "nonprofessionalization" which may go with belonging to a union, the unions' effectiveness in being able to negotiate large gains for their members is impressive. Their militancy and their willingness to strike, if necessary, have resulted in greater job security and improved salaries. The willingness of police officers, firefighters, and other government employees, even though not traditionally classified as professionals, to collaborate in their efforts, select bargaining representatives, and negotiate and administer a labor agreement with their employer has significantly changed the relationship between these employees and their employers.

Professional occupational associations and unions often perform similar functions, but associations prefer to avoid the union title. The better-known associations include the American Association of University Professors, the Association of Certified Public Accountants, the American Medical Association, and the American Bar Association. These associations perform union-type functions when they control the supply of entrants into the occupation, explicitly or implicitly determine the wage rates, or lobby for legislation that will protect or improve working conditions affecting their members.

Many professional groups do perform one or more of these activities. For instance, the American Medical Association accredits medical schools and hence controls the number of new doctors who can practice. It informally establishes standardized fees. It can impose formal penalties and informal pressures on members who do not adhere to the organization's code of acceptable behavior. On the political front, the **AMA** has one of the most active, powerful, and effective lobby groups in Washington, and it organizes impressive lobby efforts anywhere that legislative bodies seek to make changes affecting the medical profession.

Goals of Group Representation

In the previous section, we said professionals join unions in order to get the benefits that can be achieved through more aggressive and militant collective behavior. In this section, we want to focus on the mean-

GEECH　　　　　　　　　　　　　**by Jerry Bittle**

FIGURE 20-2

SOURCE: Geech, Universal Press Syndicate.

ing of these benefits for the individual and ask, Why would any worker want to join a union? Then we will review the specific goals of group representation.

Why Unions?

Reasons for unions

The seeds of the union movement lay in employees who had to work torturously long hours, received poor working conditions, and faced a rigid authoritarianism that gave management the right to hire, fire, and control employees' lives in an almost capricious manner. As recently as the 1930s, some employees were treated in a slavelike manner. While certainly not typical of the time, the following excerpt is from a contract that a young woman had to agree to before being hired as a teacher in a small school in North Carolina about fifty years ago:

> *I promise to take a vital interest in all phases of Sunday-school work donating all my time, service, and money without stint for the benefit and uplift of the community. I promise to abstain from all dancing, immodest dressing, and any other conduct unbecoming a teacher and a lady. I promise not to go out with any young man except in so far as it may be necessary to stimulate Sunday-school work. I promise not to fall in love, to become engaged or secretly married. I promise to remain in the dormitory or on the school grounds when not actively engaged in school or church or elsewhere. I promise not to encourage or tolerate the least familiarity on the part of any of my boy pupils. I promise to sleep at least eight hours each night, to eat carefully, to take every precaution to keep in the best of health and spirits in order that I may be better able to render efficient service to my pupils. I promise to remember that I owe a duty to the townspeople who are paying my wages; that I owe respect to the school board and to the su-*

perintendent who hired me; and that I shall consider myself at all times the willing servant of the school board and the townspeople and that I shall cooperate with them to the limit of my ability in any movement aimed at the betterment of the town, the pupils or the school.[2]

If employees in other sectors of the economy experienced even a small number of such demands from their employers, is there any doubt that workers would be highly motivated to join unions?

The evidence indicates that when workers are dissatisfied with their economic and working conditions and perceive that they lack the influence to change these conditions, they are more motivated to join a union.[3] This propensity is increased where workers perform routine work that offers meager *opportunities* for advancement or self-enhancement. In such cases, unions provide a means to protect and enlarge this narrow sphere. Additionally, because the required skills to perform routine jobs are often commonly available, management tends to consider workers interchangeable. Employees feel powerless and respond by seeking security against the arbitrary actions of management in such an environment. Of course, unions can only thrive if a group of employees feel dissatisfied. It is the shared opinions of workers that provide the basis for a prounion coalition.[4]

Specific Goals

We began this chapter by describing unions as organizations that seek to protect and promote their members' interests. Union protection and promotion basically revolve around four specific goals. We can say that any labor union will seek to

1. Influence the wage and effort bargain
2. Establish a security system for members
3. Influence the administration of rules
4. Obtain political power in the state and over the economy

Wages, hours, terms, and conditions of employment

Wages and Effort. We traditionally view unions as bargaining for their members in the areas of wages, hours, and working conditions. The result of this bargaining determines the amount of pay, the hours of employment, the amount of work required during a given pe-

---

[2]"North Carolina Teachers—Slaves?" *Current History,* June 1937, p. 113.

[3]Holley and Jennings, *Labor Relations Process,* pp. 16–18.

[4]Jeanne M. Brett, "Behavioral Research on Unions and Union Movement Systems," in *Research Organizational Behavior,* ed. Barry M. Shaw and Larry Cummings (Greenwich, Conn.: JAI Press, 1980), II, 181–84; and James D. Thompson, *Organizations in Action* (New York: McGraw-Hill, 1967), pp. 109–10.

riod, and the conditions of employment. The union's ability to influence final negotiations is determined by the union's power relative to that of management.

What is union power? How is it achieved? Do all unions have the same amount of power? These are important questions and deserve our attention.

Union power is demonstrated by its ability to obtain its objectives. The greater the union's power, all other things equal, the more successful the union will be in protecting and promoting the mutual interests of its members. This power is achieved through the union's efforts at creating employer dependence; that is, by developing a situation where the union controls a resource vital to the objectives established by managers for their organization. Again, all things equal, the greater the employer's dependence on the union's members, the greater the power of the union in its negotiating with that employer.

Obviously, dependence can only be achieved by reducing alternatives. If an employer needs workers in order to get the work done, and if these workers can only be secured by negotiating with a given union, that union has through control of the employer's labor supply successfully reduced the employer's options to one. The union has created power through its monopoly position.

Consistent with this description of union power, some unions must, by definition, have greater power than others. The type of security agreement the union has been able to establish with an employer will, to a large extent, define the parameters of the union's power.

Employment security

Security.   The ideal agreement, from a union standpoint, would be a situation where workers could not be hired by an employer unless, at the time of hiring, they were already members of the union. In such a case, the union is the only source of labor for the employer. Complete monopoly power can be exerted, since the employer's alternatives have been reduced to one. This type of arrangement is referred

Closed shop

to as a *closed shop* and was declared illegal by the Taft-Hartley Act in 1947. Yet, in many construction and printing jobs, and arrangement exists that closely resembles the closed shop; in those cases, it is called a hiring hall.

Union shop

The most powerful relationship legally available to a union is a union shop, which stipulates that employers, while free to hire whomever they choose, may retain only union members. That is, all employees must, after a specified probationary period—usually thirty to sixty days—join the union or give up their positions. However, in right-to-

Right-to-work states

work states, compulsory union membership is forbidden. At present, this legislation exists in twenty states, though right-to-work laws are most heavily concentrated in the South, the farm block, and the Mountain States.

FIGURE 20-3

Right-to-Work States

Alabama	Louisiana	South Dakota
Arizona	Mississippi	Tennessee
Arkansas	Nebraska	Texas
Florida	Nevada	Utah
Georgia	North Carolina	Virginia
Iowa	North Dakota	Wyoming
Kansas	South Carolina	

If a union shop does not exist, then there can be no requirement that the employee join the union. All other types of security, therefore, are clearly inferior from a union's standpoint. These other types of security arrangements include maintenance of membership and preferential, agency, and open shops.

Maintenance of membership

A *maintenance of membership* agreement states that no worker is required to join the union as a condition of employment, but it stipulates that should an employee join the union, he or she then becomes locked in. This locked-in status compels the employee to remain in the union for the extent of the contract. When the contract expires, most maintenance of membership agreements provide an escape clause—a short interval of time, usually ten days to two weeks, in which the employee may choose to withdraw his or her membership without penalty.

Preferential shop

When a union member is given preference over a nonunion member, we have a *preferential shop*. This type of agreement must be carefully monitored to ensure that preferential treatment is not interpreted to mean union members exclusively. When preference results in decisions that consistently exclude nonunion members, we do not have a preferential shop, but rather a closed shop.

Agency shop

An agreement that requires nonunion employees to pay the union a sum equal to union fees and dues as a condition of continuing employment is referred to as an *agency shop*. It was designed as a compromise between the union's desire to eliminate the "free rider" and management's desire to make union membership voluntary.

Open shop

The least desirable form of security, again from the union standpoint, is the *open shop*. This is where there is, technically, no union, but it is sometimes applied to places of work in which there is a union but membership is not a condition of employment.

Guaranteed annual income

In addition to the unions' desire to develop a security agreement with an employer, unions have recently begun also to press for job and income security for their members. Ideally, a union would like to be able to provide its members with complete job security. While union officials may use the phrase "guaranteed lifetime security" to describe their goal, what they actually want is the same kind of job security most managers have. This is not lifetime security, but rather significant reductions in the practice of instant layoffs during even minor economic slumps or cutting workers adrift when a plant or office is closed down. Unions in recent years have sought to have management vest jobs rights to union members. After a stipulated number of years of service, a worker would have earned the right to be kept on the job. Workers with high seniority could be guaranteed work even during slumps or at least be guaranteed a certain number of hours of work— or pay in lieu of work—per year.

As indicated above, security can include such arrangements as a guaranteed annual income. Probably the best-known guarantee is that between the members of Longshoremen's Union and their employers. The dockworkers in New York are guaranteed 2,080 hours of work a year so long as they meet one stipulation, that is, being available to work.[5] With current wages approximately $15 per hour, this guaranteed annual income amounts to $31,200 per worker. In other ports, the number of hours guaranteed is less, 1,900 in Baltimore for a worker with ten years' seniority, but the impact is the same. The guaranteed annual income provision costs millions of dollars.[6]

Rules.   Where a union exists, workers are provided with an opportunity to participate in determining the conditions under which they work, and an effective channel whereby they can protest conditions they believe are unfair. Therefore a union not only is a representative of the worker but also provides rules that define channels in which complaints and concerns of workers can be registered.

Grievance
procedures

Grievance procedures and rights to third-party arbitration of management-labor disputes are examples of practices that are frequently defined and regulated as a result of union efforts.

Union power

Power.   A final objective of a union is to obtain political power in the state and over the economy. The union movement has not been reluctant to exert political muscle to gain through legislation what it has been unable to win at the bargaining table.

The AFL–CIO, for example, is a potent lobbying group. No national politician can ignore the needs of the union movement as articulated by the AFL–CIO. Those who seek election to public office, or who want to maintain the positions they already hold, find that labor's interests must be heard. The winning of labor support can be a valuable aid, often a necessary requirement, in attaining important positions at the local, state, and national levels.

There is considerable debate regarding the power of a union in endorsing a particular political candidate or a specific piece of legis-

[5]*Baltimore Sun*, February 17, 1984.
[6]Ibid.

lation. The days of a union's being able to "deliver" the votes of its members are gone. Union members are under no obligation to vote in the manner recommended by their union's top officers. However, union members utilize the union as a central clearing house for the obtaining of information concerning a particular candidate's past record and current position on issues sensitive to labor. The hope of winning union endorsement and the fear of being labeled "antilabor" motivate government officials and legislators to ensure that labor's voice is heard and, often, that labor's interests are enhanced.

Unions and Occupational Associations Today

At the beginning of this chapter, we described how organized labor groups can significantly constrain managerial decision-making discretion in the area of human resources. At the same time we have shown how the union movement has ceased to be an expanding force. The figures, in fact, appear to show unions as a declining force in the American economy. Is this true? What is the status of unions and occupational associations today? In the following pages we will consider the public's current perception of American unions and assess the evidence—both pro and con—surrounding the issue of whether union influence is on the decline. It is hoped that this last section can bring into perspective the actual clout that unions bring to HRM.

Public perception of unions

The Public's Perception. It is generally believed that the public holds a dim view of labor unions today. But the evidence, expressed by Harris and Gallup polls, show something very interesting. In the late 1970s, only 15 percent of Americans gave labor leaders a favorable rating. However, in another study, the majority of Americans approve of labor unions generally and favor the right to collective bargaining for all workers.[7] These polls suggest labor's negative image is probably reserved for its leaders and not the movement itself. Americans apparently do not like labor leaders, but they do like unions. And they support union goals.

This leads us to conclude that the public is generally supportive of the union movement. In such an environment, why should unions be a declining force in the American economy? Or is that an erroneous conclusion?

Is Union Influence on the Decline?

Union decline

Since its heyday in the 1950s, organized labor has declined as a proportion of the total labor force. Unionized workers currently represent less than 20 percent of the work force, down from more than 30 percent in the mid-fifties. American unions, though, have not lacked op-

[7]*Time*, November 16, 1981, p. 124.

portunities. They have, however, failed to make their case and win representation elections. In 1950, 83 percent of the elections conducted by the National Labor Relations Board to determine union representation were won by unions; that is, the employees voted to have the union become their bargaining agent. In the early 1980s, unions lost about one-half of all representation elections.[8]

Today many labor unions are fighting for their survival. Those that evolved out of organizing largely male, blue-collar factory workers find membership declining. Service, technical, professional, and public-employee unions, on the other hand, are finding fruitful opportunities. The picture of union influence must, therefore, be somewhat cloudy. As we summarize and integrate what we have learned about unions, let us look at both the pros and the cons on the question, Is union influence on the decline?

Pros.   Size is power. Generally speaking, the larger the union movement, the greater its power. In this context, it can be argued that union influence is on the decline. Union membership as a percentage of the total labor force has been dropping. In the past few years, even the absolute number of unionized workers is down—down more than 2.5 million since 1980. The economic sectors in which union strength has traditionally been based have become stagnant, and the movement has been unable to make significant progress in organizing women or technical and professional employees. Additionally, unions have been making wage concessions, something unheard of in labor relations history.

Cons.   Unions are still the dominant force in major manufacturing industries. While it is true that their traditional strength is in industries like automobiles and steel, which are not the products of the future, it is erroneous to assume that because these industries are stagnant or declining, union power must be hurt. Union influence over these industries is very deep, and union inroads in these basic industries spill over into all other sectors. Labor agreements negotiated by the teamsters, for example, not only benefit truckers but also become a precedent for wage and benefit demands made by other unions and set the parameters for compensation packages offered by nonunionized employers. Labor agreements negotiated in the basic unionized industries are very visible and have ramifications on HRM policies for many nonunionized employers.

We cannot ignore union successes during the 1970s in organizing in the public sector. It is estimated that more than 50 percent of state and local government employees are now organized for collective bargaining. Unions similarly represent for bargaining purposes over half

---

[8]Susan R. Zacur and David A. DeCenzo, "Can a Pro-Management Film Affect Attitudes towards Unions," *Southern Academy of Management*, November 1984.

the white-collar and a whopping 85 percent of blue-collar federal government workers.[9] In spite of limitations, collective bargaining appears to be the choice of federal, state, and local government employees, and the unions have taken advantage of this rich opportunity.

Finally, we should not ignore the sophisticated lobbying efforts the union movement is able to present. Unions have friends throughout government. Many elected representatives owe their successful election campaigns to union support. Any review of union power, therefore, must also consider its ability to move issues off the bargaining table and into the public domain where it can call on the support of its many friends.

Summary

Unions have lost much of the power they enjoyed when they represented nearly one-third of the labor force and controlled the primary sectors of the economy. However, this loss has been somewhat offset by large gains in the public sector and a continued strong power base which comes from an effective lobbying organization.

For human resource managers, only the naive can afford to ignore the influence of unions. While the union movement's relative power may have declined over the past generation, it remains a major constraint on HRM decisions in absolute terms. Both directly and indirectly, union successes and failures have an impact on literally all human resource managers. Union impact on managers operating in unionized organizations is obvious. Managers in nonunionized organizations who desire to avoid unionization can never ignore the demands and achievements that unions are making in other quarters.

Conclusion

This chapter has addressed many of the fundamental aspects of labor relations, and the following chapter will explore the negotiating of the collective-bargaining contract. We noted that just because an organization does not have a union with which to contend does not mean that it can ignore the process of collective bargaining. The spillover effects are numerous, and if an organization intends to remain union free, then it must offer its employees the benefits that a union could provide without the costs associated with such an action.

In the next chapter, we will also explore a recent phenomenon in collective bargaining, wage concessions (which may be changing the course of labor relations), along with the antiunion campaigns of employers.

[9]Al Bilik, "Corrupt, Crusty, or Neither?", p. 326.

SUMMARY

1. A *union* is an organization of workers, acting collectively, who seek to protect and promote their mutual interests through collective bargaining.

2. Unions constrain managerial discretion through their impact on key sectors of the economy and through the spillover effect of their achievements on employers of nonunionized personnel.

3. The major labor legislation includes the Railway Labor Act (1926), the Wagner Act (1935), the Taft-Hartley Act (1947), Executive Orders 10988 (1962) and 11491 (1969), and the Civil Service Reform Act (1978).

4. Management is prone to fight unions because the latter
   a. Reduce management's power
   b. Increase the potential for strikes
   c. Can increase costs
   d. Create threats to efficiency
   e. Redirect employee commitment
   f. Review HRM policies

5. Many professional occupational associations perform the function of a union.

6. The goals of group representation include
   a. Influencing the wage and effort bargain
   b. Establishing a security system for members
   c. Influencing the administration of rules
   d. Obtaining political power in the state and over the economy

7. The American public is generally supportive of the union movement but does not appear to like labor leaders.

8. Union influence may have declined, but it is still a force in America today.

KEY TERMS

Agency shop
Civil Service Reform Act of 1978
Closed shop
Executive Orders 10988 and 11491
FMCS
Featherbedding
Grievance procedure
Labor Management Relations
   Act of 1947
National Labor Relations
   Act of 1935

National Labor Relations
   Board
Occupational Association
Open shop
Preferential shop
Railway Labor Act of 1926
Right-to-work laws
Taft-Hartley Act
Union
Union shop
Wagner Act

QUESTIONS FOR REVIEW

1. How do unions constrain the HRM decisions of managers in a unionized organization? In a nonunionized organization?

2. Why does management resist unionization?

3. What forces have acted to stagnate union membership in recent years?

4. Describe the major labor legislation's effect on labor-management relations.

5. Compare and contrast the Wagner Act with the Taft-Hartley Act.

6. What factors usually exist prior to the time that workers decide to join a union?

7. What is the purpose of the union movement?

8. Contrast the various types of union security agreements. Which is preferable from management's standpoint? From labor's standpoint?

9. What do union members generally think about their unions?

10. Is union influence on the decline?

QUESTIONS FOR DISCUSSION

1. "The American Medical Association is a nonunion union. It controls entry into the job and sets wages." Do you agree or disagree? Discuss.

2. Given your career aspirations, might you join a union? Why or why not?

3. Is life better today for the average North American as a result of unions? Discuss.

4. Can you think of situations where an employer might prefer to have a union representing his or her employees?

5. College faculties are increasingly turning to unions. Why? Should this trend have any effect on the student-faculty relationship? Discuss.

CONTINUING CASE: Concord General

Look for the Union Label

The nurses at Concord General are furious. Last year's cost-of-living adjustment was not given, and prospects for next year's are slim. Benefits have been cut, working conditions are worsening, and overtime is becoming mandatory. Reports from most of the department heads have revealed that in the busiest units, there are staffing shortages of up to 20 percent. Salaries too are becoming a point of contention, as the salaries of nurses at the hospital are $2.70 below those of their competitors.

Last week, after a decision to suspend a nurse for failing to clock in became known, the nurses met to discuss their alternatives. Tammy Simpson, a vocal nurse with nine years' experience, stated the following:

> We need to do something here. Our morale is at an all-time low. Our salaries are low, our benefits are being taken away, and some of the nurses are being unjustly disciplined. I went to Judy Sapp last week about our complaints and she said there is nothing she can do. She realizes we are understaffed but says that Mr. Michaels has implemented a hiring freeze. As for money, don't expect any more soon. Salary compressions are horrendous, but they say there is no money to bring salaries up to market value. Yet did you know that last month this hospital spent $378,000 to pave the parking lot that was paved last year? Sure, they had to spend their money so as not to lose their not-for-profit tax status. I think it is time we face this hospital's administration and get some answers. But to do so, we must act as one. If we separate, we'll all go down the drain.

Hearing rumors of the meeting, Judy met with John Michaels to discuss the nurses' concerns:

> John, I think we have a problem that needs immediate attention. Our nurses are upset over a lot of things. In fact, their most outspoken member is getting them to unite. You know that two hospitals in this state have won the right to unionize, and I believe if we don't act properly, we may be hit with a union campaign drive. Besides, we are now seventh out of eight hospitals in the area with regard to salary levels of our R.N.'s.

John gave his view of the situation:

Judy, you are right. We don't want a union here. But these nurses won't unionize. I don't believe a union could help them. Besides, unions are not for professional employees. Sure our pay may be low, but that is no reason to unionize. I think the nurses just need to blow off steam. So let them go. After airing their complaints, they'll come back to their senses. And hey, we are giving a fifty-cent across-the-board raise next month. I'm sure that will ease the pain.

Sure enough, the raise went into effect. But the union was contacted anyway. Authorization cards were signed, and an election was held. The election results: 214 nurses voting for the union; 387 voting against the union.

Questions

1. What problems at Concord General, do you think, led to the union election?
2. Do you think that a nurse who joins a union is losing her professional image? Explain.
3. "By the results of the vote, it is apparent that Mr. Michaels was right." Do you agree or disagree? Explain.
4. If you were Judy, what would you do to help correct the situation?

CASE APPLICATION

Grayco Resists Unionization

Scott Gray had started Grayco Film Processors more than fifteen years ago. Beginning with only $8,000 of borrowed capital, Gray had built a company employing three hundred people and doing more than $15 million of mail-order film processing a year. The firm had always paid higher wages and given better benefits than comparable employers in the community. While Gray expected "a day's work for a day's pay," he thought his employees were generally contented with the pay, benefits, and working conditions in his firm. However, about sixty days ago, Cathy West, Grayco's personnel manager, had mentioned to Gray that there were attempts under way by the Amalgamated Radio, Television and Film Technicians union to organize the firm's film processors. She said that she had seen several organizers handing out something that looked like union literature in front of the plant. West asked Gray if he would approve an information campaign to counter "the union's propaganda." Gray concurred.

It was a Monday morning and Gray was in his office early to go through the mail and memorandums that had accumulated from late in the previous week. As he went through the stack of correspondence, he found a copy of a form letter from Cathy West. A note attached advised Gray that she had sent this letter to the home of each of the 170 film processors working for the company. It read:

> Dear Employee:
>
> It has come to my attention that the Amalgamated Radio, Television and Film Technicians is currently encouraging you to join their union for the purpose of having them be your representative in collective bargaining with Grayco Film Processors. We believe you have nothing to gain by joining this union and your best interests will continue to be served by keeping Grayco nonunion.
>
> Speaking for the management of Grayco, I want to assure you we have no intention of recognizing a union as your bargaining agent. Further, you should consider this as a formal warning that any of our employees found to be supporting this organizing effort will be fired immediately.
>
> Grayco has grown and prospered by treating all of its employees fairly. We expect to continue to act in this tradition. As a result, we see no reason for you to entertain thoughts of unionization.
>
> Sincerely,
> Cathy West
> Director of Personnel

Scott Gray read the letter several times. He couldn't believe his eyes. "So this is what Cathy West meant by an information campaign!"

Questions

1. Would you consider this letter to be consistent with "an information campaign"?
2. The letter is illegal. Why?
3. How would you have worded a letter to employees that was legal?
4. What would you do now if you were Mr. Gray?

ADDITIONAL READINGS

CHAISON, GARY N., and MARK S. PLOVNICK, "Is There a New Collective Bargaining?" *California Management Review,* 28, No. 4 (Summer 1986), 54–61.

KLANDERMANS, BERT, "Perceived Costs and Benefits of Participation in Union Action," *Personnel Psychology,* 39, No. 2 (1986), 379–97.

"Labor Contract Negotiations: Behind the Scenes," *Personnel Administrator,* April 1986, pp. 55–60.

MITCHELL, DANIEL J. B., "Concession Bargaining in the Public Sector: A Lesser Force," *Public Personnel Management,* 15, No. 1 Spring 1986, 23–40.

STEEN, JACK E., "How to Win Arbitration Decisions," *Personnel,* 63, No. 3 (March 1986), 66–69.

CHAPTER 21

Collective

Bargaining

AFTER READING THIS CHAPTER, YOU WILL BE ABLE TO:

1. Describe the components of collective bargaining
2. Discuss the objectives of collective bargaining
3. Describe the collective-bargaining process
4. Identify four recent trends in collective bargaining

What's the purpose of a union? To get more! More! MORE!

—John L. Lewis

Literally hundreds of thousands of managers direct the activities of unionized employees who work under a collective agreement. In the industrial sector alone, there are nearly twenty-three hundred union contracts with firms that employ one thousand or more. In total, these contracts cover over 10 million workers. When the tens of thousands of smaller negotiations and nonindustrial contracts are added to these figures, we can see that for a large segment of managers, HRM practices are substantially determined by the results of collective bargaining.

Collective bargaining defined

The term *collective bargaining* typically refers to the negotiation, administration, and interpretation of a written agreement between two parties that covers a specific period of time. This agreement or contract lays out in specific terms the conditions of employment; that is, what is expected of employees and what limits there are on management's authority. In the discussion that follows, we will take a somewhat larger perspective than this definition in that we will also consider the organizing, certification, and preparation efforts that precede actual negotiation.

Most of us only hear or read about collective bargaining when a contract is about to expire or when negotiations break down. When a major steel contract is about to expire, we may be aware that collective bargaining exists in the steel industry. Similarly, teachers' strikes in Cleveland or auto workers striking at Ford plants throughout the United States remind us that organized labor deals with management collectively. In fact, collective-bargaining agreements cover about half of all state and local government employees and one-fifth of the employees in the private sector. The wages, hours, and working conditions of these unionized employees are negotiated for periods of usually two or three years at a time. Only when these contracts expire and management and the union are unable to agree upon a new contract are most of us aware that collective bargaining is a very important part of HRM.

Objective and Scope of Collective Bargaining

Collective-bargaining
objective

The objective of collective bargaining is to agree upon an acceptable contract—acceptable to management, union representatives, and the union membership. But what is covered in this contract? What is the acceptable scope of collective bargaining?

The final agreement will reflect the problems of the particular workplace and industry in which the contract is negotiated. The agreement may be very vague or highly specific. It may cover the obvious or what may appear to be ridiculous or irrelevant issues:

> Some maritime agreements specify the quality of meals and even the number of bars of soap, towels, and sheets that management is to furnish to the crew. Such provisions are natural subjects for negotiation, since they are vital to the men at sea, but they would make no sense in a normal manufacturing agreement.... Detailed procedures respecting control over hiring are central to collective bargaining in industries with casual employment, where employees shift continually from one employer to another, as in construction or stevedoring; but in factory and office employment, new hiring typically is left to the discretion of management.[1]

What is important on one job may therefore have no bearing on another. This fact will definitely be reflected in the demands placed by the union on management and in the subject and terms of the agreement finally negotiated.

Irrespective of the specific issues contained in various contracts, four issues appear consistently throughout all labor contracts. Three of the four are mandatory bargaining issues, which means that management must be willing to negotiate with the union. These mandatory issues are defined by the Wagner Act as wages, hours, and terms and conditions of employment. The fourth issue covered in almost all labor contracts is the grievance procedure, which is designed to permit the adjudication of complaints (see the "Contract Administration" section of this chapter). But before we progress further into collective bargaining, let us inspect our cast of characters.

Who Participates in Collective Bargaining?

Collective-bargaining
participants

Collective bargaining was earlier described as taking place between two parties. In that context, the two parties are management and labor. But who represents management and labor? And given our pre-

[1]D. C. Bok and J. T. Dunlop, "Collective Bargaining in the United States; An Overview," in *Contemporary Problems in Personnel* (rev. ed.), ed. W. Clay Hamner and Frank L. Schmidt (Chicago: St. Clair Press, 1977), p. 383.

vious discussion, would it be erroneous to add a third party—government?

Management's representation in collective-bargaining talks tends to depend on the size of the organization. In a small firm, for instance, bargaining is probably done by the president. Since small firms frequently have no specialist who deals only with HRM issues, the president of the company often handles this responsibility. In medium-sized organizations, bargaining is typically completed by the personnel manager, who is often supported by outside legal assistance. In large organizations, there is usually a sophisticated personnel department with full-time industrial relations experts. In such cases, we can expect management to be represented by the senior manager for industrial relations, corporate executives, and company lawyers—with support provided by legal and economic specialists in wage and salary administration, labor law, benefits and so forth.

On the union side, we typically expect to see a bargaining team made up of officers of the local union, local shop stewards, and some representation from the national union. Again, as with management, representation is modified to reflect the size of the bargaining unit. If negotiations involve a contract that will cover fifty thousand employees at company locations throughout the United States, the team will be dominated by national union officers, with a strong supporting cast of economic and legal experts employed by the union. In a small firm or for local negotiations covering special issues at the plant level for a nationwide organization, bargaining representatives for the union might be the local officers and a few specially elected committee members.

Watching over these two sides is a third—government. In addition to providing the rules under which management and labor bargain, government provides a watchful eye on the two parties to ensure the rules are followed, and it stands ready to intervene if an agreement on acceptable terms cannot be reached and the impasse undermines the nation's well-being.

Are there any more participants? Generally no for the most part, with one exception—the banks.[2] Most people are unaware of the presence of the financial institutions' role in collective bargaining. Although not directly involved in negotiations, the banks set limits on the amount that the company can spend in upcoming negotiations. Exceeding that amount may cause the banks to call in the loans that had been made to the company. This results in placing a ceiling on what management can spend.

While we can show that there are more groups involved in collective bargaining, our discussion will focus on labor and manage-

---

[2] If we take into account public-sector collective bargaining, then we have another exception—the public. The taxpaying voting public an influence those elected officials to act in certain ways during negotiations.

ment. After all, it is the labor and management teams that buckle down and hammer out the contract.

The Collective-Bargaining Process

We now want to consider the actual collective-bargaining process. Figure 21-1 contains a simple model of how the process typically flows in the private sector.

Organizing and Certification

Organizing workers

Efforts to organize a group of employees may begin by employee representatives requesting a union to visit the employees' organization and solicit members, or the union itself might initiate a membership drive. Either way, as established by the NLRB, the union must secure signed authorization cards from at least 30 percent of the employees whom it desires to represent. Employees who sign these cards indicate that they desire the particular union to be their representative in negotiating with the employer.

RC elections

While 30 percent of the potential union members must sign the authorization card prior to an election, unions are seldom interested in bringing to vote situations where they merely meet the NLRB minimum. Why? The answer is simple, and a matter of mathematics and business: To become the certified bargaining unit, the union must be accepted by a majority of the eligible workers. This election held by the NLRB, which is called a representation certification (RC), can only occur once in a twelve-month period. Thus the greater the number of signatures on the authorization cards, the greater the chances for a victory. But by no means is the victory guaranteed. We should not assume that management will be passive during the organization drive. In actuality, the management of most organizations can be expected to resist unions. Although there are laws governing what management can or cannot do, management will undoubtedly use a variety of tactics to protect its interest. While it is running its "stay nonunion campaign," it will be attempting to persuade the potential member to vote no. Union organizers realize that some initial signers may be persuaded to vote no. Thus unions usually require a much higher percentage on authorization cards so that they can increase their odds of obtaining a 50 percent plus one vote, a majority.

When that majority vote is received, the NLRB certifies the union and recognizes it as the exclusive bargaining representative for all employees within the specified bargaining unit. Irrespective of whether the individual in the certified bargaining unit voted for or against the union, each worker is covered by the negotiated contract and must abide by the governance.

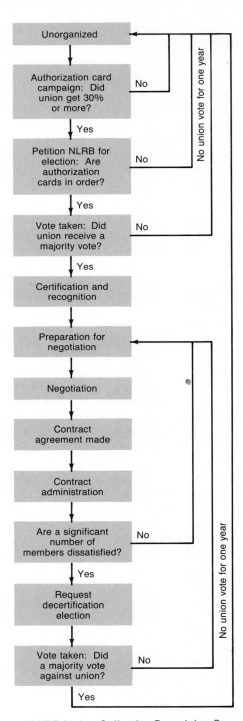

FIGURE 21-1   Collective Bargaining Process

RD elections

Once a union has been certified, is it there for life? Certainly not. On some occasions, the union members become so dissatisfied with the union's actions in representing them that they want to turn to another union or return to their nonunion status. In either case, the rank-and-file members petition the NLRB to conduct a representation decertification (RD). Once again, if a majority of the members vote the union out, it is gone. However, once the election has been held, no other action can occur for another twelve-month period. This grace period protects the employer from having employees decertifying one union today and certifying another tomorrow. And finally, and even more rare

RM elections

than an RD, is an RM or representation decertification initiated by management. The guidelines for the RM are the same as for the RD except that it is the employer who is leading the drive. While RDs and RMs are possibilities to decertify unions, it should be pointed out that most labor agreements bar the use of either decertification election during the term of the contract.

Organizing drives may be unsuccessful, but when they do achieve their goal to become the exclusive bargaining agent, the next step is to negotiate the contract. However, before attempting to negotiate the contract, advance preparation is warranted.

Preparation for Negotiation

Preparing to negotiate a contract

Once a union has been certified, both the union and management begin the ongoing activity of preparing for negotiations. We refer to this as an *ongoing activity* because it should begin, ideally, as soon as the previous contract is agreed upon or certification is achieved. Realistically, it probably begins anywhere from a month to six months before the current contract expires. We can consider the preparation for negotiation as basically composed of three activities: fact gathering, goal setting, and strategy development. Since we are interested in the role of collective bargaining in HRM, the following discussion will look at the process from management's perspective.

Information is acquired from both internal and external sources. Internal data that are needed will include grievance and accident records; employee performance reports; overtime figures; and reports on transfers, turnover, and absenteeism. External information should include statistics on the current economy, both at local and national levels; economic forecasts for the short and intermediate terms; copies of recently negotiated contracts by the adversary union to determine what issues the union considers important; data on the communities in which the company operates—cost of living, changes in cost of living, terms of recently negotiated labor contracts, and statistics on the labor market; and industry labor statistics to see what terms other organizations, employing similar types of personnel, are negotiating.

VIEWS IN THE NEWS

Dealing with Organizing: Do's and Don'ts

Faced with a declining membership base and an erosion of bargaining power, organized labor is stepping up its efforts to enlist new members from previously untapped or underrepresented segments of the labor force. Unions are focusing on women and minorities, as well as high-tech and service industry employees, as likely recruits. In planning for a "resurgence" of labor's fortunes unions also are adopting innovative tactics, such as television advertising campaigns, to rebuild their public image. In light of these developments, employers would be well-advised to review the legal ground rules governing what management can and can't do during a representation campaign.

INADVISABLE ACTIONS

The Taft Act, as enforced by NLRB and the federal courts, places certain restrictions on supervisors' statements and conduct during a union organizing drive. These rules are designed to prevent unfair labor practices that interfere with employees' right to join or support a union. Under the law, for example, supervisors cannot:

- Misrepresent the facts—Any information management provides about a union or its officers must be factual and truthful.
- Threaten employees—It is unlawful to threaten employees with loss of their jobs or transfers to less desirable positions, income reductions, or loss or reduction of benefits and privileges. Use of intimidating language to dissuade employees from joining or supporting a union also is forbidden. In addition, supervisors may not blacklist, lay off, discipline, or discharge any employee because of union activity.
- Promise benefits or rewards—Supervisors may not promise a pay raise, additional overtime or time off, promotions, or other favorable considerations in exchange for an employee's agreement to refrain from joining a union or signing a union card, vote against union representation, or otherwise oppose union activity.
- Make unscheduled changes in wages, hours, benefits, or working conditions—Any such changes are unlawful unless the employer can prove they were initiated before union activity began.
- Conduct surveillance activities—Management is forbidden to spy on or request anti-union workers to spy on employees' union activities, or to make any statements that give workers the impression they are being watched. Supervisors also may not attend union meetings or question employees about a union's internal affairs. They also may not ask employees for their opinions of a union or its officers.
- Interrogate workers—Managers may not require employees to tell them who has signed a union card, voted for union representation, attended a union meeting, or instigated an organizing drive.
- Prohibit solicitation—Employees have the right to solicit members on company property during their nonworking hours, provided this activity does not interfere with work being performed, and to distribute union literature in nonwork areas during their free time.

The above acquired information tells management where it is, what similar organizations are doing, and what it can anticipate from the economy in the near term. These data are then used to determine what management can expect to achieve in the negotiation. What can it expect the union to ask for? What is management prepared to acquiesce on?

With homework done, information in hand, and tentative goals established, management must put together the most difficult part of the bargaining preparation activities—developing a strategy for dealing with the union's demands. This includes assessing the union's power and specific tactics.

Not all unions bargain from equal power bases. The security agreement that the union has with management, the labor market, economic conditions, rates of inflation, and recent contract settlements will all affect the degree of union influence. The ability of management to tolerate a strike will also be crucial. If demand for the company's product or service has been high, management will be reluctant to absorb a strike, even one of short duration. On the other hand, if business has been slow, management may be considerably less willing to concede to union demands and may be prepared to accept a lengthy strike. These power factors will all affect the tactics of bargaining.

Negotiation

Negotiation customarily begins by the union delivering to management a long and extravagent list of demands. By initiating with extreme demands, the union creates significant room for trading in the later stages of the negotiation. It also disguises the union's real position, leaving it to management to try to figure out which demands are adamantly sought, which are moderately sought, and which the union is prepared to quickly abandon. Examples of recent demands made by unions upon management include an immediate increase in the hourly wage, special adjustments for skilled workers, cost-of-living adjustments, early retirement, free dental care, free psychiatric care, improved quality of work life, increased relief time off the assembly line, more paid holidays, extended vacations, a shorter workweek, and a guaranteed annual wage.

A long list of demands often fulfills the internal political needs of the union. By seeming to back numerous wishes of the union's members, the union's administrators appear to be satisfying the needs of the many factions within the membership. In reality, however, these will be scaled down or abandoned if the union's negotiators believe it is expedient to do so. Not surprisingly, the initial response from management is usually as extreme as the union; that is, management counters by offering little more than the terms of the previous contract. It is not even unusual for management to begin by proposing a reduction in benefits and demanding that the union take a lesser role in the organization's decision-making process.

These initial proposals are then considered by each party. This is a time of exploration—each trying to clarify the proposals of the other and to marshal arguments against them. As should be expected, political activity tends to accelerate as each group plays out various roles. Management may say, "If we concede to the union's demands, we'll be bankrupt within six months"; or union representatives may argue, "Company profits are at an all-time high, and our previous settlement has been eaten away by inflation. We must not only achieve a large raise to cover the next two years, but we must also be compensated for the loss in buying power during the past two years."

While both management and union representatives publicly accentuate the differences between them, the real negotiations go on behind closed doors. Each party tries to assess the relative priorities of the other's demands. Furthermore, each begins to combine proposals into viable packages. What takes place, then, is the attempt to get management's highest offer to approximate the lowest demands that the union is willing to accept. Hence negotiation is an activity of compromise, each group forced to give up some of its demands in order that an agreement can be reached. When an oral agreement is achieved, it is converted into a written contract. Finally, negotiation concludes with the representatives submitting the contract for ratification or approval.

This brief summary of the negotiating process tends to mask the fact that conflict is a natural part of negotiation. Given that the resources that management is being asked to increase are scarce, there is reluctance to increase settlements. Increased costs, if not offset by increases in productivity, must be either passed on in higher prices or absorbed through a lower profit margin.

From the view of the union representatives, failure to secure a satisfactory settlement can cause dissension among union members and eventually lead to pressures for union officers to resign, create a loss of union membership, or both. Therefore the union representatives have a vested self-interest in ensuring that they at least appear to have made heavy demands on management. While militancy may not be the way to win negotiations, such behavior by union representatives is often necessary to demonstrate to the rank-and-file members how hard the union is fighting to improve their working conditions and standard of living. One of the problems inherent in collective bargaining is the fact that representatives do the bargaining. A representative must be prepared to compromise, but to do so paradoxically reduces his power base with his constituency:

> *He has been placed in a leadership position because he holds the trust of the group and will be expected to represent the views held by his constituencies. But in the bargaining process, any signs shown by this leader of his willingness to compromise demonstrates weakness in the constituency's view and threatens his power position. Should he be in a position to resolve the issue so as to make his group a clear winner, at the expense of the other, he returns a hero. Should the compromise be made at his group's expense, the leader returns a loser and finds his leadership position deteriorated. Therefore, "giving in" on some of the demands of the adversary may significantly alter his leadership effectiveness with his group, but it is this compromising that is necessary to achieve resolution.[3]*

The possible preliminary outcomes from negotiation are only two. First, and obviously preferable, is agreement. The other alternative, the failure to reach agreement, may show itself in the need for the

[3]Stephen P. Robbins, *Managing Organizational Conflict: A Nontraditional Approach* (Englewood Cliffs N.J.: Prentice-Hall, 1974), p. 71.

services of a third party—a fact finder, a mediator, or an arbitrator. The role of the third party may be advisory, reviewing the areas of disagreement and pointing out unreasonable positions and areas of compromise. In arbitration, the third party hears arguments from both sides and then comes to a decision. This decision may be ignored by the parties or may be binding, depending on the prior agreement made between the conflicting parties. Of course, at the extreme, when no viable solution can be found to the parties' differences, there may be a strike or a lockout.

The union's ultimate weapon is its right to strike—to walk off the job. Paralleling this activity may be picketing of company facilities or boycotting of the company's products and services. Management, too, has its ultimate weapon. It can always lock out employees from their jobs. Clearly, however, the union's threat or actual practice of striking, picketing, and boycotting has a far more powerful impact than a lock-out or a threat of one.

Contract Administration

Administering
a contract
Once a contract is agreed upon and ratified, it then must be administered. The way it will be administered is included in the contract itself.

For instance, 70 percent of collective-bargaining contracts include management right provisions that specifically state management's prerogatives.[4] Typically, management is guaranteed the right to allocate organizational resources in the most efficient manner; to create reasonable rules; to hire, promote, transfer, and discharge employees; to determine work methods and assign work; to create, eliminate, and classify jobs; to lay off employees when necessary; to close or relocate facilities; to institute technological changes, and so forth. Of course, good HRM practices suggest that whether the contract requires it or not, management would be smart to notify the union of major decisions that will influence its membership. Such a practice will minimize disruptive effects and reduce bargaining conflicts when the current contract expires.

Probably the most important element of contract administration has to do with the spelling out of a procedure for handling contractual disputes. Almost all collective-bargaining agreements contain formal procedures to be used in resolving grievances over the interpretation and application of the contract. For instance, approximately 99 percent of all labor contracts have provisions in their agreements for resolving specific, formally initiated grievances by employees concerning dissatisfaction with job-related issues.[5]

[4]William H. Holley and Kenneth M. Jennings, *The Labor Relations Process*, 2nd ed. (New York: Dryden Press, 1984), p. 333.

[5]Ibid., p. 247.

Grievance procedures are typically designed so as to resolve grievances as quickly as possible and at the lowest level possible in the organization. As such, the first step almost always has the employee attempt to resolve the grievance with his or her immediate supervisor. If it cannot be resolved at this stage, it is typically discussed with the union steward and the supervisor. Failure at this stage usually brings in the operations superintendent, someone from the organization's industrial relations department, or the facilities' manager. When the grievance still cannot be resolved, it is usual for a third-party arbitrator to hear the case and make a ruling. In practice, we find that 99 percent of all collective-bargaining agreements provide for arbitration as the final step in an impasse.[6] Of course, in small organizations these steps tend to be condensed, possibly moving from discussing the grievance with the union steward to taking the grievance directly to the organization's senior executive or owner. Finally, management should be aware that a number of states have mediation services to assist with negotiation problems. At the national level, the Federal Mediation and Conciliation Service provides mediators and arbitrators on a no-fee basis to both public and private organizations.

Several Important Trends in Collective Bargaining

Four trends in collective bargaining have evolved over the past two decades. The first is a marked increase in rejection of agreements by union members when their representatives have presented the negotiated contract to them for ratification. The second is an increase in the militancy of public-sector employees. The third and fourth trends deal with union avoidance and concessionary bargaining, respectively.

Rejection of Agreements

Rejection of agreements

Twenty years ago when a contract had been agreed to by labor and management representatives, the contract's ratification was, for all intents and purposes, merely a rubber-stamping activity. In fact, it was not unusual for there to be no ratification vote. Not so today! We now find an increasing number of instances where the union membership turns down the final agreement resolved through negotiations and sends its representatives back to the bargaining tables. Why is this happening? Several reasons have been proposed.[7]

The most frequent reason for rejecting agreements is dissatisfaction with the size of wage and fringe benefits. Union members, like most of the work force, have suffered from the rapidly inflating cost of living. When inflation was averaging more than 12 percent a year,

[6]Holley and Jennings, *Labor Relations Process*, p. 247.
[7]Bok and Dunlop, "Collective Bargaining in the United States," p. 385.

a union settlement of anything less translates into a lower standard of living. Union members in recent years, therefore, have voiced their frustration over lower settlements by increasingly rejecting the contract terms negotiated by their representatives.

It can be argued that many union administrators have lost touch with the needs and desires of their constituencies. In some cases, for instance, union negotiators have fought hard to gain increased medical benefits, earlier retirement, and larger pensions, only to have the agreement fail ratification. It is then that many negotiators find out that the members preferred something else—such as greater immediate wage increases.

A most disturbing reason for this rejection of agreements may be political. Rejection of the agreement may be a deliberate tactic to demonstrate unity among the rank-and-file membership. The union's administrators may not actively seek ratification by the members. They may accept the rejection, then go back to management and say, in effect, "See, we told you this was an inadequate offer. We knew our members would not find it acceptable." Of course, such a tactic is not consistent with good-faith bargaining. Management becomes soured by the practice. Moreover, once management finds itself burnt by such a tactic, future bargaining will be seriously hurt. Next time around, management is likely to save its best offer for a later date, in anticipation of the first representative-derived agreement being rejected by the membership.

Finally, contract rejection can imply internal union political problems. When the rank-and-file members refuse to be persuaded by the union leadership that the tentative agreement is the best that can be achieved, they are revealing a lack of trust in their leadership. This aspect became quite evident in the 1981 coal miners' negotiation as the rank and file and the executive council of the union vetoed the contract. This action was partly responsible for the decline of the then UMW president, who was removed from office during their next election.

Public Employee Militance

Public employee militance

The second trend we have identified is the growing militancy of public employees. This is most evident in the increasing number of work stoppages and strikes in the public sector, even in the face of state laws forbidding public-sector strikes. Strikes by employees of state and local government have sometimes occurred at a rate of more than forty a month.[8] Headlines of our newspapers tell us about the more visible of these. Police and firefighters walk out in Memphis and Wichita. Teachers strike in Cleveland and Chicago. Major work stoppages occur

[8]Holley and Jennings, *Labor Relations Process*, p. 438.

in Philadelphia, Detroit, Louisville, St. Louis, Tucson, and Dayton. As with contract rejection, twenty years ago such walkouts and strikes were rare. But times have changed in the public sector.

A major part of the explanation for this phenomenon lies in the relatively recent rise of public-sector collective bargaining, which had not been widely practiced until the late 1960s. But the inflation-revenue squeeze may have been the more dominant factor in the past few years.

Inflation pushed up the price of providing government services. At the same time, Proposition 13-type taxpayer revolts spread throughout the United States. The public was saying that it wanted tax cuts or at least no increases. Yet it assumed that the level of government services could be maintained, even with inflation, by merely having public employees work harder and become more efficient. These employees did not believe that they should be expected to subsidize lower taxes by doing more work for the same or less money. The result was aroused public employees who were more adamant at the bargaining tables and more willing to accept a lengthy walkout than their peers of a decade or more ago.

FIGURE 21-2   *"You fellows about ready to strike for dinner?"*

SOURCE: GRIN AND BEAR IT by Fred Wagner © by and permission of News America Syndicate.

Union Avoidance

Avoiding unions

As we stated earlier, management is unlikely to give up running the ship without a fight simply because a union organizing campaign is under way. However, how it is fighting back has changed. Let us review the old methods and the new antiunion tactics.

A popular long-term response of management has been to support lobbying efforts for legislation at the state level that prohibits requiring individuals to be members of a union as a condition of employment. Management has a vested interest in supporting such legislation, widely referred to as "right-to-work" laws, because in states that have so-called right-to-work laws, the union shop is illegal (see Chapter 20). Employees cannot be forced to join a union if they want to work for an employer, even though employees at that location are unionized. As a result, where right-to-work laws exist, it is more difficult for unions to survive.

The above approach is unrealistic for many small organizations that can muster little political power. Moreover, when confronted with the fact that an organizing drive is currently under way, the management in small or large firms must make an immediate response. Such a response tends to take the form of a countercampaign to argue the benefits of maintaining a nonunion environment. This frequently means that management emphasizes what is has done in the past for its employees, the value of the individual ethic and the individual freedoms that workers relinquish when they become part of a collective-bargaining unit, and the costs of unionization. But management's countercampaign must be carefully thought out and implemented. The information given workers must be factual and nonthreatening. In this context, management must be careful not to engage in illegal practices. These include physically interfering, threatening, or engaging in violent behavior toward organizers; interfering with the employees involved in the organizing drive; disciplining or discharging employees for any prounion activities; or promising to provide or withhold future benefits contingent on the employees' decision regarding unionization.

The two methods mentioned above, while not obsolete, are giving way to new techniques. To meet the challenge of more-sophisticated union-organizing efforts, some companies have been engaging in two major activities: remaining nonunion through expensive antiunion campaigns or union busting.

Many companies that desire to remain nonunion are engaging in activities that inform employees that joining a union is not worthwhile. Through educational programs, these companies have tried to avoid having the campaign begin. To do so, they are implementing sound employee relations programs in their organizations. These programs are designed to provide benefits that are similar to those that unions would provide, yet without the fees associated with joining the union. These companies also have elaborate grievance procedures designed to permit the employee to settle a complaint. As stated in the epigraph in Chapter 20, "The union organizer's best weapon is poor management." Therefore these employee relations programs are designed to correct the discretionary decisions of employers toward their workers.

Companies are also using audiovisual devices to spread the word that management believes that if workers were knowledgeable about unions, understanding the facts and voting on these premises rather than emotions, unions would never win an election. Some of these audiovisual devices sell for a few thousand dollars and are owned by some of the leading companies in the United States. Do they educate the worker about unionism? Figure 21-2 lists the issues that are addressed in one popular film. Answer yes or no to each of them. When your instructor gives you the answers, see how many you got correct. It may surprise you!

Other companies that currently operate with a unionized group of employees have taken a different approach. Programs to educate the worker about why he or she should not join a union are considered useless. Instead these companies have implemented a major effort: union busting.

Union busting Busting unions is becoming a profitable venture for some individuals. Armed with a variety of tactics, these consultants are working with companies and are developing alternatives to reduce the costs associated with the union. Some are running strong decertification

FIGURE 21-3

Union Fact Questionnaire

		YES	NO
1.	The union can guarantee you higher wages.	___	___
2.	The union can increase your pay and benefits up to union standards.	___	___
3.	Where a union shop is permissible, you can still choose not to join the union.	___	___
4.	Most workers in the United States belong to a union.	___	___
5.	When the union wins an election the company *must* agree to all union demands.	___	___
6.	If the union goes on strike, the company must close down.	___	___
7.	If an employee is striking for a contract, the employee cannot be permanently replaced.	___	___
8.	Unions have a strike fund that will pay you most of your salary while you are on strike.	___	___
9.	You can collect unemployment during a strike.	___	___
10.	When a strike is over, the company must give you your old job back.	___	___

SOURCE: Thomas-Mitchell & Associates, "Working without Unions: A Guide to Getting the Facts" (Atlanta, Georgia), pp. 14–15.

campaigns, taking short-term losses in a lockout for future gains. Others are claiming that if the company does not regain more control, it will close down the plant and move. Although statistics are not readily available regarding how many companies do shut down to eliminate their union, migration to the South by many companies has occurred. Moving to an area that is traditionally antiunion, and the fact that labor costs are cheaper and expenditures for capital improvement at the existing plant approximate the costs of building a new plant, inducements for the move are evident.

In February 1984, the U.S. Supreme Court ruled that to eliminate the union contract, a company could file for bankruptcy. While this approach had been used in the airline industry in the summer of 1983 and had been threatened by others, it is difficult to determine whether the Supreme Court's decision will have a major effect on unionization. However, this decision has obviously dealt a severe blow to organized labor.

Concessionary Bargaining

Wage and benefit concessions

Ever since the Chrysler workers voted to reduce their wages and benefits in order to help the ailing car manufacturer, concessionary bargaining has been snowballing. More and more companies facing a bleak financial future are turning to the unions representing their workers and are seeking drastic changes in their labor agreements. Salaries are a prime concern, but companies are also seeking concessions elsewhere.

All of the nation's leading newspapers have published reports of unions giving back a sum of money to the company by means of cuts in wages and benefits. Most of the major industries have sought concessions. The auto workers, the teamsters, and the airline pilots are among those whose concessions have warranted top billing. But in many cases, these concessions on wages and benefits were made with the agreement that as the economic picture improved the unions would recover their share. Additionally, as the unions made concessions, so did management. In lieu of the givebacks in wages and benefits, unions received concessions from management on job and income security and were given more input in the decision-making process.[9]

Since the economy has improved, the thrust of wage concessions has diminished. In fact, unions are now demanding that some of their givebacks be returned. While there has been some increase, for the first time in modern labor history the nonunion worker has fared better in salary increases. The average annual union wage boost negotiated in 1983 amounted to only a 2.8 percent increase.[10] Slight, but the fact remains that increases are now expected.

[9]"Why Workers Are Souring on Concessions," *Business Week*, November 1, 1982, p. 29.

[10]"Unions Settle for Less in '83," *Baltimore Sun*, January 30, 1984.

Even though unions might expect salary increases to continue, the overriding issue of productivity remains. The gains that companies made in the productivity areas are not likely to be diminished. To achieve their job and income security demands, unions relaxed many of the work rules that companies argued hindered productivity.[11] This means that unions conceded to displace workers with technological advancements (robotics), to hire fewer replacements, and to work with management on quality concerns.

Finally, concessionary bargaining has placed the responsibility for labor-management relations at the source, that is, the union and the company involved. Traditional union demands were made based on what had been demanded and achieved by the leading unions. This concept was termed *pattern bargaining,* or making demands based on the patterns established in other industry union contracts. However, the concessionary bargaining has reduced the impact of this patterned bargaining and has placed more emphasis on a case-by-case issue.[12]

Conclusion

Collective bargaining has progressed from a show of strength to one where a sophisticated strategy is needed. Specific rules and procedures must be followed to become the certified bargaining unit. Once certified, a signed labor contract is the goal. However, negotiating a contract is not easy, nor is it all fun and games. Agreements are reached only after careful preparation and long days of negotiating. And when a contract has been signed, collective bargaining does not stop. Instead it just begins, as the two parties now administer the agreement.

While the traditional collective-bargaining arena has been regarded as volatile, the trends appear to be heading toward more cooperation between the parties. Management must realize that its workers are an important asset, and the workers must realize that expecting too much may ultimately shut the business down. The best in collective bargaining, we believe, is yet to come.

SUMMARY

1. *Collective bargaining* typically refers to the negotiation, administration, and interpretation of a written agreement between two parties that covers a specific period of time. It can also include the organizing, certification, and preparation efforts that precede negotiation.

2. The objective of collective bargaining is to agree upon an acceptable contract, but because situations tend to differ widely, each contract

[11]"Wages Aren't About to Explode," *Business Week,* November 21, 1983, p. 41.
[12]Ibid.

tends to be tailored to the particular workplace and industry in which the contract is negotiated.

3. The collective-bargaining process comprises the following steps:
   a. Organizing
   b. Certification
   c. Preparation for negotiation
   d. Negotiation
   e. Contract administration

4. Four recent trends in collective bargaining:
   a. A marked increase in rejection of agreements by union members when their representatives have presented the negotiated contracts to them for ratification
   b. Increased militancy among public employees, resulting in more work stoppages and strikes
   c. Increased efforts by employers to stay nonunion or to "bust" existing unions
   d. Concessions made in many of the largest industries in which unions are strongest

KEY TERMS

Arbitration	Pattern bargaining
Collective bargaining	RC
Concessionary bargaining	RD
Contract negotiation	RM
Mandatory bargaining items	

QUESTIONS FOR REVIEW

1. What is collective bargaining? How widely practiced is it?
2. What is the objective of collective bargaining?
3. What can management do to counter a union's organizing drive?
4. What are the so-called right-to-work laws?
5. Describe the collective-bargaining process.
6. Why do a union's initial demands tend to be long and extravagant?
7. What is the purpose of a grievance procedure? Describe the typical steps in a grievance procedure.
8. What is the purpose of the preparation stage of collective bargaining?
9. How can companies avoid unions? "Bust" unions?
10. What major concessions have been made by unions since 1978?

QUESTIONS FOR DISCUSSION

1. "You can predict strikes. Union administrators have to call a strike every now and then just to demonstrate to their membership that they're fighting hard for them." Do you agree or disagree? Discuss. Could the same claim be made about corporate executives in their efforts to impress stockholders with the corporation's determination to hold down contract settlements?

2. How would the existence of a union and a collective-bargaining agreement affect (a) recruitment? (b) selection? (c) compensation? (d) discipline?

3. "All that is required for successful labor-management relations is common sense, sound business judgment, and good listening skills." Do you agree or disagree? Discuss.

4. "An employer might not want to stifle a union-organizing effort. In fact, an employer might want to encourage his employees to join a union." Do you agree or disagree? Discuss.

5. "Antiunion and union-busting attempts are techniques that are causing the labor-management relationship to step back one hundred years." Do you agree or disagree? Explain.

CONTINUING CASE: Concord General

Dealing with a Full Deck

After months of experiencing continued problems with Concord General's administration, the nurses at the hospital decided again to seek representation fourteen months to the day since their last union election. Their belief that a third party could voice their concerns better to management were well founded, since more than 85 percent of the nurses voted to join the Amalgamated Meatcutters Union (AMU). With the election over, and the subsequent certification of Local 28 of the AMU, the hospital's administration is now preparing for the negotiations.

John Michaels has decided to act as the chief spokesperson for the hospital and has asked four of his aides to join him. However, he is quite concerned about the upcoming negotiations. He feels that the unionization itself was wrong, but he realizes that he must abide by the law. However, he has stated several times that he will not buckle under to union power plays and feels that he is someone with whom the union must reckon.

While sentiments between the union and John Michaels are not the best, the fact still remains that negotiations must be started in less than six weeks. Realizing this, John has asked each of his aides for information that is needed for the upcoming negotiations. Jorge Travers, the executive vice-president, has been put in charge of preparing for the upcoming sessions and developing a list of anticipated demands from the nurses. However, since Jorge is unfamiliar with the labor relations process, John has given him permission to hire you as a consultant to help with the preparations.

Questions

1. Describe how you would instruct the hospital's administration to prepare for collective bargaining. What data would you suggest that they obtain to help them achieve a comparison referent?
2. Based on the previous activities at the hospital, list the possible demands that you expect from the nurses.
3. Discuss the similarities and differences in managing the nurses now that they are unionized.

CASE APPLICATION

A Royal Flush

Timmons Fisheries in South Harbor, Maine, has been the leading distributor of fish products in the Mid-Atlantic States for the past quarter of a century. Timmons is known for its fresh fish, its frozen fish products, and its distribution of exotic fish. Until five years ago, Timmons had experienced continual growth. Although its packaging and distribution workers were unionized, Timmons had been more than willing to pass on to the workers part of the profits made. However, profits have not been very good lately. Consumer demand for Timmons' breaded fish products has severely declined as the consumer has become more weight conscious. Losing its share of that market segment has meant a financial burden. To help alleviate the burden, Timmons management has turned to the union representatives, its workers, and has asked for givebacks in wages and benefits amounting to $2.50 per hour.

The union feels that the request is unreasonable and that the rank and file will strike if the issue is pressed. Timmons's response is that if the cuts are not made—savings that would allow for retooling the production process to regain its market segment—the company will face bankruptcy. As one Timmons vice-president stated, "Two and half bucks less an hour is better than no pay at all. But those union folks cannot understand that."

Seemingly unable to compromise, the union members went on strike. After three months of striking, Timmons began to search for a new location and a new owner for the company. To avoid the impending doom, the rank and file voted for a new wage package that amounted to a $2.10-per-hour cut. On Friday, the package was ratified, and the workers returned to work.

The following Monday, the newspaper headlines read: "Union Accepts Wage Cuts, Management Gives Itself a Raise." In the evening newsstory, the president of Timmons explained that for five years while experiencing problems, no manager had been given a raise. To keep the managers from resigning, there were given an across-the-board raise. It had been planned before the strike, and "it's just too bad that it coincided with the union's wage cut."

Questions

1. Do you believe the raise given to management was an unfair labor practice? An attempt to bust the union? Discuss.
2. What impact do you believe this management action will have for the workers returning to work after a three-month strike? For the next negotiations?
3. Are the activities undertaken by management concerning management under the union's scrutiny? Discuss.
4. If you were the president of Timmons, what would you have done? Discuss.

ADDITIONAL READINGS

"Beyond Unions," *Business Week,* July 8, 1985, pp. 72–77.

"Big Labor Tries the Soft Sell," *Business Week,* October 13, 1986, p. 126.

COLLINS, R. DOUGLAS, "Agency Shop in Public Employment," *Public Personnel Management,* 15, No. 2 (Summer 1986), 171–79.

FREEDMAN, LEE, and ROBERT J. HARVEY, "Factors of Union Commitment: The Case for Lower Dimensionality," *Journal of Applied Psychology,* 71, No. 3 (August 1986), 371–76.

SOLBERG, SYDNEY L., "Changing Culture Through Ceremony: An Example from GM," *Human Resource Management,* 24, No. 3 (Fall 1985), 329–40.

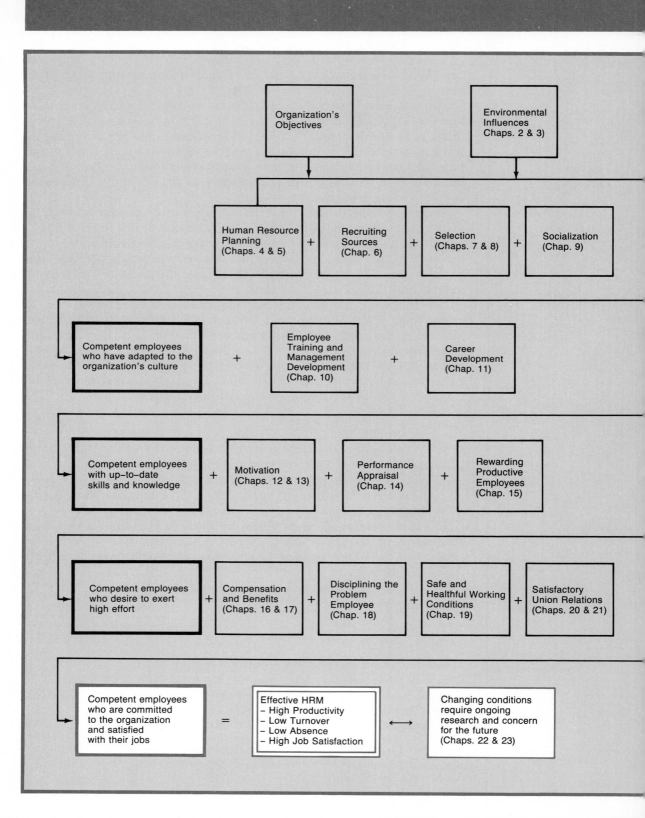

PART SIX

RESEARCH
AND
THE FUTURE

	Competent employees who have adapted to the organization's culture
=	

	Competent employees with up–to–date skills and knowledge
=	

	Competent employees who desire to exert high effort
=	

	Competent employees who are committed to the organization and satisfied with their jobs
=	

CHAPTER 22

Research

in Human Resource

Management

AFTER READING THIS CHAPTER, YOU WILL BE ABLE TO:

1. Define *research*
2. Explain why every manager should conduct HRM research
3. Define *pure research*
4. Define *primary research*
5. Identify the secondary sources of HRM information
6. Describe the most popular and relevant techniques for doing primary research on HRM topics

It's what you learn after you know it all that counts.

—John Wooden

Managers make decisions and solve problems. Additionally, we have described all managers as having responsibilities for ensuring the acquisition, development, motivation, and maintenance of their subordinates. To make decisions about personnel and to solve human resource problems, managers gather data and draw conclusions from these data. The effective manager will attempt to substitute systematic inquiry and analysis in place of intuition wherever possible. While almost all management decisions can be improved if managers appreciate and use research findings, in this chapter we want to present the benefits and methods of research as it applies to making human resource decisions.

What is Research?

Research defined   Among practicing managers, the term *research* frequently carries the connotation of academic "mumbo jumbo" or irrelevant findings that have little generalizability to practice. While this, of course, is true in a number of cases, it certainly need not be. The research process and the findings it generates can provide valuable input to a manager.

When we use the term *research*, we mean a systematic and goal-oriented investigation of facts that seeks to establish a relationship between two or more phenomena. Most of the conclusions presented throughout this book are based on systematic and goal-oriented research. For instance, you may remember that in our discussion on selection we presented the assessment center as a highly effective procedure for identifying high performers. This statement was not based on casual observation or intuition; rather, it was based on a number of research studies, the results of which led us to our conclusion.

Research, however, is not the province solely of scientists and academicians. By the time you finish reading this chapter, it will be clear to you that every effective manager should consider research—particularly human resources research—a mandatory and ongoing part of his or her job.

Types of Research

There are a number of ways to classify research, but we have made a few distinctions that are important for understanding its applicability to human resource management.

Pure versus Applied Research

Pure research

Applied research

Some research projects are engaged in for their own sake. There is no specific problem that is expected to be solved. This type of research is referred to as *pure*. In contrast, research that seeks to find an answer to a specific current problem is called *applied*.

Pure research is more likely to be conducted by scientists in laboratories—for instance, within the Bell System—than by actual managers. For the most part, it is probably fair to say that managers are, and should be, concerned only with applied research. In determining how to most effectively use the personnel within an organization, managers must confront an unending series of specific and changing problems that demand managerial action—and applied research can be helpful in suggesting ways of directing this action.

Primary versus Secondary Research

Primary research

Research can also be distinguished as being either primary or secondary. Effective managers will utilize both primary and secondary research sources.

By *primary research*, we are referring to original investigations. If you were to ask individuals in your organization to complete a questionnaire on factors they like and dislike about their supervisor, you would be conducting primary research.

Secondary research

It is usually far easier and less costly to engage in *secondary research;* that is, to rely on investigations, the source of which is outside the organization. If you have a problem to solve and look for the solution in books, journals, or trade magazines, you would be utilizing secondary research sources.

Managers should regularly review the most recent books and articles that relate to their current or potential managerial problems. In this way, they develop a mental file of where to look for secondary sources when they seek to solve these problems. But there will be times when secondary research will be done in conjunction with or superseded by primary research. If the problem is unique, or if the conditions are somewhat different from those that previous research has encountered, or if it is believed that there might be some benefits in attempting to replicate a previous study in your organization, then primary research methods will be desirable. Later in this chapter we will present sources of secondary research and discuss the more relevant primary research methods.

Why Research in HRM?

HRM research   Research can lead to an increased understanding of and improvement in HRM practices. The following examples represent a small sample of topics that can be better understood through HRM research:

- Wage surveys
- Effectiveness of various recruitment sources
- Test validation
- Effectiveness of training efforts
- Supervisor's effectiveness survey
- Development of weighted application blanks
- Recent community labor settlements
- Recent industry settlements
- Recent labor settlements negotiated by our union
- Job analysis
- Effectiveness of an assessment center
- Job satisfaction survey
- Survey of employee needs
- Performance appraisal validation
- Attitude survey toward reward system
- Areas of high accident frequency
- Areas of high reported OSHA violations
- Compliance with affirmative action goals

The above listing suggests that HRM research can provide insights for managers as they atrtempt to increase employee productivity and satisfaction while reducing absence and turnover. For instance, research findings let managers become aware of changes. The department manager who annually surveys her subordinates' attitudes about their work, her supervisory practices, and the organization in general will develop long-term data that will allow her to assess changes in her subordinates' perception of the organization's climate. Research can also identify potential problem areas. If our department manager notes an unexpected drop in her subordinates' satisfaction with a certain element of their work, she can take rapid action to correct it, preferably before it leads to resignations, increased absenteeism, shoddy workmanship, or some similarly undesirable outcome.

Managers derive other positive benefits from engaging in research. Certainly managers who keep current with what other managers are doing and with the latest HRM theories increase the probability that they will be more effective. In fact, engaging in some type of research into what is happening in the HRM discipline can be viewed as necessary for one's survival as a manager over the long term. Research can additionally help managers answer questions about the successfulness of programs—such as those for training and development—for which they may bear responsibility. For example, it can be used to determine whether a program's benefits exceed its costs.

We should also remember that some of the research findings presented in a book such as this are not generalizable to all situations. Research studies on the motivation needs of unionized automobile workers in Detroit, for example, may have little bearing if you are managing a group of nonunionized civil engineers working for the New Hampshire Department of Highways. Therefore there are benefits to a manager who understands the methodology or approach for engaging in primary research. Such research can provide answers to the unique issues and problems that managers face in their *specific* environment.

Secondary Sources: Where to Look it Up

As we noted above, a manager's long-term survival depends on staying current. We propose, therefore, that every manager should engage in ongoing secondary research.

What sources should a manager look to in order to keep up with the latest findings in HRM? The answer to that question depends on the level of sophistication desired. Obviously, research journals are directed to different audiences. Some assume the reader has a solid background in statistics and research methodology. Articles in these journals contain more details but at the expense of being more difficult to read. Other journals are meant to be read quickly. Their articles are condensed and simplified. Whether you read one type of journal or both depends on what you are looking for. The two lists below cover the major sources in HRM. We have separated the more academic or rigorous sources from the nontechnical (those focusing on translating the academic research into practical application).

In addition to the journals we have listed, other secondary sources include books, government publications, and research reports from organizations such as the American Management Association, American Society for Personnel Administrators, American Society for Training and Development, the Institute of Social Research at the University of Michigan, the International Personnel Management Association, the International Industrial Relations Association, and the National Industrial Conference Board.

Technical Journals

HRM-related journals: technical

Academy of Management Journal	Human Organization
Behavioral Science	Human Relations
Canadian Industrial Psychology	Industrial and Labor Relations Review

Industrial Psychology
Industrial Relations
Industrial Relations Quarterly
  Review
Journal of Applied Behavioral
  Science
Journal of Applied Psychology
Journal of Business Research
Journal of Human Resources
Journal of Industrial
  Psychology
Journal of Industrial Relations

Journal of Social Psychology
Journal of Vocational Behavior
Manpower and Applied
  Psychology
Occupational Psychology
Organizational Behavior and
  Human Performance
Personnel Practice Bulletin
Personnel Psychology
Psychological Bulletin
Studies in Personnel
  Psychology

Nontechnical Journals

HRM-related
journals:
nontechnical

Academy of Management
  Review
Across the Board
Arbitration Journal
Business Horizons
Business Week
California Management Review
Canadian Personnel and
  Industrial Relations Journal
Civil Service Journal
Compensation Review
Employee Relations Law
  Journal
Fortune
Harvard Business Review
Human Resource Management
Labor Law Journal
Labour Gazette
Management of Personnel
  Quarterly

Management Research
Manpower
Monthly Labor Review
Organizational Dynamics
Pension and Welfare News
Personnel and Guidance
  Journal
Personnel Journal
Psychology Today
Public Administration Review
Public Personnel Management
Public Personnel Review
Supervision
The Personnel Administrator
The Personnel Woman
Training and Development
  Journal
Training in Business and
  Industry

Primary Sources: Relevant Research Methods

We now want to turn to the more ambitious objective of providing
guidance in the conducting of primary research. The methodologies
discussed below represent the most popular and relevant techniques
for doing primary research on HRM topics.

Historical Studies

Historical studies   The easiest method for engaging in primary research is to use the records and documents that the organization already has on file. Historical studies review past information in order to identify unique patterns. For instance, assume a manager wanted to know if there were common characteristics in subordinates who voluntarily resigned within six months of being hired. The manager might use personnel records to assess whether age, sex, years of work experience, departmental affiliation, or any other characteristics differentiated those who left from those who stayed. Such information might prove highly beneficial for making future selection decisions.

An Actual Research Study.   To demonstrate how a manager might go about doing a historical study, we will present a factual example. The following research investigation took place at the Minnesota Gas Company.[1]

Over the thirty-year period between 1945 and 1975, Minnesota Gas required all job applicants to complete a job preference questionnaire that asked respondents to rank the importance of ten factors that make a job good or bad. During the thirty-year period, the utility accumulated over fifty-six thousand usable questionnaires. The questionnaire itself first asked applicants to rank, from most important (1) to least important (10), their preferences for the following ten job factors: advancement, benefits, company image, co-workers, working hours, pay, security, supervisor, type of work, and working conditions. Second, applicants were asked to rate these same factors as they thought *others* of similar age, education, number of dependents, and engaged in the same type of work would respond.

What did a historical summation of these data reveal? It was found that the rank ordering of self-preferences remained unusually consistent. This must be viewed as surprising given the major political, social, and economic changes from the post–World War II period to the post-Vietnam years. However, the rankings differed significantly between male and female respondents. Figure 22-1 summarizes the rankings by sex.

The data in Figure 22-1 indicate that Minnesota Gas's male applicants considered security the most important factor (2.5) and working conditions the least important (7.9). Ratings for the remaining eight factors were spread rather evenly between those of the top- and bottom-ranked factors. Women, however, rated their top choice, type of work, far more important (1.5) than any other factor. Their rankings of the next eight factors are closely bunched (between 4.6 and 6.9) while benefits stand alone at the bottom (8.0).

[1]Clifford E. Jurgensen, "Job Preferences (What Makes a Job Good or Bad?)," *Journal of Applied Psychology,* June 1978, pp. 267–76.

FIGURE 22-1

Median Rankings of Ten Job Factors Over a Thirty-year Time Interval

JOB FACTOR	MALES		FEMALES	
	Self-Preference Ranking	Ascribed To Others Ranking	Self-Preference Ranking	Ascribed To Others Ranking
Advancement	3.3 (2)	3.8 (3)	5.3 (5)	4.3 (3)
Benefits	6.8 (8)	5.2 (5)	8.0 (10)	5.9 (6)
Company image	4.5 (4)	6.8 (7)	4.6 (2)	7.1 (9)
Co-workers	6.0 (6)	7.7 (10)	5.2 (4)	7.3 (10)
Working hours	7.6 (9)	5.4 (6)	6.9 (9)	5.0 (4)
Pay	5.6 (5)	2.1 (1)	6.0 (7)	2.1 (1)
Security	2.5 (1)	3.6 (2)	4.9 (3)	5.4 (5)
Supervisor	6.3 (7)	7.4 (9)	5.3 (5)	7.0 (8)
Type of work	3.3 (2)	4.9 (4)	1.5 (1)	3.5 (2)
Working conditions	7.9 (10)	6.9 (8)	6.5 (8)	6.8 (7)

SOURCE: Adapted from Clifford E. Jurgensen, "Job Preferences (What Makes a Job Good or Bad?)," *Journal of Applied Psychology*, June 1978, pp. 269–70. Copyright 1978 by the American Psychological Association. Reprinted by permission.

Job preferences attributed to others differed significantly from self-preferences. Consistent with the beliefs of most lay people and many managers, respondents thought pay would be most important to others. Corporate personnel policies and the reward system at Minnesota Gas should reflect these self-preferences.

Closer analysis of the data by age, marital status, and educational level gave the utility other information that could prove valuable in shaping its HRM policies. For example, younger applicants, especially those under age twenty, placed more emphasis on the here and now, and less on factors that are more important in the long run. Younger respondents attached greater importance to co-workers, hours, pay, their supervisor, and working conditions, with less importance given to advancement, benefits, company image, and security.

When the applicants were separated as to single, married, widowed, divorced, or separated, single men were found to differ markedly from other men. Their preferences tended to be very similar to those under age twenty, which is not too surprising since the two groups overlap. Differences between married, widowed, divorced, and separated men were not significant. Marital status had no effect on female responses except for widows. This group placed more importance on advancement, benefits, and security, and less importance on co-workers, hours, type of work, and working conditions.

The level of the applicant's education also moderated the findings in Figure 22-1. As education increased, so did the importance of type of work. At the same time, however, the importance of security declined.

Summary.   Note that the above analysis and conclusions were made entirely on data that already existed in Minnesota Gas's personnel files. From these data the company's researchers were able to generate overall patterns of applicant job preferences, and to moderate the findings so as to know more about the preferences of individuals having similar characteristics. Certainly this type of research should be an important input to shaping HRM policies in the areas of selection, job design, reward allocations, and benefit offerings at the Minnesota Gas Company.

Surveys

Surveys   The most common form of primary HRM research is undoubtedly the survey. By using questionnaires or structured interviews, management is able to tap employee attitudes, assess present practices, and attempt to relate certain results to particular causes.

An Actual Research Study.   The employee survey described in this section took place in a bank.[2] The study sought to assess the two interrelated elements of employee job satisfaction and employee health. Its specific goals were to answer such questions as What is the level of employee satisfaction? How well is the bank handling alcohol, drug, marital, weight, smoking, and other personal problems of employees? Is job dissatisfaction behind personal problems? What can the bank do to improve its programs for dealing with these problems? The justification for doing primary rather than secondary research on these issues was defended as follows:

> *Before a program is developed in any organization, there should be an assessment of need in order to allow for individual differences among organizations. This assessment, of course, assumes that employee personal problems differ by organization—an assumption that research has yet to dispute. . . . to devise a specific intervention, an objective diagnostic effort should be undertaken. Along with this needs assessment, it is also possible to obtain from the employees some ideas about the optimal structure of a program.*[3]

A structured survey questionnaire was created and sent to a group of 263 employees randomly selected from the 2,000 who worked at the

---

[2]James A. Finkelstein, "Diagnosing Employees' Personal Problems," *Personnel Journal*, November 1978, pp. 633–36, 643.

[3]Ibid., pp. 633–34.

FIGURE 22-2

Employee Satisfaction at a Bank's Urban Central Office

QUESTION	CHOICES	PERCENTAGE RESPONSES[a]
1. Considering everything, how would you rate your overall satisfaction in the company at the present time?	Satisfied Dissatisfied Neither	58 26 16
2. How do you feel about the amount of work you do?	Too much Right amount Too little	27 62 11
3. How do you like your job—the kind of work you do?	Good Average Poor	62 25 13
4. I feel my job makes the best use of my abilities.	Yes No	47 53
5. How do you feel about the quality of supervision you get?	Good Average Poor	50 30 20
6. Do you feel the company is concerned about your performance?	Yes No	75 25

[a]Rounded to whole number and adjusted to equal 100.
SOURCE: "Diagnosing Employees' Personal Problems," by James A. Finkelstein. Reprinted with permission of *Personnel Journal*, Costa Mesa, CA. Copyright November 1978.

bank's main office; 115 valid responses were returned. The questionnaire's six employee satisfaction items and their results are shown in Figure 22-2.

The research found that 58 percent were satisfied with their work; 62 percent felt they had the right amount of work; 62 percent liked their jobs and the kind of work they were doing; and 75 percent felt the bank was concerned with their performance.

As to health-care problems, approximately one-third of the respondents would seek information on problems like drugs and alcohol if it were available; 26 percent knew someone who had missed work because of a personal problem; 27 percent knew someone whose work had been hindered by personal problems; and more than 70 percent of the employees felt health-care programs were a good idea and should be implemented. The great majority of employees did not feel free to speak to their supervisors about personal problems. Preference was given to a program operated within the bank.

Summary   When the data were carefully scrutinized, no relationship was found between job dissatisfaction and perceived needs. In fact, the need for problem consultation seemed independent of satisfaction. Did this mean that there were no suggestions to come out of this research? On the contrary. Recommendations generated by the study included:

1. The bank should begin a dialogue with its employees on personal problem issues through its personnel and employee relations division.
2. The bank should establish a committee to determine policies and directives regarding the personal problem situation and should make the policies known to all employees.
3. The bank should consider the implementation of personal problem assistance programs and an identification and referral service to support them. The form of these programs should satisfy the employee's concern for confidentiality and security.
4. In developing the program, the bank should be sensitive to the following concerns expressed by employees:
   a. Include family members
   b. Avoid contact with supervisors on personal, confidential matters
   c. Notify employees of available programs through written memoranda and newsletters.

Controlled Experiments

Controlled experiments

The third research methodology we will consider is the most complex and expensive but can produce the most valid and reliable findings. This is the controlled experiment. This methodology is built upon comparing two or more groups, where conditions are kept constant in one (the control group) while some intervention and modification is made in the others (the experimental groups). Assuming that the groups are alike on all relevant factors when the research begins, the maintenance of a control group allows us to conclude that any difference in outcome between the experimental and control groups can be attributed to the modification.

An Actual Research Study.   An example of how a controlled experiment might be done is a study undertaken at AT&T to assess the effects of job previews on job acceptance and turnover among telephone operator candidates.[4]

The researchers began by developing descriptive statements about the telephone operator position. These statements were pretested on a large group of incumbent operators, with only those statements that were agreed to by at least 70 percent of the incumbents surviving. The surviving statements were then categorized as favorable, neutral, and unfavorable based on incumbent ratings. The result

---

[4]Richard R. Reilly, Mary L. Tenopyr, and Steven M. Sperling, "Effects of Job Previews on Job Acceptance and Survival of Telephone Operator Candidates," *Journal of Applied Psychology,* April 1979, pp. 218–20.

was two scripts of equal length—a favorable script made up of thirty-six favorable and twenty-one neutral statements, and a realistic script with the same thirty-six favorable statements plus twenty-one unfavorable ones.

The researchers randomly assigned 325 candidates for the operator position to one of three groups: realistic, favorable, and control. The realistic group was given the script that contained a balanced job preview; the favorable applicants received the script that contained only favorable and neutral information; and the control group was given no special preview information. All the candidates went through the telephone company's normal employment process—initial interview, test taking, waiting for tests to be scored, and a final interview where a job offer was made to test-qualified applicants. Those individuals in the realistic and favorable groups were given their preview scripts during the waiting period. Interviewers were not aware of the type of preview given to their interviewees.

It was hypothesized that applicants receiving the realistic information would have the lowest acceptance rate, on the assumption that the inclusion of unfavorable statements would turn off some candidates. Additionally, it was hypothesized that the candidates receiving the realistic preview and accepting the job would have lower turnover than the other groups. Note that while the second hypothesis is consistent with the literature on realistic job previews, discussed in Chapter 8, the first is not. You will remember that the research has generally found that realistic previews do *not* adversely affect acceptance rates.

Summary.   Consistent with their first hypothesis, but contrary to most other published research findings, AT&T found that the realistic job previews did result in a lower acceptance rate: 56.1 percent versus 68.6 percent and 71.6 percent for the favorable and control groups, respectively. But the turnover hypothesis was not supported. The results showed no significant difference after six months between the three approaches. This latter finding is not in agreement with the preponderance of research on the realistic job preview. So the researchers naturally wondered why the telephone operators who received the realistic preview did not demonstrate less turnover. Their conclusion is interesting in the sense that it offers an excellent illustration of why managers should not always fall back on secondary research. What works on one job in one organization may not necessarily work in another organization or in another job in the same organization. The AT&T researchers surmised that the telephone operator job, in contrast to the type of job where realistic previews resulted in lower turnover, was a relatively simple job. They concluded that job previews can have more impact for more complex jobs, simply because a complex job requires more learning.

VIEWS IN THE NEWS

A Research Study to Find a Way to Reduce Absenteeism

The research component of Human Resource Management is extremely important. Often times, though, research is a word that practitioners look down on. The term connotates an activity best left to academicians. But in those organizations where Human Research Management research is conducted, the results can be beneficial to the organization.

The Problem: How to find a positive way to reduce absenteeism is the question. The study was conducted at The Maid Bess Corporation. Prior to the study, The Maid Bess Corporation experienced "an average absenteeism rate of approximately 6 percent, which translated into a $700,000 annual loss in sales, overtime payments, added overhead and extra employees."

The Method: Six separate plant sites of The Maid Bess Corporation were chosen. These plants ranged in size from 149 to 400 employees. In four of the plants, one of the following "attendance improvement" programs was implemented:

- Financial Incentive Program—$50 bonus to an employee with no absenteeism; $25 to an employee with one or two absences.
- Recognition Program—Employees with perfect quarterly attendance received a letter from management recognizing their perfect attendance; at the end of the year, any employee with one or two days' absence receive a gift of custom-designed jewelry.
- Lottery Program—A prize (worth about $200) was awarded quarterly. Employees with no absences had their names submitted twice for the drawing; one absence, and the name was submitted one time.
- Information Feedback Program—Employees received information in each paycheck on their attendance. This information had no positive or negative inference.

Workers in the two remaining plants served as control groups.

The Results: The following outcomes were identified as a result of the study:

- Financial Incentive Program—No real decrease in absenteeism found (.31% decrease).
- Recognition Program—Significant decrease in absenteeism found (36.9% decrease). While the program cost $10,000 to implement, absenteeism costs decreased more than $58,000.
- Lottery Program—An increase in absenteeism was witnessed. But when employees selected a prize of choice, a slight decrease was noticed. Overall, absenteeism costs were reduced approximately $650.
- Information Feedback Program—No real decrease in absenteeism found (.24% decrease).

The Implications: While it may be difficult to generalize these findings to all organizations, the recognition program appeared to work the best. This program "was associated with the largest decrease in absenteeism and the most dramatic change in employee attitudes."

Studies such as this study clearly show the relevance and necessity for conducting research. Organizations cannot exist in isolation. What worked yesterday may not work today. Organizations must constantly be searching for better ways to become more effective and efficient.

Source: Adapted from K. Dow Scott, Steven E. Markham, and Richard W. Robers, "Rewarding Good Attendance: A Comparative Study of Positive Ways to Reduce Absenteeism," *Personnel Administrator*, 30, No. 8 (August 1985), 72–83.

Conclusion

Who does HRM
research?

We will conclude this chapter by assessing who, in organizations, actually does HRM research. It would be naive and misleading on our part to imply that most managers actively engage in primary research. This just is not true. The more sophisticated, ambitious, and knowledgeable manager will undoubtedly initiate a project and seek outside consultants to provide the research expertise required to complete the project. Others do secondary research—reading the more popular nontechnical journals in HRM. But except for those managers working specifically in the personnel and labor relations area, few will read the technical articles.

Who, then, engages in primary research? Certainly we would argue that all managers can benefit at times by doing primary research, but that does not mean that this occurs in practice. Evidence indicates that the size of the organization is a major determinant of the amount of primary research that is likely to take place. Companies like AT&T, Western Electric, Sears, IBM, Xerox, Texas Instruments, General Motors, General Electric, and J. C. Penney all have personnel research departments. So do many state and federal agencies. But the number of organizations with personnel research departments appears to be slim.

So where does this leave us? We can say that, in spite of what managers actually do, they *can be* more effective in managing their human resources if they accept that doing ongoing secondary research is a vital part of their job. In those cases where the benefits exceed the cost, they should further recognize the value of initiating primary research when they seek answers to important HRM questions. Of course, because primary research is considerably more complicated than secondary, managers may want to consult internal research specialists or outside experts before initiating primary studies. Finally, we should expect to find full-time personnel research specialists in only the largest organizations.

SUMMARY

1. Research is a systematic and goal-oriented investigation of facts that seeks to establish a relationship between two or more phenomena.

2. Every effective manager should consider human resources research a mandatory and ongoing part of his or her job.

3. Pure research is engaged in for its own sake; applied research seeks to find an answer to a specific, current problem.

4. Primary research is original; secondary research relies on data collected by others outside the organization.

5. Secondary sources on HRM topics include technical and nontechnical journals, books, government publications, and institutional research reports.

6. The most popular and relevant primary research techniques for HRM problems are
   a. Historical studies
   b. Surveys
   c. Controlled experiments

KEY TERMS

Applied research
Controlled experiments
Historical studies
HRM research
Primary research

Pure research
Research
Secondary research
Surveys

QUESTIONS FOR REVIEW

1. Contrast an intuitive approach versus a research approach to HRM problems.

2. Compare pure and applied research. How applicable is each to the practicing manager?

3. Describe several types of problems that lend themselves to HRM research.

4. Why would a manager want to do HRM research?

5. What secondary sources might provide HRM research data on problems that might occur at (a) a state welfare office, (b) a pro-football team, and (c) a large oil refinery?

6. Contrast historical studies and survey research.

7. Why are controlled experiments described as "complex and expensive"?

8. Give an example of a type of problem that could better be investigated by historical studies than by a controlled experiment.

9. Contrast the HRM research role of the manager in theory and in practice.

10. One of the first steps in conducting HRM research is to formulate specific hypotheses. Develop three hypotheses for studies that could be conducted by an HRM research specialist.

QUESTIONS FOR DISCUSSION

1. "A manager should always try to do primary research, rather than secondary research, whenever possible." Do you agree or disagree? Explain.

2. If you were a senior executive at the Minnesota Gas Company, how would you use the information reported on pages 585–87?

3. Assume you are a manager and want to do some primary research that requires skills that are beyond your competence. Where would you go to find the expertise you needed?

4. Explain how an instructor might use research to improve his or her teaching effectiveness.

5. Explain how you might use research to make a better job-choice decision upon graduation.

CONTINUING CASE: Concord General

Time Management

The AMU and the hospital failed to reach an agreement after negotiating for fifteen months. Aggravated, the nurses have petitioned to decertify the union. Needless to say, too, Concord General has been experiencing a severe decline in productivity. Now, however, with the union decertification (RD) campaign over and the AMU ousted, John Michaels has decided to establish a committee to study the efficient utilization of staff resources and prescribe standard operating procedures that would make the most effective use of time.

Judy Sapp has been asked to chair the committee—as director of personnel, she has the most access to current employee personnel files. Serving on the committee with Judy are the unit supervisors of the Intensive Care Unit, recovery room, pediatric ward, and maternity ward, respectively.

Judy began the meeting by discussing the problems associated with poor productivity. She stated that this condition can result in increased costs, boredom, and, ultimately, low morale. If this committee is to meet its goals, it will be necessary to monitor activities in each unit to discover how time is being wasted and to develop procedures to solve the problem.

Although this is a long-term project and it is obvious that changes will not occur overnight, John Michaels has asked the committee to develop a preliminary action plan within three months.

Questions

1. Given the opportunity to research Concord General's productivity problem, how would you do so if you were given (a) unlimited time, (b) three months' time?
2. Develop a methodology that could be used to study the problem.
3. What action plan would you submit to John Michaels in three months?

CASE APPLICATION

KSUP Station

KSUP is an affiliate of one of the major television networks, located in Duluth, Minnesota. The station was established by Jon Jorgensen in 1980 and has grown over the years to where it employs a staff of approximately 150 people. Until 1987, the station was owned entirely by Jon Jorgensen and his wife. Pretax profits in 1986 had been $472,000.

In February 1987, Jon and his wife were killed in a car accident. Their only child, Ursula, suddenly found herself the owner of KSUP. A 1982 graduate of the University of Minnesota, with a degree in English, Ursula immediately left her copywriting job with an advertising firm in Minneapolis to take control of her family's business.

As Ursula reviewed her situation, she knew she had inherited a strong and profitable station. But she recognized that she had several major human resource problems on her hands. KSUP was under siege by several unions who sought to organize the station's employees; there were OSHA citations outstanding that criticized a number of work methods at the station; and the station was experiencing extreme difficulty in locating, hiring, and keeping skilled electrical technicians. Ursula wanted to make the right decisions but was unsure where to begin.

Questions

1. How might research help Ursula Jorgensen solve KSUP's problems with unionization, OSHA, and the shortage of skilled technicians?
2. Suggest secondary sources that might assist Ursula in resolving these problems.
3. Propose a primary research design for each of these problems that could give her important input in the seeking of solutions.

ADDITIONAL READINGS

BLANK, SALLY J., "The Future Ain't What It Used to Be," *Management Review,* July 1986, pp. 16–29.

COTTON, JOHN L., and JEFFREY M. TUTTLE, "Employee Turnover: A Meta-Analysis and Review with Implications for Research," *Academy of Management* Review, 11, No. 1 (January 1986), 55–70.

ELLIOTT, ROBERT K., "Auditing the 1990s: Implications for Education and Research," *California Management Review,* 28, No. 4 (Summer 1986), 16–29.

GRAEN, GEORGE B., TERRI A. SCANDURA, and MICHAEL R. GRAEN, "A Field Experiment Test of the Moderating Effects of Growth Need Strength on Productivity," *Journal of Applied Psychology,* 71, No. 3 (August 1986), 484–91.

"Nucor's Ken Iverson on Productivity and Pay," *Personnel Administrator,* October 1986, pp. 47–52.

CHAPTER 23

Human

Resource Management

in the Future

AFTER READING THIS CHAPTER, YOU WILL BE ABLE TO:

1. Describe the major forces for change in HRM
2. Discuss the societal trends that will have important implications for HRM in the twenty-first century

My interest is in the future because I am going to spend the rest of my life there.

—Charles F. Kettering

One of the most difficult things to get across in a book about a lively and rapidly changing subject is the dynamic nature of the subject matter itself. Because a textbook must, by definition, be a static entity, the whole field of human resource management may have a tendency to come across as similarly static. Nothing could be farther from the truth.

Human resource management has undergone extraordinary changes in the past generation—a fact we have continually noted in the previous twenty-two chapters. We suggest that the next generation will bring changes of similar magnitude. While the exact nature and direction of these changes are difficult to predict, it can be stated with little chance of error that there will be important changes. In this chapter, we will attempt to look at this future, constraining our horizon, however, to only the next ten years.

Forecasting the future carries certain risks. If one is going to make an effort, he should either limit his forecasts to the very near term (since the future is very much a product of the past), or to a time frame so far in the future that he can be sure that he will have long been buried when the results are finally in. Ten years seems a short enough time period to avoid soothsayings, yet reasonable enough to embarrass the authors when they are ten years older.

Our approach to forecasting will be to describe some of the major changes in our society and then attempt to interpret the possible implications of these changes on HRM. However, before we proceed, one point must be made. Whether or not these forecasts turn out to be accurate is not as relevant as the process itself. The key point to ponder is that human resource management is going to be a different "game" by the year 2000. Your forecast of how it will be different is probably as good as, or maybe better than, ours. But we must consider the future if only for the realization that you will work and manage in the future!

The previous twenty-two chapters have talked about "what is and what was." But you will be working with human resources in that period of time that "will be." It is our belief that the authors of a textbook such as this have the responsibility to get you to think about the future and how the subject you are studying may be different in the years ahead. That is what this chapter is all about.

The Future Reflects the Recent Past

Future reflects past   The past quarter century has seen significant changes in our society brought about by technological advancements, social alterations, economic influences, and political pressures. A short list of the more obvious would include:

- Technological:
  —Organ transplants
  —The space shuttle
  —Artificial organs
  —Fourth-generation computer software
- Social:
  —Human rights movement
  —Women's movement
  —Unprecedented growth in higher-education enrollments
  —Skyrocketing health-care costs
- Economic:
  —Dramatic rise in the average American's living standards
  —Rapid expansion of the checkless society (i.e., credit cards)
  —Highly fluctuating interest rates
  —Foreign competition
- Political:
  —The $1-trillion federal budget deficit
  —Medicare for the aged
  —Government employees allowed to bargain collectively
  —"Star Wars" space defense system

Current Trends and Implications for HRM

The changes we have listed above, however, reflect only the past. Our concern is with the future. Therefore let us extend some current trends to predict changes that are likely to occur within the next decade; and furthermore, let us consider the impact of these changes for HRM practices.

Increased Concern by Organizations With HRM

Increased concern
for HRM

The Trend.   As recently as twenty years ago, human resource management had a questionable image. It was thought that HRM involved mainly paper shuffling and arranging employee picnics. Those days are gone.[1]

Today HRM has become more important and human resource managers have become more powerful. This can largely be attributed to such factors as increasing labor costs, concern for improving worker productivity, search for compensation plans that motivate, and the need for interpreting and implementing new government laws and regulations.

The Implications.   Within the next decade, human resource managers will learn how to use their new power. Successful HRM executives will have become strong decision makers and will accept the responsibilities that go with greater influence. Additionally, because of HRM's growing importance, senior executives in the organization will be increasingly coming out of the HRM function.[2] We can expect during the next ten years that ambitious executives will use HRM—as opposed to the more traditional functions of engineering, production, finance, or marketing—as the route to the top.

Removal of Termination as a Threat

Removal
of termination
as a threat

The Trend.   Legislation regarding the appraising and terminating of employees has increasingly placed the burden of proving inadequate performance on the employer. This trend, coupled with greater demands by unions for guaranteed lifetime employment, should find more employees permanently attached to organizations.

The Implications.   Lifetime employment, whether controlled by legislation or contract, will reduce the manager's power to exact compliance through the threat of termination. There will also be a greater need for the organization to become actively involved in career development and planning with its employees.

Creation of a Bimodal Work Force

Creation
of a bimodal
workforce

The Trend.   Growth in the work force will be concentrated at two extremes of the income spectrum. There will be a greater demand for the educated professionals who earn high salaries and among low-skilled service workers who make only the minimum wage. The demise of old-line industrial jobs is eliminating the $15-an-hour job for the low

---

[1] "HRM Takes Its Place in the Executive Suite," *Training and Development Journal,* September 1984, p. 81.

[2] Ibid., pp. 82–83.

or moderately skilled person. The work force of the future will tend toward a bimodal distribution—two large groups with very different wage rates.

The Implications. Major salary and benefit structure changes will have to be made to reflect and accommodate this bimodal work force. Competition among companies for the highly skilled workers will increase, reflecting the need for even higher wages and benefits. Career development efforts will refocus toward providing forced skills retraining in an effort to enlarge the pool of qualified, educated professionals. This retooling of skills will be needed to allow the organization to adapt to the dynamic environment.

Organizations will place more reliance on institutions of higher learning to develop and train students in the high-skill areas. Accordingly, more cooperative arrangements between businesses and colleges can be expected. College professors will be spending time, or sabbaticals, in specific organizations so that they can learn about the organization's "system" and be better qualified to prepare individuals for the job. Likewise, arrangements to bring businesspeople to the classroom, to teach full time for a semester, will increase.

Because of the bimodal nature of the work force, tension between the two groups will grow. Motivating the low-paid service worker will become a major challenge. The question of how to motivate an employee who makes the minimum wage and has little opportunity for advancement will challenge both managers and academics. The answer is likely to suggest the need for more employee participation and nonfinancial rewards.

Managements' Move to Make Their Organization "Lean and Mean"

Managements' move to make their organization "lean and mean"

The Trend. As a result of deregulation, foreign competition, and the like, organizations will further act to trim the fat, or inefficiencies, from their ranks. We can expect more layoffs. Furthermore, all employees will feel less secure in their jobs. "Corporate divorce" will be the hot issue and the new buzz term of the 1990s.

The Implications. Organizations will embark heavily on dehiring practices. There will be a significant increase in emphasis, ranging from providing career growth opportunities to providing outplacement services. Organizations will be "buying out" their employees, especially older employees and senior executives. This will involve large outlays of cash, as severance pay will be required. Commitment and loyalty to the organization are likely to suffer. Employees will become more "self" oriented and will act as if they were, in fact, individual entrepreneurs.

Legal battles over being bought out involuntarily will increase.

Organizations will be required to document why a particular individual has been targeted for release. EEO considerations will be significantly challenged in the process.

Those individuals close to retirement, either by age or by years of service, will increasingly be forced into voluntary retirement. Many individuals in their middle to late fifties will find themselves back in the job market. Accordingly, unemployment rates for this group are likely to rise dramatically. Age discrimination suits can be expected to increase.

Organizations will rationalize buying out employees and forced retirements on the grounds that it is necessary to improve productivity and efficiency and to make room at higher levels for younger workers.

Dual-Career Couples

Dual-career couples

The Trend.   The women's movement and inflation have caused the proliferation of dual-career couples. The one-breadwinner household is rapidly disappearing.

The Implications.   Because of the greater number of dual-career couples, the employees' mobility will decrease. Organizations will continue to face more resistance to offers of promotions that require geographical moves.

Organizations will also have to implement better human resource planning systems. Promotion from within will become more prevalent, especially at the middle to upper levels. However, because of the leanness of organizations, there will be fewer of these positions to fill. The search for applicants will focus on the local job markets.

The increase of dual-career couples will also witness a redundancy of benefits—especially in the offering of health insurance. Companies will become more concerned about this duplication and will seek a better coordination of benefits. That is, a company will pay for the health coverage for its employee, and the spouse's coverage will be paid by the spouse's organization. Children of the marriage will usually be covered under the husband's health plan.

Benefits and Health

Benefits and health

The Trend.   To attract and keep good female employees, the organization will provide expanded day-care benefits. This will be especially true of organizations that require its employees to work evening or night shifts. Healthier work environments will become a political issue. Smoking on the job, for instance, is likely to be banished or highly restricted.

The Implications.   Operating and paying for day-care services will increase an organization's costs. To remain competitive, however, organizations will have little choice but to offer this as a benefit.

Organizations will offer programs to help employees to stop smoking, reduce weight, and the like. More and more organizations will recruit nonsmokers and make nonsmoking a condition of employment. Companies will add gymnasium facilities to their premises or offer corporate memberships at health clubs. Time off from work will be given to those who participate reflecting the organization's commitment to improving the health of its employees.

Working at Home

Working at home

The Trend.   Through the use of personal computers, more workers will be able to process information by working at home. By the year 2000, as many as 20 million people may be employed in this manner.

The Implications.   In an organization's efforts to become "lean and mean," more work will be done at home by employees. Individuals who need more flexibility in their schedule (e.g., to facilitate child rearing), and older individuals seeking to augment their retirement income, will be doing work at home that was once done on the company's premises.

The outcome of more individuals doing work at home will likely be a major restructuring of pay levels. Companies will have to determine the worth of each job and pay accordingly. This will probably result in wide variances of pay being offered to different individuals.

Working at home will also require the organization to implement new quality control measures. Performance evaluations will have to be revised, for close supervision of the work will not be possible. Monitoring techniques will have to be developed to ensure accuracy and timeliness of the work.

Matching the Environment to the Employee: Ergonomics

Matching
the environment
to the employee

The Trend.   Organizations are studying their office furniture, their work environment, and their space utilization in an effort to provide a productive atmosphere. New kinds of office furniture are being designed to ease fatigue and back strain. Experiments with various office decors are being conducted in an effort to provide a pleasant work station, one that promotes efficient work in a supportive environment.

The Implications.   The new decors, office furnishings, and space utilizations will make employees' surroundings more pleasant and more conducive to working. Work-related health problems, especially back strain, should be reduced by having offices furnished with ergonomically designed furniture.

In management's effort to make the work more satisfying for employees, the open-space office concept will become prominent. Although this may result in less privacy for workers, open-space designs will be more consistent with more open communications. The result of this concept will likely be the reduction of status differentiation within the organization, a movement toward a more egalitarian atmosphere.

Offices in the year 2000 will be characterized as spaces enclosed by movable partitions. These offices will probably be self-contained

VIEWS IN THE NEWS

Ergonomics

The term *ergonomics* has reached many organizations. In its basic meaning, ergonomics refers to the science of adapting the work place to the employees. For years, researchers and practitioners have been searching for ways to make the work environment more conducive to productive work. For instance, we've read about studies where lighting was altered in an effort to achieve this end.

Modern ergonomic studies have gone much further than just lighting. While illumination plays a vital role, research has expanded into many new areas. These areas include work stations, correct posture at work, work scheduling, body measurements and furniture design, and video display terminal glare. What impact is this research having? From most indicators, both the organization and the employee are benefiting.

For example, a study published in July 1985 focused on the many benefits realized from implementing ergonomic improvements with a study group of employees using computers. The improvements made included "ergonomically designed chairs, work station design, layouts and accessories." The outcomes identified were:

1. Absenteeism decreased from 4 percent to less than 1 percent in the study group.
2. Error rates decreased from 25 percent to 11 percent in the study group.
3. Time spent on the computer increased from 60 percent to 86 percent in the study group.

What would these outcomes mean in dollar figures? According to the researcher, improvements such as these could increase each organization's productivity by about $1,500 per employee. In an organization with "575 employees, this means the added cash flow from increased human productivity over ten years is in excess of $7 million, with a net income of $5 million. This is an after tax return on investment of over 40 percent." With these potential savings and increases in productivity, the researcher's premise is "Ergonomics can no longer be ignored."

Source: M. Franz Schneider, "Why Ergonomics Can No Longer Be Ignored," *Office Administration and Automation*, July 1985, pp. 26–29.

units (desk furniture part of or attached to the partitions), which will provide privacy while reaping the benefits of an open-space design. Colors, too, will become more important in establishing office decors. Colors that are soothing, (e.g., mauves) will be selected rather than the more vibrant colors.

The offices of the future will require more deliberation than just finding a space to place a desk. Because the environment has such an impact on employee productivity, this area is likely to become a major function within human resources.

Decline of Unions

Decline of unions

The Trend.   From a high of 35 percent in 1945, union workers now account for approximately 17 percent of the U.S. labor force. Because of the bimodal distribution of the work force, there will be even fewer employees joining unions. The unions will focus, however, on the low to moderately skilled workers.

The Implications.   Although there will be fewer people unionized, the animosity between management and unions will intensify. The presence of unions will further dichotomize the groups in the bimodal work force. This is likely to further exacerbate the tension between the "educated professionals" and the "minimum-wage service workers."

Conclusion

Certainly no one can predict the future, and we are not implying that we can. However, the evidence thus far points to a more active interest in and careful implementation of human resource management. Remember that *management* is, by definition, getting things done through people. If managers are to increase productivity, reduce costs, and improve their organization's competitive posture, they must focus on how to properly manage personnel.

As an aspiring manager, you will be charged with the responsibility for effectively and efficiently managing your subordinates. This leadership role is one that does not manifest itself overnight. It is a lengthy process. You must be willing to expend your time and energy to learn how to manage people. Managing the human resource has changed drastically from the days when managers hovered over subordinates with a stopwatch and threats of punishment. The environment in which managers work today is more dynamic than in the past. Additionally, the individuals with whom they work are increasingly diverse in intents, abilities, and motivations. The result is a future with exciting challenges and opportunities for managing an organization's most valuable resource—its people.

SUMMARY

1. Human resource management will undergo considerable change by the year 2000.

2. The four major forces for change are
   a. Technological
   b. Social
   c. Economic
   d. Political

3. The following societal trends will have important implications for HRM practices as we enter the twenty- first century:
   a. Increased concern by organizations with HRM
   b. Removal of termination as a threat
   c. Creation of a bimodal work force
   d. Managements' move to make their organization "lean and mean"
   e. Dual-career couples
   f. Benefits and health
   g. Working at home
   h. Matching the environment to the employee (ergonomic)
   i. Decline of unions

KEY TERMS

Bimodal work force   Dual-career couples
Dehiring   Ergonomics

QUESTIONS FOR REVIEW

1. Given that any discussion of the future can only be speculative, why should we spend the time to consider it?

2. What are the implications of an increased concern by organizations with HRM?

3. What are the HRM implications of the removal of termination as a threat?

4. What are the HRM implications of the creation of a bimodal work force?

5. What are the HRM implications of managements' move to make their organization "lean and mean"?

6. What are the HRM implications of dual-career couples?

7. What are the HRM implications of changes in benefits and health?

8. What are the HRM implications of working at home?
9. What are the HRM implications of matching the environment to the employees?
10. What are the HRM implications of the decline in unions?

QUESTIONS FOR DISCUSSION

1. "The future is an extension of the past." Do you agree or disagree? Discuss.
2. Will operative employees of 1997 be any different from their 1987 counterparts? Discuss.
3. What issues do you think the union movement will emphasize during the next decade? Why?
4. Do you think that the Reagan presidency has had an impact on HRM practices? Discuss.
5. Is HRM a profession? Discuss.

CONTINUING CASE: Concord General

We've Come a Long Way, Baby

Establishing an effective human resource department in an organization is a long process, one that must be monitored and updated constantly. At Concord General, you have been instrumental in helping to establish the HRM policies. From a nonexistent, unilateral process, Concord General has developed an ongoing HRM function.

But the work is not over. As you have undoubtedly noticed, problems still exist. The nurses are not by any means the happiest group of employees in the organization. But your efforts, combined with those of individuals such as Judy Sapp, have provided a foundation for HRM. However, as with any function, proper planning is necessary. One must be aware that changes do occur and that flexibility must be built into the system to allow for these changes.

Judy and John Michaels have come to you one last time for advice. Their concern is, "Where do we go from here and how do we get there?"

1. Armed with the information you have thus far, summarize the activities that have occurred in the hospital with respect to HRM. What impact do you feel these activities have had?
2. What human resource changes do you expect the hospital to encounter through the mid–1990s?
3. Develop a plan that will enable the hospital to implement the HRM practices that you envision it encountering through the mid–1990s.

CASE APPLICATION

HRM: What'll It Be in Two Thousand and Three?

Every spring the vice-president of personnel and labor relations at American Paper Corporation, B. Howard Irwin, has a three-day HRM retreat in Steam Boat Springs, Colorado. The purpose of the retreat is to bring together the company's twenty-six mill personnel managers and, in an open and unstructured environment, talk about their mutual problems and the future directions for American's HRM programs.

Near the end of last year's retreat, Irwin asked: "What do you think jobs at American will be like in ten years?" The question initiated a considerable amount of debate, but the most polarized views came from Art Lewis, manager at the Coos Bay, Oregon, mill, and Ron Crawford, from the Orono, Maine, mill.

Basically, Art's position was that the company would be fitting jobs to people: "I think jobs will be designed to increase challenge and autonomy in work. Our employees will be better educated and they'll expect more from their jobs. I also think government programs will increase so people who can't find interesting work won't have to take employment but will receive substantial unemployment benefits. So, if we want to get and keep decent people, we're going to have to make work inherently meaningful, allow employees to take personal responsibility for their outcomes from work, and provide them with ongoing feedback as to how things are going. We're going to have to design each job around the unique characteristics of each employee."

Ron Crawford couldn't have disagreed more. He saw the company as fitting people to the available jobs: "We're in the paper business. Art, you seem so concerned with our employees' psychological well-being that I think you've lost sight of the big picture. We use people to achieve the company's goals. Human resources aren't the ends; they're the means. We select and develop people to fit our needs, not the other way around. Our job is to design work for maximum economic and technological efficiency and then do whatever must be done to help people adapt and adjust. This job humanization baloney is only going to happen in isolated cases. If it were easy to install, if it fit the need of my plant and offices, and if it required only minimum capital investment or startup costs, I'd consider it. But it appears far more likely that in ten years we'll be finding people to fit our jobs rather than designing jobs to accommodate individuals.

Questions

1. If Art Lewis is right, describe what HRM practices will be like.
2. If Ron Crawford is right, describe what HRM practices will be like.
3. Who do you think is right? Why?

ADDITIONAL READINGS

BAKSHIAN, JR., ARAM, "America's Gray Wave of the Future," *Nation's Business*, April 1986, p. 4.

"Business Starts Tailoring Itself to Suit Working Women," *Business Week*, October 6, 1986, pp. 50–54.

DRUKER, PETER F., "Goodbye to the Old Personnel Department," *Wall Street Journal*, May 22, 1986, p. 1.

ODIORNE, GEORGE S., "Human Resources Strategies for the 80s," *Training*, January 1985, pp. 47–51.

TROST, CATHY, "Toddling Trend: Child Care Near the Office." *Wall Street Journal*, October 6, 1986, p. 1.

Glossary

Absolute standards. Measuring an employee's performance without comparing that employee with any other employee.

Accept error. Accepting candidates who would later prove to be poor performers.

Achievement need. The drive to excel, to strive to succeed.

Acquisition function. The function of HRM concerned with getting individuals into the organization.

Adverse impact. A consequence of an employment practice that results in a disparate rate of selection, promotion, or firing.

Advertisements. Communicating to the general public that a position in a company is open.

Affirmative action. Specific and positive action taken to eliminate the present effects of past discrimination.

AFL. American Federation of Labor, formed in 1886.

AFL–CIO. Formed in 1955 when the American Federation of Labor and the Congress of Industrial Organizations merged.

Age Discrimination in Employment Act. Passed in 1967, and amended in 1978, this act prohibits arbitrary age discrimination, particularly among those forty to seventy years of age.

Agency shop. Requires employees who do not belong to the union to pay union dues nevertheless.

Albemarle Paper Company. Landmark Supreme Court decision clarifying requirements for using and validating tests in selection.

Alienation. A feeling of one's work is meaningless and that he or she is powerless to correct the situation.

Applied research. Research that seeks to find an answer to a specific current problem.

Apprenticeship. A time—typically two to five years—when an individual is considered to be training to learn a skill.

Arbitration. The hearing and resolution of a labor dispute, usually performed by a neutral third party.

Assessment center. A facility where performance simulation tests are administered. These are made up of a series of exercises and are used for selection, development, and performance appraisals.

Attribution theory. A theory of performance evaluation based on the perception of who is in control of an employee's performance.

Attrition. A process whereby the jobs of incumbents who leave those jobs for any reason will not be filled.

Autonomy. Freedom and independence.

Behaviorally anchored rating scales (BARS). A performance appraisal technique that generates critical incidents and develops behavioral dimensions of performance. The evaluator appraises behaviors rather than traits.

Benefits. Membership-based, nonfinancial rewards offered to attract and keep employees.

Bimodal work force. A work force characterized by two extremes.

Blind advertisement. An advertisement where there is no identification of the advertising organization.

Bona fide occupational qualification (BFOQ). An applicant's religion, sex, or national origin may be used as a basis for hiring if it can be clearly demonstrated to be job related.

Bottom-line technique. A technique used to assist in the compliance of the Uniform Guidelines on Employment Selection.

Burnout. Chronic emotional stress.

Cafeteria compensation. Allows each employee to choose that total compensation package, including benefits, which best satisfies his or her current needs.

Capital accumulation programs. Pension plans that accumulate monies on a pretax basis.

Careful personality type. A personality type whereby one is characterized as being meticulous with details.

Career. The sequence of positions that a person has over his or her life.

Career development workshop. A training program designed to assist workers in managing their careers.

Career stages. An individual's career moves through five stages: exploration, establishment, mid-career, late career, and decline.

Cases. In-depth descriptions of organizational problems.

CIO. Congress of Industrial Organizations, formed in 1935.

Civilian Conservation Corps. A federal government program designed to put some of the unemployed to work on public projects.

Civil Rights Act. Passed in 1964, with several later amendments, this act prohibits discrimination on the basis of race, color, age, religion, sex, or national origin.

Civil Service Reform Act of 1978. Replaced Executive Order 11491 as the basic law governing labor relations for federal employees.

Closed shop. A union security arrangement whereby workers could not be hired by an employer unless they were already members of the union. The closed shop was declared illegal by the Taft-Hartley Act.

Coaching. A development activity where a manager takes an active role in guiding another manager.

Collective bargaining. The negotiation, administration, and interpretation of a written agreement between two parties, at least one of which represents a group that is acting collectively, that covers a specific period of time.

Collective socialization. A socialization program that processes new members in collective groups.

Commonwealth v. Hunt. A decision rendered in this case said that a union was not illegal in and of itself. The case ended the use of the Criminal Conspiracy Doctrine application to a labor matter.

Comparable worth. Equal pay for similar jobs, jobs similar in skills, responsibility, working conditions, and effort.

Compensation administration. The determination of how much an employee should be paid.

Comprehensive Employment and Training Act. Passed in 1973, this act amended the Manpower Development and Training Act of 1962.

Computer modeling. A complex computer program that simulates the work environment.

Concessionary bargaining. Wage and benefits givebacks to the employer from the union members.

Concurrent validity. Validating tests by using current employees as the study group.

Constraints. Those things that keep us from doing what we desire to do.

Construct validity. The degree to which a particular trait is related to successful performance on the job (e.g., IQ tests).

Content validity. The degree to which the content of the test, as a sample, represents all the situations that could have been included (e.g., a typing test for a clerk typist).

Contract negotiations. The process whereby management and labor agree on the details of their contract.

Controlled experiments. Comparing two groups where conditions are kept constant in one group (the control group) while some intervention and modification is made in the others (the experimental groups).

Credit union. A banklike organization that provides financial services to its members.

Criminal conspiracy doctrine. Made it unlawful for workers to organize against the power of management.

Criterion-related validity. The degree to which a particular selection device accurately predicts the important elements of work behavior (e.g., the relationship between a test score and job performance).

Critical incidents. Key behaviors that make the difference between doing a job effectively and doing it ineffectively.

Cut score. A point at which applicants scoring below that point are rejected.

Decline phase. The final stage in one's career, usually marked by retirement.

Dehiring. Getting an employee to voluntarily resign by sending out clues to the employee that his or her services are no longer necessary.

Development function. The function of HRM concerned with preparing employees to work effectively and efficiently in the organization.

Discipline. A condition in the organization when employees conduct themselves in accordance with the organization's rules and standards of acceptable behavior.

Discrimination. The use of any test or decision device that adversely affects hiring, promotion, transfer, or other employment opportunity.

Discrete selection process. The hurdle process to selection. It involves seven steps, all of which must be passed before one is hired.

Disjunctive socialization. A socialization process whereby a new recruit does not have a guide on which to model organizational behavior.

Divestiture socialization. A socialization process that focuses on stripping away certain characteristics of a recruit, enabling the recruit to make minor modifications to improve the fit between himself or herself and the organization.

Dominant personality type. A personality type whereby one is characterized as being forceful and domineering.

Dual-career couples. A situation where both the husband and the wife have distinct careers outside the home.

Duty. A number of tasks involved in one's job.

Economic Opportunity Act. This act established a new job corps to provide basic education, training, and work in urban residential centers and rural conservation camps for unemployed youths.

Effectiveness. Attainment of the goal.

Efficiency. The ratio of inputs consumed to outputs achieved.

Employee referrals. A recommendation from a current employee regarding a job applicant.

Employee Retirement Income Security Act (ERISA). Established uniform guidelines to protect employees against arbitrary pension rules and inadequately funded pension plans.

Employment Act of 1946. This act indicated that the federal government was committed to taking actions necessary to maintain employment at high levels.

Employment-at-will doctrine. Nineteenth-century common law that permitted employers to discipline or discharge an employee at their discretion.

Encounter stage. The socialization stage where the individual confronts the possible dichotomy between his or her expectations about the organization and reality.

Equal employment opportunity. Hiring workers based on job-related factors, not personal characteristics.

Equal Employment Opportunity Act (EEOA). Title VII of the Civil Rights Act, which specifically bars discrimination with respect to race, color, religion, sex, or national origin.

Equal Employment Opportunity Commission. The arm of the federal government empowered to handle discrimination in employment cases.

Equal Pay Act. Passed in 1963, it requires equal pay for equal work.

Equity theory. Individuals seek a balance between their input-outcome ratio and the input-outcome ratio of relevant others.

Ergonomics. Matching the work environment to the employee.

Establishment phase. A career stage where one begins to search for work. It includes getting one's first job.

Executive Order 10988. Affirmed the right of federal employees to join unions and granted restricted bargaining rights to these employees.

Executive Order 11246. Prohibited discrimination on the basis of race, color, religion, or national origin by federal agencies, as well as contractors who work under federal contracts.

Executive Order 11375. Added sex-based discrimination to E.O. 11246.

Executive Order 11478. Stated that employment practices in the federal government must be based on merit and must prohibit discrimination based on race, color, religion, sex, national origin, political affiliation, marital status, or physical handicap.

Executive Order 11491. Designed to make federal labor relations more like those in the private sector. Also established the Federal Labor Relations Council.

Expectancy diagram. A bar chart showing the relationship between a test score and performance on the job.

Expectancy theory. An individual's desire to produce at any given time depends on his or her goals and perception of the relative worth of performance as a path to the attainment of these goals.

Experiential exercise. Short structured learning experiences where individuals learn by doing.

Exploration phase. A career stage that usually ends in one's midtwenties as one makes the transition from school to work.

External dimension. The objective progression of steps through a given occupation.

Extrinsic rewards. Rewards one gets from the employer, usually money, a promotion, or benefits.

Fair Labor Standards Act. Passed in 1938, this act established laws outlining minimum wage, overtime pay, and maximum hours requirements for most U.S. workers.

Featherbedding. The performing of work or the creation of jobs, both of which are not necessary.

Federal Emergency Relief Act. This act required Washington to fund state-run welfare programs.

Feedback. Knowledge of results.

Fixed socialization. A socialization program that has a fixed schedule for the transition timetable.

Flex-time. Employees work a specific number of hours a week but are free to vary the hours of work within certain limits.

FMCS. Federal Mediation and Conciliation Service.

Formal socialization. A socialization program where new employees are segregated from the ongoing work setting and differentiated in some way to make explicit their newcomer role.

Four-fifths rule. A rough indicator of discrimination, this rule requires that the number of "protected group" members that a company hires must be at least 80 percent of the white male population hired.

Functional job analysis. The Department of Labor's procedure for describing what a worker does, cataloged into three general functions: data, people, and things.

Golden parachute. A protection plan for executives in the event a merger takes place. These protections were usually a severance salary or a guaranteed position in the newly created (merged) organization.

Graphic rating scale. A performance appraisal method that lists a number of traits and a range of performance for each.

Graphology. Handwriting analysis.

Grievance procedure. The steps followed for handling contractual disputes arising out of a collective-bargaining agreement.

Griggs v. Duke Power. Landmark Supreme Court decision stating that tests must fairly measure the knowledge or skills required for a job.

Group order ranking. A relative standard of performance characterized as placing employees into a particular classification, such as the "top one-fifth."

Guilds. Formed in the Middle Ages to control and regulate trade. The forerunners of today's trade unions.

Halo error. The tendency to let our assessment of an individual on one trait influence our evaluation of that person on other specific traits.

Hawthorne studies. Conducted in the late 1920s and early 1930s, these studies ushered in a human relations movement. Gave new emphasis to human emotional factors and the influence of the informal group on worker productivity.

Headhunters. Private employment agencies specializing in middle-level and top-level executive placements.

Health maintenance organization (HMOs). Comprehensive health services for a flat fee.

Herzberg's motivation-hygiene theory. A theory of motivation where one is motivated by intrinsic factors, not by extrinsic factors.

Historical studies. Reviewing past information in order to identify unique patterns.

Home work. A job design concept whereby individuals do their work at home.

Hot stove rule. Discipline should be immediate, provide ample warning, be consistent, and be impersonal.

HRM research. Research to increase the understanding of and improvement in HRM practices.

Human resource accounting. Computing the value of an organization's human assets along with its financial assets.

Human Resource Information System. A computerized system that assists in the processing of HRM information.

Human resource inventory. Describes the skills that are available within the organization.

Human resource management (HRM). A process consisting of the acquisition, development, motivation, and maintenance of human resources.

Human resource planning. The process by which an organization ensures that it has the right number and kinds of people, at the right places, at the right time, capable of effectively and efficiently completing those tasks that will aid the organization in achieving its overall objectives.

Imminent danger. A condition where an accident is about to occur.

Implied employment contact. Any organizational guarantee or promises about job security.

Incentive compensation plans. Plans that pay for performance.

Individual ranking. Ranking employees' performance from highest to lowest.

Individual Retirement Account. A planned savings for retirement.

Individual socialization. A socialization program whereby each individual is socialized independently of others.

Industrial Revolution. Phenomenon that peaked in the United States in the late nineteenth century and marked the move from an agrarian to an industrial society, from the use of hand-powered tools to mechanized tools, and from small local workshops to large factories.

Influencing personality type. A personality type whereby one is characterized as being outgoing and effervescent.

Informal socialization. A socialization program that places new employees immediately into their jobs and does not differentiate their newcomer role.

Initial screening. The first step in the selection process whereby inquiries about a job are screened.

Internal dimension. The subjective progression of steps through a given occupation.

Internal search. A promotion from within concept.

Intrinsic rewards. Rewards that one gets from the job itself and that are usually self-initiated.

Investiture socialization. A socialization process that ratifies the usefulness of the characteristics that the person brings to the new job.

Jaques's theory. A theory of equitable payment whereby fair and equitable compensation should reflect the maximum time during which the employee exercises discretion without the results being reviewed.

Job. A type of position within the organization.

Job analysis. Provides information about jobs currently being done and the knowledge, skills, and abilities that individuals need to perform the jobs adequately.

Job characteristics model. Identifies five job factors and their interrelationships, then demonstrates their effect on productivity, motivation, and job satisfaction.

Job description. A written statement of what the jobholder does, how it is done, and why it is done.

Job design. The way in which job tasks are organized into a unit of work.

Job element. The smallest unit into which work can be divided.

Job enrichment. Deepening a job by allowing employees to do more planning and controlling of their work.

Job evaluation. Specifies the relative value of each job in the organization.

Job family. A group of two or more jobs that either call for similar work characteristics or contain parallel work tasks.

Job rotation. Includes both promotions and demotions, but most often used to refer to lateral transfers.

Job specification. The minimum acceptable qualifications that a job incumbent must possess to perform the job successfully.

Job Training Partnership Act. This act amended CETA and focuses on the issues of unemployment and underemployment.

"Just cause" dismissals. Terminating an employee for a proper reason.

Labor Management Relations Act of 1947. Also known as the Taft-Hartley Act, it constrained the powers of unions.

Labor-Management Reporting and Disclosure Act. Also known as the Landrum-Griffin Act, this legislation protected union members from possible wrongdoing on the part of their unions.

Laissez faire. The view that government should not interfere in the economic affairs of others.

Landrum-Griffin Act. Also known as the Labor and Management Reporting and Disclosure Act, its thrust was to require all unions to disclose their financial statements.

Late-career phase. A career stage whereby one is no longer learning about his or her job, nor is it expected that he or she should be trying to outdo his or her levels of performance from previous years.

Layoffs. Removing workers from an organization on a temporary or permanent basis.

Learning. A relatively permanent change as a result of experience.

Learning curve. Depicts the rate of learning.

Leaves of absence. Allowing workers to take time away from work, usually for an extended period, to pursue personal interests.

Leniency error. A means performance appraisal can be distorted by evaluating employees against one's own value system.

Maintenance function. The function of HRM concerned with keeping employees by providing those working conditions that employees believe are necessary in order to maintain their commitment to the organization.

Maintenance of membership agreement. Employees do not have to belong to the union, but those who are members must remain so for the period of the bargaining contract.

Management. The process of efficiently getting activities completed with and through other people.

Management by objectives (MBO). A performance appraisal method which includes mutual objective setting and evaluation based on the attainment of the specific objectives.

Management development. Future-oriented training, focusing on personal growth of the employee.

Mandatory bargaining items. Items that must be negotiated. These include wages, hours, and terms and conditions of employment.

Manpower Development and Training Act. This act established a three-year program for the training and retraining of unemployed workers and workers whose jobs were threatened because of automation or other technological advances.

Maslow's hierarchy of needs theory. A motivational theory based on the progression through five steps—physiological needs, safety needs, love needs, esteem needs, and self-actualization needs.

McClelland's three needs theory. A theory of motivation based on the need for achievement, the need for affiliation, and the need for power.

Membership-based rewards. Rewards that go to all employees regardless of performance.

Mentor. An individual who serves as an employee's advocate and who advises and guides the new employee on how to move effectively through the system.

Metamorphosis stage. The socialization stage whereby the new member must work out any problems discovered during the encounter stage.

Mid-career phase. A career stage marked by a continuous improvement in performance, leveling off in performance, or beginning to deteriorate in performance.

Motivation. The willingness to do something, conditioned by the action's ability to satisfy some need.

Motivation function. The function of HRM concerned with activating employees by reflecting the needs of each individual.

National Industrial Recovery Act. This act was the first major effort by the federal government to plan and regulate the economy and to establish collective bargaining and wage and hour regulations.

National Labor Relations Act of 1935. Also known as the Wagner Act, it became labor's Magna Carta.

National Labor Relations Board. Established to administer and interpret the Wagner Act, the NLRB has primary responsibility for conducting union representation elections.

Norms. Tells group members what they ought or ought not do in certain circumstances.

Norris-LaGuardia Act. Labor law act that set the stage for permitting individuals full freedom to designate a representative of their choosing to negotiate terms and conditions of employment.

Occupation. A group of similar jobs found across organizations.

Occupational association. A group of professionals that performs many of the same functions as a union.

Occupational Safety and Health Act (OSHA). Passed in 1970, it set standards to ensure safe and healthful working conditions and provided stiff penalties for violators.

Open shop. Employees are free to choose whether or not to join the union, and those who do not also do not have to pay union dues.

Organizational culture. The rules, jargon, prejudices, customs, and other traditions that clarify acceptable and unacceptable behavior in an organization.

Organization development. A process of systemwide change, designed to make organizations more adaptive.

Orientation. The activities involved in introducing new employees to the organization and their work units.

Outplacement counseling. The free counseling an employer provides for a dismissed employee to assist the employee in marketing his or her services and locating a new position.

Paired comparison. Ranking individuals' performance by counting the number of times any one individual is the preferred member when compared with all other employees.

Pattern bargaining. An agreement in one company or industry sets the stage for similar agreements in other companies or industries.

Pension. A fixed payment, other than wages, made regularly to former employees or their surviving dependents.

Pension Benefit Guarantee Corporation. The organization that lays claim to corporate assets to pay or fund inadequate pension programs.

Performance. Effective and efficient work, which also considers personnel data such as measures of accidents, turnover, absence, and tardiness.

Performance appraisal process. A formal process in an organization whereby each employee is evaluated to determine how he or she is performing.

Performance-based rewards. Rewards exemplified by the use of commissions, piecework pay plans, incentive systems, group bonuses, or other forms of merit pay.

Performance index. A measure to determine if an executive's salary is commensurate with the organization's performance.

Perquisites. Attractive fringe benefits, over and above a regular salary, granted to executives.

Personnel management. The traditional functional area responsible for the management of human resources.

Piecework. An incentive pay system where the individual earns so much for every piece or every piece above some standard.

Polygraph. Records physiological changes caused by stress. Often referred to as a "lie detector" test.

Position. Refers to one of more duties performed by one person in an organization.

Position Analysis Questionnaire (PAQ). A job analysis technique that rates jobs on 194 elements in six activity categories.

Pre-arrival stage. The socialization process stage that recognizes that individuals arrive in an organization with a set of organizational values, attitudes, and expectations.

Predictive validity. Validating tests by using prospective applicants as the study group.

Preferential shop. Union members are given preference over non-union members in selection.

Preferred Provider Organizations. Using specific physicians and health care facilities to contain the rising costs of health care.

Primary research. Research involving original investigations.

Private agencies. An external source for job applicants, usually specializing in higher-caliber jobs.

Productivity. The quantity or volume of the major product or service that an organization provides. It includes capital investments, innovation, learning, and an employee's motivation.

Professional organizations. A source of job applicants where placement facilities at regional conferences and national conferences usually occur.

Programmed instruction. Material is learned in a highly organized, logical sequence, which requires the individual to respond.

Protected group. Term used to refer to those covered under EEO laws. This includes blacks, women, Hispanics, American Indians, handicapped individuals, veterans, individuals between 40 and 70, and Pacific Islanders.

Protégé. A person under the care of someone influencial who can further the person's career.

Public agencies. A public employment service; the state employment agency.

Pure research. Research for the sake of researching in an effort to further knowledge.

Quality of work life. A multifaceted concept whereby the work environment is meaningful to employees. Components include autonomy, recognition, belonging, progress and development, and external rewards.

Railway Labor Act of 1926. Provided the initial impetus to widespread collective bargaining.

RC. Representation certification election. The process of voting in a union.

RD. Representation decertification election. The process of voting out an existing union.

Realistic job preview (RJP). A selection device allowing job candidates to learn negative as well as positive information about the job and organization.

Recruitment. The discovering of potential applicants for actual or anticipated job vacancies.

Red-circle rates. A job whose pay rate is too high, meaning the individual's pay will be frozen or below-average increases will be granted until the rate is within the normal range.

Reject error. Rejecting candidates who would later perform successfully.

Relative standards. Evaluating an employee's performance by comparing the employee with other employees.

Reliability.   A selection device's consistency of measurement.

Research.   A systematic and goal-oriented investigation of facts that seeks to establish a relationship between two or more phenomena.

Retrenchment.   A mode of downsizing an organization when the organization faces an environment of decline.

Right-to-work laws.   Prohibits the requirement that an individual must be a member of a union as a condition of employment.

RM.   Representation decertification election. Initiated by management. The process of voting out an existing union, but with the initiator being management.

Roles.   Behaviors that job incumbents are expected to display.

Sabbatical.   An extended leave of absence.

Scientific management.   Proposed by Frederick Taylor in the early 1900s, scientific management viewed management as a science. Management's responsibilities were clearly distinct from those of the worker. The former planned and the latter executed.

Secondary research.   Solving a problem by using sources other than original investigations.

Self-actualization.   To become what one is capable of becoming; to reach one's full potential.

Sensitivity training.   Unstructured group interaction in which participants discuss themselves and their interactive processes.

Serial socialization.   A socialization program where an experienced organizational member guides the new recruit.

Sexual harassment.   Any unwelcome sexual advances, requests for sexual favors, or other verbal or physical contact of a sexual nature.

Similarity error.   Evaluating employees based on the way an evaluator perceives himself or herself.

Simulation.   Any artificial environment that attempts to closely mirror an actual condition.

Socialization.   A process of adaption that takes place as individuals attempt to learn the values and norms of work roles.

Social-learning theory.   A learning approach that blends both the cognitive theory of learning and the environmental perspective of learning.

Social Security.   Retirement, disability, and survivor benefits, paid by the government to aged, former members of the labor force, the disabled, or their survivors.

Standardized evaluation form.   A tool for use in interviewing whereby all applicants are evaluated on the same criteria.

Steady personality type.   A personality type whereby one is characterized as being extremely loyal to others and being predictable.

Stereotypes.   Attributing characteristics to individuals based on their inclusion or membership in a specific group.

Stress.   A dynamic condition in which an individual is confronted with an opportunity, constraint, or demand related to what he or she desires and for which the outcome is perceived to be both uncertain and important.

Stressors. Something that causes stress in an individual.

Structured interview. An interview whereby there are fixed questions that are presented to every applicant.

Succession planning. An executive inventory report indicating what individuals are ready to move into higher positions in the company.

Surveys. Research by use of questionnaires or structured interviews.

Suspension. A period of time off from work as a result of a disciplinary process.

Taft-Hartley Act. See Labor Management Relations Act of 1947.

Targeted industries. Refers to an OSHA priority for inspections whereby OSHA's attention is directed at those industries with the highest injury rates.

Task. A distinct work activity carried out for a distinct purpose.

Theory X and Theory Y. Theory X managers assume that employees dislike work, cannot be trusted, and must be closely supervised. Theory Y assumes employees do not dislike work, can accept responsibility, and can impose self-control.

Title VII. The most prominent piece of legislation regarding HRM, it states that it is illegal to discriminate against individuals based on race, religion, color, sex, or national origin.

Training. A learning experience that seeks a relatively permanent change in an individual that will improve his or her ability to perform on the job.

Training within Industry (TWI). Program during World War II to train supervisors to prepare unskilled for work in defense industries.

Transactional analysis (TA). An approach for defining and analyzing communication interactions between people and a theory of personality.

Transfer learning. Learning is enhanced when the skills learned are readily transferable to the job.

Understudy assignments. A development method whereby potential managers are given the opportunity to relieve an experienced manager of his job and act as his substitute during the period.

Union. Organization of workers, acting collectively, seeking to protect and promote their mutual interests through collective bargaining.

Union shop. Employees can hire nonunion workers, but they must become dues-paying members within a prescribed period of time.

United Steelworkers v. Weber. A landmark Supreme Court case that justified giving special preference for jobs to blacks so as to correct racial imbalances, without fear of reverse discrimination charges.

Validity. The proven relationship of a selection device to some relevant criterion.

Validity correlation coefficients. An elaborate statistical procedure showing the relationship between one's test score and job performance. These coefficients range from $+1$ to -1.

Values. Basic convictions about what is right or wrong, good or bad, desirable or not.

Variable socialization. A socialization program that does not have a fixed schedule for the transition timetable.

Vestibule training. Employees learn their jobs on the equipment they will be using, but the training is conducted away from the actual work floor.

Vesting. The permanent right to pension benefits.

Vocational Education Act. This act greatly increased support for education designed to prepare students for gainful employment in a broad selection of occupations.

Vocation Rehabilitation Act. This act extended to the disabled the same protections afforded racial minorities and women.

Wage curve. The result of plotting of points of established pay grades against wage base rates to identify the general pattern of wages and find individuals whose wages are out of line.

Wage grades. The grouping of similar jobs into a common wage category.

Wage structure. A pay scale showing ranges of pay within each grade.

Wagner Act. See National Labor Relations Act of 1935.

Walk-ins. Casual, unsolicited applicants.

Weighted application form. Items on the application form are validated against performance and turnover measures and given appropriate weights.

Worker's compensation. Payment to workers or their heirs for death or permanent or total disability that resulted from job-related activities.

Work modules. Work activities broken into two-hour task units.

Work sampling. A selection device requiring the job applicant to actually perform a small segment of the job.

Work sharing. A job design concept whereby two individuals share one full-time job.

Name Index

Subject Index